GREEKS, LATINS AND MUSLIMS IN LUSIGNAN CYPRUS

THE DEPICTION OF INTERDENOMINATIONAL RELATIONS IN THE *CHRONICLE* OF LEONTIOS MAKHAIRAS

TRAVAUX DE L'INSTITUT DES CULTURES MÉDITERRANÉENNES ET ORIENTALES
DE L'ACADÉMIE POLONAISE DES SCIENCES
TOME 12

MAŁGORZATA GLINICKA

GREEKS, LATINS AND MUSLIMS IN LUSIGNAN CYPRUS

THE DEPICTION OF INTERDENOMINATIONAL RELATIONS IN THE *CHRONICLE* OF LEONTIOS MAKHAIRAS

Harrassowitz Verlag

Warsaw – Wiesbaden

2021

Series Editor
BARBARA LICHOCKA

Scientific Editor of the volume
PRZEMYSŁAW KORDOS

Translation
KRYSTYNA KUPISZEWSKA

Proof-reading in English
JO B. HARPER

Cover photo
Magic books and scrolls in antique library
© Adobe Stock shaiith

Technical editing and revision
KATARZYNA A. CHMIELEWSKA

Layout, typesetting and graphics
MIŁOSZ A. TRUKAWKA

Bibliographic information published by the Deutsche Nationalbibliothek
The Deutsche Nationalbibliothek lists this publication in the Deutsche Nationalbibliografie;
detailed bibliographic data are available in the internet at https://dnb.de/.

© Institute of Mediterranean and Oriental Cultures, Polish Academy of Sciences (IMOC PAS / IKŚiO PAN),
Harrassowitz Verlag and Małgorzata Glinicka, Warsaw – Wiesbaden 2021

This work, including all of its parts, is protected by copyright. Any use beyond the limits of copyright law without the permission of the publisher is forbidden and subject to penalty. This applies particularly to reproductions, translations, microfilms and storage and processing in electronic systems. Printed on permanent/durable paper.
Printed in Poland

PL ISBN 978-83-963880-1-8
DE ISBN 978-3-447-11818-7
ISSN 2353-740X

Institute of Mediterranean and Oriental Cultures
Polish Academy of Sciences
72, Nowy Świat st.
00-330 Warsaw
Poland
www.iksiopan.pl
sekretariat@iksio.pan.pl

Otto Harrassowitz GmbH & Co KG
Harrassowitz Verlag
Kreuzberger Ring 7 c-d
65205 Wiesbaden
Germany
https://www.harrassowitz-verlag.de/
verlag@harrassowitz.de

In memory of Loukis Papaphilippou,
benefactor and distinguished friend of Poland

Contents

Acknowledgements 11

Introduction 13
    1. Cyprus as a meeting place of civilisations 13
    2. Object of study 13
    3. State of the art 15
        3.1. Works on the *Chronicle* 15
        3.2. Manuscripts and editions of the *Chronicle* 17
        3.3. Historical studies 19
    4. Research method 19
        4.1. 'Medieval postcolonial studies' 20
    5. The structure of the book 27
    6. Terminological comments 28
    7. List of abbreviations 30

I. Leontios Makhairas and his work 31
    1.1. Life and work of Leontios Makhairas 31
    1.2. Medieval Cypriot Greek 37
    1.3. Cypriot literature and its potential influence on the *Chronicle* 40
    1.4. Narrative singularity of the *Chronicle* 43
    1.5. Other texts relating to Cyprus 53
    1.6. The content of Leontios Makhairas' *Chronicle* 57
    1.7. The *Chronicle*'s potential audience 63
    1.8. Language of manipulation in the *Chronicle* 67
    1.9. The 'colonial' situation in the *Chronicle* 69

II. The complex depiction of Christianity in the *Chronicle* 73
    2.1. Plurality of denominations in Makhairas' Cyprus 73
        2.1.1. Christianisation of Cyprus 85

    2.1.2. Templars and Hospitallers 92
    2.1.3. The Frankish Conquest of Cyprus 98
  2.2. Depiction of the peaceful coexistence of Christians in the *Chronicle* 102
    2.2.1. Co-occurrence of relics 103
    2.2.2. Legends about the Saints 106
    2.2.3. Cult of the Holy Cross 113
    2.2.4. Coexistence of different forms of cult 120
  2.3. Conflicts in the Christian community 126
  2.4. Orthodoxy and heterodoxy. The case of Thibald 131
  2.5. Summary 134

III. The Lusignans, Genoese and Venetians in the *Chronicle* 139
  3.1. The Latins on Cyprus 139
  3.2. Depiction of Genoese-Venetian relations on Cyprus 143
  3.3. Depiction of Cypriot-Genoese relations on Cyprus 146
    3.3.1. The beginnings of the Cypriot-Genoese conflict on Cyprus................................. 147
    3.3.2. Siege of Famagusta (Ammochostos) 148
    3.3.3. Fighting for Lefkosia and Kerynia 153
    3.3.4. Genoese and Rhodians 158
    3.3.5. The role of religious figures in relations between the Latins 160
    3.3.6. The Cypriot-Genoese peace 164
  3.4. Depiction of Cypriot-Venetian relations 164
  3.5. The role of Providence 166
  3.6. Summary 169

IV. Depiction of contacts between Christians and Muslims in the *Chronicle* 173
  4.1. Christians and Muslims: two differing depictions 173
  4.2. Muslims in the *Chronicle* 184
  4.3. Depiction of Cypriot-Egyptian clashes outside Cyprus 188
    4.3.1. Depiction of contacts between Cypriots and Egyptians 188
        4.3.1.1. Siege of Alexandria in 1365 188
        4.3.1.2. In search of an accord with the sultan 192
    4.3.2. Depiction of contacts between Cypriots and Turks 198
        4.3.2.1. The defence of Gorhigos castle in 1367 198
        4.3.2.2. Retaking of Adalia in 1370 201
  4.4. Saracen attacks on Cyprus in the years 1363 and 1424–1426 202
  4.5. Other encounters between Cypriots and Saracens 205
  4.6. Cases of conversion 206

    4.7. The letters of the old man of Damascus and the story of the boy George 208
        4.7.1. Letters of the old man of Damascus 209
        4.7.2. The story of the boy George 212
    4.8. Summary 213

V. Final conclusions 217
    5.1. Imagined geography in the *Chronicle* 217
    5.2. Material reality: tradition, heritage and gifts in the *Chronicle* 219
    5.3. Depiction of denominations and religions in the *Chronicle* 221
    5.4. Function of religion in the *Chronicle* 222
    5.5. 'Others' in the *Chronicle* 224
    5.6. Nature of relations in the *Chronicle* 225
    5.7. Perception, words and emotions: ways of contacting the 'other' in the *Chronicle* 226
    5.8. Heretics, pagans and infidels in the *Chronicle* 228
    5.9. Leontios Makhairas' identity 229

Appendixes 235
    Appendix 1. Cyprus: location and chronology (1191–1432) 237
        Location of Cyprus 237
        Chronology of Cypriot history 324–1458 238
    Appendix 2. Maps 247

References 249
    Greek sources 249
        A. Editions and translations of the *Chronicle* of Leontios Makchairas 249
        B. Works inspired by the *Chronicle* of Leontios Makchairas 250
        C. Other Greek sources 250
    Other sources and translations 250
        A. Editions of translations of the *Chronicle* of Leontios Makchairas and texts based
           (directly and indirectly) on the *Chronicle* 250
        B. Editions and translations of other sources 251
    Scientific studies 256
        A. Scientific studies in Greek 256
        B. Scientific studies in Polish 257
        C. Scientific studies in other languages 262
    Websites 293

Indices 295
    Geographical index 297
    Index of persons 301

Plates 311

    List of figures 313

    Plates 315

Acknowledgements

I am deeply grateful to my PhD thesis supervisor, Prof. Małgorzata Borowska (Faculty of 'Artes Liberales' at the University of Warsaw) for her invaluable support extended to me during the writing of this dissertation. Her comprehensive feedback and suggestions allowed me to expand my research techniques and kindled a vivid interest in the literature, culture and history of Cyprus and the special features of Cypriot Greek.

I wish to thank Prof. Przemysław Kordos (Faculty of 'Artes Liberales' at the University of Warsaw), co-supervisor of my PhD thesis and scientific editor of this monograph, for his valuable guidance and help, and also for strengthening my interest in Cyprus, particularly in contemporary times.

Special thanks go to Prof. Mariusz Misztal (Faculty of Humanities at the Pedagogical University of Krakow) and Dr Łukasz Burkiewicz (Faculty of Education at the Jesuit University Ignatianum in Krakow) for important comments on the history of Cyprus and for providing access to many scholarly historical studies, and to Dr Konrad Kuczara (Faculty of 'Artes Liberales' at the University of Warsaw) for consultations on Church history.

Without the indispensable help of Dr Małgorzata Kornacka (Faculty of Applied Linguistics at the University of Warsaw) and Prof. Michał Moch (Institute of Mediterranean and Oriental Cultures of the Polish Academy of Sciences). I would not have been able to correctly transliterate Arab names, surnames and titles of works, and I am deeply grateful to them.

I was greatly helped by the comments of the reviewers: Prof. Andrzej Dąbrówka (Faculty of Polish Studies at the University of Warsaw) and Prof. Ilias Wrazas (Faculty of Philology at the University of Wrocław), whom I wholeheartedly thank.

Much gratitude goes to Prof. Elżbieta Wichrowska (Faculty of Polish Studies at the University of Warsaw), for her kindness and help in difficult moments.

A special word of thanks goes to my loved ones, Wojciech, Ignacy and Magdalena. I would also like to express my gratitude to my brother Mateusz, and last but not least to my parents for accompanying me in my scientific choices.

Introduction

1. Cyprus as a meeting place of civilisations

Because of its unique geographical location and rich history, Cyprus is an exceptional place. It has been the site of dynamic meetings between civilisations since the dawn of history. Phoenician, Hittite, Egyptian, Assyrian, Persian, Hellene, Arab and Roman elements[1] have intertwined there, creating a unique, diverse and constantly changing whole. The germ of 'Cypriot culture' can be held to be the culture of the island's original inhabitants, referred to in historical literature as 'Eteocypriots',[2] shaped already in the neolithic era (from the sixth millennium BCE). This elusive and hard to define core, influenced by constant contact with newcomers from other lands, was modified and absorbed over time by the inevitably transforming structure of Cypriot society. Along with the exogenous peoples, new beliefs also found a home on Cyprus, from the cult of the fertility goddess to the Christian faith. This small island should thus be recognised as a witness to fascinating episodes of clashes between cultures[3] and, as follows from that, a place where intensive 'religious colonisation' took place at each stage of history.

The medieval period relevant to this study saw an encounter between Orthodox Christianity, Catholicism and Islam, offering an example of interesting forms of coexistence and special types of confrontational attitudes.

2. Object of study

The main work depicting the history of medieval Cyprus is the fifteenth century chronicle Ἐξήγησις τῆς γλυκείας χώρας Κύπρου, ἡ ποία λέγεται Κρόνακα τουτέστιν Χρονικ(όν) (Description of the Sweet Land of Cyprus called *Kronaka* or *Chronicle*) by Leontios Makhairas, further cited as the '*Chronicle*', which

---

[1] Latif, Religion and Ethical Education, 46. Dilek Latif states: 'As a consequence, Cyprus has been religiously and culturally diverse since medieval times, with Greeks, Turks, Maronites, Armenians, Latins, Orthodox Christians, Muslims, Catholic Christians, Jews, Gypsies, and Lino-bambaki coexisting with their different identities.' (Latif, Religion and Ethical Education, 46). Charles Frazee explains the last term: 'The Catholic converts either to Islam or Orthodoxy got the colourful name of *linovamvaki*, meaning "linen-cotton", since they sought to combine their old Catholic faith with their present religion.' (Frazee, Catholics and Sultans, 114). Cf. Yakinthou, Political Settlements, 204 (Notes, 83).

[2] Misztal gives the origin of this term: 'The term "Eteocypriot" (*Eteokyprier*, "truly Cypriot") was coined by the linguist Johannes Friedrich in 1932 to describe the language of Cyprus' earliest inhabitants. Over time it was adapted as the adjective for the original inhabitants of the island.' (Misztal, Historia Cypru, 509, fn. 3. Translated by Kupiszewska). More information about the Eteocypriot language may be found in: Iacovou, 'Greeks', 'Phoenicians', 'Eteocypriots', 27–59; Steele, A Linguistic History of Ancient Cyprus, 99–172. James Clackson notes that the term 'Eteocypriot' was formed analogously to the term 'Eteocretan'. He writes: 'Eteocypriot has been identified in around two dozen inscriptions documented in the area around the town of Amathus, and may be preserved in a couple of later Greek glosses which attribute words to the speech of the Amathusians. Owing to the paucity of inscriptions, Eteocypriot is little understood and, like Eteocretan, it seems to bear no relation to any other known language.' (Clackson, Language and Society, 8).

[3] The desire to examine the biological consequences of the dynamic changes undergone by the Cypriot community (from ancient to contemporary times) has moved scholars to study the genetics of the Cypriot population, resulting in the following papers: Voskarides *et al.*, Y-chromosome phylogeographic analysis of the Greek-Cypriot population, and Heraclides *et al.*, Y-chromosomal analysis of Greek Cypriots.

presents the island's history from the fourth century, i.e. from the rule of Byzantine emperor St Constantine, to the 1458 accession to power of Charlotte, daughter of John II and Helena Palaiologina. In his narrative, Makhairas pays the most attention to the portrayal of Cypriot society under the Lusignan dynasty. As the historian probably died in 1432, the record of events that played out in the years 1432–1458 should be deemed to originate from some other person. The abbreviated take on issues concerning the period after 1432 would also seem to suggest this.

The text of the *Chronicle* served as the main material for this study. From the weave of the diverse subjects touched on by its author it is religion, a topic he particularly emphasises, that has been selected. The aim of this work is to analyse and interpret Makhairas' depiction of faith-related (i.e. interdenominational and interreligious) contacts in medieval Cyprus under the rule of the Frankish Lusignan dynasty: namely between the Greeks, Latins and Muslims.

The study attempts to answer the question as to whether the nature of the faith-related interactions captured by Leontios can be shown to be the consequence of Cyprus' annexation by the Franks. To this end, the technique that Makhairas uses to construct alterity is investigated and the issue of how, under the pen of the *Chronicle*'s author, two peoples perceive each other, is examined: how the native Cypriots see the Franks, and the Franks, the native Cypriots. Moreover, in the course of the analysis it becomes pertinent to ask whether the chronicler assigns a value to elements of the image that he creates.

The *Chronicle* is acknowledged here not only as a relevant historical source for the reconstruction of religious relations in the period (13th–14th century), but also as a literary depiction of these relationships, created by Makhairas for a given purpose and a given audience. The difference between literary and historical representation is a crucial one, because each is underlain by a different dichotomy: 'book-author' and 'individual-history'.[4] Thus the execution of the assumptions of this work is limited to the 'book-author' dichotomy and focuses on the depiction Makhairas offers of interdenominational and interreligious contacts in Lusignan Cyprus. The book, following Hayden White, is written from the position that the author has full control over the emerging text by passing over certain facts, subordinating selected facts to the remaining ones, repeating motifs, changing perspectives and tonations and applying 'alternative descriptive strategies'.[5] In accordance with White's concept, historical events are treated as a narrative element of a historiographic work. An attempt to capture the essence of the narrative is made following Maciej Czerwiński, who defined it as the 'human ability to order and present events as uniform cognitive systems or to order events into uniform logical sequences', thus making it a 'tool for establishing sense'; Czerwiński clearly opposes it to an 'ordinary sequence of events'.[6] It is the narrator, characterised by the scholar as the 'perceiving subject' and 'specific interlocutor who has a given linguistic and cultural competence and given ideological frame of mind', who consolidates such a sequence and imbues it with a specific meaning.[7]

We also encounter the problem of truth in a literary work or a work that we are reading as a literary depiction of a given reality (e.g. in a chronicle). Jarosław Płuciennik and Leszek Karczewski show that such truth can only be pragmatic. We cannot assume the classic theory of truth[8] to be appropriate in the context of literary studies because factors such as the 'nature of language, paradigmatic features of science, accidentality of interpretive values and goals' make it useless.[9]

Where historical facts happen to be cited, this is not done for the sake of the facts themselves, but in order to help the Reader to get an idea of the conditions in which events played out, or of their chronology.

---

[4] Gayatri Chakravorty Spivak portrays them as follows: 'When we operate with the opposition book-author, we want to avoid the kind of simple reversal whereby the critic's hands remain clean and the critic becomes diagnostic in a simple symptomatic reading. We keep ourselves within the book's field and see how far we can go when we respect that. In the second case, the individual and history, we want to see the individual consciousness as a crucial part of the effect of being a subject, which is itself a part of a much larger structure, one which is socio-political, politico-economic, psycho-sexual. Now all of these elements are discontinuous with each other so that you can't easily translate from the one to the other. But, nonetheless, all of these things are organised as narratives which reflect a sort of weave of presence and absence.' (Discussion between Gayatri Spivak and Walter Adamson in Spivak, Post-Colonial Critic, 51).
[5] Elements listed after White, The Historical Text, 84. White's ideas are the subject of Muchowski, Polityka pisarstwa historycznego.
[6] Czerwiński, Semiotyka dyskursu historycznego, 42. Translated by Kupiszewska.
[7] Czerwiński, Semiotyka dyskursu historycznego, 42–44. Translated by Kupiszewska.
[8] In this case, the semantic theory of truth formulated by Alfred Tarski is found to be useful here: 'x is a true sentence if, and only if, p' (Tarski, Pojęcie prawdy, 18), where 'In this model, any sentence may be substituted for variable p, and the name of that sentence, for variable x.' (Moroz, Czy Alfred Tarski jest relatywistą aletycznym?, 101. Translated by Kupiszewska).
[9] Płuciennik, Karczewski, Prawda w literaturze, 93. Translated by Kupiszewska.

3. State of the art

3.1. Works on the *Chronicle*

Scholarly literature mentions the phenomenon of co-occurrence in the *Chronicle* of representatives of different denominational communities (Greeks, Latins, Syrians, Armenians) and different religions (mainly Christianity and Islam, and marginally Judaism). However, the topic that mainly dominates is historical reflection on the diversity and coexistence of such groups in medieval Cyprus, with the *Chronicle* taken into account as one of the source materials. The papers by Nicholas Coureas[10] and Angel Nicolaou-Konnari[11] in the collected work *Identity/Identities in Late Medieval Cyprus* may be regarded as examples of the historical approach. The topic of denominational and religious contacts in the *Chronicle* has not itself previously been the subject of a study focused on literary research. Coureas, who based on various sources (including the *Chronicle*) undertook a study of the religious and ethnic identities of groups inhabiting Lusignan Cyprus, points out Makhairas' ambiguous attitude towards the new Frankish rulers, and moreover, the hostile demeanour with which, in his opinion, the Rhomaioi regarded Syrians and Armenians, as well as the decidedly negative description of Muslims, seen from the perspective of Christians (Coureas mainly writes about Greeks in the *Chronicle* in this context). Nicolaou-Konnari, meanwhile, examines how Makhairas perceives the problem of identity and otherness in the context of the situation in the Kingdom of Cyprus during the reign of King Peter I (1359–1369), comparing Leontios' position with the slightly differing approach of Philippe de Mézières (1327–1405).[12] As a whole, the publication *Identity/Identities in Late Medieval Cyprus*, which provides an insight into the current state of the art on Cypriot topics,

> *investigated the bewildering range of expressions of identity, be it religious, linguistic or cultural, through art, architecture, institutions and language in the composite, multi-confessional and multi-lingual society of the Lusignan Kingdom of Cyprus (thirteenth through fifteenth centuries).*[13]

The results of works by scholars investigating these topics provide, thanks to intensive cooperation between specialists from different disciplines (historians, archaeologists, art historians), a nuanced picture of identity issues in medieval Cyprus.

Nicolaou-Konnari is also the author of several other articles on the *Chronicle*. The objective of one of them, which clearly stresses the aspect of Frankish dominance, is defined by the scholar as follows:

> *This article aims at investigating [...] the way the notion of the crusades and holy war is perceived in the chronicle, something which inevitably raises many issues related to the expression of political ideology, ethnic identity, and culture conflict in the text.*[14]

Nicolaou-Konnari posits that Makhairas captures the 'kingdom's evolving character', starting from the stage of a Greek kingdom dominated by Frankish crusaders who desired influence in Jerusalem, through to a 'Cypriot society of Franks and Greeks in the fifteenth century'.[15] Next she analyses the content of the *Chronicle* for the textual presence of elements of 'the crusader ideology' or even 'crusading rhetoric',[16] examining fragments that describe, for instance, the 1099 capture of Jerusalem, Guy's purchase of Cyprus in 1192,[17] Peter I's expeditions to Muslim lands in 1365 and 1367,[18] and the Saracen attacks

---

[10] Coureas, Religion and ethnic identity, 13–25.
[11] Nicolaou-Konnari, Alterity and identity, 37–66.
[12] Nicolaou-Konnari analyses how Peter I's reign was presented in the works of Makhairas and Philippe de Mézières in the paper Nicolaou-Konnari, Apologists or Critics?, 359–402.
[13] Papacostas, Saint-Guillain, Preface and Aknowledgement, vii.
[14] Nicolaou-Konnari, 'A poor island...', 120.
[15] Nicolaou-Konnari, 'A poor island...', 126.
[16] Nicolaou-Konnari, 'A poor island...', 140.
[17] Nicolaou-Konnari, 'A poor island...', 126–127.
[18] Nicolaou-Konnari, 'A poor island...', 129–135.

on Cyprus in the years 1424–1426.[19] Nicolaou-Konnari pays much attention to the 'linguistic construction of ethnicity and alterity' and to ideological questions that are manifested in 'Cypriot self-perception' and their 'perception of the "Other"' in the *Chronicle*.[20] This article is presented here, because it links the topic of annexation during the crusades ('colonial' annexation carries a complementary meaning in this work) to ideology (in this case, religion).

A publication that is important for the comprehension of the nature and narrative structure of the *Chronicle* is a book by Nadia Anaxagorou, who emphasises that for a long time, the *Chronicle* was the object of scholarly interest only as 'a historical tapestry serving to reconstruct aspects of medieval Cyprus', and not as an autonomous, multi-layered text whose linguistic and literary features are worthy of exploration.'[21] In the first two chapters the scholar delineates the cultural background of Leontios' work, brings to the fore the social and educational factors that influenced its shape, discusses, in the form of a short presentation, Makhairas' life and works, and traces the tradition of the *Chronicle*'s manuscripts.[22] In the third and fourth chapters, as she herself explains in the preface, she uses 'perspectives offered by modern literary theory in the field of narratology' to examine the medieval text, which she accomplishes by analysing its 'narrative macrostructure' using Gérard Genette's model and via reflection, supported by the findings of William Lebov, on the structure of 'self-contained stories'.[23] Furthermore, Anaxagorou draws out the 'stylistic microstructure' and 'text connectivity' by applying Michael Halliday and Ruqaiya Hasan's 'cohesion theory' and taking into account 'coherence conditions' as postulated by Tanya Reinhart.[24] In the fifth chapter, Anaxagorou compares Makhairas' work with Byzantine and Western historiographical models. She searches the *Chronicle* for traces of features characteristic for these traditions and simultaneously attempts to emphasise the elements that prove the Cypriot text's originality.[25] Chapter 6, as she herself writes,

> *explores the features of narrative and style in the* Chronicle *in the light of data offered by recent linguistic research on oral vs. written discourse, as well as studies on the nature of orality and medieval poetics.*[26]

In one of subchapters Anaxagorou reviews the positions of scholars who propose varying conclusions concerning Makhairas' religious identity.[27] Establishing and determining this is particularly important from the perspective of the present work.

A hypothesis concerning Leontios' worldview, in the form of a discussion of his cultural identification and the ethnoreligious ideology motivating him, is also presented by Kostas Kyrris who, applying Hegelian concepts such as 'dialectics', etc., and citing the thought of Ernst Cassirer in several places, supports the (in his opinion indisputable) Greek, Byzantine identification of the chronicler and the existence of what he calls the 'Universal Christian Ideal' (defined by him as 'centred around the considerably hellenised Lusignan royal family' and 'derived from the "aboriginal" Byzantine-Greek kernel'[28]) in the medieval Cyprus of the *Chronicle*.

---

[19] Nicolaou-Konnari, 'A poor island...', 136–137.
[20] Nicolaou-Konnari, 'A poor island...', 137–143.
[21] Anaxagorou, Narrative and Stylistic Structures, xx. Anaxagorou is also an author of a bilingual book Μαχαιράς, Αναξαγόρου (Elab.), Εξηγήσεις δια αθύμησιν καιρού και τόπου, containing a presentation of the 'self-contained stories' taken from the *Chronicle* with drawings by Lefteris Olympios. This presentation emphasises the oral nature of these stories.
[22] Anaxagorou, Narrative and Stylistic Structures, xxi.
[23] The following are listed by Anaxagorou as 'self-contained stories' (Anaxagorou's term): The Story of the Finding of the Holy Cross, The Story of St Helena's Visit to Cyprus, The Story of the Extermination of the Templars in Cyprus, The Story of Godfrey de Bouillon and the Capture of Jerusalem, The Trilogy of the Holy Cross (The Story of the Theft of the Holy Cross, The Story of the Recovery of the Holy Cross, The Story of the Trying of the Holy Cross), The Story of the Adventures of the King's Sons, The Story of the Syrian Merchant Lakha and the Catalan Capitain, The Story of Queen Eleanora and Joanna L'Aleman, The Story of the Quarrel over the Grayhounds, The Story of King Peter I's Assassination, The Story of the Genoese Cruelty at Lefkosia, The Story of the Prince of Antioch's Assassination, The Story of Thibald's Victory over the Genoese, The Story of the Pilgrim Boy George. Listed after Anaxagorou, Narrative and Stylistic Structures, 164–183.
[24] Anaxagorou, Narrative and Stylistic Structures, xxi.
[25] Anaxagorou, Narrative and Stylistic Structures, xxi.
[26] Anaxagorou, Narrative and Stylistic Structures, xxi.
[27] Anaxagorou, Narrative and Stylistic Structures, 15–17.
[28] Kyrris, Some Aspects, 224.

3. State of the art

Leontios' work served Erma Vassiliou as the source material for her doctoral thesis.[29] In her dissertation, Vassiliou analyses various texts written in the demotic Cypriot dialect currently known as 'Medieval Cypriot Greek' from the perspective of syntactic typology,[30] that is by investigating word order. Vassiliou's thesis provides information on the linguistic structures used by Leontios, and also allows them to be compared with structures used in other texts written in Medieval Cypriot Greek, such as the *Assizes*, the chronicle of George Boustronios and Κυπριακά Ερωτικά Ποιήματα (Cypriot love poems).[31]

In Polish scholarship, Małgorzata Borowska's chapter in the two-volume publication *Cypr, dzieje, literatura, kultura* (2015)[32] merits particular attention as an introduction to the body of Cypriot literature in Greek from ancient to contemporary times, including Medieval Cypriot literature, with Makhairas as its most outstanding representative. Apart from Borowska's work no studies on the chronicler have been published in Polish.

3.2. Manuscripts and editions of the *Chronicle*

Three manuscripts of the *Chronicle* are extant: the Venice, Oxford and Ravenna manuscripts, copied in the sixteenth and seventeenth centuries. The Venice manuscript (hereinafter abbreviation MS V is used), dated to a period later than 1523, is kept in the Libreria Nazionale Marciana (MS Ven. Marc. gr. VII, 16, 1080, 375 f.). It contains the oldest and longest version and is also the only one to include references to Makhairas and his family.[33] In addition to the text of the *Chronicle*, it also contains George Boustronios' work.[34] The Oxford manuscript (MS O), written in Paphos in 1555, is held in the Bodleian Library of Oxford (Oxon. Bodl. Selden, supra 14, 331 f.).[35] Richard McGillivray Dawkins emphasises the presence of significant lacunae (mainly in fragments LM I 1–19, II 274–III 366).[36] Each of these versions contains some fragments that are missing from the other, or more extensive paragraphs.[37] They also differ as to vocabulary and syntax.[38] In Dawkins' opinion, the language of MS O is more colloquial and contains more words of French origin than MS V.[39] Meanwhile, the text of the Ravenna manuscript (MS R), dated to ca. 1600 and available in the Biblioteca Classense in Ravenna (Raven. Class. gr. 187, 184 f.), is far shorter.[40] MS R, as Nicolaou-Konnari writes, was first described in 1894 in Giuseppe Mazzatinti's catalogue by Silvio Bernicoli.[41]

Michael Pieris, writer, theatre scholar and literary critic, who discusses all three preserved manuscripts, has come to the same conclusions as Dawkins, who studied MS V and MS O, and Emmanuel Kriaras, who focused on MS R,[42] that these versions 'differ as regards vocabulary and syntax' (ἔχουν διαφορὲς στὸ λεκτικὸ καὶ στὴ σύνταξη), but 'are in agreement as to the events described' (συμφωνοῦν ὡς πρὸς τὰ γεγονότα ποὺ περιγράφονται).[43]

The primary source in this work is the two-volume edition Ἐξήγησις τῆς γλυκείας χώρας Κύπρου, ἡ ποία λέγεται Κρόνακα τουτέστιν Χρονικ(όν)/ *Recital Concerning the Sweet Land of Cyprus entitled 'Chronicle'*

---

[29] Vassiliou, The Word Order of Medieval Cypriot.
[30] The term 'syntactic typology' appears literally in Vassiliou, The Word Order of Medieval Cypriot, 333, 339.
[31] Vassiliou considers the best edition of these poems to be Shiapkara-Pitsillides (Ed.), Le Pétrarchisme en Chypre.
[32] Borowska, Panorama greckojęzycznej literatury cypryjskiej, 43–170.
[33] Dawkins, Introduction, 1; Nicolaou-Konnari, 'A poor island…', 120; Vassiliou, The Word Order of Medieval Cypriot, 54; Πιερής, Για μια νέα κριτική έκδοση, 343.
[34] Dawkins, Introduction, 1; Vassiliou, The Word Order of Medieval Cypriot, 55.
[35] Dawkins, Introduction, 1; Nicolaou-Konnari, 'A poor island…', 120–121; Vassiliou, The Word Order of Medieval Cypriot, 55; Πιερής, Για μια νέα κριτική έκδοση, 343.
[36] Dawkins, Introduction, 1.
[37] Dawkins, Introduction, 1.
[38] Dawkins, Introduction, 1.
[39] Dawkins, Introduction, 2.
[40] Nicolaou-Konnari, 'A poor island…', 121; Πιερής, Για μια νέα κριτική έκδοση, 343–344.
[41] Νικολάου-Κονναρή, Η διασκευή, 288.
[42] Πιερής, Για μια νέα κριτική έκδοση, 344. Pieris cites the publication Κριαράς,Ένα νέο χειρόγραφο. Moreover, as Anaxagorou underlines, Kriaras concludes that MS O and MS R are related and must originate from a common manuscript branch, separate from that of MS V (Anaxagorou, Narrative and Stylistic Structures, 26–27).
[43] Πιερής, Για μια νέα κριτική έκδοση, 343–344. Pieris has used the text of the *Chronicle* to create plays: Μαχαιράς, Πιερής (Eds), Χρονικό της Κύπρου.

prepared by Dawkins, a distinguished authority on Makhairas's work,[44] published in 1932 in Oxford. The first part contains the text of the *Chronicle* in Medieval Cypriot Greek[45] and Dawkins' translation into English, and the second, the editor's comments on the contents of the work and its linguistic layer, a glossary of important Cypriot terms used by the chronicler and an index of persons and places. Dawkins' edition, in Nicolaou-Konnari's opinion the best,[46] is based on MS V and supplemented by MS O.

Dawkins' edition is compared (where relevant) with that of Konstantinos Sathas and Emmanuel Miller: *Λεοντίου Μαχαιρά, Χρονικόν Κύπρου. Léonce Makhairas, Chronique de Chypre* (Leontios Makhairas' chronicle of Cyprus, 1882),[47] based on MS V, enhanced (unlike the first, 1873 edition) by unsystematic insertions made on the basis of MS O[48] and a French translation.[49] Sathas held the opinion that MS V must have been written right after the Turks took the island in 1570.[50]

Antros Pavlidis' 1995 edition: *Λεοντίου Μαχαιρά «Χρονικόν». Επιμέλεια Άντρου Παυλίδη*, Εκδόσεις Φιλόκυπρος (Leontios Makhairas' *Chronicle*, ed. Antros Pavlidis, Filokypros series, Lefkosia 1982¹, 1995²)[51] is also used. Like the previous ones it is based on MS V and supplemented by MS O (Pavlidis believed this version to be fuller[52]), though the publisher also mentions MS R.[53] This edition contains a translation of the *Chronicle's* text into Modern Greek, though Vassiliou underlines that it is useful rather as 'a communicative translation' than 'a translation approached diachronically'.[54]

An important edition, which takes into account all three manuscripts, is *Λεοντίου Μαχαιρά Χρονικό της Κύπρου. Παράλληλη διπλωματική έκδοση των χειρογράφων*. Κέντρο Επιστημονικών Ερευνών, Λευκωσία (Leontios Makhairas' chronicle of Cyprus. Parallel Diplomatic Edition of the Manuscripts, Cyprus Research Centre, Lefkosia 2003) by Nicolaou-Konnari and Pieris.[55]

The *Chronicle* has also been translated into French and Italian. The French translation was made by Isabelle Cervellin-Chevalier.[56] Diomede Strambaldi (Diomède Strambaldi)[57] translated the work into Italian, based on MS O.[58] As Dawkins notes, he must have possessed a better version of that manuscript than the one that has been preserved.[59]

In her newest study on the *Chronicle* manuscripts, Nicolaou-Konnari remarks that an Italian translation of MS R is also known, kept in the Vatican Library (Biblioteca Apostolica Vaticana)[60] and attributed to Strambaldi (Vat. Lat. 3941).[61] The scholar cites the discovery of sixteenth-century manuscripts (London,

---

[44] Cf. Dawkins, The Nature of the Cypriot Chronicle, 300–330.
[45] Positions discussing Cypriot Greek that are of interest include the following works by Marilena Karyolemou: Καρυολαίμου, Τι απέγινε η κυπριακή διάλεκτος, 451–492; Καρυολαίμου, Γλωσσική πολιτική, 242–261; Karyolemou, Goutsos (Eds), The Sociolinguistics of Cyprus; Καρυολαίμου, Le chypriote, 111–115. Also noteworthy is Varella, Language Contact, because of its references to Makhairas' *Chronicle*. The issue of French borrowings in Cypriot Greek has been examined by Henry and Renée Kahane, who observed that 'the Cypriote Gallicisms transmit the image of the Frankish feudal society in the Byzantine colonies' (Kahane, Kahane, The Western Impact on Byzantium, 137). Anaxagorou also draws attention to the following works: Χριστόδουλος, Γλωσσικά Ζητήματα, 237–248; Hadjioannou, The Medieval Dialect of Cyprus, 59–76; Meyer, Il dialetto delle Cronache di Cipro, 255–286 (Anaxagorou, Narrative and Stylistic Structures, 18, footnotes 101 and 102).
[46] Nicolaou-Konnari, 'A poor island…', 121 (fn. 5).
[47] Sathas, Miller (Eds, transl.), Chronique de Chypre (1873¹, 1882², 2004³). Other Sathas' edition: Σάθας (Ed.), Χρονογράφοι Βασιλείου Κύπρου. Almost all references to Sathas, Miller (Eds, transl.), Chronique de Chypre in the footnotes, are to Vol. III containing the French translation.
[48] Anaxagorou, Narrative and Stylistic Structures, 27.
[49] Dawkins, Introduction, 2.
[50] Vassiliou outlines this as follows: 'according to Sathas (in Pierides 1993) it has been written "ολίγον μετά την υπό Τούρκων άλωσιν της νήσου", "a short time after the capture of the island by the Turks" (1570, in Pierides 1993)' (Vassiliou, The Word Order of Medieval Cypriot, 54–55).
[51] Παυλίδης (Ed.), Λεοντίου Μαχαιρά Χρονικόν. Cf. Vassiliou, The Word Order of Medieval Cypriot, 57.
[52] Παυλίδης (Ed.), Λεοντίου Μαχαιρά Χρονικόν, δ; Vassiliou, The Word Order of Medieval Cypriot, 55.
[53] Παυλίδης (Ed.), Λεοντίου Μαχαιρά Χρονικόν, στ'; Vassiliou, The Word Order of Medieval Cypriot, 54.
[54] Vassiliou, The Word Order of Medieval Cypriot, 58. Cf. Anaxagorou, Narrative and Stylistic Structures, 27.
[55] Νικολάου-Κονναρή, Πιερής (Eds), Παράλληλη διπλωματική έκδοση. Cf. Nicolaou-Konnari, 'A poor island…', 121 (fn. 5).
[56] Cervellin-Chevalier (Ed., transl.), Édition critique et traduction française; Cervellin-Chevalier (Transl.), Une histoire du doux pays de Chypre.
[57] Mas Latrie (Ed.), Chroniques d'Amadi et de Strambaldi; Coureas, Edbury (Transl.), The Chronicle of Amadi.
[58] Dawkins, Introduction, 5.
[59] Dawkins, Introduction, 5.
[60] Nicolaou-Konnari, Leontios Makhairas's Greek Chronicle, 163 (Abstract).
[61] Nicolaou-Konnari, 'A poor island…', 121. The relationship between the text of the *Chronicle* (Ravenna version) and Strambaldi's text is the subject of Νικολάου-Κονναρή, Η διασκευή, 287–315.

British Library, Harley 1825) containing extracts from the Oxford version.[62] In response to a statement by Christos Papadopoulos made in 1889, she mentions a previously existing manuscript that was kept in the library of the Makhairas Monastery on Cyprus, which burned down in 1892.[63] Nicolaou-Konnari emphasises that 'the comparative study of language' of the three manuscripts and an analysis of 'name usage' shows that there are no 'significant differences' or 'ideological deviations'.[64]

3.3. Historical studies

A primary source of important information on the history of Cyprus for this study was George Hill's (1867–1948) four-volume work,[65] particularly the second volume, devoted to the period of Latin presence on the island, from the arrival of Guy de Lusignan in 1192 until the death of King Janus in 1432. Hill's study offers a comprehensive overview and organising of facts drawn from numerous source texts, both Greek and Western, as well as their interpretation. Historical details of the period of Frankish rule on the island, important for the accomplishment of this monograph's objectives, were also drawn from two publications that accessibly describe the history of Cyprus from prehistoric to modern times, by Mariusz Misztal and Katia Hadjidemetriou.[66] Łukasz Burkiewicz's book,[67] which focuses on a specific period (the fourteenth century) and contains an in-depth analysis of the island's political position in the Mediterranean world, gives an overview of the broader context of Cypriot politics. To a large extent, all the scholars mentioned above based their work on Makhairas' *Chronicle*, which is one of the fundamental sources on the history of Cyprus. The three-volume edition of Steven Runciman's work, first published in English in the years 1951–1954,[68] has also proved helpful. Material collected by Claude Delaval Cobham[69] and Louis de Mas Latrie[70] served as a substantial source of documents related to the history of Cyprus. In Polish historical literature mentions of Polish-Cypriot relations in the Middle Ages and the Renaissance may also be found.[71]

4. Research method

This work is interdisciplinary. The *Chronicle* is examined from the perspective of history of literature, with a special focus on religious and political categories, and to a lesser extent, rhetorical-literary categories. The fragments that contain a depiction of individual religious communities and the relations between them are analysed and interpreted in detail.

The monograph is based on a PhD thesis written under the supervision of Prof. Małgorzata Borowska and Prof. Przemysław Kordos (Faculty of 'Artes Liberales', University of Warsaw) and defended at the Faculty of Polish Studies of the University of Warsaw in 2018. In the PhD thesis, which was written in Polish, the author's own translation of Makhairas' text from Cypriot Greek into Polish was used, with references to Dawkins' translation (where difficulties in comprehending the Cypriot original were encountered), and the draft translation of the *Chronicle* into Polish by Prof. Małgorzata Borowska.[72] This book contains Dawkins' translation of longer fragments (alongside Dawkins's translation of MS O inserted in parentheses), which have been set off from the main text (in italics), sporadically accompanied by comments. All the remaining excerpts drawn from the *Chronicle*, translated by the author of the monograph to Polish, were translated into English by the translator (except the few situations where words and short phrases in the analysis are taken from the longer passage in Dawkins' translation, quoted earlier). Similarly, longer quotations from the *Chronique*

---

[62] Nicolaou-Konnari, Leontios Makhairas's Greek Chronicle, 163.
[63] Nicolaou-Konnari, Leontios Makhairas's Greek Chronicle, 164.
[64] Nicolaou-Konnari, 'A poor island…', 137.
[65] Hill, A History of Cyprus I, II, III, IV.
[66] Misztal, Historia Cypru; Hadjidemetriou, A History of Cyprus [Greek version Χατζηδημητρίου, Ιστορία της Κύπρου].
[67] Burkiewicz, Polityczna rola królestwa Cypru.
[68] Runciman, A History of the Crusades 1, 2, 3.
[69] Cobham (Ed.), Excerpta Cypria.
[70] Mas Latrie, Histoire de l'île de Chypre I, II, III.
[71] Burkiewicz, Σχέσεις Κύπρου-Πολωνίας, 18–47.
[72] See Machieras, Wykład o słodkiej ziemi Cypru.

d'Amadi (extracted from the main argument in italics) are taken literally from Peter Edbury and Nicholas Coureas' English translation. All the remaining references to its content (alongside translation of single words and short phrases) were created in Polish using the Italian original and occasionally confronted with Peter Edbury and Nicholas Coureas' English translation. The translator translated the Polish version into English.

An overarching theme of the deliberations is the author's life story, the language he selected for his work, the literary community, style and the potential addressee. A comparative analysis of the *Chronicle* and other texts from the period (such as the *Chronique d'Amadi*, *Le Songe du Vieil Pelerin* by Philippe de Mézières and Usāma Ibn Munqiḏ's *Kitāb al-I'tibār*) is carried out to enrich the adopted perspective. For examining contacts between different groups of Christians, the contextual approach (Stephen Bevans, Angie Pears, Stephen Coburn Pepper) and the classification of dimensions of confessional and religious reality devised by Roderic Ninian Smart have been deemed helpful. The starting point for the discussion of the contacts between Christians and Muslims is establishing the qualities of such a meeting, with reference to Hugh Goddard's concept of 'mutual perceptions', and then indicating the reasons for the chasm in contacts of this kind from the point of view of 'interreligious hermeneutics' scholar Werner Jeanrond.

Furthermore, the topic of interdenominational and interethnic relations is conceptualised in the categories of colonialism; it is discussed why the *Chronicle* may be investigated using selected concepts developed by colonial studies and the postcolonial school of interpretation. Despite an awareness that the beginnings of postcolonial criticism were in the 1950s and 1960s, when countries and regions colonised by Europeans, such as Algeria (colonised by the French in the years 1830–1962)[73] or India (colonised by the British in the years 1858–1947),[74] began to regain their independence, an attempt is nevertheless made to show that a knowledge of terminology forged by followers of this school of thought permits an apt analysis of the religious relations in Frankish Cyprus presented by the Medieval chronicler.

4.1. 'Medieval postcolonial studies'

> *Hybrid, uncanny bodies like those of the medieval giant [...] suggest that even if the period is alluringly strange, it is at the same time discomfortingly familiar.*[75]

Adepts of colonial studies and the postcolonial school have developed a number of concepts to characterise phenomena and situations that are underpinned by various forms of a nation's dominance over another. While aware of the distinct historical differences between the Middle Ages and contemporary times, medievalists have seen the application of these concepts within their discipline as an opportunity for a more in-depth understanding of phenomena occurring in the medieval age and of the literary texts describing them thanks to an extensive perspective of 'otherness'[76] and recognition of how important the voices of the subjugated are for the histories and narratives that had previously excluded them.[77] They realised the significant fact that the Middle Ages influenced processes occurring in Europe in modern times thanks to, as Lisa Lampert-Weissig indicates, the 'interrelated genealogies' of the two disciplines.[78] Helen Young writes that 'the postcolonial and the medieval are closely intertwined'.[79] Young considers that it is this 'recognition' of similarities that precipitated more intensive studies in this direction.[80]

---

[73] Benrabah, Language Conflict in Algeria.
[74] Knight, Britain in India.
[75] Cohen, Midcolonial, 5.
[76] Concepts such as the 'o/Other' and 'o/Otherness' were successfully and multifoldly adapted and used by Frantz Fanon, Edward Said, Gayatri Chakravorty Spivak, etc., which demonstrates some 'travel of concepts'. See Fanon, Black Skin, White Masks; Al-Saidi, Post-colonialism Literature, 95; Said, Orientalism; Gingrich, Conceptualising Identities, 11. Terms such as 'travel of concepts' or 'travelling concepts' have been discussed in Bal, Wędrujące pojęcia.
[77] Noteworthy works include: Biddick, The Shock of Medievalism; Holsinger, Medieval Studies, Postcolonial Studies; Mallette, European Modernity and the Arab Mediterranean; Prawer, Latin Kingdom of Jerusalem; Warren, History on the Edge. The term 'postcolonial medieval studies' often appears in the subject literature. See Lampert-Weissig, Medieval Literature and Postcolonial Studies, 19; Kabir, Williams, Introduction, 10.
[78] Lampert-Weissig, Medieval Literature and Postcolonial Studies, 20.
[79] Young, Constructing 'England', 2.
[80] Young, Constructing 'England', 2.

It is worth stressing that this subchapter discusses whether medieval texts, similar to the *Chronicle*, can be analysed applying this method. However, it should be remembered that some concepts used by this school have a longer history. For example, images of the self and the other in medieval literature have been investigated many times and the theory of the self and the other have been formulated by various philosophers and thinkers (Martin Heidegger, Edmund Husserl, Simone de Beauvoir, etc.) The colonial or postcolonial perspective narrows the spectrum of aspects (to the forms of relationships determined by the presence of representatives of one culture imposed upon those of the other) under study on the one hand and broadens it on the other (places the persons concerned in the context of larger wholes).

According to Sharon Kinoshita, for postcolonial thought it is important that the medieval history of contacts between Europe and Asia or Africa is a significant element of a longer history, of which colonialism and postcolonialism are a part (this conviction has led scholars to search for proto-orientalist elements in medieval epic literature and romances).[81] Strikingly, practically each of the scholars who have taken the courageous decision to write a more extensive work on the subject has voiced the hope that intensive exchange of thought would continue, benefiting both disciplines.[82]

Jeffrey Jerome Cohen, one of the pioneers of this type of thought and its applications, proposes the term 'midcolonial' in opposition to the term 'neocolonial' coined by Spivak, defining it as:

the time of 'always-already,' an intermediacy that no narrative can pin to a single moment of history in its origin or end.[83]

He explains the rationale for such a definition:

Just as there was never a time before colony, there has never yet been a time when the colonial has been outgrown.[84]

Here Cohen, considering tension between 'alterist approach' and 'continuist approach',[85] stresses two main problems that underpin the opposition of some historians, historiography specialists and theorists of literature to using colonial and postcolonial tools to investigate medieval texts. These are: a habit of treating the Middle Ages as dimension of the Other, a domain replete with peculiarities of all kinds and an undefined gap between Antiquity and modern times,[86] and the conviction (held mainly by followers of the postcolonial school) that common planes in the history of the Middle Ages and modern history cannot be sought. Shared by these two problems is the perception of a chasm between medieval times and other ages, and of their singularity and isolation.[87]

Patricia Clare Ingham and Michelle R. Warren opine on this matter, underscoring the dismissive attitude that scholars of colonial and postcolonial studies have towards the possibility of finding, for instance in medieval history, a similar depiction of conquests as in modern times:

postcolonial studies claim distance from premodern histories so as to deny the relevance of premodern dynamics of conquest and settlement to subsequent expansionist projects. Indeed, postcolonial critics question the very existence of colonialism in the absence of modernity.[88]

---

[81] Kinoshita, Deprovincializing the Middle Ages, 81–82.
[82] Davis, Altschul, Medievalisms in the postcolonial world. Cf. Altschul, Postcolonialism and the Study of the Middle Ages, 588–606.
[83] Cohen, Midcolonial, 3. Cohen's postulates are often cited by followers of this trend of thought, including Young, Constructing 'England', 3–5.
[84] Cohen, Midcolonial, 3.
[85] Cohen, Midcolonial, 5.
[86] Cohen uses following phrases: 'a field of undifferentiated alterity', 'hard-edged alterity', 'the West's shadowy "other"' (Cohen, Midcolonial, 3–4). Lampert-Weissig suggests that regardless of naming and accepted periodisation the Middle Ages have formed the subject of interest for many scholars and artists: 'The long, rich story of the Middle Ages is one that scholars and artists were writing even before the fourteenth-century poet Petrarch referred to a "middle time" between the glory of Rome and a better time that he saw as yet to come.' (Lampert-Weissig, Medieval Literature and Postcolonial Studies, xxxix).
[87] Cohen, Midcolonial, 3–6.
[88] Ingham, Warren, Introduction, 1.

This allegation is repeated after them among others by Lampert-Weissig and Young.[89] Ingham and Warren, accenting the problematic nature of the concept of 'colonial modernity' still more strongly than Cohen, show that anxiety or aversion towards crossing the boundary between medieval and modern is present on both sides: medievalists fear accusations of anachronism; followers of postcolonialism are impeded by the conviction that their discipline is inherently bound to modernity.[90] Cohen notes that the topic's controversiality may be related to the fact that medieval scholars have not themselves clearly set the boundaries of their discipline, which has become conducive to reflexive exclusion of further interpretations.[91] At the foundation of this aporia, conflict has arisen between those who recognise historical continuity between the Middle Ages and modernity, and their opponents. Cohen challenges the reasonability of such arguments, because 'both these metanarratives contain truths about the relation of the medieval to the modern and postmodern'.[92] Looking closer at the Otherness of the Middle Ages, Cohen refers to the concept of *extimité*, coined by Jacques Lacan as a portmanteau of the French *exterieur* and *intimité* (he himself translates it as 'extimacy' or 'intimate alterity'[93]), and compares it to the concept of abjection[94] originated and popularised by Julia Kristeva. Both these concepts point to a centre, characterised in terms of a certain alterity, which is deeply rooted in the structure of that which has achieved a definable identity, but is treated as exterior due to its differentiation from it, and which nevertheless interacts with the identified root. Cohen portrays such an intimately other being by citing the monster metaphor, which in his opinion is 'the embodiment of the medieval itself'.[95] And when considering the Middle Ages as a whole, completely exterior to modernity but intimately fused with it (not least because the processes occurring in the modern world have their source in those occurring in the Middle Ages), the attempt may be made to find the seeds of various oppositions, such as self–other, that have burgeoned in colonial and postcolonial reality, in the stuff of the medieval substrate. *Extimité* in Cohen's understanding is a marginal residue (associated with spoilage) arising after 'transformation' of 'the raw Real of the world […] into the Symbolic structure of culture'.[96] In this context, the metaphor of the monster (a figure which has numerous representations in medieval culture) is recalled. The monster is what medievality itself symbolises in this perspective: fearsome and repulsive, but also bearing undefinable closeness and propinquity.[97]

A reference to 'intimacy' also appears in the chapter on contrapuntal histories by Ingham, who, citing the results of Bruce Holsinger, literally indicates the 'intimacies' between the medieval historical method and postcolonial history.[98]

A sense of intimacy is an important factor mythologising the experience. John Noyes, who investigates 'the space of a colony' by analysing the impact of literature on 'structuring the experience of the colony'[99] states that 'colonial discourse […] creates an unlimited mobility across boundaries' and 'reconfirms these boundaries within a totalized experience of space.'[100] Noyes creates the idea of '**the mythical mastery**

---

[89] When defining the aim of her work, Lampert-Weissig notes that in order to understand concepts such as 'race' and 'hybridity', one should become acquainted with 'the premodern texts and contexts' in which they are rooted (Lampert-Weissig, Medieval Literature and Postcolonial Studies, xl). Helen Young mentions various reasons why followers of colonialism and postcolonialism dismiss the possibility that any form of colonialism existed e.g. in the Middle Ages. She also underlines that some are ready to admit that colonialism did take place at that time, but simultaneously try to set a clear boundary between its two types, while from her point of view it is 'a matter of perception rather than intrinsic differences' (Young, Constructing 'England', 1–2).
[90] The conviction, held by most followers of postcolonialism and a group of medievalists, that modernity is the determinant of postcolonialism, has been called the 'alibi of modernity' in Ingham, Warren, Introduction, 3.
[91] Cohen lays part of the responsibility for difficulties with defining the frames within which the Middle Ages should be studied on medievalists themselves. In his characteristic, vivid style he states: 'The supposed "hard-edged alterity" of the medieval for which some scholars have argued not only provides an astigmatic lens through which to examine such an enormous and heterogeneous time span, but—as Kathleen Biddick has shown—also manages to avoid confronting the colonialist traumas that mark the emergence of medieval studies as a discipline.' (Cohen, Midcolonial, 4).
[92] Cohen, Midcolonial, 5.
[93] Cohen, Midcolonial, 5.
[94] Cohen, Midcolonial, 5. See Kristeva, Powers of Horror.
[95] Cohen, Midcolonial, 5. Cohen often cites this metaphor. See Cohen (Ed.), Monster Theory; Cohen, Of Giants.
[96] Cohen, Midcolonial, 5.
[97] Cohen, Midcolonial, 5.
[98] Author e.g. of: Holsinger, Neomedievalism; Holsinger, The Premodern Condition. Ingham, Contrapuntal Histories, 51.
[99] Noyes, Colonial Space, 1. Based on literature about the German colonies established and maintained in South-West Africa in the years 1884–1915.
[100] Noyes, Colonial Space, 20.

of space',¹⁰¹ which places emphasis on the mythic function of colonial literature, giving the described phenomena of encounters with 'otherness' the status of a myth. Namely, the 'colonial' narrative is a narrative about the start of a new reality that emerges from chaos, about the meeting with an unknown and unnamed force, the crystallisation of rules of coexistence in one space of weaker conquered peoples with stronger invaders (gods vs. men) – who despite being a minority have real or imagined power – and the unavoidable confrontations between them, and finally, about the formation of a specific moral code, inherently binding in this hybrid world.

Cohen, on the other hand, takes the part of a commonsensical optic, favouring a 'localizing, perspectivist epistemology'.¹⁰² He proposes an attempt to look at phenomena occurring in the medieval world as phenomena set in a specific context. He believes it is necessary to reconsider temporal references of the term 'middleness' with respect to the Middle Ages in the same way that followers of postcolonialism strive to erase them from the prefix 'post'.¹⁰³

Ingham, meanwhile, postulates a **contrapuntal**, nonbinary look at historical and methodological differences, which

> *engage the diversities of various historical fields, so as to assess the complicated repetitions and patternings of violence and desire in various colonized spaces without thereby conflating them.*¹⁰⁴

The contrapuntal approach should thus involve many methodologies and numerous historical perspectives. It should also, according to Ingham, emphasise the fact that 'distinct histories of opposition related to and yet excluded from standard accounts of European rule' should be examined from different angles.¹⁰⁵ The scholar assumes that with respect to 'premodern cultures', it is necessary to make visible all the planes and aspects involved in the process (such as pressure, violence) of, as she terms it, the 'Making of Europe',¹⁰⁶ but also to give a closer picture of 'the multiple medieval versions of "the East"'. This multifacetedness of contexts and cultural frames implies unavoidable 'instabilities of categories such as "saracen" and "pagan"'.¹⁰⁷

The scholars who participated in this discussion have taken various perspectives: Deepika Bahri has opposed identifying colonialness with the West; Kalpana Seshadri-Crooks has moved the boundary still further, suggesting that no single geographic area should be ascribed to postcolonial studies, while Vilashini Coopan has similar thoughts concerning the temporal dimension.¹⁰⁸

An original approach is offered by the authors of the collected volume *Postcolonial Approaches to the European Middle Ages*, who are not only unafraid of charges of anachronism or improper application of methods, but also voice the opinion that they are able to provide to adepts of postcolonialism 'a rigorous historicization of their own insights'.¹⁰⁹ Its editors Ananya Jahanara Kabir and Deanne Williams define translation understood 'as a mechanism of and metaphor for cultures in contact, confrontation, and competition' as its main focus.¹¹⁰ For the authors of the publication translation is simultaneously: 'a metaphor for postcolonial writing itself, with the literal act of translation embodying the asymmetrical power relations and violence of different colonialisms' as well as 'a means of rehabilitating wonder' and 'the transfer of language, culture, and power'.¹¹¹ Such translation, the scholars claim, occurs on many planes, between disciplines (medieval and postcolonial studies) and between genres (including historiography, classical and vernacular literatures),¹¹² which once again indicates the two-directional impact of these disciplines and the research they undertake. The phenomenon of translation is associated with something

---

[101] Noyes, Colonial Space, 20.
[102] Cohen, Midcolonial, 6.
[103] Cohen, Midcolonial, 6.
[104] Ingham, Contrapuntal Histories, 54. The author of the concept of 'contrapuntal reading' is Said, who postulates: 'We must therefore read the great canonical texts [...] with an effort to draw out, extend, give emphasis and voice to what is silent or marginally present or ideologically represented [...] in such works.' (Said, Culture and Imperialism, 66). This kind of reading is forced by ambivalence manifesting on the narrative level.
[105] Ingham, Contrapuntal Histories, 55.
[106] A term that appears in Bartlett, The Making of Europe, 950–1350.
[107] Ingham, Contrapuntal Histories, 55.
[108] The positions of Bahri, Seshadri-Crooks and Coopana cited after Ingham, Warren, Introduction, 4–6.
[109] Kabir, Williams, Introduction, 7.
[110] Kabir, Williams, Introduction, 10.
[111] Kabir, Williams, Introduction, 6–7.
[112] Kabir, Williams, Introduction, 7.

what they call 'historical nostalgia', possessed of the capability to incite 'empathy', 'recognition' and 'wonder'.[113] Translation creates the multi-layered images of the Middle Ages and 'the idea of the Middle Ages itself is the product of ceaseless decenterings, displacements, and translations'.[114]

Simon Gaunt, though aware of historical differences between the Middle Ages and modernity, sees the application of a 'postcolonial perspective' as a chance for deeper analysis in the field of medieval studies, because due to the fact that it accents different aspects it elucidates 'things that were less visible or less in focus using other critical approaches'.[115]

He rightly observes that certain situations, phenomena and narratives (discourse) about events occurring in the medieval period may be interpreted as 'colonial' or 'postcolonial', because they concern possible, universal human behaviours and reactions to the imposition of a culture from the outside. The situations that are treated in this book as 'colonial' (bearing the hallmarks of a 'colonial' situation) include the takeover of Middle Eastern lands by the crusaders for an extended period (without specifying the form of that takeover, i.e. conquest, financial transaction, agreement), due to their guiding objective of using the captured areas for their own purposes and subjugating the nations inhabiting them. According to the perspective adopted in this monograph, the phenomena with 'colonial' overtones are those whose description may be analysed using theoretic literary concepts developed by proponents of the postcolonial school (such as 'self'/'other',[116] 'centre'/'periphery'[117]). Contacts between allochthons and autochthons representing differing cultures, denominations and religions are considered to be such. Finally, 'colonial' narratives are those where the above situations and phenomena find a verbal reflection.

In defining the nature of 'colonial literature' after the pioneers of the approach, it should be highlighted that according to Elleke Boehmer it **'reflects a colonial ethos'**[118] and according to Ania Loomba it emphasises the **'appropriation'** of aspects of the other's culture.[119] Loomba attributes the ability to create binary oppositions between the 'self' and the 'other' to language and literature.[120] In her opinion, colonial literature not only 'reflects' the colonial situation, but also 'creates ways of seeing and modes of articulation that are central to the colonial process';[121] contains an element of hybridity (the example given by Loomba is 'the European appropriation of non-European texts and traditions');[122] enters a dependent relationship with non-literary texts (travelogues, atlases) and 'colonial discourses and practices';[123] is subject

---

[113] Kabir, Williams, Introduction, 10.
[114] Kabir, Williams, Introduction, 10.
[115] Gaunt, Can the Middle Ages Be Postcolonial?, 175. Sharon Kinoshita notes: 'One preoccupation of the emerging field of "postcolonial" medievalism has been precisely to excavate the nineteenth-century roots of our discipline, revealing the mutual imbrication of medieval studies, colonialism and nationalism.' (Kinoshita, Deprovincializing the Middle Ages, 81).
[116] A central place in dualistic postcolonial discourse is occupied by two dichotomous and complementary concepts: 'the self' and 'the other'. Bill Ashcroft, Gareth Griffiths and Helen Tiffin see the usage of the concept of the 'other' by the creators of postcolonial theory as originating in 'the Freudian and post-Freudian analysis of the formation of subjectivity' proposed by Jacques Lacan, who made the important distinction between the 'little other' and the 'big Other (*grande-autre*)' (Ashcroft, Griffiths, Tiffin, Post-colonial Studies, 155–156). With the help of the first of these figures Lacan constructs his concept of the 'mirror stage', which refers to the identification of the subject, that is its acquiring of its 'image' (Lacan, Stadium zwierciadła, 6). Ashcroft, Griffiths and Tiffin provide a (post)colonial interpretation of these Lacanian constructs ('imperial centre, imperial discourse, or empire itself' as Other; the coloniser as Father/'the Symbolic Other') (Ashcroft, Griffiths, Tiffin, Post-colonial Studies, 155–156). Cf. Gingrich, Conceptualising Identities, 10–11. Marian Bielecki introduces the category of 'the same' which brings a new shade to this dynamic of concepts: 'Otherness exists not beyond discourse, does not originate from some absolute externality, but is located – may be located – within The Same. The Same and that which is Other remain mutually enmeshed, making possible not only communication, but also outwitting the metaphysical logic of The Same. Here opens the field of "different" and "invention" and the capacity to discover the Other through negotiation of The Same and that which is Other, that which is general and that which is individual.' (Bielecki, Kłopoty z innością, 9. Translated by Kupiszewska).
[117] Confrontation between invaders and the conquered peoples leads to the crystallisation of a 'centre' of the new world in the space arbitrarily developed by the foreigners, and a 'margin' or 'periphery' (Ashcroft, Griffiths, Tiffin, Post-colonial Studies, 32–33).
[118] However, she owns that it is hard to formulate or obtain a 'precise definition' (Boehmer, Colonial and Postcolonial Literature, 2).
[119] Loomba underlines that colonial literature is written by the colonised as well as by the colonisers, so the transfer and appropriation of aspects of both cultures is two-sided (Loomba, Colonialism/Postcolonialism, 63).
[120] In her understanding between 'a European self' and 'a non-European other' (Loomba, Colonialism/Postcolonialism, 66).
[121] Loomba, Colonialism/Postcolonialism, 66.
[122] Loomba, Colonialism/Postcolonialism, 67.
[123] Loomba, Colonialism/Postcolonialism, 70.

to interpretation and judgement by critics, who influence how it is read by a broader group of recipients;[124] and has the property of accenting the 'unbridgeable gap' between colonisers and colonised peoples.[125]

Taking into account criticisms of such an approach formulated among others by Gabrielle Spiegel,[126] Lampert-Weissig, convinced that 'ideological groundwork for colonialism was being laid well before 1492',[127] raises the same point as Kabir and Williams. Namely, that research on the Middle Ages and studies of nineteenth and twentieth-century colonialism and postcolonialism mutually influence each other, i.e. 'postcolonial theory has influenced the reading of medieval texts and contexts', and 'medievalists have provided important critiques of key terms and concepts in postcolonial studies'.[128] The author shows how many aspects must be taken into account to obtain a full picture: that colonialism has its germs in medieval times, and that later these germs were variously analysed and conceptualised,[129] and also that the very discipline of medieval studies was shaped along with this, what history has brought, thus with colonialism.[130]

To illustrate her assumptions, Lampert-Weissig examines: a medieval Iberian love poem written in Arabic and Old Spanish, *Guillaume de Palerme* (William of Palerme), an Old French romance about werewolves, Wolfram von Eschenbach's *Parsifal* epic written in Middle High German and a fourteenth-century travel narrative, *The Travels of Sir John Mandeville*, applying a postcolonial perspective.[131] Further, the scholar broadens the spectrum of her investigations to include the representatives of medievalism Juan Goytisolo, Salman Rushdie, Tariq Alegi and Amitav Ghosh in her analysis, who present Islam's contact with the West via reference to the medieval context.

Another noteworthy work, deemed a breakthrough by Suzanne Conklin Akbari,[132] is the publication *Medievalisms in the Postcolonial World*[133] edited by Kathleen Davis and Nadia Altschul, who, as Akbari writes:

lay the foundations for the second generation of such studies, in which an informed self-awareness of the stakes of an investment in the medieval past is of crucial importance.[134]

In recent years many studies have appeared whose authors applied the findings of the colonial and postcolonial school to the examination of medieval texts and phenomena. Suffice it to cite several to show how impressive has been the scope of their reflection. Young, for example, developed a postcolonial interpretation of the medieval English romance. Michael Faletra penned what he calls 'the Medieval Colonial Imagination', focusing on Geoffrey of Monmouth's *Historia Regum Britanniae* and its influence on other works (such as Chrétien de Troyes' *Eric and Enid*, John of Salisbury's *Policraticus* and Gerald of Wales' *Topographia Hibernica*).[135] José Rabasa examined the periodisation of the history of Mesoamerica,[136] Hernán G.H. Taboada described the nature of orientalism in Spain.[137] Meanwhile, Haruko Momma suggested that the Middle Ages may have influenced the sense of identity of the contemporary Japanese.[138] Both monographs and collected works are published from time to time, and each of the latter contains, next to objectives or a manifest in the introduction, at least several if not a dozen different perspectives.[139]

---

[124] Loomba, Colonialism/Postcolonialism, 74.
[125] Loomba, Colonialism/Postcolonialism, 79.
[126] Author e.g. of Spiegel, The Past as Text. The use of results from postcolonial studies to investigate medieval topics has been criticised in Spiegel, (rev.) Medievalisms in the Postcolonial World, 617–625.
[127] Lampert-Weissig, Medieval Literature and Postcolonial Studies, 2.
[128] Lampert-Weissig, Medieval Literature and Postcolonial Studies, xxxix. Cf. Young, Constructing 'England', 2.
[129] Lampert-Weissig, Medieval Literature and Postcolonial Studies, 2.
[130] Lampert-Weissig, Medieval Literature and Postcolonial Studies, xxxix. Cf. Young, Constructing 'England', 2.
[131] Lampert-Weissig, Medieval Literature and Postcolonial Studies, xl.
[132] Author e.g. of: Akbari, Seeing through the Veil; Akbari, Idols in the East.
[133] Davis, Altschul (Eds), Medievalisms in the postcolonial world.
[134] Akbari, (rev.) Medievalisms in the postcolonial world, 328.
[135] Faletra, Wales and the Medieval Colonial Imagination. In his review of this work David Rollo uses the phrase 'the burgeoning field of post-Conquest Insular studies'. Rollo, (rev.) Wales and the Medieval Colonial Imagination (https://michaelfaletra.weebly.com/wales-and-the-medieval-colonial-imagination.html, accessed 22 November 2021).
[136] Rabasa, Decolonizing Medieval Mexico.
[137] Taboada, 'Reconquista'.
[138] Momma, Medievalism.
[139] Huot, Postcolonial Fictions; Labossiere, Chosen Champions; Kinoshita, Medieval Boundaries; Frojmovic, Karkov (Eds), Postcolonising the Medieval Image; Burke, Tamm (Eds), Debating New Approaches to History. In 2014 the 49th International Congress on Medieval Studies: Postcolonial Disability in the Middle Ages (Medieval and Renaissance Studies Program, Purdue University) was held (https://scholarworks.wmich.edu/cgi/viewcontent.cgi?article=1051&context=medieval_cong_archive, accessed 19 October 2021).

Publications in languages other than English appear regularly.[140] Moreover, the discourse on theoretical applications of the tools of colonial and postcolonial studies has started to spread to other periods of history such as the Renaissance.[141]

The above positions are summarised to give the Reader an awareness that discussion of the possible ranges and results of such an application are constantly ongoing, and through them both disciplines are undergoing an enriching transformation. The assumptions of 'postcolonial medieval studies' have permitted the author to distinguish elements of the depiction of interreligious contacts in the *Chronicle* that would have not been a focal point had other critical approaches been used (such elements are considered to include an extended and multi-layered image of otherness or difference of one group versus other groups, the shaping of power dynamics and traces of the author's complex identity).

As indicated in the introduction, before the Lusignans' arrival in the twelfth century, Cyprus was influenced by multiple elements, but it was only after the Franks came that, for the first time in its history, it became the subject of such an extensive narrative detailing its occupation by representatives of a different (in this case, western) nation. Scholars such as Angel Nicolaou-Konnari and James Schryver use the term 'colonisation' for Frankish rule on the island. As Iona McCleery observes, it was the islands on the Mediterranean and Black Seas and the Atlantic that were among the first European colonies.[142]

Phenomena and situations related to Byzantine Greek-Frankish contact described in the *Chronicle* are called 'colonial', with an awareness that the term 'colonial' is used anachronistically. In no place in the monograph is it suggested, however, that Frankish Cyprus is an instance of a colony in the nineteenth- or twentieth-century sense. On the margin it should be noted that the research literature features discussion of whether the use of the term 'crusader colonialism' for the crusades and the term 'proto-colonists' for crusaders is justified.[143] In this book, the words 'colonisation' and 'colonial' are placed in quotation marks only in order to emphasise that solutions from the colonial school and postcolonial studies have been used. It is not intended to signal doubts as to the method adopted. The other approaches discussed, such as hybridisation, remain in the background, 'obscured by the postcolonial school approach' in the sense that the phenomena that can be described using them are strictly dependent on the enforced presence of the Franks.

The decision to take such a direction in the analysis of the *Chronicle*'s content was strongly influenced by the awareness of how significant the situation of its author was, having been born on an island taken over three centuries prior by the Franks, and the conviction that this position was reflected in his work and in the way in which he places hints as to his identity in the narrative. Leontios had bound his professional career with the Frankish elite and this experience shaped his personal involvement in its dealings. Makhairas' work is particularly suited for examination using this method as he was able to directly observe the coexistence on Lusignan Cyprus of two different communities: the Greek-speaking native population, that is the native Cypriots (among whom Rhomaioi made up the largest share) and the Frankish immigrant population, the Lusignans and those who had come with them, the Genoese, Venetians and smaller groups from the West.

The problem of differences between Greeks and Latins (doctrinal, institutional, ceremonial and also at the level of language, laws and customs) indicates the presence of 'oriental leanings' in the *Chronicle*. According to Edward Said 'orientalism is a style of thought based upon ontological and epistemological distinction made between "the Orient" and (most of the time) "the Occident"'.[144] In orientalist discourse representatives of the Occident get acquainted with the Orient 'by making statements about it, authorizing views of it, describing it, by teaching it, settling it, ruling over it'.[145] Such discourse has nothing in common with the truth, as Ashcroft, Griffiths and Tiffin suggest, being a form of constructing the other.[146]

---

[140] Uhlig, Quand 'Postcolonial' et 'Global' riment avec 'Médiéval', 1–24; Plaza, Paradigmas en contacto, 55–66; Weiss, El postcolonialismo medieval, 177–200.

[141] Brantlinger, Victorian Literature and Postcolonial Studies; Kaul, Eighteenth-Century British Literature and Postcolonial Studies; Raman, Renaissance Literatures and Postcolonial Studies; MacPhee, Postwar British Literature and Postcolonial Studies; Bohls, Romantic Literature and Postcolonial Studies; Patke, Modernist Literature and Postcolonial Studies.

[142] McCleery, What is 'colonial' about medieval colonial medicine?, 151–175.

[143] Slack, The Quest for Gain, 70–90 (The term 'crusader colonialism' in Slack, The Quest for Gain, 75). Prawer writes about 'European Colonialism in the Middle Ages' in Prawer, The Crusaders' Kingdom.

[144] Burzyńska, Markowski (Eds), Teorie literatury XX wieku, 552. Quotation after Said, Orientalism, 10.

[145] Said, Orientalism, 10.

[146] Ashcroft, Griffiths, Tiffin, Post-colonial Studies, 153.

A key issue is that this work is mainly concerned with analysing and interpreting the depiction of phenomena and relations of a religious nature, which gives the discussion a special direction. A quotation by Stephen Burns and Michael Jagessar from a book on the application of postcolonial theory in religious studies is apposite here:

Postcolonialism is [...] an elusive term as it resists being classified, lacking fixity and exactness. This may be one reason why it appeals to us, as much of what we have inherited in our Christian traditions is the result of attempts to neatly parcel our notions of truth and doctrine. The postcolonial is characterized by open-ended discursive practices, border-crossings and interplay.[147]

Restricting the scope of analysis is inevitable, but such phenomena and situations of a non-religious nature – provided that they contribute to the understanding of religious aspects – that concern the same planes of contact between representatives of the native culture and the settler culture are also distilled from the text of the *Chronicle* as in the case of nineteenth and twentieth century (post)colonial literature (reactions of characters from the world depicted in the literary work to 'otherness', different dimensions and manifestations of 'otherness', construction of identities by characters upon contact with the 'other', deconstruction by the literary scholar of the 'liminal' identity of the author, etc.) They are discussed with the help of concepts such as: 'the self', 'the other, 'identity', 'difference', 'alterity', 'the o/Otherness', 'othering', 'imagined geographies', 'contact zone', 'the third space', 'centre', 'periphery', 'catalysis', 'hybridity', 'ambivalence', 'narrative space', 'contrapuntal reading', 'metonymic gap', 'a colonial ethos' etc., proposed among others by Homi Bhabha, Frantz Fanon, Edward Said, Gayatri Chakravorty Spivak, Elleke Boehmer and Ania Loomba.

5. The structure of the book

The book consists of an Introduction, Chapters (One, Two, Three and Four), Final Conclusions, Appendices, Bibliography, Index of Places and Index of Persons.

The Introduction discusses the subject of the research, the state of the art, research methods and the structure of the work, and comments on the terminology used as well as a list of abbreviations are included.

In Chapter One Makhairas's life is presented, with particular emphasis on all the factors recognised to date that shaped his identity, and the content of the *Chronicle* is summarised since this work is not broadly known. An attempt is made to establish what audience the author addressed his message to and what his intended purpose was. The fact that the *Chronicle* was written in Medieval Cypriot Greek might indicate that his compatriots were its target audience. The most important features of this dialect are explained in order to emphasise its uniqueness and differences from Byzantine Greek. Moreover, the effects of the author's inquiries into the literature available on Lusignan Cyprus are shared. Next, Makhairas' work is compared with selected Byzantine and Western chronicles in terms of objective, style, language and structure so as to establish the degree of originality in Leontios' approach to the subject. Other selected sources concerning Cyprus are discussed to show how the topic was approached and how Makhairas' work is different in comparison. Further, it is verified whether the language used by the chronicler may be deemed manipulative, and finally, which elements of the *Chronicle*'s narrative caused me to interpret it as one that presents a 'colonial' situation.

The remaining three chapters, which make up the main part of this dissertation, focus on recreating, based on selected fragments of the *Chronicle*, the depiction of relations between one's own religious community and a foreign one and also on examining whether they change over time, and if so, how this is presented by the author. The way in which the Cypriot assigns the term ἄπιστοι ('infidel') to the Genoese, and how, to Muslims is treated here as a pivotal distinction.

The subject of Chapter Two is the multifaceted contact described in the *Chronicle* between Cyprus' Orthodox population, rooted in the spirituality of Byzantinum (and also in a particular place and history), otherwise called the Greeks, and the Latin newcomers (Templars, Hospitallers and representatives of the Lusignan dynasty), whose presence on the island lasted over four centuries, giving rise to far-reaching

---

[147] Jagessar, Burns, Christian Worship, 24.

processes of confrontation between these two types of religiosity. Much emphasis is placed on terms such as 'negotiations' and 'hybridisation' with respect to the nature of these relations, and also some attention has been given to models of contextual theology. This is because the author's intention is to look at the situation presented in the *Chronicle* of a multidimensional encounter between Byzantium and the West from the contextual point of view created by Stephen Bevans and built on by Angie Pears: based on the synthetic model that combines translational, anthropological and practical approaches.

In Chapter Three, in which the field of analysis is narrowed to a scope defined by Latin culture, the focus is on issues of how the *Chronicle* portrays the religiosity of groups from a single denomination (Latin), but different nations: mainly Cypriot Franks, Genoese and Venetians. The study leads to the discovery of the role that the island's conquest by the Lusignans plays in the later consolidation of the fourteenth-century Genoese and Venetian presence there (whether it facilitated their various operations on Cyprus and whether these were independent initiatives), as well as the features assigned to them by the chronicler and how he incorporates religion into the descriptions of these contacts.

Chapter Four is devoted to an analysis of selected sections of the *Chronicle* describing encounters between Christians and Muslims that bear the hallmark of a 'clash of civilisations', that is a clash of the internally heterogeneous Orthodox-Catholic world with the quite homogeneous but completely differing Muslim world. The focus is on whether Makhairas distinguishes any differences within the representatives of Islam and whether he demonstrates any knowledge about them in his work.

The book closes with the Final Conclusions, in which the findings made are summarised and some general comments are presented on the function that loyalty to the denomination (religion) inherited from one's ancestors has in intercultural contacts described in the *Chronicle*. It is (dis)loyalty to a denomination (religion), treated by the author of this book as the foundation and a significant element in the structure of events in Leontios's plot, that is the axis of this work as a whole, both in its spiritual and its political aspect. The concept of spirituality requires some caution and should be used – in this perspective – only to describe elements of the Christian faith from before the period of the 1054 schism (at the level of the *Chronicle*'s narrative these are objects or phenomena present in the descriptions of St Helena's activity, such as the Holy Cross relic, miracles, revelations).[148] Instead, terms such as 'religion' (for Christianity and Islam) and 'denomination' (for Orthodoxy and Catholicism) are used far more often.

The Appendices contain a discussion of Cyprus' geographical location and a chronology of key historical events from the fourth to the fifteenth century that are related to Cyprus and Christianity.

The Index of Persons and Index of Places respectively present a list of persons and of places that appear in the main body of the work (excepting the footnotes).

The structure of individual subchapters of the second, third and fourth chapter is tied to the study's focus on phenomena (e.g. cult of saints) and processes (e.g. conflicts and their progression from the event initiating the dispute, through battles, to attempts to make peace). Investigation of phenomena on a symbolical level provides a grasp of the key ideas of each community (e.g. the value of loyalty to God, the need to create a 'sacred space'), and the investigation of processes allows to deconstruct the depiction of the evolution of characters and groups that profess the given ideas, and the relationships between them. The meetings and confrontations described in the *Chronicle* were characterised by multilinearity, and also frequently impacted each other, forming a complicated system of relations and exchanges.

6. Terminological comments

In this work the distinction between 'denomination', used when writing about Orthodox Christianity and Catholicism, and 'religion', used for Christianity and Islam, is considered important. 'Orthodox Christianity' is understood to mean the 'doctrine of the Orthodox church' and 'Catholicism', the 'doctrine of the Latin Church'. The terms 'Greeks' and 'Latins' are adopted for believers of these two denominations and the term 'Rhomaioi' is used for citizens of the eastern Roman Empire, whose cultural identity is defined

---

[148] As Wilhelm Gräb rightly notes, 'a concept of spirituality' (*der Begriff der Spiritualität*) is 'too broad a concept' (*diffuser Containerbegriff*) (Gräb, Spiritualität, 31). According to Gräb it may be used to designate 'all forms of individualist religion' (*alle Formen individualistischer Religion*) that do not have a strict connection to institutional religion, particularly as the genesis of 'religion itself' (*ihre Genese*) and 'its meaning' (*ihre Geltung*) are connected with the individual (Gräb, Spiritualität, 31). Kupiszewska's translation from author's Polish translation of short extracts from Gräb's text.

here, after Nicolaou-Konnari, via three elements: loyalty to the emperor, the Greek rite and the Greek language.[149] In the case of Syrian immigrants and representatives of Christian denominations (Jacobites, Maronites, Nestorians) the one term, 'Syrian', is used and analogously for the citizens and members of the Eastern Orthodox denomination, who are assigned the name 'Armenian'.

The term 'Franks' is usually used in the literature for Latins of different nations, emphasising not only their denominational, but also social, economic and political affiliation. However, in this book, it is usually used to denote the population that arrived on Cyprus with the Lusignans. When writing about the inhabitants of Cyprus, the author distinguishes between 'Cyprians' and 'Cypriots'. The first refers to the population of Cyprus before the arrival of the Lusignans, and the second, to the group composed of Cyprians and Franks. Most of the Cyprian community was composed of Rhomaioi, who as Greeks spiritually belonged to the Byzantine world and used Cypriot Greek, characterised by specific regional features.[150]

The adjective 'Frankish' is used to refer both to the Lusignans, who came from Poitou in central-western France,[151] and to the group composed of representatives of various Western states such as Genoa and Venice.[152]

Where an author of Greek origin publishes in English, the anglicised version of their name and surname is used when their work in that language is cited. Place names spellings takes into account the version selected by Makhairas. Where comments of Latin authors or scholars who use the Latin version are referred to, however, this is also provided (and so instead of 'Ammochostos' the form 'Famagusta' is given; instead of 'Lefkosia', 'Nicosia' and for 'Lemesos', 'Limassol'). The Latin names of popes and patriarchs and other Latin names are given in the form in which they are used in English-language literature.

In discussing particular aspects of the *Chronicle* content, selected Cypriot terms and phrases taken from Makhairas' text are added in parentheses. Proper names, nouns in the nominative case, which in most cases perform the function of the subject – either the noun alone or combined with an adjective – are given without articles. Such insertions are systematically and selectively incorporated also in passages of Dawkins' translation. For the most part, these terms and phrases refer to the religious sphere or reflect the linguistic picture of perceptions and relationships between various religious groups as well as expose Makhairas' view on them (individuals and groups). When the content of the *Chronicle* is referred alongside Cypriot equivalents, the abbreviation 'LM' is used to indicate the place in the text where the information was taken from. When reference is made to other places of the edition (introduction, notes, indexes, footnotes), the full bibliographical address, i.e. Dawkins (Ed., transl.), Ἐξήγησις/ Recital, is cited.

Greek proper names are usually listed in the index in parentheses. The exceptions are names specified by Makhairas that are to be found in the main argument. Proper names in English are usually quoted after Dawkins, especially when the content of the *Chronicle* is approximated (with few exceptions such as e.g.: Khirokitia and Lemesos). In other cases, the ELOT 743 standard is used for the transliteration of Modern Greek proper names, unless the person concerned uses a different notation, e.g. when signing her/his article. Names of medieval historiographers are in conformity with the convention adopted in Dunphy, Bratu (Eds), The Encyclopedia of the Medieval Chronicle Online (Brill 2014–2021). Medieval proper names not present in this publication were written in the same convention. To record Makhairas' text the polytonic system of Greek orthography (after Dawkins' edition) is adopted (including the following diacritics: *acutus*, *circumflexus*, *gravis*, *spiritus asper* and *spiritus lenis*). When the last syllabe of quoted Cypriot word or phrase is accented, *gravis* has been changed into *acutus*. For Modern Greek quotations the monotonic system is used. In the subject literature the title of the *Chronicle* is used in both notations.

The following dictionaries were used to translate (or understand) words, phrases and expressions from Cypriot/Greek: Γιαγκουλλῆς, Θησαυρός τῆς Κυπριακῆς Διαλέκτου; Κριαρᾶς, Λεξικό; Liddell, Scott, A Greek-English Lexicon; Liddell, Scott, An Intermediate Greek-English Lexicon and https://www.wordreference.com/ (accessed 2013–2021).

---

[149] Nicolaou-Konnari, Greeks, 14.
[150] Nicolaou-Konnari, Greeks, 58, 61.
[151] Maddox, Sturm-Maddox, Introduction, 2. John of Arras' work tells of a legend according to which the Lusignan family were descendants of the mermaid Melusine. See John of Arras, Melusine.
[152] Michel Balard stresses: 'Because from the eleventh century in Byzantium and the Middle East all arrivals from the West, and so not just the French, but also the Italians, Catalans, Flemish, English, Germans, etc. were called Franks, I do not use the form "Frankish", which refers only to the Franks, but "Franconian" to indicate people of all western nations arriving in Byzantium and the Levant or settled there from the eleventh to the fifteenth century' (Balard, Łaciński Wschód, 15, fn. 1. Translated by Kupiszewska).

ISO UW style is used for the spelling of Arabic titles.

Dates (birth, death and ruling dates of rulers and popes) are consulted with: Hill, Hadjidemetriou, Misztal and Burkiewicz.[153]

7. List of abbreviations

The following abbreviations are used in this work:

LM = Λ. Μαχαιράς [L. Makhairas], Ἐξήγησις τῆς γλυκείας χώρας Κύπρου, ἡ ποία λέγεται Κρόνακα τουτἔστιν Χρονικ(όν) / *Recital Concerning the Sweet Land of Cyprus entitled 'Chronicle'*, R.M. Dawkins (Ed.), 2 vols, Oxford 1932.

MS V = Ven. Marc. gr. VII, 16, 1080, 375 f. {Manuscript of the *Chronicle*}

MS O = Oxon. Bodl. Selden, supra 14, 331 f. {Manuscript of the *Chronicle*}

MS R = Raven. Class, gr. 187, 184 f. {Manuscript of the *Chronicle*}

ΘΚΔ = *Θησαυρός της Κυπριακής Διαλέκτου. Ερμηνευτικό, Ετυμολογικό, Φρασεολογικό και Ονοματολογικό Λεξικό της Μεσαιονικής και Νεότερης Κυπριακής Διαλέκτου*, Κωνσταντίνος Γ. Γιαγκουλλής, δ.φ. Βιβλιοθήκη Κυπρίων Λαϊκών Ποιητών, απ. 70, Διευθυντής-Επιμελητής. Δπ. Κ.Γ. Γιαγκουλλής (Ed.), Λευκωσία 2009.

---

[153] Hill, Historia Cypru II; Hadjidemetriou, Historia Cypru; Misztal, Historia Cypru; Burkiewicz, Polityczna rola królestwa Cypru.

I. Leontios Makhairas and his work

In this chapter the biography of Leontios Makhairas is presented and selected topics regarding the linguistic and narrative layer of the *Chronicle* are discussed, such as: Medieval Cypriot Greek, Cypriot literature and its potential impact on the *Chronicle*, and the narrative of Leontios' work in the light of the Byzantine and Latin chronicle-writing tradition. Next, other texts (mainly chronicles) that present elements of Cyprus' history are detailed, it is shown what the 'colonial' situation in the *Chronicle* involves and the language of manipulation present in the text is examined.

1.1. Life and work of Leontios Makhairas

Sources state that the chronicler was born in 1360 or 1380 and died after 1432,[154] Dimitra Pavlakou describes him as a 'descendant of an eminent family of Orthodox Cypriot Greeks' (γόνος σημαντικής οικογενείας ορθόδοξων Ἑλλήνων της Κύπρου),[155] and Coureas deems him the most famous Rhomaioi to work in the Lusignan administration and underlines that in the context of Leontios' clear personal involvement in the affairs of the Frank elite, which made maintaining a critical distance impossible, his opinion on representatives of the Latin dynasty is 'highly ambivalent'.[156] Coureas notes, however, that despite holding an important post and despite strongly declared sympathy towards the Catholic rulers, Makhairas was sincerely attached to the Orthodox past of the island, which was likely due to the person of his father.[157]

Kyrris lists the elements that in his opinion made it possible for the *Chronicle*'s author to become acquainted with Latin culture. In the first place he places the close connection of Makhairas' family with the royal court and the probable education of Stavrinos' children in Latin schools.[158] He writes thus about the Makhairas family's connections:

> *So the family was closely linked with the royal family and court, and the same is true of the Greek or Greek-Syrian families of Genoese protection related with the Makhairades, e.g. the Sebacs, the Hareris, the Bilis, the Sozomenoi.*[159]

---

[154] Nicolaou-Konnari, Alterity and identity, 37. Dawkins believes 1380 to be the more likely date of Makhairas' birth, while Loizos Filippou (Philippou) supports the date 1350–1360, arguing thus 'partly on the basis of his brothers being at the siege' (Petre, The Fortifications of Cyprus, 37, fn. 128). Dawkins states: 'He seems to have been born not much before 1380; we know of him from Bertrandon de la Brocquière, as having been in 1432 at Laranda in Lycaonia on a mission from King John II of Cyprus to the Grand Karaman, Ibrahim Beg' (Dawkins, The Nature of the Cypriot Chronicle, 3). Edbury notes that Makhairas' narrative abounds in details and complex descriptions where the years 1359–1374 are concerned, the rest of the narrative is abbreviated and 'cursory'. Therefore the scholar asks: 'Did he start from scratch, or did he embellish a pre-existing account, expanding the narrative by making use of documents and oral traditions?' (Edbury, Machaut, Mézières, Makhairas and Amadi, 352).

[155] Παυλάκου, Εξήγησις της γλυκείας χώρας Κύπρου (http://digital.lib.auth.gr/record/7030/files/npa-2004-6775.pdf?version=1, accessed 18 November 2021). Kupiszewska's translation from the Polish translation by the author.

[156] Coureas, Religion and ethnic identity, 16.

[157] Coureas, Religion and ethnic identity, 16.

[158] Kyrris, Some Aspects, 169.

[159] Kyrris, Some Aspects, 168.

Kyrris, judging the Cypriot Greek used by Makhairas to be poorer and less refined than Byzantine Greek, voices the conviction that education in the Western mode likely made it impossible for the chronicler to gain a sufficient mastery of a 'richer' Greek, which, he believes, is proved by the language of the *Chronicle*.[160] The scholar concludes, that the level of this language

> *is not very much higher than that of the authors of the numerous marginal notes in mediaeval Cypriot manuscripts. It is mainly ecclesiastic-theological, of a popular character.*[161]

According to Kyrris Makhairas had not read the works of the Fathers of the Church (Byzantine or classical), as otherwise this would be evident in his text, while quotations from the Bible were provided by him only in translation to Cypriot Greek,[162] and even access to archival material and Greek, Latin and French sources could not improve this state of affairs.[163] As an example he quotes the following sentences from the *Chronicle*: 'ψέματα τῶν ψεμάτων, ὅλα εἶνε ψέματα used instead of ματαιότης ματαιοτήτων τὰ πάντα ματαιότης' (Eccles. 1, 2) or 'οὐδὲν ὠφελοῦν ἀλλὰ μᾶλλον μάλλωμαν γινίσκεται instead of οὐδὲν ὠφελεῖ, ἀλλὰ μᾶλλον θόρυβος γίνεται' (Matt. 27, 24).[164] In Kyrris' opinion Makhairas must have known the Bible in the original since, as he argues, he must undoubtedly have participated in Greek services.[165] He phrases this radical hypothesis thus:

> *[…] in view of his incontestable Orthodox-Byzantine feelings and mentality, he must, no doubt, have been attending mass in Greek churches […].*[166]

The selection of such a notation may have resulted from 'some set of principles instinctively or subconsciously functioning in his mind',[167] that is, as he explains, 'a general plan automatically imposed on him by cultural factors interplaying in the society'.[168] It was with an eye to being fully understood, the scholar argues, that Leontios selected his vocabulary, translating old-fashioned Latin and Greek expressions to Cypriot Greek, and forgoing words 'outside [the prevailing] code'.[169] The scholar further hypothesises that Makhairas' theological knowledge and philosophical formation was the result of occasional 'discussions' rather than comprehensive study.[170]

In the *Chronicle*, Makhairas refers to Stavrinos (Σταυρίας Μαχαιράς) using the expression τοῦ πατρός μου τοῦ κυροῦ Σταυρινοῦ τοῦ Μαχαιρᾶ ('my father, the honourable[171] Stavrinos Makhairas') in LM III 566 and τὸν πατέραν τὸν κύρην Σταυρινὸν τοῦ Μα(χαι)ρᾶ ('the priest, the honourable Stavrinos Makhairas') in LM IV 608. Dawkins explains the discrepancies between different versions of the translation of the word πατήρ in this second fragment:

> *From § 566 we know that this Stavrinos Makhairas was the father of Leontios Makhairas, but in this passage he is simply called* the father, *and O reads τὸν παπᾶ,* the priest, *followed by Str., p. 254, with il prete ser papa S. de M. The μου which Sathas inserts after τὸν πατέραν, thus turning* the father *into* my father, *has no manuscript authority at all. The most that can be said for Sathas is that V's reading is ambiguous.*[172]

---

[160] Kyrris, Some Aspects, 169.
[161] Kyrris, Some Aspects, 169–170.
[162] Kyrris, Some Aspects, 170.
[163] Kyrris, Some Aspects, 170–171.
[164] Kyrris, Some Aspects, 170 (fn. 11). Cf. Dawkins, Notes, 119 (§ 189.1). The first sentence from the Bible means: '[…] vanity of vanities! All is vanity.' The second sentence, which in the *Chronicle* means '[the Catalans, sensible people, seeing that] they could do nothing but rather that an argument was beginning […]' has its source in the Bible: '[So when Pilate saw that] he could do nothing, but rather that a riot was beginning.' All quotes on the basis of New Revised Standard Version (NRSV) of the Bible, https://www.biblegateway.com/versions/New-Revised-Standard-Version-NRSV-Bible, accessed August–December 2021).
[165] Kyrris, Some Aspects, 171.
[166] Kyrris, Some Aspects, 171.
[167] Kyrris, Some Aspects, 171.
[168] Kyrris, Some Aspects, 171.
[169] Kyrris, Some Aspects, 172. Information in square brackets added by Kupiszewska.
[170] Kyrris, Some Aspects, 170.
[171] Dawkins' translation: 'Master'.
[172] Dawkins, Notes, 201.

Leontios was not the only son of Stavrinos, of whom he wrote with distinct pride in LM IV 608, that as a learned (ὡς γοιὸν λόγιον) man he had become famed for his theological knowledge (ἐξ ἀκοῆς ἐγίνωσκεν πολλὴν θεολογίαν). At the royal court, three more sons had been born to the chancellor: Nicholas, Paul and Peter. The first two fought the Genoese in the siege of Kerynia in the years 1373-1374. Paul was employed until 1385 as secretary to John de Neuville, viscount of Lefkosia, while from the start of his career at the Lusignan court until 1401 Nicholas held the function of secretary to Sir John de Nores, a scion of the oldest Frankish noble family.[173] Peter, meanwhile, tried his luck as a squire of King Janus in 1427. Leontios mentions Paul with the words:

> *And at that time Sir*[174] *Galio de Dampierre (σὶρ Γγαλιώτη Ταπέρες) and Sir Bertolacci Trari (σὶρ Μπερτουλάτζε Τράρε) of Florence (Φλουρουντῖνοι) went away and took with them also my*[175] *brother, Sir Paul Makhairas (σὶρ Πὸλ Μαχαιρᾶ), their young squire*[176] *(παιδάκιν βαχλιώτην)* [...]. (LM II 110)

In LM III 499, Paul was chosen by the constable to be his squire, to 'stand in the field without fear' (νὰ στέκη εἰς τὸν κάμπον διὰ θαρούμενος) when fighting the Genoese. In LM IV 612 he was addressed, in his capacity as squire and secretary (γραμματικός) to John de Neuville, viscount of Lefkosia (σὶρ Τζουὰν τε Νεβίλες τοῦ βισκούντη τῆς Λευκωσίας), by Sir Nicol Busat who requested permission for an overseas voyage. The name 'Paul Makhairas' appears also in the Oxford manuscript of the *Chronicle*, in episode LM III 572, and refers to a servant of Queen Eleanora who was subjected to such cruel torture that he decided to commit suicide. Dawkins objects to this version, arguing that a different Paul, surnamed Marshal, was meant.[177] According to Leontios, Peter, immortalised in fragment LM V 630 as 'Machis' (Μαχής), carried keys from Lefkosia to Ammochostos in 1402.[178] The next paragraph LM V 631 mentions three of Stavrinos' sons: Peter (Περρὴς Μαχαιρᾶς), presented as a 'royal servant' (ὁ βαχλιώτης τοῦ ρηγός), Leontios (ἐγὼ ὁ Λεόντιος) and Nicholas (σὶρ Νικὸλ Μαχαιρᾶς), his elder brother (μεγαλήτερος), both secretaries of John de Nores (τοῦ [...] σὶρ Τζὰν τε Ν(όρ)ες). Together with Henry de Giblet, Peter took part in the suppression of the peasant revolt in the years 1426-1427 (described in LM V 697).[179] Nicholas turned out to be 'an excellent crossbowman' (καλὸς τζακράτορος), who 'cocked a crossbow with power' (ἐκόρδωννεν δυνατά) in fighting with the Genoese.[180] Referring to his own participation in the battle of Khirokitia in 1426, Makhairas tells how the marshal of Jerusalem forbade him (ὥρισέν με τὸν Λεόντιον τοῦ Μαχαιρᾶ, 'forbade me, Leontios Makhairas') to issue wine to anybody until supplies were replenished (LM V 679).

The *Chronicle* contains a mention of Sir Philip (σὶρ Φιλίππος), teacher and tutor of Peter II, and also 'a Latin priest who was the son of a Rhomaic nun' (ἱερεὺς λατῖνος, ὁ ποῖος ἦτον υἱὸς μίας καλογριᾶς Ρωμέσσας, LM III 566).[181] In LM III 633, Makhairas, as Coureas notes too, also mentions his sister's son (ὁ ἀνιψιός μου), Sir George Bili (σὶρ Τζόρτζε Μπιλής), who held the position of governor of Cyprus (ὁ κουβερνούρης τῆς Κύπρου),[182] and was called 'the cleverest of men' (φρενιμώττερος ἄνθρωπος) by the governor of Genoa Boucicault (Μπουτζεγκάτ) in 1403. In 1402, George took part in the preparations to retake Ammochostos from Genoese hands (LM V 630). Dawkins recreates a part of his family tree, concluding that his father was Sir Nicholas Bili (σὶρ Νικὸλ Πηλή), a tax collector (πράκτορας).[183] George's brother, Sir Badin Goneme (σὶρ Πατὴν (Γουν)νέμε),[184] belonged to a group – probably consisting of Rhomaioi[185] – that in 1426 'welcomed' (ἐπροσδέκτησαν) Saracens in Lefkosia (LM V 693). The chronicler

---

[173] Coureas, Religion and ethnic identity, 17.
[174] In ΘΚΔ we read that 'σίρ(ε)' comes from the French 'sir(e)', meaning 'master'/'sir'. ΘΚΔ, 427. After Dawkins this term is translated as 'Sir'.
[175] In the text: 'του' 'his'.
[176] Cf. Dawkins, Notes, 96. Miller and Sathas translate it as *serviteur*. See Sathas, Miller (Eds, transl.), Chronique de Chypre, 61.
[177] Dawkins, Notes, 195. Παυλίδης (Ed.), Λεοντίου Μαχαιρᾶ Χρονικόν, 441 (fn. 1).
[178] Dawkins, Notes, 209.
[179] Giblet, also Jubail. Spelling after Dawkins.
[180] LM III 475, 495.
[181] Kyrris refers to this particular fact in Kyrris, Some Aspects, 168.
[182] Coureas, Religion and ethnic identity, 17.
[183] Dawkins, Notes, 192 (comment 7 to LM III 563).
[184] See Dawkins' Family tree in Dawkins, Notes, 192.
[185] Dawkins writes: 'It is plain that the Greeks deserted the French and went out at once to make terms with the Saracen conquerors.' (Dawkins, Notes, 229; comment 1 to LM V 693).

details that they 'lit candles' (ἄψα λαμπάδες) and 'poured courage into [the invaders'] hearts' (ἔδωκάν τους καρδίαν). This would be an ignominious episode in the history of the author's distant family.

The name 'Makhairas' is also borne in the *Chronicle* (only, as Dawkins notes, in the Venice manuscript[186]) by a Cosmas[187] (Κοσμᾶ Μαχαιρᾶ), who during the fighting with the Genoese in 1374 held the post of 'quartermaster'[188] (σακκουμάνος), and changed the name of his slave Baxis (Μπαξής), a baptised Saracen[189] (who spoke French), calling him 'Antony' (Ἀντώνιος) and adding the surname 'Makhairas' (LM III 456).

Already such single references suffice to reveal a fragment of the chronicler's heterogeneous genealogy and indicate factors that influenced his personality and thus the nature and message of his work, as well as his perception and understanding of cultural difference. Makhairas writes about himself and his experience in an individual situation also in LM II 96, where he remembers the sad fate of Tsoles (Τζολές) and Tsetsious (Τζετζίους), sons of the Nestorian Francis Lakha, the second of whom 'killed a man' (ἐσκότωσεν ἄνθρωπον), and then joined the Knights Hospitaller and lived in great poverty, while the first was an itinerant village salesman[190] and a visitor of his brother. Leontios uses, as an interjection, the marked term 'poor thing' (πτωχούλλικος) with reference either to Tsetsious in his struggle with poverty, or to Tsoles in his life of hardship. Citing his own observations, he emphatically stresses: 'I saw him (i.e. the first) with my own eyes' (εἶδα τον μὲ τὰ 'μματία μου) and 'him (i.e. the second) I also saw' (εἶδα καὶ κεῖνον).[191]

Leontios started his career in 1401 as a secretary of Sir John de Nores, and was employed in 1426 as the person responsible for wine for the army (when the forces were preparing for the battle of Khirokitia). He took part in an embassy sent to Ibrahim Beg, ruler of the Karaman emirate, in 1432.[192] Nicolaou-Konnari cites the testimony of the traveller Bertrandon de La Broquière, who met the Cypriot chronicler in that same year, and had the occasion to discover his very good knowledge of French.[193] The scholar concludes:

> *We may thus consider Leontios to have been a member of that group of bilingual or multilingual civil servants and administrators who belonged to the Greek and Syrian burgesses, had access to both the Greek and the Latin worlds participating in both cultures, and acquired social and economic prominence in virtue of their education and linguistic abilities.*[194]

Nicolaou-Konnari posits the hypothesis that the chronicler's name suggests a link with villages located in the Troodos Mountains and the Makhairas Monastery[195] – a conviction shared by Anastasios Orlandos[196] – which Dawkins did not want to believe[197]. According to its etymology, μάχαιρα means 'knife', 'short sword', 'long dagger', 'kindjal', the name of a precious stone,[198] and does not necessarily have to be connected with this particular family. The Makhairas Monastery is famous for its image of the Virgin Mary Makhairotissa, that is the 'Virgin Mary of the Knife' (Μαχαιριώτισσα).[199]

---

[186] Dawkins, Index of Names of Persons, 297.
[187] Notation of the name after Dawkins.
[188] This translation of 'σακκουμάνος' is used after Polish translation ('stanowniczy') by Prof. Małgorzata Borowska.
[189] Dawkins, Index of Names of Persons, 297.
[190] Dawkins gives MS O's version: 'ἐγίνην γρουτάρης καὶ ἐγύριζεν εἰς τὰ χωργιά', and translates it as: 'he took to going round villages, peddling sweet-meats'. See Dawkins (Ed., transl.), Ἐξήγησις/ Recital, 86 (fn. 3).
[191] LM II 96. Mas Latrie (Ed.), Chronique de Strambaldi, 38 gives a changed and abbreviated version of the paragraph on Tsoles and Tsetsious, not providing any version of their names: *Li quali erano tutti duoi gran valent huomini; et quando tuolsero li Genovesi Famagosta, li tuolsero tutto quello che havevano et tutta la loro ricchezza che havevano in Famagosta tutti duoi li fratelli. L'uno venne nel'hospital et lo stoccova el sonava le campane; et l'altro devento marcer, et andava atorno per li casali.*
[192] Coureas, Religion and ethnic identity, 17. The emir's name is given after Dawkins, The Nature of the Cypriot Chronicle, 3.
[193] Nicolaou-Konnari, 'A poor island…', 122. Dawkins also cites this testimony in Dawkins, The Nature of the Cypriot Chronicle, 3.
[194] Nicolaou-Konnari, 'A poor island…', 122.
[195] Nicolaou-Konnari, Alterity and identity, 45.
[196] Reference to Orlandos' publication after Kyrris, Some Aspects, 169 (Orlandos, Ἡ Μονὴ Σαγματᾶ, 73).
[197] Dawkins clearly underlines that such a connection is unconfirmed (Dawkins, Notes, 85; comment 2 to LM I 74).
[198] See Liddell, Scott, A Greek-English Lexicon; 'μαχαίρι' in Modern Greek.
[199] This name appears in LM I 74. Konrad Kuczara explains that the origin of the name is that God sent a knife to the monks who wanted to take the icon of the Virgin Mary out from a cave (Kuczara, Kościół prawosławny na Cyprze, 320). Dawkins cites Hackett, who writes 'that some hold the name due to the sharp cold of the climate there, and others to the story that the icon of the Virgin kept there was found in a cave with a sword buried by it' (Dawkins, Notes, 85–86; comment 2 to LM I 74).

According to Pieris, Leontios must have died in 1432, because the *Chronicle* lacks any mention of the important event that was Janus' diplomatic mission to the sultan of Iconium. Pieris presents Makhairas as a man with a 'strong historical conscience' who was both a Byzantine and a monarchist.[200] According to him, the *Chronicle*'s author held the position that it was the responsibility of 'the local people of Cyprus, Greeks and Hellenized Orthodox Cypriots' to 'ensure the immutability' of their language and religious identity,[201] a thought that he phrases as follows:

> *Makhairas sees himself as Byzantine not least according to his 'natural upbringing', that is, an education founded in the emotional stocks of Byzantine popular and folk tradition. His formal learning is French, but his convictions and feelings are those of a Greek Orthodox Byzantine.*[202]

Pieris holds the opinion that the chief indication of Makhairas' Byzantine consciousness is that he invokes the person of Constantine the Great (at the very beginning of the *Chronicle*), seeing him as the 'temporal lord of Cyprus',[203] and hypothesises that the chronicler's 'profoundest wish'[204] was for the island to be incorporated into the Byzantine Empire. According to him this is particularly visible in LM I 22, where Guy de Lusignan foresees a possible rebellion of the local Greek people against the island's Latin rulers.[205] We should remember, however, that in writing about St Constantine, Makhairas is referring to a Christianity before the 1054 schism, and so a 'Byzantine consciousness' cannot literally mean an 'Orthodox consciousness'. Pieris suggests that Makhairas' Cyprians chose to accept the Franks' presence on the island to protect themselves against attacks by the Turks, who terrified them. According to this reading, Leontios would have expected that the forces of the Greeks and Latins would combine and as a result, repulse the followers of Islam.[206]

This view is contrary to Nicolaou-Konnari's position, according to which Makhairas is not interested in the possibility of a Greek-Latin reconciliation, as his narrative ignores the fourth crusade (1202–1204), which culminated in the capture of Constantinople by Western forces, and the union of the Churches brought about by John V Palaiologos in 1360.[207]

For Pieris the chronicler's 'deep religious feelings' towards the richness of Cyprus' Byzantine tradition are 'self-evident'.[208] This is proved by the following elements present in the *Chronicle* narrative: letter of the bishops, emphasising the 'saintliness' of the island, criticism of the Latins, who envy the privileges granted to Greeks (jealousy of the Holy Cross), praise for expelling the monk Peter de Thomas from Cyprus (done by the Lusignans themselves), and also emphasising the importance of efforts to preserve the faith of one's fathers.[209] Another phenomenon observed in the *Chronicle* is kind of manipulation of the facts (e.g. via omission of some of them), enlarging the role of the Greek clergy and undermining the status and importance of the activity of the Catholic priesthood and saints, both in terms of numbers and in terms of overlooking the real importance of individual figures. It is worth mentioning, for instance, that the above-mentioned Peter de Thomas, expelled from the island in anger, actually took an active part in events that played out in the Mediterranean Basin, fought bravely and tenaciously against the Muslims, and even became a saint of the Catholic Church.

Anaxagorou compares the different positions on Makhairas' 'ethnoreligious ideology' that have so far emerged. She cites two specialists, who find both Orthodox and Latin elements in the work of the *Chronicle*'s author: Konstantinos Sathas, who deems Leontios to have been a Greek who clearly cared for the Orthodox 'ancestral faith' of the island despite the strong influence of foreign rule, and Dawkins, who sees signs of sympathy towards the Frankish government in the chronicler's attitude, although he remains Greek 'deep down'.[210] Anaxagorou names George Hill, Konstantinos Spyridakis, Giannis Lefkis and Nikos

---

[200] Pieris, The Medieval Cypriot Chronicler, 108.
[201] Pieris, The Medieval Cypriot Chronicler, 108.
[202] Pieris, The Medieval Cypriot Chronicler, 108.
[203] Pieris, The Medieval Cypriot Chronicler, 108.
[204] Pieris, The Medieval Cypriot Chronicler, 109.
[205] Pieris, The Medieval Cypriot Chronicler, 109.
[206] Pieris, The Medieval Cypriot Chronicler, 109.
[207] Nicolaou-Konnari, Alterity and identity, 61.
[208] Pieris, The Medieval Cypriot Chronicler, 109.
[209] Pieris, The Medieval Cypriot Chronicler, 109–110.
[210] Anaxagorou, Narrative and Stylistic Structures, 15.

Lanitis as scholars who emphasised Makhairas' pro-Western inclinations[211] and counts Georgios Zoras, Fanis Michalopoulos, Kostas Kyrris, Alexandros Pallis, Petar Tivčev and Katia Galatariotou among scholars convinced that Leontios's worldview was Byzantine.[212] As we see on the basis of the summary presented above, the range of readings of the *Chronicle* is broad: from calling its author a 'monarchofascist', which Lanitis did by Anaxagorou's account, to Zoras' claim that Leontios' approach was Orthodox, and highly fundamentalist at that.[213]

The deeply emotional relationship of the *Chronicle*'s author to his home island is incontestable. He himself refers to it with expressions such as: 'sweet land of Cyprus' (ἡ γλυκεία χώρα Κύπρου) in the title of the *Chronicle*, 'islet' (νησσάκι, LM II 158), 'such a beautiful island' (τόσον ὄμορφον νησσίν, LM I 4), 'holy island' (ἁγία νῆσσος, LM I 30), 'precious land of Cyprus' (ἡ ἀκριβής χώρα Κύπρου, LM I 1), 'Cyprus, deserving of utmost praise' (πανθαύμαστη Κύπρος, LM I 3) and 'famous Cyprus' (περίφημος Κύπρος, LM I 31). He also notes a phrase uttered by the Frankish king, for whom Cyprus had become 'our place' (τόπος μας, LM I 17). In this narrative, the island seems dominated by the Franks, however. On the one hand, the chronicler uses the Greek names of saints, members of the priesthood and representatives of the Greek population,[214] and sometimes also Byzantine rulers,[215] but on the other he makes representatives

---

[211] Anaxagorou, Narrative and Stylistic Structures, 16.
[212] Anaxagorou, Narrative and Stylistic Structures, 16.
[213] Anaxagorou, Narrative and Stylistic Structures, 16.
[214] Makhairas does not assign the Rhomaioi/Greeks any particular characteristics that would necessitate a unilateral reading of the depiction of the group as a whole. The portrait of the Rhomaioi population is diverse and composed of mentions concerning individuals: these are usually brief references on the basis of which conclusions may be drawn about the perception by the *Chronicle*'s author of what he called the 'common folk' (τὸ κοινὸν τοῦ λαοῦ, τουτέστιν ποπλάνους, LM V 685). Among the people, Leontios includes the boy George, who had a vision of the Togni Cross (LM I 69–74), thus making him a depositary of a Christian mystery. Costas Philitsis (Κώστας ὁ Φιλίτζης) and Michael Psararis (Μιχάλ ὁ Ψαράρης) are featured in the role of Greek messengers sent to Peter I by the inhabitants of Gorhigos (LM II 114). Yafouni (Γιαφούνης), a Lefkosia shopkeeper, attempts to influence Peter I's brothers who rebelled against the ruler (LM II 275). Lefkosia resident Psilidi (Psichidis, Ψιχίδης) (LM III 399, 440) guards a constable to prevent his escape and then dies tortured by the Genoese. Dimitrios Daniel, Queen Eleonora's young secretary (ὁ γραμματικὸς ὁ μικρὸς τῆς ῥήγαινας ὀνόματι Δημήτρης Δανιέλ, LM III 427–431, 461–462, 504–508), whose tale Makhairas describes in the most detail, shows resourcefulness and loyalty to the queen. Alexis/Alexopoulos the Cretan (κύρης Ἀλέξιος ὁ Κρητικός, LM III 564, κύρης Ἀλεξόπουλλος/ὁ ποῖος Ἀλεξόπουλλος ἦτον Κρητικός, LM III 568–577), a soldier in Thibald's army who together with him brought about the death of the priest Philip, King Peter II's adviser, is thus portrayed by the chronicler: '[a man] with a bad head, who first kills a man and then says: "I will shoot you"' (κακῆς κεφαλῆς, ὅπου πρῶτα σκοτώνει τὸν ἄνθρωπον καὶ τότε λαλεῖ του: 'Βαρύνω σε θέλω!' LM III 569). Interestingly, when the crime comes to light, the queen comes to Alexopoulos' defence, trying to convince the king that Thibald had initiated the murder, because Alexopoulos, being 'foreign' (ὡς ξένος) and 'idle' (ἄπρακτος) may have been convinced that he was carrying out the king's orders (ἐφάνην ὅτι ἤτζου ἦτον ὁ ὁρισμό(ς) σου καὶ ὑποτάκτην τοῦ ὁρισμοῦ σου, LM III 573). This did not save him from death, however. Other examples include Andronikos, a resident of Gorhigos (Ἀντρόνικος ὁ Κουρουκιώτης, LM 652, 660), and Rekouniatos (Ρεκουνιάτος, LM V 657, 660), murdered cruelly by Muslims and canonised by the pope. Makhairas lists those killed at Khirokitia in 1426: Dimitris Lakas/Lakkas (Δημήτρης ὁ Λακκάς, LM V 680) and representatives of the people: the one-eyed ropemaker George (Τζο(ρ)τζής ὁ σκοινοπλόκος), George the shoemaker (Τζορτζοὺς ὁ τζαγκάρης), Phakelatos (Φακελάτος), apothecary Nicholas Primikyris (Νικόλας ὁ Πριμικύρης ὁ μυροψίος), Nicholas Safini of Markas (Νικολῆς Σαφίνης Μαργαζάνης) (LM V 685), thus giving them due honour. Also named are Sir John Laskaris (σὶρ Τζουὰν Λάσκαρης, LM II 194) and, several times, Sir George Monomakhos (σὶρ Τζόρτζε Μονομάχο, LM III 362, 563), Greek knights from Constantinople. Xenos (Ξένος), an Ammochostos resident (LM IV 626) who in 1369 sent a message from his hometown saying he would turn the town over to King James, was murdered. Charlotte's retinue includes John Rondos (Τζουὰν Ρόντος) (LM V 642). Meanwhile, John Sinklitikos, a doctor (Τζουὰν Συνγκριτικὸς ὁ ἰατρὸς, LM V 665), took part in an embassy to the son of a Damascus sheikh. Pella, the wife of a potter (κυρὰ ἡ Πέλλα ἡ μουχρουτίνα, LM V 695), who fought flames together with Khanna, prevented the Saracens from burning down Lefkosia. Alexis (ρὲ Ἀλέξης, LM V 696–697, 700), hailed king by the Greek people during the peasant uprising of 1426–1427, beats and robs the Latin bishop, brother Solomon, commits 'many evil deeds' (πολλὴν μεγάλην ἀντροπήν), and is then executed in the last year of the revolt. The last Greek character in the *Chronicle* is Karvouna (Καρβούνα), mother of the abbot of Antioch (πιούρης τῆς Ἀντιοχείας, LM VI 710); however, it should be remembered that these are fragments written after Makhairas' hypothetical death (recognised by some scholars only). The ethnic origin of Galeftira, the cook of John de Lusignan (μάγειρος τοῦ πρίντζη ὁ Γαλευτηρᾶς, LM III 419) and Khanna of Damascus (LM V 695) is unknown. The portrayal presented by the chronicler is heterogeneous. No single pattern can be found. The characters are placed in the narrative as if in passing, between other figures. Some of them are characterised by exceptional features such as: tenacity and loyalty to God (like Andronikos and Rekouniatos), courage and determination (like Pella), willingness to carry out the orders of other (like Alexopoulos), readiness to serve the king or queen (like Yafouni and Dimitrios Daniel), and others, by negative ones (like 'King' Alexis). The list of Khirokitia dead given by Leontios, often accompanied by their profession or characteristic feature (e.g. the one-eyed ropemaker George) is an important element of the narrative about the consequences of war, which gives the nameless and mute people a more pronounced personality. Drawn up based on Dawkins, Index I, 277–310 and the *Chronicle*. Dawkins notes Mas Latrie's comment that Sir John Silvani (σὶρ Τζουὰν Σουλουάνη) came from a Rhomaioi, Cypriot family (Dawkins, Notes, 208).
[215] Makhairas includes the following representatives of the Byzantine world in his narrative: St Constantine (LM I 3, 4, 6), Empress Helena (LM I 4–9), Isaac Komnenos (LM I 9), Alexios V Komnenos (LM I 18), 'Kyr' Manuel Katakouzinos (LM I 63), John V Palaiologos (LM III 344, 346–349) and Helena Palaiologina (LM VI 709, 712). Drawn up based on Dawkins, Index of Names of Persons, 277–310.

of Latin families the main movers and participants of the events described in his work. The exception is the Makhairas family to which he himself belongs. This indicates that the *Chronicle*'s author had more contact with members of the Frankish aristocracy, though his field of interest also included individuals belonging to the Greek community, whose lives were influenced by the settlers' political decisions.

1.2. Medieval Cypriot Greek

To record his history Makhairas chose the vernacular of the local population, the Cypriot dialect referred to by scholars as the 'Medieval Cypriot Greek', and by Kyrris 'the dialect of a Greek borderland'.[216] Leontios thus forwent the French language[217] used by the aristocracy, which he knew due to his high function at the Lusignan court. Pieris comments on the chronicler's choice, claiming he had taken the decision (απόφαση) to:

'να μην γράψει το έργο του στα γαλλικά τα οποία γνώριζε άπταιστα, αλλά στη γλώσσα του απλού λαού της Κύπρου, τα ρωμαίικα, τα οποία σπούδασε ως αυτοδίδακτος σε αγιολογικά, είτε άλλα θαυμαστά κείμενα της ελληνικής εκκλησιαστικής και λαϊκής παράδοσης ή, ως περιδεής ωτακουστής, τα θησαύριζε [...]'.[218]

not write his work in French, which he spoke fluently, but in the language of the simple Cypriot folk, the Greek he had learned as an autodidact using hagiographic [texts] or other miraculous works of the Greek Church and the lay tradition, or on the basis of what he heard himself [...].[219]

According to Vassiliou, the *Chronicle* is 'the largest bulk of information in the Cypriot vernacular',[220] and the dialect itself, a 'tongue of primarily oral communication'.[221] Geoffrey Horrocks, the author of a work devoted to the history of Greek, also comments on this phenomenon, suggesting that the Cypriot vernacular was the first modern Greek dialect 'in its distinctive regional guise'.[222] Stavroula Varella thus comments the language of the *Chronicle*:

This language, characterised as lively and casual, occasionally enriched with some archaising forms [...] and an abundance of Romance loanwords, is an interesting popular variety, which contains most of the distinctive peculiarities of the later Cypriot dialect.[223]

The complex, specific shape of Medieval Cypriot Greek was therefore influenced by many factors, among which we should primarily list the characteristic location of Cyprus, on the one hand at some distance from the rest of the Greek world, on the other – at the crossroads of pilgrimage routes, near the Middle Eastern lands. Vassiliou took the effort of preparing a multiaspectual list of these reasons, taking into account historical factors, those 'internal' to language and 'extralinguistic' ones:[224]

    a)   *the long detachment of the island from the Greek-speaking core of Byzantine Greece*
    b)   *the influence of the Greek language on Cypriot for many centuries mainly through NT Greek*
    c)   *the need of the Cypriots to belong to a Cypriot ideal, similar to that of the Κοινόν των Κυπρίων, which in older times was based on the ideal of material (monetary support) and on the 'Cypriot unity among Cypriots [...]*
    d)   *the need of the Cypriots to belong to wider γένος των Ρωμαίων the race of the Byzantines [...]*

---

[216] Kyrris, Some Aspects, 174.
[217] Benjamin Arbel cites, among others, the testimony of Agostina di Verona in Arbel, Intercultural Contacts, 48.
[218] Πιερής, Σταθμοί, 172.
[219] Kupiszewska's translation from the Polish translation by the author.
[220] Vassiliou, The Word Order of Medieval Cypriot, 52–53.
[221] Vassiliou, The Word Order of Medieval Cypriot, 45.
[222] Horrocks, Greek, 360.
[223] Varella, Language Contact, 32.
[224] Vassiliou, The Word Order of Medieval Cypriot, 35.

e) the strong link of Cypriot Greek to Asia Minor Greek and or any other form of Anatolian Greek [...]'[225]

It is clearly evident that the set of factors determining, directly or indirectly, the shape of the dialect, and simultaneously rendering it unique, is extremely rich, as a result of which the texts written in it, such as the *Chronicle*, may be the source of interesting analyses.

For Kyrris, Leontios' language was '"potentially" the Byzantine Greek language', but 'corrupted' by 'simplification'.[226] He notes that the chronicler translates words from many languages such as Ancient Greek, French, Latin and Arab, in order 'to be sure that all his vocabulary belongs to the accepted code of notions and symbols of his [...] readers'.[227] This technique may be taken to mean that the *Chronicle*'s author semantically cleaned each phrase and modelled it to influence the reader in exactly the way he expected it to, leaving no room for his own interpretation and conjecture. According to Kyrris there were two reasons behind this: only this language was comprehensible to compatriots 'of his own class or/and of similar classes' and only such a language could be 'efficiently and effectively' used given 'the educational and cultural realities'.[228] The scholar concludes:

> *With equal or rather far higher probability he could have translated the obsolete Greek words into intelligible Cypriot Greek to suit his general 'linguistic ideology', which did not allow him verbatin (sic!) quotations of words or phrases from any language including old, unfamiliar forms of his own national language.*[229]

Nicolaou-Konnari contrasts Medieval Cypriot Greek with the κοινή Greek carefully tended in the Orthodox Church, perceived as a 'purified' and 'fossilized' language that preserved the traditional Byzantine substance.[230] Convinced of an evident dissonance, the sense of which grew out of a particular 'linguistic mentality',[231] Nicolaou-Konnari forms a hypothesis to explain the low status of the Cypriot vernacular: first, the cult of Christian Greek contributed to the marginalisation of the dialect, and with it the whole Cyprian community; secondly, it blocked the dialect's development and possibility of transforming into a separate language that would hold the potential 'to shape a separate *Cypriot* ethnic identity'.[232] The scholar concludes:

> *This diglossia, a consciously pragmatic differentiation of forms of the same language according to the social context and function required, will be a persistent trait of Greek and Cypriot linguistic consciousness and will mirror the ambiguous, if not scornful, attitude of the Cypriots towards their dialect [...].*[233]

On the other hand, Nicolaou-Konnari stresses that later centuries saw Cypriot Greek flourish, being used not only by the Greek, but also by the French population, taking up more and more room in the intellectual space formed by the contemporary inhabitants of the island.[234] A significant role was played by the weakening of the Orthodox Church's position, and thus of κοινή Greek.[235]

In terms of originality Cypriot Greek resembles Cretan Greek, a local vernacular that took shape next to the learned Byzantine Greek, thanks, as Borowska writes, to 'a breaking of the monopoly on education according to the Byzantine model'.[236]

---

[225] Vassiliou, The Word Order of Medieval Cypriot, 35–36.
[226] Kyrris, Some Aspects, 175.
[227] Kyrris, Some Aspects, 172.
[228] Kyrris, Some Aspects, 172.
[229] Kyrris, Some Aspects, 172.
[230] Nicolaou-Konnari, Literary Languages, 10.
[231] Nicolaou-Konnari, Literary Languages, 10.
[232] Nicolaou-Konnari, Literary Languages, 10.
[233] Nicolaou-Konnari, Literary Languages, 10.
[234] Nicolaou-Konnari, Literary Languages, 13.
[235] Nicolaou-Konnari, Literary Languages, 13.
[236] Borowska, Kreta okresu renesansu, 20. Translated by Kupiszewska.

In selecting Cypriot Greek for the language of his *Chronicle*, Makhairas was guided by a special objective. Aware that Greek was losing its 'Rhomaic' shape by undergoing rapid transformation (LM II 158), he may have made an attempt – in his opinion, proper – to save it by building it a kind of monument. However, the chronicler had no illusions that, like himself, the Cyprians of his day used anything other than a 'barbarised' ('βαρβαρίσαν τὰ ῥωμαϊκά) Greek, irremediably changed (although some similarities between Cypriot and Byzantine Greek have been preserved[237]), subject to the influence of the French language, whose 'knowledge sufficed [on Cyprus]' (ἀρκέψα νὰ μαθάνουν). It is possible that Leontios noticed the hybridity discernible in many dimensions of the fifteenth-century Cypriot reality, which caused him to assume that only Cypriot Greek, in a way a 'hybrid', full of foreign loans and susceptible to change, could (unlike French) reflect that reality. Namely, this dialect was characterised, as Vassiliou terms it, with a 'creative dynamism' that furnished it with the 'potentiality to "juggle" between words and patterns'.[238] The scholar emphasises the capacity of Leontios' dialect to 'Cypriotise' foreign elements,[239] which indicates that by adopting vocabulary and expressions from other languages (Italian, French, Semite, etc.), he was really appropriating them and adapting them to his needs. Possibly Makhairas wanted to imitate medieval authors who wrote in French dialects (Provençal, Norman, etc.), attempting to pen a similar vernacular work to show thereby the originality and separateness of Cypriot literature (as well as its potential for development)[240] and lend Cypriot Greek a measure of prestige.[241] He likely also saw that his contemporaries often looked to the *Poems of Love* (for pleasure) and the *Assizes* (out of duty) and wanted to be part of this trend by penning the first narrative in this dialect.[242] It is unknown whether what he presented in the *Chronicle* was a comprehensive demonstration of his skills or an effect of the attempt to adapt to his potential addressees' expectations through stylisation. According to Vassiliou, Makhairas wished to write for 'any reader', because his language contains both formal and informal elements.[243] Leontios' language, as Anaxagorou rightly (after Dawkins) notes, is composed of words that appear sporadically, typical of an elevated style; words originating in 'the demotic common Greek'; and local and foreign terms, which is an indication of the multiple directions of his linguistic searches.[244] Certainly the choice of the vernacular (vulgar) dialect, hybrid, distinctive, subject to transformation and semantically capacious for the language of the *Chronicle*, which was to illustrate the changing Cypriot society at the meeting point of denominations, religions and cultures, is a significant indication of the brilliant mind of its author, who expresses his view of reality quite freely, but also intends to be understood by his compatriots, the Orthodox Cyprians. He primarily takes into account recipients who are less educated, unread, and have no taste for works with sophisticated narrative strategies and intellectually stimulating digressions.

Vassiliou highly stresses the social dimension of the language, which in her opinion is distinctly delineated in the Cypriot work:

> *When Makhairas discusses his views on the language spoken in Cyprus of his own times, he actually admits through the 1st person plural that this language is the language of the society.*[245]

In meeting this social requirement, Makhairas praises the deeds of Cypriot Franks, consigning much space to this task, and at the same time he selects the language of the local populace, adapting the form of his message to the needs of the Rhomaic people. He does not seem closely attached to this

---

[237] Vassiliou rightly observes: 'Bearing in mind the relative homogeneity of Greek during the Byzantine years and the Byzantine control over the island both linguistically and extra linguistically, we could assume that the language of the Cypriots did not differ much to the spoken language of the majority of the Romaii (Ρωμαίοι), the citizens of the Roman Empire of the East, who spoke the Romaiika (Romaic), the Greek of Byzantine years.' (Vassiliou, The Word Order of Medieval Cypriot, 24–25).
[238] Vassiliou, The Word Order of Medieval Cypriot, xvi–xvii.
[239] Vassiliou, The Word Order of Medieval Cypriot, 36.
[240] Gaunt, Kay, Introduction, 1–4.
[241] We may consider whether this would be 'covert prestige' as opposed to the 'overt prestige' of French. The terms 'covert prestige'/ 'overt prestige' were used by Jim Davy and Anna Panayotou with reference to the reasons for the presence of French loanwords in Cypriot Greek (Davy, Panayotou, French loans in Cypriot Greek, 117, and fn. 6).
[242] According to Vassiliou, Makhairas' *Chronicle* is the first confirmed narrative to be written from the outset in Cypriot Greek (Vassiliou, The Word Order of Medieval Cypriot, 66).
[243] Vassiliou, The Word Order of Medieval Cypriot, 66.
[244] Anaxagorou, Narrative and Stylistic Structures, 17.
[245] Vassiliou, The Word Order of Medieval Cypriot, 65.

people, however. For instance, when referring to the 1426–1427 peasant rebellion,[246] he does not pay much attention to their motivations or situation. It is hard to conclude what his true thoughts on the issue were. His ambivalent attitude was likely due to the participation of his brother Peter in the suppression of the uprising, which made full expression of his opinion impossible. He tells that the people (λᾶς) 'left their houses' (ἐσηκώθησαν –τὰ σπιτία–),[247] ravaged 'cellars' (τὲς ἀποθῆκες) and 'granaries' (τ' ἁλώνια), and committed robbery (κούρση) and 'many murders' (φόνους πολλούς).[248] He relates only certain sequences of events, and his focus is on the new leader, King Alexis ([τὴν] ρήγαν Ἀλέξην), to whose 'reign all the peasants submitted' (ὅλοι οἱ χωργιάτες ἐδόθησαν εἰς τὴν 'πόταξίν του).[249] His real attitude towards the people and his perception of its role in the history of Cyprus are unknown, however. Like in the case of other aspects of the chronicler's identity, also in this context it is possible to find different fragments in the *Chronicle* that interpreted jointly combine to form an ambiguous portrayal.

1.3. Cypriot literature and its potential influence on the *Chronicle*

The idiosyncratic style, language and form that Makhairas used guide the search for the sources of his inspiration to many places, but the significant obstacle that stands in the way of achieving an unambiguous result is our lack of knowledge about the literature available to the chronicler, already noted by Anaxagorou.[250] Difficulties with deciphering these sources of inspiration, and therefore with assessing the Cypriot writer's work, lead scholars to draw varying, sometimes surprising, conclusions. Tønnes Bekker-Nielsen for example calls Leontios 'the late Byzantine poet'.[251] When penning descriptions of the island's Christian past, particularly legends of the saints and stories of martyrs, Makhairas may have been inspired by works of various kinds that had been composed in Cyprus, such as: Ἀγκυρατός (Ancoratus, Well-anchored man) and Πανάριον κατὰ πασῶν τῶν αἱρέσεων (Medicine chest against heresies) by St Epiphanios of Salamis (Ἐπιφάνιος, 310/315–402), the life of St Spyridon of Trimythos by Theodore of Paphos, the life of St John the Almsgiver and St Simeon the Holy Fool by Leontios (7th c.), bishop of Naples,[252] like the *Chronicle* written in simple language. Other Christian writers whose works were available on Cyprus include: St Neophytos the Recluse (12/13th c.), who often touched on faith-related issues, author of Περὶ τῶν κατὰ τὴν χώραν Κύπρον σκαιῶν (On the calamities against the country of Cyprus),[253] and Gregory II (13th c.), a prolific author of theological writings, paraphrases, parables and an autobiography, and especially laudatory works chiefly praising two Byzantine emperors: Michael II Andronikos of the Palaiologos dynasty and King Hugh IV de Lusignan.[254]

A significant role in medieval Cyprus was played by the work of folk authors, who were called 'rhymesters'.[255] Chrystovalantis Kyriacou refers repeatedly to Cyprus in his study on 'the Byzantine warrior hero' in Byzantine folk songs. The scholar calls them 'Byzantine' because, as he explains, they are 'the offspring of this trinitarian blending'.[256] Kyriacou is particularly interested in various displays of 'Otherness' in these pieces. Referring to 'a homily on Christ's Burial', attributed to St Epiphanios of Cyprus, he notes, that even Christ was a 'divine other', '*xenos*' and 'subaltern'.[257] Simultaneously, he stresses that it is very difficult to find any information concerning the Cypriot folk songs[258] and postulates:

---

[246] LM V 696–697. See Nicolaou-Konnari, Schabel, Limmasol, 287.
[247] MS O after 'ἐσηκώθησαν' has 'πολλοὶ πτωχοὶ καὶ ἐκουρτζέψαν τοὺς χριστιανοὺς καὶ ἐσκοτῶσαν καὶ πολλούς.' After Dawkins (Ed., transl.), Ἐξήγησις/ Recital, 672 (fn. 5).
[248] LM V 696.
[249] LM V 696–697.
[250] Anaxagorou, Narrative and Stylistic Structures, 99.
[251] Bekker-Nielsen, The Roads of Ancient Cyprus, 59.
[252] All names, translated titles and dating after Borowska, Panorama greckojęzycznej literatury cypryjskiej, 56–57, translated into English by Kupiszewska.
[253] Borowska, Panorama greckojęzycznej literatury cypryjskiej, 63. Neophytos is the subject of the book Galatariotou, The Making of a Saint.
[254] Borowska, Panorama greckojęzycznej literatury cypryjskiej, 69.
[255] Prof. Małgorzata Borowska drew my attention to this aspect.
[256] Kyriacou, The Byzantine Warrior Hero, 103.
[257] Kyriacou, The Byzantine Warrior Hero, 102.
[258] Kyriacou, The Byzantine Warrior Hero, 103.

> [...] *it may be better to see Cyprus after the twelfth century as part of a 'late Byzantine Eastern Mediterranean' – evidently not politically, but religiously and culturally.*[259]

This includes ballads from the period of the Byzantine Empire's heyday and – as Borowska shows – the Ancient period, and above all, folk songs from the Acritic cycle (ακριτικά), composed in the ninth and tenth century on Cappadocian land.[260] The term 'ἀκρίτης', which designates the person lauded in these works, meant 'Byzantine soldier of the Roman Empire's eastern borders'.[261] According to Elizabeth Jeffreys,

> *Such songs are rather more common in Crete, Cyprus and the Asia Minor dialects than elsewhere, perhaps reflecting closeness to the Euphrates heartland of the epic.*[262]

One of the most famous figures of this cycle is Basil (Vasileios) Digenis (double-born, of double Descent, Two-Blood Border Lord[263]) Akritas, the son of the Arab emir Muṣūr who converted to Christianity and a Byzantine Greek, Irene of the Doukas (Δούκας) family.[264] Basil Digenes became the hero of several editions of adventures originating in various times, preserved in six manuscripts that differ in their textual layer.[265] Some of them were written in political verse, characteristic for demotic poetry.[266] It should be noted, after Giorgos Kechagioglou and Lefteris Papaleontiou, that it is hard to establish when the spread (χρονικές απαρχές διάδοσης) of acritic poetry as a genre (του λογοτεχνικού είδους της «ακριτικής» ποίησης) occurred.[267]

Makhairas also shares his experience of living on the border of two worlds: Christian and Muslim. He praises the deeds of brave rulers who – like Basil Digenes – fought to preserve a kingdom situated in the periphery of the Byzantine Empire. Finally, in the same manner, he touches on the question of conversion, mixes love plots with those of war and refers to folk beliefs, in this case astrology, to theological terms and to proverbs.[268]

As Borowska shows, works belonging to the Acritic cycle were adapted by their performers to the realities of the island and the needs of listeners.[269] One interesting example of such a work is the ballad *Της Αροδαφνούσας* (About Arodaphnousa), in which we can find reflected the love story of Peter I and Joanna L'Aleman, known to Makhairas and described at length by him (LM II 234–249) and which, Dawkins notes, entered the 'corpus of popular ballads in Cyprus'.[270]

An important narrative model (what has already been noted by Anaxagorou) may have been offered to Makhairas by the *Assizes* of the Kingdom of Jerusalem and the Kingdom of Cyprus, 'an unofficial set of treatises in Old French',[271] partly translated to vernacular Greek in the fourteenth century

---

[259] Kyriacou, The Byzantine Warrior Hero, 20.
[260] Borowska, Panorama greckojęzycznej literatury cypryjskiej, 57. Cf. Κεχαγιόγλου, Παπαλεοντιόυ, Το γραμματειακό 'πολυσύστημα', 19–20. The term 'Acritic cycle' was first used by Sathas in 1875. After Beaton, 'Digenes Akrites', 23. Roderick Beaton states: 'Although the different versions of the poem, and to a very much smaller extent certain folk songs, do indeed contain references to a real historical period, no convincing historical prototype for Akrites himself has been discovered [...]. What is more, "Akritas" or "Akritis" in folk song has turned out to be no more than a local preservation in Pontos and Cappadocia, with a vestigial trace in Cyprus. "Akritika" are still, however, treated as a separate category of modern folk songs [...] by all modern editors of Greek folk poetry and by most commentators on them.' (Beaton, 'Digenes Akrites', 23–24). Kyriacou indicates scholars who, in pointing out various aspects, noticed links between the Acritic tradition and the Island: Konstantinos Sathas, Henri Grégoire, Gilles Grivaud, Nikolaos Konomis (with special reference to Makhairas) and Stylianos Alexiou (Kyriacou, The Byzantine Warrior Hero, xix).
[261] Borowska, Panorama greckojęzycznej literatury cypryjskiej, 57. Borowska's phrase translated by Kupiszewska. The term 'ἀκρίτης' comes from the Greek 'ἄκρα', 'edge', 'brink', 'end'. In Κριαράς, Λεξικο, 184 we read: 'Από το ουστ. άκρα, ή και παραγ. κατάλ. – ίτης.'
[262] Jeffreys (Ed., transl.), Digenis Akritis, xv. Cf. Borowska (Transl.), Dijenis Akritas.
[263] Translation after Jeffreys (Ed., transl.), Digenis Akritis, xv. The phrase 'Two-Blood Border Lord' after Merry, Encyclopedia of Modern Greek Literature, 111. See Jouanno, Shared Spaces, 260–284.
[264] Borowska, Panorama greckojęzycznej literatury cypryjskiej, 57.
[265] Jeffreys (Ed., transl.), Digenis Akritis, xv.
[266] Borowska, Panorama greckojęzycznej literatury cypryjskiej, 58; Jurewicz, Historia literatury bizantyńskiej, 194.
[267] Κεχαγιόγλου, Παπαλεοντιόυ, Το γραμματειακό 'πολυσύστημα', 23.
[268] Merry, Encyclopedia of Modern Greek Literature, 111.
[269] Borowska, Panorama greckojęzycznej literatury cypryjskiej, 69.
[270] Dawkins, Notes, 127.
[271] Nicolaou-Konnari, Greeks, 21. We may distinguish the *Assises de la Haute Cour* (Assizes of the High Court), describing the law in force in Jerusalem, but adapted to the context of Cyprus, and the *Assises de la Cour des Bourgeois* (Assizes of the Burgess Court), concerning Jerusalem, but translated into Cypriot Greek in Cyprus in the fourteenth century. Information after Nicolaou-Konnari, Greeks, 21–22.

at the earliest.²⁷² Gilles Grivaud, citing the findings of Maurice Grandclaude, enumerates the different types of legislative writings in French (apart from *assizes* he lists *espéciaux commandements*, *remèdes* and *ordonnements de cour*) and explains that

> the word assise *designates a decision of legislative nature adopted by the king and his liegemen gathered in a council where jurisconsults were regularly present and, sometimes, bourgeois members attended in the case of jurisdiction for commoners.* [...] *The collection of the assizes thus includes both decisions emanating from distinct courts and measures passed down through oral tradition.*²⁷³

Vassiliou notices that through the translation of the *Assizes*, many French and Italian words entered Medieval Cypriot Greek,²⁷⁴ e.g.: 'αβαβοέ' (Fr *avant-voeu*, 'promise', 'wish', 'oath'), 'άλπιτρος' (Fr *arbitre*, 'arbiter') and 'ενταλιαστής' (Prov *entalhar*, 'false', 'counterfeit').²⁷⁵ Citing Dawkins, she further states that the French 'imported' to Cyprus was 'a mixture of a number of French dialects'.²⁷⁶ After Kyriakos Hadjioannou, she repeats that many French borrowings reached Cyprus via Provence, that is from Occitan (*Langue d'oc*),²⁷⁷ while Italian words had the most in common with the areas of Genoa and Venice.²⁷⁸ These were not the only loans, as Arab words may also be distinguished in Medieval Cypriot Greek:

> *These were brought into Cyprus through the various interactions (trading, commerce) between Cypriot merchants and those from Arabic-speaking countries (Syria, Egypt, etc). Most of these loans, according to Hadjioannou (1991), came with the establishment of the Maronites in Cyprus, although, presumably many words may have entered the Cypriot lexicon from 632 to 1191.*²⁷⁹

Vassiliou cites for instance the 14th century testimony of John of Verona, who in the *Revue de l'Orient Latin* (Review of the Latin East), confirms that Arabic (*sciunt saracenicum*) was used in Cyprus at that time, and the testimony of Estienne de Lusignan, who named eleven languages in currency on the island.²⁸⁰ A large role in this transmission, the scholar underlines, was played by monks based in Cypriot monasteries.²⁸¹ The close proximity of Egypt also contributed positively to enriching the native language, and furthermore the Semitic languages may have, according to Vassiliou, entered Cypriot Greek via the syntax of the Bible.²⁸² The influence of Arabic is reflected in the *Chronicle* in the lexical layer, where we can find words such as τζέρμες (from the Arab *djerm*), meaning a type of ship. In the *Chronicles* a knowledge of Arabic is demonstrated by the Catalan Carceran Suarez and the merchant Nicholas (LM V 683), and Sir Badin Goneme (LM V 693).

According to Nicolaou-Konnari, establishing the social group to which bilingual or multilingual Rhomaioi belonged is far more successful than attempts to ascertain their 'cultural identification'.²⁸³ The scholar calls government officials (such as the legate Zacharias and Makhairas), church officials (Konstantinos Anagnostes) and representatives of the intellectual elite (Georgios Lapithes) the 'language agents between the two ethnic groups'.²⁸⁴ Nicolaou-Konnari judges the thirteenth century to have been a period of intensive development of literature on Cyprus, as proved by the arrival of other Rhomaic authors

---

[272] Anaxagorou, Narrative and Stylistic Structures, 10–11; Borowska, Panorama greckojęzycznej literatury cypryjskiej, 72. Nicolaou-Konnari has established that in addition to legal texts, medical texts also used Cypriot Greek (Nicolaou-Konnari, Literary Languages, 13).
[273] Grivaud, Literature, 249.
[274] Vassiliou, The Word Order of Medieval Cypriot, 25.
[275] Vassiliou, The Word Order of Medieval Cypriot, 49.
[276] Vassiliou, The Word Order of Medieval Cypriot, 25.
[277] Davy and Panayotou, who devoted a whole article to French loans in Cypriot Greek, note that Dawkins found influences of Norman French (Davy, Panayotou, French loans in Cypriot Greek, 114, fn. 6).
[278] Vassiliou, The Word Order of Medieval Cypriot, 25.
[279] Vassiliou, The Word Order of Medieval Cypriot, 25.
[280] These were: 'Latin, Italien, Grec corrompu, Armenian, Cofte, Jacobite, Maronite, Syriaque, Indian, Iuerien, Albanois, ou Macedonic, et Egyptiaque.' (Vassiliou, The Word Order of Medieval Cypriot, 26). See Estienne de Lusignan, Description de toute l'isle de Cypre, 67. English translation: Stephen de Lusignan, Lusignan's Chorography.
[281] Vassiliou, The Word Order of Medieval Cypriot, 28.
[282] Vassiliou, The Word Order of Medieval Cypriot, 29.
[283] Nicolaou-Konnari, Literary Languages, 9.
[284] Nicolaou-Konnari, Literary Languages, 9.

1.4. Narrative singularity of the *Chronicle*

A chronicle is a literary genre belonging to historiography that presents historical events in chronological order. It was Byzantine chroniclers, Oktawiusz Jurewicz demonstrates, who brought about the division into chronographic narration, directed to a broader group of addressees, and the more precise historiographic narration.[286] Byzantine historiography evolved systematically, delivering outstanding works such as:[287] Anna Komnene's (11th–12th c.) Ἀλεξιάδα (Alexiad),[288] Ioannes Kinnamos' (12th c.) Ἐπιτομή (Epitome),[289] Niketas Choniates' (13th c.)[290] Χρονικὴ διήγησις (Historical narrative),[291] Georgios Akropolites' (13th c.) Χρονικὴ συγγραφή (Chronological writings),[292] Georgios Pachymeres' (13th–14th c.) Συγγραφικῶν ἱστοριῶν [πρώτη][293] (Historical writings), Nikephoros Kallistos Xanthopoulos' (14th c.) Ἐκκλησιαστικὴ Ἱστορία (Ecclesiastical history), Nikephoros Gregoras' (14th c.) Ῥωμαϊκὴ Ἱστορία (History of the Romans),[294] Ioannes Kantakouzenos' (13th–14th c.) Ἱστορίαι (Histories), Ioannes Kananos' (15th c.) Διήγησις περὶ τοῦ ἐν Κωνσταντινουπόλει γεγονότος πολέμου (Account of the Siege of Constantinople), Ioannes Anagnostes' (15th c.) Διήγησις περὶ τῆς τελευταίας ἁλώσεως τῆς Θεσσαλονίχης (Account of the Last Capture of Thessaloniki), Laonikos Chalkokondyles'[295] (15th c.) Ἀποδείξεις Ἱστοριῶν (Demonstrations of histories) and Michael Kritoboulos' (15th c.) Ἱστορίαι (Histories).[296] Chronographic writing, which matured in a separate niche of this historiographical intellectual space, is reflected in the works: Ioannes Zonaras' (11th–12th c.) Ἐπιτομὴ Ἱστοριῶν (Extracts of history), Konstantinos Manasses' (13th c.) Σύνοψις ἱστορική/ χρονική (Historical/ Summary Chronicle), Michael Glykas' (12th c.), Βίβλος χρονική (Chronicle of the Bible), Joel's (13th c.) Χρονογραφία ἐν συνόψει (Summary Chronicle, *Chronographia compendiaria*), the anonymous Σύνοψις χρονική (Synopsis Chronike, 12th c.) and Σύνοψις χρονική/ Σύνοψις Σάθας (Synopsis Chronike, 12th/13th c.), Ephraim's (14th c.) Χρονικὴ Ἱστορία δια στίχων ἰαμβικῶν/ Ἐφραιμίου χρονικοῦ Καίσαρες (World history in iambic verse/ Emperors of Ephraim's chronicle) and Michael Panaretos' (14th c.) Περὶ τῶν τῆς Τραπεζούντος βασιλέων τῶν Μεγάλων Κομνηνῶν (About the Emperors of Trabezond, the Grand Komnenoi).[297] Chronicles were intended to represent a less refined style, and thus to reach a broader audience, giving them respite and a basis for private reflection thanks to their accessible content.[298] Jurewicz notes:

---

[285] Nicolaou-Konnari, Literary Languages, 10–11.
[286] Jurewicz, Historia literatury bizantyńskiej, 47.
[287] In the following, works written from the start of the Komnenos dynasty's reign to the fall of the Byzantine Empire (1081–1453) are listed.
[288] Anna Komnene's complex style is analysed in detail by Penelope Buckley, who enumerates principal genres Komnene writes: tragedy and history, and subgenres Komnene writes or around which she oscillates such as: 'classicizing history [...] enlivened by the influence of novel-writing', 'Homeric epic', 'the more contemporary matter of chronicles', 'public discourse', 'imperial propaganda', 'romance', 'feminist readings', 'apocalyptic writing', 'dirge'. As Buckley sums up: 'She uses all these genres with awareness of their value-systems and systems of perception' (Buckley, The Alexiad, 10).
[289] Jurewicz, Historia literatury bizantyńskiej, 206.
[290] Harry Magoulias' comments on the writing skill of a representative of this group, Niketas Choniates, may serve to illustrate the complexity of the narrative construction technique : '[...] the reader will find that Niketas is anything but simple, and his rhetorical training brilliantly shines through the fabric of his history. In translating his monumental work, one must laboriously mine his words and phrases to expose the literary gems.' (Choniates, O City of Byzantium, xvi).
[291] Choniates, O City of Byzantium. Cf. Simpson, Niketas Choniates; Simpson, Efthymiadis, Niketas Choniates; Dąbrowska, Bizancjum, Francja i Stolica Apostolska, 6; Anaxagorou, Narrative and Stylistic Structures, 105–106.
[292] Based on Korobeinikov, Byzantium and the Turks, 8. See George Akropolites, The History.
[293] Based on Korobeinikov, Byzantium and the Turks, 8.
[294] Jurewicz, Historia literatury bizantyńskiej, 238.
[295] Stavrakos gives version 'Chalkondyles' instead of 'Chalkokondyles' in Stavrakos, Chalkondyles, Laonikos (http://dx.doi.org/10.1163/2213-2139_emc_SIM_01656, accessed 30 December 2021).
[296] List after Jurewicz, Historia literatury bizantyńskiej, 233–245. Kupiszewska's English translation of the titles after Polish translation by Jurewicz (slightly modified by the author).
[297] List after Jurewicz, Historia literatury bizantyńskiej, 208–211, 246–248. Kupiszewska's English translation of the titles after Polish translation by Jurewicz (slightly modified by the author).
[298] Anaxagorou, Narrative and Stylistic Structures, 101.

> *The chronicle writers did not care about the causes and consequences of historical events [...]. They painted portraits of eminent individuals [...]. They presented the fortunes of the hero against a broad historical background, far from precise and reliable. The narratives did not lack repetition and discrepancies [...].*[299]

Over time the genre evolved, taking different forms depending on the intellectual capacities of individual chroniclers and their literary skills. On the one hand they adopted certain motifs or ways of constructing the narrative from authors known to them, on the other, they added their own original elements, dependent on their degree of understanding of the political and social situation in which they were raised, their level and type of education, cultural context, and finally their own beliefs.

Anaxagorou compares the *Chronicle* with selected Byzantine (penned by Anna Komnene, Niketas Choniates, Georgios Pachymeres, Nikephoros Gregoras, Ioannes Kantakouzenos) and western (including the works of Geoffrey of Villehardouin, Robert de Clari, John Froissart) models in terms of building the narrative (action, description of physical and moral attributes/overcohesive explicitness, discourse connectivity, reiteration, addresses to the audience) and in terms of how the characters communicate (brief passages, collective discourse, discourse proper/brief passages, collective discourse, discourse proper, dialogue).[300] She devotes separate subchapters to sixth-century chronicler Ioannes Malalas, who was the first to write his work in a demotic variety of Greek,[301] and the *Chronicle of Morea*, which is expanded on below. The scholar judges Makhairas to have completely departed from Byzantine tradition, using the narrative and stylistic features of the western tradition.[302] At the same time, Anaxagorou (citing Alexander Kazhdan[303]) provides an interesting association of the two historiographic trends with the quality and features of the art created within the traditions from which these trends arose.[304] Although Makhairas and other Byzantine historiographers share, Kyrris states, the conviction about the 'usefulness' of history understood in a theological sense,[305] this should not lead to the conclusion that Makhairas took their work as an inspiration. A utilitarian perception of the role of historiography is actually also apparent in western and Muslim works.[306] When carrying out comparisons of this kind (confronting a particular text with representatives of individual text groups), it should be remembered that each of the models considered (here: Byzantine/western) is internally diverse, which is why we will always find both similar and differing elements. Nicolaou-Konnari underlines that there is no trace of imitation of 'Latin Eastern or Byzantine models' in the chronicler's work and correctly observes that he is 'the first Cypriot historiographer who chooses to write' about this exceptional phase in the history of Cyprus.[307] Nicolaou-Konnari summarises its form and content, emphasising the blending of traditions:

> *Leontios' chronicle borrows from many literary genres, embodying the fusion of the Byzantine and Latin Eastern worlds and transforming the crusader tradition of Latin Eastern historiography into a Greco-Frankish tradition proper to the socio-cultural reality of fifteenth-century Cyprus, but is primarily a dynastic history mainly consisting of Peter's encomium.*[308]

---

[299] Jurewicz, Historia literatury bizantyńskiej, 48. Translated by Kupiszewska.
[300] Elements in both brackets enumerated after Anaxagorou, Narrative and Stylistic Structures, 103–131.
[301] Anaxagorou, Narrative and Stylistic Structures, 103.
[302] Anaxagorou, Narrative and Stylistic Structures, 130–131. Cf. Nicolaou-Konnari, 'A poor island...', 123.
[303] Bibliographical data after Anaxagorou, 131.
[304] Anaxagorou draws these parallels: 'The two traditions of historical representation seem to be the products of the quality of Byzantine and western art of the time [...]. The decorative focus of a western church lies in the complete, plastic form of sculpture. The contemplative lyricism and psychological expressiveness of Byzantium is depicted in the "incompleteness" of mosaics and frescoes. The abstractions, leisured lyricism and elaborate rhetoric of Byzantine historiography, graspable only through individual reading, are as visually incomplete as a mosaic. At the other extreme, the French chronicles, full of movement and energy, reflect the dynamic quality of Western art. They recapture the flavour of the historical moment in the most lively manner and bring the characters to life. [...] In a similar manner the *Chronicle* of Leontios Machairas is the literary embodiment of the westernized Cypriot art of its time [...].' (Anaxagorou, Narrative and Stylistic Structures, 131).
[305] Kyrris, Some Aspects, 207.
[306] Kyrris, Some Aspects, 210.
[307] Nicolaou-Konnari, 'A poor island...', 124–125.
[308] Nicolaou-Konnari, Alterity and identity, 48.

In another article the scholar explains the above thought more precisely with the reference to literary genres, which the *Chronicle* 'resembles', the nature of sources of information ('written and oral') he used, specificity of his experience influenced by his career, and the shape of the whole narration:

> *There can be little doubt that Makhairas's career influenced his concept of history-writing, the style of his narrative, and, most importantly, the nature of the sources he used [...]. The extensive use of archival sources, which at times makes the text resemble an epistolary narrative, endows his history with credibility and documentary realism [...].*[309]

Dawkins does not doubt that the author of the *Chronicle* created a completely separate form of expression,[310] finding an application for the 'uncultivated native dialect'[311] that was 'a very local form of Greek'.[312] It is this local character of the text, resembling works of the oral tradition, that implies the lack of such connections.

According to Daniele Baglioni, the *Chronicle* was written between the years 1426 and 1432, and according to Kyrris, between 1432 and 1458.[313] Dawkins notes (as does Anaxagorou) that Makhairas' work saw the light of day at a time when Byzantine historiography was still developing:

> *At the time when Makhairas was composing his book, and even after his death, Greek historical writing in the Roman Empire of the East, certainly among the learned folk of Constantinople, was still actively practised. When the city fell in 1454* Makhairas may, though an old man, have been still alive, and in this very last days before the Turk the historians Doukas, Phrantzis, Chalkokondylis, and Kritoboulos were producing books still clearly in the current of Greek historical composition [...].*[314]

The *Chronicle*, having a singular shape, was not therefore a work that would constitute a caesura between two separate ages; nor was it a culmination of earlier narratives.

The singular shape of the *Chronicle* is thus the result of conscious action by the Cypriot chronicler, who gave it a specific form to express the message he intended. On the other hand we should remember the objective limitations (e.g. in access to a broader selection of texts) he experienced, and also all the individual and historical imponderabilia, hard to wholly and unambiguously identify, that may have significantly narrowed the spectrum of ways in which he could have described reality.

Kyrris distinguishes three concepts underlying Makhairas' narrative. These are: 'Christian Greek-Byzantine conscience', 'self-consciousness' and 'mentality of the Greek Cypriots', which coexisted with 'loyalty to the foreign régime'.[315] Emphasising this Greek-Latin confrontation, the scholar concludes that the *Chronicle* was in a certain dimension 'a "recreation" of the Byzantine approach to history "in a Latin image"'.[316] In opposition to Dawkins, Kyrris does not see the *Chronicle* as a singular, unique work, but derived from the Byzantine substratum, and simultaneously tailored to reality of the Latin world and mentality of its representatives. He attributes to the writer the tendency to balance 'the Greco-Latin microcosm of Cyprus' (and prioritise it) against 'the Byzantine macrocosm' or 'the wider Christian universe', which only gains its particular monolithic form in confrontation with Muslims.[317] The scholar thus points to the close relationship between Greek and Latin elements in the Cypriot chronicler's literary consciousness, which are therefore specifically situated and balanced in the narrative, and whose deciphering makes it possible to deconstruct the depiction of the Christian world, subjected to defragmentation by the author.

In an article devoted to eminent writers of Cypriot literature (της κυπριακής λογοτεχνίας), Pieris names Makhairas alongside Vasilis Michailidis (1849/1850–1917) and Kostas Montis (1914–2014), calling all three 'great writers of Cypriot hellenism' (μεγάλοι συγγραφοί του Κυπριακού Ελληνισμού).[318]

---

[309] Nicolaou-Konnari, 'A poor island…', 123.
[310] Dawkins, The Nature of the Cypriot Chronicle, 6.
[311] Dawkins, The Nature of the Cypriot Chronicle, 7.
[312] Dawkins, The Nature of the Cypriot Chronicle, 8.
[313] Baglioni, Language and identity, 34; Kyrris, Some Aspects, 167.
[314] Dawkins, The Nature of the Cypriot Chronicle, 4–5. Cf. Anaxagorou, Narrative and Stylistic Structures, 101.
[315] Kyrris, Some Aspects, 167.
[316] Kyrris, Some Aspects, 167.
[317] Kyrris, Some Aspects, 191.
[318] Πιερής, Σταθμοί, 170. Kupiszewska's translation of the Greek phrase from the Polish translation by the author.

As Borowska states, Michailidis is thought to be one of the greatest Cypriot poets of the twentieth century,[319] and Montis, is 'the greatest Greek-language poet and writer to originate from Cyprus, and one of the most outstanding Modern Greek poets in history'.[320]

Pieris, citing practically the same information about the chronicler's life and work as Coureas, adds that he was 'an exceptionally gifted figure' whose message is notable for its 'masterly narrative style', and whose statements are furnished with 'power of judgement'.[321] Pieris' suggestion and assessments are undoubtedly emphatic and emotionally charged and he seems to place emphasis on the historical magnitude and timeless perfection of Makhairas' literary skill.

What are the primary features of his workshop?

In the opening part of the *Chronicle* Leontios explains that he is penning his narrative to let people read it wherever they are (διὰ νὰ τὴν διαβάζουσιν ἐκεῖνοι, ὁποῦ εὑρίσκουνται). At the same time, he expresses the hope that they will find joy in reading old tales (οἱ ποῖγοι θέλουν ἀλεγριάζεσθαι τὰς παλαιὰς ἱστορίες). He modestly calls his work a 'short account' (μικρὴν ἀνθύμησιν), and the actions performed by him, 'description' (ἐξηγηθῶ), which is a manifestation of a universal human need (πεθυμοῦν ὅλοι, 'everybody wishes') to explain bygone events (τὰ γινίσκουνται ξηγοῦνται). He also shows that he is aware that 'everybody strongly wishes to hear [stories of things] passed away' (πολλὰ πεθυμοῦν ὅλοι νὰ γροικήσουν τὰ ἐδιάβησαν) and 'that [they] will discover things that have passed away, and on that basis they learn to see further' (ὅτι μανθάνουσιν τὰ πράματα τὰ ἐδιάβησαν, καὶ ἀπ' ἐκεῖνα μανθάνουσιν καὶ βλέπουντα). He emphasises that his work on old histories will help people helpless in the face of the dangers of fate 'to see what salvation they might find' (νὰ βλέπεται, μήπως καὶ γλυτώσουν) (LM I 1–2). He thus sets a clear goal for his task, according to which a chronicle is a narrative about the past that provides guidelines concerning the changes in human experience. Kyrris' interpretation would have this aim to be purely educational, and pleasure and artistic values to be far less important.[322] A different opinion is held by Dawkins, who proves that it was edification and pleasure of readers (as well as 'love of the country') that played the greatest role,[323] as in the case of other literary texts in the Greek tradition, such as fables ('folk-tales'), lives of saints and love poems (Ἐρωτόκριτος).[324] Undoubtedly the clarity and some repetitiveness of the narrative make it easier for the reader to understand its content, and the stories that break it up can give respite and a sense of inhabiting a shared Christian heritage. Comparing this clearly specified goal with what other historiographers such as Anna Komnene[325] and Niketas Choniates[326] wrote about their aims and expectations for the reception of their work, throws light on the diversity of motives governing individual authors. Guibert of Nogent (ca. 1055–1124), inspired by the anonymous *Gesta Francorum*, had an interesting definition of his goal, offering 'a model to correct or perhaps to corrupt'[327] the history presented in the *Gesta Francorum* starting from the initiation of the first crusade (organised in 1095) by Pope Urban II, up to the Ascalon victory in 1099. This work, written in simple language, encrusted with numerous references to the Bible and fragments explaining the course of events by the action of divine providence, is composed of ten 'small chapters' (*capitula*) devoted to consecutive stages of the military operation,

---

[319] Borowska, Panorama greckojęzycznej literatury cypryjskiej, 96.

[320] Borowska, Panorama greckojęzycznej literatury cypryjskiej, 119. Translated by Kupiszewska.

[321] Pieris, The Medieval Cypriot Chronicler, 107. In a footnote to his article, and thus somewhat marginally to the main discussion, Pieris mentions that Makhairas came to inspire the poet Giorgos Seferis, citing publications by Giorgos Savidis, Nasos Vayenas (Vagenas), Giorgos Kekhagioglu (Kechagioglou) and Giorgos Georgis (Pieris, The Medieval Cypriot Chronicler, 107, fn. 2). More about Seferis' connections to Cyprus in Λαγάκος, Ὁ Σεφέρης καὶ ἡ Κύπρος. It is true that Seferis is the author of the poem Ὁ Δαίμων τῆς Πορνείας (The Demon of Fornication), which is a reference to paragraph LM II 234, which describes the adultery King Peter committed against his wife Eleanora.

[322] Kyrris, Some Aspects, 206.

[323] Dawkins, The Nature of the Cypriot Chronicle, 13–14.

[324] Dawkins, The Nature of the Cypriot Chronicle, 14.

[325] Next to a clear metaphysical objective, Komnene's historiographical endeavour had a practical goal, which was to describe the deeds of her father in literary form. Anna Komnene writes: '[...] but the tale of my woes would not cause a movement in place, nor rouse men to arms and war, but they would move the hearer to tears, and compel sympathy from animate, and even inanimate, nature' (Anna Komnene, The Alexiad, 4, Preface, IV).

[326] Choniates declares: 'Historical narratives, indeed, have been invented for the common benefit of mankind [...]. In recording ancient events and customs, the narratives elucidate human nature and expose men of noble sentiments [...]. This history, having truth as its sole objective, shuns rhetorical artifice and poetic storytelling [...]. My work, then, is a continuation of their [preceding historiographers – note M.G.] written record and is interwoven to resemble a channel whose waters flow from a single source or connecting links which are added to a chain that reaches into infinity [...].' (Choniates, O City of Byzantium, 3–4).

[327] Guibert of Nogent, Deeds of God Through the Franks (https://www.gutenberg.org/cache/epub/4370/pg4370.html, accessed 12 January 2021).

of which the siege of Antioch takes the most space.³²⁸ This tendency to optimise is apparent for example in the syntax, which is more sophisticated than in the prototype.³²⁹ Robert Levine comments Guibert's editorial aspirations that this declared zeal of correction was directed towards improving 'the style of his source'.³³⁰ He wanted to write:

> *A version of this same history, but woven out of excessively simple words, often violating grammatical rules, exists, and it may often bore the reader with the stale, flat quality of its language.*³³¹

A declaration of the author's intent upon starting their work has specific consequences: on the one hand it helps form the depicted world thanks to proper, optimum use of the desired, sophisticated tools, but on the other it restricts their range, and also narrows the group of addressees. It also throws light on the author's personality.

The narrative of the *Chronicle* includes Leontios' 'authorial' comments on his intentions or obligations as regards making his message more cohesive, combining two elements (Anaxagorou calls them 'macroconnectives'³³²), for example: 'I showed you [...], [now] I will show you' (Ἐδεῖξά σας τὰς [...]· νὰ σᾶς δείξω, LM I 31), 'Let us move to the subject' (Ἄς ἔλθωμεν εἰς τὸ προκείμενον, LM I 41), 'I would not like to leave it unsaid' (Νὰ μηδὲν μείνῃ νὰ μηδὲν σᾶς πῶ ἀπόθεν, LM II 157), 'We thus interrupt the narrative' (Τὸ λοιπὸν ἀφίννομεν τὴν ἐξήγησιν, LM II 234), 'And to tell you this openly' (καὶ διὰ νὰ σᾶς τὸ πῶ φανερά, LM III 482), 'Let us go back to [...]' (Πάλε ἂς ἔρτωμεν εἰς [...], LM II 251), 'Let us move to Adalia and explain what happened [there]' (Ἄς ἔλθωμεν εἰς τὴν Ἀταλίαν καὶ νὰ ξηγηθοῦμεν τὰ γενόμενα, LM III 317), 'And if you want me to tell you how it happened that Ammochostos was taken, then [...]' (Καὶ ἂν θέλῃς νὰ σοῦ πῶ πῶς ἡ Ἀμόχουστο ἐπάρτην, LM III 482) or 'Let none of you think that I am doing so in order to praise [...]' (καὶ μηδὲν σᾶς φανῇ καὶ πολομῶ το διὰ νὰ φουμίσω [...], LM III 484) and many others.³³³ Expressions of pathos also occur: 'Now, the time has come for us to cut down the ears [of corn] of hostility' (Τὸ λοιπὸν εἶνε καιρὸς νὰ θερίσωμεν τὰ στραχίδια τῆς ἔχθρας, LM II 261). This type of comment serves to maintain contact with the reader, strengthen their attention, signalise a change of subject, emphasise one's own position and also lend fluency to the text. They show that creating a narrative is a process in which the key role is played by the narrator's dispositions (the author's cognitive attitude towards the events, his ordering of facts, direct involvement in the events described), which may also be seen in the sentences: 'I forgot to tell you' (ἐλησμόνησα νὰ σᾶς ξηγηθῶ, LM II 232) or 'I found out from' (ἐγὼ ἔμαθα ἀπό, LM II 249). Makhairas sometimes emphasises the veracity of information using the phrase 'It is true that' (Ἀληθινὰ εἶνε ὅτι/ εἶνε ἀλήθεια ὅτι/ [Ἔνι] ἀλήθεια [καὶ/ὅτι]),³³⁴ or its particular importance, as in the expression 'Furthermore, you have to know that' (Ἀκομὴ γινώσκετε ὅτι, LM III 548). Such narrative insertions are not exceptional: we find them not only in Byzantine and western chronicles, but also in Muslim ones, as demonstrated by the expressions 'As we already mentioned', 'We have already mentioned' present in the *Kitāb al-kāmil fī al-tārīḫ min afʿāl as-sulṭān Ṣalāḥ ad-Dīn* (Complete book of history. From the deeds of sultan Saladin) by Ibn al-Aṯir (1160–1233).³³⁵ In the case of the *Chronicle* these comments indicate an impact of the oral tradition.

Unlike in the case of most Byzantine and some western historians, Makhairas' discussion is devoid of scholarliness: he once (LM I 11) happens to cite the statement of a 'philosopher' (φιλόσοφος) who is not named,³³⁶ though its message is Aristotelian (due to its teleological interpretation), and another time, 'Aristotle' himself as if he were a mythical figure: 'accept these [words] as if they had been spoken to you by Aristotle' (ἐσοὺ [...] ἔπαρ᾽ τα ὡς γοιὸ νἄχε σοῦ πεῖν ὁ Ἀριστοτέλης, LM III 487). The only information to be obtained from the context of this statement is that Leontios associates Aristotle with the virtue of wisdom. The author of these words, a royal messenger, calls their addressee, a Genoese admiral, a 'sage full

---

³²⁸ Hagenmeyer (Ed.), Gesta Francorum et Aliorum Hierosolymitanorum.
³²⁹ Guibert of Nogent, Deeds of God Through the Franks (https://www.gutenberg.org/cache/epub/4370/pg4370.html, accessed 12 January 2021).
³³⁰ Levine, Introduction, 3.
³³¹ Levine, Introduction, 3.
³³² Anaxagorou, Narrative and Stylistic Structures, 118.
³³³ LM I 65, 80, 86, 88, II 90–92, 96–97, 99–101, 112, 115, 129–130, 157, 159, 173, 218, 261, 279, III 284–285, 310, 352, 443, 464, 484, 542, 549, 559, 562–563, 576, 579, 584, 589–590, IV 614, 621, V 634, 638–639, 660, 668, 678, 685–686.
³³⁴ LM I 39, 68, III 532, 571, 578, IV 605.
³³⁵ Al-Aṯir, Kompletna księga historii, 3, 15. Kupiszewska's English translation of the title after Polish translation: Al-Aṯir, Kompletna księga historii.
³³⁶ Dawkins adds the definite article ('the philosopher') in his translation.

of wisdom' (σοφὸς γεμάτος σοφίαν, LM III 487). The chronicler does not avoid simple wording and repetition. He incorporates expressions referring to theological truths and related to Christian dogma into the narrative in a way that suggests he may not have known their real meaning. In this he differs completely from Anna Komnene, whose learned excursions are full of references to philosophy, theology and mythology, or from Guibert of Nogent, the author of an erudite, multi-layered narrative filled with quotations from the works of ancient authors and the Bible.[337] Even if, as Anaxagorou claims, the *Chronicle* contains compositional elements typical for western historiographical texts and even if – as can be deduced from her analysis – it shares their narrative dynamic, it departs from these models in many respects. Makhairas does not incorporate any quotations or references to other texts, nor does he analyse theological and philosophical systems. In his aspirations he differs for example from Guibert or John Froissart (14th–15th c.).[338] Guibert not only displays the breadth of his philosophical reading and his knowledge of other nations, citing for instance the Arian heresy, Stoic and Manichean thought and compiling a catalogue-like list of the features of various societies (mentioning Chaldean pride, Greek bitterness, Egyptian filthiness and Asian instability), but also develops the style and structure of his work by constructing sophisticated metaphors such as the image of a locust swarm deprived of a king and a labyrinth of diseases afflicting the country.[339] In his work *Chronique de France, Dangleterre, Descose, Despaigne, De Bretaigne, De Flandres. Et lieux circumvoisins* (Chronicles of England, France, Spain, Portugal, Scotland, Brittany, Flanders, and the adjoining countries), Froissart[340] uses an 'antiphonal' technique,[341] involving the grouping of thoughts around binary oppositions. Makhairas much prefers frequent but superficial references to truths of the faith and theological categories, which he uses to explain the meaning of the course of events and to justify further events, which calls to mind the *Gesta Francorum*. However, he does not obsessively think, like Guibert for example, about achieving perfect style, which makes him exceptionally natural. And though he strives for stylistic and compositional simplicity, some kind of binary is also visible in his constant juxtaposition of good and evil, loyalty to God and godlessness, legendary past and living, tangible present, femininity and masculinity. Nevertheless, the Cypriot also opts to find a place for semitones and borderline situations (when he writes about the moral decay of man, it is hard to establish a particular fault).

Makhairas cites nature and atmospheric phenomena only when they are necessary to him as a significant element of events and a key component of the narrative: such a role is played by the carob tree in the tale of the hidden Holy Cross, and by the heatwave in the introduction to LM V 655: 'That day it was very hot' (Τὴν αὐτὴν ἡμέραν ἐγίνην μεγάλη πυρά), the mention of the calming of the sea (ἐποῖκεν γαλήνην ἡ θάλασσα, LM II 138), or the references to unnamed rivers in Turkish lands (LM II 125 in Ousgat, III 285) and on Cyprus (LM III 282) as well as the named one (τὸν ποταμὸν τὸν Μονοβγάτην, 'the river Monovagat', LM II 180). As a comparison, the *Chronique d'Amadi* contains references to nature and distinctly depicted topographical elements that might be important for the course of events or contribute to descriptions. We read that it is impossible to reach Famagusta from Mesaoria because a large amount of mud (*fango*) stands in the way.[342] In another passage dangerous places (*per molti lochi sinestri*) strike fear into readers' hearts, as do wide, hard to cross rivers (*gran fimnare*),[343] which are many in the text, including the Jordan, Tinnis and Rubin rivers.[344]

The Cypriot chronicler portrays characters mainly through frequent mentions of the emotions guiding them, describing their deeds and registering the positions taken by them, and especially their

---

[337] Such references are very numerous. Among ancient authors, the following are important to Guibert: Terence (2nd c. BCE), Caesar (2nd/1st c. BCE), Horace (1st c. BCE), Sallust (1st c. BCE), Lucan (1st c. CE), Juvenal (1st/2nd c. CE), Suetonius (1st/2nd c. CE). The Bible books quoted include: Genesis, Kings, Chronicles, Psalms, Proverbs, Ecclesiastes, Wisdom, Isaiah, Jeremiah, Lamentations, Gospel of Matthew, Gospel of Luke, Gospel of John, Romans, Corinthians, Ephesians, Hebrews (Guibert of Nogent, Deeds of God Through the Franks, https://www.gutenberg.org/cache/epub/4370/pg4370.html, accessed 12 January 2021).
[338] Buchon (Ed.), Les Chroniques de sir Jean Froissart; Luce, Raynaud, Mirot (Eds), Chroniques de J. Froissart; Macaulay (Ed.), Bourchier, Berners (Transl.), The Chronicles of Froissart. See Anaxagorou, Narrative and Stylistic Structures, 119.
[339] Guibert of Nogent, Deeds of God Through the Franks (https://www.gutenberg.org/cache/epub/4370/pg4370.html, accessed 12 January 2021).
[340] Who served Edward III. Information after Geary (Ed.), Readings in Medieval History, 677.
[341] This term was coined by Peter Ainsworth, who writes: '[…] the reason is rather what I call the antiphonal, conflictual (ironic) resonances of his prose, the composite elements of which unite in providing that moral and aesthetic tension so peculiar to his best writing. […] In the *Chroniques* […] we have an intermittent glimpse of an alternative way of considering the world about which they are written.' (Ainsworth, Configuring Transience, 18–19).
[342] Mas Latrie (Ed.), Chroniques d'Amadi, 151; Coureas, Edbury (Transl.), The Chronicle of Amadi, 150 (§ 279).
[343] Mas Latrie (Ed.), Chroniques d'Amadi, 157.
[344] Mas Latrie (Ed.), Chroniques d'Amadi, 197, 200, 207 ; Coureas, Edbury (Transl.), The Chronicle of Amadi, 102, 192, 195, 202 (Jordan §§ 196, 354; Tinnis § 368; Rubin § 406).

attitude to God and their moral condition. He sometimes assigns modifiers to persons and groups, as in the case of the epithet 'stupid and drunken people of Ammochostos' (ὁ μωρὸς καὶ ὁ μεθυσμένος λαὸς τῆς Ἀμοχούστου, LM III 330). Far more vivid figures were penned by the author of the *Chronique d'Amadi*, who for example writes about Nūr ad-Dīn (*Norandin*) that he was:

> *the adversary of the Christians but, according to his own faith, a religious and most righteous prince* [...].³⁴⁵

In some fragments of the *Chronique d'Amadi* the individual features of a given person are shown in a very interesting way. One of them tells of a lord from Beyrout (Beirut) who climbed to his toes when making requests of the king, in order to stand taller.³⁴⁶

Leontios is not prone to painting vivid descriptions of objects and events. He prefers to present facts and people's responses to them, which he accompanies with simple, sometimes one-sentence comments. Where he does attempt such a description, he usually focuses on naming the objects without characterising them. The *Chronique d'Amadi* presents a different picture, containing scenes that appeal to the imagination. One example is a fragment describing King Henry's arrival in Famagusta on 10 September 1310, accompanied by music, dancing and lights, where the amassed populace is depicted as wearing delightfully colourful clothing: Frank townsfolk resplendent in their 'white and red' (*bianco et rosso*), Syrians in 'red and green' (*rossi et verde*), Genoese in 'yellow and purple' (*zallo et pannazo*), Venetians in 'yellow and red' (*zalli et rossi*), and Pisans 'all in red' (*tutto rosso*).³⁴⁷ Still more interesting is a paragraph concerning a ceremony that took place after Henry's coronation as king of Jerusalem in 1286, during which, we read, the atmosphere of 'the Round Table' (*Tavola rottonda*) was recreated, featuring 'the queen of Femenie' (*la regina Femenia*) and 'knights in feminine guise, who together take part in the tourney' (*zoè cavaglieri vestiti da donne che giostravano insieme*).³⁴⁸ The *Chronicle* does contain exceptions, however: detailed, grandiose battle scenes in which complicated machinery is used and ingenious strategic solutions are adopted.³⁴⁹ Furthermore, an eloquent prop is occasionally incorporated into the narrative, which stands out conspicuously given the deprivation of detail in the descriptive layer. Such props include: painted canes belonging to the Venetians (τὰ ραβδία τοὺς ραβδούχους τοὺς Βενετίκους καὶ ἦτον καὶ ζωγραφισμένα, LM II 250) that served as tools for attack, a scarlet flag (μίαν παντιέραν παννὶν σχαρλάτον, LM III 300) flying among the amassed citizens of the Republics, 'three crowns of pearl' (γ' στέμματα μαργαριταρένα) pinned by the Genoese to their 'scarlet' (σχαρλάτα) robes (LM IV 617) and a 'marble trough whose volume was one Lefkosian modius' (μία γούρνα μαρμαρένη καὶ εἶνε ἄξαμος τοῦ μόδι τῆς Λευκωσίας), located near the church of St George of the Pulans, i.e. the Commoners, literally 'St George of the Birds' (Ἅγιος Γεώργιος τῶν Ὀρνιθίων),³⁵⁰ which Leontios mentions 'to remember the time and place' (διὰ ἀθύμησιν καιροῦ καὶ τόπου).³⁵¹

What the *Chronicle* has in common with western works is surely its concern for maintaining a suitable narrative pace. Leontios slows it down consistently with the use of 'self-contained stories', but does not include longer metaphysical or axiological deliberations to achieve this effect. Such a deceleration may be found in the *Chronique d'Amadi*, in a fragment where in 1232 the lord of Beyrout, after being instructed by the bishop to throw himself on the emperor's mercy, recounts a story with a moral about a melancholy old lion (*un gran leon vechio maladizzo et melanconico*) that wanted to eat the heart of a deer at all costs.³⁵² The 'self-contained stories' in the Cypriot work differ from the one above in that they are not exemplifications, but their function of slowing down the narrative is similar.

---

³⁴⁵ Mas Latrie (Ed.), Chroniques d'Amadi, 43: *adversario di Christiani, secondo la sua leze principe justissimo, religioso, et molto savio er prudente* [...]. Translation (here and below) from Italian into English after Coureas, Edbury (Transl.), The Chronicle of Amadi, 43 (§ 80).

³⁴⁶ Mas Latrie (Ed.), Chroniques d'Amadi, 150: *si levò egli in piedi, avanti al re* [...] *el crescendo le sue gambe con le ponte di piedi.* 'he rose to his feet before the king [...] and, making himself taller by being on tiptoe'. Translation after Coureas, Edbury (Transl.), The Chronicle of Amadi, 149 (§ 277).

³⁴⁷ Mas Latrie (Ed.), Chroniques d'Amadi, 383–384; Coureas, Edbury (Transl.), The Chronicle of Amadi, 350 (§ 725).

³⁴⁸ Mas Latrie (Ed.), Chroniques d'Amadi, 217; the expression 'Queen of Femenie' after Coureas, Edbury (Transl.), The Chronicle of Amadi, 213 (§ 452).

³⁴⁹ E.g.: LM II 250, III 561, 584, V 679–680.

³⁵⁰ Dawkins explains that 'τῶν Ὀρνιθίων' is a translation of *des Poulains* meaning pulans, children of Syrian mothers and Franckish fathers. He himself translates the expression as 'of Halfcastes' (Dawkins, Notes, 75).

³⁵¹ LM II 274.

³⁵² Mas Latrie (Ed.), Chroniques d'Amadi, 179–182; Coureas, Edbury (Transl.), The Chronicle of Amadi, 176–178 (§ 320).

Although it cannot be ruled out that Leontios applied certain narrative solutions used by other historiographers by borrowing specific techniques or motifs, it is worth focusing on his undoubted innovation: presenting a portrayal of the diverse Cypriot world, situated quite far away from Byzantium, but rooted at some level in a Byzantine past and shaped by the Latin newcomers. This specific historical and cultural residuum resulted in a work that is in many respects singular and unrivalled. As regards narrative innovation, but also due to its presentation, as Kyrris notes, of 'the encounter of two societies and cultures',[353] Makhairas' text resembles – if we wish to find similarities – Τὸ Χρονικὸν τοῦ Μορέως (The Chronicle of Morea) dated to the years 1300–1388,[354] an anonymous work showing events in Morea and Athens under the rule of the Franks (the Villehardouin dynasty) in the years 1204–1292.[355] In his preface to the publication, John Schmitt writes that the *Chronicle of Morea* is:

the chief literary monument of the Frankish period and one of the earliest, most important and extensive compositions in popular Greek.[356]

What links the two chronicles is the choice of Greek as their medium.[357]

Anaxagorou summarises the similarities between the texts. These are: the usage of popular language ('still in its infancy for literary compositions', she accents), 'syntactic similarities' and 'a common conception of historical representation' ('extranarrative addresses' and 'brief direct speech interjections').[358]

However, form is where the works differ. Namely, the Greek version of the *Chronicle of Morea* was written in political verse (πολιτικὸς στίχος), i.e. 'the Greek national verse in the Middle Ages',[359] though – as Schmitt shows with example – it departed significantly from the representative form,[360] while Makhairas' *Chronicle* was a prose work. The remaining versions of the former text, that is the French, Italian and 'Aragonese', are in prose.[361] Moreover the anonymous chronicle eschews overly popular forms and 'in common spelling he carefully avoids innovations',[362] while Makhairas does not shy from numerous neologisms originating in other languages (e.g. French, Italian, Provençal, Arabic), submitting to the exceptional flexibility of Cypriot Greek, and including frequent repetition on the other hand. Anaxagorou believes the most important difference to be sentence structure, which in the case of the *Chronicle of Morea* is 'compact and short', and 'loose' in the *Chronicle*.[363]

Schmitt recapitulates his analysis positing that, taking into account its linguistic layer, the *Chronicle of Morea* is a Greek work, but its unique literary form sets it closer to French works, as in its case two traditions are superimposed: the established literary tradition and the colloquial oral tradition[364] – which makes the work more legible for a larger group of recipients.[365] The publisher accurately describes the nature of the text in that it represents a state of fluctuation ('it was in so fluctuating a state').[366] Emphasising 'the prevailing use of paratactical construction',[367] Schmitt compares the *Chronicle of Morea* with Cypriot chronicles:

---

[353] Kyrris, Some Aspects, 167.
[354] Schmitt, Introduction, xxxvii–xxxviii. An important study of the *Chronicle of Morea* was made by Teresa Shawcross in Shawcross, The Chronicle of Morea. She analyses all four versions.
[355] Schmitt, Introduction, xlix.
[356] Schmitt, Introduction, vi. Showcross also discusses the *Chronicle* in Shawcross, The Chronicle of Morea, 224–229.
[357] Schmitt describes this tongue, as it appeared in the Middle Ages, as follows: 'The popular language of Greece in the Middle Ages is closely connected with that of the present day, much closer than the language of Chaucer is with modern English.' (Schmitt, Introduction, xxiii).
[358] Anaxagorou, Narrative and Stylistic Structures, 117–119.
[359] Schmitt, Introduction, xxxiii. Cf. Jurewicz, Historia literatury bizantyńskiej, 264.
[360] Schmitt, Introduction, xxxiv. Cf. Jurewicz, Historia literatury bizantyńskiej, 264.
[361] Shawcross, Oral Residue and Narrative Structure, 310.
[362] Schmitt, Introduction, xxxiv.
[363] Anaxagorou, Narrative and Stylistic Structures, 118.
[364] Schmitt, Introduction, xliii.
[365] Schmitt, Introduction, xlii.
[366] Schmitt, Introduction, xliii.
[367] Schmitt, Introduction, xlv.

1.4. NARRATIVE SINGULARITY OF THE *CHRONICLE*

The Chronicles which describe the feudal reign of the Lusignans in Cyprus, and form a counterpart to our Chronicle, are much inferior to it, just because they are written in humble and creeping prose.[368]

Makhairas' work, lacking official, rigid, incomprehensible vocabulary, is also addressed to the mass recipient. It depicts the 'colonial' reality in all its aspects: it contains a record of individual stages of colonisation, both in the linguistic layer, and as regards subject matter, and at the same time it registers the change involved in the gradual, slow fall of Frankish rule. The courage with which the Cypriot uses French words such as: 'γράσα' (Prov *graça*, Old Fr *grace*, 'grace'),[369] 'ματίνες' (Old Fr *matines*, 'call to prayer'),[370] 'ξόμπλιν'/'ὀξόμπλι(ν)' (Fr *exemple*, Lat *exemplum*, 'example'),[371] 'ὀνέστε' (Old Fr *honesté*, Lat *honeste*, 'honestly'),[372] 'ρεσπόστα' (Fr *réponse/resposte*, Prov *resposta*, It *risposta*),[373] etc., and Italian words such as: 'ἄττον' (It *atto*, 'act', 'deed', 'action'), 'βεντέττα' (It *vendetta*, 'revenge'),[374] 'περφόρτζα' (It *per forza*, 'out of necessity', 'surely'),[375] etc., indicate that he approached the writing of his work with still greater openness than the *Chronicle of Morea* author. This does not mean, however, that he did not reflect on whether his message would be understood: he sometimes translates certain phrases: he explains for instance in LM III 455 that the sentence Βίβα ρὲ Πιέρ! means Ζῆ ὁ ρὲ Πιέρ! ('Long live King Peter').

The two historiographers' situation in life also differed. Schmitt calls the author of the *Chronicle of Morea* 'a strong Catholic and a thorough Frenchman in his national feeling'.[376] Makhairas, meanwhile, was a Rhomaioi accustomed to the presence of the Franks, mentally or sentimentally close to Orthodoxy, as we may conclude from indirect indications present in his text. Leontios does not openly declare his faith in the manner of, for example, Gregory of Tours (538–594), who in the prologue to his *Histoire Ecclésiastique des Francs* (Ecclesiastical History of the Franks) states:

I desire first of all to declare my faith so that my reader may have no doubt that I am Catholic.[377]

However, Leontios does express his beliefs through the way he describes events and assigns specific meanings to them.

Only once does the *Chronicle of Morea* include, as Schmitt terms it, 'a reminiscence of a fantastical nature borrowed from popular Greek poetry [...] relating to weeping birds' (ref. to v. 7222).[378] Makhairas, in addition to regularly weaving legends into his narrative, frequently cites popular proverbs,[379] thus drawing closer to the common folk, who thanks to such narrative devices were, it may be assumed, able to understand the moral or the central point of a given event. Some examples: 'the same punishment is experienced by the one who holds the leg of the goat and by the one who skins it' (-τόσην πέναν ἔχει- ἀποῦ κρατεῖ τὸ πόδιν τοῦ 'ριφίου, ὡς γοιὸν ἐκεῖνον ὁποῦ τὸ γδέρνει, LM II 278), 'would that miserly [people] were not born, because greed makes devils of people' (μακάρι οἱ ἀκριβοὶ νὰ μὲν ἐγεννοῦνταν, ὅτι ἡ λύσσα τῆς φιλαργυρίας πολομᾷ τοὺς ἀνθρώπους δαιμόνους, LM III 532), 'the strong man holds me, the weak man beats me' (Κρατεῖ με ὁ δυνατός, καὶ δέρνει με ὁ ἀδύνατος, LM III 534) and many others.[380] Interestingly, Makhairas attributes one of these proverbs, 'do not have faith in every word you hear, so that you will not be thought a fool' (Μὲν πιστεύσῃς πᾶσα λόγον τὸ νὰ γροικήσῃς, μηδὲν σὲ κρατήσουν μωρόν) to the philosophers (τὸ πεῖν τοὺς φιλοσόφους).[381] The proverb 'where hurry[382] rules the law

---

[368] Schmitt, Introduction, xlvi.
[369] LM II 249, III 547. After Dawkins, Glossary, 242 and ΘΚΔ, 127.
[370] LM III 570. After Dawkins, Glossary, 255 and ΘΚΔ, 276.
[371] LM I 79, 85, III 573. After Dawkins, Glossary, 257 and ΘΚΔ, 32, 329.
[372] LM V 631. After Dawkins, Glossary, 258 and ΘΚΔ, 329.
[373] LM II 268. After Dawkins, Glossary, 265 and ΘΚΔ, 404.
[374] LM II 103, 146, 216. After Dawkins, Glossary, 240 and ΘΚΔ, 97.
[375] LM III 584. After Dawkins, Glossary, 262 and ΘΚΔ, 355.
[376] Schmitt, Introduction, xl.
[377] Grégoire de Tours, Histoire Ecclésiastique des Francs, 8: *prius fidem meam proferre cupio, ut qui legerit me non dubitet esse catholicum*. Translation after Gregory of Tours, The History of the Franks.
[378] Schmitt, Introduction, xl.
[379] Proverbs in the *Chronicle* have been studied by Phedon Koukoules in Κουκουλές, Παροιμίαι καὶ γνωμικά, 235–242. See Anaxagorou, Narrative and Stylistic Structures, 18 (fn. 104).
[380] LM II 253, III 593.
[381] LM III 412.
[382] Dawkins translates 'βία' as 'necessity'.

is transformed' (ὅπου βία πρόκειται, ἐκεῖ νόμου μετάθεσις γίνεται, LM III 591) is, Dawkins observes, an echo of the saying 'For when there is a change in the priesthood, there is necessarily a change in the law as well,' from St Paul's Letter to the Hebrews.[383] Other statements of a general nature and unspecified provenance may be found in the *Chronicle*, such as: '[The] more people, [the] greater the knowledge' (πολλοὶ ἀνθρῶποι, πολλὲς γνῶσες, LM II 253). The chronicler also records sayings attributed to other nations, as confirmed by the Genoese principle: 'As [somebody] acts towards you, so may you act towards him, and even if you are not able to do so, do not forget about it' ("ὅπου νὰ σοῦ ποίσῃ, ποῖσε του, καὶ ἀνισῶς καὶ δὲν ἐφτάσῃς νὰ τὸ ποίσῃς, μὲν τὸν λησμονήσῃς", LM II 259). Considering the authors's liking for this kind of statement, the *Chronicle* may be compared to Manasses' *Chronicle*, which was available on Cyprus during the Lusignan reign.[384] On Polish ground, similar tendencies may be encountered in Vincent Kadłubek's (ca. 1150–1223) *Chronicle of the Poles*, which includes numerous proverbs, such as: 'the rose hides prickly thorns, the grass hides a serpent'[385] or 'dismal is all slavery in apparel of carded cloth, [but still] more dismal in purple',[386] but unlike the *Chronicle* Kadłubek's work is full of erudite digressions, Biblical quotations and ancient themes. In its lack of such references, its straightforward structure and uncomplicated syntax, Makhairas's work suggests that its narrative has a popular character, and at its forefront are hagiographical miniatures, courtly romance with elements of scandal and dynamically recounted tales faithfully representing the turmoil of battle.[387]

The author of the *Chronicle of Morea* comprehensively describes 'the feudal customs', consigning less attention to details of warfare;[388] Leontios meticulously portrays battles initiated by Cypriot rulers. Both texts offer a depiction that contains several overlapping histories, the *Chronicle of Morea* presenting a fragment of 'French, Italian, Catalan, Slavic, Grecian and Oriental',[389] and Makhairas' *Chronicle*, of French, Cypriot, Italian and Muslim history.

The *Chronicle of Morea* opens with a remark by Peter the Hermit, who reports happenings in the Holy Land to Pope Urban II (1035|1088–1099),[390] which inspires the bishop of Rome to organise a crusade. The author expresses the objective of the work he has undertaken with the words: 'I wish to tell you a great tale' (Θέλω νὰ σὲ ἀφηγηθῶ σὲ ἀφήγησιν μεγάλην, v. 1), voicing the hope that it will be to the reader's liking (ὀλπίζω νὰ σ' ἀρέσῃ, v. 2),[391] which significantly differs from Leontios' intention to create a 'short account'. In another place he invokes the learnedness of those who intend to acquaint themselves with the work, suggesting that a person of knowledge will understand its content ('Ἐπεὶ ἂν εἶσαι γνωστικὸς κ'ἐξεύρεις τὰ σὲ γράφω, v. 1340), but he also does not forget the uneducated (εἴ τε εἶσαι πάλι ἀγράμματος, κάθου σιμά μου, ἀφκράζου, v. 1352), because learning and punishment are equally important to him (νὰ μάθῃς καὶ παιδεύεσαι, v. 1350).[392] In the context of this text, Makhairas' originality lies in the fact that he approaches his work with a large degree of restraint, treating the fruit of his labours, the *Chronicle* text, as a medium that will be tasked with preserving specific content for future generations in order to keep its significance from oblivion.

The Cypriot author created a singular work because no single line linking the *Chronicle* with other medieval historiographic works may be drawn in terms of form or content.

---

[383] Hbr. 7, 12. Dawkins, Notes, 197.
[384] Κεχαγιόγλου, Παπαλεοντίου, Τὸ γραμματειακό 'πολυσύστημα', 22. The presence of proverbs in Manasses' work is signalised by Jurewicz, Historia literatury bizantyńskiej, 209.
[385] Wincenty Kadłubek, Kronika polska, 33 (book I, chapter 19). Translated from Brygida Kürbis' Polish translation by Kupiszewska.
[386] Wincenty Kadłubek, Kronika polska, 169 (book III, chapter 30). Translated from Brygida Kurbis' Polish translation by Kupiszewska.
[387] Vassiliou writes about the structure of these sentences: 'Makhairas' narrative style regularly makes use of short sentences, when the initial paragraph verb is introductory with an overt S and the following verbs make up a string of V-s short main clauses.' (Vassiliou, Word Order of Medieval Cypriot, 230). 'S' stands for 'Subject', 'V' for 'Verb'.
[388] Schmitt, Introduction, xl.
[389] Schmitt, Introduction, liv.
[390] Dates after: Dopierała, Księga papieży, 157; Emmerson (Ed.), Key Figures.
[391] Schmitt (Ed.), The Chronicle of Morea, 3. Codex Parisinus.
[392] Schmitt (Ed.), The Chronicle of Morea, 92. Codex Havniensis.

1.5. Other texts relating to Cyprus

Other works that at some level present fragments of the history of medieval Cyprus are also known.

One of them is, already mentioned several times, the anonymous *Chronique d'Amadi* (The Chronicle of Amadi),[393] written in Italian and covering the period from the reign of Byzantine Emperor Heraklios (610–641)[394] to 1442, and which contains several texts about the Lusignan reign. They include: William of Tyre's *Eracles* (History of Heraclius),[395] a lost source recounting the events of 1099, *Annales de Terre Sainte* (Annals of the Holy Land),[396] Jacques de Vitry's *Historia Orientalia* (History of the East),[397] Philip of Novara's testimony,[398] *Templar of Tyre*,[399] a lost text on the reign of Amaury of Tyre (1306–1310)[400] and Leontios Makhairas' *Chronicle* (from the discovery of the Togni Cross in 1340).[401] A manuscript containing all of them, dated to the sixteenth century, belonged to Francesco Amadi,[402] who gave his name to the compilation.[403] Despite a similar content to Makhairas' *Chronicle*, the *Chronique d'Amadi* contains many changes, additional information and omissions compared to the original. An examination of the differences signalled by Peter Edbury and Nicholas Coureas in the footnotes to their translation of the *Chronique d'Amadi* may help glean a deeper meaning of the fragments of the Cypriot work that were expanded on or abridged. Some examples include comments in which the translators of the *Chronique d'Amadi* into English find distinct anti-Latin overtones in some fragments of Leontios' narrative, impossible to detect in the Italian version,[404] and a fuller and more precise description of Peter I's reign and the Cypriot-Genoese

---

[393] Mas Latrie (Ed.), Chroniques d'Amadi et de Strambaldi.

[394] More precisely, as Coureas and Edbury note, until the retrieval of the Holy Cross from Persian hands by Heraklios (Coureas, Edbury (Ed.), The Chronicle of Amadi, xiii).

[395] Coureas, Edbury describe this source in the following way: 'The author employed the Old French translation of William of Tyre and its continuation using the so-called Colbert-Fontainebleau Continuation. The French translation of William's original Latin would seem to date to around 1220 and this version of the continuation to around 1250 and with later additions.' (Coureas, Edbury, Annexe 4, 487). Fn. 1 on page 487 gives two sources: Guillaume de Tyr, L'estoire de Eracles [...] la translation, and Guillaume de Tyr, L'estoire de Eracles [...] la continuation.

[396] Coureas and Edbury write: 'The author appears to have used a version of the *Annales* akin to the "B" text as edited by Röhricht and Reynaud and a version of the *Annales* associated with the writings of Philip of Novara as found in the *Gestes des Chiprois*. It would seem that the texts employed had additional material, some of it relating specifically to Cyprus.' (Coureas, Edbury, Annexe 4, 487–488). Sources they specify: Röhricht, Reynaud (Eds), Annales de Terre Sainte, 427–461 and Paris, Mas Latrie (Eds), Les Gestes des Chiprois, 651–872, on pages 653–669 (after Coureas, Edbury, Annexe 4, 487, fn. 2).

[397] Jacques de Vitry, La traduction de l'Historia Orientalis (after Coureas, Edbury, Annexe 4, 488, fn. 1).

[398] According to Coureas and Edbury: 'The French text of Philip's account of events from the mid-1220s to the 1240s is preserved as part of the *Gestes des Chiprois*. This work was originally composed around the middle of the thirteenth century, and the text used by the *Amadi*-author clearly differed at certain points from that preserved in the unique manuscript of the French text.' (Coureas, Edbury, Annexe 4, 488). Source: Filippo da Novara, Guerra di Federico II in Oriente (after Coureas, Edbury, Annexe 4, 488, and fn. 2).

[399] Coureas and Edbury specify: 'This anonymous work forms the concluding section of the *Gestes de Chiprois* and was composed in the early fourteenth century', and give Minervini (Ed.), Cronaca del Templare de Tiro as a source (Coureas, Edbury, Annexe 4, 488, and fn. 3).

[400] The translators explain: 'It is likely that this account included material from the mid-1290s onwards and continued to the end of the reign of Henry II in 1324 and possibly beyond. It is particularly detailed for the years 1306–1311, and it is likely that the original version of that account was composed almost immediately afterwards. This narrative, especially in the earliest sections, is interspersed with material from the "Templar of Tyre" [...].' (Coureas, Edbury, Annexe 4, 488–489). See Crawford (Ed.), 'Templar of Tyre'.

[401] Edbury and Coureas provide an important piece of information regarding the version of Makhairas' *Chronicle* used by the author of the compilation: '*Amadi* clearly had a version that differed in places from all the extant manuscripts and which lacked the additional material found in the Venice manuscript of the Ἐξήγησις. It would also appear that the *Amadi* author tended to abridge Leontios's history, although buried in his narrative there are occasionally pieces of information not found in the Greek texts.' (Coureas, Edbury, Introduction, xxv). Elsewhere, Edbury states that it is impossible to prove all the connections and satisfactorily describe the layers of the relationship between these texts (Edbury, Machaut, Mézières, Makhairas and Amadi, 351).

[402] This was a copy of the manuscript. Coureas, Edbury, Introduction, xiv.

[403] In the Introduction to Coureas, Edbury (Transl.), The Chronicle of Amadi we read: 'The anonymous text known as the *Chronique d'Amadi* survives in a single, mid sixteenth-century manuscript in the Marciana Library in Venice.' What is particularly interesting, 'it begins with the emperor Heraklios recovering the True Cross from the Persians in the seventh century' (Coureas, Edbury, Introduction, xiii).

[404] Reference to LM I 67–77 in Coureas, Edbury (Transl.), The Chronicle of Amadi, 371 (fn. 4); to LM II 101 in Coureas, Edbury (Transl.), The Chronicle of Amadi, 373 (fn. 2).

war of 1373–1374, which may be found in the *Chronique d'Amadi*.[405] At some level, the latter text is treated here – like Makhairas' *Chronicle* – as a literary depiction of the historical reality (which is a product of the literary depictions contained in the eight original texts, as modified by the author or authors of the Italian compilation[406]). This is why in some places much importance is attached to the differences between how the narrative about a given event is built in Makhairas' *Chronicle* and in the part of the *Chronique d'Amadi* that was written on its basis (to bring out the specific features of the chronicler's perspective), and also the narrative concerning different events of the same character described in Makhairas' *Chronicle* and anywhere in the *Chronique d'Amadi* (e.g. the way different instances of encounters between Christians and Muslims are presented). In the opinion of Edbury, sixteenth-century chronicler Florio Bustron, the author of *Historia overo commentarii de Cipro* (History or rather commentaries about Cyprus),[407] whose narrative starts in 1489,[408] based his work on the *Chronique d'Amadi* to a large extent.

Diomede Strambaldi's *Chronique* (Chronicle)[409] is another Italian chronicle, and is a slightly modified translation of Makhairas' *Chronicle*. This work, like the *Chronique d'Amadi*, lacks sentences and fragments that in the Cypriot work reveal the author's personal attitude towards his family and home country (Strambaldi himself lived in Cyprus).[410] The absence of such sections in the Italian texts throws light on the sense and character of the information, which turned out to have no value for Italian chroniclers.

Another author of texts containing references to Cypriot themes is Philippe de Mézières (1327–1405),[411] already mentioned above, whom Nicolaou-Konnari called 'a Frenchman by birth and a citizen of Christendom by conviction',[412] and who like Makhairas served at the Frankish court, albeit during the reign of Peter I (1358–1369) and Peter II (1369–1382). His work in the French language, *Le Songe du Vieil Pelerin* (Dream of the Old Pilgrim),[413] which also includes mentions of Cyprus, is a literary tale composed of numerous allegories, recounting the consequences of the departure from the primary value that is the truth, as experienced by members of different nations. Cyprus holds an exceptional position within it, as Kevin Brownlee among others demonstrates.[414] Philip himself participated in these events as the biographer of Carmelite Peter de Thomas and Peter I's chancellor in the years 1360–1368. These facts are expounded on by Nicolae Iorga in *Philippe de Mézières, 1327–1405* where he devotes much space to Philippe's links with Cyprus, showing his role in historical events on a global scale, as well as to various facets of Frankish rule: for example, he underlines that Hugh IV (1324–1359), father of Peter I, strived to strengthen the 'Latin element' (*l'élément latin*) on the island.[415]

Le Songe has an allegorical structure. Its editor George William Coopland, who analyses the source in these very categories, writes:

> [...] *the* Songe *is based on a main allegory of a sort of divine working-party, a fact-finding commission, which is to examine the state of morals throughout Christendom* [...].[416]

---

[405] Edbury, Machaut, Mézières, Makhairas and Amadi, 351. Edbury takes into account two possibilities: either the 'author' of the *Chronique d'Amadi* possessed a different version of Makhairas' text, or his intention was not to reflect it literally (or to abridge it) (Edbury, Machaut, Mézières, Makhairas and Amadi, 351).

[406] Anne Gilmour-Bryson hypothesises that this compilation 'is presumably an Italian version of a French original from the fourteenth century, perhaps a fuller version of the *Gestes des Chiprois*' (Gilmour-Bryson, Introduction, 2).

[407] Bustron, Chronique de l'Île de Chypre; Bustron, Historia overo Commentarii de Cipro. Edbury states that the *Chronique d'Amadi* and *Historia overo commentarii de Cipro* are 'clearly related to Leontios's account of Peter's reign and the subsequent events'. He suggests that details concerning this particular reign described in the second text have been transplanted from the first one. As the second option he postulates that the author of the *Chronique d'Amadi* and Florio Bustron had access to 'a now-lost common original'. Edbury calls the first work 'much cruder' and the second one 'far more elegant and accomplished' (Edbury, Machaut, Mézières, Makhairas and Amadi, 351). Gilmour-Bryson holds the same opinion. See Gilmour-Bryson, Introduction, 2.

[408] Burkiewicz, Polityczna rola królestwa Cypru, 17.

[409] Mas Latrie (Ed.), Chronique de Strambaldi.

[410] Burkiewicz, Polityczna rola królestwa Cypru, 17.

[411] Dating after Głodek, Utopia Europy zjednoczonej. An important study on Philippe de Mézières is Blumenfeld-Kosinski, Petkov (Eds), Philippe de Mézières and His Age.

[412] Nicolaou-Konnari, Alterity and identity, 44.

[413] Philippe de Mézières, Le Songe.

[414] Brownlee, The Figure of Peter I, 165.

[415] Iorga, Philippe de Mézières, 77. Kupiszewska's translation of all Iorga's short phrases from the Polish translation by the author.

[416] Coopland, General Introduction, 29.

Apart from that there are

two large sub-allegories [...] that of the French ship of state, the Gracieuse *[...] and [...] the elaborate application of the sixty four squares of the chessboard [...] distinctive in its review of royal power and duties.*[417]

Le Songe opens with a scene showing a pilgrim (Philippe himself) sleeping in a chapel.[418] This approach resembles the strategy employed by Bergadis in the work *Ο Απόκοπος* (The Exhausted)[419] and Ioannis Pikatoros in *Ρίμα θρηνητική εἰς τόν πικρόν καί ἀκόρεστον Ἅδην* (Mournful Rhyme on the Bitter and Insatiable Hades),[420] who focus their message around the dream of the poet or narrator.[421] In Philippe's narrative the axis of the story is formed by the travel motif of the siblings 'Ardent Desire' (*Ardant Desir*) and 'Good Hope' (*Bonne Esperance*), reaching among others Nubia, India, China, Scandinavia and European countries in search of Truth (*Verite*).[422] Their stay in each of these places forms a pretext for commentary on the morality of the peoples encountered or for presenting a fragment of history.

The work closes with a scene in which Philippe,

overcome by despair at the failure of his hopes for the reform of the West as antecedent to a new crusade, lies prostrate before the altar in a chapel of the Celestines in Paris, and there expresses his private and public griefs. To him appears Divine Providence.[423]

When comparing the Frenchman's text with the *Chronicle*, many differences between the works may be observed. Already in the prologue to *Le Songe* we read that the work tightly combines elements of axiology (*moralment*), visions (*vision*), thought (*consideration*) and imagination (*ymaginacion*).[424] The narrative layer is replete with metaphors such as that of a smithy, where the personified figures hammer out coins, a ship representing France or the visualisation of 'Queen Truth' presenting the tablets of the law to Charles VI.[425] The *Chronicle*, though not completely deprived of contemplation of morality and commentaries on the events described, does not achieve this degree of abstraction. Deeper reflection is replaced in it by folk proverbs, conclusions flowing from observation of human behaviour (mainly that of representatives of the court) and a rather insightful study of human emotionality. The Cypriot chronicler undeniably prefers to operate on concrete material. Both where he recounts events that he witnessed and where he cites old stories, he is interested in human deeds and he describes them with attention to detail, to allow a correct understanding of their nature. In *Le Songe,* by giving a voice to personified ideas, Philippe introduces polyphony into his narrative, which permits a comprehensive view of phenomena such as iniquity and sinfulness of human nature, and their analysis in moral and historical terms. He gives the right to pronounce opinions about other peoples also to intermediaries such as the Genoese merchant who tells Philippe, who is on Cyprus at that point, a tale about the Hindus, forming a separate narrative about alterity within the main text.[426] Through the remarks of various figures and often also through their actions, Makhairas shows their own points of view, allowing polyphony only in the form of discussion, for example in a group of emirs who exchange opinions. Aware that he has accustomed the recipient of the *Chronicle* to diversity of opinion and numerous dialogues in the text, he intentionally emphasises situations in which a group takes a common position. This he phrases for example as follows: 'they told him with one mouth' (ὅλοι ἔναν στόμαν εἶπαν εἰς αὐτόν του, LM II 252). Elsewhere Leontios writes of 'the mouth of the people' (τὰ στόματα τοὺς λᾶς, LM II 240), thus also stressing the unanimity of the message. In *Le Songe* Philippe shows his curiosity about the world through the pilgrim's symbolical travels. He takes the same perspective as the author of the *Chronique d'Amadi*, who in a digression about Armenia states:

---

[417] Coopland, General Introduction, 29.
[418] Philippe de Mézières, Le Songe, 91; Coopland, General Introduction, 30.
[419] Borowska, Katabaza Bergadisa, 45–46.
[420] Borowska, Katabaza Bergadisa, 49.
[421] Borowska, Katabaza Bergadisa, 45–46, 49.
[422] Coopland, General Introduction, 33–37.
[423] Coopland, General Introduction, 1 (ref. to Philippe de Mézières, Le Songe, 265).
[424] Philippe de Mézières, Le Songe, 89.
[425] Coopland, General Introduction, 29, 32, 40–41, 60.
[426] Coopland, General Introduction, 70 (ref. to Philippe de Mézières, Le Songe, 223).

> *To understand the history of Cyprus in full, it is necessary to know certain things about other countries first [...].*[427]

For Makhairas the objective of his involvement in historiographic activity is to describe his beloved island of Cyprus and underline the elements that are necessary and useful for providing a complete view of the emerging picture (diplomatic or military action outside its borders).

Philippe appreciates rich, expressive images, which is why for example his depiction of a procession in Rome, with a crowd of figures with human bodies and animal or bird heads as its participants, seems so evocative.[428] He encrusts the narrative with numerous descriptions of nature, as demonstrated by a passage about beautifully coloured birds (*des beaulx oyseaulx rouges, vers et dorez, et de divers plumages*),[429] 'extensive forests' (*grant forestz*) and 'frozen rivers' (*rivieres engelees passans dessus la glace*).[430] He sets much store by complex depictions of personalities who are important for his work, often using metaphors. In a remark by the 'Queen Truth', for example, he compares Charlemagne to Moses, placing the ruler's life in a Biblical context.[431]

Nicolaou-Konnari compares Leontios with Philippe. In her opinion both historians derived knowledge in two ways: they used documents borrowed from archives as well as their own experience[432] – both of them very godly, as the scholar concludes, they built their historical position on the basis of a causal interpretation of events and they used the vernaculars.[433] Nicolaou-Konnari posits that Makhairas' vision is fuller and more 'multifaceted' than Philippe's account because Leontios shows the local, '*kypriotike* perception of history',[434] which takes into account the nuances of the functioning of the individual and of the group who chanced to meet. According to the author of this opinion, it is important that in employing this multilayered perspective, the chronicler preserves a suitable balance between a deeply rooted Byzantineness and participation in the new age that commenced for Cyprus upon the arrival of the Franks. Nicolaou-Konnari states:

> *Makhairas has a balanced sense of his wider Greek identity, that allows him to participate in the Byzantine* oecumene, *and of his particular Cypriot identity as a citizen of the Lusignan Kingdom, and this is clearly expressed in the way he employs ethnic names.*[435]

The scholar finds the Cypriot's attitude to show the hallmarks of exceptional tolerance and circumspection in pronouncing judgements, which she believes stemmed from the opportunity to draw on the experience of living in a multicultural society in which the Orthodox Church had become palpably subordinate to the Catholic Church. In her opinion, even if there did exist a 'differentiating trait' between Rhomaioi and Franks, the former held no 'ethnic and cultural antipathy' towards the latter.[436]

The Alexandrian Crusade described by Leontios and Philippe is also the primary subject of *La Praise d'Alexandrie* (The Capture of Alexandria)[437] by Guillaume de Machaut[438] (and so his work is not so much about Cyprus, but about a crusade by a Cypriot ruler).

In an account of works focusing on Cyprus that describe this extraordinary age, one more significant chronicle should not go unmentioned: Διήγησις κρόνικας Κύπρου ἀρχεύγοντα ἀπό τήν ἐχρονίαν αυνς'

---

[427] Mas Latrie (Ed.), Chronique d'Amadi, 88: *Per intender l'historia de Cypro integra, convien prima saver alcune cose de altre terre* [...]. Translation after Coureas, Edbury (Transl.), The Chronicle of Amadi, 87 (§ 159).
[428] Philippe de Mézières, Le Songe, 269. See Coopland, Synopsis, 142–143.
[429] Philippe de Mézières, Le Songe, 198.
[430] Philippe de Mézières, Le Songe, 237. Kupiszewska's translation of all Philippe's short phrases from the Polish translation by the author.
[431] Coopland, General Introduction, 29.
[432] Nicolaou-Konnari, Alterity and identity, 45–46.
[433] Nicolaou-Konnari, Alterity and identity, 46.
[434] Nicolaou-Konnari, Alterity and identity, 49.
[435] Nicolaou-Konnari, Alterity and identity, 58. Cf. Nicolaou-Konnari, Ethnic Names.
[436] Nicolaou-Konnari, Alterity and identity, 61.
[437] Guillaume de Machaut, La prise d'Alexandrie; Palmer (Ed., transl.), La Prise D'Alixandre.
[438] Cf. Iorga, Philippe de Mézières, 80, 190–200, 296. Louis de Mas Latrie asserts that Guillaume work is: *une œuvre conçue et exécutée dans son ensemble sous l' empire d'un double sentiment: d'une admiration exagérée et continue pour le roi Pierre de Lusignan, que ses voyages et ses brillantes expéditions contre les infidèles avaient rendu célèbre en Europe, et de l'horreur qu'inspira sa fin tragique, surtout dans les pays où les faits étaient moins connus* (Mas Latrie, Guillaume de Machaut et la prise d'Alexandrie, 455).

(Narrative of the Chronicle of Cyprus from 1456 AD) authored by George Boustronios (1430–1495),[439] who served at the court of King James II (1440–1473).[440] This work, covering the years 1456–1489, and thus forming in terms of narrative continuity an extension of Leontios' work, closes with the transfer of the island to Venice by Catarina Cornaro (1474–1489).

All the abovementioned texts show a different view of medieval Cyprus than the one seen in Leontios' work. Their perspectives on the Latin presence on the island and relations between denominations and interreligious contact are also dissimilar. Whether they are a translation of the *Chronicle*, a compilation in which content drawn from it is an important component, its continuation or a completely different take on one of the subjects therein, these works prove that because of its complexity and broad spectrum of themes, Makhairas' narrative was an important point of reference for non-Cypriot authors, and some differences and omissions actually provide additional information on the Cypriot chronicler.

1.6. The content of Leontios Makhairas' *Chronicle*

The text of the *Chronicle* was divided by Dawkins into six books of varying length, so that the first covers the 326–1359 period, and each subsequent one is allotted to the reign of one Frankish ruler:[441] Peter I (ρὲ Πιέρ 1328|1359–1369), Peter II (ρὲ Πιέρ, 1354|1369–1382), James I (Τζάκος, 1334|1382–1398), Janus (Ἰαννίους, 1375|1398–1432) and James II (ρὲ Τζουάνη, 1418|1432–1458).[442] However, it should be remembered that their author did not himself divide his text in any way, which is why in summarising the content of the *Chronicle* and citing individual segments of the narrative the term 'part' and not 'book' is used.

The first part of the *Chronicle* (LM I 1–89) is a kind of introduction to the Christian stage of the island's history, heralding events that will form the axis of the whole plot. Leontios explains his objective in writing the work and goes on to cite the details of the mission of holy ruler Helena (ἁγία δέσποινα Ἑλένη, 247–328), mother of Byzantine Emperor St Constantine (μέγας Κωνσταντῖνος, 272|306–337),[443] who after finding the Holy Cross in Jerusalem stopped in Cyprus, where she built many churches, establishing a firm foundation for Cypriot Christianity (LM I 4–9). Next, Makhairas gives a brief (likely due to lacunae) account of the Templar presence on Cyprus. He devotes one paragraph (LM I 12) to their unfortunate presence on the island before the Lusignans' arrival, resulting in a Cyprian rebellion, and then moves to describe the nature of their iniquity using an example, and so comes to their ruin in 1308 at the order of Pope Clement V (LM I 13–17).

In further parts of the text the chronicler mentions the capture of Jerusalem in July 1099 (LM I 18), wherein the following took part: Godfrey de Bouillon (Κοντεφρὲ ντε Πολίου, 1061–1100),[444] Pope Urban II (Ὀλβάνος), King Philip of France (ρὲ Φίλιππες, 1052|1060–1108) and Emperor Alexios I Komnenos (κύρης Ἀλέξης ὁ Κουμνηνός, 1048|1081–1118).[445] He then proceeds to mention consecutive rulers who sat on the Jerusalem throne since that time, starting with the above-mentioned Godfrey, who, however, never adopted the title of 'king' (LM I 18), through his brother Baldwin I (Μπαντουήν, ca. 1058|1100–1118), Baldwin II d'Aiguillon (Μπαντουὴν τ' Ἀγκιλίου, ca. 1060|1118–1131), Baldwin's son in law, Fulk V the Younger (Φουκᾶς, 1092|1131–1143), Fulk's son, Baldwin III, the Old (Μπαντουὴν ὁ Γερών, 1130|1143–1163), Baldwin's brother, Amaury I (Ἀμέρην, 1136|1163–1174), Baldwin IV, the Leper (Παντουὴν ὁ Κελεφός,

---

[439] Vassiliou, The Word Order of Medieval Cypriot, 62.
[440] Βουστρόνιος, Διήγησις κρόνικας Κύπρου; Dawkins (Transl., int.), The Chronicle of George Boustronios; Coureas (Transl.), A Narrative of the Chronicle of Cyprus.
[441] In the case of rulers and popes, their birth date is before the vertical bar. The dates marking the period from the beginning of the office to its end, which in almost all the cases mentioned in this book coincided with the date of death, are placed after the vertical bar. If the end of the office took place before the death the vertical bar divides the birth and death dates and the date of offices. Almost all names of offices are taken after Dawkins. To establish the birth, death and reigning dates of rulers the dating contained in: Hill, A History of Cyprus II; Misztal, Historia Cypru; Edbury, The Kingdom of Cyprus, and of popes, in Dopierała, Księga papieży have been included. Other publications are referred to occasionally.
[442] Edbury, The Kingdom of Cyprus, 38.
[443] Misztal, Historia Cypru, 657, 646.
[444] Misztal, Historia Cypru, 644.
[445] Birth and death dates after Wispelwey, Biographical Index, 42. Reign dates after: Savvides, Byzantino-Normannica, 1; Van Millingen, Byzantine Constantinople, 348.

1161|1174–1185), Baldwin V, the Child (Παντουήν ὁ παιδίος, 1177|1185–1186) and Guy de Lusignan (given as 'Hugh' in the text,[446] ρὲ Οὔνγκες, ca. 1150 or 1159/1160|1192–1194)[447] (LM I 19).

Having thus introduced the subject of the crusades, Leontios emphasises the moment of Guy's purchase of Cyprus in 1192, which had been held by the Knights Templar and Lombards, via King Richard Cœur de Lion of England (ὁ ρήγας τῆς Ἐκλετέρας [...] Λιτζάρ, 1157|1189–1199)[448] (LM I 20–21). Showing the politics of the Franks at the early stages of their rule on the island, Makhairas writes about the efforts undertaken by Guy to forge an agreement with sultan Saladin of Cairo (1138|1174–1193)[449] (LM I 22–25), the Latin settlement of the island, and the emergence of a new Latin church community (LM I 26–30). For the author of the *Chronicle* this event paradoxically became a pretext for lauding the greatness of Cyprus through an apotheosis of Rhomaic heritage reflected in tales of the lives and deeds of numerous saints buried on Cypriot land (LM I 31–40).

The chronicler uses the subsequent paragraphs to briefly lay out Guy's successors, omitting Amaury: Hugh I de Lusignan (ρὲ Οὔνγκε τε Λουζουνίας, 1194/1195|1205–1218), who according to Makhairas died in 1219, Henry I (ρὲ Χαρήν, 1217|1218–1253), Hugh II (ρὲ Οὔνγκε, 1253|1253–1267), Hugh III (ρὲ Οὔνγκε, 1235|1267–1284), John (ρὲ Τζουάν, 1259/1267|1284–1285) and Henry II (ρὲ Χαρήν, 1271|1285–1324) (LM I 41), and also to present events relating to the usurpation of the right to Henry II's throne by his brother Amaury (μισὲρ Μαρήν τε Λουζινιᾶς, ca. 1270–1310),[450] lord of Tyre in 1306, the rightful ruler ultimately losing the crown (LM I 42–58). Leontios shows the character of Amaury's short reign, interrupted in 1309 as a result of his tragic death at the hands of the knight Simon de Montolif (σὶρ Σιμοὺν τε Μουντολὶφ), after which Henry II returned to power for many years (LM I 59–63).

As regards lesser episodes, Makhairas discusses the execution of the death penalty involving the hanging of a hundred criminals upon the order of Hugh IV (ρὲ Οὔνγκε, 1293/1296–1359|1324–1358), successor of Henry II (LM I 64),[451] and natural disasters such as: the 1330 flood, the wide-scale plague outbreak in 1348 in which half of the island's inhabitants died, the locust plague of 1351 and the 1363 pestilence, with children as its victims (LM I 65–66).

In the first part of the *Chronicle* Leontios places much importance on the tale of the Holy Cross, wherein St Helena's story is only a prelude to a depiction of the Relic's further fate. He returns to the subject when he recounts the tale of the Relic's theft in 1318, carried out by Latin priest John Santamarin, and of how the cross hid itself in the roots of a carob tree and revealed itself to a shepherd in 1340 (LM I 67–71). The author raises the problem of doubts engendered in the Latins as to the genuineness of the Relic, which was placed in a charcoal-filled oven to be tested upon the order of a bishop (LM I 72–74). The chronicler also mentions work on building the church of the Holy Cross at the request of Maria d'Ibelin (τάμε Μαρία τε Πλισίε, 1294–1318),[452] with the participation of Ignatios II (Ἰγνάτιος, 1342–1353), Patriarch of Antioch[453] (LM I 75–77).

In his enumeration of Hugh IV's descendants in LM I 78 Makhairas introduces – apart from John de Lusignan (Τζουὰν τε Λουζουνίας, ca. 1329/1330–1375), prince of Antioch and constable of Cyprus, James de Lusignan (σὶρ Τζακὲτ τε Λουζουνίας, 1334–1398), constable of Jerusalem and Echive (Τζίβα, 1323–1363) – the figure of Peter de Lusignan (σὶρ Πιὲρ τε Λουζουνίας, 1328|1358–1369),[454] count of Tripoli, who would at the age of thirty ascend to the throne of Cyprus as Peter I. This enumeration seems to be a pretext for recounting a story from Peter's childhood, when together with his brother John, inspired by an encounter with arrivals from the west, he desired to 'see the world' (νὰ 'δοῦν τὸν κόσμον) and 'taste life abroad (lit. the foreignness)' (νὰ γευτοῦν τὴν ξενιτείαν). In 1349 the brothers managed to leave the island, aided among other by John Lombard (σὶρ Τζουὰν Λουμπάρη), whom Hugh IV had cruelly tortured in punishment, which involved cutting off an arm and leg (ἔκοψεν τὸ χέριν του καὶ τὸ πόδιν του), which

---

[446] Mas Latrie (Ed.), Chronique de Strambaldi, 8 also gives the name 'Ugo'.
[447] Edbury, The Kingdom of Cyprus, 23–27; Misztal, Historia Cypru, 630, 633, 643, 645.
[448] Misztal, Historia Cypru, 671.
[449] Möhring, Saladin; Çakmak (Ed.), Islam, 337.
[450] Edbury, The Kingdom of Cyprus, 30, 37; Misztal, Historia Cypru, 646–648, according to LM I 59 he died in 1309.
[451] Edbury, The Kingdom of Cyprus, 30, 37; Misztal, Historia Cypru, 646–648.
[452] Dating after Misztal, Historia Cypru, 662. Edbury postulates that they probably come from Pisa or Sardinia, although a fourteenth-century source suggests different connotations (with 'the viscounts of Chartres') (Edbury, The Kingdom of Cyprus, 39). Ibelin – a castle in the Kingdom of Jerusalem situated between Jaffa and Ascalon.
[453] Dawkins, Notes, 72.
[454] Edbury, The Kingdom of Cyprus, 30, 37.

where then hung from a pillory (ἐκρεμμάσεν τα εἰς τὴν πιλλιρήν), and ultimately hanging on the gallows (ἐφούρκισέν τον εἰς τὴν φούρκαν). Pope Clement VI (1291|1342–1352)[455] himself became embroiled in the matter, threatening anybody who helped the escapees with excommunication (μὲ ἀφορισμόν) (LM I 82–83). Finally, thanks to significant financial expenditure, the devastated father was able to bring his sons home, and punished them for their lack of thought by imprisonment in Kerynia (LM I 84–85). These circumstances contributed to the death of Hugh IV, who despite the unfortunate events managed to crown Peter as his successor on 24 November 1358 (LM 85–86).

Makhairas devotes the last three paragraphs of the first part to a discussion of the offices ('φίκκια, ὀφίκια)[456] held on Cyprus. First he explains 'how the sons of the kings ruled' (πῶς ἐκουεβερνιάζουνταν τὰ παιδία τοὺς ῥηγάδες). According to his testimony, 'the eldest son was the heir to the kingdom' (ὁ μέγας υἱὸς ἐγδέχετον τὸ ῥηγάτον), the next son received the title of prince of Antioch, and the others were granted various offices both on Cyprus and in Jerusalem (LM I 87). Further, the chronicler introduces a distinction between offices held for life, granted 'upon the coronation' (εἰς τὸ στέψιμον) of the king, which included the title of marshal, seneschal, butler and chamberlain, and temporary offices, granted upon other occasions, such as: admiral, auditor, tax collector and turcopolier,[457] though Makhairas also mentions exceptions (LM I 88). Finally he asserts that only (μόνον) three princely titles (πρίντζιδες) were granted: prince of Galilee, Jerusalem and Antioch (τῆς Γαλιλαίας; τῶν Ἱεροσολύμων; τῆς Ἀντιοχείας) (LM I 89).

The part of the *Chronicle* that describes Peter I's reign (LM II 90–281) focuses on events from the day he sat on the Cypriot throne in 1359 during a coronation ceremony in the cathedral of the Holy Wisdom of God (εἰς τὴν Ἁγίαν Σοφίαν)[458] in Lefkosia, where all subsequent rulers were crowned, and from the moment when, a year later, he accepted the Jerusalem crown from the hands of Carmelite Peter de Thomas (φρέρε Πιέρ τε Τουμᾶς, 1305–1366)[459] in the church of St Nicholas in Ammochostos (II 90, 104), up to his tragic death at the hands of his countrymen in 1369.

In LM II 91 Makhairas paints a picture of the prosperity that became the portion of the island thanks to the developing maritime trade. However, in that same paragraph he shows that some time later 'the place became the object of envy' (ἐφθονίστην ὁ τόπος) while 'the riches passed to the Saracens' (τὸ πλοῦτος ἐστράφην εἰς τοὺς Σαρακηνούς) (LM II 91). In addition to the general depiction, he gives the example of an individual instance of affluence in the tale of the banquet given by Sir Francis Lakha (σὶρ Φρασὲς Οὐλαχᾶ), a Nestorian involved in charitable works, attended by King Peter I himself together with his barons, during which guests could admire wonders such as logs of the aloe tree (γομαρία σαντὶς ξύλα) from India[460] and a large number of precious stones including pearls and very valuable carbuncles (ἀκαρπάνγκουλα), as well as coins. This same Lakha, also the founder of a Nestorian church (LM II 92–93), appears again in the next story, which recounts the arrival on Cyprus of a Catalan pirate who wished to sell a jewel to the island's inhabitants (LM II 95),[461] and also in a mention about his two sons Tsoles or Joseph, and Tsetsious or George (LM II 96).

Here, between more important incidents, comes a list of the titles and offices granted by Peter I after his coronation (LM II 97–100).

The chronicler pays much attention to the arrival on Cyprus of the papal legate, the Carmelite Peter de Thomas – the one who crowned Peter I as the ruler of Jerusalem – and his attempt to convert the Greek clergy to Catholicism by force, which failed thanks to the reaction of the Lusignans, which was reported to the pope (LM II 101–102).

Makhairas presents various lesser events occurring during the reign of King Peter I, such as putting to sea of the first galleys to fight Catalan bandits (LM II 103), and of ships on business (LM II 110), and also sending John of Verona off to enlist soldiers in exchange for the proper pay (LM II 109). Further issues included the conflict between old and new recruits, Cypriots and Syrians, which ended with the

---

[455] Pope Clement VI is not named in the *Chronicle*. See Dopierała, Księga papieży, 196; Misztal, Historia Cypru, 655; Kleinhenz (Ed.), Routledge Revivals, 234.
[456] The term ''φίκκια' is to be found in LM I 87–88, II 100, III 326. The term 'ὀφίκια' appears only once, in LM I 88.
[457] The turcopolier is the Frankish commander of Turkish or Arab cavalry units used by the crusaders for their own purposes (Dawkins, Notes, 77).
[458] Dawkins, Notes, 194.
[459] Rogge, Grünbart (Eds), Medieval Cyprus, 53.
[460] Dawkins, Notes, 91.
[461] The fragments LM II 94–95 are missing from Σάθας (Ed.), Χρονογράφοι Βασιλείου Κύπρου, 96.

perpetrators being hanged in 1360 (LM II 111), an argument between Leon d'Antiaume and John de Monstri (LM II 206), and King Peter allowing emancipation for a given sum (LM II 215).

The first significant military endeavour of Peter I described in the *Chronicle* was the aid he sent in 1360 to the fort of Gorhigos (τὸ κάστρον τοῦ Κουρίκου), which belonged to the king of Armenia and was besieged by the Turks. Gorhigos was inhabited by Christians who ultimately decided to surrender to the Cypriot king (LM II 112–115). Makhairas relates events linked to the coalition between the 'Great Karaman' (μέγας Καραμάνος),[462] that is the emir of Karaman, lord of Alaya, and the lord of Monovgat, forged for the purpose of organising an attack on Cyprus (LM II 116). The chronicler tells of Peter I's expedition against Turkey, which starts with intensive preparation (LM II 117–120),[463] and culminates in the capture on 23 August 1361 of Adalia (τὴν Ἀτάλειαν), ruled by emir Takka (Τακᾶς/Τακκᾶς); of the surrender of Alaya (τὴν Ἀλλαγίαν) (LM II 121–125); of Takka's attempts to recapture the city in 1362 (LM II 126, 128, 132–134); of the taking of the castle in Myra (εἰς τὰ Μύρα) (LM II 127); and of the selection of John Carmaïn (σὶρ Τζουὰν Καρμαήν) as captain of Adalia (LM II 129). Further episodes of the conflict with the Turks include their attack on plague-ridden Cyprus in the king's absence (LM II 137), including on Karpasi (τὴν μερίαν [...] τοῦ Καρπασίου) and Paphos (τὴν μερίαν τῆς Πάφου) in 1363 (LM II 139), burning of a Turkish galley by Francis Spinola (σὶρ Φραντζικῆς Σπινόλας) (LM II 140–141), revenge on the Turks in Kerynia (LM II 142) and a Cypriot attack on Anemouri (εἰς τὸ Ἀνεμούριν) (LM II 143). Makhairas describes another Cypriot expedition to Adalia in September 1364, a victory over the Saracens at sea (LM II 150–152), and a Cypriot-Turkish conflict caused by the mistreatment of the Saracen Khatziani (Χατζιάνης) by the island's inhabitants (LM II 159).

No small place in this part of the *Chronicle* is held by Peter I's famous Alexandrian expedition (εἰς τὴν Ἀλεξάνδραν), which took place on 9 October 1365, and resulted in a Cypriot victory (LM II 168–175). Numerous lesser episodes are described, such as the shipwreck of the royal fleet in January 1367 (LM II 191), the Christian victory at Gorhigos in 1367 (LM II 195), the rebellion of the inhabitants of Adalia and Peter I's remedying of the situation in 1367 (LM II 199–201), his announcement of peace in the city (LM II 208), the expedition, organised in 1367, to Tripoli (τὴν Τρίπολιν), Tortosa (τὴν Ταρτούζαν), Valena (τὴν Βαλίναν), Laodicea (τὴν Λαδικίαν), Malo (τὸν Μάλον), Ayasi (τ' Ἁγιάσιν) and Sidon (τὸ Σαΐτην) (LM II 209–214), the 1368 destruction of Sarepta (ἕναν χωρίον ὀνόματι Σαρφές) (LM II 220) and repelling the attack of Maghrebi (ξύλα τὰ μαγραπίτικα) ships on Ammochostos (LM II 221).

Paragraphs describing military clashes are interspersed with descriptions of tempestuous negotiations between the Cypriots and the sultan (LM II 181–185, 189, 192–194, 196–198, 202–205, 223–230) and with references to King Peter I's contacts with the West. This is because in his work the chronicler includes mentions of the voyage undertaken by the ruler in 1362 to Rhodes (τὴν Ρόδον), Venice (τὴν Βενετίαν), Avignon (τὸ Ἀβενίου), Rome (τὴν κούρτην τῆς Ρώμης), where he met Pope Innocent (Ἰνοκέντιον) (LM II 131), Avignon again, France (τὴν Φραγκίαν), Genoa (τὴν Γενούβαν), and to the German emperor (τὸν ἐμπεραδούρην τῆς Ἀλαμαινίας) (LM II 136). Makhairas underlines Peter I's contacts with the pope, describing how he gave the bishop of Rome a letter from Melek Bekhna (Μέλι Μπέχνα/ Πέχνα) in 1365 (LM II 159–163), and on his relationships with the Knights of the Hospital of Rhodes (LM II 164–167). Leontios relates that the Alexandrian victory was announced to the whole world (LM II 168–175), which encouraged most countries of the West to promise Peter that they would aid him in his struggle with the Saracens and in destroying the sultan (LM II 187, 217). Only the Venetians withdrew, putting off the crusade in fear of losing the opportunity to participate in trade with the Muslims (LM II 176–180, 188). When the sultan failed to consent to the agreement, Peter I ordered galleys to Syria (LM II 186). Moreover, the chronicler describes an episode in which a Saracen boat was captured by two Genoese (LM II 219).

In the part devoted to the reign of Peter I, Leontios also includes a description of the budding hate between Cyprus and Genoa, which came to a fore in the battle of Ammochostos in 1364 (LM II 145–149). He then discusses an incident in which the Genoese used the conflict with the Turks to strengthen their position on Cyprus and reveals details of the peace finally made in 1364, whose terms he provides (LM II 153–156). The chronicler then returns to describing the attitude of the inhabitants of Genoa, who since 1368 had been in conflict with citizens of the Republic of Venice (LM II 250).

---

[462] Miller and Sathas use the name *Le grand Karaman* in their translation, e.g. Sathas, Miller (Eds, transl.), Chronique de Chypre, 64.
[463] Σάθας (Ed.), Χρονογράφοι Βασιλείου Κύπρου, 105 lacks a significant part of paragraphs LM II 116 and 119, and is completely missing paragraphs LM II 117 and 118.

Peter I quite frequently turns to the Holy Father for help and contacts other leaders (LM II 102, 216). Innocent VI was approached by Hugh de Lusignan, prince of Galilee, who had pretensions to the throne of Cyprus, which according to him did not rightfully belong to Peter. This forced the pope to undertake fruitless attempts to solve the contentious issue (LM II 105–108). Peter himself also took into account the requests of the bishop of Rome when the pope demanded that peace be made with the sultan (LM II 218, 223). In the years 1360 and 1365 he organised an expedition to Rhodes to bring help in fighting with the Turks (LM II 190, 207).

Makhairas does not avoid writing about matters of the heart, which he does with precision, describing many aspects of the situation. He tells of Peter I's love for his wife Eleanora of Aragon (Λινόρα, 1333–1417)[464] (LM II 130), of the royal couple's marriage (LM II 233), of Peter I's romance with Joanna L'Aleman (Τζουάνα Λ' Αλεμά) (LM II 234) and Echive of Scandelion (τάμε Τζίβαν τε Στααντιλίου) (LM II 238), Eleanora's many attempts to revenge herself on Joanna (LM II 234–237), of Eleanora's romance with John de Morphou (Τζουὰν τε Μόρφου) (LM II 239), of the interference of John Visconti (Τζουὰν Βισκούντης), who informed the king about the previous fact (LM II 240–241), of how John of Morphou sent precious scarlet fabric to Joanna L'Aleman and Echive of Scandelion with the request that they should not betray the queen, of the false allegations made against Visconti by John of Morphou (LM II 245), of the visit Peter I made to Joanna, placed in a Clarisse convent by Eleanora's doing (LM II 248–249), of the search for help from advisors and of bringing about the death of Visconti (LM II 251–259). Convinced of the ruler's remarkability, Makhairas attributes Peter I's behaviour to an excess of feeling (LM II 242). He cites Peter's other emotional states, such as fear, recounting how he carried out the intention to build the moat-surrounded Margarita tower, which was to protect him from the revenge of his enemies (LM II 260), and also his rashness, seen in his arguments with James de Giblet (σὶρ Χαρρὴν τε Ζιπλέτ) and other knights. Leontios ends his description of the king's deeds with an account of his death in 1369, clearly showing that he was murdered (LM II 261–281).

In the part devoted to Peter's reign Makhairas mentions the plague that broke out in Cyprus in 1363 and caused the deaths of Echive de Lusignan (Τζίβα, 1323–1363), Hugh IV's daughter, and John Carmaïn (LM II 135).

The chronicler registers administrative changes implemented at various points of Cyprus' history, such as when King James changed the office of count to the office of prince motivated by private considerations. Leontios also writes about a change in the penal system that was then in force (LM II 97–98). He returns to the seizure of power by the Franks/Latins over the Rhomaioi/Greeks, which resulted in the introduction of new laws (LM II 99), to the formation of offices after Peter II's coronation (LM II 100), recruiting men in Lombardy in 1360 (LM II 109), and a new tax levied by King Peter in 1364 (LM II 157), etc.

The whole of this part is embellished by discussion of the languages used on Cyprus (LM II 158), the wonders seen by the emir of Karaman (LM II 115) and references to astrology (LM II 243, 251).

The part devoted to the reign of Peter II, son of Peter I, is the most substantial (LM III 282–598). At the very start Makhairas describes how the youth was hailed as king (LM III 282), but clearly stresses that the young successor only reached the age when the coronation could take place slightly later (LM III 319–324). Directly after relating the details of the ceremony he describes the procedure of granting the proper offices (LM III 326–327). The chronicler introduces the matter of the proposal made to Peter II by Emperor John V Palaiologos (Καλογιάννης ὁ Παλαιολόγος, 1332–1391), who offered Peter his daughter in marriage, which ultimately met with Peter II's refusal (LM III 344–349).

Makhairas also revisits Peter I's death, recounting how news of this event reached Pope Urban V and other rulers, how the guilty were accused (LM III 310–311), and how they were sentenced to torture and death by hanging on the gallows as a result (LM III 312–316).

In this part Makhairas clearly develops the motif of enmity between Genoese and Venetians, starting from the dispute that arose after Peter II's anointment and concerned the side of the royal horse on which the representative of each Republic would stand (LM III 325), through an argument in the banquet hall, up to more dangerous, violent offences that included an attack on the Genoese seat in Cyprus (LM III 328–342), an armed expedition by the latter to Cyprus (LM III 358–361), and the plundering of Ammochostos in 1373 (LM III 362–365). Leontios shows that these events caused the island's inhabitants to greatly fear the representatives of the Republic, resulting in a decision to return Adalia to the Turks (LM III 366–369), which was deemed a 'lesser evil' than if it had gone to the citizens of Genoa. The chronicler shows attempts

---

[464] Misztal, Historia Cypru, 640.

to reach an agreement with the Genoese through negotiation (LM III 371), which, however, did not protect the island against attacks of the invaders on the Aliki coast (LM III 377), Lemesos, Paphos, Lefkosia and Ammochostos (LM III 378–390), for instance. It is possible to distinguish numerous sequences of events in 1373 that are related to this conflict and described in the *Chronicle*, such as the king's council with other important personages concerning solutions to the problem and amelioration of the situation (LM III 391–398), taxing of the Genoese (LM III 397–398), Peter II's abundant correspondence with Constable James de Lusignan, thanks to which the latter decided to aid Kerynia (LM III 400–407), the constable's flight from Lefkosia to Kerynia (LM III 408–409), surrounding of the Ammochostos castle by the Genoese (LM III 410–412), inviting them to a council in that castle (LM III 413–424), the Genoese imprisonment of the king, his mother and the prince (LM III 416), the prince's escape in the guise of a kitchen boy (LM III 419), the constant attempts of the Republic's citizens to seize Kerynia (LM III 45), the fighting in Lefkosia on 6 December 1373 (LM III 433–443), aid brought to Kerynia by James de Lusignan (LM III 444–445), the blockade of Ammochostos by Sir Peter de Cassi (σὶρ Πιὲρ τε Κασίν) (LM III 448), attempts to recapture Ammochostos (LM III 449–458), the Genoese decision to capture Kerynia (LM III 459), two sieges of Kerynia (LM III 463–481, 483, 485–493, 495–503, 520), the making of the peace, participation in a mass celebrated on that occasion, and numerous announcements (LM III 524–534). The whole story of the Genoese presence on the island culminates in a short summary (LM III 543, 549, 550). Over thirty paragraphs on, the chronicler references another attempt they made to capture Ammochostos (LM III 584–595). To the plotline of the Cypriot-Genoese conflict Makhairas adds descriptions of the controversy between Venice and Genoa, culminating in the battle of Chioggia in the years 1378–1381 (LM III 584–593) and the construction of fortifications in Lefkosia (LM III 594–597).

The Genoese appear in the *Chronicle* one more time, embroiled in the capture of a constable who arrived in Rhodes and was at the time in mourning for his daughter (LM III 535–542, 544–547).

Queen Eleanora plays a big role in the events presented by Makhairas: during the Genoese attack she sent letters to the king via Dimitrios Daniel (Δημήτρης Δανιέλ) (LM III 357, 427–431, 504–508). She supported efforts to keep the peace in Kerynia (LM III 446–447), which she had reached by subterfuge, riding a mule (LM III 460–462). Overcome by the wish for revenge for Peter I's death, she brought about the murder of the prince of Antioch (LM III 551–554), and after this incident was sent back to Aragon in 1377 (LM III 581).

The chronicler emphasises the pope's involvement in the Cypriot-Genoese conflict (LM III 352–356, 374–376) and the intervention by the Rhodians (LM III 370).

In the narrative focused around this conflict, the figure of the youth Thibald (Τιπάτ) (LM III 556–575, 577–578) is particularly pronounced: a participant of the fighting against the Genoese who was ultimately executed for the violence and treason he committed in the country.

The second important plotline in this part is relations between Christians and Muslims. The foreground is occupied by the sultan's regular refusal to make peace in the years 1369–70 (LM III 284, 290–291, 294–309); the expedition of Ammochostos inhabitants against Syria in 1369: to Sidon (τὸ Σαΐτιν), Beyrout (τὸ Βερούτιν), Giblet (τὸ Ζίπλι), Boutron (τὸ Πετρούνιν) and Tortosa (τὴν Ταρτούζαν), travelling through the whole country to Laodicea (τὴν Λαδικείαν), Armenia (τὴν γῆν τῆς Ἀρμενίας), Ayas, Adalia, Phinika (τὸν Φοίνικαν) and Alexandria (LM III 285–286), the siege of which took place in July 1369 (LM III 287–288). The chronicler mentions an attempt by Takka to retake Adalia (LM III 317–318), and a letter from the king to the sultan and the latter's answer (LM II 292–293).

Makhairas states the opinion that the sins of the Cypriots were the reason for the loss of Ammochostos (LM III 482), discusses the differences between a woman's love and a man's love (LM III 576) and includes a long digression on cases of conversion in Cyprus (LM III 579). He cites letters and documents (LM III 511–519, 522–523).

Lesser episodes mentioned by Leontios include the visit to Cyprus of Queen Valentina (Βαλιαντίνα, 1357–1393), Peter II's wife (LM III 580–581), and the death of Admiral John de Monstri (σὶρ Τζουὰν Μουστρή) (LM III 583).

The next part (LM IV 599–627) is a description of the deeds of James I, crowned king of Cyprus, Jerusalem and Armenia (LM IV 615–616) in the presence of the Genoese, among others (LM IV 617), starting from the conclusion of an agreement with the latter and making of a peace in Ammochostos (LM IV 599–601, 610), though on terms that were not fully convenient for Cyprus (LM III 613), up to his death in 1398 (LM IV 627). Makhairas introduces the subject of the Montolif (Μουντολίφ) brothers' lack of approval for the coronation of James I (LM IV 602–605, 609–612). He analyses the administrative and fiscal system (LM IV 607–608, 618, 621, 625) and tells of the need to strengthen defences against the Venetians in that period (LM IV 614). He consistently includes information about the plagues afflicting the island in the years 1392–1393 (LM IV 622–624).

The penultimate part of the *Chronicle* (LM V 628–702) contains a detailed description of the reign of King Janus I, whose coronation took place on 11 November 1399. Leontios writes of the 1402 takeover of Ammochostos by Brother Gregory (LM V 630), about meetings between Cypriots and Genoese (LM V 634–635) and Muslims in the years 1404–1414 (LM V 636–695), Saracen invasions in the years 1424 and 1425 (LM V 651–660), fighting with representatives of Islam for Khirokitia (εἰς τὴν Χεροκοιτίαν) and for Lefkosia in 1426 (LM V 671–695), and also recounts the outbreak of the peasant rebellion (LM V 696–697). The chronicler remarks on events such as the birth of John (Τζουάν), son of Janus (LM V 641), the king's capture by Muslims, his return to Cyprus and his death in 1432 (LM V 699–702), and also the nomination of Hugh de Lusignan as cardinal (LM V 698). Two enlightening stories enrich this part: about an old sheik and his son, and a boy, George, and his mother (LM V 699–702). Information about a plague of locust in 1409 (LM V 637–639) and a different disease in 1410 (LM V 636) is also included.

The last and shortest part (LM VI 703–713) is a collection of unconnected notes from the thirty five year reign of King John II and covers only 10 paragraphs. It starts with a description of the coronation (LM VI 703). There is a mention of John's two marriages: with Empress Medea (Μετέα/Μετεγία, 1420–1440) and Queen Helena Palaiologina (Ἑλένη Παλαιολό(γ)ου, 1428–1458), daughter of Theodore II Palaiologos, the despot of Morea[465] (LM VI 704–712). The *Chronicle* ends with a proclamation announcing the ascension to the throne by John's daughter Charlotte (Τζαρλόττα, 1444–1487|1458–1464)[466] (LM VI 713).

An analysis of the *Chronicle* text allows us to conclude that Makhairas clearly focuses on events happening on Cyprus or directly related to it, but almost completely ignores other great events in the Mediterranean Basin. The exception is the reference to the 1099 capture of Jerusalem and the succession of its rulers, though it may be assumed that the chronicler made such a departure in order to explain to the audience how the Cypriot rulers came to take the title of kings of Jerusalem. All elements situated outside Cyprus, such as Muslim lands, the island of Rhodes and the places a ruler visited during his official travels, are only significant because of their link to Cypriot matters. The first part of the text covers a long period of time: from 327 to 1359, that is 1032 years, during which the events from the history of Cyprus that Makhairas finds the most important are summarised. The remaining parts, chronologically closer to the author's own life, are more elaborate, and events are organised around actions undertaken by Cypriot rulers.

1.7. The *Chronicle*'s potential audience

In writing the *Chronicle*, Makhairas likely had a specific 'image' of its audience in his mind.[467] This is indicated not only by the choice of language (the vernacular Cypriot Greek, comprehensible to a broad public),[468] but also by other properties of the text. One of them is its 'oral' character. Anaxagorou discusses this phenomenon, analysing among others the *Chronicle*'s narrative and stylistic structure, and also compares the three manuscripts in this respect.[469] Using the narratological categories, the scholar comes to the following conclusions: the main narrative abounds in regularly inserted 'self-contained stories'; historical events are only 'elliptically sketched', unlike the significantly expanded subplots drawn from local tales; direct speech takes up a significant part of the text; the narrator manifests his 'intrusive and participatory nature', which allows him to get closer to the audience.[470]

The *Chronicle*'s 'implied recipient'[471] demands primarily such content as is to some extent close to them from their previous experience. Often the sentences used in the Cypriot work call to mind expressions

---

[465] Dawkins, Notes, 232.
[466] Misztal, Historia Cypru, 636, 643.
[467] Cf. Handke, Oddziaływanie literatury, 93 (the 'image' problem of this kind).
[468] This issue has been discussed in Subchapter 1.2.
[469] Anaxagorou, Narrative and Stylistic Structures, 133–143.
[470] Anaxagorou, Narrative and Stylistic Structures, xvi.
[471] The term 'implied recipient' ('implikowany odbiorca') is used after Handke, Oddziaływanie literatury, 106 and translated by Kupiszewska.

'previously heard somewhere', though the author does not give them in the original form and does not usually provide the source he drew them from. These are usually paraphrases of Bible quotations, skilfully woven into the text as if in passing. The chronicler does not make the effort to check them and make clear their meanings. Perhaps he consciously treats them as verbal material that is susceptible to change and can absorb the new senses assigned to them in the context he puts them in, hoping that – despite the modifications – they will have a stronger impact on the reader, having previously embedded themselves in the collective consciousness. Walter Ong calls the preservation of petrified knowledge, characteristic for oral cultures, 'conservative' or 'traditionalist'.[472] The Biblical overtones help Makhairas both to express thoughts of a didactic nature, and give better focus to the image he paints. Historical figures such as Aristotle and St Cyriac[473] function in the work in a similar fashion, appearing in comparisons as half-real, half-mythical beings, and serving as a kind of *exemplum*, a point of reference. The echo of the images and concepts, whose traces may in a careful reading be found in other texts, is most fully pronounced in a discussion of the differences between the love of a man and of a woman (LM III 576), in which Makhairas uses the metaphor of a ladder (σκάλα), assigning each of these two shades of love a given number of steps (the more there are, the deeper the feelings felt by persons of a given sex) – the concept of the 'ladder' had been known, according to Dawkins, since a sixth-century popular text by Ioannes Klimakos.[474]

An important lead that could contribute to the discovery of the features of the *Chronicle*'s expected audience is the presence in it of simple, popular hagiographic tales and short mentions of holy figures, sometimes even anecdotal and surprising (the examples that stand out include the figure of Mamas milking lions in LM I 33, Diomidios running away with the head of St Triphyllios in LM I 35 or Neophytos living on a pillar LM I 38). They play the role of both historical accounts (holy relics do in fact abound in Cypriot land and are also preserved in churches and monasteries) that promote attachment to one's country, and of legends that arouse interest and are didactical.

Leontios systematically refers to the devil or demon (διάβολος), otherwise called an evil spirit (δαίμων), who is the 'cause of all evil' (ἀρχέκακος, LM II 239). In the alternating references to these two beings we may find a distant echo of the distinction functioning in Byzantine times, particularly in 'folk demonology', which Jeffrey Burton Russell sheds light on: between the devil or Satan, and the demons who imitate him but have their own individual features.[475] Makhairas says, for example: 'the devil hardened their hearts to such an extent that they could not be convinced [...]' (ὁ διάβολος ἐσκλέρυνεν τὴν καρδίαν τους τόσον, ὅπου δὲν –ἐθέλα– νὰ τζακκιστοῦν [...], LM I 52), 'the devil was putting into his heart that which had never taken up [his attention]' (ὁ διάβολος ἔβαλλεν εἰς τὴν καρδίαν του τὰ δὲν ἐννοιάζετον, LM I 61), 'once again, the devil begot another [mischance]' (πάλε ἐγέννησεν ὁ διάβολος ἄλλον, LM II 268), 'exceedingly devious, the devil sowed hate' (ὁ πανπόνηρος διάβολος –ἐπῆρεν– μῖσος, LM III 580) and 'the evil spirit was rejoicing' (ὁ δαίμων ἐχαίρετον, LM II 270). Similarly, using personification, the chronicler voices a thought about the causes and consequences of evil: 'the evil spirit of adultery assaults the whole world' (ὁ δαίμων τῆς πορνείας ὅλον τὸν κόσμον πλημελᾶ, LM II 234). In his causal analysis Makhairas employs the figure of an enemy (ἐχθρός), stating: 'the time [came] for the enemy to decide to reap the fruits whose [seeds] he had sown in their hearts' (ὁ καιρὸς ὅπου ὁ ἐχθρὸς ἐθέλησε νὰ 'σσοδιάσῃ τοὺς καρποὺς τοὺς ἔβαλεν εἰς τὴν καρδιάν τους, LM II 278). Sentences of this type, simple in structure, likely put the reader in a mood of expectation, vigilance, sense of threat, thus satisfying a certain type of sensibility.

The popular character of some parts of the *Chronicle* may be indicated by references to astrology, portents and horoscopes. The passages in which Peter I explains bad events with the unfortunate alignment of the planets are significant.[476] When he finds out about the adultery of his wife Eleanora, he states that

---

[472] Ong, Orality and Literacy, 40.
[473] Dawkins, Introduction, 12–13.
[474] Dawkins, Notes, 195.
[475] Russell, Lucifer, 49–51. According to Jeffrey Russell, the Byzantines perceived the devil as a creature of God, dependent on him (Russell, Lucifer, 29).
[476] Using the elite culture – popular culture opposition is risky, as prof. Andrzej Dąbrówka noted in his review (http://www.polon.uw.edu.pl/documents/9763960/10761134/glinicka_prof_dabrowka.pdf, accessed 28 November 2021). As I explained during my PhD thesis defence, I was influenced by the opinion of Anna Komnene, who in the sixth book of the *Alexiad* called astrology a vain study and a trifle tending 'to make people of a guileless nature reject their faith in God and gape at the stars.' (Anna Komnene, The Alexiad, 149, book VI, chapter VIII). However, Niketas Choniates, who calls astrologers 'baneful charletans' (Choniates, O City of Byzantium, 124), opines that astrology was, to put it in Magoulias' words, often 'an obsession of the emperors' (Magoulias, Introduction, xxii; see Choniates, O City of Byzantium, 55, 125, 305). He writes for instance: 'Manuel held the reprehensibe belief that the retrograde and progressive motion of stars and their positions, as well

the letter informing him of this contained such a bitter message 'because the sun had been in the sign of Capricorn when [it was] written' (ὅτι (ὁ) ἥ(λιο)ς ἦτον εἰς τὸν αἰγόκερον ὅταν ἐγράφετον), which does not stop him from invoking 'God Almighty' (παντοδύναμος θεός) and the 'King of Kings' (βασιλεὺς τῶν βασιλευόντων) in the same conversation (LM II 243). In 1426, when the Cypriot armies were encamped under Khirokitia, 'in the middle of the night' (μεσανυκτικόν) there appeared 'a sign' (σημάδιν) in the form of 'a great star [...] in the sky' (ἕναν ἄστρο μέγαν [...] εἰς τὸν οὐρανόν), which 'fell on the tower' (ἔππεσεν ἀπάνω τοῦ πύργου, LM V 678). On the margin of the Saracen attack on Cyprus, Makhairas notes the circumstances in which the king was kidnapped, describing portents (σημαδία) apparent in the animal world[477] as well as those that manifested as a fog that completely engulfed the world. He believes these signs to be true (πῶς εἶνε ἀλήθεια, LM V 690).

Thanks to its dramatic character, such a narrative, attractive and arresting, provided its recipients with many different stimuli. It provoked questions on that which governs human life and whether man is able to counteract misfortune, exonerated impotence, and showed the world as a complex cosmos in which various beings mutually impact each other. It did not require erudition and literacy, but did give a sense of participation in collective thought about the nature of the world.

The characters of the *Chronicle* are presented as vigorous, impulsive and governed primarily by emotion, which lets the reader achieve greater engagement in the story and experience it. Such a technique prompts empathy and engagement ('participation'), which is also, as Ong indicates, a feature of orality.[478] Makhairas expresses emotional states in various ways: using nouns,[479] participles,[480] quite frequently strengthened with the adverb 'very' (πολλά), and verbs.[481] The depiction of emotions in the *Chronicle* frequently becomes slightly more complex, which Leontios achieves by using vivid expressions,[482] descriptions of spectacular gestures,[483] and picturesque presentation and self-presentation of feelings.[484] Sporadically, the chronicler uses abstract metaphor, e.g. 'tree of hate' (τὸ δεντρὸν τῆς μισιτείας, LM II 271), or portrays emotions indirectly.[485] However, his preference is for descriptions of specific situations over abstract expressions and phrases, which is typical for orality.[486] He sometimes also presents the changing emotions of a single person. When Peter I found out that his wife had committed adultery, he moaned (ἀναστέναξεν), cursed (Ἀνάθεμαν τὴν ὥραν, 'Cursed be the hour'), tried not to let his feelings show (τινὸς δὲν ἔδειξεν φανόν), tried to look happy (πολλὰ ἐσφίγκετον νὰ δείξη ἀλεγρέτζαν), although he failed to do so (δὲν ἐμπόρεν) and his face was dark (τὸ πρόσωπόν του ἦτον πολλὰ δημμένον). In his grief he started to talk of bitter and poisoned (πολλὰ πικρὸν καὶ φαρμακερόν) news, a noose tightening in his heart (ἕναν κόμπον εἰς τὴν καρδίαν) and the impossibility of finding relief from anybody (δὲν ἠμπορεῖ

---

as the configurations of the planets, their proximity and distances, influence the fortunes and circumstances of human life' (Choniates, O City of Byzantium, 55). Magoulias states that Niketas retrieves from 'astrology and other forms of medieval superstitions as "buffooneries and vulgarities."' (Magoulias, Introduction, xxvii).

[477] LM V 690: 'οἱ σκύλλοι ἐγουριάζαν, οἱ πετεινοὶ ἐκράζαν ἀπὸ καιροῦ, οἱ κωρῶνες ἐγουργιάζαν, οἱ κουκκουφιάδες εἰς τὴν αὐλὴν καὶ εἰς τὰ τειχόκαστρα ἐγουργιάζαν.'

[478] Ong, Orality and Literacy, 45.

[479] Such as: 'ἔννοια' ('worry'), 'λύπη' ('grief'), 'ζῆλα' ('jealousy'), 'πικρία' ('bitterness'), 'θλίψις' ('unease'), 'θυμός' ('anger', 'wrath').

[480] Such as: 'πικραμμένος' ('embittered', 'saddened'), 'ἀνγκρισμένος' ('annoyed'), 'σπαβεντιασμένος' ('terrified').

[481] Such as: 'ταράσσω' ('I am moved'), 'φοβέομαι' ('I fear'), 'θυμοῦμαι' ('I am angry'), 'λυπέομαι' ('I grieve'), 'πλημελῶ' ('I feel zeal'), 'πεθυμῶ' ('I desire'), 'σπλαγνίζω' ('I sympathise').

[482] Such as: 'he was dying of unhappiness' (ἦτον νὰ μορίση ἀποὺ τὸ κακόν του, LM I 81), 'he would have died of anxiety' (ἔθελεν πεθάνειν ἀπὲ τὴν πλῆξιν του, LM I 95), 'they took [courage] in their hearts' (ἐπῆραν καρδίαν, LM II 152), 'anger decreased' (ἐπαρκατέβην ὁ θυμός, LM V 639).

[483] Such as: 'she cried and started to hit [her breast]' (ἔκλαυσεν πολλὰ καὶ ἐδέρνετον, LM I 47), 'then he sighed' (τότε ἀναστέναξεν, LM II 243), '[his] eyes darkened [in anger]' (ἐσκοτίσθ(ησ)αν οἱ ἀφθαλμοί, LM II 270).

[484] Such as: 'in the hour that I heard this, I almost fell pale to the ground' (τὴν ὥραν ὅπου τὸ ἐγροίκησα ἔφτασα νὰ πέσω χαμαὶ ἐλλιγωμένος, LM II 241), 'in a state where my heart is like a red hot furnace' (τὸ καμίνιν καὶ καμὸν τῆς καρδιᾶς μου, LM II 251), 'your terror should fall on you' (τὸ ἀναπάλημάν σου νὰ πέση ἀπάνω σου!, LM II 280), 'the love that [the king] had for Thibald was so great that it exceeded all other loves' (ἡ ἀγάπη ὅπου ἀγάπαν τὸν σὶρ Τιπὰτ ἦτον τόσον πολλά, ὅτι ἐδιάβαιννεν ὅλες τὲς ἀγάπες, LM III 571).

[485] E.g. with the words: 'should I kill this flea-ridden dog that defiled the pearl' (νὰ σκοτώσω τὸ σκύλλον τὸν ψωριάρην ὅπου 'πόντισεν τὸ μαργαριτάριν, LM II 253).

[486] Ong, Orality and Literacy, 48.

τίτοιον μαντάτον νὰ τὸ σάσῃ τινὰς ἄλλος) but God himself,[487] which – as we find out later – caused him to sicken (ἦτον ἄρρωστος).[488]

The subplot of Peter I and Eleanora shows Makhairas' love for spinning tales about the intrigues of the Lusignan court, and also reveals his belief that the recipient would expect such sensational reports. Much room in the *Chronicle* is consigned to Peter I's romances with Joanna L'Aleman and Echive of Scandelion, to the queen's infidelity and endeavours to hide it (John of Morphou's attempts, out of fear for the king's peace of mind, to bribe Joanna and Echive with two pieces of scarlet material), and to cruel revenge (Eleanora's torture of Joanna and the death sentence on the queen's lover, John Visconti). Leontios also weaves in scenes of plots at the royal court (two of which are noteworthy: one against Henry II, the other against Peter I) and brief trivia- or gossip-like information[489] that completes the picture of the characters' emotionality and behaviour and arrests the reader's attention (for example, the chronicler mentions in three instances that King Peter slept with his wife's shirt, LM II 130, 216, 242). Stories of this type, with a universal message and referring to universal human behaviours, faults and instincts, may have been of interest both to common people, interested in the life of representatives of high society, and those who belonged to the latter or were connected to them.

Another distinctive feature of the *Chronicle*'s style, which tells us a lot about the tastes and aesthetic preferences both of its author and his audience, is a focus on suffering, pain, agony, violence and cruelty through vivid images that move the imagination and provide powerful sensations. Makhairas expresses himself in an unequivocally pessimistic manner about the sudden ending of life and slow agony, which are constantly present in the narrative. He consistently and assuredly writes of death (θάνατον) as 'evil' (κακόν), 'unjust' (ἄδικον), 'cruel' (σκλερόν), 'unpleasant' (πικρόν) and caused with bad intentions (νὰ τοὺς κακοθανατίσουν).[490] In addition to brief hints, such as a comment about the head of St Triphyllios, which had been cut off his dead body and carried from place to place, unhealthy excitement may have been engendered in the reader by the scene of the murder of King Peter, who was brutally decapitated (in the text there appear two expressions for this act: ἔκοψεν τὴν κεφαλήν του; κομμοκέφαλον), and the painful mutilation of the body of the dead ruler, 'exsanguinating and stripped of his trousers' (τον τυλιμένον ('ς) τὸ αἷμαν του, ἀναβράκωτον) by depriving him of his masculinity (τὰ λυμπά του μὲ τὸν αὐλόν).[491] Another characteristic episode is the one in which Thibald, Alexopoulos and other Franks, having been burned with pliers (νὰ βράζουν δοντάκρες νὰ τζιμποῦν τὰ κρίατα τους) heated in a boiling kettle (ἕναν ἀσκοφύσιν μὲ τὸ λαμπρόν), were hanged on the gallows (εἰς τὴν φούρκαν).[492] A similar effect is given by the description of the murder in a privy of the usurper Amaury by Simon de Montolif[493] or the portrayal of a prince throwing Bulgarians out of a window to 'die in the vast abyss' (ἐσκοτώννουνταν εἰς τόσον κρεμμόν).[494] The imagination must also have been affected by the sophisticated torture that the furious Eleanora meted out (ἐτυράνιζεν) over a whole day to the pregnant Joanna L'Aleman, tormenting her in order to cause a miscarriage.[495] Eleanora venged herself particularly cruelly on Peter I's killer, whom she entrapped and killed without mercy right after he recognised the bloodied shirt of the dead ruler, brought in on a platter.[496] Makhairas causes the reader's emotions to escalate by describing, with anatomical precision, the feelings that must have accompanied a victim who sensed imminent death, such as panic and terror, as the sentence 'his heart was shackled'[497] (ἡ καρδία του ἦτον δημμένη) suggests. These stories, which show the real monstrosity of human nature, were in direct contrast to the schematic but uplifting and hopeful lives of the saints, and through these dynamics, high frequency and vividness they likely provided still greater stimuli. His portrayals of cruelty, calculated to appeal to the masses, are recalled,

---

[487] LM II 243.
[488] LM II 279.
[489] Cf. Anaxagorou, Narrative and Stylistic Structures, xvii.
[490] LM I 74, II 255, III 315, 418, 574, 575.
[491] LM II 280–281.
[492] LM III 574–577.
[493] LM I 63.
[494] LM III 552.
[495] LM II 234.
[496] LM III 554.
[497] Dawkins: 'as spellbound' (LM III 554).

among other places, in a passage about the pretend, though no less shocking, gouging out of Ursel's eyes in the *Alexiad*, watched by a delighted rabble.[498]

Makhairas thus carried in his mind the image of a reactive audience, who listened attentively to the words directed to them and had a preference for vivid depictions of the experiences of others, which thanks to the chronicler's adequately dynamic account played out practically before their eyes. Such an audience was satisfied with limited theological knowledge acquired during mass and from a cursory reading of the Bible, while other types of knowledge (of literature or philosophy) were not required at all. Finally, only such a reader was able to learn from such a narrative.

1.8. Language of manipulation in the *Chronicle*

Makhairas uses clear, dense language. Anaxagorou distinguishes its three functions: communicative, ideological and testimonial.[499] My greatest interest lies in those narrative elements which prove that the chronicler used language as a tool for manipulation, imposing a specific reading.

The chronicler consistently justifies the ambiguous deeds of the Christians by citing their proper, in his opinion, relationship with God or Divine action. For example, when discussing the reasons for their capture of Gorhigos castle (ἐκρατοῦσαν το, '[they] seized it') he states they did it 'out of love for Christ' (διὰ τὴν ἀγάπην τοῦ Χριστοῦ). According to the stylistic he adopts, Rhomaic and Armenian Christians were subject to numerous vile attacks, against which, being 'poor' (πτωχοί) and 'orphaned' (ὀρφανοί), they could 'find no help from anyone' (ἀποὺ πούποτες βοήθειαν).[500]

His ambiguity is visible in the skilful distribution of accents between the 'Greek/Rhomaic' and the 'Latin'. Leontios consistently expresses positive opinions about the Frankish court. On the one had, he had never experienced a different rule; on the other, he could not speak out against it. He comments on important events in Cyprus' history with praise of the qualities of individual kings, particularly Peter I. Describing the capture of Gorhigos, he writes:

> *And they remained in peril (ἐκιντύνευγαν) until the time of this King Peter. When he was crowned and the noble deeds (καλὰ ἔργα) of King Peter were heard of in all the world, they began to wish to range themselves at his side (ἐπεθυμῆσαν νὰ ππέσουν ε(ἰ)ς τὰ πλάγιά του).* (LM II 113)

Descriptions of the characters' behaviour in the *Chronicle* are often morally marked. When Makhairas denounces behaviour that he finds improper, he uses expressive adjectives, such as the word βρωμισμένος ('dirty, unclean, profaned') used to describe Amaury's scandalous practices (βρωμισμένη βουλή, 'unclean intention') and the rule of the Knights Templar (βρωμισμένη τάξις, 'dirty rule').[501] Such language, carrying a clear judgment, is extremely suggestive, as it defines the way in which the reader perceives the description of individual characters and assesses their behaviour.

The theme of tempestuous relations between Christians and Muslims was also structured in a marked way. Makhairas, attempting to give meaning to the inter-civilisational encounters, often uses phrasing which underlines that each side formed a kind of whole. Such unity is in the case of Christians linked to power and might, and in the case of Muslims gives rise to associations with an unbridled, unpredictable hostile mass that needs to be avoided at all costs, while curbing of this mass is presented as extremely heroic. And so we read that during the attack on Syria all (πασαεῖς) Christians who felt the zeal of battle were to assail the foe, portrayed as a host of enemies (νὰ συντρέξῃ νὰ πᾶσιν –κατάδικα τοὺς ἐχθρούς τους–).[502] Characteristically, Makhairas gives detailed descriptions of happenings that he had not himself witnessed: in his account, the Saracens 'shook with fear' (πολλὰ ἐτρομάξαν) and were 'overcome by great fear' (ἐπίασέν τους μέγας φόβος) at the sight of the opponent's approaching armies. While Muslims are usually portrayed in a way that negatively impacts their image, the extended passages about the valour of the followers of Christ are full of positive descriptions of their heroic deeds, supplemented with

---

[498] Anna Komnene, The Alexiad, 9 (book I, chapter III).
[499] Anaxagorou, Narrative and Stylistic Structures, 63–69.
[500] LM II 113.
[501] LM I 13.
[502] LM II 169.

an evaluation of such activities from the perspective of a God who reacts to human reality, and who in the *Chronicle* usually shows favour to Christians (ὁ θεὸς ἐποῖκει χάριταν τοὺς χριστιανούς).[503] Even the message of the letter from the sheikh of Damascus is weakened by the dismissive attitude of King Janus.

Makhairas shows the relations between representatives of these two civilisations in a way that imposes an unambiguous interpretation of the passages devoted to them. For instance, he uses this method in a fragment that shows the response of Peter I, unaware of the subterfuge, to the sultan's guarantees, stating that:

The king did not understand his treachery (τὴν παραβουλίαν), but as an honourable man believed him, and with a good heart ordered [...]. (LM II 184)

The Frankish king, whom the chronicler judges to be 'prudent' (φρόνιμος),[504] is characterised by the deeply entrenched virtue of honesty, which prevents him from perceiving symptoms of manifestly evil intentions, while the Islamic ruler is driven by unambiguously negative motives. This is not the only place in the *Chronicle* where its author attributes the intent to mislead Christians to the Muslims, because in the very next passage we read that Saracen soldiers did not shy from surreptitious, furtive 'whispers' (ψουψουρίσματα) and false praise (ἐκολακεῦγαν) when attempting to achieve their hidden goal and entrap the enemy.[505] The conversation between the emir and the sultan indicates that Christians trusted followers of Islam only because of 'the sultan's oath and an oath that he made before them (the emirs)' (–εἰς τὸν ὅρκον τοῦ σουλτάνου καὶ εἰς τὸν ὅρκον τὸν διδεῖ ἔμπροσθέν τους–), which strengthens the image of their wickedness still further when we read immediately afterwards that the oath was broken because a messenger had been slighted.[506]

The chronicler shows the Latin world to be united in the common need to combat the Muslims. This world, aware of the need for such unity, becomes active in difficult moments of uncertainty and celebrates the successes achieved. This may be seen when at the news of Peter I's victory in Syria, 'the pope [...] was overjoyed and [with him] all of Rome' (ὁ πάπας [...] ἐχάρην χαρὰν μεγάλην καὶ ὅλη ἡ Ρώμη).[507] Requests addressed both to the Holy Father and to the Cypriot king reveal the Christian conviction that they form one community, which requires an authority figure.[508] As a whole, however, the depiction of this community reveals numerous cracks, as indicated by frequent descriptions of clashes between the warring Genoese and Venetians and a narrative full of references to the impulsive behaviours of the Genoese, who fomented discord within the Cypriot universe. Makhairas formulates sentences about the citizens of the Repubic in such a way as to leave the reader in no doubt as to his own opinion or as to how scenes with their participation should be interpreted at any given point.

Leontios uses many words and expressions referring to emotional states, which is also intended to assign unambiguous traits to characters. When Peter I's sons ran away from Cyprus, this caused him sorrow (πολλὰ ἐλυπεῖτον; εἶχεν πολλὴν λύπην),[509] bitterness (ξηγηθῶ τὴν πικρίαν)[510] and unease (θλίψις).[511] The emotions thus named determine the interpretation of the portrayals both of the persons experiencing them, and of the persons causing them. When describing the attitude of Queen Isabella d'Ibelin, who asks the usurper Amaury to free Henry II and return power to him, he uses the phrases 'she wept a lot and beat her breast' (ἔκλαυσεν πολλὰ καὶ ἐδέρνετον, LM I 47) and '[she spoke] with great humility and sweet words' (μὲ μεγάλην ταπείνωσιν καὶ γλυκεῖα λογία, LM I 52) to increase the enormity of Amaury's crime.

According to Pieris, the 'basic rhetorical strategy' (θεμελιακή ρητορική στρατηγική) used in the *Chronicle* is 'frequent suspension of the narrative' (η συχνή άρση της αφήγησης) and 'the extensive adoption of direct [stage] dramatic speech' (σε έκταση υιοθέτηση του άμεσου [σκηνικού] δραματικού λόγου).[512] Pieris explains that he means exchanges 'either in the form of dialogues (exchange of words) [re-enactment of actions, or even in the form of exchange of remarks]' (είτε στη μορφή ανταλλαγής «λόγων» [αναπαράσταση

---

[503] LM II 171.
[504] LM II 190.
[505] LM II 185.
[506] LM II 202.
[507] LM II 175.
[508] LM II 175.
[509] LM II 80, 85.
[510] LM II 80.
[511] LM II 83.
[512] Πιερής, Σταθμοί, 172. Kupiszewska's translation from the Polish translation by the author. Round brackets in Greek quotations (here and below) have been changed to square brackets.

δράσεων είτε και παράσταση ομιλιών]), or 'in the form of embassy or exchanging "letters"' [declaration, or even letter representation]' (είτε στη μορφή αποστολής είτε ανταλλαγής «χαρτιών» [αναπαράσταση, είτε και παράσταση επιστολών]).[513] To illustrate these words, Pieris composes a short dramatic text using sentences taken from the *Chronicle*, reflecting the 'theatrical' elements of its narrative. The text shows a council convened by Peter I, composed of representatives of the 'nobility' (ευγενείς), which was to consider the issue of 'adultery' (μοιχεία) committed by Eleanora of Aragon, which is clearly emphasised in the Cypriot work.[514] Meanwhile, to discuss the phenomenon of 'dramatic usage of epistolary language' (δραματική αξιοποίηση του επιστολικού λόγου) visible in the narrative of the *Chronicle*, Pieris uses the motif of the letters written by Peter I to the sultan of Cairo and Babylon in 1369 (LM II 230).[515] Pieris' experiment reveals the dramatic potential of this medieval text, which may easily be read out and acted, and also its vernacular wording.

The examples given above demonstrate that the author of the *Chronicle* intentionally uses precise and easy to interpret language, which connotes issues of morality.

1.9. The 'colonial' situation in the *Chronicle*

Already at the beginning of the *Chronicle* we find out that the person who purchased Cyprus from the Templars was Guy, and soon afterwards we encounter a mention that he was accompanied by people from the West (τὴν δύσιν), including France (τὴν Φραγκιάν), England (Ἐγκλετέρραν) and Catalonia (τὴν Καταλονίαν), who formed a diverse group of Latins (πολλοὶ Λατῖνοι). These communities 'settled in Cyprus' (ἐκατοικῆσαν εἰς τὴν Κύπρο),[516] which was a 'place full of Rhomaioi' (ὁ τόπος ἦτον γεμάτος Ρωμαῖοι), expanding the new power structure.[517] In LM I 87, II 158 and III 580 the chronicler uses the verb 'take' (παίρνω) to designate the manner in which the Franks came to hold the island. He writes: 'since the time that the Latins took Cyprus' (ὅτι ἀφ᾽ ὃν ἐπῆραν τὴν Κύπρον οἱ Λατῖνοι), and so he holds the events of 1192 to be an important caesura that heralded the start of a new age for the Cyprians. In LM II 99 he returns to this subject, emphasising that 'the kingdom was taken away from the Rhomaioi and given to the Latins' (πῶς ἐστράφην τὸ ρηγάτον ἀπὲ τοὺς Ρωμαίους καὶ ἐδόθην τοὺς Λατίνους) – as if by an external force – and then 'foreigners' (ξενικούς) were brought in to 'look to the place' (διὰ τὴν βλέπισην τοῦ τόπου).[518] This situation was the result of the specific ideology of expansion adopted by the Franks. Already the mentions contained in LM I 18 and 19 about the rule of Godfrey de Bouillon, Baldwin I, Baldwin d'Aiguillon, Fulk, Baldwin III, Amaury, Baldwin IV and Baldwin V (from 1099) suggest that representatives of the western world had influence in the Middle East (moreover, these fragments provide the first information about the meeting of the Latin and Muslim world), which means that Leontios was very quick to introduce images that can be interpreted as a harbingers of the island's future conquest, and were also the first presentation of a meeting between two different cultures in the *Chronicle*. As the presence of the six rulers named in LM I 19 was the result of the first crusade, so Guy's appearance may be deemed the consequence of the next one, offering an interesting parallel. The Franks' control over the

---

[513] Πιερής, Σταθμοί, 172. Kupiszewska's translation from the Polish translation by the author.
[514] Πιερής, Σταθμοί, 174–177. Kupiszewska's translation of short Pieris' phrases from the Polish translation by the author.
[515] Πιερής, Σταθμοί, 177–179. Kupiszewska's translation of short Pieris' phrases from the Polish translation by the author.
[516] LM I 26–27.
[517] LM I 22. Nicolaou-Konnari writes that in Lusignan Cyprus the population 'is not thought to have exceeded 100,000'. The population of the Franks 'must never have surpassed one fourth of the total population' (Nicolaou-Konnari, Greeks, 14–15).
[518] Describing the comparatively passive reaction of Rhomaioi to the Frankish annexation of Cyprus Nicolaou-Konnari states: '[…] the partial disappearance through emigration and the socio-economic reduction of the remaining Greek landowning aristocracy rendered them unable or unwilling to lead any resistance against the new rulers' (Nicolaou-Konnari, Greeks, 18). The aristocracy was not allowed to grow in strength out of fear of its entrenchment, which Nicolaou-Konnari expresses thus: 'What is certain is that the Lusignans did not allow the survival of the Greek *archontes* as a social class, like in Venetian Crete, or the creation of a *special* class of Greek aristocracy, like in Frankish Morea, that might potentially threaten the stability of their regime.' (Nicolaou-Konnari, Greeks, 43). In the religious context, the aristocracy played an important role as a party supporting the Greek Church: '[…] evidence suggests that the Greek churches must have been supported financially by some important families, whatever disruption of patronage resulted from the flight of Greek nobles and the new social and financial conditions of the remaining ones' (Nicolaou-Konnari, Greeks, 46).

Cyprians is expressed in descriptions of individual events, such as when king Hugh forbids the monk Gabriel to leave the island with the Togni Cross under pain of a 'terrible death' (κακὸν θάνατον, LM I 74).

Elsewhere, however, a well-balanced explanation may be found of the motives guiding the Frankish population in their decision to move to Cyprus. In passage LM II 277 describing the council of the king's sons with lords and knights during which the decision to murder Peter I was taken, the knights argue that the first Lusignans, that is their ancestors (γονεῖς μας), who chose life on the island, also left behind 'their estates and their heritage' (τὸ δικόν τους καὶ τὲς κλερονομιές τους), and thus made a kind of sacrifice. They were persuaded to take this step by the principles that were to govern the newly-formed kingdom, such as: 'truth' (διὰ τὴν ἀλήθειαν), 'order' (διὰ τὸν ὄρδινον) and 'the laws of the *Assizes*' (-διὰ τὸν- νόμον τῶν ἀσίζων), which future kings were to 'care for and protect' (νὰ τὲς βλεπίσῃ καὶ νὰ τὲς φυλάξῃ). The goal that motivated these forebearers according to the knights was to find 'a moment of respite' (πρὸς μικρὴν ἀνάπαυσιν). This interesting interpretation shows the Franks as law-abiding lovers of values such as truth and order, peacefully inclined towards their new homeland, but who in a sense fail to take into account the rights of Cyprians, which can be seen in the evident silence concerning the latter's heritage.

As Nicolaou-Konnari also notes,[519] it is worth emphasising that, after taking Cyprus, the Lusignans settled there permanently, and could thus influence everything that went on there. This was not externally exerted control.

Nicolaou-Konnari shows that most of the Lusignans' actions, such as fighting the Saracens on their own land or Peter I's official voyages in the years 1362–1365, can be seen as a manifestation of crusading efforts,[520] and therefore – if we take into account the aspect of using force and the goal of annexing lands – colonising efforts. The Franks freely brought in goods from Muslim lands, as indicated by the mention of the 'pair of exceptionally beautiful dogs from Turkey' (ἀπὸ τὴν Τουρκίαν μίαν ζυγὴν σκυλλία λαγωνικὰ πολλὰ ὄμορφα, LM II 261) won by the knight Sir Henry de Giblet.

From the mention describing the island's conquest until the very end of the *Chronicle*, the Rhomaioi/Greeks appear infrequently. The narrative is dominated by the Lusignans, and also the Genoese and Venetians, who owed their presence on the island to the former. Peasants (χωργιάτες) participate in events sporadically,[521] mentioned by the author in further parts of the *Chronicle* rather than at the beginning, although villages, mentioned by name, and forming space for the performance of an action or an object of attack, are mentioned quite often. LM III 323 features 'Rhomaic notables' (οἱ λογάδες οἱ Ῥωμαῖοι). Also the means of contact with the Muslims selected by the Frankish (not only Cypriot) rulers is their sole choice.

Observation of how Makhairas eliminates mentions of the native population from the narrative concerning the Lusignans' foreign policy leads to the conclusion that the Latin minority had supremacy over the majority, composed of autochthons. The Franks's efforts to conquer a large part of the Mediterranean Basin, including Cyprus, date back to the capture of Jerusalem in 1099 by Godfrey de Boullion, who arrived from his native country, France (ἀπὸ τὴν Φραγγίαν), 'with a large number of people' (μὲ πλῆθος λαοῦ).[522]

It is hard to precisely define what, according to the author of the *Chronicle*, motivated Guy when he decided to take over the island. The chronicler states that by taking the Cypriot kingdom and granting privileges to allochthons, this self-styled monarch gained as his servants those who 'served him with their bodies and estates' (ἐδουλεῦσαν του μὲ τὰ κορμιά τους καὶ μὲ τὸ δικόν τους, LM I 19). In the *Chronicle*, Guy admits that he violated a place not belonging to him, and so his new subjects, who had already incited a 'rebellion' (τὴν ἀγανάκτησιν) and carried out 'a massacre in the country' (τὸν σφαμὸν εἰς τὴν χώραν), might go on rebelling (ρεβελιάσουν), and also call on help from the rulers of Constantinople and in consequence take the kingdom from his hands by force ("μὲ δύναμιν νὰ σηκώσουν τὸ ρηγάτον ἀπὲ τὰς χεῖρας μου"), as they did to with the Templars.[523] This indicates quite close links between Cyprus and Byzantium in the twelfth century, which the *Chronicle* introduces together with the eloquent foundational vision which starts with St Constantine's decision to send the 'blessed Helena' (μακαρία Ἑλένη, LM I 6),

---

[519] Cf. Nicolaou-Konnari's comment on the phenomenon of the social system introduced by the Lusignans: '[…] the nature of the social system introduced was determined, firstly, by the high pre-conquest population density and overall ethnic homogeneity of the indigenous population and, secondly, by the fact that this was not a system of colonial exploitation from the outside by a parent state governing from a distant metropolis, but one of administration from within, based on the permanent settlement of the incoming group' (Nicolaou-Konnari, Alterity and identity, 39–40).
[520] Nicolaou-Konnari, 'A poor island…', 132.
[521] E.g.: LM II 271, III 445, 448, 508, 562, V 659, 676, 685, 696–697.
[522] LM I 18.
[523] LM I 22.

his mother, to search for the Cross. These links were to decline later, however, and be renewed along with the appearance of Helena Palaiologina on the island in the fifteenth century.

On the basis of archeological material, James Schryver[524] discussed whether Cyprus had been the object of colonisation, or rather a space of coexistence. He discusses the problem of 'borderlands' and 'boundaries' within them that are 'fluid', 'porous' and constantly 'being negotiated and renegotiated'.[525] Schryver in an interesting way comments on the problems posed by the interpretation of the situation on the island in the medieval period, irrespective of the research material selected for analysis:

> *As an island, Cyprus plays a strange role in any discussion of borders and borderlands. […] From the end of the twelfth to the end of the fifteenth centuries, while the island was united under the rule of the Lusignan dynasty, these physical boundaries – the edges of the island and the two mountain chains that run partially across it – were the only ones that did not really change or evolve.*[526]

The Latins of the *Chronicle* built on Greek Cyprus a kingdom that functioned for three centuries, thanks to the support of popes and other western countries. The numerous decisions they were constantly forced to take led their dominium through consecutive stages of development, starting from the initial formation, through its heyday, up to the approaching decline.

Makhairas' text also contains a reflection of the colonial ethos of conquering kings, particularly strongly represented by Peter I and Peter II, who crave foreign lands (πεθυμημένος νὰ ἔχῃ τόπον),[527] make numerous contacts with other rulers, using the pope, treated as a great authority by western countries, to give a religious rationale to the plundering forays. The maxim voiced by Makhairas in LM I 11, Aristotelian in its message, may be applied in the *Chronicle*: 'Consider the end of the things and on the basis of the end [conclude] about the beginning' (Σκοπᾶτε τὰ τέλη τῶν πραγμάτων, καὶ ἀπὸ τὸ τέλος τὴν ἀρχήν). Based on the character of Cyprus' relations with other communities, conclusions may be drawn about the nature of the event during which the island was acquired: the island's foreign policy depended only on decisions of the Franks, who 'colonised' it.

---

[524] A similar situation involving multilayered shaping of relations between Latins and the population ruled by them may have been seen in Crete under Venetian rule in the years 1204–1669. Schryver emphasises that the 'Franco-Greek group' was not born 'immediately', but through intensification and 'gradual merging', where attributes were 'adopted and adapted' one from the other with no loss of the 'core identity'. According to Schryver the consequence of such a perspective is the necessity of redefining 'Franks' and 'Greeks' (Schryver, Colonialism or Conviviencia…?, 157). Schryver cites the works of Ronnie Ellenblum (Ellenblum, Frankish Rural Settlement; Ellenblum, Frankish Castles, 93–110), Kyrris (Kyrris, History of Cyprus; Kyrris, Cypriot Identity, 563–573), Benedict Englezakis (Εγγλεζάκης, Είκοσι μελέται; Englezakis, Cyprus; Englezakis, Studies and documents), Miltiadis Efthimiou (Efthimiou, Greeks and Latins).
[525] Schryver, Colonialism or Conviviencia…?, 133.
[526] Schryver, Colonialism or Conviviencia…?, 134.
[527] LM II 114.

II. The Complex Depiction of Christianity in the *Chronicle*

Δύο φιλούντων τὴν ἐν Χριστῷ φιλίαν
ἰσασμὸς οὐκ ἔνεστιν, ἀλλ' ἔρις μᾶλλον.

'Between two people sharing a friendship in Christ,
there is no equality but rather rivalry.'[528]
(Kassia, 9th c.)

2.1. Plurality of denominations in Makhairas' Cyprus

At the very beginning, Makhairas' work for an instant reveals a fragment of the image of Christendom in the fourth century, after which the narrative moves to the events of 1191, more than a century after the 1054 schism of the Churches, which was a very radical caesura, cleaving the Christian tradition.[529] In the *Chronicle*, members of Christian denominations are dominant in the social fabric of medieval Cyprus, which is subject to constant dynamic transformation.[530] From the way in which the chronicler expresses this diversity and multiformity, conclusions may be drawn about how he perceived the role of Cyprus in the Mediterranean world[531] and how his own identity had been shaped. He sometimes treats Christians as a whole, and sometimes as a set of various smaller communities. In this his work resembles the *Chronique d'Amadi*, where we read of 'the territory of Christianity" (*il territorio de la Christianità*),[532] 'the destruction of Christians' (*la destruction de li Christiani*)[533] and 'the mercy of Christians' (*pietà de la Christianità*),[534] only to elsewhere find 'great differences' (*gran differentie*) between the opinions of Greeks and Latins[535] or unity despite differences, visible in the presentation of Latin and Greek prelates gathered together.[536] Leontios ignores the presence of some Eastern Christian denominations such as Monophysitian Copts from Egypt,[537] thus suggesting which groups particularly occupied his attention. However, it is hard to establish the exact situation of the different Syrian denominations, as the *Chronicle* only features 'Syrians' and, independently, also Nestorians, similarly originating from Syria. There is however no direct mention of Syrian Maronites and Melkites, which does not mean that the chronicler was not referring

---

[528] Text and translation after Lauxterman, Byzantine Poetry, 261–262.

[529] In reality, as Nowosielski emphasises, even before the split there occurred 'a period of several centuries' hate' (Nowosielski, Inność prawosławia, 11. Short phrase translated by Kupiszewska).

[530] A historical perspective on denominations in medieval Cyprus was presented in Hackett, A History of the Orthodox Church of Cyprus.

[531] Nicolaou-Konnari writes that Cyprus was 'the only safe Christian territory in the East' (Nicolaou-Konnari, Greeks, 19).

[532] Mas Latrie (Ed.), Chronique d'Amadi, 49–50.

[533] Mas Latrie (Ed.), Chronique d'Amadi, 63.

[534] Mas Latrie (Ed.), Chronique d'Amadi, 64.

[535] Mas Latrie (Ed.), Chronique d'Amadi, 113–114: *Li Christiani fatto consulto hebbino gran differentie, perchè il re et li paesani et maggior parte di oltramontani et l'Hospital de Alemani et alcuni de li prelati si contentavano de accettar la offerta del soldan, el legato et el Tempio et la magior parte di prelati et li Italiani non volevano […]*.

[536] Mas Latrie (Ed.), Chronique d'Amadi, 354–355.

[537] Coureas, Religion and ethnic identity, 13; Hill, A History of Cyprus II, 3–4; Hadjidemetriou, A History of Cyprus, 164; Latif, Religion and Ethical Education, 46.

to them when he used the general name. Copts and Maronites are mentioned for example in the *Chronique d'Amadi* in the context of the decree issued in 1330 by archbishop John, who ordered an annual procession on the anniversary of flooding to be organised, composed of Latins, Greeks, Armenians, Copts, Nestorians, Jacobites and Maronites.[538]

Makhairas' account shows that Frankish settlers were able to succeed where the Templars, who bought Cyprus in 1191 from Richard Cœur de Lion, had failed, that is, to occupy the island for the three subsequent centuries, resulting in numerous repercussions, particularly in the sphere of its original inhabitants' religious life.[539] If from the *Chronicle* narrative we select the passages that describe events belonging to consecutive stages of Christianity's transformation on the island (starting from the fourth century), we encounter the same phenomenon that Dimitris Tziovas found in Greek history: 'a clash of two competing temporalities', one of which is linked to 'the notions of succession, continuity, and conservation', and the other involves 'a hybrid fusion and the coexistence of material objects from different periods'.[540]

It is impossible, on the basis of the incoherent (in religious and ideological terms) narrative of the *Chronicle*, to set a clear boundary between the identity of Rhomaioi/Greeks, representing 'the self' and the identity of 'the other' Franks/Latins. As the author himself avoids radical boundaries, the narrative strategy he adopts gives rise to questions about his own identity. This does not mean, however, that Cyprus completely loses its eastern character under Makhairas' pen, because significant elements of the Byzantine past are reborn in a landscape of new points of reference.

That the Franks and Cyprians were able to forge an interesting spiritual climate through their coexistence is indicated among others by the fact that two texts that were important for medieval religious theatre, 'The Cyprus Passion Cycle', written in Greek, and the Latin *Repraesentatio figurata praesentationis beatae Mariae Virginis in templo* (Representation in Images of the Presentation of the Blessed Virgin Mary at the Temple), have their roots in Cyprus. The first of them comes directly from Cyprus, while the second contains a detailed description of a play performed in 1372 in Avignon with the participation of Philippe de Mézières, who was a chancellor at the court of Peter I.[541]

It is surprising that despite attempts to characterise the relations between denominations in Cyprus and despite references to religion in its many aspects, Makhairas makes no mention of the highly important document that was the *Bulla Cypria* issued in 1260 by Pope Alexander IV, which regulated the position of the Orthodox Church in Cyprus, limiting the number of Greek bishoprics to four and making Greek bishops subordinate to the Latin archbishop, and all Greeks, to the pope.[542]

According to John Watkins and Kathryn Reyerson, it is possible to conclude based on archaeological evidence from this period that there occurred both disputes (negative, exclusionary component) and processes of adjustment (positive, including component) between the crusaders and the local population.[543] This comment applies, they accent, not only to relations between Christians and Muslims on the continent,

---

[538] Mas Latrie (Ed.), Chronique d'Amadi, 405. Nicolaou-Konnari writes about the degrees of 'otherness' with respect to the large number of denominations on Cyprus. Franks differed from other Franks who supported the Byzantine emperor, and from Rhomaioi, Armenians and Syrians due to religious differences. The scholar shows that according to the *Assizes* the hierarchy of denominations was as follows: the Latins first, then Orthodox Syrians (Melkites), then Greeks, other Eastern denominations, Jews and Muslims. However, she emphasises that 'the hierarchization of the various Eastern Christian denominations before the law probably reflected popular perceptions of the Other rather than the reality of a strictly stratified social system' (Nicolaou-Konnari, Greeks, 22–23). Christopher Schabel states that in terms of numbers, in the earliest period of the Franks' presence on Cyprus the situation was as follows: 'the Greeks were followed by Greek-rite Syrian Melkites, then Syrian Nestorians and Jacobites, while Armenians and Maronites perhaps figured less because they were predominantly outside the cities' (Schabel, Religion, 161). According to him, the Copts arrived together with the Ethiopians or the Abbyssinians before the island's conquest by Richard Cœur de Lion (Schabel, Religion, 163).

[539] LM I 12. Cf. Burkiewicz, Polityczna rola królestwa Cypru, 39; Hadjidemetriou, A History of Cyprus, 177; Hill, A History of Cyprus II, 34–35. Adrian Boas underlines that representatives of the Lusignan dynasty arrived on the island after the Kingdom of Jerusalem fell, which caused them to lose their spheres of influence in Syria (Boas, Crusader Archaeology, 4). This drive to occupy new lands was due to the attitude of Western rulers and popes, who after the Photian schism in the ninth century increasingly expressly started to identify 'orthodox purity' with the doctrine of the Latin Church. Information after Pelikan, Tradycja chrześcijańska 2, 176–177. Translated by Kupiszewska.

[540] Tziovas, Decolonizing Antiquity, 5.

[541] Puchner, The Crusader Kingdom of Cyprus, 19, 56.

[542] Misztal, Historia Cypru, 263. Other papal decrees concerning Cyprus have been collected in: Schabel (Ed.), Bullarium Cyprium 1, 2, 3. Schabel writes about its importance for the Greek clergy in Schabel, Greeks, Latins and the Church, 189–198.

[543] Watkins, Reyerson, Mediterranean Identities, 8.

but also between Franks and Rhomaioi in Cyprus, which is manifested in the coexistence in one space of different architectural styles.[544] In the scholars' words:

There Gothic and Byzantine architectural styles survive in juxtapositions that suggest complex negotiations of identity rather than a clash between irreconcilable communities.[545]

This 'clash' may be observed in other areas. Maria Paschali, who investigates Cypriot art from this time (based on the example of Famagustian architecture), writes about 'the confluence of religious practices'.[546] Similarly, as Ioanna Rapti shows with respect to the evolution of Cypriot manuscripts from the period ('painted books', 14th c.), it is possible to observe multidirectional phenomena (termed 'visual multilingualism' and 'fluctuant imagery')[547] indicating 'the reception of different visual languages'[548] and 'a fertile ground for the construction of complex individual and collective identities'.[549]

Most of the above conclusions may be applied to the *Chronicle* with regard to its content. This is because in his multidimensional narrative its author confronted the complicated reality he experienced in various ways, and did not fail to include rich references to Cyprus' religious tradition. From Leontios' perspective two phases of Cyprian religiosity form this tradition: Christian spirituality before the final schism of 1054 and Orthodox Christianity. The chronicler was clearly fascinated by both, even though he daily had direct contact with the Latins, who had become established on the island (at the moment of Makhairas' birth the Franks had been present on the island for over three centuries). This sentiment comes to the fore at the beginning of the *Chronicle*, when its author lists Cyprian saints with palpable pride and precisely outlines the structure of the Greek Christian community. However, the chronicler should also be seen as an individual subject to inevitable contact with arrivals, settlers and invaders, possessed of exceptional powers of observation that allowed him to describe individual encounters and to situate them both within a broader perspective of the confrontation between East and West, and in the context of the confrontation between Christianity and Islam. The *Chronicle*, as the work of a perspicacious observer, is undoubtedly a narrative about the meeting of different identities and their negotiation.

Rev. Tomasz Czernik writes that identity, which is dependent on context and takes shape within its boundaries, can be subject to constant development, and explains that in the process of negotiating identity 'its processual character' is important.[550]

The spirituality of medieval Cyprus portrayed by Makhairas should be treated as a kind of space where the differing denominational identities relevant from the perspective of the *Chronicle*'s content encounter each other. Influenced by the 'other', the Greek and Latin communities systematically acquire certain new features and characteristics, which the chronicler evokes by building individual episodes of his narrative. The way he describes the relation between Cyprians and Franks proves that he does not divide the original and the more freshly settled inhabitants of the island, that is all Cypriots, into 'native' and 'other' only, but also recognises intermediate states.

Such an intermediate state may be exemplified by the identity of Makhairas himself, which eludes attempts to define and name it. Based on a reading of the *Chronicle*, it is only possible to undertake to establish certain features of the author's identity and to describe certain fragments of the heterogeneous image of the 'inbetween' sphere ('third space' in Bhabha's nomenclature[551]), formed where the influence of different denominations (Orthodoxy and Catholicism) and different religions (Christianity and Islam)

---

[544] Watkins, Reyerson, Mediterranean Identities, 8.
[545] Watkins, Reyerson, Mediterranean Identities, 8.
[546] Paschali, Negotiating identities, 286. Paschali takes the position that: 'The Orthodox created, in essence, an imagery of very high intellectual calibre that could protect them, manage the difference between the Greek and Latin rite, and ultimately negotiate their own identity.' (Paschali, Negotiating identities, 292).
[547] Rapti, Painted Books, 328.
[548] Rapti, Painted Books, 329.
[549] Rapti, Painted Books, 330.
[550] Czernik, Tożsamość jednostkowa, 39–40.
[551] The concept of the 'third space' was conceived in Bhabha, The Location of Culture, 37–38. Mary Louise Pratt calls it the 'contact zone' ('where cultures meet, clash, and grapple'). Wonhee Anne Joh develops Pratt's notion to 'the contact zone of all relationality.' (Pratt, Arts of the Contact Zone, 34; Joh, Heart of the Cross, 62–63). The concept of the 'third space' is present in the medical sciences: 'A non-physiologic space into which fluids may pass in emergency clinical situations, the size of which cannot be calculated' (Segen, The Dictionary of Modern Medicine, 726). In descriptions of the phenomenon of 'third space' in medical literature the term 'interstitial' is also used. Cf. Marcdante, Nelson Pediatria, 132.

intersects, and where the original Rhomaian character is merged in the narrative with elements of the new Latin reality.

When engaging in a study of Leontios' text with a view to recreating the portrait of individual denominational groups presented therein, one should bear in mind the difficulties posed by the definition of identity itself, and also by the painstaking process of its decoding and interpretation. The fact that identity 'can be an imprecise and an ambiguous construct' is signalised among others by Schryver.[552] The complexity of identity as a topic is also noted by Baglioni, for whom it is not only 'a sum of elements', but 'an abstract structure of difference, whose signs are arbitrary and can change over time'.[553] Baglioni believes the media of identity in Makhairas' work to be 'ethnicity, religion and language', between which 'a perfect coincidence' may be seen,[554] however, citing the *Chronicle*, she simultaneously qualifies that 'the […] perception of language and ethnic boundaries' in this text is 'chaotic'.[555]

Given the allegation of chaos cited above, it is important to assess the extent to which in his *Chronicle* Makhairas reveals an awareness that the reality which has become his part results from the actions of foreign, Latin settlers who seized power over the previous identity of the island, and to what extent he treats the status quo as natural and not subject to judgement. In other words: the important issue is whether he consciously or unconsciously adopts the invader's way of thinking and categories, or whether he consciously distances himself from them.

Heike Peckruhn claims that every individual whose living space has been colonised can experience 'the internalisation of imposed racial and cultural hierarchies'.[556] What would help the colonised group protect itself against the loss of the capacity to distinguish between their own native and foreign heritage would, in Peckruhn's view, be postcolonial thought, understood as 'the theoretical resistance to the amnesia of the colonial aftermath – anamnesis'[557] and defined thus by Leela Gandhi, whom Peckruhn cites. She refers to Ashis Nandy's expression 'the colonization of minds',[558] which is a metaphor, but strongly rooted in postcolonial theory. It indicates the transformative aspect of colonisation, where the voice of the coloniser speaks in the mind of the colonised (in the structure of his mind, the way he acts and in the substance of his thoughts).[559] Colonisers achieve such an effect through practices that lead the colonised to confront their own value system with the foreign one. An example of such a 'colonised mind' may be seen in Makhairas himself, whose identity is extremely hard to establish based on an analysis of the *Chronicle*, and who on a certain level of his perception of reality attempted to identity with the Lusignans, which he was unable to fully achieve. Given these qualifications and having narrowed the scope of the possible forms that the invader's influence on the conquered population may take to the religious sphere, the term 'colonisation of the mind' takes on the meaning of internalisation of theological categories, religious practices and hierarchies of a Church other than one's own. In this perspective, the demands of the Catholic Lusignans touched the core of the Greek Cypriots' identity, namely the deepest layer of the beliefs of the island's community, composed mainly of Rhomaioi.[560] The Franks, as may be seen already in the beginning of the *Chronicle*, penetrated deeply into the structure of the Byzantine-rooted (in the meaning of space and Orthodox spirituality) world foreign to them by using the hierarchy of the Latin Church as the main tool of change and by taking power over the island and its relations with other countries.

---

[552] Schryver, Excavating the identities, 1.
[553] Baglioni, Language and identity, 27.
[554] Baglioni, Language and identity, 28.
[555] Baglioni, Language and identity, 36.
[556] Peckruhn, Of Bodily Anamnesis, 195.
[557] Peckruhn, Of Bodily Anamnesis, 193. In Catholicism, the Greek word 'anamnesis' refers to the moment during mass after the consecration during which the faithful confess their faith in the incarnation of Christ, his death, resurrection and future coming. In the colonial and postcolonial context this term has come to mean 'resisting amnesia', that is distortions created by official history, by discovering traces of another hidden history (Donadey, Between Amnesia and Anamnesis, 111). Cf. Lionett, Autobiographical Voices. To this end memory is required, whose importance is signalised by Prof. Andrzej Dąbrówka in his review of my PhD dissertation (http://www.polon.uw.edu.pl/documents/9763960/10761134/glinicka_prof_dabrowka.pdf, accessed 28 November 2021). In the *Chronicle* such a role is played by folk memory, preserved in tales and legends closely connected to the island's Byzantine past.
[558] Nandy, The Intimate Enemy, 11 (see 64).
[559] Dascal, Colonizing and decolonizing minds, 1.
[560] This issue should be examined bearing in mind, as Frances Giampapa notes, that 'the act of claiming identities and claiming the spaces of identity is a political act', especially as it means a 'movement from the periphery' and a 'reconfiguration of the center' (Giampapa, The Politics of Identity, 193).

The appropriate term for what happened between the twelfth and fifteenth centuries on Cyprus in the *Chronicle* is 'hybridisation',[561] because of the co-occurrence of adaptive factors and factors differentiating the Franks and Cypriots. Dimple Godiwala describes his understanding of 'hybridisation' thus:

Cultural hybridization can be assimilationist in its difference, benign in the appropriation and acceptance which underlie its identity formation [...].[562]

Hybridisation is the effect of various processes. Indicating the two poles of identification, Vanessa Guignery argues that the belief that a permanent monolithic 'essentialist' identity could exist is false, calling it a 'myth'[563] and counterposing it to hybridity, because the latter has the features of 'the composite', 'the impure', 'the heterogenous' and 'the ecclectic'.[564]

In the *Chronicle* the essentialist approach is visible only in the narrative about St Helena's performance of her foundational mission, because it is the manifestation of the immanent influence of Byzantine heritage. Many centuries and only several paragraphs of the *Chronicle* later, the Lusignans are still at the centre of the Cypriot world, while the Cyprians have been sidelined to its peripheries.

When analysing the depiction of the new order on Cyprus that emerges from the *Chronicle*, it is necessary to consider the narrative elements that show the internal diversification of communities that have been forced to share a common space. To some extent, Makhairas deprives all individuals of the right to autonomy in decision-making, irrespective of whether these are small actions or far-reaching endeavours, by subordinating the unfolding events to the supernatural intervention of Providence. Mutual relations between the world of the Franks and that of the Cyprians vary in the *Chronicle*, some being full of hostility, others neutral, and still others, friendly. They can therefore be referred to as 'mixed relationships', a term that, introduced by Steven Epstein, was used by Michalis Olympios to describe relations between crusaders and members of the Eastern churches, characterised by (such a sense was given to the term by Epstein) 'less trenchant attitudes towards the Other'.[565]

To understand the specific nature of contacts between different denominations within a single religion, it is helpful to assume an approach that takes into account the context in which its different aspects are manifested. The contextual approach has been defined for example by Stephen Bevans. He proposed a synthetic model that combines three constituent models: translation, anthropological and practical. The translation model is, Bevans explains, a paradigm, entailing the conviction that 'the essence of Christianity is supra-cultural' and can 'be separated from the language and culturally-conditioned concepts in which it is presented'.[566] It is important for defining the shared spiritual

---

[561] Kyrris quite frequently uses words such as 'hybridisation' and 'hybrid' when referring to instances of conversion in the *Chronicle*: 'Conversion to the Latin faith was the extreme end of the process of hybridisation, which our author accepted as a necessary evil in the linguistic sphere. But he rejected religious conversion though without offending or underestimating the Latin creed, which he put on the same level as his own traditional Orthodoxy.' (Kyrris, Some Aspects, 183–184). To Cypriot society in the twelfth-fifteenth century: 'The history of Lusignan Cyprus until the mid-15th century, his main theme, was for him an indivisible unity, an entity *per se* – of course in a wider context –, a *continuum* with which he was perfectly familiar. He was one of the "club", a factor of the system. As such he could lay a rightful claim to studying, researching, explaining and passing verdicts on it as a whole from beginning to end. This claim of a partner in the system and a member of the hybrid Graeco-Latin "club" of Lusignan Cyprus was, after all, the inner motive, the *élan* of his history-writing traceable in the opening paragraphs and elsewhere in the *Chronicle*.' (Kyrris, Some Aspects, 198). About the Greeks and Latins' shared way of functioning: 'The result, after long periods of struggle and interludes of conciliation, submission, apocryphy or mutual assimilation, was [...] a hybrid *modus vivendi*.' (Kyrris, Some Aspects, 198). About the declining Frankish empire in the reign of King John II and his wife Helena from the Palaiologos dynasty: 'But such as it [the Lusignan Kingdom – note M.G.] was, at least it tolerated Orthodoxy, be it a "semblance" of it, or a hybridisation.' (Kyrris, Some Aspects, 186). And finally, with regard to Latin ideology and culture: 'The tragicness of Leontios' feeling in this case has a national colour considerably transcending the legally and politically sanctioned, dominant Latin – in fact a hybrid version of Latin – ideology and culture of the "club".' (Kyrris, Some Aspects, 200). Kyrris uses these terms metaphorically, not having defined them anywhere. He sometimes treats them as describing a kind of *compositum* of different elements, and in other places as a modification of a specific being under the influence of specific, foreign external factors. Being aware of this, the terms 'hybridity', 'hybridisation' and 'hybrid' have been used in the context delimited by postcolonial theory. Costas Constantinu reaches a similar conclusion concerning hybridity and colonial practices on Cyprus in Constantinu, Aporias of Identity, 247–270.
[562] Godiwala, Postcolonial Desire, 73.
[563] Guignery, Introduction, 3.
[564] Guignery, Introduction, 3.
[565] Olympios, Shared devotions, 1.
[566] Bevans, Models of Contextual Theology, 190.

foundations and establishing a system of values. The anthropological model is based on 'a movement from culture to expression of faith in terms of culture', treating the experiences of the believers of a given denomination (or more broadly, religion) as inseparably linked with culture.[567] The practical model focuses on the assumption that 'orthopraxis', i.e. 'correct practice', is more important than 'orthodoxy', i.e. 'correct thinking'.[568] In the context of the *Chronicle* the anthropological model turns out to be useful for verifying the attitude of representatives of Western culture, who used faith (religion) to justify their actions, even though in actual fact their intentions had other, pragmatic grounds. When Makhairas writes about Orthodox Christians, he cites the names of selected Rhomaioi along with their occupations and includes short biographies of saints with one to several sentence-long descriptions of their deeds, thus placing the Orthodox faith in a specific cultural context. If we apply the practical model to the *Chronicle*, we find that it contains numerous descriptions of actions undertaken by representatives of individual communities, which are judged and evaluated in terms of their correctness and responsibility for the action performed, always with reference to a higher instance, such as God or the Holy Trinity.

When referring to the content of the *Chronicle*, which paints a complex picture of Christianity, it is possible to ask the question posed by Angie Pears in a publication devoted to the contextual nature of spirituality: whether there exists 'a Christian "orthodoxy" or a Christian "core" that can be identified within these different theologies, regardless of context'.[569]

An examination of *Chronicle* fragments that describe specific religious situations and phenomena often shows the lack of any sort of caesura dividing the followers of the two Churches. The chronicler captures different manifestations of one Christian idea, made present in the meeting of Orthodox culture with Catholic culture, making them dependent on political conditions, which is why in the Cypriot work we encounter an accumulation of interpretive contexts. Such a distribution of elements forms a specific constellation, which gives occasion to cite an interesting comment by Stephen Coburn Pepper, who stated that the contextual approach is characterised by 'a horizontal cosmology in contrast to other views' typified by a limiting 'vertical cosmology'.[570] The sense of horizontality intensifies when the *Chronicle* narrative is analysed in chronological order, which allows the evolving depiction of the contacts between Greeks and Latins to be deconstructed. This depiction does not have an exclusively horizontal dimension, however, because the author attributes different levels of importance to the two sides, allowing the ones or the others to dominate the narrative, also showing the influence they have on each other.

To establish what planes of denominational and religious reality can be distinguished in the *Chronicle*, the classification developed by Scottish religious studies scholar Roderic Ninian Smart is used, which is held to be the most consistent and exhaustive. Smart distinguishes the following aspects of religion: 'ritual-practical', 'legal-ethical', 'emotional-experiential', 'doctrinal-philosophical', 'narrative-mythic', 'social-organizational' and 'material-artistic'.[571] The depiction of denominational practices and religiosity in the *Chronicle* is practically devoid of elements that could be attributed to the doctrinal-philosophical dimension. Even authorial comments are free from such reflection. This is because while Leontios does take the variety of the characters' beliefs and attitudes into account, he primarily examines individual phenomena.

All the examples of religious life in the *Chronicle* – action done in the name of religion – had the goal of situating Greek-Latin contact within a specific context of historical and political transformation. Makhairas himself focuses almost exclusively on situations, giving practically no attention to doctrines or abstract ideas.

A fragment that reveals his knowledge of the truths of Christianity is the one that presents the reaction of the pope to a boy's account of his companion's admission ceremony to the Templar order. In horror, Clement V said:

> *Almighty God sent his beloved son; He willingly endured death and suffered, and went to heaven and sat down on the right hand of the Father, to deliver us from the hands of the devil; and He granted to us to flee from all sin that we should not pass into the hands of the devil* [...]. (LM I 14)[572]

---

[567] Bevans, Models of Contextual Theology, 188.
[568] Bevans, Models of Contextual Theology, 193.
[569] Pears, Doing Contextual Theology, 2.
[570] Pepper, World Hypotheses, 251.
[571] Smart, Ninian Smart on World Religions, xxxiv.
[572] "Ὁ παντοδύναμος θεὸς ἔπεψεν τὸν υἱόν του τὸν ἠγαπημένον, με τὸ θέλημάν του ἔδωκεν θάνατον καὶ ἔπαθεν καὶ ἐπῆγεν εἰς τοὺς οὐρανοὺς καὶ ἐκάθισεν ἐκ δεξιῶν τοῦ πατρὸς διὰ νὰ μᾶς λυτρώσῃ ἀπὸ τὰ χέργια τοῦ διαβόλου, καὶ ἔδωκέν μας νὰ φύγωμεν ἀποῦ πᾶσα ἁμαρτίαν διὰ νὰ μὲν πᾶμεν εἰς τὰς χεῖρας τοῦ διαβόλου [...]".

Another example, from an earlier period, is a remark by Godfrey de Bouillon, who did not want to be crowned king of Jerusalem and explained his decision thus:

The King of Kings, the sweet Jesus, put on a crown of thorns on His festival, the day when they crucified Him. (LM I 18)[573]

The ritual-practical dimension is manifested in references to liturgy and processions; the emotional-experiential, in the presentation of events and emotions experienced by characters involved in those events; the narrative-mythic, in tales about the island's Christian beginnings and the lives of saints and martyrs, and in fragments where references to God or objects from the sacred sphere are an important element of the presentation of events and actions of individuals or whole groups; the legal-ethical, in highlighting punishments meted out by God or man; the social-organisational, in showing the Church in its community and hierarchical aspect; and the material, in the description of cult objects and relics.[574]

Makhairas mentions Christians of different sects: Greeks (Ρωμαῖοι), Latins (Λατῖνοι), Syrians (Συριάνοι),[575] Syrian Nestorians (Νεστούροι/ Νεστούριδες)[576] and Armenians (Ἀρμένιδες).[577] The Greeks present in the *Chronicle* include: Rhomaioi (Ρωμαῖοι) and Cyprians (Κυπριῶτες), and the Latins: monastic orders such as the Templars (Τεμπλιῶτες) and Hospitallers (Σπιταλλιῶτες), Cypriot Franks (Φράγκοι), Genoese (Γενουβίσοι), Venetians (Βενετίκοι/ Βενέτικοι), Rhodians (Ροδίτες/ Ροδῖτες),[578] Florentines (Φλουρουντίνοι/ Φλουρουντῖνοι),[579] Catalans (Καταλάνοι)[580] and the citizens of Pisa,[581] Provence[582] and Naples,[583] who appear far less frequently. In LM III 377 also Bulgarians, Tatars and Rhomaioi are mentioned, and in LM III 509, Bulgarians, Tatars and Romanites (Ρωμανίτες),[584] which could suggest that the two names, 'Rhomaioi' and 'Romanite' have the same referent. They do not appear in a religious context, however.

Cyprus, with such a diverse population in terms of religion and ethnicity, was a kind of borderland, outside which lay Muslim, that is non-Christian, territory, which contributed to the view of the island's inhabitants as living on the outskirts of Christian civilisation. Such an image emerges, for example, from the testimony of Ludolf von Sudheim (14th c.), a traveller to the Holy Land, who stated that 'Cyprus is at the extremity of the Christian world' (*Cyprus est terra Christianorum ultima*).[585]

Hill, citing sources such as Makhairas' and Boustronios' chronicles, concludes that in 'racial and religious' terms the largest group was 'Graeco-Cypriote' which should be understood to mean Cyprians who were Rhomaioi. While the Syrian population had in his opinion 'fused' with the Greeks as to language, beliefs and customs, the Armenian population fully preserved their identity.[586] The latter are mentioned

---

[573] "Ὁ βασιλεὺς τῶν βασιλευόντα, ὁ γλυκὺς Ἰησοῦς ἐφόρησεν στέφανον ἀκάνθινον εἰς τὴν χαράν του τὴν ἡμέραν ὅταν τὸν ἐσταυρῶσαν".

[574] Schabel notes several planes on which the groups inhabiting Cyprus differed with regard to religion: practices, liturgical languages, rites and denomination (Schabel, Religion, 158).

[575] LM I 26–27, II 91, 111, 157–158, 391, 411, 437, 439, 654, 677, 681, 685.

[576] LM II 91–96.

[577] Armenians, described as 'Christians', appear in LM II 113.

[578] LM II 117, 119, 131, 135, 160–161, 163–166, 169, 174, 190, 201, 204, 206–209, 213, 216, 224, III 291–292, 294, 301, 370, 376, 463, 534–541, 544, 587, 589, 592, IV 612, V 642, 699.

[579] LM II 91, 110, III 334, 360.

[580] LM II 91, 95, 100, 103, 182, 189, 192, 230, 233, 255, III 291, 334, 342, 401, 508, 553, 583–584, 587, IV 630, 683, 686.

[581] LM II 91, 146.

[582] LM III 334.

[583] LM III 334.

[584] Pavlidis translates the term 'Ρωμανίτες' as 'Ἕλληνες'. See Παυλίδης (Ed.), Λεοντίου Μαχαιρᾶ Χρονικόν, 383. The same goes for 'Ρωμαῖοι' in LM III 377. See Παυλίδης (Ed.), Λεοντίου Μαχαιρᾶ Χρονικόν, 279. In a footnote he explains that they were a people 'from Romania, not Cypriots' (Ἀπό τὴν Ρωμανία, ὄχι Κύπριοι). See Παυλίδης (Ed.), Λεοντίου Μαχαιρᾶ Χρονικόν, 279 (fn. 1). According to Pavlidis, 'Ρωμανία ὀνομαζόνταν μεγάλο τμῆμα τῆς νοτιοδυτικῆς Μικρᾶς Ἀσίας, ποὺ ὑπῆρξε ἑλληνικό, περίπου ἀπό τὴν Νίκαια μέχρι τὴν Ταρσό. Συνεπῶς αὐτοί οἱ "Ρωμαῖοι" ἤσαν Ἕλληνες ἀπό ἐκεῖνα τὰ μέρη τῆς Μικρᾶς Ἀσίας, ποὺ ζοῦσαν ἤ καὶ ὑπηρετοῦσαν στὴν Κύπρο.' 'Romania was the name used for a large part of south-western Asia Minor that was Greek, approximately between Nicaea and Tarsus. And so these "Rhomaioi" were Greeks from this part of Asia Minor where they lived, or performed their military service on Cyprus.' (Παυλίδης (Ed.), Λεοντίου Μαχαιρᾶ Χρονικόν, 279, fn. 1). Kupiszewska's translation from the Polish translation by the author. Miller and Sathas use the translation *Romanites*: in Sathas, Miller (Eds, transl.), Chronique de Chypre, 291. Nicolaou-Konnari suggests that the term 'Romanites' could mean a person originating from Byzantine territory (Nicolaou-Konnari, Greeks, 56).

[585] After Dorninger, The Island of Cyprus, 77 (fn. 47).

[586] Hill, A History of Cyprus II, 1–2.

extremely rarely in the *Chronicle*, and the term used for them usually appears in the context of the name of a Lefkosian district. The *Chronique d'Amadi* refers to them far more often, describing for instance the release of the Armenians (*Armeni*) from their obligations towards the Saracens in 1099 through the intervention of Godfrey de Bouillon (*Godifredo de Bolione*),[587] or citing the contents of a letter addressed in 1290 by the sultan to a temple master, in which the Islamic ruler calls himself the 'scourge of Franks, Tatars and Armenians' (*scaciator de li Franchi, Tartari et Hermini*).[588] In this work the kingdom of Armenia (*l'Armenia*) is mentioned seventy-three times[589] – probably because the kings of Cyprus were for a long time kings of Armenia, and its citizens sometimes rebelled against the Cypriots (*Li Armeni designorono far un inganno a li Cyprioti*).[590] Also Boustronios wrote about the Armenians, usually presenting them as a group inhabiting a specific district[591] or holding vineyards in St Dometios.[592]

There are few references to Nestorians or Jacobites from Syria in the *Chronicle*.[593] The former appear in the context of charitable work and in a tale about the brothers Francis and Nicholas Lakha,[594] and it is hard to even find the Jacobites referred to by their name. There appears a piece of information about the Nestorian church (τὴν ἐκκλησίαν τοὺς Νεστούριδες) funded by Francis, which Dawkins has identified as the church of St George the Exiler (Ἅγιος Γεώργιος Ξορινός).[595] This demonstrates Makhairas' negligible interest in developing the narrative through reflection about smaller denominations, which clearly would not have, in his understanding, significantly contributed to the literary depiction of Cypriot inter-denominationality.[596]

It is quite difficult to establish where in the *Chronicles* Leontios is writing about representatives of ethnic groups, and where about followers of a Christian Church, that is whether he means ethnic or religious affiliation. When he writes about 'bishops of the Rhomaioi/Greeks' (οἱ ἐπισκοπὲς τῶν Ῥωμαίων), the situation is clear: he means the Orthodox clergy. Sometimes, however, he mentions Rhomaioi, people who come from the eastern part of the Roman Empire, that is Byzantium, and the 'land of the Rhomaioi' (Ῥωμανία).[597] Cretans also make an appearance in Cyprus: in the period of Venetian rule on Crete, which raises the question of who they were in terms of ethnicity and denomination. The same problem appears when trying to define the terms 'Syrians'[598] and 'Armenians'.

From historical studies we know that both members of the Syrian and Armenian Churches[599] and soldiers from Armenia[600] were present in Cyprus. And because they do not play a key role in the *Chronicle*, it is hard to verify based on context which group is meant. Next to the dimension of denominational and ethnic affiliation, a third is also present: affiliation with a place. Native inhabitants of Cyprus, called Κυπριῶτες by Makhairas, and referred to as Cyprians in this work, are undoubtedly affiliated with Cypriot land. Itinerant saints who arrived in Cyprus from foreign lands are incorporated into the Cypriot community because of their Christian faith, but their 'exogeneity' is underlined by Leontios with the adjective περατικοὶ. Cypriot Franks come from the outside (there is no mention of their place of origin in the *Chronicle*), but over time start being perceived as co-inhabiting the island. Makhairas refers to them separately as 'Franks', but when he refers to Franks and Cyprians taken together, for example jointly participating in a mission to attack or repel Muslims, he also uses the term Κυπριῶτες. To preserve the distinction, in this work the Frankish-Cyprian group is called 'Cypriots'. In the postcolonial optic, the name of a group of this type is created via the addition of a hyphen, which suggests the birth of a 'hyphenated identity'.[601]

---

[587] Mas Latrie (Ed.), Chronique d'Amadi, 25; Coureas, Edbury (Transl.), The Chronicle of Amadi, 25 (§ 35).

[588] Mas Latrie (Ed.), Chronique d'Amadi, 220. The word 'scourge' after Coureas, Edbury (Transl.), The Chronicle of Amadi, 216 (§ 460).

[589] Based on Mas Latrie (Ed.), Chronique d'Amadi.

[590] Mas Latrie (Ed.), Chronique d'Amadi, 378; Coureas, Edbury (Transl.), The Chronicle of Amadi, 345 (§ 714).

[591] Dawkins (Transl., int.), The Chronicle of George Boustronios, 11, 19.

[592] Dawkins (Transl., int.), The Chronicle of George Boustronios, 182.

[593] Mas Latrie (Ed.), Chronique d'Amadi, 25, 405. Cf. Baum, Winkler, Apostolic Churches; El-Cheikh, Byzantium Viewed by the Arabs; Deanesly, A History of the Medieval Church; Teule, East and West in the Crusader States.

[594] LM II 91, 93, 95–96, 452.

[595] LM II 93; Dawkins, Notes, 93.

[596] Cf. Mas Latrie (Ed.), Chronique d'Amadi, 25.

[597] LM II 183.

[598] Among Syrians it is possible to distinguish Arabic-speaking Christians, such as: the Maronites, Jacobites and Nestorians. The Jacobites and Nestorians were, as Schabel states, non-Chalcedonian Christian sects believed by Greeks and Latins to be heretical formations (Schabel, Religion, 164–165).

[599] Parker, Peter I de Lusignan; Dadoyan, Armenians in the Medieval Islamic World; Walsh, Introduction, 5–6.

[600] Parker, Peter I de Lusignan, 56.

[601] See dictionary entry 'hyphenated identity' in Chandler, Munday, A Dictionary of Media & Communication (https://www.oxfordreference.com/view/10.1093/acref/9780191800986.001.0001/acref-9780191800986-e-3201, accessed 12 November 2021).

Makhairas, born in the fifteenth century, when Christians of the Greek and Latin rites coexisted side by side, leaving behind a history of more or less tempestuous consolidation attempts, was primarily interested in contact between Catholicism and Orthodoxy. Explaining his decision to write the work, he himself invokes the name of God (ἐν ὀνόματι τοῦ [...] θεοῦ), goodness (ἀγαθοῦ) as an attribute of God, the mystery of the Holy Trinity (ἐν τριάδι προσκυνουμένου)[602] and inspiration sent by its second person, the Holy Spirit (διὰ τῆς χάριτος τοῦ παναγίου πνεύματος).[603] Beginning the *Chronicle* with an invocation of God's name bears a significant similarity to the first verses of each sūra of the Qurʾān: 'In the name of God, Most Gracious, Most Merciful.'[604] In the doctrines of both the Churches that are important to Makhairas and the content of his work, the Holy Trinity plays a key role, though they differ in their interpretation of the dogma of God in Three Persons and the role and origin of the Holy Spirit, as reflected in the famous dispute over the *filioque* question.[605] Leontios sometimes mentions the Three Persons jointly: for example when phrasing the confession of faith spoken by Guy in LM I 24; elsewhere, he features one of them separately in the narrative. He sometimes uses the expression 'name of God and the Holy Trinity' (τὸ ὄνομαν τοῦ θεοῦ καὶ τῆς ἁγίας τριάδος). It may be ventured that these places are an echo of a twofold view of the Holy Trinity, both as a single entity and as separate persons.[606] Many medieval authors invoked the trinitarian mystery, among them Philippe de Mézières, who wrote of the 'glorious Trinity' (*la glorieuse Trinite*)[607] and about the 'two persons of the Trinity, [who are known as] the Son of God, Jesus Christ, and the Holy Spirit' (*deux personnes de la Trinite, [...] du Filz de Dieu, Jesucrist, et du Saint Esperit*).[608]

Makhairas' comments contain traces of intuitions concerning the nature of the Holy Spirit and the mystery of the Incarnation, but they rather confirm that the chronicler knew about the existence of such categories than prove that he was fully aware of their meaning: even if he understood them, he did not find it fitting to include a comment or a more thorough discussion of the topic. The reference to the Holy Trinity in the opening of the *Chronicle* is the first trace of its author's religious awareness, but a full explanation of how he understood this phenomenon is not provided. We only find a declaration that he would hold the principles of Christian spirituality to be correct and important.[609] However, it should be mentioned that Leontios does not include in-depth theological thought anywhere. The Trinitarian allusions that he voices and the frequently used technique of invoking divine attributes serve only to draw the attention of the text's recipient to a strictly determined causal order, and also to provide a judgement of the conduct of characters and communities from a moral standpoint. The *Chronicle*'s author highlights his own lowliness and awareness that there is a proper hierarchy of entities. He demonstrates solid knowledge about the beginnings of Christianity on the island and the time of its takeover by western forces, and also reveals a lively interest in external aspects of spirituality, and so it may be supposed that his references to these categories are intentional. He also alludes, at the very start of his work, to the prophet David, who was highly appreciated in the Middle Ages, of whom we read in a Byzantine epigram:

Τέττιξ προφητῶν, ἡ λύρα τοῦ πνεύματος,
ὁ γῆν ἅπασαν ἐμφορῶν μελῳδίας·
ὦ πραότης, γνώρισμα τῆς ἐξουσίας.[610]

---

[602] The expression 'ἐν τριάδι προσκυνουμένου' can be found among others in Ζωναράς, Τα ευρισκόμενα πάντα, 961.
[603] LM I 1-2.
[604] Ali (Transl.), Quran; Dawkins, Notes, 41.
[605] Cf. Farrelly, The Trinity, 18–19; Pelikan, Tradycja chrześcijańska 2, 216; Pelikan, Tradycja chrześcijańska 3, 7, 24–25, 282–283, 321, 340.
[606] For perceptions of the Holy Trinity in Orthodoxy and Catholicism see Meyendorff, Teologia bizantyjska, 170, 221, 231–232, 235–237.
[607] Philippe de Mézières, Le Songe, 94, 99.
[608] Philippe de Mézières, Le Songe, 212.
[609] The reasons for the schism, which took place over three centuries (9th–11th c.) were numerous and became apparent at different points of this period. Jaroslav Pelikan names the activity of Gnostics, Montanists and Arians, believing it to be one of the reasons for the split. The divide weakened, according to Pelikan, thanks to the unification of Christians in the face of the threat flowing from the Muslim world as well as the 'centralisation of western Christianity' (Pelikan, Tradycja chrześcijańska 2, 175. Pelikan's phrase translated by Kupiszewska).
[610] Text and translation after Lauxterman, Byzantine Poetry, 203. Lauxterman states: 'The epigram can be found not only in Pisides' collection of poems, but also in a tenth-century Psalter, Barb. gr. 340.' The work is designated as 'Pisides St. 72'. (Lauxterman, Byzantine Poetry, 203). Jurewicz writes that Georgios Pisides was born in seventh-century Pisidia, his life revolved around Heraklios' court in Constantinople and he was one of twelve deacons of the Church of Saint Sophia (Hagia Sophia, Holy Wisdom) (Jurewicz, Historia literatury bizantyńskiej, 110).

*Cicada among the prophets, lyre of the Spirit,
filling the whole world with thy melody:
o gentleness, the hallmark of power.*

In his narrative Leontios often invokes the person of the Creator, naming His intervention as the explanation for the course of events or showing a correlation between historical episodes and His will. He uses the following expressions: 'God sent a terrible mortal [plague] for our sins' (ἔπεψεν ὁ θεὸς θανατικὸν μέγαν διὰ τὰς ἁμαρτίες μας, LM I 66), 'through the power of God the people of Adalia defeated Takka' (μὲ τὴν δύναμιν τοῦ θεοῦ ἐνίκησέν τον ὁ λαὸς τῆς Ἀταλείας τὸν Τακκᾶν, LM II 126), 'through the power of God he did not hurt anyone' (μὲ τὴν δύναμιν τοῦ θεοῦ δὲν ἔβλαψεν τινά, LM II 133)[611] and also the wishing form: 'may God bless him' (ὁ θεὸς νὰ τὸν μακαρίσῃ, LM I 82), 'may God forgive him' (τάμε ὁ θεὸς νὰ τοῦ συγχωρήσῃ, LM II 258). The author of the *Chronique d'Amadi* also uses a similar technique when he writes: 'with the help of our Creator and Lord God' (*per l'aiuto del nostro creator et signor Iddio*)[612] or 'with the help of God and the Holy Sepulchre' (*Iddio ci aiuti et il Santo Sepulcro!*).[613] This is a narrative strategy that was commonly accepted and used by medieval Christian chroniclers.

An important theological category with a constant presence in the narrative of the *Chronicle* is sin (ἁμαρτία). When writing about a devastating defeat of the Cypriots, the chronicler explains that the unfavourable result of the battle was due to the many evils they committed, thus going against God (κατὰ πρόσωπα τοῦ θεοῦ) in various ways.[614] In one such fragment we read:

And if you wish me to tell you how it was that Famagusta was taken, I say that this was allowed by God because of our sins. (LM III 482)

Sinfulness as a main attribute defining the condition of individuals, groups and societies is emphasised in the *Chronicle* by morally marked expressions, starting with a remark about Isaac Doukas Komnenos, who according to Makhairas was an adulterer (πόρνος),[615] through calling 'evil' (κακόν) the behaviour of the usurper Amaury's followers, who broke the oath they had made to Henry II, for which they were to suffer 'great humiliation in the world' (μεγάλη κατηγορία εἰς τὸν κόσμον) and 'eternal disgrace' (πάντα ἀντροπή),[616] to a general description of all Cypriots in moral terms. Leontios' axiology is particularly interesting in the last case. Namely, the chronicler believes that it is due to their sins – he literally writes 'our' (μας), identifying with the whole community – that Gorhigos castle was taken from them.[617] In a similar vein, he pronounces that God allowed the Genoese to take Ammochostos (ἦτον παραχώρησις θεοῦ) precisely due to evildoing. He adds with emphasis that it would be just (ἦτον δίκαιον) if 'not only Ammochostos' (ὄχι τὴν Ἀμόχουστον μοναχά) 'but [...] all of Cyprus' (ἀμμὲ [...] ὅλην τὴν Κύπρον) were taken away from them. This radical judgment is supported by a list of faults, which included: the sin of mistreatment of slaves (ἁμαρτία τοὺ(ς) σκλάβους), who were transported 'to the islands' ('ς τὰ νησία) when 'Romania was dying' (ἐχάννετον ἡ Ῥωμανία), without granting them the promised emancipation after six years;[618] the murder of Peter I, who was 'slaughtered like a pig' (ἐσκοτῶσαν τον ὡς γοιὸν ἕναν χοιρίδιν); the sending of John Visconti to his death; 'homosexual practices' (διὰ τὴν ἀρσενοκοιτίαν),[619] which were common and widespread in this town, and which were a crime against Divine law, and thus 'reprehensible' (εἰς κρῖμαν); blaspheming God (θεὸν βλασφημοῦσαν); pride (σουπερπία); and contempt

---

[611] LM II 133.
[612] Mas Latrie (Ed.), Chronique d'Amadi, 19.
[613] Mas Latrie (Ed.), Chronique d'Amadi, 115.
[614] LM III 482. Nicolaou-Konnari notes that according to the *Chronicle* 'the overall attitude of Cypriot society towards slaves in general and those from Romania in particular was very hard-hearted and this was one of the sins that caused the loss of Famagusta' (Nicolaou-Konnari, Greeks, 39). Petra Melichar indirectly discusses the problem of slaves, and directly of female slaves, in Melichar, God, Slave and a Nun, 180–291.
[615] LM I 9. The literary depiction of Isaac Komnenos is the subject of an article Neocleous, Imagining Isaak Komnenos of Cyprus, 297–338.
[616] LM I 43, 45.
[617] LM II 112.
[618] This thought is based in Hebrew law (Deut. 15: 12; Πρβλ. Δευτερονόμιον). After Παυλίδης (Ed.), Λεοντίου Μαχαιρᾶ Χρονικόν, 359 (fn. 7).
[619] The term 'ἀρσενοκοῖται', problematic and ambiguous, was coined by St Paul in 1 Cor. 6: 9. Cf. Petersen, Can Ἀρσενοκοῖται be Translated by 'Homosexuals'?, 62–66.

towards the people (ἐκαταφρονοῦσαν τοὺς λᾶς).[620] Human sins influence God's decisions concerning the fate of the world,[621] and their consequences pass down from generation to generation ("-ἡ ἁμαρτία εἶνε- ἀπάνω σας καὶ ἀπάνω τῶν παιδίων σας").[622] Makhairas writes about sin with reference to the Muslims less often, though morally marked remarks appear also in this case, as a comment about the sultan's pride shows.[623] The unforgivable displays of wickedness that the chronicler mentions generally include the sins 'of leading people to unbelief' (ὁποῦ σύρνουν τὸν λαὸν εἰς ἀπιστίαν), to which 'the lords [who govern] the people [usually] consent' (οἱ ἄρχοντες τοῦ λαοῦ ἀπομεινίσκουν το).[624]

An exhaustive study of sin combined with a conviction about the strong causal link between man's deeds and their later consequences is offered by Philippe de Mézières' Le Songe, where thanks to the pilgrimage of 'Ardent Desire' and his travelling companions, who travel through the world's many regions tirelessly searching for truth, he shows the faults and sins of the peoples encountered, which impact the current condition of the societies formed by them. This voyage, Philippe emphasises, was instigated by Providence itself (par le commandement de Providence Divine).[625] One land visited by the travellers is the country of the hard to identify Bragamains (la terre des Bragamains), whose monetary system is missing the Christian 'tau' sign (ne ailleurs ne trouva point le signe de Thau),[626] Tartary, whose inhabitants had become slaves to numerous idols (avoyent esleves plusieurs ydoles),[627] similarly to the Lithuanians (ceste gent sont ydolatres),[628] and also Persia, Media, Chaldea, etc., where different religious sects (plusieurs sectes) had emerged, such as Georgians (Georgins), Jacobites (Jacobins), Nestorians (Nachorins), those who did not believe in the virgin birth (qui ne croyent pas que la doulce fleur qui porta le fruit de vie soit vierge), and Copts (Coptins).[629] In Constantinople, meanwhile, they encounter Pride (Orgueil), Folly (Pauvrete) and Haughtiness (Obstinacion).[630] Philippe pays much attention to the schism of the Churches, that is presented as an event particularly destructive to the stability of the Christian world.[631] Here Truth also makes an interesting comment concerning Cyprus, discussing the murder of King Peter I, which she considers its main sin, in conversation with an old woman (une vieille dame) named Devotion (Devocion) and then Hopelessness (Desesperee), who leans on a cane with one hand (ung baton appuyal), and in the other holds a small booklet (un petit livret), uncovered and rat-bitten (descouvert et toute rongie de raz). It is concluded that the sin of regicide deprived Cyprus of the opportunity to strengthen its global position. In further passages the island is also compared to a goat that wastes its own milk (Ilz firent les chetiz comme la chievre, qui donne le lait, fiert du pie, et le repant).[632] Like Makhairas, Philippe believes sin to have a crucial influence on the fates of individual societies.

The author of the Chronicle starts his description of the island's history with a mention of St Constantine's[633] baptism (μετὰ τὸ βαπτιστῆναι), which presents this event as an evident turning point dividing the new stage of following the teachings of Christ from the tempestuous period of worshipping pagan gods, that is idolatry (ὄνταν ἐστράφην [...] ἀτὲ τὴν εἰδωλολατρείαν εἰς τὴν πίστιν τοῦ Χριστοῦ).[634] The Chronique d'Amadi enriches the portrayal of the emperor with new information about his doings after confirmation, stating that a church was built at the place of Christ's burial upon his order.[635] Other

---

[620] LM III 482.
[621] The phrase 'ὁ θεὸς ἐσυγχωρῆσεν το διὰ τὰ κρίματά μας' in LM II 230.
[622] LM II 271.
[623] LM II 219.
[624] LM I 73.
[625] Philippe de Mézières, Le Songe, 190.
[626] Coopland, Synopsis, 119, with reference to Philippe de Mézières, Le Songe, 225.
[627] Coopland, Synopsis, 120, with reference to Philippe de Mézières, Le Songe, 228.
[628] Coopland, Synopsis, 124, with reference to Philippe de Mézières, Le Songe, 235.
[629] Philippe de Mézières, Le Songe, 230. Cf. Coopland, Synopsis, 121–122.
[630] Philippe de Mézières, Le Songe, 234. See Coopland, Synopsis, 123.
[631] See Coopland, Synopsis, 136, 152–153, 159, 171, 173–175.
[632] Coopland, Synopsis, 135–136, with reference to Philippe de Mézières, Le Songe, 257–260.
[633] The reasons that led Emperor Constantine to decide to receive baptism and how this occurred may be found in: Alföldi, The Conversion of Constantine; Jones, Constantine and the Conversion of Europe; Odahl, Constantine and the Christian Empire; Ward, History of the Cross. An interesting overview of texts referring to Constantine has been written in Lieu, Introduction, 1–38.
[634] LM I 4.
[635] Mas Latrie (Ed.), Chronique d'Amadi, 5. We read that he converted to Christianity in Mas Latrie (Ed.), Chronique d'Amadi, 78.

authors, like Eusebius in the *Vita Constantini* (Life of Constantine) and Lactantius in *De Mortibus Persecutorum* (On the Death of the Persecutors), link Constantine with the sign of the Cross, which was to have appeared to him in a vision or dream.[636]

Constantine and Helena's special role in the Orthodox tradition is demonstrated by the text of a prayer drawn from a liturgical book called a 'Menaion', recited on 21 May, the Feast of Holy Great Sovereigns Constantine and Helena, Equal to the Apostles, at Great Vespers:

> *Thou didst give a most mighty weapon to our emperor: Thy precious Cross, whereby he reigned on earth in righteousness, shining forth in piety, and hath been vouchsafed the kingdom of heaven by Thy loving-kindness. And with him do we glorify Thy loving dispensation, O almighty Jesus, Thou Savior of our souls.*[637]

The text tells us the following about the Emperor's conversion:

> *The memory of the pious Constantine hath shone forth today, poured out like myrrh; for, desiring Christ, he spurned the idols, raising up a temple on the earth to Him Who was crucified for our sake; and in the heavens he hath received the crown of hope.*[638]

The linguistic image of Constantine's transformation recreated on the basis of the *Chronicle* is simple: we are told that at a certain point the emperor renounced idolatry for faith in Christ.[639] Only in one passage does Makhairas voice a universal thought that reveals his personal belief concerning this ruler's place in the natural order of the world:

> [...] *there are two natural rulers (δύο φυσικοὶ ἀφέντες) in the world, the one lay and the other spiritual, so there were in this little island (τὸ νησσάκιν τοῦτον)* [...]. (LM II 158)

By the 'lay', i.e. 'worldly' (κοσμικός), authority on Cyprus, the *Chronicle*'s author means the ruler of Constantinople, while the patriarch of Antioch the Great is given the designation of 'spiritual' (πνευματικός) ruler, but he specifically underlines that this division was present until the Latins' appearance on the island.[640] Leontios creates a symbolical topography of the world, identifying it with the Byzantine universe, and at its centre he places God, served by a spiritual though temporal, ruler. Although the sentence that contains this distinction and at the same time includes a thought about power formed a pretext for introducing a short discussion of the languages used on the island during the chronicler's life, such as Syriac (συριάνικα), Greek (ῥωμαϊκά) and French (φράγκικα),[641] it also gives some insight into the metaphysics and spirituality of the Cypriot, who superimposes this dual matrix on the whole world (εἰς τὸν κόσμον), convinced that such a division was natural and sufficient.[642]

The chronicler outlines the order that emerged after the conquest of the Holy Land, and later Cyprus, by the Latins, focusing on relations between followers of the two churches, and also on the reaction of Christians to terror-inspiring Muslim policy.[643]

---

[636] Maio *et al.*, *Ambiguitas Constantiniana*, 338.
[637] Commemoration of Holy Equals of the Apostles (https://www.ponomar.net/maktabah/MenaionLambertsenMay2000/0521470.html, accessed 22 November 2021).
[638] Commemoration of Holy Equals of the Apostles (https://www.ponomar.net/maktabah/MenaionLambertsenMay2000/0521470.html, accessed 22 November 2021).
[639] In his introduction to St Epiphanios' *Ancoratus*, Young Richard Kim qualifies that the world created by Constantine did not arise by itself, but was built on the foundations laid previously by earlier theologians: 'It is essential to bear in mind that the disputes over biblical exegesis, philosophical concepts, and technical vocabulary that characterized the fourth century did not suddenly emerge in the post-Constantinian world; rather, they were part of a lengthy and complicated negotiation of theology, liturgy, rhetoric, and ecclesiastical politics reaching back to the earliest days of the Christian faith.' (Kim, Introduction, 20).
[640] Kyrris uses the phrase 'binary oppositions' to designate this division into spiritual and lay ruler (Kyrris, *Some Aspects*, 174). Strambaldi translates the adjectives 'κοσμικός' and 'πνευματικός' by *seculare* and *ecclesiastico*. See Mas Latrie (Ed.), *Chronique de Strambaldi*, 63.
[641] LM II 158. In Mas Latrie (Ed.), *Chronique de Strambaldi*, 63 the word 'ῥωμαϊκά' is translated as 'greco ελλινικα'.
[642] It was at the time when the colonisation of Cyprus took place that the process of intensive conquest of Middle Eastern lands by the crusaders began, culminating in the fall of Constantinople in 1204. Information after Misztal, *Historia Cypru*, 174.
[643] LM I 10.

2.1.1. Christianisation of Cyprus

An in-depth analysis and interpretation of the *Chronicle*'s depiction of interdenominational relations should undoubtedly be prefaced with reflection concerning the image of the followers of the different belief systems that emerges from the Cypriot work.

Makhairas' narrative first takes the reader to the sources of the presence of an undivided Christianity on the island. The fact that he describes these beginnings in the way that he does raises the question of his reasons for constructing the text thus: does the analysed work express the author's authentic worldview, or does its content bear the hallmarks of any distortion? The contents of the numerous chronicles that cite the events playing out in the Mediterranean Basin – 'in the "geographical space" of the Roman Empire'[644] – between the twelfth and fourteenth centuries leave no doubt that their authors saw religion as a political tool. Leontios does not express his beliefs directly, which is why it is worth examining whether his declared conviction that St Constantine sent St Helena to Jerusalem in order to find the Holy Cross relic and spread the Christian faith is not in fact a literary device that distorts and simplifies the true sense, and if so, what lies behind it: the chronicler's lack of knowledge or intentional manipulation of the set of facts that he gathered and subjectively ordered?

The Christianisation of the island took place around 45–49 AD, as noted in the *Acts of the Apostles* (Πράξεις τῶν Ἀποστόλων). It came about through Barnabas and Saul, who, sent by the Antiochian community with the mission of sharing the truth about Christ with others voyaged to the island from Seleucia, taking their first steps in the ports of Salamis and Paphos, and teaching in Jewish synagogues there.[645] Makhairas does not mention this fact because he focuses on a later period, starting from the fourth century, but the *Chronique d'Amadi* emphasises that

> *The island of Cyprus was converted to the Christian religion through the preaching of St Barnabas the apostle, with whom the Gospel of St Matthew was found* [...].[646]

The Cypriot chronicle places a clear emphasis on the activities of St Helena, which took place in a kind of temporal void deprived of historical references.[647] He treats her mission as the deciding factor in the promotion of the Christian faith, and hence as the start of the process of shaping the island's own Christian character. In the *Chronicle* we find a detailed description of the deeds accomplished by this woman, the first to be described by Leontios and crucial to the coherence of his vision.[648] For Makhairas, Constantine's mother had become an intermediary in the Divine work of moving the Cross from Jerusalem to Cyprus, with the Cross seen both as a relic and as a symbol of a rich and multidimensional spiritual reality.[649]

---

[644] Paprocki (Transl.), Liturgie Kościoła prawosławnego, 27. Quoted phrase translated by Kupiszewska.

[645] Acts 13: 4–5. Cf. Hendrich, Negotiating and Rebuilding Religious Sites in Cyprus, 9; Misztal, Historia Cypru, 109.

[646] Mas Latrie (Ed.), Chronique d'Amadi, 78: *L'isola de Cypro, la quale si redusse alla religion christiana per le predication de San Barnaba, apostolo, apresso el quale si e trovato l'evangelio di S. Matheo*. Translation after Coureas, Edbury (Transl.), The Chronicle of Amadi, 77 (§139).

[647] Makhairas' version of the legend of St Helena, and in particular the phenomenon of the miracle in the first part of the *Chronicle*, has been analysed in the paper Glinicka, To idē to thaūma, 59–78. The story of how St Helena found the Holy Cross was cited in detail and examined in categories of a miracle. LM I 5–8, 33–34, 38–40, 50 and 67–77 were summarised, analysed and interpreted. Apart from the finding of the Holy Cross, the following categories of miracles were distinguished: local and foreign miracles, miracles of healing, events contrary to nature, miraculous places of eternal rest, miraculous admonitions, overcoming of plagues and disasters, and miracles across divides.

[648] See Taft, Women at Church in Byzantium, 27–87.

[649] Many medieval artists alluded to this event (called the *inventio crucis*). Louis Tongeren mentions Gelasius of Caesarea (4th c.), Ambrose of Milan (4th c.), Rufinus of Aquileia (4th–5th c.), Paulinus of Nola (4th–5th c.), Sulpicius Severus (4th–5th c.), Socrates Scholasticus (4th–5th c.), Hermias Sozomenos (5th c.) and Theodoret of Cyrus (4th–5th c.) (Tongeren, Exaltation of the Cross, 19, fn. 7 and 8). Tongeren emphasises that the fact that the true Cross of Christ has been found cannot be reliably confirmed (either via any other verifiable fact or in the available historical sources) (Tongeren, Exaltation of the Cross, 19). Cf. Heid, Der Ursprung der Helenalegende, 41–71; Baert, A Heritage of Holy Wood, 23–31; Drijvers, Helena Augusta, the Mother of Constantine; Ouspensky, Lossky, The Meaning of Icons, 148–150; Couchman, The Mystery of the Cross. Drijvers observes that the legend of the Cross' discovery only came to be attributed to St Helena in the second half of the fourth century (Drijvers, Marutha of Maipherquat, 56). According to Tongeren, meanwhile, this version, as the oldest, 'probably goes back to an oral tradition rooted in Jerusalem, which was committed to paper for the first time at the end of the fourth century by Gelasius of Caesarea in his ecclesiastical history, which is lost, but has been partially reconstructed' (Tongeren, Exaltation of the Cross, 19, fn. 8). Drijvers analyses the work *De inventione crucis* by Alexander Monomachos (dated to a period between the 6th and 9th c.) (Drijvers, Helena Augusta: the Cross and the Myth, 167–174). Alexander Monomachos' text was published in Nesbitt (Ed.), Byzantine Authors, 23–39 (after Drijvers, Helena Augusta: the Cross and the Myth, 168, fn. 174).

The various versions of the legend that arose at the start of the fifth century suggested that the Cross had been discovered by Emperor Claudius' wife Protonike[650] and St Cyriac (Judas Kyriakos).[651] The newest discovery with respect to the functioning of this motif was made by Stephen Shoemaker, who investigated 'the Syriac narratives of the Virgin Mary's Dormition and Assumption' preserved in fifth and sixth-century manuscripts, and particularly 'the so-called "Six-Books" narratives'.[652] Shoemaker presents the context as follows:

These Dormition traditions introduce the relics of the True Cross within a broader context of sustained conflict between Jews and Christians that pervades the narratives.[653]

Discussing versions of the legend other than the Greek, Latin and Syriac ones, Jan Williams Drijvers mentions an Ethiopian variant according to which the Holy Cross had been found by Theodoxia, the fictional daughter of St Helen and sister of Constantine, and the probable Coptic source of inspiration for the author of this variant, which tells of the discovery of Christ's sepulchre by Constantine's sister Eudoxia.[654] Drijvers also cites various Syriac texts that to some extent use the *inventio crucis* motif, such as the sermon of Jacob of Serugh (5th–6th c.), the lost *Cause of the Invention of the Cross*[655] by Henana of Adiabene (6th–7th c.) and the *Cause of the Feast of the Cross*[656] by Babai the Great (6th–7th c.).[657] The scholar notes that the presentation of the legend most popular in the Middle Ages originated with St Cyriac,[658] but it must have been deemed inauthentic because ultimately it was the legend of St Helena that became established as 'the standard version'.[659]

Recapitulating all his findings concerning the paths of development and transformation of the legend on the discovery of the Holy Cross, Drijvers states:

Fact and fiction are integral and not always easily distinguishable elements of the tradition about Helena and the discovery of the cross. This tradition has its origin in the fourth century and has developed rapidly in a multitude of lands and languages, becoming one of the most important narrative cycles in the Western as well as the Eastern traditions.[660]

Makhairas remains under the spell of the tradition that attributed the discovery of the relic to Constantine's mother, devoting surprisingly much space in his work to all the stages of the empresses' mission and treating the belief that such a mission had taken place as historical truth. Leontios writes of clear visions and calls, the readiness of God's servant to fulfil his command and the evident success of her actions, but he does not remain indifferent to the difficulties she had to overcome to carry out her holy mission:[661]

---

[650] Drijvers discusses this version thus: 'The Protonike legend (P), first known in Syriac and later in Armenian but not in Greek or Latin, is set in the first century. In this narrative, which dates from the beginning of the fifth century, the cross is not discovered by Helena but by the fictitious Protonike, wife of the emperor Claudius. P probably first circulated independently before its final version was included in the Doctrina Addai, the fictional foundation text of the church of Edessa [...].' (Drijvers, Helena Augusta: the Cross and the Myth, 151). Cf. Drijvers, Marutha of Maipherquat, 56; Tongeren, Exaltation of the Cross, 19 (fn. 8).

[651] According to Drijvers: 'The Judas Kyriakos legend became the best known and most widespread version of the *inventio crucis* tradition. It relates how the Jew Judas after initial opposition finds the cross for Helena. [...] Even though the earliest written testimony of the Judas Kyriakos legend is in Syriac, the text was most probably originally composed in Greek, possibly in Jerusalem.' (Drijvers, Helena Augusta: the Cross and the Myth, 151–152). Cf. Drijvers, Marutha of Maipherquat, 56; Tongeren, Exaltation of the Cross, 19 (fn. 8).

[652] Shoemaker, A Peculiar Version of the Inventio crucis, 75. See Shoemaker, Ancient Traditions. Drijvers, Helena Augusta: the Cross and the Myth, 153–158 cites this paper. One of the manuscripts was published in Smith Lewis (Ed., transl.), Apocrypha Syriaca; another by William Wright, in Wright, The Departure of My Lady Mary, 417–448, 108–160. Based on Drijvers, Helena Augusta: the Cross and the Myth, 153.

[653] Shoemaker, Ancient Traditions, 75.

[654] Drijvers, Helena Augusta: the Cross and the Myth, 158.

[655] Drijvers, Helena Augusta: the Cross and the Myth, 160.

[656] Drijvers, Helena Augusta: the Cross and the Myth, 160.

[657] Drijvers, Helena Augusta: the Cross and the Myth, 159–160.

[658] St Cyriac was a Jew (Παυλίδης (Ed.), Λεοντίου Μαχαιρά Χρονικόν, 5, fn. 1).

[659] Drijvers, Helena Augusta: the Cross and the Myth, 167.

[660] Drijvers, Helena Augusta: the Cross and the Myth, 174.

[661] St Helena's legendary visit to Cyprus and Makhairas' account are cited in: Burkiewicz, Polityczna rola królestwa Cypru, 19–20; Hadjidemetriou, A History of Cyprus, 108–109; Misztal, Historia Cypru, 91–92, 141, 236. Misztal notes that St Helena was already advanced in age at this time (Misztal, Historia Cypru, 91).

[...] *she departed and went to Jerusalem; and with much labour and at great costs (μὲ μέγαν κόπον καὶ πολλὴν ἔξοδον) and danger (φοβερίσματα) she found the Holy Cross (τὸν τίμιον σταυρόν) and the two crosses of the thieves besides (τοὺς ἄλλο υς β' σταυροὺς τοὺς ληστές), and the nails (καρφία) and the crown of thorns (τὸν στέφανον τὸν ἀκάνθινον) and thirty-six gouts of the blood of the Lord (λϛ' σταλαματίες αἷμαν), which dripped down and fell upon a cloth [...]. And the sainted lady Helena was filled with wonder (ἐθαυμάστην) at the sight, and made them build many churches (πολλὲς ἐκκλησίες) in Jerusalem in the name of the Living God and of the Living-giving Cross (ἐπὶ ὀνόματος τοῦ θεοῦ τοῦ ζῶντος καὶ τοῦ ζωοποιοῦ σταυροῦ), all new from the foundations (ἀπὸ γῆς) [...].* (LM I 5)

As to the presentation of the legend, the chronicler's thoroughness merits particular attention. It may be seen in the impressive precision with which he decided to reconstruct the deeds of St Helena, incorporating minute calculations of the dimensions and proportions of individual elements of the crosses into his narrative, and also providing a study of combining, in thought-out configurations, the parts of the crosses on which the two thieves died with fragments of Christ's Cross, though he prudently warns that a still more analytical description had been penned by St Cyriac. This particular *modus* of structuring the legend of Constantine's mother is repeated after Leontios by the *Chronique d'Amadi*.[662] The author must have intended to improve the credibility of the description in view of the exceptional importance of the event, its timeless message and significant force of impact: after all, it concerned the foundations of the Cyprians' Christian identity. The chronicler finds no other motivation for the empresses' actions than the intention to expand the Church community, which gave Cyprus its new identity.[663]

This vivid and very detailed depiction will be quoted below in order to show Makhairas' approach to religious phenomena:

And when St. Helena had found the Holy Cross and was instructed by the miracle of the Cross, she took the footpiece (ὑποπόδιον), to which they had nailed the holy feet (ὅπου ἐκαρφῶσαν τοὺς ἁγίους πόδας), and divided in thrice, and thus formed four slabs, and from these she cut away the sixteen corners, that is four corner-pieces from each slab; there were then left four crosses. But the Cross of Christ she left in the Holy of Holies (εἰς τὰ ἅγια τῶν ἁγίων) with much gold and many pearls and precious stones. Afterwards she unnailed the crosses of the thieves, and joined the long piece of the cross of the good thief (τοῦ καλοῦ) with the short piece of the cross of the bad thief (τοῦ πονηροῦ), and made thus one cross; in the same way she put the long piece of the cross of the bad thief with the short piece of the cross of the good thief, and she thus made the pieces into two crosses. Since they had been together so long (ἐποῖκαν ἀντάμα τόσον καιρὸν χρόνους), three hundred and nine years, it was not right to throw away (δὲν ἤτον δίκαιον νὰ ρίψουν) that of the bad thief [...]. (LM I 7)[664]

It is apparent that the author of the Cypriot work prefers a precise, detail-oriented description to attempts at a theological understanding of individual phenomena. Only the expression 'was instructed by the miracle of the cross' (ἔμαθεν ἀπὲ τὸ θαῦμαν τοῦ σταυροῦ, LM I 7) proves that he took into account also the cognitive aspect of religious mystery. St Helen's scrupulosity seems to fascinate him, as if the actions undertaken by her and also their logical course were a guarantee of the endeavour's success, simultaneously forming solid foundations for the community's growth.

In this passage, the chronicler raises many important issues, including: the appearance of a prophetic dream with a message (ἕναν ὅρωμαν), the consequences of the Cross' disappearance and the mission to build a Church based on the foundational process that took place in Jerusalem (ὡς γοιὸν ἐποῖκες εἰς τὴν Ἰερουσαλὴμ καὶ ἔκτισες πολλοὺς ναούς, ἤτζου ποῖσε καὶ ὧδε, LM I 8). The motive of a visionary message

---

[662] Mas Latrie (Ed.), Chronique d'Amadi, 78–79.
[663] Analysing various texts presenting the reasons for St Helena's expedition, Drijvers lists plausible motivations for her mission: 'To restore stability and acquire loyalty for Constantine's rule, to gain support for Constantine's policy of christianizing the empire according to the Nicene doctrine, and to advertise the Christianity of the court were the reasons why Helena was sent to the East.' (Drijvers, Helena Augusta: the Cross and the Myth, 141). However, he stresses that whatever the nature and aims of Helena's journey, it was important in spreading the practice of pilgrimage (Drijvers, Helena Augusta: the Cross and the Myth, 146).
[664] Dawkins comments: '[...] in several versions, notably a twelfth-century English account published by Napier, it is what was left on the beam of the sacred triple tree after the Cross had been made from it, that was divided by St Helena and sent into the four parts of the world' (Dawkins, Notes, 43).

is also present in other medieval historiographic writings. The *Chronique d'Amadi* is one example, telling of Peter the Hermit who believed he had seen the Lord Jesus sending him on a mission.[665] Makhairas also emphasises supernatural phenomena such as 'a pillar of fire [rising] from earth to the heavens' (στύλλον λαμπρὸν ἀπὸ τὴν γῆν ὡς τὸν οὐρανόν), the discovery of one of four small crosses on the river bank (εἰς τὸ πλευρὸν τοῦ ποταμοῦ τὸν ἕναν μικρὸν σταυρόν), 'a voice from heaven' (φωνὴ ἀπὸ τὸν οὐρανόν) giving the order to build the Church of the Holy Cross in Togni, which St Helena faithfully carried out, and furthermore, on her own initiative, built a bridge and embellished the cross with precious stones.[666] The *Chronique d'Amadi* concludes a similar picture with the words: 'Next [St Helena] prayed and at that moment it started to rain.'[667]

All the elements that Makhairas decided to include at the beginning of his *Chronicle* combine to give a consistent image of the process of how Christianity on the island took shape, showing a kind of two-stage strategy of marking sacred space by disseminating relics[668] and building churches.[669] The foundational work of St Helena freed Cyprus from the drought that had plagued it for thirty-six years and from numerous harmful phenomena that forced the local populace to resettle, which in effect prevented these lands from dying, because

> *the people heard of it and returned to their dwellings* (LM I 8)[670]

> [...] *for it is commanded* (ὁρισμὸς εἶνε) *that in this same land men shall dwell until the end of all things* (νὰ κατοικοῦσιν ἀνθρῶποι ἕως τῆς συντελείας), *and it shall not be destroyed for all ages* (νὰ μὲν ξηλειφθῇ εἰς τοὺς αἰῶνας). (LM I 8)[671]

In the *Chronique d'Amadi* the same thought is expressed as follows:

> [...] *for it was the will of God that the island should be inhabited and made a homeland once more.*[672]

A key role in Makhairas' narrative about how the material groundwork of the Church on Cyprus was laid is played by information about the erection of further churches. They are preceded by comments about the selection of an appropriate location (e.g. Mount Olympus, now known as Stavro Vouni),[673] carrying particular symbolism (mountain associated with the name of the Good Thief). The chronicler also gives the names of these churches (e.g. 'Church of the Holy Cross') and describes the custom of incorporating relics into them, as illustrated by the placement of a fragment of Christ's Cross 'at the heart' (εἰς τὴν καρδίαν) of an ordinary wooden or metal cross.[674]

---

[665] Mas Latrie (Ed.), Chronique d'Amadi, 15: *dapoi fatta la sua oration, dove li parse veder il nostro signor Jhesu Christo imponerli l'imbassata che doveva fari.*

[666] LM I 8.

[667] Mas Latrie (Ed.), Chronique d'Amadi, 79: *et poi orò a Dio; et dalhora comminciò a piovere.*

[668] The topic of dissemination of relics is discussed among others in: Bredero, Christendom and Christianity; Quigley, Skulls and Skeletons.

[669] Charles Anthony Stewart states that 'Early Christian churches on Cyprus (fourth to sixth centuries) were similar to constructions in the surrounding regions, such as Palestine, Anatolia, and Syria. Dozens of early basilicas have been excavated, and much is known concerning their superstructure and design. They usually featured a rectangular ground plan divided into aisles with three apses on the eastern end, covered by a wooden roof.' (Stewart, Domes of Heaven, 2).

[670] According to Cyprian the drought lasted seventeen years. Cf. Hackett, A History of the Orthodox Church of Cyprus, 8.

[671] Dawkins explains that the drought was a punishment for the martyrdom of St Catherine under Maxentius (Dawkins, Notes, 41). Cf. Hackett, A History of the Orthodox Church of Cyprus, 8.

[672] Mas Latrie (Ed.), Chronique d'Amadi, 79: *perche la volunta de Dio era che l'isola fosse habitata et repatriata.* Translation after Coureas, Edbury (Transl.), The Chronicle of Amadi, 77 (§141).

[673] Dawkins explains that 'Olympia' or 'Olympus' are older names of Mount Stavro Vouni (Dawkins, Notes, 44). Komodikis writes: 'Ὁ Μαχαιρᾶς γράφει ὅτι τὸ βουνό, πάνω στὸ ὁποῖο κτίστηκε ἡ Μονὴ τοῦ Σταυροβουνίου, ὀνομάστηκε Ὀλυμπία, διότι ἐκεῖ βρέθηκε, μετὰ ἀπὸ θαῦμα, ὁ Σταυρός τοῦ καλοῦ ληστῆ, ποῦ ὀνομαζόνταν Ὀλυμπᾶς, ὅταν εἶχεν ἐξαφανιστεῖ κατὰ τὴν παραμονὴ τῆς Ἁγίας Ἑλένης στὴν Κύπρο.' 'Makhairas writes that the mountain on which Stavro Vouni Monastery was built was called Olympia, because the cross of the Good Thief, named Olympas had been miraculously discovered on it after it disappeared during St Helena's stay on Cyprus.' (Κωμοδίκης, Οἱ Πληροφορίες τῶν Βραχέων Χρονικῶν, 235–236. Kupiszewska's translation from the Polish translation by the author). Schabel observes that at the time of Cyprus' conquest by the Franks, the Stavro Vouni monastery was Greek, and from 1254, Benedictine (Schabel, Religion, 188). Σάθας (Ed.), Χρονογράφοι Βασιλείου Κύπρου, 56, contains an explanation: 'διὰ τὸν σταυρὸν τὸ Ὀλυμπάτο ὄνομα τοῦ καλοῦ ληστοῦ'.

[674] LM I 8.

2.1. Plurality of denominations in Makhairas' Cyprus

The passage below best expresses these individual stages:

[...] *she saw a dream (εἶδεν ἕναν ὄρωμαν), that a young man said to her: 'My lady Helena [...] build a church in the name of the Venerable and Lifegiving Cross (κτίσε ναὸν εἰς τὸ ὄνομαν τοῦ τιμίου καὶ ζωοποίου σταυροῦ) [...]' [...] And lo the miracle! one of the big crosses was gone. And she sent to search for it, and it was found on the mountain called Olympia (τὸ βουνὶν τὸ λεγόμενον Ὀλυμπία) [...]. And she built a church of the Holy Cross, and set in the heart of the cross a fragment of the Holy Wood (μερτικὸν ἀπὲ τὸ τίμιον ξύλον). Afterwards she saw a pillar of fire which reached from the earth to the sky, and went to see the marvel (θαῦμα), and found on the bank of the river one of the four small crosses. And a voice from heaven said to her: 'Helena, cause a church to be built here in this very place, the name of which is Togni'.* (LM I 8)

In the opening passages of his work in LM Leontios presents the original situation of the island, namely 'deserted' (ἔρημον) land, deprived of anybody's presence (χωρὶς τινάν)[675]. The term χώρα, as Keimpe Algra underlines, was one of three most widespread terms in Greek philosophy to indicate place alongside τόπος and κενόν ('the void').[676] Although in Makhairas' language only the word κενόν to describe place is not present, we realise that in his picturing the island – in this particular instance, as microcosm – resembles the void, out of which something would emerge. Helen Saradi, who cites Algra's constatation, adds to these terms Plato's definition of space, stressing its unique quality of 'partaking in' something (μεταληπτικόν).[677] Leontios' space takes part in directly recalling the Passion of Christ and its role in giving the new life. At the instigation of the empress, people started to arrive, returning from the places to which they had fled from the disaster. Makhairas even ventures that 'the people on the island multiplied' (ὁ λαὸς ἐπλήθυνεν εἰς τὸ νησσίν).[678] This symbolism calls to mind the words of the prophet Isaiah read in the Orthodox Church on the day that St Constantine and St Helena are remembered:

You shall no more be termed Forsaken, and your land shall no more be termed Desolate; but you shall be called My Delight Is in Her, and your land Married; for the Lord delights in you, and your land shall be married. For as a young man marries a young woman, so shall your builder marry you, and as the bridegroom rejoices over the bride, so shall your God rejoice over you.[679]

The significance of empty land as a transcendent space where the sacred manifests its presence is emphasised among others in the works of Edwyn Bevan and Louis Dupré.[680] Romanian religious studies scholar Mircea Eliade also investigated this topic, arguing that through sanctification empty space was transformed:

In the homogeneous and infinite expanse, in which no point of reference is possible and hence no orientation can be established, the hierophany reveals an absolute fixed point, a center.[681]

It would be hard to state with all certainty that the introduction of this motif was an intentional device, though it should be acknowledged that Makhairas rather suggestively underlines this extinction of human presence and the demise of community life, as well as the miracle of repopulation thanks to the supernatural power of the Cross. This approach is important for an understanding of the *Chronicle* because it shows that the sanctification which took place in Cyprus occurred thanks to the presence of the relic, which gave the space a new structure and allowed people to develop and inhabit it.

---

[675] LM I 4.
[676] Algra, Concepts of Space in Greek Thought, 31–71.
[677] Saradi, Space in Byzantin Thought, 88.
[678] LM I 9. Hackett writes that St Helena 'invited settlers from all the surrounding countries, from Arabia, Syria and Anatolia, and to induce colonization bestowed estates upon them with exemption for a certain time from all taxation. Many of these new comers are reported to have been natives of Telos and others of the Sporades.' (Hackett, A History of the Orthodox Church of Cyprus, 9–10).
[679] Isa. 62: 4–5 (New Revised Standard Version; fragment located thanks to http://www.liturgia.cerkiew.pl/pages/File/docs/festum-30-konstantyn.pdf, page 2, accessed 23 December 2021).
[680] Bevan, Symbolism and Belief, 122; Dupré, Symbols of the Sacred, 79. The symbolism of empty land was important also in other cultures, e.g. in Buddhism, where 'empty space' symbolised the way in which the Buddha is present in the world. See Okumura, Living by Vow.
[681] Eliade, The Sacred and the Prophane, 20.

The chronicler states that Cyprus was deserted as a result of a devastating drought, which should be interpreted as a consequence of God's wrath, incited by the immensity of sinful deeds committed by its inhabitants. Plagues, diseases and disasters appear cyclically in Leontios' writings. Their significance has been broadly discussed in Christian literature, starting from the biblical *Book of Joel* 1,1–2,27. A similar situation takes place in the *Chronique d'Amadi*, where misfortunes of this type are treated as signs foretold in the Bible (*i segnali che dice il Vangelo*).[682] Under great cataclysms it includes the 1170 earthquake (*un terremoto grande*) in the East,[683] and in 1269 in Armenia,[684] a plague of locusts in 1178 on the day of the Holy Cross,[685] and the co-occurrence of these disasters in 1267,[686] and moreover a large failure of wheat and other grains in 1308 (*mancho le biave et altre semenze*),[687] the flooding of the Lefkosia river in 1330 (*gran ruina... imperochè il finme de Nicosia*)[688] and events of a similar nature in 1348 (*una gran mortalità*),[689] 1363 (*morbo*),[690] and 1409 (*morbo*).[691] In terms of the amount of destruction, the *Chronique d'Amadi* considers 1308 to have been the worst year.[692] In Boustronios' work we encounter a mention of a severe famine in 1469, which King James II attempted to mitigate by buying large amounts of corn to save his subjects, and also of a 1470 plague which caused the deaths of a third of Cyprus' population.[693] The high frequency of such themes, even though they reflected the true historical situation, is evidence that Christian authors used iterative narration to emphasise defenceless mankind's dependence on nature, which is governed by a punitive God.

Emptiness in the *Chronicle* is thus a consequence of evil but also, due to its specific nature, provides an opportunity for that which is empty to be refilled. Makhairas does not transfer his deliberations to the 'cosmic' sphere, but focuses on Cyprus, a specific location on Earth, which according to Jerzy Nowosielski is a distinctive feature of Orthodox Christianity.[694] What gives a more universal sense to the message is a close link between the phenomena occurring on the island with the decisions and emotions of God, including anger, which Konstantinos Komodikis describes at length, mentioning the presence in medieval chronicles of the motifs of 'wrath of God' (θεομηνίες) and 'divine signs' (θεοσημίες) manifested in catastrophes: earthquakes (σεισμοί), plagues (λοιμοί), famine (λιμοί) and cataclysms (κατακλυσμοί).[695]

One more eloquent portrayal of the destruction brought about by nature is present in the *Chronicle*: the description of the invasion of locusts in LM V 639, which 'completely despoiled the gardens of Kalamoulli' (τοῦ Καλαμουνίου τα περιβόλαια [...] ἐξήλειψέν τα παντελῶς), 'left the trees bare' (ἐμεῖναν τὰ δεντρὰ γυμνά) and 'dried [them] very much' (ἐξεράναν πολλά). In Leontios' opinion, it was the visit of Helena Palaiologina, the namesake of Constantine's mother, which alleviated the locust attack and caused 'its anger to weaken' (ἐπαρκατέβην ὁ θυμός της). When juxtaposed with the image of 'empty land' from the opening of the *Chronicle* and the motif of 'sacred' support granted to Cyprus by St Helena to avert the consequences of the natural disaster, the image contained in one of the last fragments of the text gains eloquence: that of a priest who, having gone out alone into a field to curse the mass of insects infesting Cypriot land, died attacked by a 'swarm of locusts' (ἔναν κοπάδιν ἀκρίδα). Despite this failure, however, it is religious acts such as 'processions' (μὲ λιτανεῖες), 'intercessory prayers' (ἐλεημοσύνες) and 'imploratory prayers' (παρακάλησες) that had the desired result, though the liberation process lasted two years.

At the end of the *Chronicle*, in MS O, we read that during the raging plague King James and his wife Helvis, who initially wanted to hide from death, asked rhetorically:

---

[682] Mas Latrie (Ed.), Chronique d'Amadi, 10.
[683] Mas Latrie (Ed.), Chronique d'Amadi, 42.
[684] Mas Latrie (Ed.), Chronique d'Amadi, 210.
[685] Mas Latrie (Ed.), Chronique d'Amadi, 45–46.
[686] Mas Latrie (Ed.), Chronique d'Amadi, 209.
[687] Mas Latrie (Ed.), Chronique d'Amadi, 292.
[688] Mas Latrie (Ed.), Chronique d'Amadi, 404–405.
[689] Mas Latrie (Ed.), Chronique d'Amadi, 407.
[690] Mas Latrie (Ed.), Chronique d'Amadi, 412.
[691] Mas Latrie (Ed.), Chronique d'Amadi, 498.
[692] Mas Latrie (Ed.), Chronique d'Amadi, 292.
[693] Dawkins (Transl., int.), The Chronicle of George Boustronios, 31.
[694] Nowosielski, Inność prawosławia, 22–23.
[695] Κωμοδίκης, Οι Πληροφορίες των Βραχέων Χρονικών, 195 (and fn. 664).

If they all die (οὖλοι πεθάνουν), what profit have we in the island, when the men themselves are dead (πεθανίσκουν)? [...] (LM IV 624)[696]

This example shows that existence on the island has a concrete meaning only when it is teeming with the life of its inhabitants.

The motif of the Holy Cross' discovery may be encountered in many Christian texts, which differ as to their narratives and emotional temperature. Its role as a motif in Christian writings is emphasised among others by Joanna Tokarska-Bakir, who cites the South Slavic *Legend of the Wood of the Cross* and several versions of the *Song of the Discovery of the Cross*.[697] The scholar terms this relic 'the genealogical tree of Christian religiosity', and considers that the legends form 'an improbable tapestry of motifs, allusions, topoi, in which the quest of the myth towards unity of place, time and person is the most fully marked'.[698] When reading the *Chronicle* it is impossible to overlook this genealogical aspect of the Cross, in this particular interpretation of that aspect. If it were not for the presence of the Holy Cross in Cyprus, no community would have formed there; neither would further generations of its members have appeared, including the saints, martyrs and church officials Makhairas describes, forming the genealogy of the Cypriot Church. The depiction that emerges from the narrative shows the process of how the structure of Cyprus' spiritual community was established, formed on the one hand by the relics dispersed across the island, and on the other, by the extensive institutional system. Such a delineation of sacred space gives it a specific identity. The Cross's transfer from a place occupied by the enemy to one inhabited by Christians should be deemed a separate motif. According to the *Chronique d'Amadi*, this was accomplished by the Byzantine Emperor Heraklios (*Eraclio*, ca. 574|610–641), who brought about the death of the Sassanid dynasty's ruler Khosrow II Parviz (*Codros, Codre*, 590–628) and in 629 conquered Persia, which allowed him to retrieve the Holy Cross and bring it back to Jerusalem,[699] Khosrow having run away with it during the capture of Jerusalem in 614 (*portò vie etiam la vera croce*).[700] It was in order to regain the relic for Christians and to expand the Church that the empress undertook her voyage to Jerusalem, stopping in Cyprus on her return voyage.

The image painted by Makhairas of the individual stages in which she carried out this particular mission is ascetic. It is restricted only to clear and distinct symbols: the cross, crown of thorns and nails. There is no place in it for a broad perspective allowing reflection on the dual nature of Christ or the paradox of God's death. All the above-named objects, used to impart suffering, are visible like theatre props. The chronicler focuses on the life-giving symbolism connected to them, manifested among others in that they ultimately served as foundations for a newly-formed, permanent institution. An echo of the death of the Son of God will be embodied in further parts of the *Chronicle* in scenes of martyrdom, serving, like the Holy Cross relic, to give birth to a new entity.

St Helena's arrival at the dawn of Cyprus' Christian history allowed its transformation into sacred space, filled with new meanings and symbolism. Emptiness turned out to be useful due to its potential openness to new content because, as Paul Tillich states, it is the 'holy word of God'.[701] It is the word of God and the physical presence of a relic that had been in contact with the tortured body of Christ that started the process of the island's repopulation, which several centuries later was to become a multicultural and multi-denominational melting-pot. A particularly important part in the process of organising the desolated space anew was played by the physical growth of the Church, involving the construction of different churches to allow performance of the 'religious system function', for which, according to Niklas Luhmann, man needs the 'system of religious communication called the Church'.[702] The tale of the peregrinations of Constantine's mother, who stopped in Cyprus on her return voyage from the Holy Land, which is a reflection of the symbolic journey to a holy spring, is simultaneously a harbinger of the island's role as a stopping and resting place for Christians from other lands, connecting Europe with the Middle and Far East, accessible to all followers of Christ. The character of St Helena herself lacks any distinctive features, which allowed the chronicler to show a prototypical figure of a saint, and thus strengthen the universal message of the legend.

---

[696] Dawkins (Ed., transl.), Ἐξήγησις/ Recital, 612 (fn. 2); Παυλίδης (Ed.), Λεοντίου Μαχαιρᾶ Χρονικόν, 478 (fn. 6).
[697] Tokarska-Bakir, Obraz osobliwy, 181–190.
[698] Tokarska-Bakir, Obraz osobliwy, 181–182. Quoted phrases translated by Kupiszewska.
[699] Mas Latrie (Ed.), Chronique d'Amadi, 1. Dating after Mas Latrie (Ed.), Chronique d'Amadi.
[700] Mas Latrie (Ed.), Chronique d'Amadi, 2; Coureas, Edbury (Transl.), The Chronicle of Amadi, 1 (§ 1). The form 'Codros, Codre' in Mas Latrie (Ed.), Chronique d'Amadi, 1–3.
[701] After Baek, Tadao Ando, 23.
[702] Luhmann, Funkcja religii, 58. Quoted phrase translated by Kupiszewska.

2.1.2. Templars and Hospitallers

Makhairas' account contains an evident omission of a large part of historical events after St Helena's stay on the island. Only three passages separate the account of her foundational deeds and the mention of the Templars' appearance on Cyprus in the twelfth century.

In the intervening paragraphs LM I 9–11 the author of the *Chronicle* mentions the terror-inducing intentions of the Saracens and an episode in which one of the stones situated on Cypriot land was given the name of 'freedom stone' (λίθος ἐλευθερίας). This gap in the narrative is due to the presence of lacunae. It is therefore unknown to what extent the stages of Cypriot history that played out in the meantime, such as the period in which Byzantium and the Arabs co-ruled the island, and its economic growth, occupied the chronicler's attention and to what extent he was completely uninterested in events before the Lusignan dynasty's reign.[703]

Leontios' historiographic vision shows the Templars as being linked to the Lusignans both by the same faith and by the transaction of the island's purchase. They are the first Latins in the *Chronicle* to unsuccessfully try to 'colonise' Cyprus.

The *Chronique d'Amadi* provides a far more complex depiction of the Templars than is seen in Makhairas' writings. It follows their history from 1119, when they received for their disposal, from the second king of Jerusalem, Baldwin II (of Bourg), part of a palace with a space adjoining the temple,[704] until the death of brother Haume de Seliers in 1316 (already after the dissolution of the order).[705] We read that they received their rule (*la regula*), white habit (*l'habito bianco*) and crossless cloak (*el mantelo senza croce*)[706] in 1128 from Pope Honorius II (*papa Honorio secondo*, 1124–1130) and patriarch Stephen of La Ferté (*Estiene de la Forte*, 1128–1130).[707] This is the rule and habit that Makhairas would call 'dirty' (βρωμισμένος).[708]

Leontios clearly explains that the monks sold the island, which did not belong to them, because at that time nobody was taking proper care of it (διατὶ ὁ τόπος ἀφέντην δὲν εἶχεν), and 'the emperor was far away' (ὁ βασιλεὺς ἦτον μακρά), 'fighting great wars' (ἦτον εἰς μεγάλες γέρρες) and 'was busy' (ἦτον σκολισμένος). This allowed the knights to turn the land over as a 'foreign thing' (πρᾶμαν ξένον) as soon as they felt its possession to be troublesome, because they were not closely tied to it.[709]

It is a matter well-known from the island's history that like the Knights of the Hospital, that is the Order of the Knights of the Hospital of Saint John of Jerusalem (Lat *Ordo Militiae Sancti Johannis Baptistae Hospitalis Hierosolimitani*),[710] the Templars, known as the Knights of the Temple, Poor Fellow-Soldiers of Christ and of the Temple of Solomon (Lat *Fratres Militiae Templi, Pauperes Commilitones Christi Templique Salomonis*), played an important role, becoming part of the system that was Cypriot society in the twelfth century. It is worth mentioning that in no place in the *Chronicle* does either of these formations appear under its full name. Neither does the Cypriot work contain any mention of a third Order of Brothers of the German House of Saint Mary in Jerusalem, known as the 'Teutonic Knights'. The *Chronique d'Amadi* provides far more information about them. Burkiewicz emphasises that the failure to distinctly mark the presence of this organisation in texts may be caused by the fact that they supported Frederick II Hohenstaufen in his dispute with the Frankish knighthood.[711] In addition to the ones named by Makhairas, Iorga mentions several other military orders (*ordres militaires et religieux*) that participated in the crusades, such as: the Teutonic knights (*les chevaliers Teutons*), the Order of Santiago in Spain (*les*

---

[703] Stewart states: 'The Cypriot Church's three-hundred-year building tradition was disrupted in 649, when the Arab armies invaded. From that time until the Byzantine reconquest of 965, the island was a neutral state within the political sphere of both the Arab Caliphate of Damascus and the Byzantine Empire. This era is referred to here as the "period of Cypriot neutrality"' (Stewart, The First Vaulted Churches in Cyprus, 163).
[704] Mas Latrie (Ed.), Chronique d'Amadi, 29: *Baduin dal Borgo, secondo re do Hierusalem, li ha concesso una parte del suo palazo, con una spiagia al Templum Domini, per servirse*.
[705] Mas Latrie (Ed.), Chronique d'Amadi, 398.
[706] Mas Latrie (Ed.), Chronique d'Amadi, 29; Coureas, Edbury (Transl.), The Chronicle of Amadi, 30–31 (§ 55).
[707] Dating of both based on Mas Latrie (Ed.), Chronique d'Amadi, 29.
[708] LM I 13.
[709] LM III 527.
[710] See Kelly (Ed.), The Rule, Statutes and Customs of the Hospitallers; Burgtorf, The Central Convent of Hospitallers and Templars; Nicholson, Templars, Hospitallers, and Teutonic Knights; Nicolle, Crusader Castles in Cyprus, Greece and the Aegean; Riley-Smith, Hospitallers; Riley-Smith, The Knights Hospitaller in the Levant; Olsen, The Templar Papers. Also noteworthy is Luttrell, Sugar and Schism, 157–166. Cf. LM II 96, III 463, V 642.
[711] Burkiewicz, Polityczna rola królestwa Cypru, 88.

chevaliers de Saint-Jacques en Espagne) and the Order of the Passion of Christ (*la Chevalerie de la Passion de Jésus-Christ*),[712] but there is no testimony indicating that they had an impact on the island's history.

Passage LM I 12, undated, shows only fragmentarily, due to the chronicler's lack of knowledge or presences of a lacuna, the consequences of an unpleasant change in the relations between the brothers and the people (ὄχλος), which likely refers to a clash between the Rhomaioi and the Templars right after the latter's purchase of Cyprus – this would mean 1191. The reaction of the Rhomaioi population was 'regret' (λύπη) and 'lamentation' (κλάμαν),[713] and of the Templars, 'grief' (ἐλυπήθησαν), which the chronicler describes:

> *And when Monday dawned and the Brethren came out before the people (ἐξέβησαν [...] τοῦ ὄχλου), lamentations and weeping began, as much for the women, as for the men who had been killed. The Brethren were in sore grief and distress to think in what way they could escape from this trouble.* (LM I 12)

The *Chronique d'Amadi* gives a more detailed explanation of the course of the conflict, which was rooted in a burdensome tax levied on the Rhomaioi: on trade carried out on Saturdays 'in a time when the Templars held Cyprus [in their hands]' (*nel tempo he li Templieri tenivano Cypro*).[714] When they were attacked by the native inhabitants of the island, the grand commander of Cyprus, Arnold Bochard (Arnaud Bouchart) sent them to the castle in Lefkosia, which could not, however, give them sufficient safety. Despite the monks' desperate pleas to be allowed to leave the island (*abandonarge la terra*), the Cypriots were determined to massacre them (*li volevano amazzar tutti in vendetta*) to avenge the kin they had killed. The Templars decided to give battle the next day, right after mass, which ended in a series of bloody clashes. The brothers did not spare even the people taking part in mass. The *Chronique d'Amadi* states that the slaughter was so cruel that 'blood flowed with the river current down to the Seneschal's Bridge' (*ch'el sangue corse in fino a la fiumara, al ponte del Syniscalco*).[715]

In Makhairas' description the brothers are significantly less efficient. The chronicler avoids expressions that would emphasise their might or their advantage over the Greek population. It is hard to unambiguously state whether the conflict concerned doctrine and an attempt undertaken by the Rhomaioi to defend the purity of the Greek Church's teaching, or was due to objections against the appropriation of their living space. By citing common opinions about the monks and underlining their negative descriptions, Leontios shows that this Latin formation provoked an atmosphere of scandal on the island. He thus expresses the conviction that during this contact no change in the Cypriots' identity occurred, it being established and deeply grounded.

With respect to the hierarchic structure and the various roles that monks of both orders played on the island in its socio-political sphere, Makhairas distinguishes: the grand master (μέγας μάστρος),[716] deputy to the grand master (ὁ τοποκράτωρ τοῦ μεγάλου μαστόρου)[717] and lesser offices: constable (κοντοσταύλης),[718] marshal (μαριτζάς),[719] admiral (ἀμιράλλης),[720] commander (κουμεντούρης),[721] castellan (καστελλάνος),[722] and friars or brothers (φρέριδες, ἀδελφοί),[723] united by a shared order,

---

[712] Iorga, Philippe de Mézières, 74. Cf. Edbury, The Military Orders in Cyprus. Edbury argues that the Templars and Hospitallers held significant lands on Cyprus up to 1291: 'the Hospitallers had Plataniskia, Kolossi, Monagroulli, Phinikas, Palekhori, Kellaki and Trakhoni before 1291 as well as property in Nicosia, Limassol and at Mora to the east of Nicosia, while Templar estates included Khirokitia, Yermasoyia, Phasouri, Psimolophou, Gastria and presumably Templos, as well as houses at Nicosia, Paphos, Famagusta and Limassol' (Edbury, The Kingdom of Cyprus, 78).

[713] Σάθας (Ed.), Χρονογράφοι Βασιλείου Κύπρου, 58: 'τὸ κλαῦμαν'.

[714] Mas Latrie (Ed.), Chronique d'Amadi, 83.

[715] Mas Latrie (Ed.), Chronique d'Amadi, 84. Cf. Coureas, Edbury (Transl.), The Chronicle of Amadi, 82–83 (§ 149).

[716] The grand master of the Templars appears in: LM I 13–14, 16, 20, the grand master of the Hospitallers, in: LM II 117, 166–167, 190, 207, 209, III 292, 301–302, 356, 463, 536–537. In LM I 47, 55 Makhairas writes about the grand master of the Hospitallers, even though we know based on other sources that the man in question was the grand master of the Templars. Cf. Dawkins, Notes, 76.

[717] LM III 536, 538, 540–541.

[718] LM II 119, III 536–541, 544–545.

[719] LM III 370, 376, 537–538. Cf. ΘΚΔ, 273.

[720] LM II 117, 166.

[721] LM I 56, III 391, V 638. Cf. ΘΚΔ, 226.

[722] LM II 117.

[723] The word 'brothers' is used for the Templars in LM I 12–13, and for the Hospitallers, in: LM II 117, 166–167, III 535, 537–541, 544–545.

sometimes appearing as a collective entity, e.g. 'Rhodians',[724] and sometimes as specific individuals, such as: the grand master of Rhodes, brother Raymond Berenger (ὁ μέγας μάστρος τῆς Ρόδου [...] ὁ φρὲ Ραμοὺν Μπελινγκιέρ),[725] brother (Raymond) de Lescure (φρὲ Ρεσκουρήν), prior of Toulouse (ὁ πιούρης τῆς Τουλούζας) and commander of the Hospital on Cyprus ([ὁ] κουμεντούρης τῆς Κύπρου)[726] or brother James Pelestri (φρέρε Τζάκε Πελεστρή).[727]

In LM I 13–15 the negative depiction of the monks, portrayed in a separate 'self-contained story', provides a demonstration of their immoral way of living. Pavlidis dates it to 'after 1300' (μετά 1300), and the passages LM I 16–17 that follow, recounting their destruction, to 1307.[728]

Makhairas uses the following phrases to portray them: 'they shared among them a great heresy' (εἶχαν μεσόν τους μεγάλην αἱρετικίαν) and '[they shared among them] the most unclean rule' (πολλὰ βρωμισμένην τάξιν), which involved betrayal of the basic principles of professing the faith, and emphasises that they did so 'in hiding' (εἰς τὸ κρυφόν),[729] far from potential observers. He thus underlines their duplicity and the speciousness of their actions. He does not treat them as followers of the same God as the Cypriots, but as schismatics, who under the guise of false righteousness and orthodoxy completely distorted the holy rite and the desired attitude to the truths of the faith. From Leontios' work it seems that they were the first Christian group to disturb the island's functioning, almost as successfully as the Saracens themselves. At this point, we encounter no comment or mention indicating that a true relationship of ideas or dogma existed between the knights and the Greeks or Latins. The author of the *Chronicle* focuses on emphasising deviations from the Christian faith, which in turn shows which principles he himself believed true and correct. A kind of symmetry and framing device may be seen in the structure of these parts of the *Chronicle*, which preface an episode (bearing in mind that passages LM I 13–17 actually concern a later period) that describes the arrival of Guy de Lusignan. It is visible in the placement, at their beginning and in their final part, of the symbol of the Holy Cross, and more exactly in the evocative description of its apotheosis by St Helena and the study of its profanation by the brothers. Here, the chronicler appears as a fierce defender of Christian values, who objects to the destruction of the existing order created by the Cyprians together with the Franks.

The author of the *Chronicle* augments the unilaterally negative view of the Templars' conduct with a brief but eloquent account of their destruction. He places this event on a metaphysical plane. This device allows him to play the situation out on many levels of meaning. From his account it seems that members of the Order had become a great burden on God and it was by his decision that they were destroyed. A large role in this picture is played by a description of Pope Clement V, whose decisions led to the killing of the monks, and at once justified and lent legitimacy to this event. Leontios shows that the cruel extermination of the knights was to an extent part of the providential plan:

> [...] *for God had closed their eyes so that they could not see him, in order that their doings might be discovered* (γιὰ ν' ἀποσκεπαστοῦσιν). (LM I 13)[730]

Makhairas expresses the conviction that the Templars used the Christian faith's most important symbol, the Cross duplicitously, to carry out their wicked intentions, which were completely contradictory to that faith. To construct a reliable picture of what the monks did 'surreptitiously' (κρυφά) and show how they used the substance of the Christian *sacrum* to achieve their purposes, the figure of a boy is introduced into the middle of the events. He is worried about the fate of another boy, who came from his own village and who 'desired to become a brother according to the Templar rule' (ἐπεθύμησεν νὰ

---

[724] LM II 166, III 370, 463, 539.
[725] LM II 207.
[726] LM V 638.
[727] LM V 655.
[728] Pavlidis comments: 'Οι Ναΐτες πίστευαν πως ο Χριστός ήταν ένας επαναστάτης, απέρριπταν τον λόγο των ευαγγελίων και είχαν απόκρυφες τελετές και διατάξεις. Ο πάπας τους αφόρισε, χαρακτηρίζοντάς τους ειδωλολάτρες, ωστόσο η διάλυση του Τάγματός τους έγινε με υπόδειξη του βασιλιά της Γαλλίας Φίλιππου Δ' Οι πραγματικές δοξασίες και φιλοσοφικές προσεγγίσεις, αλλά και οι γνώσεις των Ναϊτών, απασχολούν έως σήμερα πολλούς μελετητές.' 'The Templars believed Christ was a rebel, dismissed the message of the Gospel, had secret ceremonies and rules. The pope excommunicated them, calling them "idolaters", but the dissolution of their order came [only] at the direction of King Philip IV of France. The true position and philosophical beliefs, but also the wisdom of the Templars, are a subject of interest to scholars even today.' (Παυλίδης (Ed.), Λεοντίου Μαχαιρά Χρονικόν, 11, fn. 8. Kupiszewska's translation from the Polish translation by the author).
[729] LM I 13.
[730] LM I 13.

γενῇ ἀδελφὸς εἰς τὴν τάξιν τοὺς Τεμπλιῶτες). It is this young man who witnessed what the ritual held in the temple under cover of night really consisted in, and all this was possible because 'God covered their [the Templars'] eyes' (ὁ Θεὸς ἐσφάλισεν τὰ μάτια τους) and 'they could not perceive him' (δὲν τὸν εἴδασιν).[731] During the ceremony the brothers forced the boy to act and speak in a way that was supposed to be a reaction to the Cross and was to reveal his true attitude to it. To this end, they used a copper cross (σταυρὸν χαρκόν) with Jesus Christ crucified on it (ὁ Ἰησοῦς Χριστὸς σταυρωμένος ἀπάνω εἰς τὸν σταυρόν). The priest (παπᾶς) leading the initiation ceremony asked whether the adept believed that 'the Crucified was the son of God, as people say' (ὁ σταυρωμένος ἔνι υἱὸς τοῦ θεοῦ, ὡς γοιὸν λαλοῦν οἱ λᾶς). If the boy said that this was an 'image of Jesus Christ, the Living God' (τούτη εἶνε εἰκόνα τοῦ Ἰησοῦ Χριστοῦ τοῦ θεοῦ τοῦ ζῶντος), they would 'ordain' him (ἐχεροτονοῦσαν τον) and 'send him to war' ('πέμπαν τον εἰς τὸν πόλεμον), to 'end his life' (ἐσκοτώννετον). When, however, instead of professing that the figure on the crucifix was the 'image of the Lord' (εἰκόνα τοῦ Κυρίου), he unhesitatingly said that it showed someone who was a 'false prophet' (ἕνας ψεματινὸς προφήτης), and then, after this blasphemous declaration, 'ripped the venerable cross out of his [the priest's] hands' (ἐπίασεν τὸν τίμιον σταυρὸν ἀπὸ τὸ χέριν του), 'threw it on the ground' (ἔριψέν τον χαμαί) and 'insulted it horribly' (ἐποῖκεν του πολλὺν ὑβρισμόν), the brothers knew that he could be accepted. During this intensive dialogue there appear references, important from the Christian perspective, to the relationship between the Father and the Son, and thus indirectly to the mystery of the Holy Trinity, and the mystery of the Passion, which, however, are transposed to something that has no meaning, that is semantically and theologically empty: to practices aiming to affront and deform them by changing their sense. This is why Makhairas refers to an 'unclean habit of an unclean rule' (τον τὰ βρω(μι)σμένα ροῦχα τῆς βρωμισμένης τους τάξις). After an exchange of oaths, a ceremony of gestures takes place, involving a rather graphic demonstration of joy by the brothers at the admittance of a new person. This joy was expressed through a kiss placed by each monk on the head, forehead, mouth, navel and buttocks (τἄπισα ἐφίλησάν τον εἰς τὴν κεφαλὴν εἰς τὴν κορφὴν καὶ εἰς τὸ στόμαν, καὶ εἰς τ' ἀφάλιν, καὶ εἰς τὸν κῶλον) of the novice.[732] This was a harbinger of homosexual practices, which are described further on: 'those who wanted to could fornicate with him' (ὅσοι ἐθέλαν ἔχα νὰ φτιάσουν μετά του) and…

> … he promised them that every time they sought him, he would be ready and would in no way resist any one. (LM I 13)

The ceremony culminated in the new brother being paraded around the town (ἐγυρίσαν τον τὴν χώραν), having been gifted with silver (ἀσήμιν), gold (χρυσάφιν) and ample clothing (φορίχιες πολλά). Thanks to the other boy, a report of these events was received by Clement V, who caused the Order to be dissolved.

At one point, Makhairas does justice to the 'rule of the Order' (τὸ βιβλίον τῆς τάξις) itself, it being 'to the greatest degree wise and venerable' (μὲ μεγάλην φρόνησιν καὶ τιμήν), which – by way of contrast with how the Templars were described earlier – underscores their lack of credibility and thus completely condemns them. The rule assumed that 'outside, before people, they are to spread the truth of the Church' (ἔξω εἰς τοὺς ἀνθρώπους νὰ κρατοῦν τὴν ἀλήθειαν τῆς ἐκκλησίας), publicly showing 'their food, drink and clothing' (τὸ φᾶν τους, τὸ πγεῖν τους, τὴν ἐντυμασιάν τους), 'they lack pride' (μὲν ἔχουν σουπερπίαν), 'they have patience whatever one says to them' (νὰ ἔχουν ἀπομονὴν ὅ,τι τοὺς πῇ ὁ πασαεῖς ἀπομονητικοί) and, as the chronicler says, it '[contained] many other good instructions' (πολλὰ ἄλλα καλὰ μαθητεμένοι).[733] However, Leontios does not doubt that their actions are in fact contrary to these

---

[731] Dawkins and Pavlidis' edition has 'ἐμπῆκεν κρυφὰ μεσόν τους εἰς τιτοῖον μόδον, ὅτι κανένας δὲν ἐπῆρεν σκοπόν' ('[he] crept into them secretly in such a way that nobody noticed him'). Σάθας (Ed.), Χρονογράφοι Βασιλείου Κύπρου, 58, gives it as: 'ἐμπῆκεν κρυφὰ μεσόν τους εἰς τὴν σύνοδον, ὅτι κανένας δὲν ἐπῆρεν σκοπόν' ('[he] crept secretly into them to the meeting so that nobody noticed him'). Kupiszewska's translation from the Polish translation by the author.
[732] LM I 13. Misztal underlines that Pope Clement V, under influence of King Philip IV the Fair of France (on whom he was dependent), and being indebted to the Templars issued the *Pastoralis Praeeminentiae* bull (22 November 1307), in which he ordered 'to arrest the Templars and confiscate the Order's property to give it to the Church' (Misztal, Historia Cypru, 550, footnotes 85 and 86 to p. 213). Misztal points to the sources: Gilmour-Bryson, Testimony of Non-Templar Witnesses in Cyprus, 205–211; Gilmour-Bryson, The Trial of the Templars in Cyprus; Illieva, The Suppression of the Templars in Cyprus, 212–219; Frale, Templariusze (Misztal, Historia Cypru, 550, footnotes 85 and 86 to p. 213).
[733] LM I 13.

assumptions, and the discrepancy between their deeds and their declarations appears as a stark opposite to the consistent attitude of St Helena, who is a personification of loyalty to the true God and of spiritual vigilance in the *Chronicle*.

Unlike Makhairas, the *Chronique d'Amadi* describes a different, beneficial, case of conversion: that of John d'Ibelin, who was led to become a Templar with a 'quiet soul' (*con quieto animo*).[734]

Leontios gives a one-sided view of the situation, focusing much attention on the pope's part in the act of destruction, likely in order to plausibly present the faith of the Cypriots against a background of the sinfulness of another group, whose representatives were altogether foreign to the chronicler. The *Chronicle* gives prominence to the violent, emotional reaction of the pope, who wished to save Christian values from blasphemous acts and enjoined each Western ruler to exterminate members of the Order in his country, otherwise 'the wrath of God will fall on him, as it fell on Judas' (νὰ σοῦ ἔλθη ἡ ὀργὴ τοῦ θεοῦ ὡς γοιὸν ἦλθ(ε)ν εἰς τὸν Ἰούδαν), which is an exemplification and manifestation of the attitude of all followers of Christ. However, there is another explanation for Clement V's behaviour: he had been personally betrayed by the grand master of the Temple, who had been his friend (φίλος μου).[735] Moreover, as we read slightly further on, there appeared voices ('some say', κάτινες λέγουσιν) that private matters were in play, and the religious reasons were just a pretext (ἀφορμή), but right afterwards the chronicler quickly returns to assurances that the issue was Divine anger.[736] The destruction is thus described by Makhairas:

> *And he did as the pope said* (ἐποῖκεν τὸν λόγον τοῦ πάπα) *in all Cyprus, and slew them all* (ὅλους ἐσκότωσέν) *on the day of Pentecost* (τὴν ἡμέραν τῆς Πεντηκοστῆς). *Some say that the pope was angry* (ἀνκρισμένος) *with the Master of the Temple because he had done something to vex him* (ἐποῖκεν του ἀγανάκτησιν). *But the reason why the wrath of God fell upon them was* (ἡ ὀργὴ τοῦ θεοῦ ἔππεσεν ἀπάνω τους) *this,*[737] *that He was sorely angered with them* (πολλὰ ἀνγκρισμένος μετά τους) *because of their sins* (διὰ τὰς ἁμαρτίας τους): *and it was for this reason they were all destroyed in one day* (ἐκαταλύσαν τους ὅλους μίαν ἡμέραν), *and not one of them escaped* (δὲν ἐγλύτωσεν κανένας); *and if God had had to deal with clean men* (καθαρούς), *he would have saved them* (ἔθελέν τους γλυτώσειν): *and this was the wrath of God. And when the mass* (λειτουργία) *of Pentecost was ended, in every town they opened the sealed letter, and all heard what it said. And when they heard the command of the pope* (τὸν ὁρισμὸν τοῦ πάπα), *straightway before the dinner hour they killed all the Templars in the place* [...]. (LM I 16–17)

It was clearly important to Makhairas for this event, like many others described by him, to be placed in a moral context and within a causal sequence, and so he treats it as the effect of the brothers' sin, which caused God's vehement anger and led this anger to be vented in the form of a harsh punishment. An important role in the *Chronicle* is played by the category of cleanliness. This is indicated by expressions such as the already mentioned adjective 'unclean' (βρωμισμένος) and the chronicler's radical statement: 'if God held them to be clean, he would have wanted to save them' (ἂν εἶχεν ἔχειν καθαροὺς ὁ θεός, ἔθελέν τους γλυτώσειν), which forms a point of reference in issuing moral judgements. Makhairas forewent historical time frames, and instead used the liturgical calendar, which allowed him to move the description of the whole incident to the symbolical plane. Pavlidis commented on this as follows:

> Δεν έγινε έτσι αστραπιαία η διάλυση των ισχυρών Ναϊτών. Αντιθέτως, ακολουθήθηκαν πολύπλοκες διαδικασίες, δίκες, συλλήψεις, φυλακίσεις κλπ., που κράτησαν χρόνια.'[738]

> *The eradication of the influential Templars did not take place so instantaneously* [and] *in such a fashion. On the contrary,* [they] *were subjected to complex court action, processes, arrests, imprisonment, etc. which went on for years.*

---

[734] Mas Latrie (Ed.), Chronique d'Amadi, 184.
[735] LM I 14.
[736] LM I 16.
[737] Author's proposition of a slightly different translation: 'because [he] did something that enraged him, and that this was the cause. And the wrath of God fell on them, because [He] was angered at them for their sins.'
[738] Παυλίδης (Ed.), Λεοντίου Μαχαιρά Χρονικόν, 15. Kupiszewska's translation from the Polish translation by the author.

The *Chronique d'Amadi* offers a different version of the events of 1308, when the lord of Tyre, implementing a papal letter against the Templars, sent Balian d'Ibelin to carry out their arrest (*in execution della lettera del Apostolo contra li Templieri*).[739] That same year, the confession of 'the holy Catholic Christian faith' (*tutti li articuli de la santa fede catholica christiana*) made by the Templars was read out loud in Lefkosia, and then translated into French (*la interpretava in francese*) and thus read out. In it they stress, i.a., that: their death has a religious dimension (*morendo per la santa fede catholica*), they have acted as apostles and protectors of Christianity (*sempre campioni et deffensori de la santa christianità*), and never turned to any other religion and never believed in anything but what had just been read out (*che mai non erano de altra fede ne credevano altro che quello fu letto alhora*).[740] At night, the lord of Tyre, in the presence of prelates, barons, people of the faith and townsfolk, read out Pope Clement V's letter, which called the brothers 'heretics and infidels against the Catholic faith of holy Christianity' (*trovati in heresia et mescredenti contra la catholica fede della santa christianità*),[741] which coincides with Leontios' opinion.

In further parts of the *Chronicle* the Templars are only referred to by name when Makhairas mentions their purchase of Cyprus in 1191 and its sale to Guy in 1192, and the rebellion of the Rhomaian population.[742] In one instance 'brother Jacques de Molay' (φρέρε Τζάκε τε Μιλᾶ) is named, the last Templar grand master, incorrectly dubbed a Knight of the Hospital.[743]

A different fate awaited the Hospitallers, who had according to the *Chronicle* demonstrated greater distance, caution, religious comportment and obedience towards the pope, which was why they, after the events of Pentecost, took over all the estates and heritage (ὅλα τους τὰ καλὰ καὶ κλερονομιὲς) of the Templars (εἴ τι εἴχασιν ἐδόθησαν εἰς τὸ Σπιτάλλιν).[744] When after receiving the news about Templar practices Clement V requested the grand master of the hospital to ordain (νὰ χεροτονήσῃ) a second boy in his presence, he did so 'immediately' (παραῦτα), without hesitation, and so the Hospitallers were judged 'good Christians' (καλοὶ χριστιανοί). As the Templars caused the Holy Father to feel deeply embittered (πολλὰ τὸ ἐπικράνθη), so the action of the Hospitallers' representative caused him great joy (ἐπῆρεν ὁ πάπας μεγάλην χαράν).[745] Also Tsetsious, the son of a Nestorian, entered the Hospitaller order (ἔμπηκεν εἰς τὸ σπιτάλλιν): this is the only instance of a conversion from the Syrian to the Latin faith in the *Chronicle*. All we know about his time in the order was that because of his poverty he rang the hospital bells (ἐσημάνισκε τὲς καμπάνες εἰς τὸ σπιτάλλιν), for which he was given food.[746] From this story on, the Knights of the Hospital appear as inhabitants of the island of Rhodes. Information about their presence in Cyprus appears sporadically. We read, for example, that the grand master of Rhodes, who came to Cyprus in 1374 to discover why no news was arriving from the island, which was in the throes of a conflict with the Genoese, died of worry and was buried in the Lefkosian Hospital.[747] Leontios also writes of a Hospitaller commander in Cyprus and a Hospitaller knight from Paphos.[748]

The chronicler, who demonstrates evident dislike towards the Templars, maintains an almost neutral stance versus the Hospitallers, unlike Boustronios, who underlines the cruelty with which they murdered a youth named Tsarra.[749] In the *Chronique d'Amadi* the Hospitallers have no distinctive features. They usually participate in various events, sometimes together with the Templars. However, there appear mentions that indicate their capacity for cruelty towards people of other religions and civilisations. One such passage recounts how on 16 January 1264, together with the Templars, they destroyed Lajjun (*Ligon*) and captured three hundred and sixty people, both men and women, while another tells how they burnt down whole acres of land up to Ascalon (*arseno [...] tutta la terra fino Ascalona*).[750] They also demonstrated courage when they came to defend their lands against a foreign invader, for instance during the Turkish

---

[739] Mas Latrie (Ed.), Chronique d'Amadi, 283; Coureas, Edbury (Transl.), The Chronicle of Amadi, 265 (§ 567).
[740] Mas Latrie (Ed.), Chronique d'Amadi, 286; Coureas, Edbury (Transl.), The Chronicle of Amadi, 267–268 (§ 570).
[741] Mas Latrie (Ed.), Chronique d'Amadi, 287; Coureas, Edbury (Transl.), The Chronicle of Amadi, 268 (§ 570).
[742] LM I 20, 22, 27, III 527.
[743] LM I 47.
[744] LM I 17.
[745] LM I 14–15.
[746] LM II 96.
[747] LM III 463.
[748] LM V 638, 697.
[749] Dawkins (Transl., int.), The Chronicle of George Boustronios, 3.
[750] Mas Latrie (Ed.), Chronique d'Amadi, 206–207; Coureas, Edbury (Transl.), The Chronicle of Amadi, 202 (§ 406).

attack on Rhodes in 1311–1312.[751] For Makhairas it is Rhodes that came to be the permanent place of the Hospitallers' residence. The *Chronicle*'s author forgoes descriptions of their attributes and religious behaviours, and only underlines their presence in the social and political life of the Cypriots, whom they supported almost to the same degree as the pope did. More about the relations between Rhodes and Cyprus is written in Subchapter 3.3.4 in the context of the evident involvement of Rhodians in the conflict between Cyprus and Genoa, placing the main emphasis on the problem of how the Cypriot constable was received on Cyprus. In this episode we encounter brothers who feel lost, torn, scared and forced to make a hard choice between loyalty to the Cypriot king, and fear of the Genoese and threats to their safety.

Neither the Hospitallers nor the Templars, however, are presented in the Cypriot work in a way that would allow them to be perceived as fully-fledged participants of interreligious dialogue.

2.1.3. The Frankish Conquest of Cyprus

The first Latins who, despite initial difficulties, were able to establish themselves on Cyprus were members of the Lusignan family. When describing their first meeting with the Rhomaioi, Makhairas initially takes no definite position; it is unknown what he himself thinks about the appearance of the island's new owners. He does not fail to underline that the takeover of the island happened with the significant participation of other Western nations, though he does not give their description or assign any specific features to them as a group. In fact, every historiographer portrays them differently. Thekla Sansaridou-Hendrickx notes for example that the Franks who conquered the area of Epirus and Morea were viewed by the author of the anonymous fifteenth-century *Chronicle of the Tocco* as a diverse and separate ethnic group,[752] composed of brave warriors approaching 'the [...] ideal image of a knight',[753] and their role was limited to warfare.[754]

The Lusignans appear, as the second Latins in the *Chronicle* after the brothers of the Temple, in LM I 20. In an episode recounting the takeover of Cyprus by Guy de Lusignan (Guy himself makes his appearance a passage earlier) we read:

> *And when this King Guy (ρὲ Οὔνγκε) had bought (ἐγόρασεν) Cyprus from the Templars and the Lombards (τοὺς Λαγκουβάρδους), he was told of the trouble (τὴν ἀγανάκτησιν) which they had had (from the Greeks) and of the slaughter (τὸν σφαμόν*[755]*) which there had been in the town; he was much concerned (εἰς μεγάλην ἔννοιαν) and took thought (ἐννοιάζετον) what he should do to avoid vexation (κακόν) in Cyprus, for all the country was full of Greeks (ὅλος ὁ τόπος ἦτον γεμᾶτος Ρωμαῖοι): for he was saying to himself: 'Whenever they choose to rebel against me (νὰ ρεβελιάσουν κατὰ μένα), they can do it, and they will have the emperor of Constantinople (βοήθειαν τὸν βασιλέαν τῆς Κωνσταντινόπολις) to help them, and they can forcibly take my kingdom out of my hands (ἐμποροῦν μὲ δύναμιν νὰ σηκώσουν τὸ ρηγᾶτον ἀπὲ τὰς χεῖρας μου)'.* (LM I 22)

When analysing the way Makhairas describes how Christianity took root on the island on the one hand, and on the other, the circumstances of how the Latins took power over the Greek island after the schism, a stark contrast may be seen between the spiritual context of the former event, and the material, political context of the latter. It should nevertheless be noted that both took place many years before the chronicler's birth, and he himself uses various types of sources and archival material. He writes the following about negotiations concerning the handover of Cyprus:

> *And the Master of the Temple came and begged them for the love of God to take Cyprus off their hands (ἐζήτησέν τους [...] νὰ ἐβγάλῃ τὴν Κύπρον ἀπὲ τὰ χέργια τους). –And he, Richard, learned what had befallen the Templars, and made a bargain with King Guy, the king of Jerusalem, and sold him Cyprus– for a hundred thousand gold ducats. And he, Guy, borrowed a large sum from*

---

[751] Mas Latrie (Ed.), Chronique d'Amadi, 393; Coureas, Edbury (Transl.), The Chronicle of Amadi, 358 (§ 752).
[752] Sansaridou-Hendrickx, The World View of the Anonymous Author, 68–70, 73.
[753] Sansaridou-Hendrickx, The World View of the Anonymous Author, 68.
[754] Sansaridou-Hendrickx, The World View of the Anonymous Author, 70–73.
[755] Author's proposition of slightly different translation: 'about the rebellion that broke out against them [among the Rhomaioi]'.

the Genoese and bought the country according to the terms of the Templars. [...] And this man was the first king (πρῶτος ῥήγας) of Jerusalem and Cyprus [...]. (LM I 20–21)

Makhairas shows that the rulers of the newly formed Kingdom of Cyprus enforced their vision of government, introducing significant changes to the power structure.[756] This self-willed act caused the Cyprians to rebel. Guy, fearing that the Rhomaioi population would turn to the emperor of Byzantium for help, desperately looked for aid from sultan Saladin.[757] Leontios precisely describes the actions of the Latins intended to disorganise the functioning of the Greek clergy and condemn Cypriot priests (τοὺς ἀρχιερεῖς τῆς Κύπρο) to 'an impoverished life' (στενή ζωή). As an illustration:

And (the tithes (δέκατα) and) the villages (χωριά) which had belonged to the Greek[758] dioceses (ἐπισκοπὲς τῶν Ρωμαίων), they (took away and) gave to the Latins (ἔδωκάν τα τῶν Λατίνων). [...] Whatever was in the hands of the Greek bishops[759] has been taken away (ἐσηκῶσαν) and given to the Latins. (LM I 29)[760]

Leontios gives these details with unexpected diligence, which indicates that he was aware of the changes that his home country had undergone at the start of Lusignan rule, and that he wanted to express this awareness. His emotional distance actually seems quite strange if we juxtapose the passage above with the presentation of the merciless annihilation of the Templars. This precision and restraint may however have been due to a fear of the current authorities and official respect towards the royal court, inherited from his father.

On the margin, a remark by Burkiewicz is worth citing, commenting on the takeover of power in the Holy Land and in Cyprus by representatives of the Frankish dynasty:

In 1099, the Greek Church in the Levant was the richest and best-organised of all the Christian churches present there. However, with the arrival of the Franks it became exposed to affront due to the ecclesiastic unity that the Latins tried to impose.[761]

The Cypriot shows that the structure of the Orthodox Church became distorted and suffered material harm, to ultimately become only a small fraction of what it had earlier been. The result of the Frankish rulers' actions in this respect was the enacting of new laws in the form of the *Assizes*, deterioration of quality of life and transfer of lands belonging to Greek dioceses to the Latins.[762] In the *Chronicle* we find enumerated the direct consequences of the Franks' 'colonisation' of Cyprus, which were as follows: the rulers of the Western world (France, England and Catalonia are named) were notified by letter, via envoys, about the annexation, mighty landowners were sent guarantees of numerous privileges (προβιλίζια) allowing them to settle on the island together with promises of silver, gold and hereditary lands that would fall to their lot and that of their sons. The crowning argument used by the Lusignans to encourage the desired population to come was a rumour that in the new location they would find an abundance of 'holy relics' (διὰ τὰ ἅγια λείψανα) and live in the close proximity of Jerusalem (ἦτον κοντὰ τὸ Ἱεροσόλυμαν εἰς τὴν Κύπρον), which – as MS O has it – was the 'home of Christ' (τὸ σπίτιν τοῦ Χριστοῦ).[763] As an additional benefit that capped this promise, they declared that there would be a monthly payment (μηνία), rents (ρέντες), lands to be leased (ἀσενιάσματα),[764] and appointment of judges (κριτάδες), both in Cyprus and in the lands of Jerusalem (εἰς

---

[756] Makhairas does not explore the subject of Richard Cœur de Lion's reign in 1191. Cf. Nicolaou-Konnari, Greeks, 13.
[757] LM I 22–25.
[758] Rhomaioi.
[759] Rhomaian.
[760] At this time, also the 'bishop's palaces in Lefkosia' (*corte di vescovi in Nicossia*) were built and the construction of the Cathedral of Saint Sophia (*cominciorono Santa Sophia*) started. See Mas Latrie (Ed.), Chronique de Strambaldi, 11.
[761] Burkiewicz, Polityczna rola królestwa Cypru, 82. Translated by Kupiszewska.
[762] LM I 29. Makhairas would refer to the *Assizes* then enacted many times: LM I 29, II 99, 106–107, 269–271, 277–278, III 315, 327. After reducing the number of Greek bishoprics and after 'the amalgamation of the old dioceses with the four remaining ones that started in the 1220s', as Nicolaou-Konnari shows, new church offices came to be formed: *protohiereus/protopapas, deutereuon, hiereus, chartophylax, anagnostes, protonotarios, notarios, sakellarios, nomikos, taboullarios* (Nicolaou-Konnari, Greeks, 55).
[763] Dawkins (Ed., transl.), Ἐξήγησις/ Recital, 116 (fn. 1); Παυλίδης (Ed.), Λεοντίου Μαχαιρά Χρονικόν, 96 (fn. 5). Mas Latrie (Ed.), Chronique de Strambaldi, 51 gives *la casa de Iddio* as a translation of this expression.
[764] Παυλίδης (Ed.), Λεοντίου Μαχαιρά Χρονικόν, 23: 'σ' ἄλλους παραχώρησε γή'.

τὲς χῶρες τῆς Ἱερουσαλήμ).⁷⁶⁵ For 'those of the common people' (τοὺς πιὸν χαμηλούς) they established forms of freedom (ἐλευθερίες) and 'possibility of manumission' (μιαμουνάτα διὰ νὰ φριαντζιάζουν).⁷⁶⁶ Still other privileges were given by the Franks to Syrians, whom they also invited to settle there. All these efforts indicate that the Lusignans had a personal goal in this, which was to entrench their power and to strengthen the structures of the new state they were forming. As a result, as Makhairas states,

> [...] *many Syrians (πολλοὶ Συριάνοι) and many Latins (πολλοὶ Λατῖνοι) came (ἤρταν) and settled (ἐκατοικῆσαν) in Cyprus.* (LM I 27)

The new state of affairs required a change in the law, and the new law, as the *Chronicle* shows, created a clear material boundary between Greeks and Latins, where the native Orthodox population, presented as 'poor' (πτωχοί; λαὸς ὁ πτωχός), appears from this perspective as the side responsible for provoking conflict:

> *And remembering the trouble the Greeks (ἀθυμοῦνταν τὴν ἀγανάκτησιν τὴν ἐποῖκαν οἱ Ρωμαῖοι)⁷⁶⁷ had given to the Templars, they prayed (ἐζητῆσαν) the king that they should have this privilege (νὰ ἔχουν ἐλευθερίαν), not to be judged like the men of the land (νὰ μὲν κρινίσκουνται κατὰ τοὺς τοπικούς), and that if they said aught about the poor men of the land (εἴ τι ποῦν διὰ τοὺς πτωχοὺς τοὺς ἐντόπιους) they should be believed (νὰ τοὺς πιστεύγουν), and if the poor folk said aught (εἴ τι ποῦν οἱ πτωχοί), that they should not be believed (νὰ μὲν τοὺς πιστεύγουν)* [...]. (LM I 27)

Makhairas explains that the aim was to stifle, in advance, the negative reactions of the Cyprians, of whom the majority were Rhomaian – that is, 'locals' (τοπικοί), whom he also describes as '[belonging to that] place' (ἐντόπιοι) – to the takeover of power by the Frankish court and the effects of the unexpected 'colonisation'. Such a reaction was unavoidable if we consider the internal motivation of the autochthons, interpreted by the chronicler as arrogance (σουπερπία). Fear of consequences caused the Franks to bring into existence a new legal system to protect themselves, in the words of the chronicler, 'for their benefit' (εἰς τὸ διάφορός τους), sanctioned by the proper ritual that moved political action to the metaphysical plane:

> *This was done (because the Greeks were many (διατί οἱ Ρωμαῖοι ἤτον πολλοί) in Cyprus, and) in order to bring down their pride (γιὰ νὰ καταλύσουν τὴν σουπερπίαν τοὺς Ρωμαίους),⁷⁶⁸ that they might not rebel (νὰ μὲν ρεβελιάσουν)* [...]. *And they made assizes for their advantage (εἰς τὸ διάφορός τους), and made the king, when he would put on the crown in the church, swear upon the (holy) Gospel (νὰ 'μόσῃ ἀπάνω εἰς τὸ (ἅγιον) Εὐαγγέλιον) to accept (νὰ κρατήσῃ) and to maintain (νὰ στερεώσῃ) the assizes and all the good customs (ὅλα τὰ καλὰ συνηθία) of the said kingdom, and to maintain the privileges (νὰ στερεώσῃ τὰ προβιλίζια) of the holy church of Christ.* (LM I 27)

The quoted passage offers an image of Latins who view the Cyprians with superiority, from the position of a higher instance judging a conquered people in moral categories. This is indicated among other things by the phrase 'to tame arrogance' (γιὰ νὰ καταλύσουν τὴν σουπερπίαν), used to justify the pressure they exerted. The Lusignans used the Rhomaioi for their own purposes, paralysing their readiness to fight for their native land, that is to protect their own space and identity, and did so in the name of their Catholic faith, treating the Church of Christ as their demesne, and not as a good common both to them and to the Greeks.

To strengthen their position, the Franks, who had from the times of Clovis I (ca. 466–511)⁷⁶⁹ considered themselves to be Christians,⁷⁷⁰ undertook many endeavours to build their religious might and hierarchy in Cypriot lands, which Makhairas describes as follows:

---

⁷⁶⁵ LM I 26. This whole passage is missing from Σάθας (Ed.), Χρονογράφοι Βασιλείου Κύπρου, 65.
⁷⁶⁶ Consulted with Borowska's translation. Pavlidis' translation is as follows: 'δικαίωμα ψήφου' ('electoral rights'). See Παυλίδης (Ed.), Λεοντίου Μαχαιρᾶ Χρονικόν, 23.
⁷⁶⁷ Rhomaioi.
⁷⁶⁸ Rhomaioi.
⁷⁶⁹ See Budden, True Stories Fom Ancient History, 317–318. The entry 'Clovis I' in Waldman, Mason, Encyclopedia of European Peoples, 270–271.
⁷⁷⁰ Who perceived the Greeks and the Syrians as 'spiritually as well as politically subject to them' (Coureas, Religion and ethnic identity, 14).

Whilst this was on foot, the Latins had no one, neither archbishops (ἀριπίσκοπους⁷⁷¹) nor clerks (λογάδες), to chant in the holy church of God (νὰ ὑμνολογοῦν τὴν ἁγίαν τοῦ θεοῦ ἐκκλησίαν). The kings one after another (ὁ ἕνας ὀπίσω τοῦ ἄλλου) sent to the most holy pope (εἰς τὸν ἁγιώτατον πάπα) telling him to send a bishop (πίσκοπον), metropolitans (μητροπολίτες) and priests (παπάδες). (LM I 28)

This fragment shows that, according to the chronicler, the Lusignans – in this case Amaury⁷⁷² – treated the Orthodox faith as a foreign one. To rid themselves of this feeling of religious alienation, they endeavoured to build a new church structure, as well as recreate hierarchical relationships, on the island. This situation had two causes. On the one hand it was due to the dramatic consequences of the 1054 schism of the Churches, which led to a deep rupture between the communities, and on the other, to the Lusignans' linguistic isolation. Faced with such a state of affairs, Makhairas adopts an ambiguous position. He describes the aloofness, coolness and tendency of the Cypriot Franks to distance themselves from the rest of the Cyprians, as well as their unwillingness to take advantage of the space they had created for mutual contact, for instance to participate in joint religious ceremonies, but at the same time he is not indifferent to similarities, glorifying saints of both rites. The perspective adopted by the *Chronicle*'s author does not ultimately reveal whether the isolation had its source in unbelief, failure to recognise Orthodox spirituality and its foundations, or whether it served to underline their separateness.

Right after describing the process of the Catholic seizure of influence on Cyprus, Makhairas calls it a 'holy island' (ἁγία νῆσσος), thus returning – likely by way of contrast – to the motif of the island's sanctity before the conquest, present in the first part of the *Chronicle*. He calls for its praises to be sung (χρῆσι εἶνε 'νὰ φουμίσωμεν')⁷⁷³ and assures that such apotheosis will not be empty and ungrounded focusing on the irrelevant (πεῖν ψέματα). This short introduction to passage LM I 30, containing a mention of the country's excellence, forms a space for a natural justification of the choice to present further writings in the form of a catalogue of important, from the perspective of Cypriot tradition, figures. This allows Makhairas to name, in a businesslike and uncontrived manner, the seats of fifteen Orthodox bishops, though he himself writes of 'fourteen archbishops' (ἀρχιεπισκόπους ιδ').⁷⁷⁴ The *Chronique d'Amadi* states that the fourteen Greek bishoprics were divided into four Latin and four Greek bishoprics.⁷⁷⁵

Interestingly, the names of the representatives of the Greek clergy are listed right after the conquest of Cyprus is described, and before longer parts of the text completely devoted to Lusignan rule, where it is already clear that the fate of the island would over time undergo a radical change. Makhairas thus endeavours to emphasise the character of spirituality in these lands in order to make apparent – via narrative dissonance – what transformations took place as a result of the 'colonising' situation.

The first hierarch named by Leontios is 'St Barnabas' (ἅγιος Βαρνάβας), whom he considers an 'apostle of Christ' (ἀπόστολος Χριστοῦ).⁷⁷⁶ It should be assumed that his person and deeds must have made a huge impression on his successors, as two of his continuators took the same name, which is clearly proved by Leontios' list. The chronicler does not explain, however, who exactly they were, but simply uses the modifier 'other' (ἕτερος) for both.

A numerous group was composed of the forty-seven bishops – though he writes about twenty six archbishops (ἀρχιεπίσκοποι) and twenty one bishops (ἐπίσκοποι) – of individual Cypriot towns: starting with St Barnabas (ἅγιος Βαρνάβας), one of the Apostles, through to Tykhikos of Lemesos (Τυχικοῦ τοῦ

---

⁷⁷¹ Of the archbishops/bishops.
⁷⁷² Dawkins, Notes, 53.
⁷⁷³ From 'φημίζω' ('announce', 'make known').
⁷⁷⁴ LM I 30. According to his testimony, the archbishoprics were: Salamina (Makhairas writes: 'Cyprus'), Tamasia, Kition, Amathus (Lefkara), Kourion, Paphos, Arsinoe, Solia, Lapithos, Kerynia, Kythraia, Trimythos, Karpasi, Lefkosia, Lemesos. Dawkins states that Germanos was the last archbishop of the Orthodox rite on Cyprus during Lusignan rule (Dawkins, Notes, 54). Dawkins cites a list of sixteen bishop's seats created by Hackett, adding Naples and Theodosiana. Pavlidis translates 'ἀρχιεπίσκοποι' as 'Ἕλληνες ἀρχιεπίσκοποι' in Παυλίδης (Ed.), Λεοντίου Μαχαιρᾶ Χρονικόν, 25, and Miller and Sathas, as *évêchés*, i.e. 'bishoprics' in Sathas, Miller (Eds, transl.), Chronique de Chypre, 20.
⁷⁷⁵ Mas Latrie (Ed.), Chronique d'Amadi, 85.
⁷⁷⁶ Barnabas is known from the Bible (Acts, Cor., Gal.) The *Apolytikon* devoted to the apostle Barnabas mentions Cyprus: 'Τὸ μέγα κλέος τῆς Κύπρου, τῆς Οἰκουμένης τὸν κήρυκα, τῶν Ἀντιοχέων τὸν πρῶτον τῆς χριστωνύμου κλήσεως ἀρχιτέκτονα, τῆς Ῥώμης τὸν κλεινὸν εἰσηγητήν, καὶ θεῖον τῶν ἐθνῶν σαγηνευτήν, τὸ τῆς χάριτος δοχεῖον τοῦ Παρακλήτου Πνεύματος τὸν ἐπώνυμον, Ἀπόστολον τὸν μέγαν, τὸν τοῦ θείου Παύλου συνέκδημον, τῶν ἑβδομήκοντα πρῶτον, τῶν δώδεκα ἰσοστάσιον πάντες συνελθόντες σεπτῶς οἱ πιστοί, τὸν Βαρνάβαν ἄσμασι στέψωμεν, πρεσβεύει γὰρ Κυρίῳ, ἐλεηθῆναι τὰς ψυχὰς ἡμῶν. Ἀπολυτίκιο Ἀποστόλου Βαρνάβα – Ἦχος α,' (https://apostolosvarnavas.weebly.com/, accessed 10 December 2021). Apocrypha: *Acts of Barnabas, Gospel of Barnabas, Epistle of Barnabas*. Barnabas' grave is located near Salamis in the Turkish part of Cyprus.

[...] ἐπισκόπου Νέας Πόλεως Λεμεσοῦ). The information concerning Lazaros, an ordinary from Kition in today's Larnaca District[777] (Λαζάρου [...], ἐπίσκοπον Κιτταίων), is particularly interesting. The author of the *Chronicle* identifies him, without substantiating his position, with the Biblical Lazarus, resurrected from the dead by Jesus (ἀνέστησεν ὁ κύριος ἐκ νεκρῶν),[778] whom St Luke described as a 'poor man [...] covered with sores',[779] and St John, as a man who was 'ill, Lazarus of Bethany'.[780] No remark in the Bible suggests, however, that this man held any church office.[781] Most bishops are given – in accordance with the tradition of Orthodox and pre-Chalcedonian synaxaria – the modifier 'most holy' (ἁγιώτατος). Only Afxivios (Ἀξιβίος)[782] is characterised using the expression 'the most blessed' (μακαριώτατος).

By giving such a detailed catalogue of figures, Makhairas may have wanted to do justice to a tradition of honouring holy persons or to emphasise the exceptionality of the island's clergy and its particular feature of having numerous eminent administrators of the Orthodox Church. Interpretation of this passage is made more difficult by a lack of comment by the author, who does not explain his intention anywhere; nevertheless it seems obvious that he is thus creating the genealogy of the Cyprian Church. Via this technique he was also able to emphasise the entrenchment of the Greek Church on Cyprus in history (tradition), community, and an organised – to some extent – hierarchy, possessed of solid foundations formed by notables called for that purpose. At the same time, he demonstrated that it was this strong, coherent structure, based on centuries-old values, that the Latins penetrated with their own vision of Christianity, disparate from the one recognised and worshipped on the island.

It cannot go unnoticed that in the *Chronicle*, the Cyprians, confronted with the 'Otherness' of the Franks, show a greater ability to adapt to new conditions than the latter. It is they who took on, out of necessity, the burden of the imposed rule and did not bow under its yoke, and at the same time managed to build up their own position in the new reality. The Lusignans meanwhile unceremoniously entered foreign ground, occupying the centre of the Rhomaian world and seizing for their own use its various elements, with no thought for the attitude of the conquered people and their way of understanding and professing their faith, which could help enrich their own. Of the basic elements in Makhairas's account of the Greek Church's fate in the sphere of Latin influence, tradition turns out to be the most important one, expressed among others in the succession of bishops.

2.2. Depiction of the peaceful coexistence of Christians in the *Chronicle*

At the start of the *Chronicle*, Christians form a homogeneous entity, free from internal discord. Starting from LM II 12, the division into a Church of the Greeks and a Church of the Latins accomplished in 1054, the dynamic coexistence and the deep-seated differences between the two groups are already shown as a fact. The chronicler does not refer to the schism of the Churches even in allusion. The opposite approach is taken by Philippe de Mézières in *Le Songe*, where the event, its nature, causes and consequences are broadly analysed, and the author's personal opinion is provided.[783] The evolution of mutual contacts is displayed and a variety of attitudes of clergy and church dignitaries is exposed and thoroughly

---

[777] Kition – located within today's Larnaca District.
[778] See Lk 16: 19–31; J 11: 1–44. It seems unlikely to have been the same Lazarus, however. Cf. Dawkins, Notes, 55. Hackett explains why there are so many scenarios for the further fate of the resurrected Lazarus: 'Lazarus, after his resurrection at Bethany, was placed by the Jews, so the tradition runs, in a leaky boat at Joppa, with his two sisters and other companions, and committed to the mercy of the winds and waves. From this point, however, there is great divergence in the various legends. The Cypriots affirm that he was wafted to their shores near Kition and consecrated first bishop of that town by all the Apostles on the occasion of their alleged visit. There he eventually died and was buried after presiding over the See for thirty years.' (Hackett, A History of the Orthodox Church of Cyprus, 411). A discussion of Lazarus' presence in sources is contained in Hackett, A History of the Orthodox Church of Cyprus, 412–413.
[779] Lk 16: 20.
[780] J 11: 1. Contemporary Greek Cypriots give him the worship due to him. He is the object of particular cult in Larnaka, where the church of his name houses his earthly remains and once a year, during the Easter festivities, a procession of his image is held.
[781] Mentioned in Rohrbacher, Storia universale della Chiesa cattolica, 257–258.
[782] Dawkins comments: 'Makhairas' form of the name *Axivios*, Ἀξίβιος, represents the popular pronounciation, which cannot endure three consecutive consonants, unless one be a liquid; *fks* therefore becomes *ks*.' (Dawkins, Notes, 55). Mas Latrie (Ed.), Chronique de Strambaldi, 12 has 'Saint Eutychius' (*Santo Eutichio*).
[783] E.g. Philippe de Mézières, Le Songe, 354–359, see Coopland, Synopsis, 171.

analysed.⁷⁸⁴ In the *Chronicle* narrative it is possible to find passages describing mutual acceptance or simply coexistence. The narrative components showing these tendencies include: co-occurrence on Cypriot land of the relics of Orthodox and Catholic saints, unanimous glorification of persons who during their lives showed exceptional moral qualities, apotheosis of persons martyred for their faith and the painstakingly described cult of the Holy Cross.

2.2.1. Co-occurrence of relics

An important aspect of the spirituality presented in the *Chronicle* and which unites all the Christian denominations, is relics, in the form of physical remains of individuals believed to be holy ([τὰ] σώματα τῶν ἁγίων).⁷⁸⁵ Located all over the Cypriot land, they can be used to argue for an inherently Orthodox character of the country, because through the bodily remains, constantly present and enduring, the sacred sphere embeds itself in matter, which coincides with the Greek Church's 'theomaterial perception of reality'. This way of seeing the world is discussed by Nowosielski.⁷⁸⁶ According to him, in the Orthodox faith these two dimensions, the worldly and the supernatural, are inextricably bound, while in Catholicism, focused on activity and responsibility for the world, they are separate.⁷⁸⁷

Using a device that involves listing cult objects such as relics, Makhairas shows that the Franks, in 'colonising the island', violated a sacred space that had been constructed long before and had an established identity. In doing so, they demonstrated significant determination in incorporating their own elements, which changed the meaning of that space and the significant points of reference in the sacred sphere. On the land they seized, they found themselves a spiritual niche, fertile ground on which they were able to build their own Church, though despite the expansion of their spiritual domain in the conquered country they constantly had to live among the remains of Rhomaian saints and other artefacts significant to that people. Such conclusions may be reached when the legends about the early Christian history of Cyprus are juxtaposed with descriptions of subsequent forms in which Greek religiosity was manifested during Lusignan rule. Everything that had a meaning for the island in the spiritual dimension melts into the sacred topography of the 'colonised' universe.

The *Chronicle*'s narrative suggests that in Makhairas' home country both Cyprians and arrivals from foreign lands met their ends. The chronicler introduces the subject thus:

> *When the Saracens seized the Land of Promise (πῆραν τὴν γῆν τῆς ἐπαγγελίας), then the poor Christians (πτωχοὶ οἱ χριστιανοί) who had escaped, departed and went wherever they found a place of refuge (ὅπου ηὗραν καταφυγίν): there were archbishops (ἀρχιεπισκόποι), bishops (ἐπίσκοποι), priests (ἱερεῖς) and laymen (λαϊκοί), and they went where they could (ἐπῆγαν ὅπου 'φτάσαν). And a company (μία συντροφία) who were three hundred persons came (ἤρταν) to the famous land of Cyprus (τὴν περίφημον Κύπρον) (lit. called [a group of] 'three hundred' (τ' ὀνομάτοι)).* (LM I 31)

As the *Chronicle* recounts, the allochthons soon received information that the country had been seized by pagans (Ἕλληνες ἐφεντεῦγαν τὸν τόπον [...]), evidently causing them to 'fear' (φόβον), and as a result, to change their places of stay.⁷⁸⁸ They usually found shelter – wandering about in pairs or groups of three – inside the earth and they...

---

⁷⁸⁴ E.g. Philippe de Mézières, Le Songe, 354–359, see Coopland, Synopsis, 171.
⁷⁸⁵ Cf. Mt 27: 52: 'καὶ τὰ μνημεῖα ἀνεῴχθησαν καὶ πολλὰ σώματα τῶν κεκοιμημένων ἁγίων ἠγέρθησαν'. Cf. also Olympios, Institutional Identities, 216–219.
⁷⁸⁶ Nowosielski, Inność prawosławia, 52. This is the 'theomaterialism of the liturgy and mysteries'. Quoted phrases translated by Kupiszewska. The topic of relics in Orthodoxy is discussed in the papers: Klein, Eastern Objects and Western Desires; Krueger, The Religion of Relics; Nagel, The Afterlife of the Reliquary; Robinson, Beer, Harnden (Eds), Common Ground; Schädel, Die Häupter der Heiligen; Schriemer (Ed.), Relieken.
⁷⁸⁷ Nowosielski, Inność prawosławia, 45.
⁷⁸⁸ Dawkins reviews the opinions of scholars concerning the historical situation in question in the fragment about the group of 'Three Hundred'. According to Sathas, he informs, it may refer to the Saracen occupation of Cyprus in the seventh century; according to Manardos, the migration from the Holy Land after the fall of Jerusalem in 1187; according to Estienne de Lusignan, the group of 'Three Hundred' accompanied John de Montfort in his deeds after the fall of Acre in 1291; while according to the *Synaxarion of St Athanasios the Wonderworker* it was composed of German Greeks who worked for the crusaders but converted and ran away to Cyprus in search of shelter (Dawkins, Notes, 56–57).

...dug into the earth (ἐσγάψαν τὴν γῆν) and lived there (ἐμπῆκαν μέσα), and offered their prayers to God (ἐπροσεύχουνταν τῷ θεῷ) [...]. (LM I 31)

Their holiness was usually revealed posthumously 'through an angel' (δι' ἀγγέλου) or by means of particularly momentous miracles (διὰ τὰ θαυμαστὰ θαύματα). Makhairas underlines the fact that his contact with the relics of these exceptional people was that of an eyewitness because, as he writes, he was able to 'see' with his own eyes (εἶδα) and 'hear' (ἔμαθα) accounts of their burial places (πολλὰ κοιμητήρια). These passages seem to present a vision that is fairly ascetic in its message, but in fact they form an important element of Leontios' narrative. In contrast to this perspective, the *Chronique d'Amadi* contains only two mentions of relics: one of them concerns the body of St Nicholas, moved from Myra to Bari,[789] and the other, the moment when the amassed populace along with their material goods and relics entered Kerynia in 1373 together with Takka to take possession over it.[790] Meanwhile, the part of the *Chronique d'Amadi* that was written on the basis of Makhairas' text was deprived of such fragments.

An important role in crystallising the image of the sacred space, determined by the tangible, palpable presence of Christians, is played by physical signs of this presence in the form of relics (λείψανα) and groups of graves (κοιμητήρια). After the list of bishops discussed above, Makhairas builds another list in the form of a kind of 'catalogue of bodily remains', placing in it the names of forty prelates and bishops to whom those remains belonged, as well as their affiliation with specific places and their posthumous location,[791] which he uses to establish the separate spiritual tradition, strong enough to survive the invasion of the arrivals. Even if in the *Chronicle* we do find the names of persons affiliated, due to their origin, with another country, in terms of numbers Cyprians form the majority.

Leontios' record contains thirty-nine saints from different places,[792] including lesser-known figures such as St Eirenikos of Zotia (πρὸς τὴν Ζωτίαν ὁ ἅγιος Εἰρηνικός) or St Kassianos of Glyphia (εἰς τὴν Γλυφίαν [...] τοῦ ἁγίου Κασιανοῦ). The Revealed Saints (Ἅγιοι Φανέντες)[793] of Casa Piphani (μία περνιέρα γεμάτη λείψανα) are an interesting phenomenon, resting, Makhairas writes, under stone flags (μία περνιέρα γεμάτη λείψανα). According to the chronicler's account, and likely according to the legend his tale is based on, their remains dried out miraculously (λείψανα ἐστεγνῶσαν), becoming hard (ἐκολλῆσαν ὥσπερ πέτρα) and heavy as stone (ἂν ἐβγῇ κανέναν βαρὺ ὡς γοιὸν πέτρα). These exceptional men belonged to the so-called group of 'Three Hundred' (εἶνε ἀποὺ τ(οὺ)ς τ') mentioned above.[794] The author of the *Chronicle* states that the group also included St Olvianos (ἅγιος Ὀλφιανός), whose name was given to a monastery in the village of Larnaka.[795]

Makhairas closes this enumeration by stating that there are still many other saints who, though they have not revealed themselves (ὅπου οὐδὲν ἐφανερωθῆσαν), may be the addressees of Cypriot (and particularly Cyprian) prayers for liberation of their island from the Muslims, Agarenes, whose main

---

[789] Mas Latrie (Ed.), Chronique d'Amadi, 53; Coureas, Edbury (Transl.), The Chronicle of Amadi, 53 (§ 98).
[790] Mas Latrie (Ed.), Chronique d'Amadi, 441; Coureas, Edbury (Transl.), The Chronicle of Amadi, 401 (§ 893).
[791] LM I 32.
[792] In LM I 32. Here are the saints mentioned in the *Chronicle* in addition to those included in the main text: St Anastasios at Peristerona on the Mesaria plain (εἰς τὴν Περιστορόναν τῆς Μεσαρίας ὁ ἅγιος Ἀναστάσιος), St Constantine at Ormidia (εἰς τὴν Ὁρμετίαν ὁ ἅγιος Κωνσταντῖνος), St Therapon at Sinda (εἰς τὴν Σίνταν ὁ ἅγιος Θεράπων), St Sozomenos in Potamia (εἰς τὴν Ποταμίαν ὁ ἅγιο(ς) Σωζόμενος), St Epiktitos at Casa Piphani (πρὸς τοῦ Κάζα Πιφάνη ὁ ἅγιος Πίκτητος), St Hilarion the Younger in the castle of St Hilarion [the Elder] (εἰς τὸ κάστρον τοῦ Ἁγίου Ἱλαρίου ὁ ἅγιος Ἱλαρίων νέος), St Epiphanios at Kythraia (πρὸς τν Κυθρίαν ὁ ἅγιος Ἐπιφάνιος), Sts Heraklios, Lawrence, Elpidios, Christopher, Orestes and Dimitrianos at Kophinou (Εἰς τὴν Κοφίνουν ὁ ἅγιος Ἡράκλειος ἐπίσκοπος, ὁ ἅγιος Λαυρέντιος, ὁ ἅγιος Ἐλπίδιος, ὁ ἅγιος Χριστόφορος, ὁ ἅγιος Ὀρέστης, καὶ ὁ ἅγιος Δημητριανός), St Euphemianos at Lefkoniko (Εἰς τὸ Λευκόνικον ὁ ἅγιος Ἐφημιανός), Sts Barnabas and Hilarion at Peristerona (εἰς τὴν Περιστερόναν τοῦ κούντη τε Τζάφ ὁ ἅγιος Βαρνάβας καὶ ὁ ἅγιος Ἱλαρίων), Sts Heliophotos, Afxouthenios, Pamphoditis, Pammegistos, Paphnoutios, Kournoutas at Akhera (εἰς τὴν Ἀχεράν ὁ ἅγιος Ἡλιόφωτος, (ὁ) ἅγιος Αὐξουθένιος, ὁ ἅγιος Παμφοδίτης, ὁ ἅγιος Παμέγιστος, καὶ ὁ ἅγιος Παφνούτιος, ὁ ἅγιος Κουρνούτας), St Therapon at Kilani (εἰς τὸ Κιλάνιν ἄλλος, ὁ ἅγιος Θεράπων), Sts Theodosios and Polemios at Morphou (εἰς τοῦ Μόρφου ὁ ἅγιος Θεοδόσιος, καὶ ὁ ἅγιος Πολέμιος), St Barnabas the Monk at Vasa (εἰς τὴν Βάσαν ὁ ἅγιος Βαρνάβας), St Kassianos at Avdimou (Ἕτερος ἅγιος Κασιανὸς εἰς τὴν Αὐδίμουν), Sts Alexander, Khariton and Epiphanios at Axylou (εἰς τὴν Ἀξύλου ὁ ἅγιος Ἀλέξανδρος, ὁ ἅγιος Χαρέτης, καὶ ἕτερος Ἐπιφάνιος), Sts Pigon and Christopher at Kourdaka (εἰς τὸν Κούρδακαν ὁ ἅγιος Πήγων καὶ ὁ ἅγιος Χριστόφορος), Sts Kalandios, Agapios and Barlaam at Aroda (εἰς τὴν Ἀρόδαν ὁ ἅγιος Καλάντιος, ὁ ἅγιος Ἀγάπιος, καὶ ὁ ἅγιος Βαρλάμ), and Sts Basil and Dimitrianos at Pera in Tamassos (εἰς τὴν Ταμασίαν, εἰς τὰ Πέρα, ὁ ἅγιος Βασίλειος [...] καὶ ὁ ἅγιος Δημητριανός [...]). Enumeration after LM I 32.
[793] Miller and Sathas translate 'Ἅγιοι Φανέντες' as *saints Fanentes (Apparus)*. See Sathas, Miller (Eds, transl.), Chronique de Chypre, 25.
[794] LM I 36.
[795] LM I 36. Mas Latrie (Ed.), Chronique de Strambaldi, 15 gives the name *Olchiano*.

attribute is godlessness (νὰ ἀποβγάλῃ τὴν αὐτὴ νῆσσον ἀπὸ τοὺς ἄθεους -Ἀγαρηνούς-).⁷⁹⁶ In this place the difference between the chronicler's treatment of the Franks and the completely foreign Muslim invaders becomes evident. He sees no reason to pray for liberation from the Latin arrivals, who are closer to the Orthodox in terms of identity, but looks to them unconditionally for spiritual consolation during attempts to overcome the Turkish and Saracen threat.

In his narrative Makhairas focuses on the principles of placing earthly remains and fragmenting bodies,⁷⁹⁷ though he does not explain the significance of these practices. Following his argument, it may be sensed that the outlined topography of the relics' resting places was intended to present the Christian community as a living organism, whose individual parts have been endowed with a particular symbolism. This fits the Christian concept of the Mystical Body of Christ, which was how the community of members of the Church was perceived.⁷⁹⁸ Scholars agree that circulation of relics allows members of the community to continually live with the dead,⁷⁹⁹ whose earthly remains remind them of their sanctity and hence, their relationship with God. In Makhairas' portrayal, relics are to some extent equivalent to the persons of the saints whose bodies they formed during their life. This aspect of equivalence of human remains is emphasised by Cynthia Hahn.⁸⁰⁰ The depiction of the cult of relics in the *Chronicle* contains no indication that their division was carried out in the Orthodox⁸⁰¹ or the Catholic manner or that their form of worship had a character typical for either of the rites.

Makhairas is clearly interested in leading the narrative in a way that would let the reader closely link the presence of bodily fragments of God's servants and their locations with God's will, and through this association acknowledge their raison d'être. When applied to the dimension of relations between people of different denominations but the same religion, the significance of relics, which are an authentication of supernatural contact, is of key importance and can be disregarded only by infidels. Only one passage in the *Chronicle* could be found – containing the legend of St Diomidios⁸⁰² – that would show any sort of reaction by the representatives of a foreign civilisation and religion, the Muslims, to the effects of Christian remains. However, Makhairas frequently displays the living faith of Cypriot Christians, who place trust in the causative power of blessed particles of matter, and also in their capacity to reverse the impact of negative events, both individual ones and those that affect the whole community. Nevertheless, in Leontios' view they always function as an evident sign of God's will and confirmation of the righteous life of the saints.⁸⁰³ Moreover, the way in which the author of the *Chronicle* lists dates, names and resting places of the saints' bodies, enriching his account with additional historical details, brings these passages closer in style and form to western martyrologies and eastern menologia and synaxaria.⁸⁰⁴

---

⁷⁹⁶ LM I 32.

⁷⁹⁷ Books that discuss this topic include: Bynum, Fragmentation and Redemption; Hillman, Mazzio, The Body in Parts; Benthien, Wulf, Körperteile.

⁷⁹⁸ A statement that is found to be particularly apposite here was made by Scott Montgomery, who sees the phenomenon as having the following object: 'Just as Christ is held to be fully present in every consecrated host, so to the fragmented body of the saint possesses the total presence and potency of the living saint. In being able to self-translate after death, the saint manifests his/her ability to effect miracles of all manner.' (Montgomery, Securing the Sacred Head, 83).

⁷⁹⁹ See Geary, Living with the Dead in the Middle Ages.

⁸⁰⁰ Hahn phrases this as follows: 'the faithful *identified* ashes as *valuable* and *equivalent in meaning to a holy human being*' (Hahn, Objects of Devotion and Desire, 9). Already early Christian thinkers and theologians shared this perception. John Chrysostom, for example, who held the position that relics abound in the grace of the Holy Spirit and thus participate in sanctity, further believed that they serve as a reminder of the death of Christ, are a testimony to imitation, function as altars where the Liturgy of the Church is celebrated, and also inspire others (Christo, Martyrdom, 120–122).

⁸⁰¹ Charkiewicz, Relikwie świętych w prawosławiu, 3–11. Describing the role of relics in Orthodox Christianity, Jarosław Charkiewicz indicates that they are a 'place of the particular presence of a saint via grace' and 'testimony and justification of the Incarnation', guarantee immortality of the soul through the indestructibility of the body to which a given soul is linked, and also the current presence of the saint on Earth, irrespective of the degree of the body's preservation (Charkiewicz, Relikwie świętych w prawosławiu, 3–11). Furthermore, they prompt similar praiseworthy acts, 'increase the sense of unity with the invisible heavenly Church in the faithful' and demonstrate God's mastery over matter (Charkiewicz, Relikwie świętych w prawosławiu, 35–36). Dividing relics is possible because grace is present in each particle irrespective of its dimensions and dispersion which, Charkiewicz underlines, reveals their wonder still further (Charkiewicz, Relikwie świętych w prawosławiu, 57). All Charkiewicz's quoted phrases translated by Kupiszewska.

⁸⁰² LM I 35.

⁸⁰³ Cf. Mas Latrie (Ed.), Chronique d'Amadi, 151–152.

⁸⁰⁴ The most famous examples of synaxaria include among others: Synaxarion of Constantinople and Ethiopic Synaxarion. See Delehaye (Ed.), Synaxarium ecclesiae Constantinopolitanae; Wallis Budge (Transl.), The Book of the Saints of the Ethiopian Church.

The image that emerges from Makhairas' account shows the process by which the spiritual community structures of Cyprus became established, built on the one hand of physical fragments of human bodies dispersed around the island (in whose neighbourhood a miracle-working artefact may sometimes be found, as in the mention of the well with water[805]), and on the other, of an extensive institutional system in the form of the 'archbishoprics' mentioned above. Such a delineation of sacred space gives it a specific identity. Furthermore, individual features that characterised a saint during their life impact the form and implications of the miracle after their death, though simultaneously – an expression coined by Katherine Allen Smith and Scott Wells will be used here – there occurs an 'eradication of the "real" identity' of the saint through the expansion of their 'symbolic presence'.[806] The exceptional life of a saint lends credence to everything that is still yet to happen in a given place. It is also worth noting that each such sacred place occupies a specific space in the topography of the island. All these spheres, their locations and scope also remain in relationship to each other. If one considers that also Latin saints are buried in early Christian and Orthodox resting places, one may imagine such a situation as an expression of negotiating fragments of a shared space. To some extent, this is how the author tries to portray the similarities between different Christians. However, he does not hesitate to indicate differences, for instance when telling of the 'Three Hundred' saints.

2.2.2. Legends about the Saints

The *Chronicle* features a very extensive list of holy individuals, in many cases lacking detailed information about the course of their existence, type of death and fate of their earthly remains. Moreover, we receive one joint catalogue for Greek and Latin saints, because these were saints who mainly lived in the times preceding the schism of the Churches. A simple listing in one place of their names and places of origin indicates recognition of the similarities between them and equal respect for their uniqueness regardless of any differences.[807]

The word 'legend' is used here with one qualification. It is used to designate hagiographic tales which to Leontios could (though not necessarily must) have been true stories, and which regardless of their (in)authenticity had a real impact on the island's spiritual heritage.

In passage LM I 33 Makhairas introduces a precise distinction between 'saints who arrived from different lands' (ἅγιοι περατικοί) and 'holy Cyprians' (ἄλλοι Κυπριῶτες). Next to figures such as: St Photeini (ἁγία Φωτεινή), St Diomidios (ἅγιος Διομήδιος) and St Triphyllios (ἅγιος Τριφυλλίος)[808] we also have three foreigners: St John de Montfort in Lefkosia (Σὰν Τζουάνης τε Μουφόρτε εἰς τὴν Λευκωσίαν εἰς τὸ Πιάλεκε), St Mamas from Alaya in Asia Minor (ἅγιος Μάμας ἀπὲ τὴν Ἀλλαγίαν)[809] and St Photios (ἅγιος Φώτης)[810] belonging to the group of 'Three Hundred' who sheltered on the island, fleeing from the Saracens. The figure of John de Montfort, venerated both in the Orthodox, and in the Latin Church,[811] is accompanied by one sentence – this French citizen (ἀφέντης Φραντζέζης) had the miraculous ability to heal (πολομᾷ ἄξια θαύματα) the sick (εἰς τοὺς ἀστενεῖς), particularly those in the throes of fever (εἰς πύρεξες).[812]

---

[805] LM I 34.
[806] Smith, Wells, Introduction, 13.
[807] Kyrris writes about these fragments as: 'hagiological paragraphs, full of both Byzantine and local Greek Cypriot patriotism and pride, folk piety and popular metaphysics and theological thinking' (Kyrris, Some Aspects, 201).
[808] LM I 34–35.
[809] Hackett describes one Mamas (a different one than in the *Chronicle*) as follows: 'Mamas […] is traditionally reported to have suffered martyrdom at Caesarea in Cappadocia during the reign of Aurelian, A.D. 274. […] According to the Greek authorities he was born about A.D. 260 in the prison of Gangra in Paphlagonia, where his parents were at the time incarcerated for their profession of Christianity. […] he was adopted by a rich Christian lady named Ammia. From his birth to his fifth year he remained without the power of speech.' (Hackett, A History of the Orthodox Church of Cyprus, 415). The scholar lists how Mamas was persecuted: thrown into the sea, (whence he was miraculously rescued, and then fed by hinds), laid on hot coals, thrown to wild beasts to eat, and ultimately pierced with a spear (Hackett, A History of the Orthodox Church of Cyprus, 415).
[810] LM I 34.
[811] Of this saint, Pavilidis writes: 'Ὁ ἅγιος Ἰωάννης ντε Μοντφόρτ δὲν ἦταν Κύπριος ἀλλὰ τιμήθηκε ἰδιαίτερα καὶ ἀπό τοὺς Ὀρθοδόξους τῆς Κύπρου.' 'Saint John of Monfort was not a Cypriot, but is particularly venerated by Cypriot Orthodox Christians.' (Παυλίδης (Ed.), Λεοντίου Μαχαιρᾶ Χρονικόν, 29, fn. 1. Kupiszewska's translation from the Polish translation by the author).
[812] LM I 33.

Makhairas devotes significantly more space to St Mamas, following the tendency known from Orthodox tradition to create hagiographic tales of this type.[813] Drawing on legends, in currency in the Christian community, the chronicler lists the primary activities that the saint performed during his life: these included capturing and milking lions (ἐπίαννεν τοὺς λέοντας καὶ ἐγάλευέν τους), making cheese of their milk (ἐπολόμαν τυρίν) and bringing food to the poor (ἐτάγιζεν τοὺς πτωχούς).[814] In this legend, the milk became a symbol of fertility and growing in strength and generosity, while its spilling and loss foretold misfortune and martyrdom.[815] And such was, Makhairas tells us, the fate of Mamas, because he fell into the hands of the Turks, who were highly hostile towards him, 'giving chase' (ἐσκοντύλισεν) and ultimately causing his death by torture (ἐμαρτύρησεν). As a result of their attack, Mamas dropped the receptacle holding the milk, which spilled. The author tells us that to this day in Alaya we may find the 'place of the milk' (τόπος τοῦ γαλάτου), that is the place where the white liquid touched the ground.[816] Further we also find information about the martyr's parents, who 'laid him in his coffin' (ἐβάλαν τον εἰς κιβούριν) themselves. His sanctity was proved not only by his miracle-filled life, but also by supernatural phenomena after his death. Makhairas preserves an extraordinary balance between description of the martyr's life and remembrance of the fate of his remains. He therefore recounts how, through the good will of God (διὰ χάριτος κυρίου), the coffin with Mamas' remains ended up on a beach in Morphou (εἰς τὸν γιαλὸν τῆς τε Μόρφου), a town in the north-west part of Cyprus. A certain man, dubbed 'good' (καλός) in the *Chronicle*, was commanded by God in a revelation (ἐπικαλύφθην) to move the chest with the body. Obedient to his vision, the man took a team of oxen and his four sons, tied a rope around his find and tried to lift the coffin with their help. They were able to lift it 'as if it [were] a small thing' (ὡς γοιον ἔναν μικρὸν πρᾶμαν), even though in actual fact it was disproportionately heavy (τὸ ποῖον ἦτον πολλὰ βαρετόν). When they reached their goal, it became impossible to lift once more, and so 'nobody was able to move it' (δὲν ἠμπόρησεν τινὰς νὰ τὸ σαλέψῃ). At its final destination a church was built (ἔκτισα ναόν). Following the founding of the new temple, 'great miracles' (μεγάλα θαύματα) started to happen, famous 'in all the world' (εἰς οὖλον τὸν κόσμον), from the extrusion of an oil (βρύει μύρος), to the curing of 'hard to heal wounds' (πληγὲς ἀγιάτριευτες). The frequently organised pilgrimages with St Mamas' image that regularly travelled to towns and settlements such as Lefkosia, Lemesos, Ammochostos and Klavdia[817] translated into a growth in the number of extraordinary healings (ἰάματα). The author of the *Chronicle* ends this passage with the hyperbolic statement:

[...] *if I were to write the cures he has worked, I should not make an end as long as I live.* (LM I 33)

The legend of St Mamas is also one of the first references to the aggression with which the Turks attacked the island's inhabitants, and particularly devout Christians, sentencing many to a martyr's death. Using such stories, the chronicler endeavours to show his negative attitude to Muslim nations.

By presenting the lives of the saints, Makhairas builds his narrative in a manner typical for medieval texts[818] – according to a set model. He underlines their special attributes or properties, places and objects linked to them, exceptional decisions that they took, the role of supernatural influences and the miracles that embody the consequences of living according to the rules of the faith despite the dangers resulting from confrontation with non-Christians. He thus creates a depiction of a sacred space. Further on, he lists a functioning chapel (βῆμαν) in the village of St Andronikos of Kanakaria in Akrotiki (εἰς τὴν Ἀκροτίκην

---

[813] Given, The Archaeology of the Colonized, 137.
[814] LM I 33.
[815] The milk motif frequently appears in the Bible among others: as food for a journey in Gen. 18: 8; as a symbol of wealth and abundance in Ex. 3: 8; 13: 5; 33: 3; Lev. 20: 24; Num. 13: 27; 14: 8; 16: 13–14; Deut. 6: 3; 11: 9; 26: 9, 15; 27: 3; 31: 20; 32: 14; Josh. 5, 6; Jer. 11: 5; 32: 22; Ezek. 20: 6, 15; as the drink of warriors in Judges 4: 19; 5: 25; milk as the symbol of seed in Job 10: 10; as a symbol of perfection in Song 4: 11; as man's basic food in Prov. 27: 27; Ezek. 25: 4; as a food of the weak and babies in 1 Cor. 3: 2; Heb. 5: 12–13; Isa. 28: 9, 2; 2 Macc. 7: 27; as a symbol of blessings and prosperity in Gen. 49: 12; as a transitional substance in Prov. 30: 33; Isa 7: 22; as a metaphor of ideal white in Lam. 4: 7; Song 5: 12; as spiritual food in 1 Pet. 2: 2; feeding oneself with milk in Ezek. 34: 3; Song 5: 1; as fruit of labours in 1 Cor. 9: 7; as an element of a pagan ritual in Ex. 23: 19; 34: 26; Deut. 14: 21; Rev. 19: 30; in the first vision of paradise we have rivers of milk (next to those flowing with honey), in a sermon by Pseudo-Chrysostom, who compares a speech block to a block in mother's milk. Cf. Valiavitcharska, Rhetoric and Rhythm in Byzantium, 176.
[816] LM I 33.
[817] Klavdia – village located north-west of Larnaka.
[818] See Buzwell, Saints in Medieval Manuscripts.

εἰς τὴν κώμην τοῦ Ἁγίου Ἀνδρονίκου τῆς Κανακαρίας),[819] built over the grave of St Photeini (τὴν [...] ἁγίαν Φωτεινήν), which was hidden in the ground (ὁ τάφος της εἶνε κάτω τῆς γῆς),[820] and a tank filled with 'holy water' (νερὸν ἁγίασμαν). At this point, he pens a vivid picture, the like of which is not encountered in other parts of the *Chronicle*:

> *And the water is very deep: and when the moon changes, the water on the surface sets in a film as ice sets, and they take it off, all the frozen part, as if it were a piece of plank, and after some time it breaks up and becomes fine like dust, and the blind have their eyes smeared with it and are cured.* (LM I 34)

Kyriacou referring to 'the water ceremonies' in Leontios' work accents 'the collective participation of the created cosmos in Christian worship' and '"sacred materialism" of Byzantine Orthodox spirituality', linking it with Palamite Hesychasm.[821]

Makhairas is also no stranger to the interruption of decay processes in corpses. We find out that such a fate met the body of St Triphyllios, whose resting place was in a church of the Hodegetria in Lefkosia.[822] His unspoilt body (τὸν ἅγιον τοῦ θεοῦ σωστόν) was discovered by the Saracens who viciously cut the head off the corpus. Their intention to immediately burn their find was impeded by other tasks, of which a boy named Diomidios (τὸ παιδάκιν ὁ ἅγιος Διομήδιος) took advantage. This pupil of St Triphyllios stole the defiled 'holy head' (τὴν ἁγίαν του κεφαλήν) of the divine servant and ran away with it. The Saracens tried to find the lost body part and to make this task easier, they placed the remaining part of it in the place where a baptismal font (βαπτιστήρα) was later located, that is, the chronicler specifies, where '[Christians] carry out baptisms (lit. give light)' (ὅπου φωτίζουν). The device frequently used by the *Chronicle*'s author of defining words and explaining them is repeated in a further passage, which tells us that the chase caught up with the boy, who hid in a place where a gallows stood (εἰς τὴν φούρκαν),[823] that is, in a place where, it is explained, 'thieves are hanged' (ὅπου κρεμμάζουν τοὺς κλέπτες). The tale ends with a vivid and didactic moral about the well-deserved punishment that met the infidels. The important feature of this narrative is that Diomidios, despite courage that was remarkable for his young age, feared the Saracens, and found strength in supplication to God:

> *And when he saw that they were pressing hard (ἀναγγαστοί[824]) upon him, he grew frightened, and breathed upon them in the name of the Lord Jesus (ἐφυσῆσεν τους ἐπὶ ὀνόματος κυρίου Ἰησοῦ); and at once they swelled up and fell to the ground, and he took the head and came safely to Lefkomiati.* (LM I 35)[825]

This legend shows that according to Makhairas it was possible to curse one's enemies in the name of God and cause Providence to send a particularly painful ailment upon them as a punishment for destroying Christian heritage. It is only when the enemy humbled themselves and desisted from the intention to continue their negative actions that the curse was lifted, which is apparent in a further part of the tale:

> *And the Saracens who had thus swollen up, came little by little to Lefkomiati, and besought him to cure them, and promised him that they would not come to Cyprus to harm them: and he cured them.* (LM I 35)

This passage is consistent with Leontios' vision of causal order. Therein, only giving honour to the person injured by the perpetrators can reverse the curse that has befallen. Soon after this episode, Makhairas goes on to mention Diomidios' death (ἐκοιμήθην –ἐκεῖ– ὁ ἅγιος). As in the case of other saints, a church was erected also in his resting place, and its special provenance guaranteed participation

---

[819] Dawkins and Pavlidis situate Akrotiki on the Karpasi peninsula, but Dawkins emphasises that this name may only be found in Makhairas' writings. See Dawkins, Notes, 65; Παυλίδης (Ed.), Λεοντίου Μαχαιρά Χρονικόν, 29.
[820] St Photeini together with St Photios of Atienu is numbered as one of the Three Hundred.
[821] Kyriacou, The Byzantine Warrior Hero, 127. As he stresses the concept of 'sacred materialism' has been elaborated by Fr. Nikolaos Loudovikos.
[822] Dawkins, Notes, 65.
[823] Φούρκα – from Lat *furca*.
[824] Pavlidis translates ἀναγγαστοί as απειλητικοί ('inspiring terror'). See Παυλίδης (Ed.), Λεοντίου Μαχαιρά Χρονικόν, 31.
[825] A village that no longer exists (Dawkins, Notes, 65).

in 'numerous miracles' (πολλὰ θαύματα). Furthermore, the use of the expression 'to this day' suggests that the Cypriot historian knew not only the history and past, but had also obtained information about the current functioning of the tale, which in turn is an indication of these legends' endurance and the close consonance between the sacred and the profane sphere. The chronicler leaves no literary traces suggesting that he believed this legend to be only a myth or fantastic tale, as he clearly treats it as part of the island's history. It is one of the first places in the work where the image of a Muslim appears as an evident illustration of evil and hostility: a perspective that will be particularly apparent in further parts of Leontios' writings.

Already at the level of citing these local histories the narrative method chosen by Makhairas may be observed: he readily selects stories that show meetings between Christians and Muslims, who are a threat to Christian society on Cyprus as a whole. An encounter between the aggressors and a saint leads to conflict, culminating in the victory of the latter.

There occurred sporadic incidents of aggressive behaviours by representatives of the Christian world towards blessed individuals, but the extent of the damage done by them was local and did not place the whole community in danger. An example of such a situation is offered by the story about a painting of the Mother of God (ἡ εἰκόνα τῆς [...] Θεοτόκου) in the Kykko monastery in the Marathasa valley (εἰς τὴν Μαραθάσαν εἰς τὸν Κύκκον)[826] located in the Troodos Mountains, an image that Leontios refers to as portraying 'the most holy' (ὑπεραγίας). The creation of the icon has its origins on a day when in the Marathasa valley (εἰς τὰ ὄρη Μαραθάσας) there occurred an unfortunate meeting between the monk[827] Isaias (πτωχὸς γέρος [...] ὀνόματι Ἠσαΐας), a 'poor old man' (πτωχὸν γέρον), and a lord, the hostile Manuel Voutoumitis (τοῦ κυροῦ Μανουὴλ τοῦ Βουτουμήτη). As a consequence of the dispute, which happened against the clergyman's will, the defiant Voutoumitis was affected by sciatica.[828] Forced to humble himself, he bowed down before the monk and asked for his blessing (νὰ λάβῃ εὐχήν), and thus for the curse to be lifted. A specific revelation is also linked to this.[829] Because of the clear structure of this passage, a symmetry is apparent between curse and blessing: both have the nature of a wish and each leads to the abolition of the other. This tale is exceptional because it shows an evident connection between the religious history of Cyprus and the history of Byzantium. Namely, Isaias had a vision:

> *And the Mother of God (Θεοτόκος*[830]*), (the Virgin of Trikoukkia (Τρικουκκιώτισσα),) revealed herself (ἀπεκαλύφθην) to the monk, telling him to seek the picture (νὰ ζητήσῃ τὸ εἰκόνισμαν) which is in the palace of the emperor in the City (εἰς τὴν Πόλιν) and that they should bring it here.* (LM I 37)

MS O tells the further story in more detail. In it, we find out that the monk headed to Constantinople, where he healed the daughter of the basileus, to then return to the island with the miraculous Trikoukiotissa icon.

From the numerous group of divine servants, the chronicler also mentions a young monk, Neophytos of Lefkara (ἅγιος Νεόφυτος [...] ἀπὲ τὰ Λεύκαρα), who was a stylite (στυλλίτης) in the monastery in Englistra (εἰς τὴν Ἔκλειστραν) – according to Michael Angold he hid in a cave for seven years[831] – and led such a god-fearing life that even after his death his grave performed numerous miracles.[832] Makhairas evidently uses this strange and unobvious tale to construct the image of the saint's otherness, with interactions with this saint bearing fruit that reinforce the identity of the whole Cypriot community.

Just as the atypical earthly life of the persons Leontios portrayed was important to him, the same went for the various forms of their posthumous cult. An example of this may be found in the story

---

[826] The history of the image portraying the Virgin and Child (*Kykkotissa*) is presented in Kouneni, The Kykkotissa Virgin, 95–107. Σάθας (Ed.), Χρονογράφοι Βασιλείου Κύπρου, 72 has the form 'εἰς τὸν Κύκον'; Sathas, Miller (Eds, transl.), Chronique de Chypre, 22 (Vol. II) has the form 'εἰς τὸν Κύκκον'.
[827] Dawkins (Ed., transl.), Ἐξήγησις/ Recital, 36 (fn. 5).
[828] Sathas reads the name of the disease as 'ψατίκα'. See Σάθας (Ed.), Χρονογράφοι Βασιλείου Κύπρου, 72.
[829] LM I 37.
[830] Mas Latrie (Ed.), Chronique de Strambaldi, 16 gives the Virgin's epithet as 'Our Lady Trikoukiotissa' (*la Nostra Donna detta Tricucchiotissa*). Strambaldi continues the story, and there we read of the healing of the emperor's daughter, who then regretfully returns the icon (*immagine*). The tale ends with the statement that the icon was written by the apostle Luke (*la qual è depenta da San Luca*). A church was built on Cyprus to commemorate it. See Mas Latrie (Ed.), Chronique de Strambaldi, 16.
[831] Angold, Church and Society, 292.
[832] LM I 37.

of the two heads (δύο κεφαλάδες) of Cyprian and Justina (τοῦ ἁγίου Κυπριανοῦ καὶ Ἰουστίνης),[833] which the *Chronicle* recounts briefly, enumerating in detail but with no unnecessary information about its key elements. Although they were martyred in Antioch, their bodies were brought to Cyprus and laid to rest in a small church in Meniko near Akaki.[834] The culmination and confirmation of their god-fearing life was a spring situated in the northern part of the island, whose waters came to be used as a medication for diseases of the eyes and fever. The author of the *Chronicle* describes it thus:

> *It is true that the water is very brackish and ill to drink, but it is marvellous for healing.* (LM I 39)

As Makhairas says, this place became so famous that even 'Peter the Great' (ὁ ρὲ Πιὲρ ὁ μεγάλος) was healed by its power, and decided to demolish the old church and build a new one on its very foundations (ἐποῖκαν ἐκλησίαν ἀποὺ γῆς). To complete the work, the king ordered that the heads of the venerable martyrs be covered in silver (ἀργύρωσεν τὰς β' κεφαλάς), 'and at [their] top left a place with lids, so as to [make it possible to] give praise to the remains' (εἰς τὴν κορυφὴν ἀφῆκεν τόπον μὲ πόρτες νὰ προσκυνοῦσιν τὰ λείψανα), a move that allowed the faithful to come close to them.[835]

Makhairas' work is an expression of the tendency to focus on the deceased and to place hopes for a transformation of the present reality in their deaths and legends concerning their lives. A large role is played in it by the human body as matter that is subject to change, which takes on various functions in this approach. Materiality is a feature of bodies (σώματα), their parts (κεφαλή in LM I 32, δύο κεφαλάδες in LM I 39), remains (λείψανα), artefacts in the form of burial places (κιβούριν in LM I 33, τάφος in LM I 38, κοιμητήριν, κοιμητήρια in LM I 31–32, 35) and the substances that cover the remains (ἀργύρωσεν in LM I 39). The surroundings of these physical objects are also important because the relics are sometimes crowded together, placed in elaborate casings in a church, like in LM I 39, and at other times, left partly 'in the wilderness' (εἰς μοναξίαν), that is 'in places that have become empty' (οἱ τόποι ἐρημώθησαν), as in the case of St Epiphanios' grave in LM I 32. Remains are sometimes moved from place to place, like the head of the said St Epiphanios, 'located in a safe place in Koutsovendi' (εἰς φύλαξιν εἰς τὸν Κουτζουβέντην) or the heads of Sts Cyprian and Justina, brought from Syria in LM I 39. On the one hand, matter serves the saint as an absorptive, malleable, flexible substance that they themselves can use to shape their nature, and on the other, as a physical building block of a space that is becoming the property of the Church. The body, understood by Makhairas as a tool for action also in other contexts, can be subjected to a symbolical moral judgement. The dirty, sinful hands of the Genoese pause over the host in a gesture of false piety,[836] the tongue of Alice of Champagne is first tied, then untied,[837] Joanna L'Aleman's womb resists attempts to cause a miscarriage,[838] while the body of Peter I is maimed and defiled in an execution planned by people close to him.[839] The body of a saint can also be hurt and destroyed, as the problem of martyrdom described in the *Chronicle* demonstrates. In his references to this phenomenon, Makhairas may have modelled his work after religious texts present in Cyprus in the fourteenth and fifteenth centuries, such as the poems of Makarios Kalorites[840] and Neophytos the Recluse.[841] Other historians also had a fondness for this topic. The *Chronique d'Amadi* states that 'many saints suffered martyrdom and punishment for Our Lord' (*molti santi sofferseno martiri et pene per el nostro Signor*).[842] It also gained a symbol in the form of the sign of a red cross featured on the Templar robe (*portavano [...] la croce rossa in signification del martirio*)[843] since the times of Pope Eugene III (1145–1153).[844] The Italian text contains

---

[833] Cf. Foxe, The Acts and Monuments of the Church, 66. Catrien Santing and Barbara Baert have an interesting perspective on the 'chopped off heads' of the holy individuals. They emphasise the belief of the representatives of medieval and early modern cultures that the head is the crucial human bodily fragment (Baert, Santing, Introduction, 1). Cf. Jones, Martindale, Morris, The Prosopography of the Later Roman Empire.

[834] Meniko, a village 20 km west of Lefkosia, between the villages Poliometocho, Akaki and Peristerona.

[835] LM I 39.

[836] LM III 416.

[837] LM I 74.

[838] LM II 234.

[839] LM II 281.

[840] Nicolaou-Konnari, Literary Languages, 11.

[841] Nicolaou-Konnari, Literary Languages, 12.

[842] Mas Latrie (Ed.), Chronique d'Amadi, 274. Translation identical to that of Coureas, Edbury (Transl.), The Chronicle of Amadi, 258 (§ 554).

[843] Mas Latrie (Ed.), Chronique d'Amadi, 30.

[844] Dating after Coureas, Edbury (Transl.), The Chronicle of Amadi, 30.

multiple references to the phenomenon itself, and certain characters express their personal readiness to make such a sacrifice.[845] Interestingly, it lacks the translation of the *Chronicle* fragments that pertain to martyrdom, which speaks to the specific character (strong Byzantine overtones) of the Cypriot work.

The cult of martyrdom is connected to the essence of the faith as it was understood by both Churches. However, Makhairas makes no reference to its complex theological interpretation, according to which it means the union of man with Christ in his sacrifice, allowing him to participate both in the temporal and the ahistorical mystery of death. Nevertheless, it is not the process of dying that is relevant in the *Chronicle*, but the agentive function of matter, which through the saint's actions takes on certain features, such as the capacity to modify reality. No incidents involving the death of one Christian at the hand of another are encountered: only the 'infidels' are responsible for them.

In Greek and Latin hagiography a particular role is played by the type of death suffered by exceptional servants of God, and by the extraordinary qualities that allowed them to take away the suffering and fear of the rest of the community, and also to restitute a previous – seemingly irrecoverable – situation. Faithful to this tradition, the chronicler thus cites St George slain by the Sword (Makhairomenos) in St Liondis (Achlionta) (ἅγιος Γεώργιος ὁ Μαχαιρωμένος εἰς τὸν Ἀχλίοντα), 'a local miracle worker' (τοπικὸς θαυματουργός),[846] St Athanasios Pendaskinitis of Pendaskinon (ἅγιος Ἀθανάσιος ὁ Πεντασκοινίτης, ἀπὲ τὸ Πεντάσχοινον),[847] who specialised in healing (βρύει ἰάματα), John Lambadistis in Marathasa (Ἰωάννης ὁ Λαμπαδιστῆς εἰς τὴν Μαραθάσαν), whom he calls 'the Great' (μέγας), a deacon in the Marathasa parish (διάκος εἰς τὴν ἀνορίαν τῆς Μαραθάσας) and an exorcist (δώχνει τὰ δαιμόνια) and St Sozondas (ἅγιος Σώζοντας), a small shepherd (παιδὶν βοσκαρίδιν) from Plakoundoudi (εἰς τοῦ Πλακουντουδίου).[848] Notably, the exorcist is the only one in this group to have contact with the spiritual, and not just the bodily element. Makhairas pays special attention to the shepherd, recounting his confrontation with the Muslims, who accomplished their work of destruction and murdered the boy, though as we find out the fruit of his life was not ultimately erased, as the fragment below shows:

> [...] *and the Saracens pursued him* (ἐτρέξαν το), *when they burned the picture of the Mother of God in the monastery* (τὴν εἰκόναν τῆς Θεοτόκου εἰς τὴν μονήν), *and (the picture) was imprinted on the stone slabs and is so even to this day.* [...] *and he was running away (holding the vessel with the milk in it:) and he stumbled, and the vessel was broken and the milk was spilled, and what is taken for the place –is to be seen to this day.– And he went into the cave, (himself) and the other*

---

[845] Mas Latrie (Ed.), Chronique d'Amadi, 274–275, 282, 457, 502.

[846] On the Greek-language site we read: 'Ὁ Ἅγιος Γεώργιος ὁ Μαχαιρωμένος εἶναι ἕνας Κύπριος Ἅγιος που σήμερα εἶναι άγνωστος στον περισσότερο κόσμο. [...] Ὁ Καταλιόντας ήταν ένας μικρός οικισμός, ένα χλμ. νοτιοανατολικά του χωριού Αναλιόντα. [...] κοντά στον εγκαταλελειμένο οικισμό Καταλιόντα, υπάρχουν τα ερείπια της αρχαίας εκκλησίας του Αγίου Γεωργίου του Μαχαιρωμένου. [...] Η φήμη της εκκλησίας αυτής συνδέεται με τη θαυματουργή εικόνα του Αγίου Γεωργίου του Μαχαιρωμένου, η οποία για αρκετά χρόνια κοσμούσε την κύρια εκκλησία του χωριού Αναλιόντας, την Αγία Μαρίνα.' (http://www.saint.gr/1513/saint.aspx, accessed 23 December 2021). 'St George Makhairomenos belongs to [those] Cypriot saints who are still not universally known worldwide. [...] Katalionda was a small settlement [located] a kilometre to the south east from the village of Analionta (Achlionta). [...] Near the abandoned settlement of Katalionta the ruins of the old church of St George Makhairomenos may be found. [...] The fame of its church is due to the famous icon of St George Makhairomenos, which for many years was an ornament of the main church of Analionta, [the church of] St Marina.' (Kupiszewska's translation from the Polish translation by the author).

[847] 'Ὁ Ἅγιος Ἀθανάσιος ὁ Πεντασχοινίτης ήταν γέννημα θρέμμα της Κύπρου. Καταγόνταν από το χωριό Πεντάσχοινον που τώρα δεν υπάρχει, αλλά κείται σε ερείπια νοτίως του χωριού Άγιος Θεόδωρος της επαρχίας Λάρνακος. Εκεί σώζονται επίσης τα ερείπια εκκλησίας αφιερωμένης στον Άγιο [...]. Ο Ναός του Αγίου Αθανασίου του Πεντασχοινίτου καταστράφηκε από σεισμό την Κυριακή 24 Απριλίου 1491 μ.Χ. [...] τοιχογραφίες της μορφής του Αγίου Αθανασίου του Πεντασχοινίτου που υπάρχουν στην Ιερά Μονή Αμασγούς στο Μονάγρι και στο τοιχογραφημένο παρεκκλήσι του Αγίου Σωζομένου στο χωριό Γαλάτα, παριστάνεται σαν διάκονος.' (http://www.saint.gr/4341/saint.aspx, accessed 23 December 2021). 'St Athanasios Pendaskinitis was a native Cypriot. He came from the village of Pendaskinon, which now no longer exists, but [its] ruins may be found south of the village of St Theodore in the Larnaka eparchy. There [also] the ruins of a church of this saint survive [...]. The church of St Athanasios Pendaskinitis was destroyed during an earthquake on Sunday 24 April 1491. [...] the [commonly recognised] depictions of St Athanasios Pendaskinitis on murals that may be found in the Holy Monastery of [Mary] Amasgous in Monagri and on murals in St Sozondas's chapel in the village of Galata portray a deacon [...]' (Kupiszewska's translation from the Polish translation by the author).

[848] 'Ὁ Ἅγιος Σώζων εἶναι ἕνας τοπικός Ἅγιος της Πάφου και μάρτυρας της Κυπριακής Εκκλησίας [...]. Τα ερείπια της εκκλησίας του Αγίου Σώζοντος στην Ασπρογιά υπάρχουν μέχρι σήμερα. Η εικόνα του Αγίου σώζεται στη Μονή Χρυσορρογιάτισσας. Λείψανα του Αγίου σώζονται στην Μονή Μαχαιρά και στη Μονή Χρυσορρογιάτισσας.' (http://www.saint.gr/4338/saint.aspx, accessed 30 June 2021). 'St Sozondas is a local saint from Paphos and a martyr of the Cypriot Church [...]. The ruins of St Sozondas's church in Asprogia survive to this day. An icon of the saint is preserved in the Monastery of Chrysorrogiatissa [lit. 'Our Lady of the Golden Pomegranate']. Relics of the saint have been placed in the Makhairas Monastery and the Monastery of Chrysorrogiatissa.' (Kupiszewska's translation from the Polish translation by the author).

> *boys with him: and the Saracens put fire to it (ἐβάλαν λαμπρόν) and burned them (ἐκάψαν τα). And a church was built, and the -holy relics- (τὰ ἁγιάσματα) put in it, and they heal all diseases.* (LM I 36)

According to the interpretation in the *Chronicle*, there are no differences between Christians themselves concerning the right to participate in this mystery, but it sets them apart from those who are not able to accept this phenomenon. Faith in God in situations where one's life is in danger and willingness to make a sacrifice of oneself help repel the enemy. The constant presence of remains in Cypriot land and preservation of martyrs' testimonies in collective memory remind the Cyprians of the supernatural dimension of human action and encourage them to form a community, which thus undergoes rapid growth, manifesting its power in the face of the unbelievers. The omissions in the *Chronicle* lead to the belief that its author intentionally skips over historical and doctrinal topics, seeking only to present figures that experience a given religious phenomenon and to emphasise the advantages of this for all Christians. However, one should not disregard the places in the narrative that suggest that Latin saints were for the most part absorbed by the structure occupied by Orthodox saints: observations of this type are a significant hint that may be useful for defining the hidden convictions of the author, and thus for establishing his identity.

Passages LM I 31–39, hagiographic in their message, distinctly show the pathway that, according to Makhairas, the Greek Church in Cyprus followed during its development. Although most of the saints described lived before the schism, they form the strong foundation on which the Orthodox community was erected. From its manner of presentation by the chronicler, focused around local churches, it should be concluded that it was not subject to the centralisation observed for Catholicism. The uniform structure of the Greek Church as its distinctive feature has been described by Richard Kieckhefer.[849] Simultaneously, the chronicler sees the operation of saints on the island as an instance of activity by a single cohesive organism that draws its strength from active participation in a small local community and in a heritage passed down over many generations.

The Cypriot text does not answer the question of whether these blessed individuals received any reward after death, but only discusses the real and imagined effects of their presence, such as the erection of a kind of symbolical defensive wall against the invaders. We do find out, however, in what ways the community worshipped them: this was done primarily by selecting the proper place for their cult to develop, often derived from the manifest will of the saint. Every such *locum*, which can be found on the map of Cyprus via the village or town name provided in the *Chronicle*, was assigned a church building, giving it the features of a transfigured space and at the same time, a space controlled by an institution. This transfiguration was cemented by the presence of a sanctified body. Makhairas' saints never leave the persons who encountered them indifferent. They always cause a reaction, in various forms: worship, hope, contempt, fear. The chronicler's attention concentrates on holiness in action, on the quality of the attitudes adopted by the individual, and on interactions with others. This perspective calls to mind Kieckhefer's conclusions concerning the cult of saints, which is rooted in 'the Christian notion of personality'.[850] Neither the *Chronique d'Amadi* nor the works of Philippe de Mézières or Boustronios depict the phenomenon of holiness as having such characteristics.

It is unknown whether the chronicler personally encountered the phenomenon of holiness or martyrdom but by addressing these topics, adopting the given style and manner of building the narrative he certainly became part of a hagiographic trend. Moreover, into this structure of a spiritual world erected on sacrificial land inhabited by hosts of Greek imitators of Jesus Christ Makhairas weaved single instances of Latin saints, thus unifying their depiction. Next to the saints from before the schism mentioned above, such as St Mamas (3rd c.) or St Diomidios (4th c.), we encounter a mention of the Catholic John de Montfort who, as Dawkins states, died in 1248: already after the separation of the Churches.[851] This technique contributed to a minimisation of the role of Latin saints, among others because of their limited numbers, which in turn strengthened the sense of a specific Cypriot – or even 'Cyprian' – identity that took shape on Cyprus before the Frankish period. At the same time, the greater number of saints from before the schism is clearly marked in the text, which is proof that initially, a coherent form of experiencing Christian spirituality prevailed on the island.

---

[849] Kieckhefer, Imitators of Christ, 10.
[850] According to Kieckhefer the history of holiness as a phenomenon focuses on four main topics: 'the development of ways to honor the saints', 'the increasing control of their cult by the institutional Church', 'recurrent opposition to their veneration' and 'a theological and historical response to that opposition' (Kieckhefer, Imitators of Christ, 1–2).
[851] Dawkins, Notes, 62.

2.2.3. Cult of the Holy Cross

A special role is played in the *Chronicle* by the Holy Cross. It appears as the impatiently awaited Relic that St Helena set out to find. Its arrival was so anticipated that the building of 'towers from Jerusalem to Constantinople' (ἀπὸ τὴν Ἰερουσαλὴμ εἰς τὴν Κωνσταντινόπολιν [...] πύργους) was ordered, situated so as to be highly visible and 'for one to be perceptible from another' (v' ἀποσκεπάζῃ ἕνας τὸν ἄλλον), with people keeping watch day and night on each, waiting in readiness (ὅτοιμοι) for 'the blaze of fire or smoke from Jerusalem' (λαμπρὸν ἢ καπνὸν εἰς τὴν Ἰερουσαλήμ). Later, should the empress manage to reach the Venerable Tree, they 'were to lift a torch' (νὰ ὑψωθῇ νὰ γινῇ φανός) in triumph to let Emperor Constantine himself know of it.[852]

The Holy Cross sanctifies everything that is near it. The chronicler explains this phenomenon using the example of the thief's cross. Since this cross, he expounds, lay 'together' (ἀντάμα) with the Relic 'for three hundred and nine years' (τόσον καιρὸν χρόνους τθ'), 'it would not be proper to discard it' (δὲν ἦτον δίκαιον νὰ ῥίψουν).[853]

The symbol of the Holy Cross appears in the *Chronicle* many times, among others in the tales about St Helena, the Templars and Cypriot saints, the theft of the Cross from Togni by a Latin priest and further fate of the Relic. This motif, related to Jesus' crucification and termed 'Divine κένωσις',[854] that is 'Divine emptying' by Vladimir Lossky is important in many Christian texts, though variously presented and does not always play the same role.

In Philippe de Mézières' *Le Songe* there regularly appears the theme of moral assessment of a given community through the perspective of its attitude towards the sign of the cross: whether it is respected, sidelined, or completely eliminated.[855] The *Chronique d'Amadi* describes several events in which the Holy Cross or its replica appears, for example in the passages recounting the entry of Christian armies bearing the Holy Cross (*la verace croce*) into Ascalon (*città de Scalona, de Ascalona*), conquered in 1154 by Baldwin III,[856] about a procession with a cross that belonged to Syrians[857] and about a presentation of a cross to Louis IX (*re Aluise de Franza*),[858] which the ruler received in 1267.[859] The most interesting story concerns 1193, when the king of England, Richard Cœur de Lion, and the French King Philip conquered a Muslim fortress, attempting to force the Saracens to return the Cross, lost by the Christians in 1187 during the battle of the Horns of Hattin, where Guy was captured. Sultan Saladin declined to return his prize, which led to the beheading of sixteen thousand Muslims. As the author of the source states, the Islamic ruler became so angry that he ordered Ascalon to be demolished in order to destroy the most accessible route from Syria to Egypt. This account is a valuable supplement to the text of the *Chronicle*, because it shows that the holy Relic remained in the hands of the followers of Islam for some time.[860]

In Leontios' view the Holy Cross undoubtedly has the power to bolster human strength and increase the wellbeing of the whole island, which chimes with Nikolas Vasiliadis' comment that the greatest Sacrifice of Christ, and thus also its material monument in the shape of the Cross, has the function of giving life to creation.[861] St Helena bringing the Relic from Jerusalem to Cyprus is an event equivalent to the formation on the island of sacred space, and everything that is connected with the sacred. The crucifixion of the Son of God is a fact that is practically omitted in the *Chronicle* – being used only in the story of the Templars – a fact that happened in the past, is significant for the growth of the faith, explains the mechanism of its appearance on the island and is of interest primarily because of its material remains, and also calls to mind selected details of what happened at the dawn of Christianity (mention of the concurrent death of the two thieves). The sacrifice of the martyrs mentioned above could have been born of the wish to imitate Christ's offering, though in the Cypriot work none of the saints refer to this directly. Notably, the Passion of the Son of God is more profoundly suggested by some descriptions of the nails and crown of thorns than of the Cross itself.

---

[852] LM I 6.
[853] LM I 7.
[854] Łosski, Teologia Mistyczna, 138.
[855] E.g.: Philippe de Mézières, Le Songe, 225.
[856] Mas Latrie (Ed.), Chronique d'Amadi, 34.
[857] Mas Latrie (Ed.), Chronique d'Amadi, 68.
[858] Mas Latrie (Ed.), Chronique d'Amadi, 198.
[859] Mas Latrie (Ed.), Chronique d'Amadi, 209.
[860] Mas Latrie (Ed.), Chronique d'Amadi, 83; Coureas, Edbury (Transl.), The Chronicle of Amadi, 82 (§ 147).
[861] Vasiliadis, Misterium śmierci, 133, 135–139.

When portraying the phenomenon of Cross relic worship in Cyprus, Makhairas mentions other crosses that contain a fragment of wood from Christ's Cross. He thus mentions: 'the Cross of Olympas, which they call the Great' (ὁ σταυρὸς τοῦ Λυμπᾶ ὁ ποῖος κράζεται ὁ Μέγας), 'the Revealed Cross' (ὁ σταυρὸς ὁ Φανερούμενος), and also the 'Cross [from] Psoka' (ὁ σταυρὸς τῆς Ψόκας), Cross from Kouka or Kokas' Cross[862] (τοῦ λεγομένου Κοκᾶ) and the 'Cross of Lefkara' (ὁ σταυρὸς τῶν Λευκάρων). MS O contains the sentence:

(And these were built by St. Helena,) and they all contain Wood of the Cross (τίμια ξύλα), and work marvellous miracles.[863]

The empress may have constructed these crosses herself or ordered them to be built. However, Makhairas usually uses the form ἔκτισεν to indicate that a church had been erected (and not ἐποῖκεν), and so he may be suggesting a connection between these several crosses and specific churches.

Like saints' graves (tombs), places featuring wood from the Cross gradually started appearing all over the island. They all had a common feature: they were tied to extraordinary miracles (θαυμαστὰ θαύματα), such as exudation of miraculous oils (βρύει μύρον) that affected the senses, and thus tangibly marked the presence of the sacred sphere.[864]

Komodikis refers to this perspective, writing that:

'Στην Κύπρο υπήρχαν και εξακολουθούν να υπάρχουν και σήμερα πολλοί ναοί αφιερωμένοι στον Τίμιο Σταυρό. Στο χωριό Κουκά, σύμφωνα με τον Κυπριανό, βρίσκεται ναός του Ζωοποιού Σταυρού, στον οποίον η Αγία Ελένη τοποθέτησε κομμάτια από το ζωοποιό ξύλο. [...] Άλλοι ναοί αφιερωμένοι στον Τίμιο Σταυρό είναι οι εξής: ο ναός του Τιμίου Σταυρού στα Λεύκαρα, ο ναός του Σταυρού στο Όμοδος, η Μονή του Σταυροβουνιού, ο ναός του Σταυρού στην Τόχνη και τέλος το μοναστήρι του Σταυρού του Φανερωμένου. [...] ο Σταυρός του Ολυμπίου, που αναφέρεται από την πηγή, μπορεί κάλλιστα να ταυτιστεί με τη μονή του Σταυροβουνιού. Τέλος, η εκκλησία του οσίου Αθανασίου Πεντασχοινίτου βρίσκεται κοντά στο χωριό Κοφίνου, όπου υπάρχει ένα μικρό ποτάμι με το όνομα Πεντάσχινος.'[865]

In Cyprus numerous churches devoted to the Holy Cross were built and survive to this day. According to Cyprian, in the village of Kouka there is a church of the Life-giving Cross in which St Helena placed fragments of the life-giving wood. [...] Other churches devoted to the Holy Cross include the Church of the Holy Cross in Lefkara, the Church of the Cross in [the village of] Omodos, Stavro Vouni Monastery, the Church of the Cross in Togni and finally the Monastery of the Revealed Cross. [...] Olympas' Cross, which levitated over water, may best be identified with Stavro Vouni Monastery. Finally, the church of St Athanasios Pendaskinitis is located in the village of Kofinou, where there is a small river called Pendaskinos (analogously to the form 'Pendaskinitis' given by Dawkins).[866]

As Christianity grew on the island, as presented in the *Chronicle*, there was a gradual increase in the number of extraordinary places made famous for their particular objects of worship, such as the Great Cross (τὸν σταυρὸν τὸν μέγαν) or the Small Cross of Togni (τὸν μικρὸν εἰς τὴν Τόγνην). Physical objects endowed with the power of relics are present in the narrative like strongly outlined stage props, playing the role of elements that recall the great Orthodox heritage.

In passage LM I 67 the chronicler returns to the subject of the Cross in another 'self-contained story', recounting its theft in 1318 by a Roman Catholic priest (ἕνας παπᾶς λατῖνος), John Santamarin (σὶρ Τζουὰν Σαρθαμαρήν). Makhairas says that he:

---

[862] The whole phrase 'ὁ σταυρὸς τῆς Ψόκας, τοῦ λεγομένου Κοκᾶ' is problematic. For Pavlidis it means: 'ὁ Σταυρός της Ψόκας, ο Σταυρός του λεγόμενου Κοκά' ('the Cross from Psoka, the Cross from so-called Kouka'). He holds Psoka to have been a settlement in the Troodos Mountains, and Kouka, a village in the Lemesos district. See Παυλίδης (Ed.), Λεοντίου Μαχαιρᾶ Χρονικόν, 35 (fn. 4). Dawkins translates it as 'the Cross of Psoka, the Church of the Cross of the man called Koka'. See Dawkins, Notes, 39. Miller and Sathas interpret it as: *la croix de Psocas surnommé Kouca* ('the Cross of Psokas who was called Kokas'). See Sathas, Miller (Eds, transl.), Chronique de Chypre, 27.
[863] Dawkins (Ed., transl.), Ἐξήγησις/ Recital, 39 (fn. 2); Παυλίδης (Ed.), Λεοντίου Μαχαιρᾶ Χρονικόν, 34 (fn. 1).
[864] LM I 38.
[865] Κωμοδίκης, Οι Πληροφορίες των Βραχέων Χρονικών, 235–236.
[866] Kupiszewska's translation from the Polish translation by the author.

[…] put it underneath his coat, and went to the shore where the boat was waiting to take him off, and he embarked on the boat and they set sail. Oh the miracle! at once a (great) storm arose and they were like to be drowned, and they put him out upon the land. And he (took the cross and) stripped off the jewels and (the silver and) all the pearls and took them with him, and the Life-giving Wood (τὸν ζωοποιὸν ξύλον) he threw into the midst of the carob tree of Avra at the village of Kalamoulli […]. (LM I 67)

Coureas and Edbury notice a strong anti-Latin message in this version, in contrast to the one present in the *Chronique d'Amadi*.[867]

According to the account of the *Chronicle*'s author, the Cross remained in the crown of a carob tree (τὴν κερατζίαν)[868] for twenty two years. The historian emphasises that it was the will of the Cross to reveal itself at (ὄνταν ἐθέλησε νὰ φανερωθῇ) the proper moment to a chosen boy who was herding cattle (ἕνας […] βοσκαρίδιν τῶν σφακτῶν),[869] which may be related to an apotheosis of childness, wherein children are attributed moral and cognitive purity.[870] The second aspect of the choice made by the Cross is that the person selected was a slave (σκλαβοποῦλλον), and thus a person on a lower rung of the social hierarchy, which is in accordance with the Christian practice of recognising the weak and the poor. In a sense, Leontios attributes volition to the Cross, and thus personifies it. When the boy attempted to carry his vision to the villagers and inform them of his discovery, they did not believe him, suggesting that what he had experienced was only an illusion (Εἶνε φαντασία!). In his vision a voice called him by his name (ἐλαλοῦσαν του τ' ὄνομάν του),[871] George (ὀνόματι (Γ)εώργιος) of Kalamoulli (ἀπὲ τὸ χωργιὸν τὸ Καλαμούλλιν).[872] One day, the youth heard the portentous words, promising him remarkable treasure (θησαυρόν):

Come to me and I will give you a treasure which will not fail you (ἀποῦ νὰ μὲν σὲ λείψῃ). (LM I 69)

Makhairas paints a vivid picture of this event:

It befell -after a few days-, as he was feeding the beasts, that he grew tired and lay down to sleep near the carob tree, in which the Cross was […] and he sees a carob on a branch of the carob tree. He got up and wanted it to eat. And he […] throws his staff to knock down the carob, and the staff caught in the branches. Then he took a stone and threw it to knock down the staff, and as he went to throw the stone, he sees a fire (λαμπρόν) in the middle of the carob tree and grew frightened. (LM I 70)

As the chronicler tells it, at the shepherd boy's request the inhabitants hurried to help with water (νερόν) and axes (ξινάρια), cut the tree, and from the incision there came an aroma (μυρωδία) reminiscent of musk (τὸν μοῦσκον). The boy allegedly shouted:

Now my visions (τὰ 'ρώματά μου) are fulfilled (ἐτελειῶσαν): behold ('δέτε) the Cross of the Lord (τὸν σταυρὸν τον κυρίου!) (LM I 70)

Makhairas continues this tale consistently following the hagiographic convention, introducing the element of miracles that forms a permanent fixture in his narrative building, such as the healing

---

[867] Coureas, Edbury (Transl.), The Chronicle of Amadi, 371 (fn. 4).
[868] The carob tree (*Ceratonia siliqua* L.) grows in Mediterranean countries, including on Cyprus. It has a 'broad, semi-spherical crown and a thick trunk with a coarse brown bark and strong branches', with long alternate leaves and numerous small flowers 'spirally arranged along the inflorescence axis in catkin-like racemes borne on spurs from old wood and even on the trunk' (Battle, Tous, Carob tree, 9–12). The fruit of the carob tree (pod) is called 'St John's bread'. It is used to make a meal called carob or carob gum. 'The locust tree, carob tree, carob, ceratonia (*Ceratonia siliqua* L.) is also often called St John's bread, though the last name is more commonly used for the edible pods of the tree rather than the whole tree, or St John's tree' (Jazurek-Gutek *et al.*, Zapomniane walory, 306. Translated by Kupiszewska). From the second half of the thirteenth century, carob was also, next to wheat, wine, olive oil, legumes, salt and sugar, a main export product (Coureas, Economy, 103, 106, 108–109).
[869] LM I 69.
[870] See Hos. 11: 1–4; Mt. 18: 4.
[871] The motif of God calling a person by name appears in the Bible many times, e.g.: 'Lift up your eyes on high and see: Who created these [stars – M.G.]? He who brings out their host and numbers them,/ calling them all by name' Isa. 40: 26; 'from the rising of the sun he was summoned by name.' Isa. 41: 25; 'Do not fear, for I have redeemed you,/ I have called you by name, you are mine.' Isa. 43: 1; '[…] it is I, the Lord/ the God of Israel, who call you by your name.' Isa. 45: 3.
[872] Kalamoulli – a settlement in the Kakoratsia region on the road from Lemesos to Lefkosia.

of twelve people (ιβ´ ἀστενεῖς) and curing of attacks (λαμπαχίον), hemorrhages (ἐπηγαῖνναν αἷμαν), illnesses of the disabled (στραβοί), paralysed (λωροί) and others (ἄλλοι), which brought acclaim to the event (λόγος) all over the country (περίχωρα).[873] In a sense, the figure of George plays a similar role to that of St Helena. This is because he took part in a discovery of the Cross, though unlike St Constantine's mother he did so unwittingly, as the terror experienced by him and the people from the village indicates. The aid of the bishop of Lefkara was needed to interpret the significance of the find. As Makhairas says, it was the bishop who deduced that the object and the stolen Cross from Togni were the same. In these two stories the Relic remains hidden for some time. And what distinguishes them is the scale of the event: the empress came to Cyprus together with other members of an expedition, and her mission had not only a religious significance, but primarily a political one. Meanwhile, George discovered the relic accidentally, during a tiring day, not expecting what was about to happen, and was forced to explain the course of events to others. Even the king required him to recount and explain the unfathomed phenomenon:

> *The king put it in his house, and seeing the many miracles that were being worked by it, wanted to keep it in his house (ἐπεθύμησε νὰ τὸν κρατήσῃ εἰς τὸ σπίτιν του): and he kept it for eleven days. And in the night as he was asleep the king saw a very evil vision (ἔναν ὅρωμαν πολλὰ κακόν), and took fright and called for George and gave him the Cross. And they sought for him to go to Kerynia (because of sick people there), and he took the Cross there and worked many miracles. [...] and he was tonsured as a monk (ἐκουρεύτην μοναχός), and they called him Gabriel (ἐκράξαν τον Γαβριήλ).* (LM I 71)

The Cross as possessing volition, next to the motifs that underline the relic's features such as giving of life, the ability to teach, capacity to bestow gifts and infallibility, appears one more time in the *Chronicle*: in the mention about the cross of Olympas (ὁ σταυρὸς τῶν Λυμπίων), that is the Great Cross (τουτέστιν ὁ μέγας), which descended of itself from the mountain of Olympia (Stavro Vouni) in 1426 in order to avoid meeting the Saracens attacking the country, keeping the Venerable Tree (τὸ τιμίου ξύλου) and the gold covering it (χρυσάφιν) untouched.[874] The object thus depicted by Makhairas represents the reified will of God and notably, from the point of view of this work, most frequently appears during encounters between two denominations or religions.

Not insignificant is the fact that the chronicler introduces the carob tree, so important in the life of the island's inhabitants, into his narrative. Carob is known from Jewish literature as a subject of rabbinic disputes.[875] It appears in the tale of Honi (Ḥoni, ha-meʿaggel, 'He who draws a circle'), a sage from the first century BCE who fell asleep for seventy years, i.e. the period needed for the tree to bear fruit.[876] In another, the rabbi Eliezer moves a carob tree from place to place.[877] Both these stories come from the Babylonian Talmud (the first from *Taanit* 23a, the second from *Bava Metzia* 59b).[878] The motif found in the *Chronicle* of the carob tree providing shelter in which the Life-giving Cross hides may be compared to that of the Tree of Life, known from the Bible (Gen. 2, 9; Rev. 22, 2).[879]

To provide the Christian community with an indestructible foundation for correct functioning and growth, the church notables in the *Chronicle* placed great weight on the authenticity of the Relic found by George. When at one point some Latins began to cast doubt on its genuineness, the customary test for discovering the truth was immediately ordered. The decision concerning its procedure was taken by representatives of the royal court together with the Catholic bishop of Ammochostos Fra Marco (Φρὲ Μαρά), which is important for an understanding of the essence of interdenominational contacts in the work. Makhairas builds a dialogue between the notables, putting the following words in the mouth of the Church hierarch: 'you and I will give an account of this to God' (ἐγὼ καὶ σοὺ θέλομεν δώσειν λόγον τοῦ θεοῦ).[880] The motif of measuring the Cross' authenticity, shown from a Catholic perspective, gives

---

[873] LM I 70. In Mas Latrie (Ed.), Chronique de Strambaldi, 29 we read: *Et venero subito sacerdoti, et in quel istante si sanorono 12 persone amalate de più loro malatie; li duoi erano inspiritati donne che avevano il mal de Santa Martha, orbi asserati.*
[874] LM I 68.
[875] Cf. Eisenberg, Jewish Traditions, 679–680.
[876] Horst, Pious Long-Sleepers, 102–103.
[877] Dan (Ed.), Studies in Jewish Thought, 55.
[878] After Visotzky, Sage Tales, 173; Dan (Ed.), Studies in Jewish Thought, 55.
[879] Lanfer, Allusion to and Expansion of the Tree of Life, 96–108.
[880] LM I 73.

the reader an essential narrative binding device that integrates the two Christian branches. The conversation between the bishop and the ruler of Cyprus is as follows:

> '[…] we hear that in our midst (μεσόν μας) some boy (ἔναν κοπέλλιν) has carved a cross (ἐπελέκισεν ἔναν σταυρόν), and is saying that it is a part of the Cross of Christ (ἀπὸ τὸν σταυρὸν τοῦ Χριστοῦ), (and many foolish things (πολλὲς πελλάρες) are being said,) and we are suffering it (μεῖς βαστοῦμεν το).' The king said to him: 'What must be done?' The bishop said to him: 'We must examine it (Νὰ τὸ ἐξετάσωμεν), to see if it is of the wood of the Life-giving Cross (ἂν ἦνε ἀπὸ τὸ ξύλον τοῦ ζωοποιοῦ).' The king said to him: 'Must I try the mysteries of the church (τὰ μυστήρια τῶν ἐκκλησιῶν)?' The bishop said to him: 'No, it is I, it is I who am concerned (ἐμέναν, ἐμέναν ἐγκίζει!). But', said he, 'without your help I cannot do it.' The king said to him: 'Do what is needful in my presence (ὀμπρός μου), and no one shall condemn you.' (LM I 73)

Makhairas places emphasis both on the element of community and on the complementarity of the religious and political spheres. The first aspect may be discerned in the scene in which George is heard out by the members of his community. It is likely because of their common religious bond that they ultimately believe him. Such an interpretation is suggested by the words of a church notable, who states that the boy comes 'from among them' (μεσόν μας). In the second case, the following relationship appears: the bishop protects the 'mysteries of the Church' (τὰ μυστήρια τῶν ἐκκλησιῶν) and issues all decisions related to this, while the head of state is tasked with ensuring he has the proper conditions to do so through his presence and protection against the interference of others. The church leader's expression 'without your help' (χωρὶς τῆς βοηθείας σου) reflects a division of duties, but also indicates the supportive role of the lay authorities, who demonstrate their readiness to cooperate with the church authorities. By his presence, the Frankish king guarantees security and rule of law.[881]

In the *Chronicle*, verifying the authenticity of relics involves the use of the indisputably destructive power of fire (διὰ πυρός) and the special properties of blood (διὰ αἵματος), which Makhairas describes thus:

> 'Lord, you must know that wood of the Holy Cross (τίμια ξύλα) is tried (ἐξετάζουνται) by fire (διὰ πυρός) and by blood ([διὰ] αἵματος): by fire (διὰ τὸ λαμπρόν), you put in the wood (ξύλον[882]), and if it be burned (ἂν καγῇ) it is not wood of the Holy Cross, but if it abides without injury (χωρὶς βλάβην), it is of the wood of the Holy Cross. Also if blood be flowing from any one, and you lay it thereupon, the blood stops and dries up (στέκει τὸ αἷμαν καὶ πήσσει).' The king said to him: 'Do what you think good.' (LM I 73)[883]

The test was carried out using a 'large, four-sided royal furnace' (τὸ μέγαν κανούνιν τὸ ρηγάτικον τὸ τετρακάντουνον), filled with charcoal (ἐγέμωσάν το κάρβουνα). Despite the merciless work of the flames, the Cross showed no destruction of any kind and moreover, as the chronicler tells, caused the tongue of Queen Alice of Champagne to become untied after she had been cursed to remain in protracted silence in punishment for insubordination (she had entered Makhairas church despite a ban).[884] Freed from the cumbersome infirmity, the woman was said to solemnly profess her faith: 'I believe, oh Lord, that this wood is of Christ's Tree' ("Πιστεύω, κύριε, ὅτι τοῦτον τὸ ξύλον εἶνε ἀπὸ τὸ ξύλον τοῦ Χριστοῦ"), and this *credo*, though incomplete in its significance, since it concerns faith in the origins of a material object, with no fuller exploration of the mystery of the Holy Cross, delivered her from suffering.[885] The king gave the cross to the monk Gabriel, allowing him to depart with it, on the condition that he would not leave Cyprus with it: in such a case, he would be risking a 'cruel death' (κακὸν θάνατον).[886] As before, the offered Relic once again became the reason for erecting yet another church, this time – upon the initiative of Maria of Plisie, and more precisely d'Ibelin (τάμε Μαρία τε Πλισίε).[887] Obedient

---

[881] LM I 73.
[882] Παυλίδης (Ed.), Λεοντίου Μαχαιρά Χρονικόν, 59: 'Με την φωτιά, τοποθετώντας σ'αυτήν το ξύλο' ('With the fire, placing the wood in it', Kupiszewska's translation from the Polish translation by the author).
[883] Παυλίδης (Ed.), Λεοντίου Μαχαιρά Χρονικόν, 59: 'το αίμα πήζει και η αιμορραγία σταματά' ('blood congeals and the flow of blood stops', Kupiszewska's translation from the Polish translation by the author).
[884] Fn. 4 in Παυλίδης (Ed.), Λεοντίου Μαχαιρά Χρονικόν, 58. See Mas Latrie (Ed.), Chronique de Strambaldi, 30.
[885] LM I 74.
[886] LM I 74.
[887] LM I 75.

to these commands, Gabriel prayed and with 'the blessing of the bishop of Lefkosia' (μὲ τὴν εὐχὴν τοῦ ἐπισκόπου Λευκωσίας)[888] received guidance telling him of an 'isolated place' (ἕνας ἀναπαμένος τόπος) for the church, located between the town and the land of St Dometios (νὰ τὸν 'γείρουν [ὅπου εἶνε εἰς τὴν γῆν] τοῦ Ἁγίου Δομετίου).[889] As a result of these actions, we find out from the *Chronicle*'s author, a church dedicated to the Revealed Cross (ὁ Σταυρὸς ὁ Φανερωμένος) was built, and a monastery (μονή) with cells for monks (κελλία διὰ μοναχούς) was erected, painted (ζωγραφίσαν την) and furnished with icons (ἐβάλαν τὰς εἰκόνας) in the church pews (εἰς τὰ στασιδία),[890] and silver vessels (ἱερὰ ἀργυρᾶ) and books (βιβλία) were brought in. The cross, decorated with silver (μὲ τὸ ἀσήμιν), gold (χρυσίον), pearls (μαργαριτάριν) and precious stones (πέτρες πρετζιοῦζες), was placed in a chest (ἕναν σεντούκιν) at the centre of the church.[891] Analysis of this image allows us to observe the remarkable precision with which the chronicler approached the portrayal of individual parts of this event, which indicates the great significance that this tale had for him, particularly when passages confirming his interest in the Greek tradition are placed in the context of what is known about his life story, rooted in the firmly entrenched Latin tradition. One cannot fail to see that it is these elements that arouse many positive feelings in the *Chronicle*'s author, that they had a particular value for him, and thus this is the place where one should look for material hints concerning his worldview and identity. The Holy Cross is featured at the centre of the world presented in the Cypriot work as a valuable object with its own history, and is the pride of the island and the whole Cyprian community. The fragments that refer to it are undoubtedly a sign of Makhairas' sense of belonging to the land on which the events described played out. They consolidate the image of Cyprus as a primarily Christian island, where concern for the Relic or the dream to possess it is a feature of both the Orthodox population and the Latins; furthermore, they do not allow the place where its cult began to be forgotten.

This discussion also moved the chronicler to underline the need to carefully, scrupulously store holy objects according to the established rules. For example, he describes how the patriarch of Antioch, Ignatios (πατριάρχης τῆς Ἀντιοχείας [...] Ἰγνάτιος), ordered the building of a structure in the form of a cross made of walnut wood (ξυλένον κάρυνον) five and a half spans long and four fingers wide, then consecrated it, sprinkled it from top to bottom with three kinds of holy oils (γ' λοές), placed inside it a small shard of the Holy Cross and the Body of Christ obtained from the consecration performed on Maundy Thursday (τῆς ἁγίας Πέφτης μέσα) and also recorded the Ten Commandments (τοὺς δέκα ὁρισμούς) and a fragment from the Gospel of St John (τὸ Εὐαγγέλιον τοῦ κατὰ Ἰωάννην) read on Great Friday (τῆς ἁγίας Πέμπτης) on it. Finally, in a silk-covered (χολέτραν) groove at the back of the cross he placed forty six relics of the saints: Epiphanios, archbishop of Cyprus (τοῦ ἁγίου Ἐπιφανίου ἀρχιεπισκόπου Κύπρου), Triphyllios, bishop of Lefkosia (τοῦ ἁγίου Τριφυλλίου ἐπισκόπου Λευκωσίας), Sozomenos, bishop of Potamia (τοῦ ἁγίου Σωζομένου Ποταμίας), Herakleides (τοῦ ἁγίου Ἡρακλειδίου), forty martyrs of Sevasteia (τῶν ἁγίων μ' μαρτύρων τῶν ἐν Σεβαστεία) and Euthymios of the Monastery of the Priests (τοῦ ἁγίου Εὐθυμίου μονῆς τῶν ἱερέων). The cross itself was stored – according to the rules and to preserve its mystery – 'under the eaves of that church' (εἰς τὸ κουβούκλιν τοῦ αὐτοῦ ναοῦ). When giving these details, Makhairas also cites the source of the guidelines for such organisation of sacred space, calling it 'the book of that Cross' (τὸ βιβλίον τοῦ αὐτοῦ σταυροῦ).[892] Like in earlier fragments, the material facet of Christianity comes to the fore: a fragment of the Cross is present, the Body of Christ is present, the remains of saints are present. However, in no place does an explanation appear of what this 'concretism' serves, why it is important. Similarly, a purely material meaning is connected to the engraving of the Ten Commandments and extracts from the Bible without an explanation of their content and sense: the fact that Makhairas stopped at this point indicates his passion for cataloguing objects linked to the Church as an institution and to registering data. The relic concealed in the newly built church was intended to propitiate God and mitigate his anger, expressed by plagues, diseases and cataclysms:

> *And when there is a plague (θανατικόν) or locusts (ἀκρίδα) or a drought (ἀβροχία), they shall make a procession (λιτήν) and bring out the cross, which is called the Cross made Manifest (τὸν φανερωμένον σταυρόν), and shall carry it in procession round the church (νὰ τὸν λιτανέσσουν τριγύρου τῆς ἐκκλησίας), and shall make holy water (νὰ ποίσουν δρόσος νὰ τὸν βουττήσουν) and*

---

[888] In Mas Latrie (Ed.), Chronique de Strambaldi, 30: *con la benidittione del vescovo di Nicossia greco*.
[889] LM I 76.
[890] Παυλίδης (Ed.), Λεοντίου Μαχαιρᾶ Χρονικόν, 61: 'τοποθέτησαν καὶ τις εἰκόνες στα στασίδια' ('they also placed the pictures on the pews').
[891] LM I 76.
[892] LM I 77.

dip it in it (νὰ τὸν βουττήσουν), and sprinkle it over against the sky (νὰ τὸν ραντίσουν κατὰ τὸν ἀέραν), and God will remove His wrath (νὰ σηκώσῃ τὴν ὀργήν) as we have just said. (LM I 77)

From the above-quoted *Chronicle* passages, it is clearly apparent that in the place where Christ's Cross is located, a centre of Christian faith and culture forms. The fragments discussed allow the depiction that emerges to be interpreted using concepts of postcolonial theory. This is because the actions of the Franks presented there, endowed with a 'colonising' momentum, were directed at what in the spiritual sense was common both to the Orthodox and the Catholics, but what initially – spatially, materially and chronologically – belonged to the Rhomaian people. The Latins endeavoured to obtain from the Greeks that what was good for themselves under the pretext of exercising the right to what was held in common. At this point, there appears the theme, not stated explicitly but suggestively implied, of the seizure by the Lusignans of double authority, over territory and the cultural and religious affiliation of the island's inhabitants, the pretext for which was provided by Christianity's most important Relic. In the *Chronicle* Cyprus owes its identity to its presence, which is apparent since the introductory passages that, together with tales of the saints and martyrs, introduce a concrete religious dimension. In turn, the themes that highlight the Franks' interest in the Holy Cross show that its placement on the island made it easier for them to 'colonise' it because they did not have to change the core convictions rooted in the Cyprians' consciousness to achieve their goal. Undoubtedly in this case the nature of Orthodox faith is important, portrayed by Makhairas in a way that gives it the capacity to play a foundational role on the island, potentially ready to receive new, though still Christian content. This phenomenon is explained by Paul Hedges:

Christian orthodoxy, in a historically nuanced and ecumenical context, does not consist in adherence to a single dogmatic formula, whether this be Chalcedon orthodoxy or anything else, and various factors such as political debates have shaped notions of 'orthodoxy' and 'heresy'.[893]

It is only political factors, the interference of secular actions in the sacred sphere, that form an impulse for religious diversification.

The universality of the Holy Cross and its cult is demonstrated by numerous medieval testimonies from different parts of Europe. The apotheosis of this most sacred Relic was expressed among others in a text preserved in a manuscript located in the Italian abbey of Farfa:

[...] *Crux parvulorum custos, Crux virorum caput* [...], *Crux lumen in tenebris sedentium, Crux regum magnificentia, Crux scutum perpetuum* [...], *Crux libertas fervorum, Crux Imperatorum Philosophia, Crux lex impiorum* [...], *Crux martyrum gloriatio, Crux monachorum abstinentia* [...], *Crux idolorum repulsio* [...], *Crux invalidorum virtus* [...].[894]

[...] *The Cross* [is] *the guardian of the poor. The Cross* [is] *the commander of men* [...]. *The Cross* [is] *light for those sitting in darkness. The Cross* [is] *the magnificence of rulers. The Cross* [is] *an eternal shield* [...]. *The Cross* [is] *the freedom of the enslaved. The Cross* [is] *the philosophy of emperors. The Cross* [is] *the law* [meted out against] *the godless* [...]. *The Cross* [is] *the exaltation of martyrs. The Cross* [is] *the temperance of monks* [...]. *The Cross* [is] *the rejection of idols* [...]. *The Cross* [is] *the strength of the weak* [...].[895]

Here, the Cross seems a remedy to every evil and the crown of humankind's moral and cognitive capacities. What fragments of the *Chronicle* share with the quotation above is the conviction that the presence of the Cross gives man an opportunity to change and provides real help in social and personal life, strengthens certain states, confirms whether an action is proper, and indicates a forthcoming transformation. As a part of the world depicted, it is a potent testimony of God's presence in the life of individuals and a reference point for all the decisions of man.

At the start of this chapter, Nandy's expression 'colonisation of the mind' is cited. Is using it with respect to Cyprus appropriate? On the one hand, we have no cause to believe that Makhairas' Franks confronted

---

[893] Hedges, Controversies in Interreligious Dialogue, 87.
[894] 'Item Joan. Chrysostom. in Homilia 13. de Cruce Dominica' in Goldast, Collectio constitutionum imperialium, 169.
[895] Kupiszewska's translation from the Polish translation by the author.

the Greeks with their own assumptions about God. On the other, however, it is clearly apparent that they found it surprisingly easy to reach the Greeks' religious awareness thanks to the idea and significance of the Holy Cross, which formed the same foundation for their beliefs as it did for the Rhomaioi Cyprians. In the *Chronicle* the Latins show an ambiguous attitude towards sharing their spiritual reality with the Greek population. Emotions present in the text are expressed, jealousy and desire to possess being the strongest. The highlighted impulses that lead to shameful deeds (such as the greed of the Catholic priest Santamarin, which moved him to steal the Cross) show that the Franks did not unanimously accept a single coherent vision unifying the two Churches. In this particular light, the Franks' 'colonisation' of Cyprus may be perceived as an attempt to gain an advantage over the Orthodox population by acquiring the sole right to derive benefits from possession of the Relic.

2.2.4. Coexistence of different forms of cult

As the *Chronicle* states, with time the Franks settled on Cyprus worked out a form of coexistence with the Cyprians involving the acceptance of differences that unavoidably arose during the formation and establishment of their religious identities. One of the components of such an attitude is hospitality, in the sense of a non-judgemental mindset that is an attempt to find a plane of agreement with the 'other'. It does not mean the synthesis of both paradigms of faith.

In Leontios' world joint action by the Latins and Greeks undertaken to achieve a specific goal is most clearly manifested in the face of the cyclical plagues, epidemics and catastrophes that endanger all Cypriots without exception. For each of the sides, mutual contact, being a meeting with the 'other' who is never completely known, carries a certain element of uncertainty that creates tension, which often transforms into hostility as a result. It is no accident that at the basis of the phenomenon of negotiating identity is the dialectic relationship of hospitality and hostility. The latter is usually caused by fear of excessive submission and the loss of something significant.

In studies of the topic, the etymological reflection by Richard Kearney and James Taylor is noteworthy. The scholars conclude that

> *The common root of hospitality and hostility* – hostis – *carries this sense of primary wager between welcome or exclusion.*[896]

These two phenomena thus hold the same weight of becoming aware of the 'other' and carry an involuntary attempt to visualise and accept the manifestation of his presence.

The Rhomaioi's silence about the Franks in the *Chronicle* is neither an expression of complete hospitality nor of hostility. Marianne Moyaert calls such duality (simultaneous acceptance and rejection of another faith) inclusivism.[897] In Leontios' portrayal of these two attitudes we find reflected the double identity of the chronicler who, loyal to the royal court, expresses himself particularly diplomatically and subtly about Lusignan rule, recounting events with detachment and sophistication. A factor that contributed to the chronicler's approach was that he was born three centuries after the Lusignans had taken over the island. Loyal to his employer, having no experience of a different situation, he clearly takes pride in the careers of his family members at court, such as his father's participation in the selection of the king. On the other hand, aware of the dynasty's creeping decline, he vividly and daringly presents Cyprus' Byzantine past, and most importantly he does so in the Cypriot dialect.

The depiction of how identities are negotiated in Cyprus presented in the *Chronicle* shows a phenomenon that can be interpreted as a manifestation of inclusivism, i.e. to paraphrase Marianne Moyaert's definition, a position involving concurrent acceptance and rejection of another religion. According to Leontios, what Greeks and Latins on the island shared was, to use George Lindbeck's[898] terminology, 'a common core experience' in the presence of the relic of the Cross, as well as ritual forms of functioning, such as masses (λειτουργία/ λουτουργία),[899] processions and the sacrament of penance. To illustrate the process of negotiating identity as it occurred on Cypriot territory, approached from a different – namely architectural – perspective

---

[896] Kearney, Taylor, Introduction, 1.
[897] Moyaert, Fragile Identities, 22.
[898] After Moyaert, Fragile Identities, 147.
[899] The former word appears in the *Chronicle* four times (LM I 16, 17, III 416, 524), and the latter twice (LM III 524).

than the one seen in Makhairas' writing, a statement by Margit Mersch may be used. She identifies elements that indicate this process in the history of the church of Saints Peter and Paul in Famagusta.[900] Meanwhile, Paschali, having investigated with a particular focus on the fourteenth century the history of the church of St George of the Greeks, that is 'the ostentatious Orthodox cathedral of Famagusta',[901] describes masses concelebrated by the Latin clergy with Greek priests and joint prayers for a reversal of the adversities caused by plague, drought and flooding.[902] These comments reveal how rich the heritage experienced by the chronicler was and what impression the denominational and cultural mix in which he came to live must have made on him. Furthermore, his impressions and sensations had to be condensed and restricted by the lack of a broader perspective, because he had spent most of his life on the island.

Makhairas emphasises the important differences between the Latins and the Greeks in their religious practice and the cult forms practised by them that he was able to observe, for example in the sacrament of penance, though he does not use this word. The passage of the *Chronicle* relating to this sacrament is of interest for several reasons. First, it shows that at its basis was a common idea that was important to both Churches. Secondly, it highlights differences in the external form in which it was practised. Thirdly, it touches on the issue of sin, very important for the content of the *Chronicle*, and whose consequences include plague, disease, disaster, conflicts between communities and defeats in wars, as well as on absolution of sins. Fourthly, it is one of the few instances where the chronicler briefly reveals his views on the human fate after death, which he does not do either when discussing the significance of the Holy Cross or the phenomenon of the Relic. He introduces the notion of purgatory and hell, using the expressions: 'purgatorial fire' (πῦρ καθαρτήριον) and 'eternal fire' (πῦρ τὸ αἰώνιον), but makes no mention of heaven. He suggests that burning incense (τὸν φυμιατόν)[903] was a shared practice, while the use of holy water (νερὸν τοῦ ἁγιασμοῦ) appeared later. This distinction appears in a marked statement of Fra Marco, bishop of Ammochostos, who is 'jealous' (εἰ(ς) ζῆλαν) of the Cross found by the shepherd boy George. Motivated by 'great spite' (μὲ μεγάλην κακίαν), he said to the king:

> '[...] there are sins (ἁμαρτίες) which are pardoned (συγχωροῦνται) by the burning of incense (μὲ τὸν φυμιατόν)'[904] – now the Latins have water of sanctification which they make on Saturday (νερὸν τοῦ ἁγιασμοῦ τὸ πολομοῦν τὸ σαββάτον), and say they are pardoned by the holy water (συγχωροῦνται μὲ τὸ δρόσος[905]), – 'other sins are pardoned by prayer and fasting (διὰ προσευχῆς καὶ νηστείας), and others by the fire (διὰ τὸ λαμπρόν) which we call the fire of purgatory. But the sins which lead the people into unbelief (ὁποῦ σύρνουν τὸν λαὸν εἰς ἀπιστίαν), and the rulers of the people abide it (ἀπομεινίσκουν το),– these men go unpardoned into the everlasting fire (τοῦτοι πᾶσιν ἀσυμπάθητοι εἰς τὸ πῦρ τὸ αἰώνιον)'. (LM I 73)

In this passage, along with a discussion of the remission of sins, Makhairas demonstrates the ability to look at an issue from different perspectives, thus giving diversity a voice. At the same time, he does not resolve which group is right or which method he holds to as his own. With the expression 'the Latins have' (οἱ δὲ οἱ Λατῖνοι ἔχου) he establishes a caesura between the practices of the Greeks and of the Latins. It is Catholics who are convinced that certain sins and transgressions require purification in purgatory, which is an extension of the belief that each action should be judged, and each sin punished.

By following Makhairas' exposition, the reader can become acquainted with the way that the Christian community grew: the chronicler's attention is focused particularly on the religious situation prevalent under the rule of the Lusignan court. Namely, the *Chronicle* regularly features Catholics such as consecrated

---

[900] Mersch, Hybridity, 241–280.
[901] Paschali, Negotiating identities, 282.
[902] Paschali, Negotiating identities, 284.
[903] Sathas gives this as 'τὸν ριμιατόν'. See Σάθας (Ed.), Χρονογράφοι Βασιλείου Κύπρου, 87. In Mas Latrie (Ed.), Chronique de Strambaldi, 30, the whole fragment reads as follows: *son delli peccati, li quali si perdonano per pregheri, et sono delli pecati che si assolveno con il foco, cioè il purgatorio. Ma li peccati che tirano la gente in infideltà et li ricchi della gente permetteno questi, vanno, senza nissuna remissione, nel foco eterno*. Compared to Makhairas' text this is an abbreviated version.
[904] For more about the symbolism of incense in Christianity, see Harvey, Scenting Salvation. This book covers interesting matter of linking a given scent with the identity of the person exuding it (Harvey, Scenting Salvation, 125–134).
[905] The sequence 'καὶ λέγουν, συγχωροῦνται' is missing from Σάθας (Ed.), Χρονογράφοι Βασιλείου Κύπρου, 87.

persons from different orders, including the Dominicans,[906] Augustinians[907] and Franciscans[908] (including Clarisses[909]). We additionally encounter a nun (κολογριά) from the monastery of St Mamas (εἰς τὸν Ἅγιον Μάμαν),[910] brother (ἀδελφός) Wilmot, the canon (Χλιμὸτ ὁ τζανούνης)[911] and the Frankish monk (μοναχός) Gregory (φρὲ Γκικάλ).[912] This indicates that Catholicism expanded systematically and peacefully and that the Latins found space for their activity and a place within the structures of Cypriot society. Komodikis notes the presence of the following monastic orders (μοναχικὰ τάγματα) on Cyprus: Benedictines, Cistercians, Templars, Joannites (Hospitallers), Dominicans, Franciscans, Carmelites and Augustinians,[913] which shows how diverse the Catholic community of Cyprus was at the time.

Few direct mentions about the peaceful coexistence of Greeks and Latins in the form of a description of specific events or situations may be encountered in the *Chronicle*. These are usually brief pieces of information intended to signalise the phenomenon. We can assume that the chronicler is referring to the theme of such coexistence and mutual acceptance from a comment about a promise made by King Peter I to give thanks to God for safe return to Cyprus after a difficult military expedition, which was to involve visits to all monasteries of both rites located on the island,[914] and King Peter II's proclamation of 1373 forbidding both Greek and Frankish priests to sound a bell or semantron before dawn (οὐδὲ νὰ σημάνη καμπάνα, οὐδὲ σήμαντρον ὡς τὸ ξημέρωμαν, LM III 383).[915] Both these places indicate that Makhairas is attempting to depict the hybrid nature of the Greek and Latin formation, though he does this somewhat in passing.

A similar convention is used in the *Chronicle* to mention the issue of marriages contracted between persons who grew up in two different Christian traditions. As an example, the chronicler cites the matrimonial proposal made to King Peter II by the ruler of Constantinople, John V Palaiologos, in the name of his daughter.[916] Also of interest is a passage directly connected to the life of the author who, when mentioning Sir Philip (σὶρ Φιλίππε), states that he was:

a Latin priest (ἱερεὺς λατῖνος) and the son of a Greek nun (μίας καλογριᾶς Ῥωμέσσας), who was a cousin (ἐξάδελφη) of my father, Master Stavrinos Makhairas. (LM III 566)

An analysis of the above examples suggests that Makhairas perceived certain phenomena and situations as complementary and coinciding. The coexistence and co-functioning within the *Chronicle* narrative of spiritual elements belonging to different orders are indicated by the numerous cult objects it mentions. It systematically features icons placed in sanctuaries, for example in the already mentioned description of the monastery built at the wish of Queen Alice next to the church of the Revealed Cross,[917] and images (κυράδες).[918] Those presenting

---

[906] The *Chronicle* features: two Dominicans as messengers (δυὸ καλογήρους τοῦ Σὰν Τομένικου, LM I 53, 56); a confessor of the king (ὁ πνευματικὸς [...] ὀνόματι φρὲ Τζάκε τοῦ Σὰν Τομένικου, LM II 260); a superior of Dominican nuns (τὸ τοῦ πριούρη τοῦ Σὰν Τομένικου, LM III 394); the Dominican brother Matthew (φρὲ Ματαίου [...] ἀποὺ ὄρδινον τοῦ Σὰν Τομένικου, LM V 628); brother Angelo of St Dominic (φρὲ Ἄγγελος τοῦ Σὰν Τομένικου, LM V 699); and brother Solomon from the order of St Dominic, bishop of Tortosa (φρὲ Σαλάμος ἀπὸ τὸν ὄρδινον τοῦ Σὰν Τομένικου ἐπίσκοπος Ταρτούζας, LM VI 706).

[907] Leontios mentions only one Augustinian monk (ἕναν καλόγηρον Αὐγουστίνον, LM III 360).

[908] Franciscans, under the name of 'Friars Minor' (εἰς τοὺς Φρὲ Μενούριδες) appear in LM III 289, 330.

[909] The *Chronicle* contains the expression 'a Clarisse from St Photeini' (εἰς τὴν Ἁγίαν Φωτεινήν, LM II 237). A more detailed description may be found in: LM II 248–249, 265. The following publications deal with St Photeini, that is St Clare, and her namesakes: Constanelos, Christian Faith and Cultural Heritage, 14; Swann, The Forgotten Desert Mothers; Spetsieris, The Hermitess Photini. See Dawkins, Notes, 128.

[910] LM III 570. According to Dawkins this cannot be 'the St Mamas of § 429, which lie seven miles from Lefkosia. It must be the church of that name in the town [...].' (Dawkins, Notes, 194).

[911] LM IV 599.

[912] LM V 630.

[913] Κωμοδίκης, Οἱ Πληροφορίες τῶν Βραχέων Χρονικῶν, 48.

[914] LM II 246.

[915] Dawkins explains: 'In the Levant people are summoned to church very often not by bells but by a *semantron*, a clapper; either a specially shaped plank or a curved metal hoop: both are suspended by a cord and struck with a mallet. These clappers are used specially in monasteries, and for the less festive occasions: when the Turks later forbade bells, they permitted the use of the *semantron*.' (Dawkins, Notes, 158).

[916] LM III 346.

[917] LM I 76.

[918] The image of St Christopher (ἕναν εἰκόνισμαν τὸν ἅγιον Χριστόφορον μάρτυραν), LM I 40, the icon of St Nicholas (τὴν εἰκόναν τοῦ μεγάλου Νικολάου), LM II 127; 'images' (εἰκονίσματα) in the plural, with no details of what they portrayed, LM IV 623. Nicolaou-Konnari draws attention to the intensive practise of writing icons in medieval Cyprus. She writes: 'A study of icon painting in Cyprus in the thirteenth century points to a prolific output of icons produced on the island and intensive

the Virgin Mary merit particular attention, including: 'the icon of the Most Holy Mother of God' (ἡ εἰκόνα τῆς ὑπεραγίας Θεοτόκου) of the Kykko monastery in Marathasa (εἰς τὴν Μαραθάσαν εἰς τὸν Κύκκον),[919] 'the miraculous icon of Kouroukiotissa (the Virgin of Gorhigos), an icon of the Mother of God' (ἡ θαυμαστή εἰκόνα τῆς Κουρουκιώτισσας εἰκόνα τῆς θε(οτόκ)ου)[920] or 'the icon of the Mother of God of Cyprus written by the Apostle Luke' (ἡ εἰκόνα τῆς Κύπρου Θεοτόκου, τὴν ἐζωγράφισεν ὁ ἀπόστολος Λουκᾶς).[921] In popular reception, the first of these three icons is the best-known. Hans Belting describes it thus:

> *The Virgin of Kykkos [...] reverses the roles of Mother and Child in that the Mother presses the Child to her face, while the Child tries to tear himself free from her with impatient kicking and a violent grab at her veil. The rhetorical figure inherent in the motif of kicking (periskirton) occurs in texts on the presentation of Jesus in the temple, which make the Child break away from his Mother to leap into the arms of Simeon.*[922]

The chronicler does not cite any specific features of the image, but he does provide precise information about it, allowing the portrayal to be identified and the history of its creation to be discovered. When he wrote about the icon of the Virgin written by the hand of St Luke,[923] Makhairas likely meant the iconographic model of 'Our Lady of the Way' or 'She Who Shows the Way',[924] that is the *Hodegetria/Hodigitria* (Ὁδηγήτρια).[925] By focusing on the period in which the Cypriot community recognised this portrayal to be particularly important, he indicates that his convictions and feelings may be rooted in Orthodox Christianity. On the margin, it should be added that Doula Mouriki argues that the image is of Cypriot origin.[926] According to MS O, Peter I ordered the creation of the icon in the Church of Mercy at the top of Margaret tower.[927] The term εἰκόνα in the meaning of 'image' other than an 'icon' in the technical sense was used by Leontios in LM I 13, in a passage telling of the Templars, to indicate a crucifix: 'image of Jesus Christ, the Living God' ([ἡ] εἰκόνα τοῦ Ἰησοῦ Χριστοῦ τοῦ θεοῦ τοῦ ζῶντος) and 'image of the Lord' ([ἡ] εἰκόνα τοῦ Κυρίου).

However, the author of the *Chronicle* does not give much prominence to the person of the Virgin Mary. Comments about the icons are basically the only pretext for referring to her. In the narrative we encounter no statements of the type that may be found in Machaut's work, where King Peter I turns to the Virgin in his suffering:

> *De Dieu ancelle,*
> *Vierge, glorieuse pucelle,*
> *Vierge pucelle, Vierge mere,*
> *Mere dou fil, et fille au pere [...]*[928]

> *Handmaid of God,*
> *Glorious virgin and maiden,*
> *Virgin girl, virgin wife,*
> *Mother of the Son and daughter to the Father [...]*[929]

---

private Greek patronage. The existence of some 20 large icons, designed for public use in churches, reflects a context of Greek patronage rich and powerful enough to maintain both the activity of artistic workshops and the development of a "self-sustaining local manner", the *maniera Cypria* [...].' (Nicolaou-Konnari, Greeks, 48).

[919] LM I 37. Cf. Carr, Morrocco, A Byzantine Masterpiece; Ryder, Micromosaic Icons.
[920] LM II 114-115.
[921] LM III 368. Pavlidis' comment suggests that this is the first icon found on Paphos, which arrived from Anatolia. See Παυλίδης (Ed.), Λεοντίου Μαχαιρᾶ Χρονικόν, 269.
[922] Belting, Likeness and Presence, 290.
[923] Woods, Encountering Icons, 136.
[924] Shabliy, Representations of the Blessed Virgin Mary, 136.
[925] The *Hodegetria* is one of the four main icon types, next to 'Orans', 'Eleusa' and 'Akathist' (Charkiewicz, Ikony Matki Bożej, 153-154). As Victor Lasareff demonstrated, this was 'one of the commonest iconographic types in Byzantine art' (Lasareff, Studies in the Iconography, 46).
[926] Mouriki, A Thirteenth-Century Icon, 403.
[927] LM II 260. Cf. Dawkins (Ed., transl.), Ἐξήγησις/ Recital, 240 (fn. 2); Παυλίδης (Ed.), Λεοντίου Μαχαιρᾶ Χρονικόν, 192 (fn. 3).
[928] Guillaume de Machaut, La prise d'Alexandrie, 271 (v. 8762).
[929] Translation after Palmer (Ed., transl.), La Prise D'Alixandre, 411.

In the *Chronicle*, icons that signalise the holiness of the personages they depict have, similarly to relics, significant power and perform an important function. While human remains usually rested only in selected spots and were the foundation for erecting churches, icons could be moved regularly (at cyclical intervals) from place to place in processions in order to propitiate God so that he would reverse an undesirable state of affairs. In several places Makhairas cites events that moved the Cypriots to organise thanksgiving and propitiatory processions. The most frequent reason for such decisions was plagues, particularly plagues of locusts, which with other disasters Makhairas calls a 'deadly [plague]' (θανατικόν). During one such unfavourable episode King Hugh ordered an icon (ἕναν εἰκόνισμαν) depicting St Christopher (τὸν ἅγιον Χριστόφορον) the Martyr (μάρτυραν), St Tarasios (τὸν ἅγιον Ταράσιον), the patriarch of Constantinople (ὁ πατριάρχης Κωνσταντινουπόλεως), and St Tryphon the Martyr (ἅγιον Τρύφον μάρτυραν) to be written (ἐζωγραφῆσαν). The chronicler comments thus:

> [...] *and they sent it* [the icon – note M.G.] *to Palokythro, where the plague was. And he*[930] *told them that when the locust hatched they should carry the picture in procession* (νὰ λιτανεύουν τὸ εἰκόνισμαν) *and say mass* (νὰ λ(ει)τουργᾷ), *and the Lord will protect the crops* (ὁ κύριος νὰ φυλάξῃ τοὺς καρπούς).
> (LM I 40)

Iconographic depictions thus gained an agentive significance: they awoke the awareness of the presence of selected saints and appealed for constant intercession.

In the *Chronique d'Amadi* we also encounter mentions of icons. In one of two such descriptions, the Italian text presents Benedictine nuns from the Holy Cross monastery, later called the 'Monastery of Our Lady of Tortosa' (*le monache della Nostra Donna de Tortosa*), as they prepare to receive 'the image of Our Lady' (*per la immagine della Nostra Donna*) at Pentecost in 1308. As the translator of the *Chronicle* into Italian emphasises, thanks to the image (*per la qual figura*) the monastery received high alms (*molte helemosine*).[931] To read the next comment featuring an icon, a move to 1362 is necessary, when the turcopolier went to Myra with his fleet, whence he took the image of St Nicholas (*la immagine del signor San Nicolò*). No mention is made there about its properties or powers.[932] Based on these two – and only! – examples it may be seen that icons did not have any particular importance for this author who had read Makhairas' vision of history.

When examining how Leontios mentions icons and the context in which he places them, one may conclude that mainly their presence is important to him, which is why they are not described in detail. In his theoretical sketch, Jesús Castellano Cervera OCD discusses the aspect of the icon's meaning, emphasising that the living presence is the feature that gives the whole liturgy its value.[933] Another aspect of Marian iconography that is important from the perspective of this work and the analysed text is its ecumenical character, as cited by Zdzisław Józef Kijas OFMConv: a feature that he believes to 'flow from its very internal structure'[934] because it connects the material and the non-material sphere.[935] When mentioning the author of an image, Makhairas sets the holiness of this figure next to the significance of the portrayal for the whole Christian community. This particular manifestation of the cult of the icon in the Cypriot text recalls another statement by Kijas, who claims that the ecumenical nature of an image is expressed in the experience of its mystery because it unites the Churches 'on a plane that is both extremely important and extremely difficult: the cultural'.[936]

Icons that according to tradition were written by St Luke, a figure worshipped by Greeks and Latins alike, played a particular role also because their evident part in the process of Christianity's establishment on the island was a guarantee of their exceptionalness. It was they that, as further reading of the *Chronicle* will prove, would greatly contribute to repelling the might of the Saracen invader.

---

[930] Ignatios, patriarch of Antioch.
[931] Mas Latrie (Ed.), Chronique d'Amadi, 292; Coureas, Edbury (Transl.), The Chronicle of Amadi, 272 (§ 580).
[932] Mas Latrie (Ed.), Chronique d'Amadi, 412.
[933] Cervera, Teologia i duchowość, 41. Cervera emphasises that the Virgin Mary is a 'pure image of God' and 'clarity of the Spirit' (Cervera, Teologia i duchowość, 44. Cervera's Polish expressions translated by Kupiszewska). As Tadeusz Dionizy Łukaszuk OSPPE notes, the icon is closely linked to the mystery of the Incarnation (Łukaszuk, Wcielenie fundamentem ikony, 26).
[934] Kijas, Perspektywy ekumeniczne, 75. Kupiszewska's translation from the Polish translation by the author.
[935] Kijas, Perspektywy ekumeniczne, 75–76.
[936] Kijas, Perspektywy ekumeniczne, 86. Kupiszewska's translation from the Polish translation by the author.

Next to icons and the Relic, artefacts also hold an important function in Makhairas' work. These can be both small objects with a symbolical meaning such as a nail from the church of St George of the Pulans (ἔναν καρφὶν εἰς τὸν Ἅγιον Γεώργιον τῶν Ὀρνιθίων),[937] and churches of both rites that share the same space[938] – next to Catholic churches of Santa Sophia (Ἁγιά Σοφιά),[939] St Nicholas (Ἅγιος Νικόλαος)[940] and St Dominic (Σὰν Τομένικο),[941] Rhomaioi churches (τὰς ἐκκλησίας τῶν Ρωμαίων) are mentioned,[942] such as the church of St Mamas (τοῦ Ἁγίου Μάμα).[943] The case of other objects that have no detailed description in the *Chronicle* is similar.

Also feasts and prayer times turn out to be important to the author, being an element that unifies the two denominations. Under this heading the following events mentioned by Makhairas are counted: 'the feast of the Virgin Mary' (τὴν ἡμέραν τῆς Θεοτόκου),[944] events related to the Holy Week,[945] eves of other holidays such as 'the eve of St Nicholas' day' (τὴν παραμονὴν τοῦ ἁγίου Νικολάου)[946] and 'St Antony's eve' (τὴν παραμονὴν τοῦ ἁγίου Ἀντωνίου),[947] and also masses celebrated in the name of various aspects of the Creator, for example in the name of the Holy Trinity (λουτουργία εἰς τὸ ὄνομαν τῆς ἁγίας Τριάδος),[948] those related to making various kinds of oaths: on the Body of Christ (ἐποῖκεν καὶ ἐλειτουργῆσαν, καὶ ἀπάνω εἰς τὸ κορμὶν τοῦ Χριστοῦ)[949] or on the Bible (ὠμόσαν ἔμπροσθεν τοῦ ρηγὸς ἀπάνω εἰς τὰ ἅγια τοῦ θεοῦ εὐαγγέλια).[950] In the *Chronicle*, time is measured by holidays, 'forefeasts' (παραμονή),[951] i.e. eves, and periods delimited by different holidays, such as 'Mid-Pentecost' (μεσοπεντήκοστον), which has Orthodox overtones because in the Greek Church this day is celebrated as a separate holiday.[952]

In the *Synaxaria of the Pentecostarion* the verses contain the following fragment:

Standing in the midst of the teachers
Christ the Messiah teacheth at Mid-feast.[953]

In the *Chronique d'Amadi* the situation is similar. We read of 'the feast of St Agatha' (*la festa de Sancta Agatha*),[954] 'St Luke's day' (*el di de San Luca*),[955] 'All Saints' Day' (*Davanti la Tusans*),[956] 'St John's

---

[937] LM I 65. Miller and Sathas translate this as *un clou dans l'eglise de Saint-Georges des Poulains*. See Sathas, Miller (Eds, transl.), Chronique de Chypre, 40. Cf. Κωμοδίκης, Οι Πληροφορίες των Βραχέων Χρονικών, 209–210.

[938] Makhairas mentions also the churches of: St George of the Pulans (ὁ Ἅγιος Γεώργιος τῶν Ὀρνιθίων, LM I 51, II 274, 276); St George in Dadas (ὁ Ἅγιος Γεώργιος τῆς Δαδᾶς, LM II 192); Mercy (–ναὸν ὀνόματι– Μιζερικορδία, LM II 260); St George of Adalia (κατὰ πρόσωπα τοῦ Ἀταλιώτη, LM IV 607); St Epiktitos (ἀπὸ τὸν Ἅγιον Πίκτητον, LM IV 611); St Reginos (τὸ μερτικὸν τοῦ Ἁγίου Ρηγίνου, LM IV 620); St Sergios (εἰς τὸν Ἅγιον Σέργιον, LM III 448, V 654); St Antony (εἰς τὸν Ἅγιον Ἰωάννην, LM III 470); St Eugnomon (εἰς τὸν ναὸν τοῦ Ἁγίου Εὐνομένος, LM III 524); St George (εἰς τὸν ναὸν τοῦ Ἁγίου (Γ) εωργίου, LM III 332); St Afxivios (εἰς τὸν Ἅγιον Εὐξίφην, LM III 377, IV 613); St Marina, near Adalia (εἰς τὸ ναὸν τῆς Ἁγίας Μαρίνας πλησίον τῆς Ἀταλείας, LM III 283).

[939] LM II 90, 101, III 310, 324, 570, V 628, 698–699, VI 706, 708, 710. See Andrews, Santa Sophia, 63–80; Andrews, Conveyance and Convergence.

[940] Both the church of Santa Sophia in present-day Nicosia and the church of St Nicholas in Famagusta are currently used as mosques.

[941] LM I 63, 86, III 427, 554, IV 627.

[942] LM I 72.

[943] LM III 429, 570.

[944] LM I 41.

[945] 'Holy Thursday' (ἁγία Πέμπτη, LM I 77); 'Easter Day' (ἡμέρα τοῦ πασχάτου, LM II 104); 'Holy and Great Sunday of Easter' (ἁγία καὶ μεγάλη κυριακὴ τοῦ πάσχα, LM II 219); 'Holy Sunday' (ἁγία κυριακή, LM II 220); '[Great] Lent and Holy Week' (σαρακοστή; τὴν ἁγίαν ἑβδομάδαν, LM II 260); 'Paschal Week' (ἑβδομάδα τοῦ Πασχάτου, LM III 569); 'Tuesday of the Paschal Week' (τρίτη τῆς Λαμπρῆς, LM III 570); 'Holy Lent' (ἁγία σαρακοστή, LM IV 607, 609); 'Easter Sunday' (ἁγία κυριακή, LM V 630).

[946] LM III 549.

[947] LM II 279.

[948] LM III 524.

[949] LM III 551.

[950] LM III 526.

[951] E.g.: LM II 279, III 549. The term 'forefeast (Gr paramone)' is given in the Orthodox context by Fr Alciviadis Calivas in Calivas, Oddawanie czci Bogu, 66.

[952] LM V 700.

[953] Vaporis (Ed.), The Divine Liturgy, 246 (https://www.goarch.org/-/the-divine-liturgy-of-saint-basil-the-great, accessed 24 November 2021).

[954] Mas Latrie (Ed.), Chronique d'Amadi, 36.

[955] Mas Latrie (Ed.), Chronique d'Amadi, 39.

[956] Mas Latrie (Ed.), Chronique d'Amadi, 74.

eve' (*la vigilia di San Joanne*)⁹⁵⁷ and 'St Martin's day' (*il dì de san Marti*).⁹⁵⁸ An oathmaking combined with a mass also appears in Boustronios' chronicle.⁹⁵⁹

The author of the *Chronicle* mentions architectural facilities that took their appellations from saints' names. Among them he lists bridges, for example 'the bridge of the Holy Apostles' (τὸ γιοφύριν τοὺς Ἁγίους Ἀποστόλους, LM III 434, 436) and 'the Bridge of St Dominic' (τὸ γιοφύριν τοῦ Σὰν Τεμένικου, LM III 571), public gates, such as the gate of St Parskevi and the gate of St Andrew (β' πόρτες καθολικὲς […] τῆς Ἁγίας Παρασκευῆς καὶ τοῦ Ἁγίου Ἀντρέα),⁹⁶⁰ towers, including 'the tower of St Andrew' (ὁ πύργος τοῦ Ἁγίου Ἀνδρέου, LM III 424), and also other public buildings, like 'St Augustine's inn' (ὁ ξενοδοχεῖον τοῦ Σαντ Ἀκοστή, LM V 642).

All these forms of cult, buildings with a sacral function⁹⁶¹ or even those called after a saint, belonging to both rites, coexist in the *Chronicle* and are an expression of inclusivism in its accepting aspect. The concurrent functioning of Greek and Latin components becomes possible particularly where 'a common core experience' is realised (Mystery of the Passion, cult of saints, celebration of holidays focused on personal and collective participation in the mysteries of the Gospel). At the centre of this experience are objects that are the target of special worship, whose very presence is sufficient to call up an image of community and to designate the boundary along which the two Churches' spheres of influence adjoin and the space where they are both present.

2.3. Conflicts in the Christian community

Makhairas recounts that the appearance of the Franks on the island led to the disorganisation of the previous order, which was directly due to their takeover of power and the gradual strengthening of their position: not only by creating their own state structure and issuing new laws, but also by erecting religious buildings, gifting land and transferring bishoprics from Greek into Latin hands. Hill, based on the *Histoire de l'île de Chypre* by Mas Latrie and Ernoul's testimony (12th c.),⁹⁶² emphasises that as early as in the time of Guy in his role of King Richard Cœur de Lion's vassal there occurred in Cyprus a gradual transformation of the social and religious structure,⁹⁶³ which he phrases thus:

> […] *the transplantation into Cyprus of a society of feudal customs and Christian faith inevitably meant that those customs, laws and cults were carried with them into their new land.*⁹⁶⁴

Hill concludes that the originator and proponent of introducing and establishing the Latin church on the island was Amaury, Guy's brother and constable of Jerusalem.⁹⁶⁵ The donation to the Knights Templar was made during his reign, on 29 September 1195, but as Hill stresses,

> *anything like a regular establishment to balance, or overbalance, the Greek Church, there was not, until Aimery took steps to inaugurate it.*⁹⁶⁶

Further on, Hill mentions Pope Celestine III's bull of 20 February 1196,⁹⁶⁷ addressed to the clergy, lords and population of Cyprus, announcing that Amaury had sent the Archdeacon of Laodicea to Rome

---

⁹⁵⁷ Mas Latrie (Ed.), Chronique d'Amadi, 77.
⁹⁵⁸ Mas Latrie (Ed.), Chronique d'Amadi, 92.
⁹⁵⁹ Dawkins (Transl., int.), The Chronicle of George Boustronios, 45–46, 58, 278–59.
⁹⁶⁰ Gate of St Parskevi, LM III 395, 408, 434, 437, 594, IV 623; Gate of St Andrew, LM III 395, 433, 436–438.
⁹⁶¹ Also objects connected to spiritual life are present throughout the *Chronicle*, such as: monastic habits (μοναχικὸν σχῆμα), silver vessels (ἱερὰ ἀργυρᾶ), books (βιβλία), a cross of walnut wood (ἕναν σταυρὸν μέγαν, ξυλένον κάρυνον) steeped in perfume (ἐμύρωσέν τον μὲ γ' λοὲς), a cross in silk under a canopy, etc. LM I 77.
⁹⁶² Mas Latrie, Histoire de l'île de Chypre I, II, III.
⁹⁶³ Hill, A History of Cyprus II, 43–44.
⁹⁶⁴ Hill, A History of Cyprus II, 43.
⁹⁶⁵ Hill, A History of Cyprus II, 44–45.
⁹⁶⁶ Hill, A History of Cyprus II, 45.
⁹⁶⁷ Mas Latrie, Histoire de l'île de Chypre III, 599: *Bulle de Célestin III prévenant le clergé, les grands et le peuple de Chypre, qu'à la demande d'Amaury, seigneur de l'île, le saint siège a délégué l'archidiacre de Laodicée et Alain, chancelier de Chypre, pour régler tout ce qui pouvait concerner l'établissement et la dotation de l'église catholique en ce pays, jusqu'ici schismatique.*

in order 'to bring the schismatic Greeks back to the true fold'.⁹⁶⁸ As a result of the decree the Latin Church was organised as the archdiocese of Lefkosia with three suffragan dioceses covering the area of the former Greek dioceses:⁹⁶⁹ Paphos with Arsinoe,⁹⁷⁰ Lemesos with Kourion and Amathus, and Ammochostos with Mesaoria proper and the Karpasi peninsula.⁹⁷¹ Hill himself uses the term 'diminution' to describe what happened to the property of the Greek Church.⁹⁷²

As regards the issue of restricting the rights of Rhomaian bishops, according to the medieval texts that Hill uses as his source it was not immediate, occurring only in 1222.⁹⁷³ Listing the decisions of a different papal bull of 13 December 1196, the scholar indicates that it contained a clear announcement of forthcoming control: a list of penalties, principles for taking over inherited rights in cemeteries, a prohibition against building churches without the bishop's permission and against taking the position of priest or chaplain without permission of bishop.⁹⁷⁴ In another place, he reflects that if Cyprus had not fallen into Lusignan hands, it would have gone to the Armenians.⁹⁷⁵

The depiction of the island's conquest by the Franks in LM I 20–21 is particularly ascetic. Its consequences appear in further parts of the *Chronicle*. In the narrative about the Latins, Makhairas introduces the persons of several popes, choosing only a few of the twenty-four notables to hold this office between the twelfth and fifteenth century⁹⁷⁶ and leaving unspoken his attitude towards them. This is how he describes the takeover of spiritual power in Cyprus:

> *Then the kings and the lords one after another built churches and many monasteries (and courts for the bishops in Lefkosia; and they began Santa Sophia). And they made the assizes, and arranged that they should have their revenues to live upon. And (the tithes and) the villages which had belonged to the Greek dioceses, they (took away and) gave to the Latins. Then when the emperor saw the penury of the (Greek)⁹⁷⁷ bishops of Cyprus (τὴν στενὴν ζωὴν τοὺς ἀρχιερεῖς (τῶν ἐπισκόπων Ῥωμαίων) τῆς Κύπρου), that they had no church tithes, (the kings) made concessions (ἐσυγκατέβησαν), and he gave them villages and other revenues (χωργιὰ καὶ ἄλλα εἰσσοδέματα), to each one of them as seemed good to him (τοῦ πασανοῦ κατὰ τοῦ ἐφάνην). And in such a manner the kings took away the property of the bishops under pretexts (ἐσηκῶσαν τα οἱ ρηγάδες ἀπὲ τοὺς ἐπισκόπους διὰ ἀφορμές), and they hold them even to the present day, and give them as gifts to the knights (χαρίζουν τα τοὺς καβαλλάριδες), (and they give them to the clerics and to whom they please). Whatever was in the hands of the Greek⁹⁷⁸ bishops has been taken away and given to the Latins.* (LM I 29)

This fragment clearly proves the attention to detail of the author, an official at the Lusignan court, as well as his caution in expressing opinions. He presents the actions of the settlers as a natural consequence of the 'colonial' situation. Apart from interfering with the Cyprian administration, politics and society, Makhairas' Cypriot Franks also challenged the religious beliefs of the native Rhomaian population, and motivated by jealousy (ἐζηλεῦγαν) and envy (φθονοῦν; διὰ φθόνον), accused them of perfidy, which can be seen in the attitude of bishop Fra Marco, already mentioned (pp. 116, 121). The above comment indicates

---

⁹⁶⁸ Hill, History of Cyprus II, 46. Mas Latrie, Histoire de l'ile de Chypre III, 600: *Sane, quia, sicut ex tenore litterarum dilecti filii nobilis viri A. domini Cipri, perpendimus evidenter, ipse Dei scientiam, ejus inspiratione dumtaxat, in singularitate fidei possidet, et romanam ecclesiam, caput et magistram ecclesiarum omnium recognoscens, Cipri insulam, cujus dominium divina potius credimus quam humana ei potestate collatum, a suis tandem erroribus suo diligenti studio revocatam a beluato fermentatorum scismate ad unitatem ortodoxe matris ecclesie reducere studio se contendit, sicut per dilectum filium magistrum B. archidiaconum Laodicensem, nuntium suum, virum utique providum et discretum, nobis est manifestius intimatum [...]*.
⁹⁶⁹ These Orthodox dioceses were: Lefkosia, Kition, Kerynia, Kithraia, Lapithos, Solia, Tamassos and Trimythos. After Hill, A History of Cyprus II, 46.
⁹⁷⁰ Dawkins, Notes, 55.
⁹⁷¹ Hill, A History of Cyprus II, 46–47.
⁹⁷² Hill, A History of Cyprus II, 47.
⁹⁷³ Hill, A History of Cyprus II, 47.
⁹⁷⁴ Precise quotation after Hill, A History of Cyprus II, 48.
⁹⁷⁵ Hill, A History of Cyprus II, 130.
⁹⁷⁶ Celestine III, Innocent III, Honorius III, Gregory IX, Celestine IV, Innocent IV, Alexander IV, Urban IV, Clement IV, Gregory X, Innocent V, Adrian V, John XXI, Nicholas III, Martin IV, Honorius IV, Nicholas IV, Celestine V, Boniface VIII, Benedict XI, Clement V, John XXII, Benedict XII, Clement VI. Listed after Dopierała, Księga papieży.
⁹⁷⁷ Rhomaioi.
⁹⁷⁸ Rhomaian.

that not all passages of the *Chronicle* are free from an emotional attitude and that in these few fragments the chronicler finds the courage to express his more radical and decided opinion about the invaders:

> *When the Latins saw this they were jealous and were saying that it is no miracle of the cross, but the Greeks[979] were working miracles by magic arts. Others said: 'Nay, but the miracles are worked by the cross.'* (LM I 67)

And another passage with the same message:

> *And because the Latins envy the Greeks,[980] they hide (κρύβγουν[981]) the miracles that are worked by the icons and by the pieces of the Holy Wood in the churches of the Greeks:[982] not because they disbelieve, but because they are envious. For this reason the Latin churchmen (κλησιαστικοὶ λατῖνοι) used to say that the Cross is not of the Holy Wood (ὁ σταυρὸς δὲν εἶνε τίμιον ξύλον), but the miracles are worked by craft (τὰ θαύματα γινίσκουνται ἀπού τέχνες).* (LM I 72)[983]

Jealousy is one of the strongest emotions expressed in the *Chronicle*. It reflects the feeling of having encountered 'otherness', that is core alterity, and the consciousness of lacking something that the 'other' possesses, which in turn engenders anxiety about losing (spiritual and material) influence and significance. One interesting expression, 'not for lack of faith, but for envy' (ὄχι δι' ἀπιστίαν, ἀμμὲ διὰ φθόνον) plainly expresses Makhairas' belief that the Greek and the Latin denominations have both substance that is shared and substance that is separate. In LM II 99 Makhairas returns to the issue he raised in LM I 29, summarising the course of the transaction pursuant to which the island was sold, and which heralded the new state of affairs:

> *I have now told you how the kingdom was turned away (ἐστράφην) from the Greeks[984] and given (ἐδόθην) to the Latins, and how they brought strangers (ἐφέραν ξενικούς) to govern the country, and how they made the Assizes and how the king and the knights swore (ἐμόσαν) to maintain them (νὰ τοὺς κρατοῦν), and how they brought Latin clerks (ἐφέραν λογάδες λατίνους) and built churches, and many matters (πολλὰ πράγματα), and the order of the kings until King Peter (πῶς οἱ ρηγάδες ἐγέννοντο ὡς τοῦ ρὲ Πιέρ). And beginning from him I shall tell you all that in the world God grants that men may tell (ὅσο νὰ δώσῃ ὁ θεὸς νὰ τὸ ξηγοῦνται εἰς τὸν κόσμον).* (LM II 99)[985]

In this passage, the key word is βλέπιση ('control', 'oversight, 'guarding') meaning observation of the newly-conquered place in order to keep in check the vitality and action of the 'colonised' population. This passage eloquently shows that the Franks appropriated land belonging to the Cypriots without their consent, and power over the latter was seized by 'strangers' (ξενικοί). This is one of the places in the *Chronicle* where the (post)colonial overtones are the most legible.

Fractures in the Christian community were due to various factors. Makhairas describes incidents that illustrate the Greek-Latin conflict. On their basis it may be speculated that in his opinion a significant role in mutual misunderstandings was played by fear of the unknown, of a deformation of the familiar world and the rules governing it, and by lack of knowledge, manifested by both sides.

The chronicler notes a case of forced conversion from the Greek to the Latin faith when he recounts the arrival in Cyprus of the papal legate, a monk from the order of the Virgin Mary from Mount Carmel. He clearly specifies that this newcomer's aim was to 'convert' (νὰ τοὺς κουφερμιάσῃ) the Rhomaian

---

[979] Rhomaioi.
[980] Rhomaioi.
[981] Σάθας (Ed.), Χρονογράφοι Βασιλείου Κύπρου, 87: 'τὸ κλαῦμαν'.
[982] Rhomaioi.
[983] Kyrris comments this fragment as follows: 'Leontios refers here to an incident of 1340, when Mark the Latin bishop of Famagusta contested the genuineness of the cross of Tokhni, one of the crosses allegedly brought by Helena to the island [...]' (Kyrris, Some Aspects, 187). In Mas Latrie (Ed.), Chronique de Strambaldi, 29 one of the reasons for the Latins' reaction is also fear: *Et per il timor delli Latini, tenivano secretti li miracoli che facevano le immagini et li honorandi legni delle chiese greche; et non per infideltà, ma per invidia, et dicevano che la crose non era falta dal santo legno, et questi erano li clerici latini, ma che li miracoli venivano fatti per arte.*
[984] Rhomaioi.
[985] This fragment does not appear in Strambaldi's text.

population.⁹⁸⁶ Belief in a common God shared by the two Churches did not prevent the zealous Latin from undertaking individual efforts to bring the Greeks closer to what he believed the truth. Such an approach may have been related to the legate's misunderstood concern for other individuals, and thus the desire to take responsibility for them; it may also have been an expression of pride, consisting in placing himself above others. Leontios does not comment on the monk's behaviour or judge it, but relates the course of events in detail.

Brother Peter de Thomas (φρέρε Πιέρην τε Τουμᾶς) arrived on the island at a transitional moment, when the understanding between the faithful of different Christian denominations on Cyprus was still forming. The papal legate's visit initially promised dialogue and respect, heralded the strengthening of the Cyprians in their faith and was also a chance for the whole community to participate in the creation of a shared spiritual universe. Rhomaian bishops received the arrival in a friendly manner, with due respect and all honours, unconscious of the threat he posed to the community they headed. When under the Carmelite's influence the Franks decided to barricade the Greek clergy in the cathedral of Santa Sophia, there was an 'uproar' (τὴν ταραχήν). Makhairas clearly emphasises that the hidden intentions of the stranger were in opposition to the Rhomaian clergy's beliefs about the object of his visit. Peter attempted to impose the new faith by force, which in turn caused the local population to intervene using battering rams, and also by starting a fire. The whole incident was described as follows:

> *On Monday the eighth of December 1359 there appeared in the harbour of Kerynia a galley fully fitted out, and in her came a legate from the pope (ἕνας ληγάτος τοῦ πάπα), whose name was Brother Peter de Thomas of the order of Carmel: and he came to Lefkosia. And King Peter and all the lords received him with great honour (ἐπερίλάβαν τον πολλὰ τιμημένα). And his intention was to make the Greeks⁹⁸⁷ Latins (νὰ ποίσῃ τοὺς Ῥωμαίους Λατίνους), and he wanted to give them confirmation (κουφερμιάσῃ); and there arose a great uproar (μέγαν σκάνταλον⁹⁸⁸) between the Greeks⁹⁸⁹ and the Latins. And he sent to fetch the bishops and abbots (and priests),⁹⁹⁰ and they (all) came one day to Santa Sophia, and the bishops did not know of his intentions (δὲν ἔξευραν τὸ θέλημάν του). And when they had gone into the church the doors were shut. -And they seized upon¬ a priest,⁹⁹¹ whose surname was Mantzas (Μαντζᾶς): and the rest of the people resisted (ἐδιαφεντεύγουνταν), and the Franks ¬tried to confirm them by force (ἐδυναστεῦγαν), and a great uproar arose.¬ The people heard the tumult and ran to go into Santa Sophia,⁹⁹² and they did not allow them, but bolted themselves in. Then they went and brought a great beam to break down the doors, and others kindled a fire (to burn them). When the king heard what had happened, he sent his brother the prince and the admiral and the sheriff of Lefkosia, and they gave orders for Santa Sophia to be opened, and restrained the people, who drew back to one side. And at once they brought out the Greek bishops (and abbots) and priests, and bade them continue to act as they were accustomed (ὥρίσαν τους νὰ πολομοῦν κατὰ τὸ ἦσαν συνηθισμένοι). And the legate they ordered to leave the island (τον νὰ 'φκαιρέσῃ τὸ νησσίν). (LM I 101)*

A multilayered image emerges from this fragment. According to Makhairas, Peter de Thomas came at the express order of Pope Innocent VI, well-prepared for the expedition, his boat being 'equipped with

---

⁹⁸⁶ LM II 101 (examples of voluntary conversion are to be found in: LM III 579, IV 599). Olympios cites the figure of Peter de Thomas, accenting that he died on the island and was buried in Famagusta. Peter I requested chancellor Philippe de Mézières to record the monk's life, which was to become an important document in his canonisation process, but the Carmelite's case met with a negative decision and the murder of King Peter I curbed the process aimed at sanctioning the cult of this person in Cyprus. As Olympios emphasises after Philippe de Mézières, various 'schismatics' and 'unbelievers' participated in the funeral ceremonies, treating the monk as a saint, and in order to illustrate this statement he quotes a fragment of his life authored by Philippe, in which he writes about: 'schismatic Christian people', and enumerates 'the Greeks, Armenians, Georgians, Jacobites, Copts, Maronites' and attributes them vicious practices (Olympios, Shared devotions, 12).
⁹⁸⁷ Rhomaioi.
⁹⁸⁸ Pavlidis enlarges the Carmelite's agency, stating that it was he who 'caused the great commotion' (προκλήθηκε μεγάλη αναστάτωση). See Παυλίδης (Ed.), Λεοντίου Μαχαιρά Χρονικόν, 79.
⁹⁸⁹ Rhomaioi.
⁹⁹⁰ Prof. Małgorzata Borowska translates the term 'γουμένους' as 'igumeni' (hegumens). Mas Latrie (Ed.), Chronique de Strambaldi, 39 lists: *li vescovi et abbati et preti*. The hegumen is a superior of a monastery in the Orthodox Church lower in rank than an archimandrite (Rygorowicz-Kuźma, Terminologia prawosławna, 405). Miller, Sathas give 'γουμένους' as *les supérieurs des couvents*. See Sathas, Miller (Eds, transl.), Chronique de Chypre, 57.
⁹⁹¹ The Rhomaian priest. MS O adds 'καὶ παπάδες'. See Dawkins (Ed., transl.), Ἐξήγησις/ Recital, 90 (fn. 1). In Mas Latrie (Ed.), Chronique de Strambaldi, 39, *prete*. In Sathas, Miller (Eds, transl.), Chronique de Chypre, 57, *les prêtres*.
⁹⁹² Cathedral of Saint Sophia (Hagia Sophia, Holy Wisdom).

weapons' (ἀρματωμένον), which increased his effectiveness in achieving his goal and carrying out his plan. The real objective of the legate was to 'make Latins of Greeks' (νὰ ποίση τοὺς Ρωμαίους Λατίνους) and their 'conversion' (νὰ τοὺς κουφερμιάση). The Rhomaian clergy remained calm and neutral until they became aware of the stranger's true intentions (δὲν ἔξευραν τὸ θέλημάν του). Makhairas describes what ensued after the Greeks came to understand the true aim of Peter's visit as a 'great [mutual] affront' (μέγαν σκάνταλον). The events that took place during the papal emissary's stay in Cyprus show that Rhomaian hospitality and openness were insufficient to stifle their strongly rooted awareness of their own spirituality and the tradition they cultivated. The Carmelite's visit and his self-confidence are proof that the island taken over by the Lusignans, was wide open to other Catholics, who decided they had a right to take arbitrary action on it.

A very suggestive picture is painted by the last fragment of this narrative:

And all those whom he had confirmed (ὅσους ἐκουφερμίασεν), threw down the cotton (ἐρίψαν τὸ πανπάκιν) and spat upon it (ἐπτύσαν το). (LM I 101)[993]

This sentence is proof that the priests, obedient to their Orthodox faith, surprised by the unforeseen intervention and confronted with a difficult situation, fell prey to various negative emotions such as fear, disorientation and agitation. Having met with duress and violence, they resisted strenuously, thus manifesting their attachment to their own beliefs and forms of expressing them. However, a part of the Greek clergy, giving in to the monk's persuasion, consented to conversion and betrayed the rite shaped by their tradition. Although the conversion was within one religion, the Rhomaian priests did not hide their bitterness when they understood their mistake. Ashamed of their acquiescence, they cast off the coarse robes they had donned for the confirmation and spat on them in contempt, thus expressing grief and anger at their credulity and impotency in that moment of danger.[994]

The *Chronique d'Amadi* also mentions the monk Peter and discusses the same situation. Its author comments as follows: 'the people took it badly, but that was what the emissary wanted' (*il che hebbe il populo a mal, et si volse esso legato*). In anger, an attempt was made to burn him in the Santa Sophia cathedral, but these efforts were stopped.[995] However, the *Chronique d'Amadi* contains still further mentions of the Carmelite, concerning his boat in 1361[996] and a mass he celebrated during the conquest of Alexandria in 1365.[997] It is also worth mentioning that according to sources he died in 1366 in Cyprus and was later canonised in the Catholic Church.[998]

The most attention to Peter de Thomas was paid by Philippe de Mézières, who devoted a biography written in Latin to him, the *Vie de Peter Thomas* (*Vita S. Petri Thomasii*).[999] Iorga underlines the legate's participation in later endeavours, particularly in Peter I's Alexandrian crusade. He draws a figure of a zealous clergyman by emphasising his inexhaustible strength, calling him the 'Carmelite enthusiast' (*le Carmélite enthousiaste*),[1000] 'holy person' (*le saint personnage*)[1001] and a brave warrior who helped the Latin armies face the 'neccessity of the sacred passage' (*de la nécessité du saint passage*).[1002] Iorga also cites the conversion of Rhomaian bishops, that is 'schismatics' (*commença par convenitr les schismatiques*)[1003] described in the *Chronicle*, which 'work

---

[993] This sentence is missing in Mas Latrie (Ed.), Chronique de Strambaldi, 39. Pavlidis explains that 'this was the cotton material used to carry out confirmation' (Επρόκειτο για το βαμβάκι με το οποίο τους είχε δοθεί το χρίσμα). See Παυλίδης (Ed.), Λεοντίου Μαχαιρά Χρονικόν, 79 (fn. 3).

[994] This incident was not without its consequences. In LM II 102 Makhairas writes that a request was sent to the pope asking him not to send emissaries who caused riots (νὰ μὲν πέψη τους ληγάτους νὰ γενοῦν σκάνταλα). In MS O the respective sentence is as follows: 'καὶ νὰ τοῦ ποῦν καὶ τὴν πελλάραν τὴν ἐποῖκεν ὁ ληγάτος' ('and to stop him and the madness that the legate had committed'). Dawkins (Ed., transl.), Ἐξήγησις/ Recital, 90 (fn. 7); Παυλίδης (Ed.), Λεοντίου Μαχαιρά Χρονικόν, 78 (fn. 7). Strambaldi translates this in the following way: *et referri ancora la materia che fece il legato in Cipro*. See Mas Latrie (Ed.), Chronique de Strambaldi, 40.

[995] Mas Latrie (Ed.), Chronique d'Amadi, 410; Coureas, Edbury (Transl.), The Chronicle of Amadi, 373 (§ 814). Translation consulted with Coureas and Edbury' translation.

[996] Mas Latrie (Ed.), Chronique d'Amadi, 411; Coureas, Edbury (Transl.), The Chronicle of Amadi, 374 (§ 819).

[997] Mas Latrie (Ed.), Chronique d'Amadi, 414–415; Coureas, Edbury (Transl.), The Chronicle of Amadi, 377–378 (§ 830).

[998] Cf. Philippe de Mézières, The Life of Saint Peter Thomas.

[999] Cf. Iorga, Philippe de Mézières, 105, 216, 237, 344–346, 473.

[1000] Iorga, Philippe de Mézières, 106.

[1001] Iorga, Philippe de Mézières, 106.

[1002] Iorga, Philippe de Mézières, 216.

[1003] Iorga, Philippe de Mézières, 105, 108, 110.

of conversion' (*l'œuvre de conversion*) he found to be 'very successful' (*réussi si bien*).[1004] Furthermore, he writes about the monk's visit to the Latin bishopric of Coron in Greece,[1005] where he went to confront the 'new schismatics' (*nouveaus schismatiques*). He proceeds to describe many of his other acts[1006] up to his death in Ammochostos in 1366.[1007] The lack of these elements in the *Chronicle* shows that its author endeavoured to expose the least praiseworthy act of the legate's life, portraying him as having ultimately been banished from the island, and to strengthen the picture of persecuted Rhomaian clergy via contrast.

This incident also reveals the existence of diverse attitudes among the Franks, some of whom joined in the forced conversion (ἐδυναστεῦγαν), pushing the Greeks to defend themselves (ἐδιαφεντεύγουνταν), while others, and these were the representatives of the royal court, put a stop to the endeavour, setting the Greeks free. Later, when informing the pope of his coronation, Peter I requested him 'not to send legates who spread disorder' (νὰ μὲν πέψῃ τοὺς ληγάτους νὰ γενοῦν σκάνταλα).[1008]

The examples above reveal a second, next to acceptance of similar elements, side of inclusivism as understood by Moyaert, which is manifested in the *Chronicle* in the guise of rejecting a foreign tradition to cultivate one's own, despite similarities. Where the two sides do not agree to a change that would reach the deepest level of their identification and undermine their connection to their heritage (for the Rhomaian population this heritage was the holy land of Cyprus, full of saints' remains and inhabited for centuries by the Rhomaioi), negotiating identity occurs very slowly and encounters barriers that are hard to overcome. Despite sharing a 'common core experience', Makhairas' Greeks and Latins cannot always adapt to each other as regards respect for the other side's faith and way of life. The Greeks do not seem to mind living on the periphery of the Kingdom of Cyprus (in the sense of participating in decisions taken by the Franks regarding the political fate of the island), on the condition that they can preserve their tradition. The Cypriot work presents the struggle for power over the religious space shared by all Christians and the right to recognise the story of the Relic's discovery as one's own. Granting such a right would bring prestige and confirm the infallibility of the members of a given group in their more or less radical daily decisions.

Nicolaou-Konnari reads many of Makhairas' statements as a criticism of the overzealous Catholic clergy. She quotes the chronicler's sentence about 'the old hate between Franks and Rhomaioi (τὴν παλαιὰν μιστείαν τοὺς Φραγγοὺς μὲ τοὺς Ρωμαίους).[1009] Coureas holds a similar opinion, expressing the view that the Cypriot author clearly stands against the Latin clergy, though he praises the pope.[1010] However, the manner in which the *Chronicle* presents the function of the bishop of Rome in general and the way in which the depictions of individual popes are shaped should be examined separately.

Mentions of cooperation and hostility in the early parts of the *Chronicle* alternate or occur simultaneously. In his narrative, Makhairas begins to introduce more and more static images, indicating stabilisation and pacification of relations, but also, and not insignificantly, his attention moves increasingly towards the theme of confrontation with the Muslims. This narrative muting of tensions and unification of the image of Christians is how the author illustrates the Franks' rising fear of the Saracens and Turks.

2.4. Orthodoxy and heterodoxy. The case of Thibald

At this juncture, the question returns of the presence in the Cypriot work of the author's thoughts about the concept of 'orthodoxy' in the Christian sense and, it follows, of establishing which side represented a 'heretic' attitude. LM III 579 is held to be one of the most important fragments that raise the problem of heresy and say much about Makhairas' own convictions. In it, he writes about the conversion of the Rhomaioi Thibald Belfarage (σίρε Τιπάτ Πελφανάντζα)[1011] to Catholicism. This figure plays an important role in the *Chronicle*. He first

---

[1004] Iorga, Philippe de Mézières, 110.
[1005] Iorga, Philippe de Mézières, 110.
[1006] Iorga, Philippe de Mézières, 11, 206, 214, 225, 233, 251, 260–265, 280, 304, 329.
[1007] Iorga, Philippe de Mézières, 311.
[1008] LM I 102.
[1009] Nicolaou-Konnari, Alterity and identity, 61.
[1010] Coureas, Religion and ethnic identity, 16–17.
[1011] Dawkins argues for Thibald Belfarage's Syrian origins, unlike Mas Latrie, who thought him a Greek (Dawkins, Notes, 191). Pavlidis follows this lead, stating that 'he came from a Syrian family' (καταγόταν οικογένεια τῆς Συρίας) (Παυλίδης (Ed.), Λεοντίου Μαχαιρά Χρονικόν, 427, fn. 1).

appears in passage LM II 214, and for the last time in LM III 581, and thus is present in the awareness of the text's recipient for quite some time, though he is mentioned relatively rarely. Makhairas constructs a complex portrayal of Thibald. We come to know him gradually because the chronicler reveals his extraordinary qualities sparingly though systematically. He initially served Peter I as one of his many knights (LM II 214). Over two hundred paragraphs later, in LM III 403, he is introduced in the narrative as a 'beloved' (ἠγαπημένος) emissary of Peter II who delivers a 'confidential letter' (ἕναν χαρτὶν τῆς ἐμπιστιοσύνης) to the constable. The measure of confidence placed in him is indicated by the Cypriot ruler's stipulation that the information brought by the youth should be treated as the 'truth' (ἀληθῶς), as if it were they (i.e. the king) themselves who spoke it (ὡς γοιὸ νὰ σοῦ τὄπαμεν μὲ τὸ στόμαν μας, 'as if it were spoken by our lips'). In LM III 404 Leontios calls him a 'wise man' (γνωστικός) because he was able to calm a raging crowd of Lefkosians who were throwing stones at him. In LM III 556–557 he calls him 'Hypatios' (Ὑπάτιος), perhaps wanting to emphasise his Rhomaian identity.[1012] This passage, recounting a successful clash with the Genoese, shows the crowning point of Thibald's abilities, into whose 'heart the spirit of the Lord had entered' (ἐνέβην πνεῦμα κυρίου εἰς τὴν καρδιάν -του-), which Peter II expressed 'God put it in [his] mind' (ἔβαλέν το ὁ θεὸς εἰς τὸν νοῦν -σου-). Makhairas argues that Thibald's 'mind' (νοῦς) and 'heart' (καρδιά) – the chronicler evidently makes no distinction between these faculties – were inspired by a supernatural act of a God who actively reacts to events (ἐνέβην, ἔβαλέν).[1013] This is not only a legible example of how Providence affected happenings in Cyprus, but also an expression of its concrete impact on the deepest core of an individual. Thanks to this inspiration Thibald, as an 'embattled warrior' (καλὸς πολεμιστής), weakened the position of the Genoese who were occupying Ammochostos,[1014] which earned him the king's profound affection. He received numerous gifts from the grateful ruler, which Peter II himself talks about in detail in a statement included in MS O: from burgher, he made him a knight and then raised him to the rank of turcopolier of Cyprus. He endowed him with many lands: Trimithia (τὴν Τριμιθείαν), Petra (τὴν Πέτραν) and Elia (τὴν Ἐλιάν), which only increased his desire to seize the most important royal estates (what Pavlidis calls 'βασιλική ιδιοκτησία'[1015]) (LM III 566).[1016] The verbs used by the king, 'I made' (ἐποῖκα) and 'I gave' (ἐδωκά),[1017] indicating his generosity and goodwill, are not without significance. Thibald, however, desirous of the most precious, unachievable gift, Gorhigos castle, was unable to be satisfied with what he had received.[1018] Driven by increasing bitterness, he started to systematically check who advised Peter II against giving him Gorhigos. Then, having identified the culprit to be the priest Philip,[1019] he murdered him together

---

[1012] Comment by Prof. Małgorzata Borowska.

[1013] LM III 556–557. Pavlidis translates the second sentence in the following way: […] 'αυτή την ενέργεια την έβαλε ο Θεός στο μυαλό σου', where the ambiguous 'ενέργεια' can be interpreted in many ways, as 'energy', 'enthusiasm', 'strength', 'vitality', etc. The publisher adds meaning, making it marked. See Παυλίδης (Ed.), Λεοντίου Μαχαιρά Χρονικόν, 427.

[1014] LM III 559–562. The expression 'καλὸς πολεμιστής' in LM III 560.

[1015] Παυλίδης (Ed.), Λεοντίου Μαχαιρά Χρονικόν, 435 (fn. 2).

[1016] Dawkins (Ed., transl.), Εξήγησις/ Recital, 566 (fn. 1).

[1017] LM III 568. Παυλίδης (Ed.), Λεοντίου Μαχαιρά Χρονικόν, 436 (fn. 5).

[1018] LM III 565.

[1019] This was a distant relative of Makhairas' father, the son of a Rhomaian nun, already mentioned (pp. 33, 122). Pavlidis provides an interesting description of Philip, emphasising how unique his ethnic origin was in the context of his service at the royal court and influence on the ruler's decisions and the course of events. 'Αυτός ο ιερέας Φίλιππος, γιός Ελληνίσας καλογριάς όπως λέγει ο συγγραφέας, ήταν μέλος της Λατινικής Εκκλησίας και μάλιστα "δάσκαλος" (=σύμβουλος, παιδαγωγός, πνευματικός) του ιδίου του βασιλιά. Έχουμε λοιπόν, μία περίπτωση ενός ανθρώπου ελληνικής καταγωγής, τουλάχιστον από την πλευρά της μητέρας του, ο πατέρας του δεν αναφέρεται ποιος και τί ήταν, με άμεση επιρροή στο ανάκτορο. Μέσω ανθρώπων τέτοιων κατηγοριών ήταν που εβοηθούντο και άλλοι Έλληνες της Κύπρου να ξεφύγουν από την κατώτατη τάξη των δουλοπαροίκων και να ανέλθουν κοινωνικά. Ο ιερέας Φίλιππος φαίνεται ήταν το ίδιο πρόσωπο που πιο πριν (παράγρ. 40) παρουσιάζεται ως σύμβουλος και πληροφοριοδότης του συγγραφέα για το έργο του.' This priest, Philip, the son of a Rhomaian nun, as the chronicler writes, was a member of the Latin Church and most likely a "teacher" (i.e. an advisor, tutor, confessor) of the king himself. We thus have a case of a man of Rhomaian origin, mainly on his mother's side – there is no mention of his father, neither who he was nor what he was [that is, what his profession/religion was – note M.G.] – who had direct influence on [matters of the royal] palace. Among people of this kind who were advisors there were also other Rhomaioi from Cyprus, who had been able to emancipate themselves from the lowest class of serfs and rise to a higher social position. Father Philip seems to be the same person as [a character appearing] far earlier (LM I 40), introduced in the chronicler's work as an advisor and informant.' (Pavlidis (Ed.), Λεοντίου Μαχαιρά Χρονικόν, 435, fn. 1. Kupiszewska's translation from the Polish translation by the author). Thibald's story thus shows a constellation of figures 'from the borderland'. Thibald, who converted to the Latin faith from the Greek without any known reason, the 'foreign' Rhomaioi Alexopoulos, unacquainted with the situation on the island (whom, Pavlidis states, Thibald had brought from Venice, 437, fn. 1), the Latin priest Philip with Rhomaian roots, and above all this, Makhairas himself, a very distant relative of Father Philip, whose identity was not fully revealed, but who carefully observed the goings on of the Cypriot court. The fact that the two 'hybrid' characters that were close to Peter II, of whose attention Makhairas may have been jealous, ultimately met a cruel fate is rather significant. Leontios may have also felt disoriented, not being able to fully identify any person, and searched genealogies and kinship for guidelines that would allow him to understand and explain certain events and interpersonal relationships.

2.4. Orthodoxy and heterodoxy. The case of Thibald

with Alexopoulos.¹⁰²⁰ According to Queen Eleanora, who commented the occurrence, he had committed blatant murder (εἶνε φόνος), was the perpetrator (ὁ πγοιός ἐγύνην ἀπό τόν Τιπάτ) and 'cause' (ἀφορμή) of the tragedy, and moreover had 'persuaded' (ἐπῆρεν) Alexopoulos and other Franks to do evil.¹⁰²¹ Makhairas thus depicts the moral fall of a young man from a loyal friend of the king who had been elevated to high office (and was so close to God as to be sent salutary inspiration by him), changed into a money-seeking parvenu deceived by courtly dazzle, and finally into an enemy of the king – Peter II began to fear that Thibald might enter into a pact with the Venetians or Saracens that would be unfavourable to the Lusignan kingdom¹⁰²² – and ultimately ended up as a common traitor and murderer sentenced to torture and death. Thibald himself owned in LM III 575 that together with Alexopoulos they had been the ones to sin against the ruler (πταῖσθε(ς) σου). Looking for mercy from his lord, he attempted to show himself in a favourable light by various means. He even laid the blame on Queen Eleanora, whom he maligned as a 'dirty and evil harlot' (βρωμισμένη καὶ κακὴ πολιτική), claiming that he had not wanted to return her advances so as not to 'dishonour the house of the lord' (ποίσω ἀντροπὴν ἔσσω τοῦ ἀφέντη).

Leontios explains Thibald's painful fall with his conversion from the Greek (Rhomaian) to the Latin faith, which he comments with the words: 'he abandoned hope placed in God' (ἐσήκωσεν τὴν ἐλπίδαν ἀπὲ τὸν θεόν), 'he trusted in his mind' (ἐθάρησεν εἰς τὸ νοῦν του), 'he [trusted] in the king's love' (εἰς τὴν ἀγάπην τοῦ ρηγός) and came to be influenced by the 'vanity of the world' (διὰ τὴν ἔπαρσιν τοῦ κόσμου). These four reasons for Thibald's bad decision listed by the chronicler show his attitude to the act of conversion: man should not place hope either in himself, or in his own mind, or in another person. The same 'mind' (νοῦς) that had been recognised by the author to be God-inspired in LM III 557 was then led astray in LM III 579. It may seem that Makhairas thus declares his affiliation with the Greek Church, especially as he preserves a certain detachment when writing about the Latins. This is not unambiguous, however. The last sentence of paragraph LM III 579 takes on a special significance: '**Latins** belong to the **apostolic** [Church], [while] the **Greeks** form the **catholic** [Church]' (Ἀποστολικοὶ οἱ Λατῖνοι, καὶ καθολικοὶ οἱ Ρωμαῖοι). Such a remark indicates that the chronicler is blurring the boundaries, treating both denominations as valid. In this statement he shows a convergence with the words of the Niceno-Constantinopolitan Creed from the Divine Liturgy of St John Chrysostom: '[I believe] in one holy, catholic, and apostolic Church'¹⁰²³ In the Greek version they are as follows: 'Πιστεύομεν [...] εἰς μίαν ἁγίαν καθολικὴν καὶ ἀποστολικὴν ἐκκλησίαν'.¹⁰²⁴ Whether he is intentionally referring to these specific words or whether it is only an echo of what he heard at some point, there is no doubt (judging by the whole structure of Thibald's tale and the bravely inserted discussion) that he had given thought to the concept conveyed in the *credo* and was expressing something that was important to him. He writes that the choice of denomination should be decided by the 'faith of the fathers' (ἡ πατρική του πίστη),¹⁰²⁵ which the young man 'abandoned' (ἐγκατέλιπεν), and that it should be the deciding factor as regards such affiliation. The term 'faith of the fathers' may be understood twofold: relating to the faith of one's ancestors (fathers, forefathers)¹⁰²⁶ or to the faith transmitted by the Fathers of the Church. Makhairas asks two questions, which from his point of view are rhetorical: 'What is the sense (ἀμμὲ ἴντα χρῆσι) of a Greek

---

¹⁰²⁰ LM III 567–571.
¹⁰²¹ LM III 573. Παυλίδης (Ed.), Λεοντίου Μαχαιρᾶ Χρονικόν, 440 (fn. 7).
¹⁰²² LM III 566.
¹⁰²³ Symbol of Faith.
¹⁰²⁴ After Kelly, Early Christian Creeds, 297–298. John Kelly comments the specific nature of the 'Nicene-Constantinopolitan symbol': 'Its hybrid title combines the popular but erroneous tradition that it is none other than the true Nicene creed enlarged with the theory, widely held since the middle of the fifth century at any rate, that the occasion of its enlargement was the second general council, held at Constantinople in 381. Of all existing creeds it is the only one for which ecumenicity, or universal acceptance, can be plausibly claimed. Unlike the purely Western Apostles' Creed, it was admitted as authoritative in East and West alike from 451 onwards, and it has retained that position, with one significant variation in its text, right down to the present day.' (Kelly, Early Christian Creeds, 296).
¹⁰²⁵ In Mas Latrie (Ed.), Chronique de Strambaldi, 245 this expression is not present.
¹⁰²⁶ Cf. Prayer of the priest in the *Divine liturgy of St Basil the Great*: 'And unite us all to one another who become partakers of the one Bread and the Cup in the communion of the one Holy Spirit [...] forefathers, fathers, patriarchs, prophets, apostles, preachers, evangelists, martyrs, confessors, teachers, and every righteous spirit made perfect in faith.' (Vaporis (Ed.), The Divine Liturgy, https://www.goarch.org/-/the-divine-liturgy-of-saint-basil-the-great, accessed 24 November 2021. Cf. H. Paprocki (Transl.), Liturgie Kościoła prawosławnego, 156). Pavlidis comments: 'Αὐτή η αναφορά του Μαχαιρά ενισχύει την άποψη ότι ο Θιβάλτ ήταν ελληνικής καταγωγής. Ο Μαχαιράς εννοεί εδώ πάντως ότι αρχικά ήταν Ορθόδοξος, ανεξαρτήτως εθνικότητος.' 'This remark by Makhairas strengthens the conviction that Thibald was of Rhomaian origin. In this place Makhairas means, at least, that he was initially an Orthodox [Christian], regardless of his ethnic origins.' (Παυλίδης (Ed.), Λεοντίου Μαχαιρᾶ Χρονικόν, 447, fn. 1. Kupiszewska's translation from the Polish translation by the author).

becoming a Latin' (εἶνε Ῥωμαῖος νὰ γενῇ Λατῖνος)?[1027] and 'Should an orthodox Christian betray one faith and adopt another?' (Ἐπειδὴ ὀρθόδοξος χριστιανὸς εἶνε χρῆσι νὰ καταφρονήσῃ τὴν μία νὰ μπέσῃ εἰς τὴν ἄλλην)? He then turns directly to the reader, 'Do you repudiate [your] previous [faith]' (Καὶ καταφρονεῖς τὴν πρώτην)? He explains that after all, Thibald 'was not a heretic who had become orthodox' (Δὲν ἦτον αἱρετικὸς καὶ ἐγίνην ὀρθόδοξος).

In MS O this thought is completed:

[...] *thought that the God of the Latins is different from the God of the Greeks.*[1028] *And if a man thinks thus and changes his allegiance, God loves him neither in this world nor in the other. Men should therefore not despise the orthodox*[1029] *faith.* (LM III 579)[1030]

According to the author of the *Chronicle* Christianity is the paramount value, while the second important value is affiliation to a faith inherited from one's ancestors. The story of Thibald has a particular significance because it is the tale of the moral fall of a man who served the king faithfully as a Greek, heroically saving Cyprus from Genoese intrusion, and after conversion to the Catholic faith underwent a degradation, making material demands of the king and ultimately causing the death of a priest and his own execution. His fault was not that he betrayed God – for Makhairas, this was one and the same God! – but that he betrayed his own nation, its traditions, ancestors, heritage, which should decide a man's identity forever. The discussion of the pointlessness of conversion (only from the Orthodox to the Catholic faith) may have been a pretext for Makhairas to show that in his view a departure from Orthodoxy was an event that transformed and destroyed an individual's identity. However, it is more likely that he believed searching for a different road to be destructive if the original road had already been paved by glorious ancestors. This place in the *Chronicle*, LM III 579, should be considered the most symptomatic and the most telling about the chronicler, his views and his identity.

2.5. Summary

In the *Chronicle*, the Orthodox identity is forcibly confronted with the Catholic one, whose presence on Cyprus began with the imposed rule (although Makhairas writes laconically about a transaction, there is no doubt that the Franks manifested their power when taking the island despite the hostility of the Rhomaian people), which had various consequences in different contexts considered by the author. It is most clearly visible in the example of Thibald's existential disorientation: his sense of religious 'self' came to be split. He became 'the other' not only to the Frankish king, but also to himself, having lost the instinct that may have protected him from annihilation. Makhairas is not as radical in his presentation of this otherness as Neophytos the Recluse, for example, who – as Seyit Özkutlu notes – describes the Franks using blunt, pejorative expressions.[1031]

Comparing the perspectives of Makhairas and Philippe de Mézières, Nicolaou-Konnari notices that it is not possible to satisfactorily analyse the encounter between Cyprians and Franks without placing the former in the context of the Eastern Byzantine culture, and the latter, in the context of the Western Latin culture.[1032] The scholar observes that the Lusignans saw the Cypriot population as different primarily in terms of religious affiliation.[1033]

[1027] Mas Latrie (Ed.), Chronique de Strambaldi, 245 expresses this paticular idea as follows: 'And why would the God of the Latins be better than the one of the Greeks?' (*Et perochè l'Iddio de Latini è miglior de quello delli Greci?*). Furthermore, Makhairas' version is more extensive.
[1028] Rhomaioi.
[1029] right.
[1030] LM III 579: 'καὶ ἐθάρησεν ὅτι εἶνε ἄλλος θεὸς τοὺς Λατίνους παρὰ τοὺς Ῥωμαίους. Καὶ εἴ τις πολομᾷ τίτοιαν στίμαν καὶ ἀλλάσσει τὸ σέβεται, ὁ θεὸς δὲν τὸν ἀγαπᾷ οὐδὲ ὧδε οὐδὲ ἐκεῖ· καὶ διὰ τοῦτον δὲν πρέπει νὰ καταφρονοῦν τὴν ὀρθὴν πίστιν'. See Dawkins (Ed., transl.), Ἐξήγησις/ Recital, 576 (fn. 7); Παυλίδης (Ed.), Λεοντίου Μαχαιρᾶ Χρονικόν, 446 (fn. 3).
[1031] Özkutlu, Medieval Famagusta, 212.
[1032] Nicolaou-Konnari, Alterity and identity, 39.
[1033] Nicolaou-Konnari, Alterity and identity, 40.

2.5. Summary

An attempt to reforge the link between the Byzantines and the Franks in the form of the matrimonial proposal was made in 1372 by John V Palaiologos (who offered his daughter's hand to Peter II), whose emissaries emphasised that 'many were the ties of kinship between Rhomaioi and Latins' (πολλὲς συνμπεθθερίες ἐγίνουντα ἀνάμεσα τῶν Ρωμαίων καὶ τῶν Λατίνων), 'like between the king of France and the emperor of the City' (ἀπὸ τὸν ρήγαν τῆς Φραγγίας μὲ τὸν βασιλέαν τῆς Πόλεως). The fame of Peter II's rule (ἡ φάμα τῆς ἀφεντιᾶς) had in fact reached the Rhomaian state. This was an opportunity for the Lusignans to gain 'many castles in Hellas' (κάστρη πολλὰ εἰς τὴν Ἑλλάδαν) and to establish a firm relation between emperor and king along the lines of a father-son relationship, which would doubtless have had an impact on the relationship between Churches.[1034]

The fact that we receive a rather unclear position concerning the Cyprians' opinions about Lusignan rule may be a manifestation of the chronicler's lack of knowledge or lack of interest in this subject, or an expression of political correctness, but may also be due to his position in life, tightly linked to the entrenched 'colonial' reality, which made it difficult to take a different perspective. We do not know whether Leontios himself experienced what Komodikis calls 'difficult relations between Franks and Cyprians' (δύσκολες σχέσεις μεταξύ των Φράγκων και των Κυπρίων).[1035]

The Greek-Latin universe presented in the *Chronicle* forms a kind of 'third space' (as understood by Bhabha), where different identities meet: followers of the Latin Church and of the Greek Church, who are dominated by the former. What connects these two groups is a 'core common experience' in the form of the cult of the Cross and relics of saints who died before the 1054 schism of the Churches, respect for Cypriot hagiography, and fighting plagues, diseases and cataclysms with the help of masses, processions and icons. To analyse this topic, it is possible to apply a dynamic of acceptance and rejection, and thus inclusivism as understood by Moyaert (p. 120), involving the adoption of certain elements of a foreign culture and a rejection of others in a continuous process of negotiating identities.[1036]

In the *Chronicle*, affiliation with the Christian religion is the only common plane for Greeks and Latins, though doctrinal, institutional and ritual differences may be distinguished (though there exist more broadly understood concerning language, laws and customs). For the chronicler each attempt to convert from the Greek to the Latin faith is, despite his awareness that they have common foundations, controversial. The Rhomaioi in the *Chronicle* evidently rebel against Peter de Thomas' attempts to convert them. Thibald voluntarily adopts Catholicism, but this leads to his moral fall and agonising death. In the Cypriot work, the line between what is familiar and what is other is marked on several different levels. Though the common core made colonisation easier for the invaders, it was no guarantee of full mutual comprehension. The Latins (Lusignans together with other Franks and the Syrians), having imposed

---

[1034] LM III 346.
[1035] Κωμοδίκης, Οι Πληροφορίες των Βραχέων Χρονικών, 48. Nicolaou-Konnari, meanwhile, notes that the inhabitants of Cyprus entered into a pattern of behaviour with representatives of the Lusignans, like with Richard Cœur de Lion, that was neutral or collaborating, and the only symptoms of rebel attitudes were in her opinion the protests against Richard's governors and the Templars (Nicolaou-Konnari, Alterity and identity, 39).
[1036] To explain the development of the contacts between Cyprians and Franks portrayed in the *Chronicle* it is worth investigating whether one of Schryver's models may be applicable in this case. This scholar proposed a theory that analytically explains the consequences of contact between the two groups on Cyprus – a theory that he formed based on analysis of archaeological evidence – over time and successive generations. The theory is as follows: 'Interactions between the Franks (Group A) and the Greeks (Group B) occurred with increasing regularity in certain spheres of everyday life as time went on. These increased interactions would eventually result in a mixed cultural group of Franco-Greeks or Franco-Cypriots (Group AB). The period of time needed for this to occur would have been relatively short, perhaps one to three generations. As time continued on, more interactions between different members of this new group AB would simply increase its mixed nature, perhaps creating what we might symbolize as group AB2.' (Schryver, Excavating the Identities, 2). This model cannot be applied to the depiction of Latin-Greek contact and shaping of identity in the *Chronicle*, as in no place do we encounter in it a mention of a figure or collective entity to whom Makhairas would have assigned a mix of features typical of both groups. At most, there are uncertain identities, where there is a lack of sufficient data. Schryver's idea is very interesting because of the concepts he uses to investigate the situation on medieval Cyprus based on archaeological sources. The scholar builds a new model, introducing two variables to designate the groups, A and B, calling them 'fluid bodies', and then analysing the relations occurring within them and between them. The conclusions he reaches make him reject the ultimate formation of a hybrid, because the first generation is not described with the formula AB, but A1 and B2, while the second generation can be recorded as A12 and B12. This model should be read as constant negotiation and renegotiation of boundaries, with the assumption that identity is both a constant and a variable, and its interpretation depends on the situation and recipients (Schryver, Excavating the Identities, 6–9). If this last model is applied to the text of the *Chronicle*, it may be observed that the author creates a depiction of Cypriots who are accustomed to constant exchange with the Franks, but who have preserved their identity, and Franks who on the one hand impose their presence on them, and on the other, respect differences. Both the Cypriot and Frank groups remain separate, though slightly changed: the ones by the presence of the others.

their presence, deprived the Greeks of their priority right to Cyprus, situated on the pilgrimage route to the Holy Land, and took advantage of the 'abundance of relics' that was the property of the Cypriots. For Makhairas, the space and land inherited from ancestors take precedence over other elements that define identity, which means that by invading Cyprus the Franks colonised the very thing that determined Cypriot identity. That the atmosphere on the island was not always conducive to peaceful coexistence is indicated for instance by the rebellion of Rhomaioi peasants in the years 1426–1427, and the fear and anxiety of the Lusignans towards the local populace, which remained for some time.

All these circumstances point to the presence of an 'oriental deviance' in Cyprus. Leontios limits his perspective because he does not often give the Rhomaian population a voice to allow them to legibly and unambiguously express their opinion about the Franks' arrival and rule. However, some conclusions may be drawn based on descriptions of their reactions to some events. Guy, the first ruler of the Lusignan dynasty in Cyprus, presents the Rhomaioi as unpredictable, inclined to rebel, and maintaining a close relationship with the emperor of Constantinople. In reality, the only clear echo of their protest is emphasised at the start of the *Chronicle*, when the Rhomaioi rebel against the brothers of the Temple, whose 'otherness' they perceive through the prism of their domination and which they treat as a threat: however, the Templars die not at their hands, but two centuries later upon the pope's command. From the start, the Franks at the royal court attempt to keep significant privileges for themselves, asking the king to believe only them if they say something against the island's inhabitants, and under no condition believe the other side if they say anything about the Franks. Even the repetition of the adjective 'poor' (πτωχοί) with respect to the local population indicates a specific perception of them imposed by the Franks. In many instances, representatives of the Latin clergy question the reliability of the Greeks, accusing them of working miracles through magic and different types of tricks, of cheating the people and leading them to heresy while fraudulently claiming that the cross that is in their possession contains the Wood of the Life-giving Cross, of being like pagans and telling of unrighteous and untrue things. In a conversation with King Hugh, bishop Fra Marco speaks slightingly about the shepherd boy who found the Cross of Togni in the crown of the carob tree, insinuating that 'he carved some cross' (ἐπελέκισεν ἕναν σταυρόν) and was trying to talk others into believing it to be genuine. MS O additionally contains the sentence: 'and rattle out many other absurdities' (καὶ λαλοῦν πολλὲς πελλάρες) with reference to the Greeks.[1037] Also interesting is that the Latins place themselves in the position of the victims, which is visible in the remark 'and we bear it' (μεῖς βαστοῦμεν το), which is intended to amplify the inconveniences provoked by the Rhomaioi and to show the Franks in a positive light (LM I 73).

The Franks' disparaging attitude towards Cyprus may be seen among others in the words of emissaries who explain to the pope that their fathers (γονεῖς μας) 'had not left their homes' (δὲν ἀφῆκα τὰ σπιτία τους), 'their kin' (τοὺς συνγκενάδες τους) and 'their inherited lands' (τοὺς κλερονομιές τους), in order to 'live on some rock among the seas' (νὰ ἀπλικέψουν εἰς μίαν πέτραν μέσα εἰς τὴν θάλασσαν), and emphasise that only the *Assizes*[1038] and contracts (στοιχήματα) can give them a sense of security (νὰ ἦνε θαρούμενοι) on this isolated patch of land.[1039]

Makhairas himself describes the revolt of Rhomaioi peasants from a pro-Western perspective, taking the official position of a functionary at the Frankish court, which he in fact was. He calls the rebels 'wolves' (λύκοι) and 'damned peasants' (καταραμένοι χωργιάτες), doing 'evil' (κακοσύνη) and 'evil things' (κα(κά)), and committing 'treachery' (ἀπιστίες) (LM VI 697). The radical opinion of the author, who does not usually express himself negatively about the Rhomaian people, was likely due to his brother's participation in putting down the rebellion, a fact that he attempted to neutralise. In most cases, the chronicler presents these negative elements of the image of the Greeks that emerge from this fragment, as perceived by the Latins and constructed according to their own vision and needs, in order to underline the latter's desire to gain an advantage over the former, either from a need for dominance or to guarantee themselves protection. However, he is not free from hypocrisy when he tries to diminish the importance of the Rhomaian rebellion to hide his true source of discomfort.

[1037] Dawkins (Ed., transl.), Ἐξήγησις/ Recital, 66 (fn. 4).
[1038] The *Assizes of Jerusalem*: Σάθας, Ἀσίζαι; Coureas (Transl.), The Assizes. Cf. Burkiewicz, Polityczna rola królestwa Cypru, 55; Hill, A History of Cyprus II, 52.
[1039] LM II 106.

2.5. Summary

In the *Chronicle*, the problem of denominational 'otherness' is enmeshed in the problem of ethnic 'otherness', which leads to the formation of various planes and scopes of alterity.[1040] Franks were 'others' to the Cyprians (they came from elsewhere and represented a different denomination), but thanks to long cohabitation and common religious elements they had become 'native', unlike Rhomaioi and other Latins (e.g. the Genoese and Venetians) from outside the island.[1041]

The impact of the Franks' presence in Cyprus in the *Chronicle* may also be assessed on the basis of a noticeable change in the ontological status of the sacred, which starting from LM I 41[1042] is subject to rapid narrowing and transcendentalisation. On Byzantine-period Cyprus the sacred is omnipresent, but this omnipresence does not consist in a chaos of signs, gestures or rituals,[1043] but in a pure, phenomenological potentiality of contact with God. The whole island is taken in the possession of St Helena (building churches, distributing fragments of the Life-giving Cross) who forges a personal relationship with the sacred through visions (the vision motif also appears in the allegorical tale of the Alexandrian lad George). Makhairas enhances this image by listing places where relics of the saints have been laid to rest (repetition of the adjectives 'holy' and 'most holy' additionally strengthens the picture), and thus by showing the places of their constant material presence, and also by retrospectively allowing several of them to speak by portraying their attitude to sacred space in hagiographic stories and by showing that prayers directed to them help preserve a link with the sacred. The transcendentalisation of the sacred in the part of the *Chronicle* that describes Lusignan rule takes the form of a phenomenon that Andrzej Dąbrówka terms sacramentalism[1044] (the sacred is reduced to the sacraments and sacramentalia) and defines after Rolf Sprandel as 'a form of religiosity based on a formalised system of rules whose observance under the strict direction of the Church is sufficient for salvation'.[1045] Dąbrówka adds that sacramentalism limits man's contact with the sacred to several turning points over the course of their life.[1046] In the Cypriot work a movement is visible from the presence of the sacred in every inch of matter and the 'holy time period'[1047] undefined by the chronicler, to the exclusive presence of the sacred in the signs of the Eucharist and coronation ceremonies, consecrations, blessings and processions, accompanied by clergy, cult objects (e.g. altars), and also the word (prayers, Bible).[1048] From omnipresent churches that are sanctuaries of the Life-giving Cross to church buildings administered by priests and objects called after saints but with no spiritual status. This is undoubtedly an example of a colonising change that took place

---

[1040] According to Ashcroft, Griffiths and Tiffin '**alterity**' (as opposed to '**difference**' whose character is 'epistemic'), that is 'otherness in the moral sense', is a handy category, useful for the analysis of cases of contact between representatives of different cultures that are characterised by an unequal level of complexity (religious, linguistic and political) (Ashcroft, Griffiths, Tiffin, Post-colonial Studies, 9–10).

[1041] The compulsory situation of dealing with settlers evokes different reactions on the part of the original inhabitants, such as hospitality and hostility, subjugation (willingness to conform) and mimicry (emulation). Although the Greeks gained familiarity with this 'otherness', the *Chronicle* does not contain any narrative elements that could be read as a record of 'colonial mimicry' involving an imitation of the arrivals' religious behaviours by the local population. 'Mimicry' is a term introduced by Bhabha to designate a situation in which the colonised imitates the coloniser's customs. As Ashcroft, Griffiths and Tiffin write, 'the result is a "blurred copy" of the colonizer that can be quite threatening. This is because mimicry is never very far from mockery, since it can appear to parody whatever it mimics.' (Ashcroft, Griffiths, Tiffin, Post-colonial Studies, 125). In another place they stress that colonial discourse 'never really wants colonial subjects to be exact replicas of the colonizers [...].' (Ashcroft, Griffiths, Tiffin, Post-colonial Studies, 11).

[1042] Here Leontios lists earlier kings of the Lusignan dynasty.

[1043] Andrzej Dąbrówka defines the phenomenon of sacramentalism as follows: 'From all the chaos of signs, places, behaviours, objects, gestures, rituals that spread the sacred in such a way that it started to become almost omnipresent, polymorphous and common, the most necessary and important signs were selected to protect it from banalisation, the rest being moved to an open class of phenomena that can be described as a protective zone for the truly holy sacred, in which its operation is non-communicational, does not consist in any defined exchange or is outside the Church' (Dąbrówka, Teatr i sacrum w średniowieczu, 111. Translated by Kupiszewska).

[1044] Dąbrówka, Teatr i sacrum w średniowieczu, 110. Dąbrówka names Peter Damiani as one of the main architects of sacramentalism. He also states that the differences between the sacraments and sacramentalia were indicated by Ivo of Chartres, and the 'canonical shape' of these arguments was given to them by Hugh of St Victor (Dąbrówka, Teatr i sacrum w średniowieczu, 110).

[1045] Dąbrówka, Teatr i sacrum w średniowieczu, 108. Translated by Kupiszewska.

[1046] Dąbrówka, Teatr i sacrum w średniowieczu, 312.

[1047] Dąbrówka, Teatr i sacrum w średniowieczu, 123. Translated by Kupiszewska.

[1048] Dąbrówka emphasises the aspect of the 'communicativeness of the sacraments' in the West (Dąbrówka, Teatr i sacrum w średniowieczu, 181. Quoted phrase translated by Kupiszewska).

in the Rhomaian dominion, involving disparagement of that original sacredness. This process gained impetus from the formalisation of religion and through state control.[1049]

Another sphere expanded, however: the sphere of contact with forces governing the universe, which is manifested in the free use of astrological findings. The Franks experience fear when faced with their ignorance of the operations of fate and the relationships between different phenomena. During one of his tirades in which he calls on God four times and once begs for the grace of the Holy Spirit, Peter I states: 'I was born in the sign of Capricorn and crowned under the planet Kronos' (εἰς τὸν αἰγόκερον ζῴδιον ἐγεννήθηκα, καὶ εἰς τὸν πλανήτην –τὸν καιρὸν– ἐστέφθηκα), thus making the astrological art of reading signs in the heavens equivalent to the Divine truths.[1050] The superstitious nature of the Cypriots is revealed in the position of King Peter II, who desiring to build a castle in Lefkosia called the archbishop to 'bless the foundations' (εὐλογήσῃ τὸν θεμέλιον) of the building under construction because he associated the erection of new walls with frequent deaths of builders. The chronicler writes that the cause of such deaths was unknown and that it is difficult to pronounce with certainty whether it was brought about 'by the laying of the first stone' (εἰς τὸ κάτζιμον τῆς πρώτης πέτρας), 'by human destiny' (εἰς τὴν ὀσκίαν[1051] τοῦ ἀνθρώπου), or even 'by coincidence' (εἰς τὴν συντυχίαν).[1052] Leontios aptly sums this up:

> *For if the craftsmen (τεχνίτες) knew, they would choose (στοιχειώννειν) their enemies to be the spirits to guard the building.* (LM III 596)

The sacred, which had previously been strongly linked to the land made holy by the close location of Jerusalem, partly gives way to the abstract sphere, governed by hypothetical laws. Moreover, the connection with the divine takes an impersonal aspect.

[1049] Cf. Dąbrówka, *Teatr i sacrum w średniowieczu*, 219.
[1050] LM II 251.
[1051] Pavlidis translates this word as 'ἡ μοίρα'. See Παυλίδης (Ed.), Λεοντίου Μαχαιρᾶ Χρονικόν, 458.
[1052] LM IV 596.

III. The Lusignans, Genoese and Venetians in the *Chronicle*

Ahi Genovesi, uomini diversi
d'ogni costume e pien d'ogni magagna,
perché non siete voi del mondo spersi?

Ah, Genoese! ye men at variance
With every virtue, full of every vice
Wherefore are ye not scattered from the world?[1053]
(Alighieri, Inferno, Canto XXXIII, v. 151–153)

3.1. The Latins on Cyprus

This chapter differs from the others (the second and fourth) because it primarily concerns the *Chronicle*'s depiction of the single, internally diverse community of Latins, composed of Cypriot Franks, Genoese and Venetians. Makhairas, retrospectively referring to the events (he could not have witnessed them himself) in which they participated, devotes a lot of space to them in his narrative, even though their greater presence on the island was of relatively short duration. The diversity of the Latin world is expressed in the plurality of behaviours, intentions and actions of these two groups described by the chronicler, which caused the narrative concerning the Cyprians themselves to be more restricted, and also determined how contacts between Christians and Muslims were presented, though denominations and religiosity play a very limited role in this picture. This is because the axis of the narrative concerning the relationships between different nations in the *Chronicle*'s Latin universe is the conflict between Cyprus and Genoa.

Peter Lock, who investigated the character of intercultural encounters between the Franks and Byzantines based on numerous Western and Greek sources, asks who the Frankish settlers were. In his answer he specifies five nations inhabiting the area of the Aegean Sea, that is: Venetians (in Constantinople, Thessalonika, Thebes and Corinth, on Crete and in Messenia), Genoese, merchants from other merchant republics, Catalans, and mercenaries from Gascony and Navarre.[1054]

Apart from the citizens of Genoa and Venice, Leontios sporadically mentions single Catalans or larger groups of them[1055] but he never describes them in the context of a separate identity; moreover, he never attempts to portray how they manifested their religious beliefs. A similar tendency may be found in the *Chronique d'Amadi* and Boustronios' work.[1056]

[1053] Italian text after Chimenz (Ed.), Tutte le opera, 311. Translation after Alighieri, Inferno, 112.
[1054] Lock, The Franks in the Aegean, 10–11.
[1055] Mentions of Catalonia appear in: LM I 26, II 91, 233, III 583–584, 587, V 686, and of Catalonians in LM II 95, 103, 182, 189, 192, 230, 255, III 291, 334, 342, 401, 508, 553, V 630, 683.
[1056] The former source most often mentions individuals such as the merchant *Alfonso Ferando*, who collaborated with Queen Eleanora (Mas Latrie (Ed.), Chronique d'Amadi, 435–436), the knight *Francesco Saturnino* (449, 478) and *Calceran Suares* (507–508, 514), and a young Catalan (*un zovene catelan*, 496). Francesco Saturnino also appears under the name Saturno (478). For information about versions of this surname see Cardinali, Costa, Dizionario della lingua italiana, 661. In the *Chronique d'Amadi* there also appear mentions of Catalonia as a geographical region (488) and about a group of Catalans (498), as well as two comments about objects belonging to them, that is a Catalan galley (*galie de Catalani*, 488) and ships (*nave de Caellani*,

Although in the literature on the medieval period all these communities are referred to as 'Franks', Makhairas avoids using this term with respect to nations other than the one that had arrived in Cyprus with the Lusignans. In the *Chronicle*, descriptions of the Genoese community are predominant, which proves that it made a far greater impression on the island's character in the period discussed by the author than the Venetians did.

The chronicler frequently uses the term 'community' (κουμουνί) to describe both the Genoese and the Venetian populations as a group. David Abulafia, who is interested in the structure of Genoese society, argues that like the Pisans, the Genoese organised themselves into communities called 'communes', 'city-republics' or finally 'companies'[1057] that were, he writes, public institutions 'embracing the whole community'. Simultaneously they were treated as separate formations, full of 'private enclaves'[1058] belonging to monastic orders and the nobility.[1059] In the *Chronicle* the Genoese not only besiege Cyprus, but partly also inhabit the island of Chios (Χίος),[1060] which, as Dawkins writes, had been 'a Genoese colony' since 1346.[1061]

Makhairas does not seem interested in whether and to what extent the Genoese and Venetians were religious, or in the course of their relationships with the church hierarchy. In this respect the narrative of the *Chronicle* is restrained and economical. In effect, we get a sparse image of the faith followed by these groups, a limited understanding of their concept of God and a meagre outline of religious practises. The chronicler usually focuses on the involvement of the Republic's citizens in trade and on conflict situations in which they often became embroiled. He does sometimes emphasise their affiliation with the Catholic Church by describing the influence repeatedly exerted on them by the pope. The Cypriot work, like the *Chronique d'Amadi*, Philippe de Mézières's text and Boustronios' work, shows that both states had their impact on events in the Christian world, also those directly linked to contact with followers of Islam, among others due to the significant profusion of their citizens in many countries of the Mediterranean Basin.

Staying on the subject of the evident Genoese presence outside Genoa, it is worth citing, after John Yousey-Hindes, the account of the notary Bonaventure of Savio, who in 1294 started out by ship on an expedition to the 'overseas': through the Straits of Messina, the Greek islands and Cyprus, to the Levant.[1062] He observed that the Genoese had spread worldwide and learned to gather into new clusters in foreign lands,[1063] though some of them – he himself being the best example – later returned to their native regions.[1064] Apart from the Turkish Ayas, the traveller visited Famagusta, which at that time was the seat of the Genoese clergy.[1065] According to Yousey-Hindes, who comments this report, the Genoese were divided into three groups: the first consisting of 'those that were virtually sovereign', the second, of those who lived in Muslim lands, and the third, of those who had settled 'in Christian territories'.[1066] If we adopt this division, in the *Chronicle* we encounter only the third group. Yousey-Hindes notes that many rulers of such foreign lands, the members of the Lusignan dynasty in Cyprus among them, had 'nominal control' over Genoese settlements, as was the case in Ayas and Cilician Armenia.[1067] The scholar thus describes the voyages made by the Republic's citizens and the role of religion in this process:

> *For Genoese traders looking to establish and maintain permanent settlements on foreign soil, the freedom to practice their faith must have been a significant matter. Access to familiar religious services [...] was certainly important at certain crucial moments, like immediately before and after death. [...] The presence of Genoese priests and churches helped tie the settlements together into*

---

517). All these examples were featured in the part of the narrative covering the 1372–1441 period. In Boustronios we encounter only two similar comments. See Dawkins (Transl., int.), The Chronicle of George Boustronios, 34, 52.

[1057] Abulafia, The Great Sea, 275–276.
[1058] Abulafia, The Great Sea, 276.
[1059] Abulafia, The Great Sea, 276.
[1060] LM II 145–146, III 376, 542, 563.
[1061] LM II 145. Dawkins, Notes, 108.
[1062] Yousey-Hindes, Living the Middle Life, 165.
[1063] Yousey-Hindes, Living the Middle Life, 165.
[1064] Yousey-Hindes, Living the Middle Life, 166–167.
[1065] Yousey-Hindes, Living the Middle Life, 166.
[1066] Yousey-Hindes, Living the Middle Life, 170.
[1067] Yousey-Hindes, Living the Middle Life, 172.

a specifically 'Genoese' network. [...] Just like in neighborhoods back home in Genoa, churches in the settlements were focal points of activity and symbolic emblems of their communities.[1068]

This idea of imperceptible dominium of Genoa is also reflected in literature, such as this poem by an anonymous author:

E tanti sun li Zenoexi
e per lo mondo sì distexi,
che und'eli van o stan
un'atra Zeno age fan.[1069]

And so many are the Genoese
And so scattered the world round
That wherever one [of them] *goes and stays,*
There he forms another Genoa.

The multidimensional activity of the Genoese[1070] and Venetians[1071] in the Mediterranean Basin and the Middle East is restricted in the *Chronicle* to Cyprus itself and to the role that the citizens of these small states played in its history: in the internal life of the island, trade contacts and numerous martial expeditions and political endeavours of the Frankish rulers, often making their presence strongly felt.

The start of relations between Cyprus and Genoa fell in the reign of Alice of Champagne, who granted this group many privileges, as communicated by the document of July 1218.[1072] The decree guaranteed 'freedom to buy and sell' (*libertas emendi et vendendi*) and also 'freedom to export and import on land and sea' (*[libertas] adducendi et extrahendi in terra et in mare*), consented to a free judiciary in all matters, 'excepting treason, rape and homicide' (*exceptis proditione, rapina et homicidio*), and also offered 'two pieces of land, that is one in Limassol, the other in Famagusta' (*duas pecias terre, scilicet unam apud Nimociam,*[1073] *aliam vero apud Famagustam*) with the right to build, and also the right to 'preserve integrity of persons and effects' (*personas et res eorum indemnes conservare*) in case of shipwreck.[1074] As Hill comments on these arrangements, the agreement had advantages for both sides: Cyprus obtained the support of the Genoese fleet while the inhabitants of Genoa could expand commerce and ensure their security.[1075] Earlier, in 1155, they had been granted the relevant rights ('commercial and fiscal privileges')

[1068] Yousey-Hindes, Living the Middle Life, 173.

[1069] Quotation drawn from Epstein, Genoa and the Genoese, 166. Kupiszewska's translation from the Polish translation by the author. Quoted and translated also in Yousey-Hindes, Living the Middle Life, 165.

[1070] Cf. Runciman, A History of the Crusades. The Genoese took efforts to actively extend their influence as traders, which Runciman emphasises, listing among others after Raymond of Aguilers' *Historia Francorum qui ceperunt Jeruzalem* (History of the Franks who captured Jerusalem) (11th c.) and after the *Gesta Francorum* their activity in Antioch, mobilisation to defend Jerusalem in 1099 and their part in building siege towers (v. 1, 218–219, 282, 284). It was thanks to them, the scholar states after Radulf of Caen (11–12th c.), Anna Komnene, Caffaro (12th c.) and Albert of Aix (12th c.), that Tancred, regent of the Principality of Antioch, cut Laodicea (Lattakieh) off from Cyprus in 1103 (v. 2, 34). They participated in the siege of Tripoli in the years 1103–1109 (v. 2, 56–70). During their activities they formed many colonies, conquering over a dozen settlements for their purposes. Runciman lists Jaffa, Acre, Caesarea, Arsuf, Tyre, Beyrout (Beirut), Tripoli, Jubail (or Jebail, Giblet), Laodicea (Lattakieh), Saint Siméon (Symeon) and Antioch (v. 2, 294). The texts used by Runciman as sources thus show them to have been active participants in many events related to the crusades.

[1071] Cf. Runciman, A History of the Crusades. The scholar bases his statements about the Venetians among others on sources such as *Translatio Sancti Nicolai in Venetiam* (Transfer of [the body of] St Nicholas to Venice) and *Historia ducum Venetorum* (History of the leaders of Venice) by anonymous authors (13th c.) and the chronicles of Albert of Aix, Fulk (Fulcher) of Chartres (11–12th c.) and William of Tyre (12th c.). Citing the aspect of the undoubted self-sufficiency of this Republic's representatives in setting valuable, in their view, objectives, he gives an account of how the influence of Venice expanded systematically thanks to various events in which its citizens took part. The deciding moment was 1100, when Godfrey de Bouillon, convinced by the Burgundian duke Warner of Gray, decided to grant the representatives of St Mark's standard the right to free trade in the whole state of the Franks, and the right to possess their own sacred building, marketplace and up to one third of the area in each jointly conquered town (v. 1, 312). In 1119, with the pope's consent, their aid was sought by Baldwin II after the 'Field of Blood' defeat (v. 2, 166). The Venetians took part in the attack on the island of Corfu, then in Byzantine hands, in 1122, on Acre in 1123 and in the siege of Tyre a year later (v. 2, 166–170).

[1072] Mas Latrie, Histoire de l'île de Chypre II, 39.

[1073] Nimocia is another name for Limassol, Lemesos. Information after Collenberg, État et origine, 197.

[1074] Mas Latrie, Histoire de l'île de Chypre II, 39. Cf. Hill, A History of Cyprus II, 85.

[1075] Hill, A History of Cyprus II, 85–86.

by Emperor Manuel I Komnenos.[1076] A similar honour had been awarded to the Venetians already in 1092 further to a decision ('the chrysobull') by Emperor Alexios I Komnenos.[1077] The task of defining anew and crystallising the mutual relationship with the Venetians was undertaken by Amaury de Lusignan in 1306 in Lefkosia. He ruled that 'Venetians and Venetian subjects and residents' (*Veneti et subjecti et districtuales Veneciarum*) should be given privileges that would make their functioning on the island easier, and moreover 'should have their own church, loggia, bath and accessible street in Lefkosia, Limassol and Famagusta' (*habere debeant in Nicossia, Limesso et Famagosta ecclesiam, logiam, domum pro bajulo et plateam convenientem non clausam*). Amaury guaranteed many other accommodations, which promise he sealed with the assurance that he did not want anything in exchange and that citizens of the Republic would always remain his friends.[1078]

The first mention – apart from the information about the Genoese participation in Guy's 1192 purchase of Cyprus[1079] – about the presence of representatives of merchant communities on the island appears in the *Chronicle* in the description of Cypriot ports,[1080] which explains the reasons for the diversity of products appearing on the islands, such as spices (σπετζίες).[1081] Based on this fragment, conclusions may be drawn about the causes of the islanders' prosperity at the time. Leontios compares Venetian ships with Genoese, Florentine, Pisan and Catalan ones. The riches they carried (τὴν πλουσιότηταν τὴν εἶχαν) were so imposing that the chronicler consciously refrains from further description of them: as he owns, his words lack sufficient power to do them justice (δὲν μπορῶ νὰ γράψω). At this point, the account is spontaneous, personal, and thus deprived of detail: Makhairas does not focus on specific features but on a general image of the 'beginnings' of Genoese and Venetian citizens' presence on the island, which is conducive to a reading of this passage as conveying a depiction of a kind of idyll, of the Latins' coexistence and cooperation, which brought prosperity and distinct harmony in mutual relations, to be later transformed into an ambiguous, hard to assess, often controversial form. In this passage the motif of the port as a gate is employed. Through it foreigners from distant lands arrive in Cyprus, enriching the multicultural community with new elements. In this description, the author does not convey the sense of threat from the sea that can be felt in the depiction of the Alexandrian port in the *Chronique d'Amadi*, where we read that 'the sea near the town was highly perilous' (*il mare apresso la cità è molto pericoloso*),[1082] and in another passage, where the waters touching the outskirts of Alexandria are called agitated (*il mare era grosso*).[1083] This vision is also a nod to the civilisational advances made by man, such as ships and vessels that made it possible to reach distant regions of the world (for purposes other than warfare) and communicate with foreign nations. The people 'who arrived from the West were deemed beautiful and good' (οἱ ἐρχομένοι ἀπὸ τὴν δύσιν ὄμορφοι καὶ καλοί) by the young brothers Peter and John de Lusignan.[1084] Western merchants who happened to 'be in that place' (ὅπου εἶχεν ὁ τόπος) were sometimes used to adjudicate local disputes.[1085]

The chapter examines the contacts between Cypriot Franks, Genoese and Venetians in the *Chronicle* in three dimensions of relations: between Genoese and Venetians, Cypriots and Genoese, and Cypriots and Venetians. It thus starts by showing what attitude in Makhairas' work the two communities that were the closest in the historical sense had towards each other, and finishes with the relationship that he described the most economically. The study devotes the most space to analysis of the Lusignans' confrontation with the citizens of Genoa, whose portrait the chronicler draws with exceptional attention to detail.

[1076] Jacoby, Byzantium, the Italian Maritime Powers, 677.
[1077] Frankopan, Byzantine Trade Privileges to Venice, 135–160.
[1078] Mas Latrie, Histoire de l'île de Chypre II, 102–108. Kupiszewska's translation of the Latin phrases from the Polish translation by the author.
[1079] LM I 19–20.
[1080] A detailed list of Cypriot ports is contained in Özkutlu, Medieval Famagusta, 328–330.
[1081] LM II 91.
[1082] Mas Latrie (Ed.), Chronique d'Amadi, 41. 'Perilous' has also been the word chosen by Coureas, Edbury (Transl.), The Chronicle of Amadi, 42 (§ 74) as a translation of the word '*pericoloso*'.
[1083] Mas Latrie (Ed.), Chronique d'Amadi, 193.
[1084] LM I 79.
[1085] LM III 334.

3.2. Depiction of Genoese-Venetian relations on Cyprus

The relations between the Genoese and the Venetians portrayed in the *Chronicle* manifested themselves in tensions, skirmishes and rivalry caused by the desire to take possession over a given area and derive benefits from unlimited control over it.[1086] Despite the initially, as the work suggests, peaceful coexistence of the Genoese and Venetian nations on Cyprus, their relations presented in further parts of the text change gradually. At certain moments the interests of the two countries seem closely convergent, at others they are clearly contradictory. Mentions of both the Genoese and of the Venetians are an important component of the narrative, though usually these formations appear to be in constant conflict.

The first trace of hostile relations is found in LM III 325, during an unfortunate incident during which a custom was violated. The Venetians, who were escorting Peter II together with the Genoese after his coronation ceremony in 1372, desired to hold the reins on the right side (τὸ ῥέτινον [...] τὸ δεξιόν) of the royal horse, which had previously, 'in accordance with the privilege' (κατὰ τὴν φραντζίνζαν), been done by representatives of the other community, with the Venetians taking the left side (ἀριστερά). Makhairas explains that the Venetians decided to commit this act of insubordination 'because [they] were many' (διατὶ ἦτον πολλοί). The 'great confusion' (μία ταραχὴ μεγάλη) that ensued was contained by the prince (the king's uncle) and the lord of Arsuf.[1087] The *Chronique d'Amadi* cites the same episode of course.[1088]

Right after this incident came a dinner held to celebrate the coronation, with tragic consequences: during it a duel was fought, and then a battle (ἡ ταραχὴ ἦτον πολλὰ μεγάλη), joined also by the populace of Ammochostos, who attempted to force their way into the Genoese loggia.[1089] Leontios uses the following legible, suggestive metaphor to describe the hostility demonstrated during the feast by the two communities:

[...] *as they were eating, the one Republic was threatening (ἐφοβέριζεν) the other, and they were grinding their teeth (ἐτρίζαν τὰ δοντία τους).* (LM III 328)

The events outlined in LM III 328–343 show the escalation of mutual dislike. During this dinner there took place a fierce fight with naked swords, which led to the deaths of several persons.[1090] According to the chronicler, this happened because a convenient opportunity occurred: that is, the king left the hall. The Venetians unfurled their war flag, thus signalising their readiness for battle, and the maddened crowd started raiding shops in panic.[1091] It is in this description of the failed banquet, which cast a shadow on other events of the celebrations such as the tournament (τζοῦστες),[1092] that the reasons for the increasing disagreement growing between the Lusignans and the citizens of Genoa may be found. As a higher instance, Pope Gregory XI (1328|1370–1378) had the king and his council confiscate the assets of the Venetians responsible for the turmoil, calling them 'murderers' (τοὺς φονιάδες).[1093]

An important factor in the shaping of Genoese-Venetian relations was whose side would be taken by the Franks, who stood at the head of Cypriot society and were at the centre of events. The island conquered by them in the twelfth century gradually took on the role of a space of bitter conflict and rivalry between different Western nations. In passages of the *Chronicle* that show the complicated (and very numerous) links between the three groups that made up the Latin denominational community, the island's Greek character is almost completely lost. When describing these links Makhairas puts the Orthodox population to one side, thus making room for a discussion of the different forms of coexistence between the Catholic

---

[1086] The citizens of the two Republics usually fought each other for control over a given area, and Cyprus was not the only location involved. In the years 1204–1211 they were involved in bitter conflict for influence in Crete, for instance (Borowska, *Kreta okresu renesansu*, 13). In the discussion of their aggressive behaviour in other territories that were in the sphere of influence of the two states, Runciman cites the murder of a Genoese merchant at the hand of a Venetian in Acre in 1250 and the two states' claims towards the monastery of St Sabas located on Montjoie hill in Acre, dividing the zones occupied by the two communities (Runciman, *A History of the Crusades* 3, 282).

[1087] LM III 325.

[1088] Mas Latrie (Ed.), Chronique d'Amadi, 432–433.

[1089] LM III 330.

[1090] Makhairas informs us that the bodies of the dead were transported out of Ammochostos on carts to St George's church and buried there.

[1091] LM III 331.

[1092] LM III 333.

[1093] LM III 353.

communities on Cyprus: both the positive ones that brought prosperity to the island and the destructive ones that weakened the potential brought by cooperation and were related to the struggle for influence.

In the *Chronique d'Amadi* we encounter a similarly complicated image. The two groups were united in 1242 in helping to repel the Lombard siege of Tyre,[1094] and in 1310 decorated Tyre together with the Pisans during preparations of a ceremony to welcome King Henry on his return after the end of fighting with the Armenians.[1095] In their presence Pope Urban V encouraged King Peter to forge peace with the sultan in 1368[1096] and ultimately they both played an equal part in the agreement King Janus concluded with the Islamic ruler in 1426.[1097] However, it is the spectacular incidents that make up the feud, mentioned in the *Chronique d'Amadi*, that seem more strongly accented: they include the dispute about the house of St Sabas in Acre in 1256 and the continuation of the conflict thus engendered a year later,[1098] the maritime battle between fleets belonging to the two Republics in 1292–1293,[1099] the events following the fatal banquet at the conclusion of King Peter II's coronation[1100] and the battle of Chioggia in the years 1378–1381, which had great repercussions.[1101] Terms of interest present in this source that negatively describe the nature of the mutual relations between the two states' citizens and the resulting actions include: 'hostility' (*inimicicia*),[1102] 'great battle' (*gran battaglie*)[1103] and 'disorder' (*romor*),[1104] which in terms of meaning coincide with the ones found in the *Chronicle*.

From the sequence of events portrayed by Leontios, it seems that as the rulers of Cyprus, the Frankish sovereigns had the power to pronounce judgements if one of the groups living on Cypriot land disturbed the peace of the general populace, which is seen among others in the attitude of Peter II and the prince, who accused the potestate of Genoa, Antony de Negrone (μισὲρ Ἀντίνιος τα Νεγροῦ), of intentionally participating in the Genoese-Venetian conflict.[1105] In revenge, the latter accused Peter II of rashly sending many Genoese to their deaths without making a full reconnaissance and in violation of the terms of the agreement concluded between the Republics and the Kingdom of Cyprus.[1106] In Leontios' account, Antony de Negrone used the right means of persuasion, emphasising the undeserved suffering of his fellow citizens, whom the Lusignans, following a policy of favouring the Venetians, treated with violence, disregarding the aid that the Genoese had previously offered them.[1107] The Genoese leader's words are an instance of evident manipulation, because he alleged that the Frankish authorities acted to the advantage of the Republic of Venice, which would prove their duplicity. The chronicler skilfully shows how this trick of persuasion helped the potestate influence the king's decision: after hearing the accusations he apologised immediately and forbade any harm to be done to the Genoese under pain of losing one's right hand, freed the Genoese prisoners, made his amends to them,[1108] and moreover consented to their movement on the island and to expeditions beyond it, e.g. for purposes of trade.[1109] The consequence of this verdict was that the citizens of the Republic sailed away unnoticed 'so that they were not seen' (δὲν τοὺς ἐνῶσαν) in treasure-filled ships to tell their countrymen of the matter.[1110]

The Lusignans treated the two Republics not as uniform wholes, but as heterogeneous collectives composed of individuals who were responsible for their own deeds. This is confirmed by specific cases of persons named by the chronicler and by the legal provisions discussed below, which distinguish and define different forms of belonging to the Genoese community. This is particularly evident in those places where Makhairas makes a distinction between the Genoese who are guilty and those free of guilt

---

[1094] Mas Latrie (Ed.), Chronique d'Amadi, 189–194; Coureas, Edbury (Transl.), The Chronicle of Amadi, 187–189 (§§ 344–345).
[1095] Mas Latrie (Ed.), Chronique d'Amadi, 380, 383–384; Coureas, Edbury (Transl.), The Chronicle of Amadi, 347, 350 (§§ 718, 725).
[1096] Mas Latrie (Ed.), Chronique d'Amadi, 419; Coureas, Edbury (Transl.), The Chronicle of Amadi, 381–382 (§ 844).
[1097] Mas Latrie (Ed.), Chronique d'Amadi, 514; Coureas, Edbury (Transl.), The Chronicle of Amadi, 465 (§ 1075).
[1098] Mas Latrie (Ed.), Chronique d'Amadi, 204–206; Coureas, Edbury (Transl.), The Chronicle of Amadi, 200 (§§ 394–395).
[1099] Mas Latrie (Ed.), Chronique d'Amadi, 230–233; Coureas, Edbury (Transl.), The Chronicle of Amadi, 225–227 (§§ 482–483).
[1100] Mas Latrie (Ed.), Chronique d'Amadi, 432–435; Coureas, Edbury (Transl.), The Chronicle of Amadi, 392–395 (§§ 872–877).
[1101] Mas Latrie (Ed.), Chronique d'Amadi, 488–490; Coureas, Edbury (Transl.), The Chronicle of Amadi, 442–444 (§§ 997–1002). Edbury and Coureas explain that this referred to rule over the island of Tenedos on the Aegean Sea (Coureas, Edbury (Transl.), The Chronicle of Amadi, 443, fn. 2).
[1102] Mas Latrie (Ed.), Chronique d'Amadi, 230.
[1103] Mas Latrie (Ed.), Chronique d'Amadi, 233.
[1104] Mas Latrie (Ed.), Chronique d'Amadi, 432.
[1105] LM III 336.
[1106] LM III 328, 336.
[1107] LM III 336.
[1108] LM III 337.
[1109] LM III 338.
[1110] LM III 339–340.

or mentions letters sent to the government stipulating that the innocent Genoese can go on working and have the right to retain...

> ... *their freedom (τὴν ἐλευθερίαν) at all times (πάντοτε) in all [...] island, according to their use and wont (κατὰ τὸ συνειθισμένον τὸ ἔχουν).* (LM III 335)

The descriptions of the events discussed are not directly connected to religion. However, they are a reflection of a sort of the relations within the Latin community in Cyprus. An analysis of these incidents shows that belonging to the same religion, denomination or culture does not imply that shared goals will emerge, while lack of unanimity in this respect leads to an evident breach that has dangerous consequences. Disputes resulting from such discord do not have to have a religious nature to effectively split the inherent structure of the Western world, stunting the care for fellow worshippers that is necessary for its cohesiveness and continuity of tradition.

In the *Chronicle* it may be seen that in situations where there was no chance of reaching a convenient solution, alliances were formed between the three state entities, Genoa, Venice and the Kingdom of Cyprus established by the Franks, where countries granted each other the right to administer places and facilities (e.g. castles) that were important from their point of view. To back up this claim: during the Genoese-Venetian battle of Chioggia (Κλόζαν), fought at the turn of the years 1379–1380, the citizens of Genoa ceded Ammochostos, an important object of their interests, to the Cypriot king, because they feared that it would become the property of their enemies.[1111] The same passage reveals the game that the Genoese played with the Venetians, involving close observation of their moves and using moments of their inattention to demonstrate their triumph at an auspicious moment. Namely, using a drop in the vigilance of their opponent, busy searching for a lost ship, they captured Chioggia, a town that, as the *Chronique d'Amadi* states, the Venetians believed 'noble' (*nobile*).[1112]

The defeat at Chioggia determined the long-term position of the Venetians, who 'seeing their weakness' (θωρῶντα τὴν ἀδυναμιάν τους) acquiesced to the demands of the Genoese, sending them a 'blank sheet' (χαρτὶν ἄγραφον) in recognition of their defeat. The latter, taking advantage of the circumstances to demonstrate their disdain, proposed a list of demeaning and humiliating wishes, the most important being the opportunity to 'plunder Venice for three days' (νὰ κου(ρ)σεύσουν μέσα τὴν Βενετίαν γ΄ ἡμέρες), and also set 'many other reprehensible conditions' (ἄλλα πολλὰ στοιχήματα ἄπρεπα). To make their portrayal still more ambiguous, Makhairas states that they pretended to temper their expectations by spreading out the destructive actions over time. Although the Venetians managed to regain Chioggia thanks to the elderly Victor Pisani (Βιτὸρ Πιζάνης), who had been liberated from prison and whom the *Chronicle* describes as a 'wise old man' (ἕναν γνωστικὸν ἄνθρωπον γέροντα), their level of fear and distrust was so high that for a long time they doubted that the triumphantly flying flag of St Mark (τὸ φλάμπουρον τοῦ ἁγίου Μάρκου) that Carlo Zeno (Κάρλο Τζὲτ) used to announce his victory when approaching Venice was real. Carlo was a representative of the younger generation (ἑνός παιδίος), who 'out of hate' (διὰ τὴν μισιτείαν) for the Genoese agreed to Peter II's proposal to aid him in combating them.[1113] Having returned from his expedition 'in the East' (ἀπὸ τὴν ἀνατολήν),[1114] he first went to Venice and then set off for Chioggia to support Victor Pisani, which hastened the victory. Peace was made on condition that Chioggia be destroyed (νὰ χαλάσουν τὴν Κλόζαν) so that '[they] will fight no more' (μηδὲν πολεμίσουν).[1115]

It should be emphasised that none of the episodes discussed is strictly related to religion, although mentions are frequent in the text of Pope Gregory XI's intervention in the events described by providing counsel or relevant commands. Leontios, focusing on the political dimension of the conflict, credits individual groups with having the protection of God, who evidently favourises this or that community depending on their current merits. When the representatives of one of them betray His will – and it may be noted that this will is not precisely defined anywhere in the *Chronicle* – they are punished for it. Makhairas himself frequently finds it hard to judge whether the act of one person or group is righteous from a human perspective, and thus he does not usually reveal his own beliefs.

[1111] LM III 584–586.
[1112] LM III 588. See Mas Latrie (Ed.), Chronique d'Amadi, 488.
[1113] LM III 584.
[1114] LM III 591–593.
[1115] LM III 593.

3.3. Depiction of Cypriot-Genoese relations on Cyprus

The *Chronicle* shows that the emergence of the relationship between the Cypriots, that is the community composed of Franks and Cyprians on the one hand, and the Genoese on the other was quite a tempestuous process, which is reflected in different parts of the narrative.

Leontios assigns pejorative descriptors to the citizens of the Republic, including: 'unfaithful people of the Genoese' (ἡ ἄπιστος γενεὰ τῶν Γενουβίσων),[1116] 'unfaithful Genoese' (ἄπιστοι Γενουβίσοι),[1117] 'unfaithful and treasonous Genoese' (οἱ ἄπιστοι Γενουβίσοι οἱ παράβουλοι)[1118] or 'enemies of God, the Genoese' (οἱ ἐχθροὶ τοῦ θεοῦ οἱ Γενουβίσοι).[1119] This also pertains to expressions describing the complex sphere of their activity, such as: 'false oaths of the Genoese' (οἱ ψεματινοὶ ὅρκοι τῶν Γενουβίσων),[1120] or marked sentences concerning their immoral conduct, like: 'betrayal [committed] by the Genoese of the people who had left the town' (τὴν ἀπιστίαν τοὺς Γενουβίσους μέσα εἰς τοὺς λᾶς ὁποῦσαν ἔξω τῆς χώρας).[1121] In one passage Makhairas describes them as 'having knowledge' or otherwise 'gifted in cognitive facilities' (γνωστικοί), but this designation only seemingly praises their intellect, serving rather to underline their craftiness and guile in using a Greek priest for their own ends in January 1374, and then killing him cruelly.[1122] In another fragment, the author of the *Chronicle* calls them 'people inclined to grill [others]' (ἀνθρῶποι τζιγαριστάδες),[1123] who are…

> …*never content but when toiling after riches* (δὲν παίρνουν ἄλλην ἀνάπαυσιν παροὺ εἰς τὸ πλοῦτος καὶ εἰς τὸν κάματον). (LM III 558)

In various places of the *Chronicle* the citizens of Genoa are compared to Armenians, like in the remark:

> […] *there are no people* (καμίαν γενιά) *more given to faction* (νὰ ζηλεύγουν) *than the Genoese and the Armenians, both of them cursed folks* (δύο καταραμένοι) […]. (LM III 520)[1124]

In yet another paragraph Leontios writes:

> […] *the Armenians had two hundred castles and towns and lost them through (their pride* (τὴν σουπέρπιαν τους) *and) factiousness* (ἀπὸ τὴν ζήλαν τους ἐχάσαν τα). *And this same thing we trust in God will befall this Republic as well* (τὸ ποῖον ἤτζου θέλει γινεῖν καὶ τοῦτον τὸ κουμούνιν, θαροῦμεν εἰς τὸν θεόν). (LM III 520)

The Genoese trait of deceitfulness, combined with arrogance and a tendency to work towards permanently destabilising the island's wellbeing, underlined in the *Chronicle*, is accented in the research of Nicolaou-Konnari, who notes that the terms and expressions used by the chronicler to describe this group are more numerous than the vocabulary with which he portrays the Muslims and their connotations are more negative.[1125]

[1116] LM III 538.
[1117] LM III 421, 423, 538, 545.
[1118] LM III 473–474.
[1119] LM III 443.
[1120] LM III 546
[1121] LM III 443.
[1122] LM III 468.
[1123] Dawkins explains the meaning of the noun 'τζιγαριστάδες': 'By a metaphor […] it means people who keep their neighbours, as it were, in a pan over a fire of trouble, and, as a cook stirs the meat with a fork, so keep them perpetually on the move with fresh forms of vexation.' (Dawkins, Notes, 191).
[1124] Dawkins, citing a medieval Greek proverb and two lines by the Byzantine poet Kassia, argues that Armenians were perceived as troublemakers and traitors (Dawkins, Notes, 182). A negative attitude towards Armenians, not only in Makhairas' *Chronicle*, but also in Nilos' work, was noted by Coureas, in Coureas, Religion and ethnic identity, 23.
[1125] Nicolaou-Konnari, Alterity and identity, 53–54.

3.3.1. The beginnings of the Cypriot-Genoese conflict on Cyprus

We find one of the first mentions of Cypriot-Genoese contact in the *Chronicle* in LM II 145, on the margin of the events that played out in 1363 in the shadow of the conflict between Christians and Muslims. Leontios begins the narrative concerning this subject with a tale of two sailors who are crew members on galleys sent 'to guard the island' (διὰ φύλαξιν τοῦ νησσίου) against a potential attack by the Saracens.[1126] As the chronicler writes, the Genoese affiliation of these guards was revealed through their own declaration ('διαφεντεύτησαν διὰ Γενουβίσον). The conflict flared when the men, despite having received remuneration for the work contracted from the Cypriot government, ran away without having fulfilled their duties, and after being captured suffered the punishment of losing their right ears. At the same time a different Genoese galley had been in port, and on hearing of this affront its crew murdered a large number of Cypriots in a gesture of revenge, which in turn led to the arrest of all the Genoese upon the order of the regent of Cyprus, the prince of Antioch, James de Lusignan.[1127] In vengeance, the potestate commanded the tongue (γλῶσσαν) of the Pisan 'who had found a pretext to [pretend that he] was Genoese' (ηὗρεν τὸν ἀφορμὴν πῶς ἤτοι Γενουβίσος) to be cut off.[1128] This incident depicts an escalation of violence, originating in an individual decision and then gradually coming to involve more and more innocent people who were forced to suffer its consequences.

In the context of this particular sequence of events, a comment by the potestate to Cypriot admiral John de Sur is noteworthy. He noted the dispersal of the Genoese population outside the borders of Cyprus and that its members, linked by ties of cooperation and support, were carriers of memory about injury and the thought of revenge.[1129] The potestate expresses this thought thus:

'Do not think, my lord, that if you cut down (κατακόψῃς) the Genoese who are in Famagusta, that you are killing (σκοτώννεις) all the Genoese in the world (ὅσους ἔχει εἰς τὸν κόσμον); there are many more in the world of our blood (ἀπὲ τὸ αἷμαν μας), and they will avenge themselves (ἀποῦ θέλουν πάρειν βεντέτταν ἀπὸ 'ξ αὐτῶν) on the murderers (τοὺς φονιάδες): do not think that we are your serfs (χωργιάτες σου).' (LM II 146)

The vision of the Genoese community's dispersal 'in the world' (εἰς τὸν κόσμον) – this general description of place is contained in the quoted fragment twice – is consistent with Yousey-Hindes' remark cited at the start of this chapter.[1130] The words that appear in the potestate's statement, such as 'cut down' (κατακόψῃς) and 'kill' (σκοτώννεις), call up an image of the expected potential actions of the admiral, suggest that even taking part in a massacre, of which the Cypriots are capable, will be insignificant in the context of the sheer numbers of Genoese connected by ties of blood to their fellow citizens who might be killed on the island. The expression 'of our blood' (ἀπὲ τὸ αἷμαν μας) refers to the category of heritage and family, within which memory about an injury passes from generation to generation and demands retribution for the many murdered compatriots.[1131]

The events discussed in the *Chronicle* were not without serious repercussions. The Cypriot authorities realised that the tragedy and mutual recriminations occurred due to a lack of knowledge about the real identity of the negligent workers, which left room for interpretation and as a result, vigilante justice. In their attempt to deal with this, the potestate and the Lusignans issued two contradicting decrees (διαλαλημοί). The first commanded that 'all Genoese leave Cyprus' (ὅλοι οἱ Γενουβίσοι νὰ 'φκαιρέσουν τὴν Κύπρον),[1132] while the second allowed them to remain 'without fear for their persons or material effects' (χωρὶς φόβον τὸ κορμίν του καὶ τὸ δικόν του), and thus took into account the freedom (θέλημάν) to choose, which in Makhairas' opinion had previously always existed (κατὰ τὸ συνήθιν).[1133]

[1126] LM II 145.
[1127] LM II 145.
[1128] LM II 146. Σάθας (Ed.), Χρονογράφοι Βασιλείου Κύπρου, 117, lacks part of LM II 146 and all of LM II 147–149.
[1129] LM II 146.
[1130] Fragment discussed above in Yousey-Hindes, Living the Middle Life, 165.
[1131] LM II 146–147.
[1132] LM II 147.
[1133] LM II 148.

The uncertainty with which the Frankish court approached the drafting of specific legal provisions indicates the complexity of the situation in which Makhairas' Franks had found themselves. This situation was affected both by their expectations, such as the need to ensure their safety in the face of political threats, in this case mainly from the Turks. The Cypriot king, invariably desirous of 'defeating the infidel Saracens' (νὰ κατακόψῃ τοὺς ἀπίστους Σαρακηνούς), adopted a conciliatory attitude because he did not want to become embroiled in a conflict with the Genoese and irritate them (νὰ τοὺς ἀγκρίσῃ). In effect, confronting, as the chronicler termed it, 'numerous differences' (πολλὲς διαφορές) and 'contested issues' (ζητήματα), he brought about the adoption of 'legal articles' (κεφάλαια τοῦτα), recorded in Latin (λατίνικα),[1134] for 'reaching an accord' (νὰ συντύχουν),[1135] which regulated the presence of citizens of the Republic on the island and set out the permitted scope of their functioning, based on a precise vocabulary, chosen so as to minimise the risk of tragic misunderstandings as far as possible.[1136]

These articles contain the requirement of true and permanent peace (ἀγάπη νὰ ἦνε ἀληθινὴ καὶ στερεωμένη), the establishment of which was to be facilitated by specially selected 'envoys' (μαντατοφόροι). A command was included to 'define' (νὰ καθαρίσουν), 'who the Genoese are' (ποῖγοι εἶνε Γενουβίσοι), 'who those that use the name "Genoese" are' (ποῖγοι εἶνε ὅπου κράζουνται Γενουβίσοι),[1137] which individuals are Genoese as a result of emancipation (ἦνε ἀπουλεύθεροι τῶν Γενουβίσων), and which are 'of the emancipated' (ἀπὸ ἐλευθέρους),[1138] what the situation of 'those who live on Genoese lands' (ὅλοι ὅπου εἶνε εἰς τὸν τόπον τοὺς Γενουβίσων) is, what freedom may be obtained by those who 'use the name "Genoese"' (οἱ κραζομένοι Γενουβίσοι), what should be done with those who are 'people of the king' ([οἱ] ἀνθρῶποι τοῦ ρηγός) 'because of their poverty' (ἀπὸ τὴν πτωχιάν τους), what right to enter Cyprus appertains to 'all Genoese' (ὅλοι οἱ Γενουβίσοι) and to 'those who are called "Genoese"' (οἱ λεγομένοι Γενουβίσοι), who should hold the right to the 'Genoese loggia' (λότζαν τῶν Γενουβίσων), upon what basis such membership should (νὰ τοὺς δεκτοῦν μετὰ χαρᾶς) be extended to a man 'from Genoese lands' (ἀπὸ τόπους γενουβίσικους)[1139] and many others.

These articles show the interpretational difficulties involved in establishing the scope of the name 'Genoese', which originally meant a 'citizen of Genoa', and thus in ascertaining the identity of such a person and defining the principles of participation in the Genoese community. An interesting distinction lies at the basis of the juxtaposition of Genoese in truth (ποῖγοι εἶνε Γενουβίσοι), and thus in blood, and the so-called White Genoese, who 'were Genoese in name' (κράζουνται Γενουβίσοι), i.e. by convention, which proves that in this case strict rules of inheritance were not observed, and above all that religious issues were not a constituent of this identity.

3.3.2. Siege of Famagusta (Ammochostos)

The *Chronicle* states that one of the main objects in contention between the Genoese and the Cypriots was the port of Ammochostos (Ἀμόχουστος, Αμμόχωστος), called Famagusta by the Latins.[1140] This port town located in the eastern part of Cyprus and important for international trade had existed, as Nicola Coldstream notes, before the arrival of the Lusignans.[1141] It drew the attention of the citizens of the Republic because of its particularly advantageous location. According to the *Chronique d'Amadi*, citizens of Genoa received houses there as early as 1232.[1142]

[1134] LM II 153.

[1135] LM II 153, MS O. See Dawkins (Ed., transl.), Ἐξήγησις/ Recital, 134 (fn. 6); Παυλίδης (Ed.), Λεοντίου Μαχαιρᾶ Χρονικόν, 110 (fn. 8).

[1136] Pavlidis notes that: 'Ὁ Μαχαιρᾶς δίνει πολύ αλλοιωμένα τα ονόματα των 12 Γενουατών εκπροσώπων.' 'Makhairas provides many incorrect names [of persons] in the group of twelve Genoese representatives.' (Παυλίδης (Ed.), Λεοντίου Μαχαιρᾶ Χρονικόν, 113, fn. 2. Kupiszewska's translation from the Polish translation by the author).

[1137] Sathas, Miller (Eds, transl.), Chronique de Chypre, 84: *Qui se disent Génois*.

[1138] LM II 154. MS O. See Dawkins (Ed., transl.), Ἐξήγησις/ Recital, 136 (fn. 2); Παυλίδης (Ed.), Λεοντίου Μαχαιρᾶ Χρονικόν, 112 (fn. 1).

[1139] LM II 154.

[1140] Ammochostos, the town presently known also as Gazimağusa and Mağusa. Located in north Cyprus, on territory inhabited by the Turkish population.

[1141] Coldstream, Preface, xxvii.

[1142] Mas Latrie (Ed.), Chronique d'Amadi, 167.

Makhairas tells that right after the hostile encounter between the Genoese and Venetians when they were together at the royal table during the post-coronation dinner, there occurred rioting, with far-reaching consequences. Initially, the representatives of the Genoese nation remained patient (μὲ τὴν ἀπομονήν) and prudent ([μὲ] τὴν φρόνησιν), but after the situation calmed down they sent letters to the king of Aragon and the lords of Barcelona explaining that it had been the queen of Cyprus, Eleanora of Aragon, who had requested them to undertake an expedition to the island 'in order to avenge' (νὰ πάρουν βεντέτταν) King Peter I, her murdered husband.[1143] This step shows that they were acting intentionally and were able to gauge the situation and use it for their ends.

The Genoese started preparing the expedition to Cyprus in 1372, when they received permission from the pope.[1144] Shortly after the first attack, they kept circling Ammochostos, unsuccessfully attempting to enter the port.[1145] Leontios speaks out on the Lusignans' side, attaching no blame for these incidents to them, as indicated by his negative assessment of the Genoese multitude besieging the town on 12 May 1373. The surrounding of Ammochostos was a consequence of earlier Cypriot-Genoese strife and the aggressors' response to their demands not being met.[1146] Commenting this fact, Makhairas refers to them as 'devious' (πονηροί) because, as he explains, 'they [acted] deviously' (πονηρὰ ἐκαταστῆσαν). On the day in question they started plundering the port, entering it 'from the side of Oxen Island' (εἰς τὸ νησσὶν τῶν Βοϊδίων), as Dawkins explains, one of the two nearby islets (LM III 362).[1147]

The *Chronicle* familiarises us with many episodes of the evolving crisis, which Makhairas describes in his characteristic manner, in the form of sequences of different persons' actions.

The climax is the tale of how the Genoese, endeavouring to seize the 'heart' of Ammochostos, that is to win the castle, deceived John of Morphou, prince of Rukha (Edessa). To do this they plotted an intrigue that used their knowledge about the claims of the pretender to the Cypriot throne, Hugh, prince of Galilee, the son of Guy, constable of Cyprus and grandson of Hugh IV of Cyprus,[1148] who was also the son in law of John of Morphou, and to whose father, Guy, Hugh IV had promised the throne (which was then taken by force by King Peter I).[1149] The Genoese envoys told John in secret from Peter II, who was then in his chamber, that Hugh himself was on their ship (he was actually fighting against the Lombards in Neapolis),[1150] and was waiting to take over the kingdom. Despite the difference in opinions between the members of the hastily called council and Raymond Babin, butler of Cyprus, whom John persuaded to agree to open the gates of the castle to the Genoese, the decision was made to allow them in. The plot culminated in a siege of the castle, and thus the whole town.[1151]

John of Morphou's outmanoeuvring of Raymond Babin is compared by the chronicler to the scene in paradise where Adam and Eve are led astray by Satan:

And he acted towards him (ἐποῖκεν εἰς αὐτῆς του) as the devil acted to Eve and Adam (ὣς γοιὸν ἐποῖκεν ὁ διάβολος μὲ τὴν Εὔαν καὶ τὸν Ἀδάμ) [...]. (LM III 412)

Leontios writes that they rued their lack of caution. MS O contains an additional piece of information comparing their sorrow to that of Judas (ὡς γοιὸν ἐμετάνωσεν ὁ Ἰούδας μὲ τὸν Χριστόν).[1152]

Continuing this interpretation, Makhairas writes that John, who 'became blind because of their sinfulness' ('κάθετον τυφλὸς διὰ τὴν ἁμαρτίαν τους), and Raymond:

[...] allowed themselves to be deceived (ἐκομπώθησαν) for the sake of gain (κέρδος), and all of them were cheated (ὅλοι ἐτζενιάστησαν) and brought the island to ruin (ἐκλῦσαν τὸ νησσίν). How many

---

[1143] LM III 354.
[1144] LM III 358.
[1145] LM III 362.
[1146] See LM III 352–424.
[1147] Dawkins, Notes, 152. The occupation of Ammochostos in the years 1373–1464 is mentioned among others in: Arbel, Venice's Maritime Empire, 184–185; Coureas, Taverns in Medieval Famagusta, 69; Coureas, Economy, 155; Hill, A History of Cyprus II, 387; Varella, Language Contact, 60.
[1148] LM III 409.
[1149] Dawkins' addition in brackets in LM III 412.
[1150] LM III 409.
[1151] LM III 414.
[1152] Dawkins (Ed., transl.), Ἐξήγησις/ Recital, 394 (fn. 10); Παυλίδης (Ed.), Λεοντίου Μαχαιρᾶ Χρονικόν, 304 (fn. 8).

women were widowed (χῆρες) and how many children were orphaned (ὀρφανοί), and the Genoese (took away their goods,) and they became beggars! (LM III 413)

In these passages we encounter references to Biblical figures and the motif of beguilement, which is part of the semantic field of the devil. It is the Cypriots' sinfulness (διὰ τὴν ἁμαρτίαν τους) that determined the failure of their relations with the Genoese, whose object was 'benefit' (διὰ τὸ κέρδος), that is tangible material goods. Makhairas uses the verbs 'τζενιάζω' ('cheat')[1153] and 'κλύζω' ('mill round', 'flow in', 'cumulate')[1154] to describe what the citizens of the Republic had done to the island's inhabitants. ΘΚΔ gives 'πλημμυρίζω' as a synonym of 'κλύζω', which should be translated as 'swarm' and 'inundate'. These meanings seem significant for reconstructing the image of how the island was taken by the Genoese masses, resembling rapid flooding, entrapping it or a teeming inside it. This portrayal can be interpreted as a metaphor of a flood of rough waters engulfing the country or a plague of locusts spreading all over the land.

A demonstration of the conviction held by the representatives of the Republic that they had priority rights to the Cypriot town and that the course of events unfavourable to the Cypriots was the result of their sins may be found in the following passage, containing a statement from 1374 made during a specially summoned council.

'Sirs, we have now come (ἥρταμεν –νὰ κάμωμεν,–) here –to Cyprus,¬ and God has given (ἔδωκέν μας) us Famagusta; now that we have come to try to take Kerynia, we are afraid that we may lose the sweet for the sake of the sour (φοβούμεσταν μὲν χάσωμεν τὰ ἥμερα διὰ τὰ ἄγρια). By the grace of God (μὲ τοῦ θεοῦ) we are holding (ἔχομεν) Famagusta, and let us not lose (μὲν χάσωμεν) Famagusta for the sake of Kerynia [...].' (LM III 449)[1155]

It is evident that the Genoese treat the port as a gift from God and want to keep this particular gift as rightfully theirs, even though the capture of another Cypriot town, Kerynia, would have given them complete power over the island. There appears in this place, like in others, an incongruity between the Cypriots' belief that their control over the island was granted by God, and the firmly expressed conviction of the Genoese that they were receiving supernatural aid.

When relating these events, Makhairas finds an interesting though indirect way of showing the differences in understanding the question of otherness. This may be seen in the description of Peter II's deliberations concerning who was the greater threat, and thus the greater evil, to his plans and the prosperity of Cyprus as a whole: the Genoese, who though close to the Franks in terms of religion and culture destroyed that unity through impulsiveness, unpredictability and lack of respect for their common heritage, or the Turks, who belonged to a completely different civilisation, followed a different religion but were perhaps willing to reach some kind of agreement because of their strategic thinking. The king, though unable to extend his protection to Turkish Adalia, was afraid both that it would be captured by the Genoese, who would use it as an outpost for attacks (ἐζητῆσαν το νὰ τὸ δηγοῦν), and that due to an interruption in reinforcements and the impassability of roads (ζωοτροφίαν, καὶ ἂν χάσουν τὴν στράταν) it would fall to the Turks. He thus stood before a difficult choice that was to decide the further fate of the town and in effect the degree of influence the Lusignan dynasty would have on its development. Notably, he ultimately chose the Saracens, followers of a different religion (stipulating that Adalia should fall under the care of the emir Takka).[1156] This interesting juxtaposition of Cyprus' two different opponents, belonging to two differing civilisations, Christian and Muslim, and also the king's contemplations on which of them a town with such importance for the functioning of the Cypriot state should be ceded to, shows how serious a threat the Genoese were.

The conflict with members of the Republic allowed the Cypriots to perform self-identification. When upon the pope's request the marshal of Rhodes attempted to reconcile the two sides, they felt forced to put forward defensive arguments that went beyond the material sphere because next to declarations such as: 'the kingdom is poor' (τὸ ρηγάτον εἶνε πτωχόν), 'our lord the king is an orphan' (ὁ ἀφέντης μας

[1153] ΘΚΔ, 469.
[1154] ΘΚΔ, 208.
[1155] Cf. LM III 482.
[1156] LM III 366.

ὁ ρήγας εἶνε ὀρφανός), 'what he holds is so little' (τὸ ἔχει εἶνε πολλὰ ὀλλίγον), there appears the comment: 'we live among the infidel Turks and Saracens' (εἴμεστεν ἀπλικιμένοι μέσον τοὺς ἀπίστους Τούρκους καὶ Σαρακηνούς).[1157] This last argument shows how depending on current needs the characters of the *Chronicle* invoke the civilisational differences that imply the incommensurability of religion that is obvious to the chronicler: when threatened, when other means of rescue have been lost, to underline the moral superiority they represent, or else in order to elicit pity from the recipient of the information, for example by emphasising their immense vulnerability and the importance of the virtues that they cultivate, such as righteousness and faith in a common God.

The Genoese, like the Cypriots, use a specific kind of persuasive language that involves weaving references to theological categories into their statements. Their commanders by manipulating the earthly and the spiritual orders make the island's inhabitants aware that at the start of their relationship they had been received with much goodwill and that this happened with God's knowledge (πέτε του, ὁ θεὸς τὸ ξεύρει, πολλὰ μετὰ χαρᾶς ἐδεκτήκαμεν τὸ ἔλα σας).[1158] Gradually, as they suffer further setbacks, they reformulate their claims and next to requests for material objects, such as a fort or castle, they start to emphasise other values, such as the figure of the pope, the sacredness of the crown (εἰς τὸ θάρος τοῦ ἁγίου σου στεφάνου, τὸ ἐστέφθης παρὰ θεοῦ) or the trust placed in respect for strictly defined peace terms (ἄδικα χωρὶς καμίαν ἀφορμήν). They try to elicit specific reactions from the Cypriots, threatening that they will be suspected of the sin of obstinacy and omission (νὰ μπέσης εἰς κουντουμαντζιόαν), attempting to place the burden of responsibility on the island's rulers. They skilfully place themselves in the role of a people slighted and humiliated by the experience of death, the sense of being deprived of honour and a miserable life spent in prisons. They emphasise that they are treated 'like mortal enemies and [people] without a lord' (ὡς γοιὸν ἐχθροὺς θανατήσιμους καὶ ἀνάφεντους) and this type of unjust stigmatisation should be replaced by sound judgment.[1159]

At the end of their stay on the island they express the belief that it was King Peter II who had been the 'cause of the whole dispute' (ἡ ἀρχὴ τῆς μάχης) and had started the violations of the agreement concluded in the presence of the pope, and that 'God would avenge them' (νὰ μᾶς ποίση βεντέτταν ὁ θεός).[1160] The ruler of Cyprus, attempting to assuage their anger, responds to the accusations they make in the same vein, swearing an oath on the Bible and citing the peace agreement, which should be concluded for the glory of God (δόξα σοι ὁ θεός). He also admits that he has previously assured the citizens of Genoa of his love for them and adds:

'[…] *If you wish to make peace* (νὰ ποίσετε ἀγάπην), *glory be to God: if not, do as you please.* […]'
(LM III 374)[1161]

When reading similar fragments of the *Chronicle* it is impossible not to become convinced that references to God appear in it as an adroit tool of manipulation. Of the Christians present in Makhairas' work, it is the Latins who have the greatest skills of persuasion. This helps them to convincingly explain their own actions and justify endeavours such as an attack on somebody's land or fighting for rights in areas not belonging to them.

Citing religious values is also a feature of peace negotiations, used as a method of verifying intentions and serving to move mutual relations to another plane. The chronicler particularly emphasises this matter when describing in detail an incident where during a Catholic mass the Genoese confirmed their desire to reconcile. The establishment of the new state of affairs was only sanctioned after an oath on the Sacred Body of Christ (τὸν ἅγιον σῶμαν τοῦ Κυρίου, τὸ κορμὶν τοῦ Χριστοῦ) made in the church of St Nicholas

---

[1157] LM III 370.
[1158] LM III 371.
[1159] LM III 372.
[1160] LM III 372.
[1161] As a result, six Genoese were thrown into the Lord of Tyre's prison, and with them a Cypriot citizen of Genoese origin, whom the blessed kings (οἱ μακαρισμένοι οἱ ρηγάδες) set free. Those protesting against the inappropriate treatment included free Genoese from Syria (also called White Genoese), the Gurrich, Bibich, Danielich and Gulich families, who came from Giblet, Acre, Caffa, Chios and Galata, and claimed that they should not be counted as Genoese nationals. See Dawkins, *Notes*, 156.

(τὸν Ἅγιον Νικόλαν)[1162] on the coast beyond Ammochostos.[1163] Makhairas describes this significant fragment of the liturgy thus:

> *And when the priest (παπᾶς) had lifted up (ἐσήκωσεν) the Body of Christ, it was left on the holy paten (εἰς τὸν ἅγιον σκούτελλον), and the Blood of the Lord (αἷμαν τοῦ Κυρίου) in the chalice (εἰς τὸ ποτήριον), and the Genoese, the admiral and the captains, laid upon them their pestilent hands (μιαρά τους χέργια) [...].* (LM III 416)

The author of the *Chronicle*, consciously using paradox, operates within the semantic field of crime, highlighting it via a glaring contrast between the sanctity of the Body of Christ and the hands of the Genoese, which he calls 'pestilent', 'defiled', raised over consecrated bread and wine. He precisely shows the duplicity of the citizens of Geneva evident in their actions, which are in opposition to their declared intentions.[1164]

The purity of the Body of Christ and the requirement of moral purity of the persons coming into physical contact with Him are familiar motifs in the Christian tradition. According to the Divine Liturgy of St John Chrysostom, the Body of Christ is 'most pure'.[1165] In the Ethiopian Anaphora of Jacob of Serugh we read:

> *Thou hast taken bread in thy holy hands*
> *to give it to thy pure apostles.*
> *Thou who then hast blessed*
> *Also now bless this bread.*
> *And again (thou wast) mixing a cup of wine with water*
> *to give it to the disciples.*[1166]

In the passage of the *Chronicle* describing the mass we read that the Genoese, who professed their goodwill during it, imprisoned the members of the royal family right after the service ended.[1167] Likely in order to strengthen this image, the chronicler gives a voice to Galeftira, prince John de Antioch's cook, who seeing his master in stocks calls on the power of God in despair. The prince on hearing his words responds that things will happen 'as God wishes it' (ὡς τὸ δώσῃ ὁ θεὸς ἂς γενῇ).[1168] In this description the author shows strong emotions and voices a radical judgement of how the citizens of the Ligurian state behaved, through which he expresses a lack of consent to the violent operations carried out to capture Ammochostos.

Although the Eucharistic test in LM III 416–417 turned out to be ineffective, over a hundred paragraphs further on, in LM III 523–524, Makhairas once again uses the motif of mass and an oath made in the presence of the sacrament. This is because no other ritual could lend legitimacy and ultimate validity to the gestures and words of the arrivals from Genoa. This is clearly evident in the 1374 letter by Constable James de Lusignan:

> [...] *May God keep (νὰ βλέπῃ) the Genoese fleet from coming near me! [...] tell the admiral to send to Kerynia –two– Genoese (of importance, in person,) to swear to me (νὰ μοῦ μόσῃ) on the Body of Jesus Christ (εἰς τὸ κορμὶν τοῦ Ἰησοῦ Χριστοῦ), when the priest lifts up the Body of the Lord and His Blood (ἄντα νὰ ὑψώσῃ τὸ σῶμαν τοῦ Κυρίου καὶ τὸ αἷμαν), that they will do me no hurt (νὰ μὲν μοῦ ποίσουν καμίαν ζημίαν) and not prevent me from going on my way (οὐδὲ νὰ μὲ ξηλώσουν ἀπὲ τὴν στράταν μου).* (LM III 523)

[1162] The church of St Michael, a thirteenth-century Gothic cathedral, was turned into the mosque of Lala Mustafa Pasha in the sixteenth century.
[1163] LM III 415–416.
[1164] LM III 416.
[1165] H. Paprocki (Transl.), Liturgie Kościoła prawosławnego, 117. Quoted expression translated by Kupiszewska.
[1166] Polish version taken from Paprocki (Transl.), Liturgie Kościoła prawosławnego, 29. English translation after the quotation from Euringer (Ed., transl.), Die äthiopischen Anaphoren quoted in Hofrichter, The Anaphora of Addai and Mari, 7. Henryk Paprocki notes that this text is of Syrian origin (Paprocki (Transl.), Liturgie Kościoła prawosławnego, 29).
[1167] LM III 416–417.
[1168] LM III 419.

The passage above shows that for a Christian, an oath on the Body and the Blood in the presence of the Eucharistic miracle guaranteed peace and signified hope that a possible tragedy would be forestalled. This may be interpreted as an expression of particular trust in that no Latin would be capable of perjury, which makes the Eucharist the only possible deceit-free, credible means of guaranteeing an agreement. The Eucharist also becomes an instance that confirms whether a person truly merits the name of Christian.

Makhairas presents a detailed description of the ceremony. He states that the oath demanded by the constable was made at the end of mass (ἄρχεψεν ἡ λουτουργία), which was celebrated 'in the name of the Holy Trinity' (εἰς τὸ ὄνομαν τῆς ἁγίας Τριάδος). The priest lifted the Host (ὁ ἱερεὺς ὕψωσεν τὴν ὄσταν) and the Blood (αἷμαν), and then placed them on the holy altar (εἰς τὴν ἁγίαν τράπεζαν). On the step (εἰς τὸ βῆμαν) were placed letters by the admiral and the soldiers, and Sir Damian Cattaneo and Sir James de St Michel laced their hands on them as they respectively said:

I [...] swear (ὀμνύω) by the Body of Christ [...] without any knavery (χωρὶς καμίαν κακουργίαν) of wicked intention (κακῆς ἀφορμῆς). (LM III 524)

[...] I swear to you (μόννω σου) upon the venerable Body and Blood of the Lord (εἰς τὸ τίμιον σῶμα καὶ αἷμαν τοῦ Κυρίου) [...] as I am a Christian (ὡς χριστιανὸς ὅπου εἶμαι) [...]. (LM III 524)

After each oath the priest repeated the phrase:

So may God help you (νὰ σοῦ βοηθήσῃ)! (LM III 524)

Making an oath in the presence of the sacrament is an extremely important element of political games in the *Chronicle*, forcing the opponent to declare his attitude to the postulated arrangements and transferring the burden of perjury onto him. It is also an expression of religious, and thus also civilisational unity: for a Frank, the Genoese is an unbeliever, but one who is able to swear to the same God, which was not possible in the case of a Muslim. This is evidently a case of blurring between the perspectives of Greek and Latin culture by examining the conflict using the same religious symbols and values. Another example of a ceremony of this kind is offered by an event where an admiral and captains of a ship swore on the Gospel before the king (ἀπάνω εἰς τὰ ἅγια τοῦ θεοῦ εὐαγγέλια).[1169]

Passage LM III 524 clearly indicates the chronicler's belief that the Genoese were capable of slighting that which was common to all Christians. In letters to Luke d'Antiaume and Peter II, the constable reminds them that Ligurian merchants 'deceived them many times, despite oaths' (διὰ πολλὲς φορὲς μὲ ὅρκους ἐκονπῶσαν μας).[1170] This comment, discrepant with the Cypriots' belief in guarantees of this kind expressed many times in the *Chronicle*, is evident proof that they lacked other tools they could use to ensure their safety.

3.3.3. Fighting for Lefkosia and Kerynia

The next towns to draw the attention of the citizens of Genoa were Lefkosia (Λευκωσία)[1171] and Kerynia (Κερυνία),[1172] the largest on the island after Ammochostos, Lemesos and Paphos.[1173] Full of Gothic buildings erected over the ages by the Lusignans, Lefkosia lies on the Mesaoria (Dawkins: 'Mesaria') plain. Its exceptional location at the heart of the island protected it from the direct and unexpected external attacks to which other port towns were particularly susceptible. Genoese activity in Lefkosia and towards residents of Lefkosia (Λευκωσιάτες/ Λευκωσίτες), to some extent successful, but for the most part chaotic, was as follows according to the *Chronicle*:

[1169] LM III 526.
[1170] LM III 523. Consulted with Borowska's translation.
[1171] Today Lefkosia (otherwise Nicosia) is the country's capital, divided by the Green Line into a Cypriot and a Turkish part (Tur Lefkoşa).
[1172] Kerynia (Tur Girne) is currently under Turkish rule.
[1173] Κωμοδίκης, Οἱ Πληροφορίες τῶν Βραχέων Χρονικῶν, 47.

> *And on Tuesday the sixth of December 1373 after Christ the Genoese tried to deprive the men of Lefkosia of their arms (νὰ σηκώσουν τὰ ἄρματα) by force (δυναστικῶς), beginning in the Armenian Quarter (ἀπὸ τὴν Ἀρμενίαν). And great tumults arose (ἀρχέψαν ταραχὰς μεγάλες). And the men of Lefkosia seized the keys of the Gate of St Andrew by force (δυναστικῶς), and blocked the passages with planks and stood ready to fight (ἐστάθησαν ἕτοιμοι εἰς τὸν πόλεμον). And they killed (many) Genoese, because (they were elated and) so confident in their safety, that they were wandering about the town, scattered here and there like sheep (σκορπισμένοι ὡς πρόβατα). [...] And the men of Lefkosia made a brave venture and went and snatched the keys of the Market Gate from the hands of the Genoese.* (LM III 433)

Quite apart from the way in which in Makhairas' opinion Providence governs events, thanks to the internal tensions rife in Lefkosia the Genoese managed to achieve significant advances in gaining influence there (ἐμπῆκαν παραμπρός).[1174] The uneasy atmosphere that settled over the town should primarily be blamed on the categorical decree issued by Queen Eleanora, forbidding Genoese residents 'to interfere in matters of the crown' (μὲν γυρεύγουν τὲς δουλεῖες τὲς ρηγάτικες) under pain of beheading.[1175]

Like in passage LM III 412–413, which calls up a vision of swarming locusts, in fragment LM III 433 Makhairas uses the expression 'they rambled around the town spread out like sheep' (ἐτριγυρίζαν τὴν χώραν σκορπισμένοι ὡς πρόβατα), which creates the image of a chaotic, roaming flock, making the portrait of the Genoese extraordinarily evocative.

Leontios shows that the main goal that motivated the citizens of Genoa besieging Ammochostos and later Lefkosia in 1373 was actually capturing Kerynia, a town located in northern Cyprus, separated from its internal part by the Kerynia Mountains, with a castle structure dating to Roman times located in the eastern part of the old port, which had been later modified by the Byzantines and Lusignans.[1176] On 15 March 1374 the island's inhabitants finally repelled the attack,[1177] which justifies Makhairas' conviction, expressed elsewhere, that 'the Cypriots always won thanks to the power of God' (μὲ τὴν δύναμιν τοῦ θεοῦ οἱ Κυπριῶτες πάντα εἶχαν τὴ νίκην).[1178]

On the margin of these events discussed in detail in the *Chronicle*, Leontios singles out one incident that was favourable for the Genoese, namely the capture in 1373 of Akrotiki (Ἀκροτική), a fertile region on the Karpasi peninsula. This was where in his opinion, taking into account the dominating features of their portrayal in the *Chronicle*, the merchant collective demonstrated their 'first heroic feat' (πρώτη ἀντραγαθία).[1179] He adds however with absolute conviction that this was an isolated incident – and here he expresses the same comment as in LM III 481 – because...

> *...always when they fought (πάντα τὸ νὰ 'βρέθηκαν εἰς τὸν πόλεμον) the Cypriots were victorious (ἐνικοῦσαν οἱ Κυπριῶτες).* (LM III 448)

This statement appraises the recipient of the starting point that Makhairas selected for his presentation of events: the core message is the conviction that it was the Cypriots who deserved victory.

At the centre of events concentrated around Lefkosia and Kerynia the *Chronicle*'s author places the queen of Cyprus, Eleanora of Aragon, who in various ways guards the wellbeing of Cyprus. In one of her letters, for example, she asks Constable James de Lusignan 'to drive out the Genoese in ignominy' (τοὺς Γενουβίσους ἂς τοὺς δώξουν μὲ ἀντροπήν).[1180] The representatives of the merchant Republic realise that the queen cheated them, doing 'something contrary' (κατάδικον) to what they had agreed with her. Namely, they arrived on the island to help her take revenge on the murderers of Peter I, which is particularly visible in the following words:

[1174] LM III 433.
[1175] LM III 433.
[1176] Mirbagheri, *Historical Dictionary of Cyprus*, 95.
[1177] LM III 520.
[1178] LM III 481.
[1179] LM III 448.
[1180] LM III 430.

My lady, we placed our hope (ἐλπίδα μας) in God and in you that we should be helped in avenging you on your enemies (νὰ ἔχωμεν βοήθειαν νὰ σὲ ἐκδικήσωμεν ἀπὸ τοὺς ἐχθρούς σου), and now we have found the contrary (κατάδικον), and you have brought us here (ἀπέσωσές μας ὧδε) for them to kill us (νὰ μᾶς σκοτώσουν). (LM III 433)

The Genoese emphasise that they left their country and abandoned their possessions (ἐμεῖς ἀφήκαμεν τοὺς τόπους μας καὶ τὸ δικόν μας) in order to avenge her injury (ποίσωμεν ἐκδίκησιν) by fighting her enemies (that is the constable and the prince), to safeguard (νὰ -τὴν βλέπωμεν-) the kingdom 'for her beloved son' (διὰ τὸν ἠγα(πη)μένον σου υἱόν), and above all to change to existing state of affairs 'for her own good' (διὰ ἀλλόγου σας).[1181]

As the chronicler shows, Queen Eleanora is so afraid that her beloved island will be enslaved that she often turns to various kinds of 'tricks' (μὲ τὲς τέχνες σου).[1182] One example: the attempt she makes to escape the Kerynian castle unseen, under vigilant Genoese eyes, on the mule of her husband Peter I.[1183] In the chronicler's account the mother of King Peter II appears to be a dynamic, ruthless person, determined to prevent his enemies from enslaving (αἰχμαλωτευθεῖν) Cyprus.[1184] Meanwhile her son, who at the time of the Cypriot-Genoese conflict was quite a young man, is presented in the *Chronicle* as a weak, passive and submissive being. However, being aware of the Genoese danger he uses emotionally marked expressions like his mother. In his statements we encounter for example the verb 'clung' (ἐκολλήθησαν) to describe how he perceives the enemy's operational strategy, which gives rise to associations with an alien, sticky and invasive substance.[1185]

The numerous descriptions of acts of aggression committed by the two sides found in the Cypriot work present a whole spectrum of manifested feelings – from dislike to hate – experienced by the two culturally close peoples. It is worth emphasising that not only the citizens of the Republic are assigned negative traits, but also the local population. The fragment below observes this particularly distinctly:

Others (ἄλλοι λᾶς), too, from Trakhona (ἀπὸ τὸν Τράχοναν[1186]) and from the graveyard and from Voni (Βονιάτες[1187]) rose (ἐσηκώθησαν) and pursued them (ἐκαταδιωξάν), and began to pillage (ἀρχέψα νὰ κουρσεύσου) as far as the Bridge of the Pillory (ὡς τὸ γιοφύριν τῆς Πιλλιρῆς). And there they joined battle (ἐσμίξαν πόλεμον), and there was much violent fighting (πολλὺς καὶ δυνατός) [...]. And when the Genoese went to the king's court, the men of the town (τοπικοί) went and pillaged (ἐκουρσεῦσαν) the houses of the White Genoese (τὰ σπιτία τοὺς Γενουβίσους τοὺς ἄσπρους) and of the Lefkosia men who had had friendly relations with the Genoese (ὅπου εἶχαν ἀγάπην μὲ τοὺς Γενουβίσους). And the poor helpless handicraftsmen (οἱ πτωχοὶ χεροτεχνίτες οἱ ἀνήμποροι) went into their houses and locked themselves in, and the town was as if it had been deserted (ἐπόμεινεν ἡ χώρα ὡς ἔρημη). They also set fire (ἐβάλαν λαμπρόν) to the houses of the Genoese [...]. (LM III 436)

The images that emerge from this passage[1188] bluntly show the well-organised, strategically inclined newcomers, who do not hesitate to attack not only the native islanders and the Cypriot-Frakish community, but also individuals belonging to other nations, including the Syrians. A fragment in which the chronicler describes the massacre of Syrians in one of Lefkosia's towers indicates a conflict on this line.[1189] The effectiveness of the Genoese was primarily the effect of their superior numbers, since despite

---

[1181] LM III 459.
[1182] LM III 470.
[1183] This mule was even given a name: Margaret (Μαργαρίτα). The Cypriot describes this event vividly: 'And when the queen came to the hill, she made the sign to Putsurello, and he turned his foot and put on her spurs, and she pressed her mule and was off. Then they shouted: "Let him come with us who will come, and he who will not, let him go hang!" And immediately the queen fell in with the (constable's) army, and they received her with great honour.' (LM III 460. Dawkins' translation). George Seferis' poem *Three Mules* (1955) is devoted to this fragment. Seferis, Complete Poems, 48–49.
[1184] LM III 461.
[1185] LM III 512.
[1186] Pavlidis explains that Trakhona (Τράχωνας) is a settlement north of Lefkosia, situated in its very close proximity. See Παυλίδης (Ed.), Λεοντίου Μαχαιρᾶ Χρονικόν, 325 (fn. 3).
[1187] Voni (Βώνης), a village close to Kithraia, north-east of Lefkosia. See Παυλίδης (Ed.), Λεοντίου Μαχαιρᾶ Χρονικόν, 325 (fn. 5).
[1188] Leontios describes these events with great care for detail, discussing battle principles, taking into account the numbers of the aggressors and the victims, and also relating the course of skirmishes as if he himself had been at the centre of events.
[1189] LM III 439.

having lost seventeen soldiers they were able to replace murdered or tired companions with others, unlike their opponents. The account of this incident is as follows:

> *One of them, whose name was Nasr (Νάσαρις), saw this: he stood there fighting hard with his sword and defending himself as long as he could endure. Then he sees two Genoese standing by a battlement (εἰς ἕναν προμοχιόνιν*[1190]*): he dashes forward and flings his arms round them, and all three of them fell down on the inner side of the wall into the town, and died at once. This he did because they had cut down all his fellows.* (LM III 439)

Makhairas uses an interesting technique where he gives the name of one of the Syrian soldiers, which he does not do for the Genoese soldiery: apart from their commanders they remain anonymous until the end, which may be a mark of the open disdain that he had for them. It seems to be an intentional narrative strategy and also expresses his opinion of the two groups involved in the conflict. Also not without import is that in the description of the brave Syrian's deeds, even those that involve killing, Makhairas underlines his loyalty towards his companions. Meanwhile, the Genoese act without noble motivation and they do not cease to murder the defenceless even after having achieved their goal.

Such examples showing the great dishonesty and perfidy of representatives of Genoa are very numerous in the *Chronicle*. Their negative image is made complete by the story of the Rhomaioi Psilidi (Psichidis, Ψιχίδης) and his fifty companions who, deceived by a proclamation offering them safe conduct to their homes, were attacked by the Genoese and brutally murdered. As Leontios tells, they were killed by hanging, having previously been laid on carts and burned with hot tongs.[1191] Further blemishes on the portrait of the Genoese community are added by the mention of a man who returned home from war convinced that this would not endanger either himself or his wife Vergilina (Virginella) (Βεργιλίνα). They both died, however: she, burned in the Coach builder's district (εἰς τὸ Ἀμαξαρεῖον), he, hanged on the gallows – because unaware of her spouse's decision, the woman had tried to convince the men questioning her that he was absent.[1192]

In the description of the actions undertaken by the citizens of Genoa attention is focused primarily on the factors that make it easier for them to achieve victory in confrontations. These include: well-organised troops, superior numbers and savage cruelty towards each opponent, no matter who he is and which group he belongs to. However, they do not always show the same fervour in their actions. When fortune turns against them, they start wondering how to change the existing situation. As Makhairas states, they noticed that 'in each fight many [of them] fell' (πᾶσα πόλεμον χάννουνται πολλοί) and they were 'fewer each day' (καθημερινὸν ὀλλιγανίσκουν), and so 'they did not want to take [further] part in battle' (δὲν ἐθέλησα νὰ ποίσουν πόλεμον),[1193] thus expressing their awareness that the resources they held were gradually running out.

The chronicler emphasises that all the defeats they suffered should be attributed to greed (ἀκριβοί, 'misers'), a grave sin, and the effect of 'God's judgement' (κρίσις θεϊκή),[1194] which the *Chronicle* mentions also elsewhere, in the description of the siege of Kerynia on 3 March 1374:

> *And now you shall see the judgement of God! Down comes a missile from the trebuchet and hits the platform tied to the galleys, and carries it away and hurls it into the sea; and the Genoese fled away from the harbor with loss and disgrace.* (LM III 498)

To the Genoese methods of dealing with the Frankish court mentioned above Makhairas adds manipulation. This was how the Genoese influenced the decisions of its representatives. A fragment where this is evident describes an exchange of demands between them and Peter II on 14 January 1374, which was as follows:

[1190] Pavlidis translates 'προμοχιόνιν' as 'προμαχῶνα' ('bastion', 'fortification', 'wall'). See Παυλίδης (Ed.), Λεοντίου Μαχαιρᾶ Χρονικόν, 327.
[1191] LM III 440.
[1192] LM III 443.
[1193] LM III 438.
[1194] LM III 451.

'Your uncles (θεῖοί σου) have divided (ἐδιαμερίστησαν) Cyprus amongst themselves: one has taken St. Hilarion and the other Kerynia: what is left for you (ἐσέναν ἴντα σούμεινεν)?' He said to them: 'And what can I do, a poor orphan (πτωχὸν ὀρφανόν), held as a prisoner in your hands (ἀποκλεισμένον εἰς τὰ χέργια σας)? What can I do?' They said to him: 'Come out with us ("Ἔβγα ἔλα μετά μας), –and we will go to attack (–νὰ τὴν πολεμίσωμεν–) Kerynia.'– He said to them: 'I am at your orders (Εἰς τὸν ὁρισμόν σας).' (LM III 465)

A sophisticated game played out between the Genoese and the king. The Ligurian citizens made use of his words, in which he unequivocally called himself an 'orphan'.[1195] They intentionally referred to this statement, accenting Peter II's compassion-worthy condition, and also using the moment of understanding thus born to further their goals: they led Peter II to the castle in Kerynia with the aim of retaking the fortress. The chronicler vividly writes about the way they did this, underlining that they led the king 'as if he were an animal intended for the slaughter' (ὡς γοιὸ νὰ εἶχεν εἴσταιν σφακτό), that is one 'that is being led to be butchered' (ὄνταν τὸ παίρνουν νὰ σφάξουν),[1196] in order to actually 'slay' it (νάχα θέλει νάχαν τὸ σφάξειν).[1197] Using the rhetoric peculiar to him, the author of the *Chronicle* calls the Cypriot ruler an 'orphan without a guide' (ὀρφανόν, ἀνακέφαλον), and by comparing him to a sacrificial animal he reveals his helplessness and passivity.[1198] The representatives of the Republic manipulated Peter II, juggling phrases that alternated expressions of goodwill towards the king with overt dislike, and trying to distort his perception of the situation as a whole.

The hot-tempered, devious Genoese used the same methods not only in their treatment of individuals from the royal family, but also of the whole populace of Kerynia, whom they rather skilfully incited to fight through persuasion and persecution. However the means they selected, lacking proper balance, did not wholly bring the desired results and sometimes prompted violent objections. When, for example, they accused the Cypriots of lack of nobility, the latter responded sharply:

You lie (Ψέμα λαλεῖτε), you scum of the market (λᾶς τῆς μέσης), you scurvy curs of fishermen (λύκοι ψαροπούλιδες[1199]); indeed we have noble knights (καβαλλάριδες εὐγενικούς), lieges and burgesses, men of the best nurture (πολλὰ καλὰ ἀναγιωμένους). You rascally sailors (ναῦτες κατεργάριδες) in your galleys, how can you dare to speak ill of the nobly nurtured men of Cyprus? But if you have an appetite for this sport, fix a lance in the ground, and let it be a sign of fair play, and put a banner on the lance, and then we will come out to run a course with you (νὰ ἐβγοῦμε νὰ παρδιαβάσωμεν). (LM III 499)

In the mouths of the Cypriots this decided response is also an act of affirmation of the values linked to affiliation with the Cypriot community. It expresses a radical judgement of the conduct of merchants who systematically came to the island under the guise of furthering their trading interests, but in reality behaved like invaders, who lied habitually, 'saying evil things' (κακολογᾶτε), and held the only form of demonstrating their position to be confrontation in battle. The courage that the citizens of Genoa showed was according to the *Chronicle* only in seeming and sporadical, and therefore not their distinctive feature.

While representatives of the Republic tried to oppose the Cypriots and Syrians, the chronicler relates that they lived in fear of the Bulgarians. Makhairas evocatively describes the confrontation of the Genoese oppressors with the Bulgarian people, leading to the 'shaming and ruin' (ἀντροπὴν καὶ ζημίαν) of the former,[1200] which aroused in them the sense of being involved in a situation with no solution.[1201] This worry was not without real grounds, as the Genoese had already previously been able to witness the injury done to their companions at the hands of the redoubtable Bulgarians: to depict it, the chronicler paints a vivid but blunt picture of 'cutting into pieces' (κατακόβγουν μας).[1202] Fragments containing a narrative thus shaped enrich and deepen the detailed, multifaceted portrait of the citizens

---

[1195] LM III 465. Cf. LM III 370.
[1196] Dawkins (Ed., transl.), Ἐξήγησις/ Recital, 452 (fn. 9); Παυλίδης (Ed.), Λεοντίου Μαχαιρᾶ Χρονικόν, 348 (fn. 8).
[1197] LM III 470.
[1198] LM III 470.
[1199] 'market-day rabble, wolves selling fish (wolfish fish sellers)!'
[1200] LM III 466.
[1201] LM III 446–467.
[1202] LM III 467.

of the Republic, which is based on a deconstruction of individual representations of their contacts with different groups present in Cyprus.

Through its inviolable majesty, the Kerynian castle, imposing and unconquered, gained in the chronicler's eyes the rank of blessed (εἰς τὴν εὐλογημένην Κερυνίαν),[1203] like the island as a whole.

The portrayal of the Genoese in the *Chronicle* is wholly negative: they are intruders who penetrated the Cypriot community as an unvanquished force in order to take advantage of the opportunity to steal the buildings and whole towns that they captured from the Lusignans. By selecting as the main subject of a part of his work the confrontation between citizens of the Republic and non-Cypriot Christian groups like the Syrians and Bulgarians, Makhairas attributes specific traits to the former and reveals his own attitude towards them, and also provides some insights about the latter communities.

3.3.4. Genoese and Rhodians

The Cypriot-Genoese conflict extensively described in the *Chronicle*, which took place mainly over the years 1373–1375, had a clear impact on Cypriot-Rhodian relations, because the rulers of Rhodes, the second instance after the pope to intervene at various points when Cyprus was in difficulty, played a significant role in the life of its inhabitants (which may be seen for example in paragraphs LM II 163–166 and LM II 206–209). Pavlidis explains that the Knights of the Hospital, that is the 'Joannites of Rhodes' (Ἰωαννίτες τῆς Ῥόδου), the rulers in question, were commanded by Pope Gregory XI to 'observe' (παρακολουθοῦν) the tense situation on Cyprus and to 'adjudge' (διαιτητεύσουν) disputes, and the Franks expected them to do so.[1204] Already LM II 117 contains a mention that Peter I sent an envoy to them with a request for support, convinced that the grand master was 'obliged to help the poor' (κρατούμενος νὰ ἐλεμονοῦνται τοὺς πτωχούς).

The way how the chronicler describes the relations between the merchants of Genoa and the brothers from Rhodes is noteworthy: in the eyes of the monks, the former primarily appear as 'bad Christians' (οἱ κακοὶ χριστιανοί) and 'works of the devil' (τὰ ἔργα τοῦ διαβόλου), which may be seen in the following fragment:

> *But the Brethren of Rhodes (ἀδελφοὶ τῆς Ῥόδου), I mean the Frères (φρέριδες), were in great fear of the Genoese (εἰς μέγαν φόβον διὰ τοὺς Γενουβίσους), for they knew their pride (τὴν σουπερπίαν) and the mischief (κακόν) they had done to Cyprus, and so they sent word to the constable to go away on his journey, because they could not stand out against (δὲν δύνουνται νὰ ἀντισταθοῦν) the Genoese, men who were bad Christians and creatures of the devil [...]. (LM III 537)*

The *Chronique d'Amadi* also cites this incident, underlining the Rhodians' fear (*gran paura*), which Makhairas mentions.[1205] It additionally sheds light on a previous episode of the Rhodian-Genoese feud, describing the exploits of a citizen of Genoa, Vignol, who in 1306 spied on the inhabitants of Rhodes in order to take over Rhodian facilities at an opportune moment.[1206]

As the *Chronicle*'s narrative unfolds the consequences of Genoese action, leading to a rupture in the Western world, become increasingly apparent, being quite clearly marked in fragments that show the change which occurred in relations between the two islands.

When in the year 1373–1374 gruelling fighting, full of 'bloody clashes' (ταραχές) and 'delays' (ἀργίσματα), was going on in Cyprus between inhabitants and newcomers for its finest towns such as Ammochostos, Lefkosia and Kerynia, the Rhodians, with their grand master foremost, noticed that no Cypriot had arrived at their shores for several months. Having received a message that the Genoese 'had plundered the kingdom' (ἐκατακουρσέψαν τὸ ῥηγάτον) of Cyprus, exposing it to acute poverty experienced primarily by the 'fearful' (ἐννοιασμένοι) people (τίποτες δὲν εἶχαν οἱ λᾶς),[1207] the brothers had to take a firm position on the issue. The Hospitallers had to confront the problem and their fear all

---

[1203] LM III 464.
[1204] Παυλίδης (Ed.), Λεοντίου Μαχαιρᾶ Χρονικόν, 271 (fn. 4). This is particularly evident in LM III 356.
[1205] Mas Latrie (Ed.), Chronique d'Amadi, 474.
[1206] Mas Latrie (Ed.), Chronique d'Amadi, 254–259; Coureas, Edbury (Transl.), The Chronicle of Amadi, 242–243 (§ 523).
[1207] LM III 463.

3.3. DEPICTION OF CYPRIOT-GENOESE RELATIONS ON CYPRUS

the sooner because of a visit by Constable James de Lusignan, who came to Rhodes to request support (this expedition is also described in the *Chronique d'Amadi*[1208]) and greeted them with the words:

> [...] *I gave thanks to God* (ἥτζου εὐχαρί(στη)κα τοῦ θεοῦ) *who had put me into (your) good hands* (ὁποῦ μ' ἔβαλεν εἰς -καλὰ- χέργια); *and will you refuse to have mercy upon me* (νὰ μὲν θελήσετε νὰ μοῦ σπλαγχνιστῆτε), *and to cover me with your protection* (μὲ σκεπάσετε ἀπουκάτω τὸ σκέπο(ς) σας), *and be afraid rather of the faithless Genoese, and not help me as the Order of the Brotherhood* (ὀρίζ' ἡ τάξι τῆς ἀδελφοσύνης) *bids you?* (LM III 538)

This fragment is a show of rhetorical flair, full of subtle persuasion and references to values held by the addressees, such as compassion and obedience to the monastic rule. An important term that appears in two fragments of Leontios' work, LM III 489 and 538, is σκέπος, which may be translated as 'care', 'protection' and 'cover'. Repetition of the stem in the related verb σκεπάσετε strengthens the implications and force of the noun.

The Rhodians, more than any other Christian group, are attributed a particular trait: care for those who most need support. An expectation of such help may be seen in some other words by the constable, who quite emotionally says:

> *My dear Christian brethren* (Ἀκριβοὶ ἀδελφοὶ χριστιανοί), *you who are the protection of the weak* (σκέπος τοὺς ἀδυνάτους), *now is the time for you to help me and to take me ⌐out of the hands¬ of the Genoese*. [...] (LM III 539)

This statement shows that citing compassion and brotherhood is a permanent rhetorical element in conversations between Cypriots and Rhodians. ΘΚΔ explains that synonyms of the verb 'ἀποβγάλλω' include 'ἀπολύω' ('free', 'liberate') and 'ἀπαλλάσσω' ('free', 'remove', 'get rid of', 'avoid').[1209] According to the chronicler it is those who share Christian values that should liberate their brothers in the spirit from entrapment and stand between (πρόσωπον) them and the enemy. James de Lusignan's statement indicates that relations between the people living on Rhodes and citizens of Cyprus were positive, and negative between each of these groups and the Genoese. However, this is not a comprehensive presentation of mutual relationships that could serve as proof of full cooperation between the two islands' inhabitants. The Rhodians were in a difficult position, as they were not wholly able to provide help selflessly, with no thought for their own safety. Having a critical attitude towards the citizens of Genoa, they also had a well-founded fear of them, knowing their pride and bad deeds, and so they behaved ambiguously.[1210] This ambivalence is apparent already in the deceitful ritual of greeting the constable who had come to their land. The Rhodians received the Cypriot notable in accordance with the requirements of hospitality, which was not, however, dictated by scrupulosity in observing etiquette, but by strong anxiety (φοβούμεθα, 'we fear') concerning control over how the situation would unfold. Makhairas explains that if the brother of Peter I, who was accused of regicide, declined their offer of hospitality, it would shame the Rhodians (ἔνι μεγάλη μας ἀντροπή) and encourage the enemies who might come (μηδὲν ἔλθουν οἱ ἐχθροί σου καὶ πάρουν σε) to carry out an attack.[1211] Counting on support, the constable invoked the great deeds of his ancestors and communion of values: personal sentimental attachment to the island of Rhodes as if it were his own country, faith in God's causative power, which allowed him to safely land on Rhodian shores, the weight of compassionate acts and the ideals of the Order.

At this point Makhairas introduces significant ambivalence, which modifies the positive or simply neutral depiction of Rhodians as bringing support in danger. The brothers, placed in an awkward position, took the decision to escort the constable to Venice.[1212] Near Mandraki they handed him over to the Genoese, convinced of their honest intentions that were supported by the special oaths the latter had made 'on the seven sacraments of the Church' (μὰ τὰ ζ' μυστήρια τῆς ἐκκλησίας) and 'the Divine Gospel of God' (εἰς τὰ θεῖα τοῦ θεοῦ εὐαγκέλια).[1213] The *Chronicle* states that the citizens of the Republic

---
[1208] Mas Latrie (Ed.), Chronique d'Amadi, 474–475.
[1209] ΘΚΔ, 69.
[1210] LM III 537.
[1211] LM III 535.
[1212] LM III 538.
[1213] LM III 541.

swore twice on the Body of Christ and three times on his Blood and on the Gospel, promising that they would not harm the notable. Makhairas' phrasing, 'the Divine Gospel of God', emphasises the exceptional importance of the Bible, thus strengthening the significance of the oath. Given the adoption of such a perspective and in juxtaposition with the text of their promise, the later imprisonment of the constable and seven other knights by the Genoese in a prison in Mala Paga and the Lighthouse Tower lays bare the evil nature of the oathbreakers. The chronicler writes thus:

> *But the poor Cypriots (οἱ πτωχοὶ οἱ Κυπριῶτες) are much-enduring people (βαστάννουν πολλά), and God in His mercy (μὲ τὴν ἐλεμοσύνην του) avenges them (ἐκδικᾷ τους) [...]. (LM III 545)*

The Rhodians presented in the *Chronicle* turned out to be gullible, rapidly giving in to the Genoese. Their motivation for handing the notable into the hands of his enemies is unknown. Were they persuaded to believe the Genoese? Was their act deliberate, and if so, why did they do it? Was it out of fear for their own safety or expectation of tangible benefits? It is worth noting that for Cyprus they were only an external ally, not directly involved in its problems, and thus their responsibility was in actual fact smaller.

The description of how the brothers saw the members of the Genoese community does not differ from the Cypriots' perception. Its significant feature is the conviction about the dishonesty of the inhabitants of Genoa and their use of holy symbols and expressions known to all Christians for their own deceitful purposes, which were wholly unconnected to the sacred dimension. In his depiction of Cypriot-Rhodian contacts in the *Chronicle*, Makhairas introduces an important category, brotherhood, which was cited many times in attempts to achieve the desired effects. This brotherhood was understood as a commonality of goals and fighting against the same enemy, and above all, as a source of potential help in case of danger. However, as may be seen from the constable's story, these assumptions and values were no guarantee of protection and support.

3.3.5. The role of religious figures in relations between the Latins

In many places in the *Chronicle* there appear representatives of the clergy, who play a significant role in political events on the island: some act deliberately, while others become involved in them by accident. Therefore, it is justified to discuss the way that they are portrayed by the chronicler in the chapter on conflicts within the Latin world because these figures usually act within the confines of this very world. However, we should not forget that clergymen who take part in encounters with Muslims also sporadically appear.

Of all religious figures, the one who plays the most important role in the depiction of politics in the *Chronicle*'s Roman Catholic world is the pope, called the 'helper of Christians' (τῶν χριστιανῶν ἡ βοήθεια) and the 'scales of justice' (τὸ ζύγιν τῆς δικαιοσύνης) (LM III 352). In the *Chronique d'Amadi* the head of the Church has a large decision-making role. In Boustronios' work he also holds an elevated position: he decides for instance about matters such as the coronation of a king and the location of a ruler's sarcophagus.[1214] In Leontios' text an unambivalent interpretation is difficult, however.

Leontios repeatedly voices deep respect for the supreme pontiff. He often underlines that many decisions concerning the island depend on his will, and that certainly many leaders draw on his advice. Meanwhile, his attitude towards Latin priests is ambiguous. He sometimes reports incidents in which the Catholic clergy do not appear in a positive light, but usually he simply notes their existence.

In the years 1192–1432, that is from the Lusignans' taking of power on Cyprus to the probable date of Makhairas' death, the papal office was held by thirty-two bishops. In his narrative, the author of the *Chronicle* introduces only eight of them: Urban II (ca. 1035|1088–1099),[1215] Celestine III (ca. 1105|1191–1198),[1216] Boniface VIII (ca. 1235|1294–1303), Benedict XI (1240|1303–1304),[1217] Clement VI

[1214] Dawkins (Transl., int.), The Chronicle of George Boustronios, 31–32, 34.
[1215] LM I 18.
[1216] LM I 28.
[1217] LM I 13–17.

(1291/1292|1342–1352),[1218] Innocent VI (1282|1352–1362),[1219] Urban V (1310|1362–1370),[1220] Gregory XI (1329|1370–1378).[1221] Of these he mentions Urban [II] (Ὀλβάνος),[1222] Urban V (τον πάπα Οὔρπαν πέμπτον)[1223] and Innocent [VI] (Ἰνοκέντιον)[1224] by name. LM II 136 contains a mention of Innocent VI's death and the election of Urban V, that is of the transfer of power from one notable to the next.[1225] The *Chronique d'Amadi* also refers to this event[1226] and talks of other such cases, like the death of Celestine IV, the election of Innocent IV in 1243[1227] and the adoption of the name Alexander IV by Rinald, bishop of Ostia in 1255.[1228]

Sometimes it is uncertain which pope is meant.[1229] The chronicler happens to extend the office to 'all of Rome' (ὅλη ἡ Ῥώμη)[1230] or to reduce its function to the office of the 'pope of Rome' (ὁ πάπα τῆς Ῥώμης).[1231] Makhairas gives the epithet 'most holy' (ἁγιώτατος) to five popes: Urban II,[1232] Celestine III,[1233] Innocent VI,[1234] Urban V[1235] and Gregory XI,[1236] although he most often uses it with respect to Urban V, whom he also mentions particularly frequently.

Nevertheless, the *Chronicle* does not contain any such intimate portrait of a pope like the one in Machaut's *La Prise d'Alixandre*, which depicts Peter I's meeting with Urban V:

Li sains peres l'envoia querre
Et il vint à li sans enquerre
Qu'il li voloit, que oubeissance
Li faisoit et grant reverence.
Li papes par la main le prist,
Et lez li doucement l'assist,
Et li dist moult courtoisement
Et moult tres amiablement:
'Biaus fils, il est chose certeinne
Que vous avez heü grant peinne
Eu service Nostre Seigneur,
De quoy li grant et li meneur
Et chascuns heüreus vous clainme;
Et je croy bien que Dieux vous aimme [...]'.[1237]

'The holy father ordered him sought out,
And he came to him without inquiring
What he wished because he accorded the pope
Obedience and great respect.
The pope seized his hand
And gently seated him by his side

[1218] LM I 83.
[1219] LM II 91, 101–102, 104–108.
[1220] LM II 129, 131, 160, 174–175, 206–207, 214, 216–218, 223, III 290, 292–293, 300–301, 310–311.
[1221] LM III 342, 352–353, 355–356, 372, 512, 529.
[1222] LM I 18.
[1223] LM II 136.
[1224] LM II 105.
[1225] LM II 136.
[1226] Mas Latrie (Ed.), Chronique d'Amadi, 418.
[1227] Mas Latrie (Ed.), Chronique d'Amadi, 197.
[1228] Mas Latrie (Ed.), Chronique d'Amadi, 203.
[1229] Boniface VIII and Benedict XI LM I 13–17; one of them LM I 62; LM II 129.
[1230] LM II 175.
[1231] LM II 206.
[1232] LM I 18.
[1233] LM I 28.
[1234] LM II 91, 105–106.
[1235] LM II 160, 223, III 290, 292, 300, 310–311.
[1236] LM III 352, 372, 512.
[1237] Guillaume de Machaut, La prise d'Alexandrie, 236–237 (v. 7648–7661).

*And spoke quite courteously to him
And with much amity:
"Sweet son, certain it is
That you have suffered greatly
In the service of Our Lord,
For which those of high and of low degree
To a man consider you fortunate.
And I am convinced that God loves you [...]"*.[1238]

The pope appears in many places in Machaut's[1239] work as an embodiment of holiness, dignity and humility (*sa sainté et sa dignité/ et sa très grant humilité*).[1240] The *Chronique d'Amadi* clearly shows the efforts and care of the pontiffs of Rome for the success of the Western world in endeavours organised in the Middle East and for the well-being of members of the Church. We read that the pope (Gregory IX) strongly urged the Emperor Federick II to take the area of Syria under his protection,[1241] and that (Nicholas IV) supported Cyprus after the loss of the Holy Land in 1291 because Christians had taken refuge there and the Sultan was heading that way.[1242]

In the conflict between the Cypriots and Genoese in the *Chronicle* a large role is played by Gregory XI, even though the chronicler does not mention his name. The two sides vie with each other to provide him information about their opponent with their own commentary.[1243] This pope, despite being termed 'most holy' (ἁγιώτατος) three times and, in the world depicted by Makhairas, inspiring awe in rulers of Western countries, gives the appearance of an undecided person who lacks confidence in his convictions and changes his opinions, one who issues judgements based on the evidence and testimonies collected on the one hand, but on the other is unable to make a clear decision. The depiction of this particular pope provided in the narrative is therefore blurred and ambiguous. Either the author does not mind this lack of consistency, or he intentionally manipulated Gregory XI's portrayal. The example of the dispute between the envoys Sir Peter Le Petit (σὶρ Πιὲρ Λε Πέντιτη) and Sir William of Charni (σὶρ Λιάμε τε Τζερνή) may be given to illustrate this finding. Having heard the report of the Genoese side, the pope decided that the fault lay with the Cypriots, but when told the arguments of the latter, he changed his declaration and laid the responsibility on the representatives of the Republic, with the proviso that the injury was unintentional (πρᾶγμαν [...] ἀθελῶς).[1244] If we consider the positive aspects of this event, the dignitary's faltering should be interpreted as an attempt to properly weigh out, to the extent that he was able, the blame and to establish the proper form of compensation. Detrimental to his image, however, are his indecision and changeability of opinion, and also his rash formulation of judgements revealed in the words:

> *and we do not ascribe blame either to the one (οὐδ' ἑνοῦ διδοῦμεν ἀφορμήν) or to the other (οὐδὲ τοῦ ἄλλου).* (LM III 353)

Such a construction of the pope's description leads us to conclude that the chronicler did not see him as an authority. After all, as Makhairas shows the very presence of the Genoese on the island was due to his consent. We find out in further parts of the text that he did not make the decision about this matter independently, but acquiesced to the request of another person: in this case, he listened to Queen Eleanora, being unaware of her true intentions, that is her desire to avenge the death of her husband with the help of the Republic, and her efforts to gain the throne for her son, Peter II. To obtain a kind of blessing for these intentions, the ruler sent suitable gifts to the bishop of Rome, and her father, Peter of Aragon, convinced him to join the expedition to Genoa. These examples bring to the fore such traits of Gregory XI as: gullibility, susceptibility to persuasion and the capability of accepting material gratification, which runs counter to what is usually imagined of authority figures. He demonstrated greater initiative when

---

[1238] Translation after Palmer (Ed., transl.), La Prise D'Alixandre, 365.
[1239] Guillaume de Machaut, La prise d'Alexandrie, 238–239 (v. 7712–7739), 240 (v. 7768–7773), 245 (v. 7924–7935).
[1240] Guillaume de Machaut, La prise d'Alexandrie, 238 (v. 7718–7719).
[1241] Mas Latrie (Ed.), Chronique d'Amadi, 121; Coureas, Edbury (Transl.), The Chronicle of Amadi, 121 (§ 231).
[1242] Mas Latrie (Ed.), Chronique d'Amadi, 228; Coureas, Edbury (Transl.), The Chronicle of Amadi, 224 (§ 477).
[1243] LM III 340.
[1244] LM III 352–353.

he asked the Rhodian master of the Order[1245] for help, and thus showed himself a thorough observer of events in the Mediterranean Basin, who had under his care many nations that were connected through the link of baptism, and as a mediator who attempted to avert both internal and external conflicts for the good of Christendom and to uphold his rule.

Interestingly, Makhairas treats the attitude of different groups or individuals towards the commands he issues as an important measure in his assessment of their conduct. The chronicler judges the citizens of Genoa negatively because in his opinion they revealed a lack of consistency in their actions, manifested in the discrepancy between their declared willingness to listen to the words of the pope, and their actions, which went against his commands whenever they had the opportunity to find themselves outside his line of vision. They thus betrayed the ideal of peaceful coexistence, an important requirement of Christianity, by declaring war with Cyprus in 1372 in Genoa, which the *Chronicle* terms 'damned expedition' (καταραμένη ἀρμάδα)[1246] since it took place without the consent of the Head of the Church. Furthermore, the Genoese manipulated the pope's words, placing themselves in the role of an injured party, forced to look on the acute suffering of their countrymen injured in the loggia. They made a promise to obey the words of the pope under the condition that the king would himself listen to his requests, pledging that they would refrain from all destruction (καμίαν ζημίαν) and desist from improper grievance (κανέναν φαστίδιον).[1247] As befits a spiritual master who watches over the Catholic world, Gregory XI played a role in the departure of the Genoese from the island. Despite his faults, he was treated as the only permanent link connecting the feuding sides, though he was not always obeyed and did not always refer to theological categories in his statements.

The importance of individual popes and their significance for the situation in Cyprus may be seen in the *Chronicle* in single sentences spoken by different figures under the influence of emotion, recorded at various points in the narrative, and usually expressed in the context of danger, such as 'as you are not getting what you wanted, all you can do is appeal to the pope' (ἄντα νὰ μηδὲν ἔχετε τὸ θέλετε, νἄχετε τὸ ποίσειν νῶσιν τοῦ πάπα),[1248] and other similar statements. When the newcomers from Genoa became particularly cumbersome, representatives of the Cypriots asked the constable to go to Rome and express, in the presence of the head of the Church, an objection against their presence on the island and the destruction they wrought.[1249]

It might seem that the assessment of the persons holding the papal office voiced by figures of the *Chronicle* is usually positive. However, based on the way in which Makhairas structures their portraits, conclusions that preclude an unambivalent interpretation may be drawn, because Leontios does not give the reader an insight into how they thought. We may, however, judge the decisions taken, the commands issued and the attitudes assumed, as in the case of the clumsy attempts at mediation made by Gregory XI, who demonstrated a lack of the ability to explore the true essence of the problem. The style adopted by the chronicler in passages recounting the actions of the bishops of Rome is characterised by the same restraint that is seen in fragments describing the deeds of Western rulers, which lack an assessment of their conduct.

Most religious figures involved in the Cypriot-Genoese conflict used their special position to carry out a specific task that was to help resolve a critical situation. Among those who had some impact on the course of these clashes, Makhairas includes a Greek priest, who unaware of a ruse led the Genoese, at their request, to unarmed men, thus contributing to both their deaths and his own,[1250] and a confessor (πνευματικός) from the church of St Augustine in Lefkosia, who acted as an intermediary, passing letters from Queen Eleanora.[1251] These individuals are not endowed with any exceptional traits. Although Makhairas includes only scant information about their profession and reveals his conviction about their inferior role in the events, he deliberately emphasises the presence of the clergy in general, which is conducive to highlighting the concept of Providence and the presence of God in the sequence of events.

[1245] LM III 356.
[1246] LM III 358.
[1247] LM III 359.
[1248] LM III 374. Consulted with Borowska's translation.
[1249] LM III 512.
[1250] LM III 468–469, 476.
[1251] LM III 504–505.

3.3.6. The Cypriot-Genoese peace

In the *Chronicle*, the Cypriots make many attempts to free themselves from the acute problem that is the Genoese presence by expelling them for good (τοὺς ἐξόδους τοὺς Γενουβίσους νὰ πᾶν εἰς τὸ καλόν). During a council convened for that purpose in 1372, Peter II proposed that the island's inhabitants give the troublesome merchants their material goods as a tribute – and himself unhesitatingly decided to give up a part of his property – in order to save the kingdom (ρηγάτον), which 'was falling apart from day to day' (καταλυέται καθημερινόν). To encourage his subjects to cooperate, the authorities decided that they would put a strong 'fear of God' (μὲ φόβον θεοῦ) in the population under their rule, as well as making them aware of the debt they allegedly had towards the court (ὡς χρέος ἀγρωνιζάμενον εἰς τὴν αὐλήν).[1252]

The conclusion of the peace between Cyprus and the Genoese was something of a higher necessity intended to interrupt the ruinous clashes that brought nothing to either side, either from the material or from the political point of view. As Makhairas says, the proclamation announced on 8 January 1374 on the conclusion of the 'good peace' (καλὴν ἀγάπην), called a 'command of God and the king' (ὁρισμὸς τοῦ θεοῦ καὶ τοῦ ἀφέντη μας), was addressed to everyone: 'small and large' (μικροὶ μεγάλοι), 'rich and poor' (πλούσιοι καὶ πένητες), 'clergyman and layman' (κλησιαστικοὶ καὶ λαγικοί), and contained an encouragement to 'undertake trade, travel beyond [the land] or on land, wherever they would, according to their wishes, as they were wont to, as was their custom' (νὰ πραματευτῇ, νὰ πάγη πέρα ἢ τῆς γῆς ὅπου νὰ θελήσῃ εἰς τὴν ὄρεξίν τους, ὡς γοιὸν ἦτον συνειθισμένοι).[1253]

Like other events described in the *Chronicle*, also this agreement (σασμός), together with the terms of the peace and orders (τὴν ἀγάπην καὶ τοὺς ὁρισμούς), was deemed 'valid' (ἐξαζόμενα) and 'confirmed' (στερεωμένα) by the relevant authorities. The efforts were sealed by an oath on the 'holy Gospel of God' (εἰς τὰ ἅγια τοῦ θεοῦ εὐαγγέλια) to make them eternal: the terms of the contract, being timeless, were to remain in force 'forever' (πάντοτε).[1254]

For the chronicler this was undoubtedly a victory that meant the restoration of balance on the island, with implications that were more political than religious. Makhairas returns to the Genoese issue one more time: when he tells of the agreement concluded 'to the great detriment of the kingdom' (εἰς τὴν μεγάλην ζημίαν τοῦ ρηγάτου) between the Genoese and King James (he who had come to Rhodes as a constable in 1374), in exile in Genoa in the years 1383–1385. Seized 'by the desire, which they have, to travel to the East' (ἀπὸ τὴν περιθυμίαν τὴν εἶχαν νὰ ταξειδεύγουν εἰς τὴν ἀνατολήν) they forced James to grant them rights to Ammochostos in exchange for bringing him back to Cyprus, thus confirming their modus operandi (and object of interest) already known from previous incidents.[1255]

3.4. Depiction of Cypriot-Venetian relations

Relations between Cyprus and Venice, both outside the island and those that took shape within its territory, were peaceful for a long time. In the *Chronicle* we read for example that Peter I visited Venice at the turn of the years 1364–1365 during his travels through Rhodes and the towns of Italy on his way to Avignon.[1256] The other merchant Republic next to Genoa was frequently a source of justified anxiety because of its excessive interference in relations with the Saracens, which was due to its quest to save trade in Syria by any means possible.[1257] A 1366 letter addressed by the Cypriot king to Sir Peter Monstri expressly contains phrases of respect and adoration towards '[our] beloved friends the Venetians' (τοὺς ἠγαπημένους μας φίλους τοὺς Βενετίκους)[1258] and stipulates that for their good the sultan of Cairo, at that

---

[1252] LM III 452.
[1253] LM III 525.
[1254] LM III 526.
[1255] LM IV 613–614.
[1256] LM II 161.
[1257] LM II 176.
[1258] LM II 180.

time Al-Ašraf Zayn ad-Dīn Šaʿbān (which we are not told in the *Chronicle*)[1259] should not be provoked to take unexpected steps because this might damage their interests.

The relations with the Egyptian ruler described by Leontios are at the centre of the Venetians' actions. It was they who were frequently sent to him as envoys with gifts and various requests.[1260] Because of the foresight demonstrated by Peter I, who did not want to undermine their interests, other Western countries abandoned their plans to set out (παζάριν) for the Middle East, accusing Cyprus of having believed those who had done 'a great injury to Christians' (μεγάλη ζημία εἰς τοὺς χριστιανούς) through their efforts. One ruler, the Count of Savoy Amadeus VI, disappointed by such a turn of affairs, hastened to the 'land of the Rhomaioi' (τὴν Ρωμανίαν) to help the ruler of Constantinople, John V Palaiologos.[1261] In MS O we read that the emperor, 'having embarked against the Turk, crushed him' (πηγαίνοντά του κατά πρόσωπα τοῦ Τούρκου ἐτζάκισέν τον).[1262] From various narrative elements of this type there emerges the image of a diverse Christian civilisation, within which individual nations were unable to communicate with each other.

Because of this fragmentation, the sultan was able to interfere in matters of the Christian world, and constantly delayed his final consent for the conclusion of the peace treaty, first agreeing to it and then going back on his promises. The Mamlūk ruler found advantages in the chaos reigning in the West, and thus, despite his intentions to the contrary he deviously underlined that he desired to stabilise mutual relations with the Republics (and the Catalans).[1263] The Venetians, who for some time remained unaware that they had been deceived, endeavoured to gain his favour, losing the trust of other Western countries. Furthermore, unaware of the undesirable developments, they set off to Syria in good faith, risking their lives in doing so.[1264] In turn, Peter I convinced the peace would be signed, 'was disappointed' (ἐπικράνθην πολλά) when he discovered the truth.[1265]

The *Chronicle* discusses the course of the peace talks in detail. On 24 August 1368, an embassy was sent to Cairo, composed of Genoese and Venetians.[1266] On 6 August 1370 another effort at mediation was made, which against hopes and expectations resulted in the Venetian Peter Giustiniani being cast into prison.[1267] Makhairas describes the involvement of Pope Urban V, some of whose decisions were motivated by 'love for the Republics' (διὰ τὴν ἀγάπην τῶν κουμουνίων).[1268] In their contacts with followers of Islam, both merchant communities hold a position equivalent to that of the Cypriots: they are fighting the same enemy and they have the same desire to stabilise the situation, although this is not always dictated by concern for the other communities.

The other events that transpired in Cyprus with significant involvement of the Venetians, less painstakingly presented in the *Chronicle*, include the sending of letters by the Lusignans to Venice asking them to help liberate Cyprus from the Genoese arrivals[1269] and recruitment of an army composed of representatives of many nations in Venice by Thibald.[1270]

Makhairas' comments about the Venetian presence on the island and contacts between Cypriots and Venetians in the Mediterranean Basin are far fewer than descriptions of Genoese activity. This Republic's citizens are sometimes presented in the *Chronicle* as having a peaceful mindset, focused on their trade activities, which they use as the measure for their choices and decisions, and sometimes as criminals who are responsible for the Genoese-Cypriot conflict and (which is demonstrated in the fourth chapter) as Latins who cooperate with the Muslims. The depiction that emerges from Leontios' work is of a people who have good contact with the pope, born of a natural attachment to him: the supreme pontiff often becomes their confidant and an instance that protects their interests. However, in no place do the Venetians manifest their personal attitude to God, and where they fight for peace they also do so for prosaic political and trade reasons.

[1259] Freeman-Grenville, Chronology of World History, 314.
[1260] LM II 181.
[1261] LM II 183. See Dawkins, Notes, 118.
[1262] LM II 183. Dawkins (Ed., transl.), Ἐξήγησις/ Recital, 162 (fn. 4); Παυλίδης (Ed.), Λεοντίου Μαχαιρᾶ Χρονικόν, 132 (fn. 6).
[1263] LM II 192.
[1264] LM II 188.
[1265] LM II 186.
[1266] LM II 223–230.
[1267] LM II 303.
[1268] LM II 300.
[1269] LM II 512.
[1270] LM III 559.

3.5. The role of Providence

In creating his multidimensional depiction of Cypriot-Genoese relations, Makhairas hides his private opinions under the sequence of events he reports, whose course he attributes to Providence (this concept is inferred from the contents of the work: the word 'Providence' is not used there) and its operation in terms of cause and effect. We receive a legible providentialist vision of Divine control exerted over the Latins, who are dependent on the supernatural power that decides their fates. References to this aspect form both a permanent component that links all the motifs in the *Chronicle*'s narrative, and an important element of the rhetoric used by figures of the portrayed world. The chronicler's intuitions regarding the consequences of human sins bring to mind the deliberations of Thomas Aquinas, who combines two concepts: of providence and causation.[1271]

There are many instances where the chronicler demonstrates this approach. He explains the outcome of the battle of Chioggia by a deliberate act of God, who 'threw [the Genoese under the feet of the] Venetians' (ὁ θεὸς ἀποκούππισεν τοὺς Βεννετίκους), and argues that this happened because 'God does not listen to the arrogant, [but] grants victory to the meek' (ὁ θεὸς ὑπερηφάνους δὲν γροικᾷ, τοὺς ταπεινοὺς διδεῖ νίκος).[1272]

Describing the taking of Ammochostos by the Genoese and the ceremonial opening of the gates, he puts the following into the mouths of the knights and people of Ammochostos: 'This came about because of our immense evil [deeds] – hence the devil blinded them' (τοῦτον ἐγίνετον διὰ τὰ πολλά μας κακά, ὅπου τοὺς ἐτύφλωσεν ὁ διάβολος),[1273] which expresses a moral judgement of their own actions. Citizens of the merchant state voice the belief that they took control of the port due to the will of God, but are simultaneously aware that they could lose it, which ultimately happened. A change in destiny is presented in the tale of the youth Thibald,[1274] who after seeing the Genoese forces in Ammochostos in 1375, two years after its siege, wanted to send an expedition to recapture the port at his own expense.[1275] Here Makhairas accents the role of the 'spirit of the Lord' (πνεῦμα κυρίου)[1276] which inspired him, though it is hard to tell whether he understands the theological interpretation of this phrase or treats it as a rhetorical figure used to strengthen the impression of causative force and presence of a supernatural element in the portrayed events. This mystical experience had far-reaching consequences. As an individual with a calling, Thibald gathered a large throng of valiant men, composed of Lombards, Germans, Hungarians, Franks, Cretans, Englishmen and people of Savoy: because the nations involved in the fighting are listed, we gain an insight into the diverse community of Latins who achieved the victory against the enemy.[1277] From the day on which this group met the opponent in battle, 'Ammochostos was closed' (ἐσφαλίστην […] ἡ Ἀμόχουστος) because none of the Genoese who remained there dared to make demands of the king.[1278] Makhairas explains the mechanism of Divine intervention in simple terms: 'God wished to help the poor Cypriot kingdom' (ὁ θεὸς ἐθέλησεν νὰ βοηθήση τοῦ πτωχοῦ τοῦ ρηγάτου τῆς Κύπρου) because he was 'the one who punishes and heals' (ὁ παιδεύων καὶ πάλιν ἰατρεύει).[1279] The final resolution of the conflict shows that even if God allowed a temporary victory by the enemy, he did so only to punish and instruct him, and then return the Cypriots' property to them.

Cyprus' exceptional importance in the eyes of God may be illustrated by the vivid, emphatic (and partly manipulative) exchange between an envoy of the constable and a Genoese admiral during the fighting over Kerynia, which Makhairas embellishes with references to religion:

> *For this island is built* (εἶνε θεμελιωμένον) *upon a rock* (ἀπάνω εἰς μίαν πέτραν) *in the midst of the sea* (μέσα εἰς τὴν θάλασσαν) *and is surrounded* (τριγυρισμένον) *by the infidels* (τριγυρισμένον ἀπὸ τοὺς ἀπίστους), *Turks and Saracens, and you have punished us* (ἐποίκετε εἰς αὐτόν μας κρίσες) *and done many injustices* (πολλὰ ἄδικα) *to the inhabitants* (τοὺς λᾶς τοὺς κατοικισμένους), *who are subjects of the realm* (ἀποῦ εἶνε ἀπουκάτω εἰς τὴν βασιλείαν) *under the king's protection* (εἰς τὸ σκέπος

[1271] See Łukasiewicz, Opatrzność Boża, 119.
[1272] LM III 590–593.
[1273] LM III 420–421.
[1274] The story of his transformation and fall is discussed in detail in Subchapter 2.4.
[1275] LM III 556.
[1276] LM III 556.
[1277] LM III 559–561.
[1278] LM III 562.
[1279] LM III 560.

τοῦ ῥηγός). And beyond all this you want to hunt down (νὰ γυρέψετε) the king in his poverty (τὸν πτωχὸν) and deprive him of his kingdom unjustly (ἀπὸ τὸ ῥηγάτον του νὰ τὸν ἀδικήσετε). And in this matter you should fear God, and know that death must come upon both you and upon us (πῶς μέλλει ν' ἀπεθάνετε καὶ σεῖς καὶ μεῖς) [...]. (LM III 489)

This passage shows how in the convention he adopts Makhairas situates different nations that are not faithful to God on the religious map that he envisions. He undoubtedly holds Muslim peoples to be an external enemy that besets the island from all sides, while the Genoese are an internal enemy that intensively harries the Cypriots, but which remains within the fold of the Christian civilisation, a position that grants them access to the life that pulses at the centre of the Frankish domain as well as influence on the processes occurring there. As Leontios shows, for the aggressors themselves the consequence of having decided of their own free will to penetrate territory under the rule of a different power was fear caused by the awareness of the effects of crossing a boundary set by Providence. Reaching that untouchable core primarily involved plundering the two most powerful towns on Cyprus, which were protected by God: 'admirable Ammochostos' (θαυμαστὴ Ἀμόχουστος) and 'noble Lefkosia' (εὐγενικὴ Λευκωσία).[1280]

The image of Providence and the concept of its causative power are also invoked by the constable who travelled to Rhodes in search of help and was grateful to be placed 'in good hands' (εἰς -καλὰ- χέργια).[1281]

Two dimensions in which Makhairas perceives and interprets the events that occurred may thus be distinguished: the plane of operations by Providence, which directs the course of history in a manner contingent on the measure of sins of the two sides of a conflict, and the plane of God's influence on individuals via inspiration, which causes them to influence the flow of events. Leontios juxtaposes the inevitability and omnipotence of this supernatural involvement with the petty and thus grotesque-seeming endeavours of the Genoese made to overcome the inevitable (in the case of the fighting for Ammochostos these were: enlarging the walls, transporting seawater and pouring it out around the town to transform it into an island, plundering the opulent apartments of prince John de Lusignan, kidnapping his wife and ultimately murdering him). He shows their determination, expressed in the fact that even the riches they seize 'do not suffice to satisfy the Genoese and cause them to leave' (ἦσαν ἀκανητὸν νἄχαν κουντεντιαστεῖν οἱ Γενουβίσοι καὶ νἄχαν πάγειν).[1282]

In the *Chronicle*, the Cypriots envisage an outcome unfavourable to them, taking the position that since it was highly probable that they would be defeated and deprived of the means for safe existence, and perhaps even lose their lives in one of the many battles fought in their homeland, their enemies would meet the same fate. Makhairas expresses this in a statement by an envoy, addressed to the Genoese admiral, which underlines that if the interlocutor desires to deprive the king of his heritage (ἔχετε τὸ θέλημα νὰ καθαρίσετε τὸν ῥήγα ἀπὸ τὴν κληρονομίαν του), 'the God of the heavens will not bear it' (ὁ θεὸς τοῦ οὐρανοῦ δὲν θέλει τὸ βαστάξειν)[1283] and 'the God of the heavens will hold judgement [over them]' (ὁ θεὸς ὁ ἐπουράνιος θέλει ποίσειν κρίσιν).[1284] Every deed of man that distorts the balance of life on the island impacts God's decisions and forces him to react.

The Genoese use the same framework as the Cypriots in their argumentation, adapting the providentialist discourse to their needs. Interestingly, Makhairas does not hesitate to put in their mouths words that destroy the painfully idealistic image of his countrymen. Namely, they refer to the murder of Peter I and the attempt to place the blame for this act, which was the responsibility of individuals, on the whole Cypriot community. The commander of the Genoese fleet Peter de Campo Fregoso, who speaks in the name of the whole Republic, gleefully paints a picture of the islanders' wickedness, accusing them of having sent their ruler to his death 'in the beauty of his body' ((εἰς) τὴν ὀμορφίαν τῆς σαρκός του) and adding that this was the reason for their punishment, i.e. defeat. In his opinion, the moral consequences of this sin went further still because the perpetrators were 'excommunicated' (ἀφωρισμένοι), 'excluded from the Church' (ἔξω τῆς ἐκκλησίας τοῦ θεοῦ) and 'damned by God' (καταραμένοι ἀποὺ τὸν θεόν).[1285] According to the admiral, it was the Cypriots who had wrought the greatest desolation in their own country, though they ineptly tried to lay the blame on the Muslims. The ghost of Peter I's murder torments

---
[1280] LM III 489.
[1281] LM III 538.
[1282] LM III 450–451.
[1283] LM III 489.
[1284] LM III 492.
[1285] LM III 490.

Makhairas the most, which is visible in his many references to the event (LM II 280–281, III 355–356, 482). In a comment on this conversation he presents his assessment of the situation, where he calls the words of the commander 'empty' (εὔκαιρα λογία), and him a 'man without value' (ἕνας οὐδετιποτένος),[1286] discounting the allegations against his own countrymen. However, by touching on the problem and refraining from excessive idealisation of the Cypriots, he gives his message the appearance of accuracy and impartiality.

Makhairas ends the Cypriot-Genoese episode with a brief summary in which he states that the citizens of the Republic 'laboured in vain' (ψέματα ἐκοπιάσαν). The pointlessness of their efforts was due, as we might guess, to God's plan and his response to their actions. Leontios claims that at the end of these events '[they] were sad' (θλιμμένοι), retreated 'with moaning' (μὲ ἀναστεναγμούς) and were 'filled with pain' (μὲ πόνους).[1287]

Elements of theodicy may be found in the *Chronicle* where its author debates the causes for the successes of evil in the context of the constant operation of Providence: the explanation for God's attitude, wherein he allows situations that are ambiguous and evil from the moral point of view, is his plan to use human sin for higher purposes, though the chronicler does not say what these might be or interpret them in any way.[1288] The description of Genoese cruelty when hanging a priest named Elias (Γλίακα) may serve as an illustration of such conduct:

> [...] *(they seized) also a certain Elias, a priest of Christ* (ἱερέαν τοῦ Χριστοῦ) [...] *they took him and hanged him at midnight. The faithless bastards* (ἄπιστοι κοπέλλοι) *who denounced them* (ὅπου τοὺς ἐδεῖχναν)! *And how could the righteous Judge endure it* (πῶς τὰ ἐβάσταξεν ὁ δίκαιος κριτής)? *But (all these things were done) because of the many sins, beyond all reckoning* (ἀμέτρητες), *(which were in the island, and) God allowed* (ἐπαραχώρησεν) *(the people to be chastened by the Genoese.)* (LM III 441)[1289]

The rhetorical question asked by Makhairas indicates that he has an evident emotional attitude to the information he transmits. The chronicler links Providence and human morality with the category of the enemy, as seen in the following example:

> *And no man may boast in his own strenght, for the Lord will make him weak* (διότι (ὁ) Κύριος ἀστενεῖ τον), *to cause his enemy to prevail in strength* (διὰ νὰ δυναμώσῃ τὸν ἐχθρόν του). (LM III 421)

According to him, the enemy is always lurking near man like a thief (κλέπτης), waiting for a moment of inattention. Man's defencelessness is all the more acute since he does not know (δὲν ἠξεύρ(ει)) 'in what hour it will come' (ποίαν ὥραν ἔρκεται).[1290] At the same time, Makhairas voices the general thought that evil in the moral sense will be overcome by righteousness: this is indicated by the following sayings: 'after the storm comes good weather' (μετὰ τὴν σκλερίαν ἔρχεται γαλήνη) and 'water flows away and the sand remains' (τὸ νερὸν πάγει, καὶ ὁ ἄμμος μεινίσκει).[1291] This unpredictability of fate and lack of coherence between human expectations and reality is bluntly expressed by the constable, who shouts: 'These are your promises and your oaths! Praise be to you, oh Lord!' (τοῦτα εἶνε τὰ προυμουτιάσματά σας καὶ οἱ ὅρκοι σας; Δόξα σοι ὁ θεός!) when it turns out that the Genoese he meets at sea do not want to hurt him but only accompany one who is 'of royal blood' (αἷμαν ρηγάτικον) in reaching harbour safely.[1292]

The chronicler shows that each individual human act is linked to the operation of Providence and only a detailed examination of all the aspects of a given event allows the true will of God to be established. Of course, this perspective also covers relations between Christians and Muslims, but its multiformity

---

[1286] LM III 491–492.
[1287] LM III 458.
[1288] Cf. LM III 482.
[1289] Pavlidis comments: '[...] αυτός ο ιερέας ήταν ένας από τους συντρόφους του Ψυχίδν [...] που προδόθηκε αργότερα'. 'This priest was one of the companions of Psilidi, who [...] later suffered a defeat.' (Παυλίδης (Ed.), Λεοντίου Μαχαιρᾶ Χρονικόν, 329, fn. 2. Kupiszewska's translation from the Polish translation by the author). This is yet another example of a priest in the *Chronicle* who meets a tragic fate.
[1290] LM III 402.
[1291] LM III 492.
[1292] LM III 534.

is most fully revealed in descriptions of episodes involving a single though diverse and internally divided religious community.

3.6. Summary

The portrayal of Cypriot-Genoese, Cypriot-Venetian, and also Genoese-Venetian relations in the *Chronicle* is extremely dynamic, though religiosity is not the main plane of interpretation. The appearance in Cyprus of representatives of the two Catholic Republics was in some ways a natural progression as a consequence of the crusades and an expression of the Western states' belief that the island was available to them for their benefit and aims (since the Lusignans had previously carried out its systematic 'colonisation' from within). The image of the Franks battling each other for the island, which initially belonged to representatives of the Orthodox culture inherently foreign to them, appeals very strongly to the imagination. If we examine the reality presented in the Cypriot work, we may notice that both the Genoese and the Venetians are only beginning to mark their territory, looking for the space they need to extend the scope of their activities.[1293] In the description of these events, the Orthodox elements characteristic of the narrative about the earlier period of the island's history disappear and the Cypriots' distinctive identity is overshadowed, making room for a new series of events with the participation of figures from the Western world.

A precise timeframe of the Genoese presence on Cyprus – they arrived on 30 April 1373 with seven galleys and departed a year later on that same date, causing much evil and destruction in the meantime (πολλὺν κακὸν καὶ ζημίαν)[1294] – shows how short the period in which they managed to capture the island's important locations was. Of course, this refers only to the Genoese who came to Cyprus solely in order to plunder it, and not those living there permanently. The Cypriot-Genoese conflict additionally coincided with an intensive dispute between Genoa and Venice, which led to the escalation of aggressive behaviours, notably leading to the battle of Chioggia.[1295] In his assessment of the effects of Genoese actions, Makhairas shows that in the post-Genoese reality his beloved country became a place that had been orphaned,[1296] widowed and made beggarly.[1297]

The Genoese specified their goal openly:

> [...] *we shall get into our power (εἰς τὴν ἐξουσίαν μας) the whole kingdom of Cyprus.* (LM III 459)

They justified their endeavours by treating them as a response to past 'injuries' (τούτην τὴν ζημίαν), 'daily slaughter' (σκοτωμοὺς καθημερινόν) and 'fear' (φόβον), and as Makhairas writes, the solution that they chose made everybody happy (τοῦτος ὁ λόγος ἄρεσεν ὅλους).[1298]

In the *Chronicle* three identities (apart from the less highlighted ones) come within the scope of 'Latinness': Frankish, Genoese – regardless of whether we are talking about 'Genoese in truth' or 'Genoese in name' – and Venetian. Fragments describing the actions of the Lusignans, Genoese and Venetians show that representatives of the same religion interpreted the will of God in their own favour, even if their objectives were mutually incompatible, and thus granted themselves a greater right to His help. Furthermore, all the parties regularly invoked the decisions of the pope, who was both an intermediary and the ultimate instance.

The portrait of the Genoese painted by the chronicler presents a chaotic group of individuals foreign to Cyprus who claim the right to benefit from the rapid changes occurring – also under their influence – on Cypriot land. They do not hesitate to provoke conflict situations in contacts with its inhabitants or to fan the flames of discord between them and the Venetians. Although Makhairas perceives the representatives

---

[1293] Svetlana Bliznyuk underlines that Genoese forces were not yet established before the 1373–1374 war (Bliznyuk, Diplomatic Relations, 279).
[1294] LM III 543.
[1295] LM III 588–593.
[1296] The theme of orphaning as an element of ideological manipulation is raised by Nicolaou-Konnari in the article Nicolaou-Konnari, 'A poor island...', 119–145.
[1297] LM III 414–415.
[1298] LM III 459.

of this other Republic as more helpful towards the Franks than the Genoese are, they nevertheless still act with their own good in mind to the extent that they interfere in Cypriots contacts with the Muslims.

In the contextual layer of the *Chronicle* good and evil appear as basic, complementary axiological categories. The image of evil as correlated with the nature of the Genoese is complex and may be gleaned from how the chronicler presents their actions and the epithets he attributes to them. Leontios perceives them primarily as infidels (ἄπιστοι), that is those who betray God, are deceitful (παράβουλοι), use invalid banners,[1299] and furthermore are cowardly, because they fear the consequences that might come 'as a result of the injuries' (διὰ τὲς πολλὲς ἀδικίες) that they have inflicted. He explains that they tyrannised (τοὺς τυρανισμούς) the impoverished people (οἱ πτωχοὶ οἱ λᾶς) of Cyprus, scaring them as they had no right to (τὲς ἀδικὲς ἀπειλές).[1300] The methods they use are compared to a plunge into chaos (ἀνακατώθησαν μεσόν τους)[1301] and filling people with fear (ὁ λαὸς ὅλος ἐφοβήθησαν).[1302] With each subsequent event in the *Chronicle* the reader discovers new traits in the personalities of the merchants and notices an evident contradiction between their behaviour versus the faith they declare and affiliation with the Catholic Church. The murder of father Elias proves that the Genoese, inclined to brutal behaviour, knew how to hide their crimes from others, and thus how to protect themselves from their judgement.

The chronicler paints an emphatic picture of the cunning Genoese, who as a 'haughty' (σουπέρπιον) and 'treacherous' (παράβουλον) people (γένος) were able to use the Cypriot-Turkish conflict for their aims. In doing so, he uses the verb 'looked for a chance' (ἀφορμολογοῦσαν) for the way they worked so as to further accentuate the deviousness and calculation behind their successes. In his opinion, this *modus operandi*, dictated by cunning, had been effective since time immemorial (πάντα), and the citizens of Genoa themselves turned out to be extremely consistent in their behaviours, which he expresses thus:

> *So the Genoese people, haughty and treacherous, who were for ever trying to get Cyprus (into their hands) (ὁποῦ πάντα 'πλημελοῦσα νὰ πάρουν τὴν Κύπρον) and trying to find pretexts for this (ἀφορμολογοῦσαν), found a pretext (ηὖραν ἀφορμὴν) in this quarrel (τοῦ μαλλωμάτου), and sent letters to Genoa, where King Peter was, and made claims against him for the wrong (ἀγγαλέσαν ἀπὸ τὸ ἄδικον) which had been done to them in Cyprus [...].* (LM II 153)

The chronicler clearly sees the mistakes and faults of his community, treating them as a painful manifestation of the fall and moral deficits of its individual members, but simultaneously he has faith in God's mercy and the special, God-granted status of Cyprus as an island belonging to the Cypriots only, that is to the Franks and the Cyprians. Adding an explanation of the term 'Cypriots' is significant. It suggests that Leontios has become used to the 'colonial' situation or that he is censuring himself due to his position as a state official at the Lusignan court.

One of the many intrigues where the Genoese play a main role is used by Leontios to show that we have no influence over the evil that affects us. Citing words drawn from the Bible, he states:

> *But we will not allow any single one of the faithless (ἀπὲ τοὺς ἄπιστους) and traitorous (τοὺς παράβουλους) Genoese to enter, as to whom we pray God (ὅπου παρακαλοῦμεν τὸν θεόν) to look upon (νὰ 'δῇ) our humility (τὴν ταπείνωσίν μας) and to do away their pride (νὰ σηκώσῃ τὴν σουπερπίαν τους). The scripture (γραφή) saith: Fear not the proud man, for if he is to-day, to-morrow he is not (μὲν φοβηθῇς ἀποὺ ἄνθρωπον σουπέρπιον, ὅτι ἂν ἤνε σήμμερον αὔριον δὲν εἶνε).* (LM III 473)

The above statement refers to ethical dispositions of the human being, such as humility (ταπείνωσις) and its opposite – pride (σουπερπία). It expresses the belief that God controls human attitudes and an unwavering certainty as to the inevitability of death. That every situation requires humility is expressed in the following fragment:

[1299] LM III 474.
[1300] LM III 442.
[1301] LM III 558.
[1302] LM III 417.

[...] *you must not think that I am doing this in any way to make a boast (διὰ νὰ φουμίσω) of our Cypriot armies as against the Genoese armies, because I often tell you –how the Genoese slaughtered (τοὺς μακελλεμοὺς ὅπου ἐμακελλεύγουνταν) the Cypriots.–*[1303] (LM III 484)

As in the account of the Franks' rule, also in this case references may be found to the themes of mercy,[1304] the Divine ability to work with extremes (transforming evil into good, a strong person into a weak one), protection,[1305] giving of life[1306] and God's knowledge. This last attribute is particularly visible in the words of the constable spoken on Rhodes, the place where his daughter had just died:[1307]

God knows (γινώσκει) that I shall be very glad (εὑρίσκομαι εἰς μεγάλην πεθυμία) to finish the affair (νὰ τὸ τελειώσω), but my only daughter has fallen very sick [...]. (LM III 536)

In his description of Cypriot-Genoese relations, the chronicler alludes in many fragments to the hostility between the two groups, which he places in a religious context: it is usually the Genoese who are the enemies of the Cypriots. Thanks to the contrast that he obtained by juxtaposing representatives of these two groups, his depiction of the former was strengthened.

Both in the case of the Cypriot-Genoese conflict and Cypriot-Venetian relations in the *Chronicle* religion takes a secondary position as a permanent but not a determining aspect, and is merely a pretext that legitimises intentions and efforts, offensive (Genoese) and defensive (Cypriots). It is hard to find a place in the *Chronicle* that would show the two Republics' citizens to be truly interested in Catholic doctrine or individual practices. Although the figure of the pope is an instance of appeal, he also serves as a tool for manipulation, endowed with the highest authority, which may be used to influence the opponent's way of thinking and emotions. The political language of the Genoese features the notion of a vigilant God, a God that grants victories and a punishing God, which they invoke in moments they deem appropriate. Makhairas does attribute words related to religion to them and himself embellishes his narrative with similar terms, but he does so only in order to show that the newcomers from Genoa were playing a game with the Cypriots and the Venetians intended to draw their attention away from their strictly political objectives.

By including these two communities in his work, the chronicler expands the image of Latin society, and more importantly, shows the differences within it, and simultaneously he does not allow the reader to forget that also Greeks, Syrians and Armenians fought for the good of the island.

Meanwhile, by showing the role of Providence with respect to the actions of Catholics he strengthens the contrast between the Lusignan period, in which man interpreted the nature of specific interventions by God and used his beliefs in this respect in practice, and the Byzantine period, when God made direct contact with man, leaving no place for conjecture.

[1303] MS O has additional information: 'ἐμακελλέψαν καὶ οἱ Γενουβίσοι τοὺς Κυπριῶτες'. See Dawkins (Ed., transl.), Ἐξήγησις/ Recital, 466 (fn. 10).
[1304] LM III 393, 545, 548.
[1305] LM III 401.
[1306] God as the giver of 'happy life' (-μακαρίαν- ζωήν) in LM III 492.
[1307] LM III 535.

IV. Depiction of contacts between Christians and Muslims in the *Chronicle*

Does not God
Know best
All that is
In the hearts of all Creation?[1308]
(Qurʾān, Sūra XXIX, The Spider [Al-Ankabut], v. 10)

4.1. Christians and Muslims: two differing depictions

A significant role as regards the perception of the religious 'other' is played in the *Chronicle* by the Cypriot Christians' attitude to Muslims. Usually, contact of this kind, between worlds with incompatible histories, is based on the image that the representatives of one of them creates of the other one's representatives in situations where they happen to encounter each other. Hugh Goddart calls such a phenomenon 'mutual perceptions',[1309] and they involve becoming acquainted with each other through words, actions and observation. All these forms are dependent on the degree of 'commensurability of phenomena',[1310] which should be understood as the occurrence of certain identical foundations on which each of these worlds builds its specific experience. Substance permeates between the non-coherent realities that coexist in the universe created by Makhairas even on small, seemingly unnoticeable planes.

In Leontios' narrative, neither party, Christian nor Muslim, has sufficient knowledge about the opponent, and at the same time neither expresses the desire to change this state of affairs or shows willingness to come to know the enemy. This kind of ignorance, visible also in other Christian and Muslim texts from the period, is manifested in the way how medieval authors use general statements about the 'religious other'. In Arab historiography such a trend may be seen for example in the chronicle *Kitāb al-kāmil fī al-tārīḫ min afʿāl as-sulṭān Ṣalāḥ ad-Dīn* (Complete history. From the deeds of sultan Saladin) by Al-Aṯir ('Alī 'Izz ad-Dīn Ibn al-Aṯir al-Ǧazarī, 1160–1233),[1311] where we read:

The Franks had religious motives that honed their anger, so despite difficulties they set off by land and sea from all distant corners.[1312]

This fragment reflects the author's simple assumptions about the motivation governing the Latins who decided to go to the Middle East, expressed without in-depth analysis. Transferring this thinking to the *Chronicle*, we may notice that in paragraphs about the followers of Islam there are many deficiencies and omissions, including in the quite lengthy (LM II 176–230 and LM III 284–309) descriptions of peace

---

[1308] Ali (Transl.), Quran, 1031.
[1309] Term coined by Hugh Goddart in Goddart, A History of Christian-Muslim Relations, 56.
[1310] The concept of 'commensurability of phenomena' appeared with regard to culture in Tambiah, Racjonalność, relatywizm, przekład, 54. Translated by Kupiszewska.
[1311] Al-Aṯir, Kompletna księga historii, xxiii–xxxii.
[1312] Al-Aṯir, Kompletna księga historii, 5. Translated by Kupiszewska.

negotiations with the sultan, where the name of the Muslim ruler is not given even once. This example permits one to conjecture that this perception of phenomena concerned only those forms of manifestation of the 'other's' attitudes and habits that were possible to verify personally, without deeper cognitive interference in the internal dynamics of his world.

In the *Chronicle* the centre of gravity is naturally located on the Christian side, and the position of the adherents of Islam may be ascertained mainly through their statements and letters, probably reconstructed by Makhairas on the basis of the documents available to him. The mood and sense of the correspondence and thus its reception primarily depend on the reliability of the Cypriot chronicler.

From the point of view of this book's assumptions, it is paramount to consider how the course of these relations was impacted by the 'colonial' situation on Cyprus, which led to differences within the Christian community and to a transformation of the social structure during the three centuries of Lusignan rule. Also important is whether representatives of Islam in the *Chronicle* hold the Cypriots (and Christians in general) to be a monolithic religious group, or whether they notice the difference between the Franks and the Cyprians.[1313]

The Christian and the Muslim worlds portrayed in the *Chronicle* are called 'civilisations' because they are composed of people occupying a common space, fostering the same values and expressing themselves in a way that unequivocally identifies them, building their sense of identity on the foundations of a given religion. In the *Chronicle* these worlds are formed by individuals or easy to distinguish groups (Cypriots, Genoese and Venetians vs. Turks and Egyptians) under the standard of one religion – each side speaks in the name of the God it professes – and in order to multiply the greater good. Faith demarcates the boundaries of military action and forms a pretext for aggressive behaviours, directed towards conquering new lands. These circumstances force the individual to redefine their identity, assess the value and the usefulness of their connection to other people who belong to the same or a culturally related nation, define their place in collective religious life and observe the fate of the civilisation of their affiliation (how it is made present in the world).

Christians and Muslims in the *Chronicle* are aware of the differences between them, which they interpret almost exclusively as discrepancies in their perception and worship of God. The important role of religion in defining civilisations has been emphasised by thinkers such as Sigmund Freud, Russell Kirk and Samuel Huntington.[1314] Werner Jeanrond, a scholar of 'inter-religious hermeneutics', explains the difficulties experienced by a person who is rooted in their own beliefs when trying to understand the way of thinking of a believer of a different religion:

> *Interreligious hermeneutics thus is faced not only with the task of understanding the religious other, but also with the task of developing a hermeneutics of suspicion to be applied to any project of imagining both the religious self and the religious other.*[1315]

Jeanrond's statement implies that the categories used to define one's own system of beliefs are insufficient for the description and assessment of the behaviour of such believers. Figures from the *Chronicle* are unable to move beyond their own understanding of God, their own duties and forms of demonstrating their faith, which is why they cannot reach 'the religious other'. This difficulty must have also been the experience of Makhairas when he attempted to recreate in his narrative the correspondence between the Christians and the Muslims using documents available in the archives. Under the chronicler's pen, the wording used by the sultan in the letter to King Janus is deprived of its 'Arab' character, as it combines categories that can be linked to Islamic doctrine with the sense carried by a statement written in the Cypriot dialect.

It is worth noting that all contacts (intercultural and intercivilisational) are conducive to observation of the world and redefining one's own identity. The clash of the Christian East and West with the Islamic civilisation that occurred in the Middle Ages took place through trade, via fighting for territory, in disputes concerning spiritual values and also at the level of interpreting the norms of social functioning and customs. Makhairas refers to all these elements. He writes about the vibrant ports of Cyprus and Egyptian Alexandria, about the rituals of receiving envoys and about Cypriot-Saracen fighting in Cyprus and

---

[1313] According to Seyyed Hossein Nasr, from the doctrinal point of view the main difference between Christianity and Islam is that for the former, God is a mystery, while according to the latter man 'is veiled from God' (Nasr, Ideals and Realities of Islam, 8, http://traditionalhikma.com/wp-content/uploads/2015/02/Ideals-and-Realities-of-Islam.pdf, accessed 9 November 2021). The similarities between the religions named by Nasr are: emphasising the immortality of the soul, importance of inner life and compatible eschatological perspectives (Nasr, The Heart of Islam, 42).
[1314] Freud, Kultura jako źródło cierpień; Kirk, Civilization without Religion?
[1315] Jeanrond, Toward an Interreligious Hermeneutics, 47.

the Middle East. However, he blurs these differences, penning frugally worded descriptions of situations in which certain behaviours, like the attitude of rulers of both sides to envoys, are extremely similar: King Peter I and the sultan were capable of showing both the courtesy desired in such situations and outbursts of anger that went against the code of hospitality.

When analysing the differences between the Christian and the Muslim civilisations in the Middle Ages, we may see that the main levels of 'otherness' were defined by: a specific way of thinking about God, which was used to interpret the nature of one's attitude to other peoples, geographical separateness, language, grounding in laws and holy books, the hierarchy of power and ways of using force. They all have their proper reflection in the Cypriot work. Namely, on its basis we are able to deconstruct the image of a collective that believes in a different God than the inhabitants of Cyprus, who is represented by the prophet Muḥammad; recreate the geographical division of the world into the Cypriot land known to Leontios and the distant, faraway overseas lands inhabited by the enemies of Christ's followers; note differences in language; find the names of the most important religious texts and determine the legal codes used, and also to observe glaring examples of the merciless resolve with which the Saracens interfere in the life of Christians on the island.

By examining how Makhairas describes contact between Christians and Muslims, the chapter reflects on what for him as a representative of the Cypriot community Islam really is and how the differing civilisational features of Christians and Muslims dominated the Cypriot-Saracen and Cypriot-Turkish contacts he described. Before this topic is analysed, some information about the assumptions underlying the doctrines of Islam is provided to give an outline of the rudimentary concepts which will be later used.

Erwin Rosenthal, one of the greatest experts on the subject, defined Islam as follows:

Islam is a religious way of life which contains diverse elements all bound together in a certain unity of outlook by the common belief in God and his prophet who had received a revelation – the final revelation – in the form of the Qur'ān, 'the precious Book'.[1316]

This faith in God, the prophet and the Qur'ān was the basis for the shaping of political reflection that defined relations between the Muslims and representatives of other civilisations, contingent on the specific course of events. As Rosenthal states, this happened through evolution of the initial set of beliefs and their adaptation to current requirements ('systems, theories and ideas which are brought to Muslims from without').[1317]

A reference to the Qur'ān and the prophet is made in the Chronicle only once, but this single case, combined with frequent references to God made by the adherents of Islam, allows the roots shared by Muslim peoples such as the Turks and the Egyptians to be noted and discerned. A more in-depth conceptualisation of this community remains practically unexpressed in the Cypriot work. Unlike Leontios' text, the *Chronique d'Amadi* starts with a reference to Muḥammad (*Maomet*), calling him an 'emissary of the devil who styled himself a prophet sent by [the sole] God' (*messo del demonio, et se feva intender esser propheta, mandato da la parte de Dio*).[1318] It calls the new religion spreading in the Eastern lands and all Arabia (*sparsa per tutte le parte de Oriente et medemamente in Arabia*) 'false Mahometan faith' (*la falsa fede mahomettana*). It contrasts Muḥammad with Heraklios, the emperor on the Byzantine throne at the time, whom it considers a 'good Christian' (*bon christiano*).[1319] Philippe de Mézières also writes about the prophet.[1320]

The depiction of Islam in the *Chronicle*, and particularly its image that is shaped by Christian attempts to describe and name its followers may be interpreted as reflecting the idea of unity. This unity, however, is a superstructure appended over a community composed of smaller nations such as the Turks and Egyptians (Tatars also make an appearance, LM III 377, 509). Once again a statement by Rosenthal may be cited, according to which 'the Islamic' empire was 'made up of pre-Islamic Arabian, Byzantine,

---

[1316] Rosenthal, Political Thought in Medieval Islam, 2.
[1317] Rosenthal, Political Thought in Medieval Islam, 3.
[1318] Mas Latrie (Ed.), Chronique d'Amadi, 1; Coureas, Edbury (Transl.), The Chronicle of Amadi, 1 (§ 1).
[1319] Mas Latrie (Ed.), Chronique d'Amadi, 1; Coureas, Edbury (Transl.), The Chronicle of Amadi, 1 (§ 1).
[1320] Philippe de Mézières, Le Songe, 90: *O, tu Pauvre Pelerin, combien que en ta jeunesse tu ayes este ung tres grant et public pecheur, toutesfoiz pour la bonne voulente que tu as eu et monstre des ta jeunesse que la sainte cite de Hierusalem et la Terre Sainte fussent delivrees de l'ydolatrie et souilleure de la faulcete de Mahommet et des ennemis de la foy et ramenees a la sainte foy catholique, par laquelle deliverance tu as assez travaille ung long temps [...].*

Persian and Roman elements'.¹³²¹ This comment allows us to understand why different groups of Muslims, clearly distinguished by the chronicler and referred to by name, are treated as a single elemental force that receives specific appellations in the Cypriot text. Namely, we cannot fail to note that Makhairas skilfully uses the categories of unity and diversity to encompass the whole of the unknown, foreign civilisation and highlight the exceptional courage and effort of the island's inhabitants in their fight against this might on the one hand, while on the other he describes skirmishes with different nations, giving the invaders individual treatment, as if he wanted to tame his own fear of meeting an undefined and unpredictable force. Despite numerous references to smaller communities, in the *Chronicle* the emphasis is placed on the aspects of these nations' community, on their 'being Muslims' (μουσθουλμάνοι).

Halim Bakarat underlines that 'the Arab world' should be seen as an 'overarching society, rather than a collection of several independent nation-states that increasingly, and particularly in times of crisis, assert their differences and separate identities',¹³²² underlining the fact that there is 'the potential for both unity and divisiveness'.¹³²³ A similar opinion is expressed by John Saunders, who claims that Islam is 'an element of cohesion' uniting tribes.¹³²⁴ Of Polish scholars, Marek Dziekan investigates the topic, highlighting in his work the diversity existing within Muslim civilisation and the fact of Islam's supremacy and domination 'as a religious and legal factor'.¹³²⁵

When presenting a specific group of Muslims such as the Egyptians or Anatolian Turks, Makhairas treats them as a body, distinguishing only individuals who hold power, such as the sultan (σουλτάνος; σουρτάνος)¹³²⁶ or emir (ἀμιρᾶς).¹³²⁷ Experts on Islam would say that he expressed the postulate of subordinating the individual to the community, so important in medieval Islamic political thought.¹³²⁸ The chronicler undoubtedly notices the differences in government existing between the two civilisations, which is particularly apparent when he describes a meeting of Cypriot, Genoese and Venetian delegates with emirs, and thus realises that the followers of Islam form a state that differs in type from the Byzantine or Western one. By discussing such meetings in detail and even recreating the proceedings of an emirs' council, Makhairas paints an image of individuals involved in the matters of their state, in which hierarchy played a large role. This touches on certain intuitions clearly expressed by Ibn Ḥaldūn (332–1406), 'the scientist, the polymath, the thinker',¹³²⁹ an Arab who lived slightly earlier than the author of the *Chronicle*. He considered the state to be an overriding structure that was helpful in defining Muslim civilisation as, in Rosenthal's words,

> *an end in itself with a life of its own, governed by the law of causality, a natural and necessary human institution* […].¹³³⁰

Rosenthal underlines that for Ibn Ḥaldūn the state was also 'the political and social unit which alone makes human civilization possible'.¹³³¹ The Arab thinker himself, who cites Aristotelian thought in his explanation of the sense of civilisation, which is itself an interesting example of the intercivilisational reception of an important concept, states:

> *Social organisation is a necessity for man. Philosophers express this fact using the words: 'Man is "political" (urban) in nature'. This means that the social organisation which philosophers termed "town" is necessary to him.*
> *This is the sense of civilisation (al-umran).*¹³³²

---

¹³²¹ Rosenthal, Political Thought in Medieval Islam, 31.
¹³²² Bakarat, The Arab World, xi.
¹³²³ Bakarat, The Arab World, xi.
¹³²⁴ Saunders, A History of Medieval Islam, 40.
¹³²⁵ Dziekan, Klasyczna kultura arabsko-muzułmańska, 235–249.
¹³²⁶ The variant 'σουρτάνος' appears in LM II 189, V 636, 661.
¹³²⁷ These figures, usually nameless, appear in the following places in the *Chronicle*: LM II 125–126, 133, 144, 159, 188, 196, 198, 202–203, 208, 225–227, III 287, 291, 296, 303–306, 317, V 636, 664.
¹³²⁸ Which is emphasised in Crone, Medieval Islamic Political Thought, 393.
¹³²⁹ Fromherz, Ibn Khaldun, 2.
¹³³⁰ Rosenthal, Political Thought in Medieval Islam, 84.
¹³³¹ Rosenthal, Political Thought in Medieval Islam, 84.
¹³³² Ibn Chaldun, Wybór pism, 92–93. Translated by Kupiszewska.

In the *Chronicle* Muslims are distinguished not only by a particular state structure, but also by the way in which they mark their presence and in which they strive towards their goals, usually by using force. They manifest it by attacking envoys, repaying them for losses incurred, and seeking to conquer new lands at all costs. This is how they organise their expeditions to distant lands. Makhairas highlights a particular Muslim trait, which Rosenthal attributes to them after Ibn Ḫaldūn: the ease of using force, understood as 'the basis of the state and the necessary instrument of that restraining authority without which man cannot exist'.[1333] Many scholars, including Rosenthal[1334] and Alper Dede,[1335] cite the emblematic claim that in the Islamic view religion and temporal force are 'twin' phenomena, as expressed by the great Arab philosopher and Sufi al-Ġazālī (ca. 1058–1111).[1336]

To make fully clear Makhairas' notions about the true nature of the force used by the Muslims and the determination they showed in conquering the enemy, either through direct attack on his lands or defence of their own territory, and to realise that he was not alone in his impressions and conclusions, fragments of works by the Arab poet Abū Tammām (805–846) will be quoted:

The sword is more veracious
    than the book,
Its cutting edge splits earnestness
    from sport. [...]
Knowledge lies in the bright spears
    gleaming between two armies [...][1337]

And elsewhere:

The lives of ninety thousand [warriors]
    [fierce] as Mount Shara's lions
Were ripe for plucking before the ripening
    of figs and grapes.
How many a bitter soul was sweetened when
    their souls were plucked from them [...][1338]

Abū Tammām perceives war as an awaited event that one should prepare for appropriately and which should be welcomed with gladness because it would speed the process of maturation towards a glorious, final passing:

A conquest for which
    the sky opened its [flood] gates
And the earth appeared bedecked
    in new attire.
You left the fortune of the Banū al-Islām
    Ascendant
And in decline the fortune of idolaters
    and their abode.[1339]

In this short passage we may observe both the functionality of the category of inheritance and the handiness of the adjectival noun 'idolaters', which is used to describe members of other civilisations and which Christians and Muslims in the *Chronicle* also use for each other. Like for Makhairas, who finds the clearly expressed will of the Supreme in the wars fought by the Cypriots, also for the Arab poet the reality of war is shaped and prepared by God:

[1333] Rosenthal, Political Thought in Medieval Islam, 87.
[1334] Rosenthal, Political Thought in Medieval Islam, 39.
[1335] Dede, Islamism, 210.
[1336] See Griffel, Al-Ghazali's Philosophical Theology, 19–60.
[1337] Stetkevych, The Poetics of Islamic Legitimacy, 156.
[1338] Stetkevych, The Poetics of Islamic Legitimacy, 162.
[1339] Stetkevych, The Poetics of Islamic Legitimacy, 157.

> *For centuries God churned fat butter for us*
> *which fell prey to famished wolves.*[1340]

And further:

> *If only Infidelity had known*
>   *how many ages*
> *This outcome lay in ambush*
>   *amidst the spears and swords.*[1341]

Makhairas does not take as radical a perspective as Abū Tammām does. He does not speak in the name of all Greeks and Latins, but only in the name of the participants of the Cypriot spiritual microcosm, though he emphasises a certain mythical prehistory of Christian faith, where God creates sacred space through man.

From the outset the Muslim belief system valued people in a binary way as believers (*mu'min*) and unbelievers (*kafir*).[1342] This is undoubtedly, as J.S. Jensen realises, consistent with the method of using 'sharp' and 'rigorous divisions' that characterise 'Islamic doctrine'.[1343] However, the issue of distinguishing who is really *mu'min* and who is really *kafir* is far more complex.[1344] A more elaborate analysis is carried out by Jean Jacques Waardenburg, who exposes a number of concepts which had been used to classify and 'qualify' other religions (in terms of deviation from morality, 'logical/doctrinal errors' and '"exaggerations"'). Muslims' judgements of Christians, treated by them simultaneously as 'people of Scripture' (*ahl al-kitāb*) and 'infidels' (*kuffār*) in opposition to what Waardenburg conceptualizes as 'true primordial monotheistic Islam',[1345] have evolved over time[1346] gaining meticulous and intricate classifications.

Historical data indicate that the features of Muḥammad's successors named above – particularly their military attitude related to the conviction of Islam's superiority – were confirmed in the history of contacts between Muslims and the rest of the world. Examples include wars with Byzantium, which resulted in spectacular though short-lived successes, won mainly, as Janine and Dominique Sourdel underline, by Mu'āwiya (602|661–680),[1347] Al-Walīd (ca. 668|705–715) and Suleiman the Magnificent (Sulaymān, 1494|1520–1566),[1348] and the attack on Cyprus in 649,[1349] which was the start of the Umayyad claims to maritime hegemony in the eastern part of the Mediterranean Sea.[1350]

Ahmad Nazmi, who analyses the attitude of Muslims to the Western world based on source texts, shows how they perceived various geographical locations, for example the Mediterranean Sea, which in the *Chronicle* was the focal point of actions carried out by the two civilisations' representatives, and of contacts between them. Among the expressions they used for it he names: 'Western Sea', 'Al-Maġrib Sea', 'Greek Sea' and 'Baḥr ar-Rūm'.[1351] He cites the vision of Ibn Ḫaldūn contained in the work *Al-Muqqadima* (Introduction):[1352]

[1340] Kupiszewska's translation based on Danecki (Select., elab.), Klasyczna poezja arabska, 82.
[1341] Stetkevych, The Poetics of Islamic Legitimacy, 160.
[1342] Danecki (Select., elab.), Klasyczna poezja arabska, 46.
[1343] Jensen, Towards Contemporary Islamic Concepts, 202.
[1344] Laliwala, Islamic Philosophy of Religion, 143–145.
[1345] Waardenburg, Muslims and Others, 192.
[1346] Waardenburg, Muslims and Others, 193.
[1347] Danuta Madeyska informs that Mu'āwiya or Mu'āwiya Ibn Abī Sufyān (661–680) was a scion and founder of the Umayyad dynasty, a branch of the Quraysh (Madeyska, Historia świata arabskiego, 155).
[1348] Sourdel, Cywilizacja Islamu, 55. Mu'āwiya's activity is described in Hadjidemetriou, Historia Cypru, 146–150, and that of al-Walīd I, in Hadjidemetriou, Historia Cypru, 153–154.
[1349] See Beihammer, The First Naval Campaigns, 47–68. This event is mentioned in Hadjidemetriou, Historia Cypru, 146.
[1350] Beihammer, The First Naval Campaigns, 55. Cf. Saunders, A History of Medieval Islam, 60.
[1351] Nazmi, The Muslim Geographical Image, 220–221. Nazmi interprets the name 'Baḥr ar-Rūm' as the equivalent of the whole Mediterranean Sea. The author explains that the term 'Rūm' means 'Roman', a word that denoted European Christians, Catholic and Orthodox (Nazmi, The Muslim Geographical Image, 220, fn. 4). Brauer, Boundaries and Frontiers also offers an interesting perspective on the perception of the world and on boundaries in Arab-Islamic geography.
[1352] *Al-Muqqadima* is the introduction to the *Kitāb al-'ibar* (Book of Allusions) (Masad, The Medieval Islamic Apocalyptic Tradition, 37, fn.).

As for its border, Ibn Ḫaldūn states that to the south it is bordered by the coast of the Maġrib, beginning with Tangier at the straits, then Ifrīgīya, Barqua and Alexandria. To the north, it is bordered by the shore on which Constantinople is located, then Al-Banadiqqah (Venetians), Roma (Rome), Ifringa (Franks), the Andalus (Spain), and finally back to Ṭarifa on the Strait of Az-Zuqāq, opposite Tangier.[1353]

Inaccuracies in nomenclature, and in particular the use of the adjectives 'western' and 'Greek' to denote the Mediterranean Sea,[1354] indicate that the Muslim ability to distinguish between the Latin and the Greek world was incomplete. The word 'al-rūm' appears for instance in the work of Al-Aṯir, translated as 'maritime countries belonging to the Franks and Greeks'.[1355]

Nadia Maria El-Cheikh believes the twelfth and thirteenth centuries to be 'crucial' in the development of the Muslim civilisation because they were a time when evident 'political fragmentation' occurred. In her opinion, Byzantium was undergoing a military and political weakening, particularly visible when compared to the increasing power of the Crusader states.[1356] As El-Cheikh notes, activity of crusaders was what contributed to the 'multifaceted image' of Byzantium in Muslim perception,[1357] particularly as its representatives were often confused with the Latins.[1358] Gradually the two groups started to be recognised as separate, which was also reflected in the practice of using different terminology.[1359]

It is not possible to recreate on the basis of the *Chronicle* the way in which Christian territories were perceived by inhabitants of Turkish and Arab lands with the same level of detail as seen in Ibn Ḫaldūn's work. The lack of relevant expressions revealing the Saracens' convictions may mean that Makhairas wanted to emphasise their lack of knowledge or was convinced that they saw this world as uniform. However, he certainly believes Muslims to be hostile towards all of Christendom. The reader has the opportunity to encounter not only the author's vision of the behaviour of the followers of Islam, but also the attitude of Cypriots towards unbelievers, presented in the narrative. The chronicler leaves some hunger for more information in this respect because he does not describe the situation before the arrival of the Lusignans: the exception is passage LM I 9, where he states that after St Helena set off for Constantinople, people:

[…] *fell to thinking of the coming of the godless Saracens (ἔλα τῶν ἄθεων Σαρακηνῶν), how that many times they led the said island into captivity (αἰχμαλωτεῦσαν τὸ αὐτὸ νησσὶν)* […]

The Franks' intrusion into a world that was based on Orthodox beliefs added a further layer, superimposed over what had previously existed: the conflict of the Byzantine world with the world of Islam. In the twelfth century the Franks conquered the Mediterranean Basin, taking Ascalon, Mosul, Aleppo and Damascus in 1153, two of which were Christian according to Christopher MacEvitt.[1360] The scholar cites the opinion of Emmanuel Rey, who in his book *Les colonies franques de Syrie aux XIIme et XIIIme siècles* (1883) termed the Franks' presence in the Levant 'colonies',[1361] and stated:

[1353] Nazmi, The Muslim Geographical Image, 221.
[1354] The Arab philosopher calls it the 'Rūmī Sea' and 'Šāmi Sea'. He names Cyprus (Qubruṣ) as one of the islands located there, next to Crete (Iqrītiš), Sicily (Ṣaqallyya), Mallorca (Mayūrqa) and Sardinia (Sardīnyya). Names and spelling after Nazmi, The Muslim Geographical Image, 221. Nazmi underlines that it was probably only Mastawfi who used the term 'the Sea of Greeks and Franks', while Muslims termed it the 'Sea of Constantinople' (Nazmi, The Muslim Geographical Image, 222). Nazmi states that the Muslims gained 'much accurate information' about different islands in this sea, and also in the Indian Ocean, the Malay Archipelago and in the Far East. He emphasises that geographers had high familiarity with all the islands they had taken over during the reign of the Umayyad and Abbasid dynasty (Nazmi, The Muslim Geographical Image, 248). Obviously Cyprus also came within their sphere of interest.
[1355] Fn. 16 in Al-Aṯir, Kompletna księga historii, 4. Phrase translated by Kupiszewska.
[1356] El-Cheikh, Byzantium through the Islamic Prism, 55.
[1357] El-Cheikh, Byzantium through the Islamic Prism, 55.
[1358] El-Cheikh, Byzantium through the Islamic Prism, 56.
[1359] El-Cheikh, Byzantium through the Islamic Prism, 56.
[1360] MacEvitt, The Crusades, 3. The capture of Ascalon by King Baldwin is mentioned in Mas Latrie (Ed.), Chronique d'Amadi, 33–37.
[1361] MacEvitt, The Crusades, 15.

Scholars, however, began to turn away from the image of an integrated Levant as two issues gained attention: an increased emphasis on Christian-Muslim conflict, and a growing sense of the influence of French colonialism on crusade historiography.[1362]

According to MacEvitt, what allowed followers of different religions to function side by side in the Levant was a state in which coexistence 'without the legal or social structures of control' was based on 'ignoring difference', which in turn, the scholar emphasises, ensured peace on the one hand but led to acts of extreme cruelty on the other.[1363] This state of affairs shaped relations that MacEvitt calls 'rough tolerance',[1364] characterised by the 'unspoken, undefined, and amorphous', as well as 'absence', 'permeability' and 'localization'.[1365] MacEvitt writes:

Both local Christians and Franks chose not to know, to forget, or to overlook those aspects of the other which had the most power to control and define the other.[1366]

This statement is interesting among others because it makes visible the relations between the Latins and Christians belonging to other churches, a situation similar to the one on Cyprus.

Waardenburg shows, based on literature from the period, that mutual distrust between Christians and Muslims grew. He refers to a polemical correspondence between the patriarchs of Constantinople and the caliphs, for example: Photios I the Great (ca. 820–891) and Al-Mutawakkil (821|847–861) in 855–856, and between Nicholas I Mystikos (852–925) and Al-Muqtadir (895|908–932) around 913.[1367] The increase in tensions between the two civilisations and the accumulation of disputes came, according to Waardenburg, in the tenth century,[1368] but at that point Cyprus was slowly undergoing its separation from Byzantium. In the literature that was developing at the time it is possible to cite: Greek treatises against Islam, popular literature and texts by Christians living on land belonging to Muslims.[1369] Similarly lucid were polemical texts authored by: Al-Ġazālī,[1370] Al-Qarāfī (1228–1285),[1371] Saʿīd ibn Ḥasan al-Iskandarānī (b. after 1320),[1372] Ibn Taymīya (1263–1328)[1373] and Ibn Qayyim al-Ǧawziyya (1292–1350),[1374] which challenged the main tenets of Christianity.[1375] According to Waardenburg, after the eleventh century an increase in knowledge about Islam was observed in Byzantium.[1376] Mrożek-Dumanowska indicates that the literature of the period was mainly apologetic, defending its own importance and calling for conversion. Christian theologians expressed themselves in the form of letters to a Muslim,[1377] while Arab-speaking Christians and Muslims penned dialogues in which the argument was structured on the basis of the principles of Greek logic.[1378] Similarly, the fourteenth and fifteenth century abounded in literature presenting various forms of Christian-Muslim relations and the opinions of the ones about the others. Among the many examples the following are of note: Εὐχή ἐκφωνηθεῖσαι ἐπὶ τῇ εἰς τὴν Ἐφέσον εἰσόδῳ ἡμῶν ('Prayer to be spoken at our entry to Ephesus') by Manuel Gabalas (1271/72–1359/60), metropolitan of Ephesus who died

---

[1362] MacEvitt, The Crusades, 16.
[1363] MacEvitt, The Crusades, 21.
[1364] MacEvitt, The Crusades, 21.
[1365] MacEvitt, The Crusades, 22–23.
[1366] MacEvitt, The Crusades, 23.
[1367] Waardenburg, Muslims and Others, 140–141.
[1368] Waardenburg, Muslims and Others, 141.
[1369] Waardenburg, Muslims and Others, 141–142.
[1370] MacDonald, The Life of Al-Ghazzali.
[1371] More about the defence of Islam according to Al-Quarāfi and more about the thinker himself may be found in Sarrió Cucarella, Muslim-Christian Polemics, 41–45.
[1372] The author of *Masālik al-naẓar fī nubuwwat sayyid al-bashar* ('Ways of discernment, concerning the prophethood of the master of mankind'); *Al-muḥīṭ*, ('The all-embracing'). David Thomas states that al-Iskandarānī was a bitter opponent of Christians and Jews and a proponent of closing churches and synagogues (Thomas, Saʿīd ibn Ḥasan al-Iskandarānī, 775–777).
[1373] Memon, The Struggles of Ibn Taymīya.
[1374] Waardenburg, Muslims and Others, 141–142. See Schumm, Stoltzfus, Disability in Judaism, Christianity, and Islam, 58; Renard, Islam and Christianity, 128.
[1375] Waardenburg, Muslims and Others, 143.
[1376] Waardenburg, Muslims and Others, 143.
[1377] Mrożek-Dumanowska, Islam a Zachód, 84.
[1378] Mrożek-Dumanowska, Islam a Zachód, 84.

in Constantinople, from 1339,[1379] the *Il Decameron* ('Decameron') by Giovanni Boccaccio (1312–1375),[1380] *Kitāb al-Sinaksār al-jāmiʿ li-akhbār al-anbiyāʾ wa-l-rusul wa-l-shuhadāʾ wa-l-qiddīsīn al-mustaʿmal fī kanāʾis al-karāza l-marqusiyya fī ayyām wa-āḥād al-sana l-tūtiyya* ('The Synaxarion: A collection of reports about the prophets, apostles, martyrs, and saints, used in the churches of the See of St Mark on weekdays and Sundays of the Coptic calendar year'),[1381] *Taʿrīf al-tabdīl fī taḥrīf al-Injīl* ('Intimation about substitution concerning falsification of the Gospel') by Ibn al-Durayhim[1382] (1312–1360/61), a text written between 1330 and 1360,[1383] *Le livre* ('The book') by Ioannes Mandeville from the years 1351–1371,[1384] Ἱστοριῶν βιβλία τέσσαρα ('Four books of history') by Ioannes Kantakouzenos (ca. 1295–1383)[1385] and Λόγοι τέσσαρες κατά Μωάμεθ ('Four orations against Muḥammad') by the same author,[1386] or *Fuṣūl al-qidr* ('The rite of the jar'), containing guidelines concerning a Coptic Arab ritual of return to the faith by a person who had abandoned that faith from 1374,[1387] and many others.[1388] Each of them presents a different aspect of Christian-Muslim relations, a different context and has a different purpose. Among texts of this type from the fourteenth and fifteenth centuries we may mention those connected to Cyprus, such as the *Legenda Sancti Antonii* ('Life of St Antony'), found by Alfons Buenhombre, Dominican and bishop of Marrakesh, in a Coptic monastery in Ammochostos in 1341 and translated by him from the Arabic.[1389] Another interesting text is certainly *The Coeur-de-Lyon Romances*, written in Middle English between 1200 and 1400. It refers to the moment, important for the *Chronicle*, of Richard's acquisition of Cyprus and then its sale, and above all, pays much attention to Saladin.[1390] Letters from the sultan of Egypt Barsbāy (Al-Malik al-Ashraf Abū l-Naṣr Barsbāy, d. 1438) to Byzantine rulers (in connection with a Byzantine embassy sent in 1426 to prevent attacks on Cyprus)[1391] and *The Martyrdom of Rizq Allāh ibn Nabaʿ of Tripoli* from the fifteenth century, recounting the story of the murder by Muslims of a Christian professionally connected with Tripoli, whose body was buried in Cyprus,[1392] show a critical escalation of negative relations between Christians and Muslims. One edition of the *Kitāb al-majāll* ('Book of rolls'), that is the *Jalayān Buṭrus* ('Apocalypse of Peter'), with many alternative titles, among them *Iktishāf Shimʿūn* ('Apocalypse of Simon') and *Kitāb al-sarāʾir al-maktūma* ('Book of the hidden secrets') from the ninth-tenth century was stored in the residence of the bishop of Lefkosia.[1393] Nothing indicates that Makhairas had any knowledge on this subject; or at least he does not share it with the reader.

Examples from other medieval texts serve to vividly illustrate such encounters, starting with a fragment of the *Kitāb al-Iʿtibār* (Instructions),[1394] the memoirs of Usāma ibn Munqiḏ (1095–1188),[1395] an Arab

---

[1379] Information and title of the work after Pahlitzsch, Manuel Gabalas, 71–73. Johannes Pahlitzsch writes: 'If this prayer was actually uttered when Gabalas entered Ephesus, it is a very rare example of such a liturgical text, expressing the feelings of Byzantine Christians who lived under Turkish rule.' (Pahlitzsch, Manuel Gabalas, 73). Manuel Gabalas also authored letters 54, 55, 57 written in the years 1339–1341 about the fates of Christians in Turkish lands (Pahlitzsch, Manuel Gabalas, 73).

[1380] Morosini, Giovanni Bocaccio, 82–88. Connected with the name of Boccaccio is the text *Zibaldone Magliabechiano* which Roberta Morosini calls 'Boccaccio's notebook', containing *De Maumeth propheta Saracenorum, Venetus*, that is the life of Muḥammad copied from the *Gesta Machumeti et Saracenorum* by Paolino Veneto (Morosini, Giovanni Bocaccio, 80). In turn, Morosini stresses, Veneto used the *Speculum historiale* (Book XXIII, 39–67, *Libellus in partibus transmarinis*) by Vincent of Beauvais (Morosini, Giovanni Bocaccio, 80).

[1381] Swanson, The Copto-Arabic Synaxarion, 92. The Synaxarion contains quite a few lives of saints and martyrs, which are important from the perspective of Christian-Muslim relations (Swanson, The Copto-Arabic Synaxarion, 92–100).

[1382] Yarbrough gives the full name: 'Tāj al-Dīn Abū l-Ḥasan ʿAlī ibn Muḥammad ibn ʿAbd al-ʿAzīz ibn Futūḥ al-Thaʿlabī or al-Taghlibī al-Shāfiʿī al-Mawṣilī' (Yarbrough, Ibn al-Durayhim, 138).

[1383] Yarbrough, Ibn al-Durayhim, 140.

[1384] Higgins, John Mandeville, 149–158.

[1385] Todt, John V Cantacuzenus, 165, 168–171.

[1386] Todt, John V Cantacuzenus, 173–176.

[1387] Otherwise: *Ṣalat al-qidr* ('The prayer of the jar'), *Qānūn li-man jaḥada l-īmān* ('The ritual for one who has denied the faith') (Swanson, The rite of the Jar, 179–180).

[1388] All of above encyclopedia entries are part of Thomas, Mallett (Eds), Christian-Muslim Relations 4, 5, which are only one part of a seven-volume edition containing bibliographical addresses of texts presenting Christian-Arab relations from both the Christian and the Muslim point of view.

[1389] Biosca, Alfonso Buenhombre, 67–69.

[1390] Larkin, The Coeur-de-Lyon Romances, 268–271.

[1391] Kolditz, Barsbāy, 366–368.

[1392] Swanson, The Martyrdom of Rizq Allāh ibn Nabaʿ of Tripoli, 526–527.

[1393] Grypeou, Kitāb al-majāll, 634.

[1394] Title according to Mallett, Usāma ibn Munqidh, 764–768.

[1395] Usāma ibn Munqiḏ, Kitāb al-Iʿtibār. This text is cited among others by Nalborczyk, Obraz Europejczyka, 17–25.

leader living at the turn of the eleventh and twelfth centuries, which describe the reflections of a Muslim who encountered Christians – Franks and Templars – in Jerusalem. The memories of a follower of Islam, forming a counterweight for Makhairas' narrative (a kind of 'inverse narrative image'), confirm the Cypriot chronicler's observations concerning the intensity of negative feeling engendered by the appearance of the 'other'. Ibn Munqiḏ presents one encounter as follows:

Here is an example of the thick skin and bad customs of such people – may Allah disfigure them. Once when I was visiting Jerusalem I stepped into the al-Aqsa mosque. Next to it there stood also a small mosque, changed by the Franks into a church. Went I was going to al-Aqsa mosque – and some Templars, my friends were there – they left me alone in this small mosque so that I may pray there. So I went in there one day, recited: 'Allah is great' and stood immersed in prayer. Suddenly one of the Franks threw himself on me, seized me and turned me to face the east and shouted, 'Pray like this!' Several Templars dashed to him, caught him and dragged him away from me, and I returned to my prayer. He however distracted their attention for a moment and threw himself at me again, turned me to face the east and shouted, 'Pray like this!' And once again the Templars returned, jumped on him and dragged him away from me. They apologised saying, 'This is a foreigner who has just arrived from the land of the Franks and has never seen anybody pray otherwise than turned towards the east.' I said, 'I have had enough of this prayer,' and left the mosque. I was very surprised by the behaviour of this Satan, how his face changed, how his body trembled and what happened to him at the sight of prayer towards Qibla.[1396]

His second tale is as follows:

I saw one of them. He came to Emir Muʿīn ad-Dīn – Allah be merciful to him – when he was in as-Sakhra mosque and asked him, 'Do you wish to see a small God?' Muʿīn ad-Dīn answered, 'Yes!' The Frank stood before us and showed us a picture of Mary with the small Messiah – peace be with him – on her knee and said, 'Here is the small God.' Exalted is Allah above what the infidel say, infinitely exalted![1397]

The first of these accounts presents a conflict rooted in a lack of understanding for the form taken by a confession of the faith, the other concerns dogma. Apart from references to similar historical phenomena, what Ibn Munqiḏ's writing shares with Makhairas' work is a homologous attack on the heterodoxy attributed to the opponent, a complete lack of understanding of the principles of the other faith, and also a lack of desire to become acquainted with its dogmas and the significance it has for the persons who profess it. Ibn Munqiḏ voices his opinion about the noble influence that infidels experience by interacting with followers of Islam in the form of a statement that those who recently arrived from the 'country of the Franks' conduct themselves worse than those who have already 'become close with Muslims'.[1398]

Al-Aṯir in turn describes the mood prevailing after the loss of Jerusalem by the Christians as a result of its capture by Saladin:

They created an image of the Messiah, peace be with him, together with an image of an Arab beating him, and they made bloodied the figure of the Messiah, peace be with him, and they told them, 'Here is the Messiah being beaten by Muhammad, the Prophet of the Muslims, verily he has injured and killed him!' Then this agitated the Franks, so they gathered and prepared everyone to fight, even women.[1399]

Saladin's retaking of Jerusalem is described in the *Chronique d'Amadi*, which portrays him as absorbed in prayer, sprinkling the thresholds of the temple occupied by Christians with rose water (*acqua rosa, aque rose*) brought from Damascus and taking down a gold-plated cross from the wall (*zoso una croce*).[1400]

Unlike Ibn Munqiḏ, Ibn Wāṣil (1208–1298), the author of the thirteenth-century chronicle *Mufarriğ al-Kurūb fī Aḫbār Banī Ayyūb* (The Dissipater of Anxieties on the Reports of the Ayyūbids),[1401] follows,

---

[1396] Usama Ibn Munkiz, Kitab al I'tibar, 236–237. Translated by Kupiszewska.
[1397] Usama Ibn Munkiz, Kitab al I'tibar, 237–238. Translated by Kupiszewska.
[1398] Usama Ibn Munkiz, Kitab al I'tibar, 236. Short phrases translated by Kupiszewska.
[1399] Al-Aṯir, Kompletna księga historii, 3–4. Translated by Kupiszewska.
[1400] Mas Latrie (Ed.), Chronique d'Amadi, 73; Coureas, Edbury (Transl.), The Chronicle of Amadi, 72 (§ 128).
[1401] Hirschler, Ibn Wāṣil.

as Konrad Hirschler writes, the happenings of the Christian world with interest;[1402] however, this is an exception. Hirschler argues thus:

> [...] *his description of the court in southern Italy was far from the standard approach towards the 'Franks' in other chronicles, which varied between hostility and disregard.*[1403]

In Western chronicles, expressions of the Muslims' hostility and cunning are at the forefront. Once again, a legible message is offered by the *Chronique d'Amadi*, which compares 'the evil Saracen thieves' (*li malvagii ladri Saracini*) and the 'poor [Christian] pilgrims' (*poveri peregrini*).[1404] The adjectival noun 'infidels' (*infideli*) makes multiple appearances.[1405] Other significant epithets include the phrase 'enemies of our faith' (*li inimici de la nostra fede*).[1406] The first depiction of the Muslim community in the *Chronique d'Amadi* appears at the very start, where the Arab prince 'Umar ibn al-Ḥaṭṭāb (*Homar, figliolo de Harap*, ca. 591|634–644), 'third after Muḥammad' (*terzo dapoi el Mahometto*), came to Palestine 'with such a great number (lit. a multitude) of people that they covered the entire land' (*con tanta moltitudine de gente che coperse tutta quella terra*).[1407] Of particular import are three fragments, two relating to 1187 and one to 1269. The first tells of an aged Saracen woman sitting on a donkey (*una vechia saracina che cavaleava sopra un asino*), tortured by Christians (*Li nostri la ligorono et comminciorono a tormentar [...]; Li Christiani la tormentorono più aspramente [...]*), who was 'very scared and did not know what to say' (*che fu grandemente oppressa dal timor, non sapeva che responderli*).[1408] The second shows Muslims throwing powder (*polvere*) with a spade to make it blow into the eyes of the Christians (*a dar in li ochi alli Christiani*).[1409] From the third we find out that the Saracens stole the head of St George and burned the body of St Christinus.[1410] These examples show the great cruelty of both sides. Makhairas' work, unlike the Italian text, contains many omissions concerning the faults of the Christians. In Sansaridou-Hendrickx's dissertation about the chronicle of the Tocco family already mentioned (p. 98), we find the information that for its anonymous author the Muslims cause 'collective fear' in Christians,[1411] though he himself considers the Turks to be 'wise and cunning',[1412] and their individual representatives, 'the primordial enemies of the Christians',[1413] 'a military power'[1414] and 'a political power'.[1415]

In his way of speaking about the followers of Islam, Makhairas is part of this trend, highlighting the intensity of encounters with them and their tangibility. He treats them as an infidel force that would be capable of seizing a large part of the Mediterranean world, and thus also Cyprus, if the Christian peoples were not able to repel it by all means.

[1402] Hirschler, Medieval Arabic Historiography, 82.
[1403] Hirschler, Medieval Arabic Historiography, 83.
[1404] Mas Latrie (Ed.), Chronique d'Amadi, 28–29.
[1405] Mas Latrie (Ed.), Chronique d'Amadi, 4, 6, 7, 11, 13–14, 23, 26, 28, 34, 51, 68, 92, 103, 106, 112–113, 184, 188, 197, 207, 220, 226, 228, 239, 257, 259, 318, 399, 401, 418, 443, 463, 501.
[1406] Mas Latrie (Ed.), Chronique d'Amadi, 415.
[1407] Mas Latrie (Ed.), Chronique d'Amadi, 1; Coureas, Edbury (Transl.), The Chronicle of Amadi, 1 (§ 2).
[1408] Mas Latrie (Ed.), Chronique d'Amadi, 62; Coureas, Edbury (Transl.), The Chronicle of Amadi, 61–62 (§ 112).
[1409] Mas Latrie (Ed.), Chronique d'Amadi, 66–67; Coureas, Edbury (Transl.), The Chronicle of Amadi, 66 (§ 118).
[1410] Mas Latrie (Ed.), Chronique d'Amadi, 209.
[1411] Sansaridou-Hendrickx, The World View of the Anonymous Author, 40.
[1412] Sansaridou-Hendrickx, The World View of the Anonymous Author, 43.
[1413] Sansaridou-Hendrickx, The World View of the Anonymous Author, 44–46.
[1414] Sansaridou-Hendrickx, The World View of the Anonymous Author, 46–51.
[1415] Sansaridou-Hendrickx, The World View of the Anonymous Author, 51–53.

4.2. Muslims in the *Chronicle*

The Muslims (μουσθουλμάνοι) who appear in the *Chronicle* are a massive, hostile force directed against Christendom as a whole, regardless of the internal divides within it.[1416] Among adherents of the Muslim religion the chronicler includes Arabs (ἀράπιδες),[1417] Moors (μαῦροι),[1418] Ishmaelites (Ἀγαρηνοί),[1419] Turks (Τοῦρκοι),[1420] who appear under the name of Bahriyyah or Bahri Turks (Τοῦρκοι Βαρσαχίδες),[1421] that is the 'personal guards of the sultan', from whom the Mamlūk dynasty originated,[1422] and Turks from Barbary ([οἱ Τοῦρκοι] τῆς Βαρβαρίας),[1423] who came from the Maghreb countries in North Africa. The appellation 'Saracens' (Σαρακηνοί)[1424] is usually attributed to the Egyptians, as evinced by the juxtapositions 'on one of their sides are the enemies of God, the Saracens, and on the other, the Turks' (ἀπὸ τὴν μίαν μερίαν εἶνε οἱ ἐχθροὶ τοῦ θεοῦ οἱ Σαρακηνοὶ καὶ ἀπὸ τὴν ἄλλην οἱ Τοῦρκοι),[1425] 'by infidel Turks and Saracens' (ἀπὸ τοὺς ἀπίστους Τούρκους καὶ Σαρακηνούς).[1426] Leontios often combines the term 'Saracens' with modifiers that have negative connotations, such as: 'vile' and 'faithless' (ἄπιστοι)[1427] while 'Turks' are often called 'damned' (παράνομοι).[1428] The noun 'Hagarenes/Ishmaelites' (Ἀγαρηνοί) appears twice.[1429] The term 'χαρφούσιαδες', which is difficult to translate, is used once: Pavlidis has it as 'Turks' (Τοῦρκοι), though he stipulates that,

---

[1416] Cf. e.g. LM II 169. Other forms: 'μουσθουλμάνοι' (LM III 287), 'ἐμουσθλουμάνισεν' (LM II 203), 'μουσθλουμανίσειν' (LM V 660), 'τοῦ μουσθλουμανίου' (LM II 226), 'τοῦ μουσθλουμανείου' (LM V 664).

[1417] LM V 672.

[1418] The *Chronicle* features a Moorish slave in LM IV 611 and Ibrahim Maur in LM IV 642. Ross Brann notes that, 'Unlike relatively stable terms of Roman provenance inherited by Christians such as Arab, Ishmaelite and Saracen, *Moor* is problematic because of its shifting significance. [...] Later documents authored in the Christian kingdoms attest to the complete transformation of *Moor* from a term signifying "Berber" into a general term referring primarily to Muslims living in recently conquered Christian lands and secondarily to those residing in what was still left of al-Andalus.' (Brann, The Moors?, 307–318, 311).

[1419] LM I 32, III 346.

[1420] LM I 33, II 91, 112–114, 121, 126, 133, 137, 139–144, 150, 152, 157, 180, 183, 195, 199, 203, 212, III 283, 317, 366, 368, 370, 417, 488.

[1421] LM II 196. See Moravcsik, Byzantinoturcica, 87. Other terms are: 'βαρσάκιδες', 'βαράχιδες', 'βαροχιδες', 'βαρνάκιδες', 'βαρσᾶκιδες'. Dawkins and Pavlidis give the form 'Βαράχιδες'. See Dawkins (Ed., transl.), Ἐξήγησις/ Recital, 176 (fn. 4); Παυλίδης (Ed.), Λεοντίου Μαχαιρᾶ Χρονικόν, 144 (fn. 1). Dawkins translates this term as 'Baharide' (Dawkins (Ed., transl.), Ἐξήγησις/ Recital, 177, LM II 195). Pavlidis underlines that they were part of 'ἐκλεκτό και ειδικά εκπαιδευμένο (από εφηβική ηλικία) στρατιωτικό σώμα', i.e. a 'select, specially trained ([composed of young men] around the age of puberty) military troop'. They were the sultan's guard (Παυλίδης (Ed.), Λεοντίου Μαχαιρᾶ Χρονικόν, 145, fn. 2).

[1422] Dawkins, Notes, 120.

[1423] LM II 219. The expression 'in Barbary' (εἰς τὴν Μπαρπαρίαν) in LM V 701. Cf. Dittenberger, Orientis Graeci Inscriptiones Selectae, 292; Lorenti, Geographia, 3, 407; Stephanos Byzantios, Ethnicorum quæ supersunt, 158. Ramzi Rouighi explains who the Berbers were in Rouighi, Berbers of the Arabs, 49–76.

[1424] LM I 9–10, 19, 21, 31, 35–36, 68, II 90, 144, 153, 159, 171, 175, 183, 188, 193, 210, 212, 219–220, III 285, 292, 295, 302, 308–309, 370, 417, 489, 566, V 636, 645, 651–652, 654, 656–659, 661–665, 673–674, 676–678, 680–683, 686–689, 691, 693, 695, 702.

[1425] LM II 91.

[1426] LM III 489.

[1427] LM I 9, II 153, 158, 188, III 370, 489.

[1428] LM II 152.

[1429] LM I 32, III 346. The term Hagarenes/Agarenes comes from Hagar, Abraham's Egyptian slave, the mother of Ishmael who is considered, Alexios Savvides states, the 'progenitor of most Arab races' (Savvides, Some Notes, 90). Fergus Millar explains that both names 'Ishmaelites' or 'Hagarenes' originates in the belief that the peoples of the steppe are descendants of Hagar and her son Ishmael (Millar, Rome's 'Arab' Allies, 201). Savvides concludes: 'The biblical term was later used to denote the Arabs/Moslems particularly of the Emirate of Crete as well as of North Africa in the 9th, 10th and 11th centuries, but, mainly, to signify the major Turkish dynasties of the Late Middle Ages (i.e. Seljuks and Ottomans) from the 11th to the 16th century; a scarcer use of the term connects it with the Mongols/Tatars from the 13th century onwards, while of importance is also its use in relation with Seljuk and Turcoman raids in north-western Anatolia in the early 13th century. The *Agarenoī* who had accepted Orthodox baptism in the 2nd part of the 12th century during the Patriarchate of Lucas Chrysoberges (1157–1169/70) were most probably Seljuks and Turcomans.' (Savvides, Some Notes, 90–91). Meanwhile, other terms such as *Ismaelītai* or *Ismaelitikōn phylon* (Ishmaelite race) are associated by Savvides with Arabs from before the Islamic period, with Muslim Arabs who appear in Byzantine texts, and also a Turkish people living in the eleventh to the sixteenth century (Savvides, Some Notes, 92). The last term discussed by Savvides, *Sarakenoī*, comes in his opinion from *sharq/shark* and *sharqiyun* or *saraka*. While the last term has negative connotations with thievery, pillaging, etc., the first words mean the East and inhabitants of the East. This is, Savvides underlines, the term most often used in medieval literature, starting from Claudius Ptolemaeus, Ammianus Marcellinus and Marcian of Heraclea, who called Scenite Arabs Saracens (Savvides, Some Notes, 94). In addition to Arabs, since the eleventh century Turks, i.e. the Seljuks and Ottomans, were termed thus (Savvides, Some Notes, 95). Savvides also indicates the anonymous *Byzantine Short Chronicles*, which he believes to be important. The word used in them, *Agarenoī*, refers to Turkmens from west Anatolian emirates, the so-called beyliks,

'Χαρφούσιαδες' δεν σημαίνει 'Τούρκοι' αλλά η παρουσία των Τούρκων στο εκστρατευτικό εκείνο σώμα του σουλτάνου (ή ορθότερα Τουρκομάνων), μαρτυρείται από άλλες πηγές (Amadi, Φλ. Βουστρώνιος).[1430]

[The word] *'χαρφούσιαδες'* does not mean *'Turks',* but [refers to] *the participation of Turks in the sultan's expeditionary corps (properly Turkmens),* [which was] *supported by other sources (Amadi, F. Bustron).*

In his accounts of individual groups such as Turks and Egyptians Makhairas gives no details about their culture or the topography of their lands, in which he differs from other chroniclers. The author of the *Chronique d'Amadi* expressly writes:

Because we have spoken of the Turks and must speak of them often, it is fitting that we should say where these people originally came from and how it was they became so numerous.[1431]

Right after this introduction he builds a detailed description. Initially, the Turks were, according to the author of the *Chronique d'Amadi*, 'very miserable and dissipated' (*assai nude et scostumate*), and also 'lacking a country or any permanent seat' (*non havevano alcun paese ne alcuna sedia certa*). When describing their life, he emphasises the fellowship resulting from their lineage (*lignagio*) or kinship (*parentado*), which inspires them to keep moving and to form a hierarchy.[1432] He states that this fellowship did not unite the community as whole, however, but only individual groups, which is why for a long time its members were not aware of how numerous they were (*un gran numero et moltitudine de gente*). However, when they had obtained a full view, we read in the *Chronique d'Amadi*,

they realized that no land would accept them nor could they all remain in one city [...].[1433]

As their first king they chose a Seljuk (*Selduc*),[1434] an Oghuz Turk, and with his help they quickly conquered Persia (*Persia*), 'all Arabia' (*tutta l'Arabia*), 'other territories in the East' (*altre terre in Oriente*), Egypt (*Egipto*) and Jerusalem (*Hierusalem*).[1435] This period, the *Chronique d'Amadi* says, involved a complete fall of Christian values: fear of God, faith in Jesus and charity.[1436] The terrifying Biblical scenario, which foretold annihilation, cruel disasters, plagues, the degradation of customs and lack of religious sensitivity, indicating service to the devil (*con gran solicitudine de servir al diavolo*), was coming to a pass.[1437] Here we receive a vivid, strongly marked image showing that the changes in the Christian and the Muslim worlds (fall of values in one versus an increase in power of the other) were occurring concurrent.

In the *Chronicle* the first mention of the Saracens is encountered in LM I 9, where we read that after St Helena departed from Cyprus, the Cypriots so 'feared the arrival of the Godless Saracens' (ἐννοιάστησαν τὸ ἔλα τῶν ἄθεων Σαρακηνῶν), who had previously 'many times enslaved' (πολλὲς φορὲς αἰχμαλωτεῦσαν)

---

e.g. in the context of the crusade to the Balkans in 1307. It was also used for Ottomans involved in the siege of Bursa in 1326 and İzniku (Nicaea) in 1331 (Savvides, Some Notes, 91–92). As regards the word *Ismaelītai*, in the *Short Chronicles* it refers to Seljuks and Ottomans (Savvides, Some Notes, 93). In this source, *Sarakenoī* is consistently used for Arabs from Africa and Sicily, the Ayyūbids led by Saladin, and Mamlūks. In the context of the last-named, a reference is made to the attacks of the Mamlūks on Cyprus in the years 1425 and 1426 (Savvides, Some Notes, 96).

[1430] Παυλίδης (Ed.), Λεοντίου Μαχαιρά Χρονικόν, 511 (fn. 5).
[1431] Mas Latrie (Ed.), Chronique d'Amadi, 8: *Perchè havemo parlato de Turchi et haveremo da parlar spesso, convien che diciamo d'onde tal gente sia venuta prima et dove feceno così gran numero de homini*. Translation after Coureas, Edbury (Transl.), The Chronicle of Amadi, 8 (§ 13).
[1432] Mas Latrie (Ed.), Chronique d'Amadi, 8; Coureas, Edbury (Transl.), The Chronicle of Amadi, 8–9 (§ 13).
[1433] Mas Latrie (Ed.), Chronique d'Amadi, 9: *pensorono che nessuna terra non li accettaria, ne potevano tutti star in una città*. Translation after Coureas, Edbury (Transl.), The Chronicle of Amadi, 9 (§ 13).
[1434] Coureas and Edbury translate it as 'Seljuq'. Coureas, Edbury (Transl.), The Chronicle of Amadi, 9 (§ 14).
[1435] Mas Latrie (Ed.), Chronique d'Amadi, 10; Coureas, Edbury (Transl.), The Chronicle of Amadi, 10–11 (§ 15).
[1436] Mas Latrie (Ed.), Chronique d'Amadi, 10: *non si trovava più alcuno che temesse Idio col core; la fede di Jhesu era del tutto anihilata; de carità non si parlava niente*.
[1437] Mas Latrie (Ed.), Chronique d'Amadi, 10–11; Coureas, Edbury (Transl.), The Chronicle of Amadi, 10–11 (§ 15).

the island and its people, that they wanted to ask the emperor to take them under his protection and send his guards. In the next passage we read:

> [...] *in Jerusalem there were Saracens, and they had four giants as well.* (LM I 18)

Meanwhile, a clear piece of information about the conflict between the Cypriots, who were under the rule of the Franks, and the Saracens appears when Guy, isolated in his fear of losing the recently acquired Cyprus, asks the sultan for help should the ruler of the Rhomaioi attack him (ὁ βασιλεὺς τῶν Ῥωμαίων νὰ ποίσῃ ἀρμάδαν νὰ ἔλθῃ ἀπάνω μου), which shows that at the start of the twelfth century the difference between the Orthodox population and the Catholic arrivals was significant. The new ruler justifies his request by stating that the island's inhabitants and the Muslims are neighbours (ὅτι εἶσαι γεῖτος μου), and thus should conclude an agreement (ἔχωμεν δῆμμαν μεσόν μας). He strengthens his willingness to establish closer relations with an assurance that he accepts such a development (τζετιάζω το). The sultan agrees to grant the required aid on the condition that Guy will convert to Islam, 'entrusting himself to God and the great prophet Muḥammad' (νὰ βουθοῦμεν τοὺς πιστοὺς τοῦ θεοῦ καὶ τοῦ μεγάλου προφήτη τοῦ Μαχομέτη), and will 'lift a finger' (νὰ ψηλώσῃς τὸ δακτύλιν σου),[1438] which would mean Guy's express submission to 'the only God' (ἕναν μόνον θεόν).[1439] This statement indicates that only community of religion, as the necessary condition of an alliance, gave a purpose to the fight against a common enemy (θέλω εἴσταιν κατάδικος τοὺς ἐχθρού(ς) σου).[1440] Saladin offered a change of perspective, but also gave a choice, and thus seems to have been faithful to Quranic prescriptions such as: 'If it had been thy Lord's will, they would all have believed – all who are on earth!' (Sūra X, *Jonah* [Yūnus], v. 99), 'Let there be no compulsion in religion' (Sūra II, *The Cow (Heifer)* [Al-Baqara], v. 256) and 'Let him who will believe, and let him who will, reject (it)' (Sūra XVIII, *The Cave* [Al-Kahf], v. 29).[1441] This requirement turns out to be too difficult for the Frankish ruler to accept due to his attachment to his own religion. In his refusal he cites the Holy Trinity (–δὲν θέλω ἀρνηθεῖν– τὴν ἁγίαν Τριάδαν) and confesses faith in the Father, Son and Holy Spirit (πιστεύω πατέρα, υἱὸν καὶ ἅγιον πνεῦμα).[1442] This exchange may be considered a concise presentation of the doctrinal differences between the worldviews of Christians and Muslims in the *Chronicle*, explaining the reasons for their lack of agreement. By describing three centuries of Cypriot-Saracen contact, Makhairas showed the great extent to which these communities were focused on their religious heritage, which defined their identity.

Sometimes in addition to the references to 'peace' (ἀγάπη) that frequently appear in connection with the onerous conciliation negotiations, the relations between Christians and Muslims are presented in the *Chronicle* with phrases such as: 'bond' or 'covenant' (δῆμμαν),[1443] 'oath' (ὅρκος),[1444] 'agreement' (συμπαμμός)[1445] and 'word' (λόγος), which indicate different forms of contact signalising willingness to come to an understanding and herald the renunciation of hostile intentions. Usually, however, situations

---

[1438] In a comment on their translation of this place, Miller and Sathas state that the expression pertaining to the lifting of a finger is an expression usually used in colloquial language (*une locution usitée surtout dans le langage vulgaire*). According to the scholars, the Turks call the index finger '*chehadet parmaghe*', which they themselves translate '*doigt de la profession de foi*' ('the finger that serves the faith') (Sathas, Miller (Eds, transl.), Chronique de Chypre, 16, fn. 1).

[1439] Saladin may have used the adjective 'μόνος' to emphasise his belief that there exists only one God. It may, however, have served to distinguish Islam and Christianity. Meyendorff writes: 'Both Christianity and Islam professed to be universal religions, at the head of which there stood the Byzantine emperor and the Arab caliph, respectively. But in the psychological war accompanying this confrontation Islam unceasingly claimed to be the newest, and so the highest and most pure manifestation of the God of Abraham, and constantly accused the Christian teachings about the Holy Trinity and the practice of icon worship of polytheism and idolatry.' (Meyendorff, Teologia bizantyjska, 56. Translated by Kupiszewska). A confirmation of this observation about the Muslim focus on monotheism is found in a fragment of Sūra XXV of the Qur'ān entitled *The Criterion* [Al-Furqān], v. 2: 'He to Whom belongs the dominion of the heavens and the earth: no son has He begotten, nor has He a partner in His dominion' (Ali (Transl.), Quran, 926). This conviction was also expressed in a collection of the hadiths of Al-Bukhārī (al-Bukhārī, 9th c.), among others in the pledge of Al-'Aquaba, whose text was dictated by 'Allah's Apostle' (Muḥammad): 'Swear allegiance to me for: not to join anything in worship along with Allah' (al-Bukhārī, Ṣaḥīḥ Al-Bukhārī, Hadith 18).

[1440] LM I 23.

[1441] Ali (Transl.), Quran, 509, 103, 738.

[1442] LM I 24.

[1443] LM I 22–23. In Σάθας (Ed.), Χρονογράφοι Βασιλείου Κύπρου, 64: 'δῆμαν'.

[1444] LM V 651.

[1445] LM V 701.

where the efforts of the two sides collide are referred to by expressions with the reverse sense,[1446] such as: 'he broke agreements' (ἐτζάκκισεν τὰ στοιχήματά),[1447] and also words such as 'fight' (μάχη)[1448] and 'hostility' (ἔχθρα).[1449] In the numerous descriptions of fighting and confrontations in the *Chronicle* the Muslims are usually shown in the context of plundering (κοῦρσος)[1450] or impatient watching for an opportunity to seize foreign land. Leontios makes references to the strategic movements made by them, indicating an evident ingenuity (aimed at entrapping, methodically tightening the ring of their presence around Christian habitations), which can include hiding from the island's populace 'behind fences' (ἐ(ι)ς τοὺς φραμούς) and 'in the reeds' (εἰς τὰ καλαμερά).[1451]

An example of the Cypriots' attitude in the face of the threat by the Muslim peoples is the expression uttered by the envoys of the Byzantine emperor, John V Palaiologos, who arrived to conclude a prenuptial agreement between the ruler's daughter and Peter II:

> [...] *may God increase your years (ν' αὐξήσῃ τὰ ἔτη σου) and give you strength against (νὰ σοῦ δώσῃ δύναμιν κατάδικα) the Hagarenes.* (LM III 346)

This is one of the few fragments in the *Chronicle* that show that the Franks and the citizens of the Byzantine Empire united in their fight against the enemy of their shared religion. In this whish there is an echo of the belief that the power necessary to valiantly stand against (κατάδικα) the fearsome, powerful opponent is the main desire of a ruler of a country situated in the periphery of the Christian world. Leaving no doubt as to the real nature of Christian-Muslim relations, Makhairas thus portrays the transformation of attitudes towards the other side, their point of departure being a lack of willingness to understand on the one hand, and irreconcilable differences on the other.

> [...] *from long-standing dissension and strife (ἀπὸ παλαιὰν ταραχὴν καὶ μάχην) is born enmity (γεννᾶται ἔχθρα), and from enmity is born hate (ἀπὸ ἔχθραν γεννᾶται μῖσος), and because of hatred men transgress the commandment of God (ἀπὸ τὴν μισητείαν διαβαίννουν τὴν ἐντολὴν τοῦ θεοῦ), and the evil thoughts and then the evil intentions of men follow, the one upon the other (ἀλλάσσουν), and men turn obstinately to wicked passions (μεταστρέφουνται εἰς τὰ πάθη μὲ πεῖσμαν).* (LM II 273)

This passage can truly be taken as a demonstration of the postulate about the evolution and escalation of evil: the slow transformation of an initial dispute or misunderstanding into a permanent inability to respect another people. From the cause-effect perspective the seed of iniquity takes on increasingly sophisticated forms and thus is accomplished the slow fall of man, whose internal impulses and inclinations completely change him, causing havoc. It is in evil thoughts (κακοὶ λογισμοί) and evil intentions (κακιὲς συνείδησες) that Makhairas sees the roots of evil in this world.

A completely different image emerges from passage LM I 22–25 already mentioned, where Guy de Lusignan attempts to manifest his sympathy towards the sultan of Cairo in order to win his help in case of a threat from the Byzantines:

> *He formed the plan of an alliance (νὰ δηθῇ) with the sultan of Cairo, and sent envoys to him with this request: 'Always it is the will of God that peoples should love their neighbours, and by the grace of God we are neighbours: I beg you to let us make and alliance (δῆμμαν)[1452] between us, and I promise you that I will always be your hearty friend (ἤμαι φίλος σου σπλαγχνικός), and I will hold your friends as my well beloved friends (νὰ κρατῶ τοὺς φίλους σου διὰ ἀγαπημένους μου φίλους) and your enemies as my deadly enemies (τοὺς ἐχθρούς σου ὡς θανατήσιμούς μου ἐχθρούς). And I beg of you, in case the emperor of the Greeks (βασιλεὺς τῶν Ῥωμαίων)[1453] makes an expedition to attack*

[1446] LM II 159, 183–185, 188–189.
[1447] LM V 662.
[1448] LM II 202, 225, V 636.
[1449] LM II 200.
[1450] LM II 182, 210, III 295.
[1451] LM II 210. Cf. Hill, The History of Cyprus II, 353.
[1452] Covenant.
[1453] Rhomaioi.

me, to lend me help and strength (βοήθειαν καὶ δύναμιν), and I will be your servant (ὑπόδουλός σου). And if he chance to send an expedition against you, you shall have warning[1454] to be on your guard (νὰ ἔχῃς νῶσι νὰ β(λ)έπεσαι).' (LM I 22)*

Guy, wishing to influence the decision of sultan Saladin and to achieve a political goal that was important for Cyprus, commands the envoys to allude to the category of God during the talks. He attempts to confer the status and sense of universal rules upon the Christian truths of faith so that they would, through skilfully applied rhetoric full of religious arguments, effectively speak to his opponent's imagination. To this end, he uses emotionally charged verbs typical of persuasive speech such as 'I beg' (παρακαλῶ) and 'I swear' (προυμουτιάζω) to reveal his helplessness to the sultan. He also cites the dichotomy of friend and enemy.

Guy's message is proof that from the narrative of the *Chronicle* there emerges an image of a divided world of Christians who are unable to judge which 'other' is a greater threat to them (a Christian of another denomination or a representative of another religion?).

4.3. Depiction of Cypriot-Egyptian clashes outside Cyprus

According to what the pages of the *Chronicle* show, the Cypriots mainly encountered two Muslim groups, that is Egyptians and Turks: these were predominantly encounters of an unambiguously military nature. Fighting took place in Egyptian Alexandria, Armenian Gorhigos, Turkish Adalia and in Cyprus. The peace negotiations connected to these events required high personal dedication from the many envoys involved in the issue and had various effects. A particular feature of these contacts is that both sides believed themselves orthodox worshippers of the true God and unequivocally treated their opponents as 'infidels' (ἄπιστοι).

4.3.1. Depiction of contacts between Cypriots and Egyptians

The course of the contacts between Cypriots and Egyptians, as presented from Leontios' point of view, may be divided into two stages: the siege of Alexandria in 1365[1455] and the many months of peace negotiations with the sultan.[1456] All these events fell in the period of King Peter I's reign. Both the dynamic phase of war, filled with military clashes, and the phase of talks, characterised by a slowing of the narrative and a certain serenity, show the nature of these relations, and also permit a closer look at the depiction of the two civilisations. According to Nicolaou-Konnari, the motif of religion is not dominant in these events in the *Chronicle*, which she phrases thus:

Makhairas does not justify Peter's expeditions in terms of war sanctioned by God for the restoration of Christian jurisdiction, neither does he demonize his adversary by attributing to the Mamluks intentions of launching a holy war for expansion of Islam when they invade Cyprus [...].[1457]

Therefore, examples will be used to trace how the religious element is actually manifested in Cypriot-Egyptian relations in the *Chronicle*.

4.3.1.1. Siege of Alexandria in 1365

The 1365 Cypriot attack on Alexandria, the pride of the Mamlūk sultanate, called the 'old port' (ὁ λιμνιώνας ὁ παλαιός) in LM II 171, should be considered an expression of one of the most characteristic conflicts described in the *Chronicle*. The series of passages devoted to this event makes fully apparent

---

[1454] Vigilance.
[1455] LM II 159–175.
[1456] LM II 176–230.
[1457] Nicolaou-Konnari, 'A poor island...', 130.

4.3. Depiction of Cypriot-Egyptian clashes outside Cyprus

Makhairas' image of Christians' and Muslims' universal knowledge of the art of war, which channels his extraordinary perspicacity and liking for topics of military strategy.

To understand the significance of this episode in the history of medieval Cyprus, one should remember that the Alexandrian port was among the most magnificent of its time. This is demonstrated in the words of the traveller Ibn Baṭṭūṭa (1304–1377), who came to the town in 1326, and was entranced by its beauty:

> *In Alexandria there is a magnificent port, and I have not seen its like anywhere in the world apart from Kaulam and Calicut in India, the port of the infidels in Sudaqin in the land of the Turks and port Zaitun in China* [...].[1458]

At one point, the author of the *Chronicle* states that Alexandria

> [...] *is the strongest of all* (εἶνε περίτου δυνατὴ παρὰ οὗλες) *(the towns) which the Saracens have by the sea*. (LM II 171)

Already the plan to capture such an exceptional city is an indication of some measure of audacity in Peter I and other Western rulers, and the faith they had in their own powers and in Providence.

The *Chronique d'Amadi* presents the events during the siege briefly, in less detail than Makhairas' text:

> *On 9 October, the fleet left Rhodes and headed for Crambousa; from there it went to Alexandria. Many Saracens had come to the shore there to oppose the Christians and obstruct their descent* [...]. *The following day, 10 October, they assaulted the city, which they captured, sacked and later set on fire. There the legate celebrated mass, offering thanks to God.*[1459]

This image is economical in words, though it gives some idea of the course of the expedition and the author's conviction concerning God's participation.

An extended description of the Egyptian port was written by Guillaume de Machaut, who devoted his whole chronicle, the *La Prise d'Alexandrie* to it. Guillaume approaches the subject with more attention to detail than the author of the *Chronique d'Amadi*,[1460] enthusiastically praising Peter I's deeds and still more clearly showing that the conquests were sanctioned by God. John Froissart's account is similar.[1461]

Muslim testimonies also exist, for example authored by the previously mentioned Ibn Wāṣil[1462] and An-Nuwayrī al-Iskandarānī, who in his work *Kitāb al-ilmām bi-al-iʿlām fī mā ǧarrat bi-hi al-aḥkām wa-al-umūr al-muqḍīyya fī waqʿat al-Iskandarīyya* (The Book of Gleanings Relating what Occurred in the Events of the Fall of Alexandria) accents the destruction done by the Franks.[1463]

Before Leontios moves to a description of the conquest of Alexandria, he relates the vast contacts between Cyprus and Western states, which were to help the Cypriots prepare for the expedition. He emphasises that there had been differences of opinion between its participants, which is expressed in the attitude of the Venetians, who took a differing position to the Lusignans. The protest of the Venetian citizens against harrying the Saracens was connected to the close commercial relations that they regularly established with them. To earn more authority, they had to cite – being aware of the effectiveness of persuasion of this kind – shared values derived from religious thought:

> [...] *we beg you* (παρακαλοῦμέν σε) *by the baptism wherewith you have been baptized* (εἰς τὸ βάπτισμα τὸ εἶναι βαπτισμένος), *to stay your fleet from going to Syria, but rather to make the peace for which the sultan asks, and when we have got our goods away safely, (then) do as you please.* (LM II 177)

[1458] Ibn Battuta, Osobliwości miast i dziwy podróży, 8. Translated by Kupiszewska.

[1459] Mas Latrie (Ed.), Chronique d'Amadi, 414–415: *A di 9 octubrio, essendo partita ditta armada da Rhodi et andata a Cambruse, de li andò in Alessandria, a la riva del qual loco venero molti Saracini contra li Christiani, per devedarli el discender* [...] *a di 10 di octobrio assaltarono la cità, et la preseno et messeno a sacco et poi a foco. In ditto loco, il legato cantò messa, ringratiando Iddio.* Translation after Coureas, Edbury (Transl.), The Chronicle of Amadi, 377–378 (§ 830).

[1460] Callin, A Poet at the Fountain, 205–206.

[1461] Rigby, Knight, 54.

[1462] Hirschler, Ibn Wāṣil.

[1463] Steenbergen, The Alexandrian Crusade, 125–132. Al-Iskandarānī's account has been investigated in Wrisley, Historical Narration and Digression, 451–476.

The Venetians, endeavouring to achieve the desired effect, cited baptism and the sense of spiritual community connected to it. At the same time, the chronicler reveals the true reason for the fears of the citizens of the Republic, stating that the problem was the uncertain fate of their own trade contacts and material goods.

As for the numbers of the groups taking part in the attack and national affiliation of the persons in them, it is possible to conclude on the basis of a list of lesser rulers (ἡ νοματολογία τῶν ἀρχόντων) given in the *Chronicle* that it was large.[1464] Burkiewicz states, after Philippe de Mézières, that a significant role in these events was played by the Carmelite legate Peter de Thomas,[1465] who, though mentioned by Makhairas in the context of the attempt to convert the Orthodox inhabitants of the island, is not named in his version of the Alexandrian events.

In Makhairas' account economic and political goals are somewhat obscured by the postulated religious motives. While according to him all actions of the Latins in the Mediterranean Basin were dictated by an arbitrary and ambiguous reading and understanding of the will of God, not all historiographers express the same belief. Guillaume de Machaut, who so glorifies Peter I, the main initiator of the expedition, takes the view, Misztal states, that the intent was economically motivated.[1466] Hill expresses a conviction about the more religious nature of their aspirations and motivations, citing the legend of the vision experienced by the king in Church of the Holy Cross on Mount Stavro Vouni:[1467]

> *One thing distinguishes these expeditions from all other Crusades, the fact that the impulse and execution were due not to any western personality or Power, but to one who lived on the frontiers of the Sultan's dominions. In another aspect, the way in which the whole adventure centres on a single individual, as in the intensity of the religious enthusiasm which inspired that leader, it has its nearest parallel in the Crusades of St Louis.*[1468]

Makhairas focuses on the actions of the Cypriots and the task of describing their excellent battle attitude, as well as on properly accentuating the cruelty and godlessness of their opponents to such an extent that he does not bother to mention Ğanġara (Ğanġara, Janghara), the second-in-command of Alexandria's ruler, who played a significant part in these events. An-Nuwayrī (1279–1333) does do so, however.[1469] The chronicler also does not elaborate overly on the moral implications of the behaviour of the Christian multitudes who charged at innocent people who were unaware of their danger. He juxtaposes two uncompromising forces: the believers of Christ and the followers of Muḥammad, without emphasising the doctrinal differences between them.

Makhairas illustrates the Christian military forces as approaching in the form of an 'army' (φουσάτον).[1470] He assigns the same term to Muslim troops that attack, and also to the militaries of the Western countries that fight amongst themselves. In the perspective he presents, the Saracens are depicted unfavourably, as thoughtless and lacking the ability to anticipate events. Leontios writes that the sight of the approaching aggressors caused fear in the inhabitants of Alexandria. To express this he uses the phrases 'shook with fear' (πολλὰ ἐτρομάξαν) and 'were in a state of great terror' (ἐπίασέν τους μέγας φόβος) in order to strengthen the image of the attackers' might by emphasising the feeling of horror experienced by the followers of Islam. The Egyptians' carelessness is revealed in the moment when they descended from the walls and shouted 'many unpleasant and prideful words' (πολλὰ ἄπρεπα λογία καὶ σουπέρπια)[1471] all night, only to feel fear at the sight of the host of armed men brought in by Peter I on the following day.

Although the Alexandrians hid 'within the port walls' (εἰς τὰ τειχόκαστρα) and defended them bravely (μὲ θάρος νὰ τὴν διαφεντέψουν), the Cypriots were victorious, having demonstrated relentless

---

[1464] LM II 162–163.
[1465] Burkiewicz, Polityczna rola królestwa Cypru, 228, 238, 242, 244–245.
[1466] Guillaume de Machaut, La prise d'Alexandrie, 9–21 (v. 259–660). See Misztal, Historia Cypru, 222.
[1467] Hill, History of Cyprus II, 319.
[1468] Hill, History of Cyprus II, 319.
[1469] Hill, History of Cyprus II, 331.
[1470] According to ΘΚΔ, 514 the noun 'τὸ φουσάτον' comes from the Lat *fossatum*, otherwise 'στράτευμα' ('military force'), 'πλῆθος' ('mass').
[1471] LM II 171.

determination: they burned down part of the city gates (ἐκάψαν τες πόρτες τῆς χώρας), and punched through the others with galleys (τὰ κάτεργα ἀπὸ τὴν πόρταν) to let the land army (τὸ φουσάτον τῆς γῆς) march inside freely (ἐδῶκαν ἔσσω). Makhairas, invoking the conviction about the supernatural mandate of events entrenched in the *Chronicle*, comments this with the words: 'God showed favour to the Christians' (ὁ θεὸς ἐποῖκει χάριταν τοὺς χριστιανούς).[1472] An evident pride in the success achieved by his countrymen shines through in this statement. Leontios provides no moral assessment of the Christians' cruelty because he does not treat their conduct as a sin, and even seems to claim that the manifestations of aggression by non-Muslim countries have a specific value and importance for the fates not only of Cyprus, but also the whole world. Namely, even a single advance in the clash with the followers of Islam increases the might of all Christian countries, irrespective of whether Greek or Latin.

Culminating the narrative about the fall of the Mamlūk city with a religious comment is a manifestation of Makhairas' belief in the supernatural triumph of Christians over Muslims. We read that the armies commanded by the Franks reacted to the victory they achieved with 'great joy' (ἐχάρησαν χαρὰν μεγάλην) and gratefulness to God (εὐχαρίστησαν πολλὰ τοῦ θεοῦ),[1473] expressed in prayers (παρακάλεσες), celebration of a mass in the name of the Holy Trinity (ἐλειτουργῆσαν εἰς τὸ ὄνομαν τῆς Ἁγίας Τριάδος) and blessing the fallen Christians (ἐμακαρίσαν [...] τοὺς χριστιανοὺς ὅπου 'σκοτώθησαν εἰς τὸν πόλεμον).[1474] Afterwards, the king of Cyprus sent letters to Pope Urban V and other Western dignitaries (οἱ ἀφέντες τῆς δύσις), to Ammochostos (τὴν Ἀμόχουστον), St Ayia Napa (τὴν Ἁγία Νάπαν), Paphos (τὴν Πάφον), Rhodes (τὴν Ῥόδον),[1475] Genoa (τὴν Γένουβαν) and Rome (τὴν Ῥώμην)[1476] to inform them of the triumph of the whole Latin and Greek world.

An analysis of the *Chronicle*'s content allows us to recreate the complex image of relations between the two civilisations: both the alliances taking shape and the growing divisions. The Christians are presented as vigilant allies of other Christians, observing the situation in the Mediterranean Basin and where necessary taking action to support nations of a kindred faith. In confrontations with the 'other' they see an opportunity for development and blossoming of the whole community. To strengthen this message, Makhairas writes that even the pope was gladdened by such a turn of affairs, accepting the undertaken steps, while the Western rulers 'felt a zeal' (ἐζηλέψαν) and set out to help the Cypriot king in his operations in Syria. Their involvement is also visible in the evident disappointment upon finding out in 1366 that a peace treaty had been concluded between the king and the sultan.[1477]

An interesting passage about the siege of Alexandria is contained in the work of Guillaume de Machaut, who as a Frank shares his impressions of the event:

Il veoient le grant desroy
Des annemis Dieu qui traioient
A eaus, et pierres leur gettoient
Fort et dru et espessement,
Et si très felonessement
Que ne le vous saroie dire.[1478]

They saw the great horde
Of God's enemies who were shooting
At them and throwing stones at them
Forcefully, often, and thickly,
And with such perfidiousness
I could not tell you.[1479]

[1472] LM II 171.
[1473] LM II 171.
[1474] LM II 172.
[1475] LM II 174.
[1476] LM II 175.
[1477] LM II 175.
[1478] Guillaume de Machaut, *La prise d'Alexandrie*, 154 (v. 5079–5084).
[1479] Translation after Palmer (Ed., transl.), *La Prise D'Alixandre*, 253.

The similarity between the images created by Makhairas and Machaut is striking. Both accounts concern the way in which Christians perceived the 'other', and both may be interpreted as a consequence of perceiving Muslims as the enemies of God, and thus as infidels. Both chroniclers voice the same belief that in the eyes of the invaders, the Egyptians were seen as wicked. Interestingly, none of the characters of the presented world seemed to notice that the conduct of the Alexandrians was dictated solely by the need to defend the lands belonging to them. Finally, both authors focus on the participation of God in the events, as if his presence *in media res* and the fulfilment of his will were their chief component.

The author of the *Chronicle* disregards the evident contradiction involved in underlining Christian values and going against them, which is visible in acts of Peter I, who is highly glorified. He also criticises the inability of the Saracen soldiers to carry out assessments that would be correct from a commonsensical perspective, and on the other hand he praises the ingenuity and intelligence of the Cypriots, who for their own material and political gain subjugate others.

4.3.1.2. In search of an accord with the sultan

Makhairas describes in detail the peace negotiations between the Cypriots and the sultan that took place in 1366 already after the previously ongoing fighting ceased. Their course reveals the specific features of the attempts at dialogue and the ways the two sides communicated.[1480] Nicolaou-Konnari expresses the conviction that the passages devoted to these events were written on the basis of archival sources.[1481]

Christian-Muslim peace negotiations constitute an important subject in medieval historiographic literature. This may be seen in the *Chronique d'Amadi*, for instance, which references the positive, negative or ambivalent relations between Charlemagne (*Charlomagno*, 742/747|768–814) and Hārūn ar-Rašīd (*Aaron Ressit*, 763|786–809),[1482] Romanos III Argyros (*Romano Eliopolitan*, 1028–1034) and caliph Aḏ-Ḏāhir (*Daher*, 1005|1021–1034),[1483] Romanos IV Diogenes (*Romano Diogene*, ca. 1020–?|1068–1071) and the Seljuk sultan Alp Arslan (*Belfith*, 1029|1063–1072),[1484] Amaury and Nūr ad-Dīn[1485] and finally King Richard and Saladin.[1486]

The *Chronique d'Amadi* briefly tells that the peace negotiations in 1366 came about 'at the request of the Venetians' (*ad instantia di Venetiani*). Slightly further we encounter a comment that the terms of the peace were not to the king's taste (*Vedendo il re che la pace che si trattava non era a suo modo*), so he rejected them (*si sdegnô*)[1487] and set off with a large fleet to the sultan. However, he was obstructed in reaching his goal by a storm that dispersed his army, scattering soldiers around the island. Part of the king's companions managed to reach the goal, which forced the Muslim ruler to work towards a peace settlement, which was concluded on 10 February 1366.[1488] In a later part of the text, the *Chronique d'Amadi* returns to the subject of the negotiations, initiated in 1368 after fighting for the Armenian castle of Gorhigos, the events in Adalia and the conquest of Tripoli and Tortosa by Western forces. In this case, it was Urban V who appealed for an agreement at the urgent request of the citizens of Genoa and Venice.[1489] The sultan agreed to mend relations on the condition that prisoners be mutually released. However, when the Christians met these demands, he withdrew without hesitation.[1490] We find out that after Peter I's death in 1369 the Egyptian king did not attach any weight to relations with the Cypriots

---

[1480] Hill, after Guillaume de Machaut among others, presents in detail how complicated this endeavour was by showing individual stages of negotiating the possible solutions and conditions of the agreement (Hill, History of Cyprus II, 338–359).
[1481] Nicolaou-Konnari, 'A poor island…', 135.
[1482] Mas Latrie (Ed.), Chronique d'Amadi, 4; Coureas, Edbury (Transl.), The Chronicle of Amadi, 4 (§ 6).
[1483] Mas Latrie (Ed.), Chronique d'Amadi, 7; Coureas, Edbury (Transl.), The Chronicle of Amadi, 7 (§ 12).
[1484] Mas Latrie (Ed.), Chronique d'Amadi, 11; Coureas, Edbury (Transl.), The Chronicle of Amadi, 11 (§ 16).
[1485] Mas Latrie (Ed.), Chronique d'Amadi, 36–43; Coureas, Edbury (Transl.), The Chronicle of Amadi, 37–44 (§§ 68–80).
[1486] Mas Latrie (Ed.), Chronique d'Amadi, 86; Coureas, Edbury (Transl.), The Chronicle of Amadi, 85 (§ 154).
[1487] Mas Latrie (Ed.), Chronique d'Amadi, 415; Coureas, Edbury (Transl.), The Chronicle of Amadi, 378–379 (§§ 831–833).
[1488] Mas Latrie (Ed.), Chronique d'Amadi, 415; Coureas, Edbury (Transl.), The Chronicle of Amadi, 378–379 (§ 833).
[1489] Mas Latrie (Ed.), Chronique d'Amadi, 416–419; Coureas, Edbury (Transl.), The Chronicle of Amadi, 379–382 (§§ 834–844).
[1490] Mas Latrie (Ed.), Chronique d'Amadi, 419; Coureas, Edbury (Transl.), The Chronicle of Amadi, 381–382 (§ 844).

(*feva poca stima délia pace de Cyprioti*).[1491] The peace was concluded on 20 September 1370 after meetings that were recommenced many times and whose course had dramatic consequences.[1492]

Makhairas devotes a lot of space to the subject of the negotiations (55 paragraphs, as Nicolaou-Konnari rightly notes).[1493] According to his account, various countries of the West became involved in the tedious process of reaching an agreement with the Egyptian ruler – a process that influenced the politics of the Mediterranean world as a whole.[1494] Only some passages in the *Chronicle* indicate that the conflict with the sultan (σουλτανίκιν)[1495] had, in Makhairas' opinion, also religious undertones, as indicated by sentences interjected at different points in the narrative, such as: 'with the help of God they burned them all' (ἐκάψαν τα οὖλα μὲ τοῦ θεοῦ τὴν βοήθειαν).[1496] In this perspective, every Christian country had differing expectations concerning relations with the sultan, which is seen from the various reactions of Western rulers to the news about a peace or lack of it. However, the prevalent belief was that renouncing attacks on Muslim lands was 'greatly injurious to Christians' (μεγάλη ζημία εἰς τοὺς χριστιανούς).[1497]

Makhairas consistently employs the concept of a God who intervenes in the course of events in his narrative, treating it as a point of reference for his authorial comments. His use of such a strategy is dictated not only by the convention, but above all by his belief in the information he gives. He does not attempt to understand the otherness of the Saracens, which should serve to explain why he has a positive view of the Greeks and Latins' improper conduct towards them. He evidently shows that there is no point in considering the category of mercy with respect to followers of Islam as they are outside the universe of Christian civilisation, and thus beyond the moral system that applies within its confines. Meanwhile, the Muslims impacted the fates of the Greeks and Latins only when God allowed them to, wishing to punish the ones or the others for their sins. The author of the *Chronique d'Amadi* agrees with this belief held by Makhairas, writing that:

> *The Christians for their sins remained continuously under the thumb and power of the infidels for 490 years, but not always in the same manner: sometimes bad and sometimes worse, depending on the kindness of the lords they had.*[1498]

Makhairas shows in detail how the meeting of representatives of two different civilisations looked using the example of relations between the king of Cyprus and the sultan, revealing certain traits of their personalities. He cites with emphasis the devious nature of the Muslim ruler, who deceitfully, by resorting to treachery (τὴν παραβουλίαν), withdrew from the intention to make peace. He is forbearing in his explanation of the reckless and uncritical behaviour of Peter I, in his opinion a good, honourable and gullible man, who ceased to be vigilant under the influence of the inconsistent actions of the Mamlūks. The attitude of the Islamic ruler, chimeric and unfaithful to his promises, becomes a pretext for undermining the credibility of the whole Muslim community, which is caused primarily by the fact that Makhairas' Christians perceive the Muslim world of Saracens and Turks as a homogeneous whole and thus interpret the act of an individual as the deed of the group. For instance, the Cypriot king voices the fear that the sultan may change his mind (μηδὲν μετανώσῃς) concerning the peace agreement, 'as he previously did in other conditions' (ὥς γοιὸν ἐποῖκες καὶ τὲς ἄλλε(ς) φορές),[1499] which most fully shows this uncertainty. The chronicler shows in a broader perspective the general nature of the Saracens, manifesting itself in various situations: when deceiving the Christians, they communicated true information to each other in whispers, used false praise[1500] and broke their promises. The expression 'the perfidy of the infidel Saracens' (ἡ ἀπιστία τοὺς ἀπίστου(ς) Σαρακηνούς) and the description of the Christian reaction to the Egyptians

---

[1491] Mas Latrie (Ed.), Chronique d'Amadi, 427; Coureas, Edbury (Transl.), The Chronicle of Amadi, 388 (§ 858).
[1492] Mas Latrie (Ed.), Chronique d'Amadi, 429; Coureas, Edbury (Transl.), The Chronicle of Amadi, 389–390 (§ 862).
[1493] Nicolaou-Konnari, 'A poor island...', 135.
[1494] LM II 177–188, 197–198, 202–203.
[1495] LM V 664.
[1496] LM II 180.
[1497] LM II 183.
[1498] Mas Latrie (Ed.), Chronique d'Amadi, 4: *Per li peccati de Christiani el tempio stete in man et potentia de infideli 490 anni continui, ma non sempre ad uno modo; ma hora mal, et quando pezo, secondo la bonta dei signori ch'avevano* [...]. Translation after Coureas, Edbury (Transl.), The Chronicle of Amadi, 3–4 (§ 8).
[1499] LM II 225.
[1500] LM II 185.

breaking their word: 'they were all bitterly moved' (ἐπικράνθησαν ὅλοι τους πολλά) serve to strengthen this negative portrait.[1501]

We read of the cunning disposition of the Muslims also in the *Chronique d'Amadi*, which gives the example of a 'malicious infidel' (*infidele maligno*) who hated Christians (*che odiava grandemente li Christiani*) and placed in a despicable act a dead dog in the central hall of 'the Temple of God' (*Templum Domini*) to wake the 'anger' (*ira*) of those who would arrive in that temple, and whom the chronicler also terms 'infidels' (*de li infideli*) – which interestingly accents the perspective unequivocally adopted by the Christians and Muslims of seeing the 'other' as an 'infidel' – to bring them to their deaths (*a la morte*).[1502]

The *Chronique d'Amadi* provides extended and varied descriptions of Muslim rulers far more often than Makhairas' work does. A comparison of the portrayals of the Abbasid caliph Hārūn ar-Rašīd (*Aaron Ressit*, 763|786–809) and the Fatimid caliph Al-Ḥākim bi-Amr Allāh (*Chetan*, 985|996–1021) may serve as an example. We read that the first of them was:

> *so courteous, liberal and generous in all good practices that he was praised throughout the infidel territories just as much as Charlemagne was praised in France* [...].[1503]

Meanwhile, the author of the Italian work writes of the second of them that:

> *This man resolved to surpass in cruelty and malice those who were cruel and malicious. He himself was considered by his own people to be insane, disloyal and iniquitous. Among other the perfidies he committed, he issued orders for the destruction of the church where Our Lord Jesus Christ was entombed.*[1504]

A recreation of the peace talks described in the *Chronicle* allows one to trace the dynamic of subsequent meetings and follow how the attitudes of the king of Cyprus and the sultan changed. We thus gain the chance to analyse both emotionally marked statements and rationally balanced words. Leontios' narrative, deprived of comments about the topography of towns and descriptions of meeting places, requires effort from the reader, as well as intensive work of the imagination necessary to envisage individual scenes from which would emerge the figures important to Makhairas who issued specific decisions with tangible consequences. Into the main plot of the peace negotiations are threaded side plots, such as the murder of Emir El Bogha el Azizi (Υἱοπέχνα ἐλλ Ἀζεζή), the regent of Egypt, who counselled the sultan to make peace.[1505]

The chronicler shows how the representatives of the two sides acted to the detriment of their opponent, repaying each other with further injuries. He refers to various incidents, which form an illustration of the systematically incited hostility, creating a sequence of images that give the reader some idea about the nature of the relations between the two sides. Makhairas tells how the Christians captured a Saracen boat just before dawn on 'great and holy Easter Sunday' (τῇ ἁγίᾳ καὶ μεγάλῃ κυριακῇ τοῦ πάσχα), how they destroyed Sarepta village (Σαρφές), which caused the Saracens to scream in anguish (ὀφωνάξαν),[1506] and finally how the sultan avenged the plunder of his country and casting Muslim envoys into prisons in Cyprus.[1507] In the Cypriot text we find many instances of scenes with such confrontations, similar in terms of structure and message, and thus limiting the examples provided only to several is justified.

Leontios builds tension skilfully. He shows the desperation of the Christians who beg the Islamic ruler to make concessions to them so as 'to show reluctance to injure or destroy Christians' (νὰ μὲν θελήσῃ τὴν ζημιάν του καὶ τὴν ζημίαν τοὺς χριστιανούς), to 'rein in his anger' (νὰ πάψῃ τὸν θυμόν του), to 'have

---

[1501] LM II 188.
[1502] Mas Latrie (Ed.), Chronique d'Amadi, 6; Coureas, Edbury (Transl.), The Chronicle of Amadi, 6–7 (§ 10).
[1503] Mas Latrie (Ed.), Chronique d'Amadi, 4: *cosi cortese, liberale et generoso in tutti li boni costumi, che in tutta la pagania era lodato come era lodato in Franzia Charlomagno* [...]. Translation after Coureas, Edbury (Transl.), The Chronicle of Amadi, 4 (§ 6). Coureas and Edbury provide a version of the name 'Haroun al-Rashid'.
[1504] Mas Latrie (Ed.), Chronique d'Amadi, 5: *Il quale deliberò passar di crudeltà et malignità quanti son stati mai crudeli et maligni. Costui era tenuto da li soi proprii per forsennato, disleal et iniquo; et tra le alter dislealtà che fece fare commando che fusse ruinata la chiesia dove era sepolto el nostro signor Jhesu Christo* [...]. Translation after Coureas, Edbury (Transl.), The Chronicle of Amadi, 5 (§ 8). Coureas and Edbury provide a version of the name 'al-Hakim'.
[1505] LM II 196.
[1506] LM II 220.
[1507] LM II 221.

mercy on his own people' (ἅς λεμονηθῇ τοὺς δικούς του), to 'allow his ill will to rest' (ἅς κοιμήσῃ τὴν κακοσύνην του).[1508] All these requests refer to universal values that are important to both civilisations, and primarily to mercy.

Once again, we encounter the concept of a God who intervenes in the course of events characteristic for the *Chronicle*. We see that he shapes human attitudes for his purposes, influencing via inspiration the thoughts and decisions of individuals. According to Makhairas, he also has an impact on the sultan's will, because it was he who 'hardened his heart' (ἐσκλήρωσεν τὴν καρδιάν του) 'as he did with the Pharaoh' (ὡς γοιὸν τοῦ Φαραῶ), and thus took away his will to do good (δὲν ἔθελε νὰ ποίσῃ ἀγάπην).[1509] It is not completely certain whether the chronicler is referring to ruthlessness and obstinacy resulting from human sinfulness or whether he assumes that God has the power to shape human impulses both in the positive and the negative sense, which would be indicated by the incorrect decisions of popes, who sometimes had evident problems with discerning the true nature of individual incidents.

In the *Chronicle* the sultan repeatedly refuses to make peace, claiming that he wants to conclude it primarily with Peter I, which shows that he treats the Frankish king as the main representative of the Christian world.[1510] The latter, meanwhile, gives his response via the commander of the cavalry, turcopolier James de Nores,[1511] sent 'in the name of Christ' (εἰς τὸ ὄνομαν τοῦ Χριστοῦ),[1512] who lectures the Muslim ruler that sovereign monarchs should avoid indecision with respect to promises of peace. He thus manifests the lack of consent on the part of the Western countries to instability and political unreliability, encouraging the Egyptians to apply all efforts to mend the uncomfortable situation, with no heed for the difficulties involved. The allegations of the envoy are phrased in a way intended to make the reader see the sultan as a person with negative traits, who manipulates events and postpones (ν' ἀποδιαβάζῃς) the peace.

Makhairas, expanding on the subject of peace talks, gives the reader an insight into the Saracen community, and by introducing scenes of discussions between emirs into the narrative he enriches the portrait of the sultan, who is forced to interact with them. The council provides a pretext for the chronicler to achieve a polyphony and is an opportunity to present many points of view, the effect of which is an image of some diversity within the Muslim group. During this meeting, one dignitary revealed his opinion about the ruler's decision, suggesting that he should depart from the code of behaviour accepted in their country.[1513] He encourages him to look into the chronicles, that is 'the books of the sultans' (τὰ βιβλία τὰ σουλτάνικα),[1514] and verify whether any of his predecessors acted in the same way (τίτοῖον πρᾶμαν), treating a captive dishonourably ('τιμάζεται) or using physical punishment (παιδεύγεται). At this point, he emphasises that also the death penalty (τὸν θανατώσουν) is unacceptable. The only thing that the sultan can do in the case of improper behaviour by an envoy, for instance one who uses 'inappropriate vocabulary' (ἄπρεπα λόγια), is to send a letter of admonishment to the king of the country whence that legate comes (LM II 202). The episode that shows the discussion of the emirs, though not indicative of a lack of coherence on a higher level, nevertheless plays an important role in an analysis and picture of Cypriot-Egyptian relations. During the council, voices appear that encourage the Saracen ruler to fight Cyprus: both emotionally charged ones and those calming that zeal, grounded in rational reasons. However, what the participants of the meeting had in common was a conviction about the might and ruthlessness of the Western armies and the threat they therefore posed to the whole Muslim world. During the exchange, the following significant, almost prophetic, words were said by the emir:

> *Sir, I vow to you upon my faith* (τάσσομαί σου εἰς τὴν πίστιν μας) *that, if you do not conclude the peace* (ἂν δὲν τελειώσῃς τὴν ἀγάπην), *such an army (from the king) will come upon you, that both you and the poor merchants as well will be utterly destroyed* (θέλουν σὲ ξηλοθρεύσειν). (LM II 225)

[1508] LM II 189.
[1509] LM II 189.
[1510] LM II 197.
[1511] LM II 193–202.
[1512] LM II 198.
[1513] The emir expressed his doubts with respect to the fact that the Christians were overly confident in expediting their treasures (τόσον λογάριν), goods (πραματεῖες) and merchants (πρα(μα)τευτάδες) and took a position on the treatment of hostages.
[1514] Miller and Sathas' translation: *les livres des sultans*. See Sathas, Miller (Eds, transl.), Chronique de Chypre, 112.

This statement garnered an immediate reaction from an older emir, who decidedly expressed his view about Western rulers, judging that they sowed destruction:

Sir, do not listen to him who speaks to you for his own profit (μηδὲν γροικᾷς ἐκείνου ὅπου σοῦ λαλεῖ διὰ τὸ δικόν του διάφορος), but rather listen to him who speaks to you for the profit of all (διὰ οὕλους τὸ διάφορος). [...] Know that the king of Cyprus is in the West and is collecting an army (συνπιάζει φουσάτον) from the Christian rulers (ἀπό τοὺς ἀφέντες τοὺς χριστιανούς), and they are coming utterly to destroy your land (ἔρχουνται νὰ ξηλοθρεύσουν τὴν γῆν σου). [...] (LM II 226)

His speech ends with a pathos-filled phrase that emphasises the indivisibility of the community, for which even one lost prisoner should be a disgrace, and the importance of the blood ties that connect all individuals:

[...] I have told you this for the sake of my ancestors (διὰ τοὺς γονεῖς μου) and for the profit of the Moslem (διὰ τὸ διάφορος τοῦ μουσθλουμανίου).[1515] *I promise you, for the sin of the blood which will be shed (τὸ κρίμαν τοῦ αἵματος ὅπου νὰ χενωθῇ) and of the captives who will be led into captivity (τοὺς αἰχμαλώτους ὅπου νὰ αἰχμαλωτευτοῦσιν), God for their sakes will demand an answer of you, and of those who are preventing you from making peace (ἀπὸ κείνους ὅπου σὲ κωλύουν νὰ μηδὲν ποίσῃς ἀγάπην).* (LM II 226)

The emirs' statements echo with fear and the awareness of their opponents' real power, which is a threat to their unity, over which in their belief God stands. From the way in which the author of the *Chronicle* shows their point of view it may be concluded that lower-ranked Egyptians considered the need for peace to be the most important issue, because without it they would be unable to preserve political, and especially spiritual unity.

Similar values, such as regard for tradition and the lives of fellow believers, inspired Makhairas' Christians, though they did not always adhere to them in their lives. Peter I, for example, felt the need to speak the truth (τὴν ἀλήθειαν) and expressed the desire to behave nobly, but his good deeds resulted only from the fear that the liberties of Christians (ἡ ἐλευθερία τοὺς χριστιανούς) could be threatened.[1516] Nowhere does anything suggest that he himself considers these postulates to be binding and inalienable in a universal dimension, either in the Christian or in the non-Christian world. How strong the emotions stirring the Cypriot king were may be seen in the ambiguous descriptions of his actions. On the one hand, he tried, the chronicler claims, to gain the favour of the Egyptian ruler; on the other he did not hesitate to suggest in many places that the Saracens are 'enemies of God' (οἱ ἐχθροὶ τοῦ θεοῦ).[1517] This abundance of contradicting feelings is best reflected in the letter to the Muslim monarch, which is full of meanings:

To our loved friend the Sultan of Babylon (Πρὸς [...] τὸν σουλτάνον Βαβυλωνίας): your own friend the King of Cyprus, (King Peter,) sends many greetings (πολλὰ χαιρετίσματα). Know that I feel myself much aggrieved by you (ὅτι γνώθομαι πολλὰ βαρυμένος ἀξ αὐτόν σου), because you by your own desire (μὲ τὴν ὄρεξίν σου) and your own seeking (εἰς τὴν ἐζήτησιν) wrote to me to make peace (ἄλλην μετανώθεις): and this I did at the request of the Genoese and the Venetians and also of the Catalans [...]. And one moment you ask for peace (ζητᾷς τὴν ἀγάπην) and at another you change your mind (ἄλλην μετανώθεις) and make long delays (μακρυνίσκεις). This is not done by noble rulers (τοὺς καλοὺς ἀφέντες); you let it be seen that you are a ruler who has been raised up by fortune (ἕνας ἀφέντης ὅπου σ' ἐψήλωσεν ἡ τύχη). And since God has allowed this to (ἐσυγχώρησεν το) be because of our sins (διὰ τὰ κρίματά μας), and has given you this lordship, you should do as rulers do who are kings, having their lordship in virtue of their birth (ἀπὸ γεννήσεώς τους). First take the advice of your council and of your own people, and then all alone by yourself examine your heart [...]. I swear to you on my faith as the Christian I am, that the rulers of the West made an order to their officers to prepare a great expedition (μεγάλην ἀρριάδαν) to come to attack you (νὰ κατεβοῦν ἀπάνω σου), but I was misled by the Venetians, and I misled my good kinsmen the rulers, saying to them

---

[1515] Islam.
[1516] LM II 226.
[1517] LM II 91.

that there is now a firm peace between us [...] I believed your words as being the words of a king, and delivered my Saracen slaves from the prisons and sent them to you, whilst you are keeping the Christians in prison. For this reason, if God grant it as I wish, [...] and my faith is in God, that he will give me the victory. Also you are vexatious to me (πλημελεᾶς με), and I shall write to you no more, except at the fit time and place. (LM II 230)

The letter starts with the application of a rule of linguistic etiquette: 'Πρὸς τὸν ἠγαπημένον μας φίλον [...] πολλὰ χαιρετίσματα' ('To our loved friend [...] many greetings'), and differs in its message from the rest of the missive. In his correspondence the Cypriot king expresses his emotions, which include 'grievance' (πολλὰ βαρυμένος), and underlines that his addressee is governed by improper motivation, namely 'desire' (τὴν ἐζήτησιν). Peter I attempts persuasion by citing the stereotypical virtues of rulers. He then refers to God, phrasing his declaration in the form of a credo: 'I swear to you on my faith as the Christian that I am' (Τάσσω σου εἰς τὴν πίστιν μου ὡς χριστιανὸς ὅπου εἶμαι), and touches on the problems of the consequences of sin, the Divine provenance of power, and duty. He contrasts power that is granted and power that is inherited and emphasises the difference between them, which places his statement within the semantic field of heritage. The chronicler uses an interesting device involving employment of the same verb twice in Peter I's statement, once in the passive and once in the active voice: 'I was misled' (ἐκομπώθηκα) and 'I misled' (ἐκόμπωσα). Through the passive voice the Cypriot king can indicate that he feels he is the victim, and more precisely, the object of somebody else's action, while through the active voice he expresses the conviction that he also deceived someone. The order in which the forms appear shows that the ruler was first the victim of the deception, and then started to deceive others. As a result of the false communication from the sultan, who pretended that there was peace between Cyprus and Egypt, a number of undesirable actions came to a pass (ἐπίστευσα; ἔβγαλα; ἔπεψά). Peter I, using the imperative mood and means of persuasion (ἐπίστευσα εἰς τὰ λογία σου ὡς λογία ἀφέντη), encourages his addressee to take the proper course of action, including the admonition to independently consider everything in his mind (μόνος καὶ μοναχός σου καὶ 'δὲ τὸν νοῦς σου). In the summary he portrays what might happen to the sultanate in the future if God decides to participate and grant him victory (δώσῃ ὁ θεὸς ὡς θέλω, ἔχω θάρος εἰς τὸν θεὸν νὰ μοῦ δώσῃ τὸ νίκος). Moreover, he makes the recipient of the letter, the ruler of Babylon, aware of how he is affected by his attitude (πλημελεᾶς με) and so decides to suspend contact for an undetermined period (χωρὶς νὰ ἦνε καιρὸς καὶ τόπος). MS O contains one more sentence, which is a moral assessment of the sultan's deed: 'these are actions of despicable people' (εἶνε πράματα τοὺς χοντροὺς ἀνθρθώπους).[1518] In this version we also find Peter I's declaration:

[...] (I shall go by His power to the West, and you wait for me;) I shall come down upon you (to visit you,) and will give you to know what kind of man I am (θέλεις ἀγνωρίσειν ἴντα ἄνθρωπος εἶμαι) [...]. (LM II 230)[1519]

The Cypriot king's statement and its complexity give us reason to believe that we are dealing with different semantic fields: friendship (φίλον), rule (ἀφέντες; ἀφέντη ἀφέντης; τὴν ἀφεντίαν), destiny (τύχη) and judgement (κρίματα, βουλή), as well as a rather extensive axiological argument (δικός; δική; ἀγάπη; καλοί).

The interesting phenomena connected to Christian-Muslim relations depicted in the *Chronicle* undoubtedly include that of formulation by some Christians of questions sent in secret to 'their friends' (τοὺς φίλους τους) – fellow believers and Saracens (τοὺς χριστιανοὺς καὶ Σαρακηνούς) – requesting advice as to 'what road they should take in the hope for conclusion of a blessed peace' (νὰ τοὺς βουλεύσουν ἴντα στράτα νὰ κρατήσουν, μήπως καὶ τελειωθῇ ἡ εὐλογημένη ἡ ἀγάπη).[1520] This shows that also among the representatives of the Muslim civilisation trustworthy persons who were friendly to selected followers of Christ were to be found.

[1518] Dawkins (Ed., transl.), Εξήγησις/ Recital, 212 (fn. 4); Παυλίδης (Ed.), Λεοντίου Μαχαιρά Χρονικόν, 170 (fn. 7). Mas Latrie (Ed.), Chronique de Strambaldi, 91–92 presents an abbreviated form of this letter, free from such strongly marked wording.
[1519] MS O's phrases after Dawkins (Ed., transl.), Εξήγησις/ Recital, 212 (fn. 5); Παυλίδης (Ed.), Λεοντίου Μαχαιρά Χρονικόν, 172 (fn. 1).
[1520] LM III 304.

Makhairas shows the culmination of these long-winded negotiations, which took place in 1366 and took the form of a symbolical ceremony wherein the sultan and the Cypriot, Genoese and Venetian envoys conclude the peace agreement, in which an important role was played by oaths 'on the Qur'ān' (εἰς τὸν Κόραν) and 'on a 'naked sword' (εἰς τὸ σπαθὶν τὸ γυμνόν), and 'on the Bible' (εἰς τὸ ἅγιον Εὐαγγέλιον). This gave the declarations a supernatural guarantee, and the two holy books assuring that the promises would be kept were placed on an equal footing.[1521] The chronicler writes that despite 'numerous differences' (πολλὲς διαφορές) peace was made with the wish that 'this hour be good and blessed' (νὰ ἦνε εἰς καλὴν καὶ εὐλογημένην ὥραν). Emirs were sent with letters to Cyprus and all Christians held in Syria and Muslims captive in Cyprus were released from prisons.[1522]

In further parts of the *Chronicle* the figure of the sultan returns in the account of King Janus' war with the Saracens in the years 1424–1426. Makhairas once again introduces the element of diverse attitudes within the Muslim community, in the face of which the conciliatory attitude of the sultan at that time, Barsbāy (Μπαρσμπάι, Μελέκ ἐλ-Ἀσράφ, 1421–1438), the eighth of the Mamlūk dynasty,[1523] was conducive to increasing unity.

Leontios' tale of the peace negotiations may be read portraying the clash of two civilisations, represented by specific leaders and their subordinates, and also by envoys. It presents both a dynamic exchange of thoughts, and the impossibility of departing from ingrained ways of thinking.

4.3.2. Depiction of contacts between Cypriots and Turks

The contacts between Cypriots and Turks presented in the *Chronicle* were characterised by a more dynamic course of events than the encounters with the Egyptians. Long descriptions of peace negotiations are not featured here, and neither is the complicated issue of diplomatic relations. The chronicler's narrative covers the episodes of the defence of Gorhigos in Cilicia, the fighting for Turkish Adalia, the massacre in Armenia and also battles at sea and in Cyprus.

4.3.2.1. The defence of Gorhigos castle in 1367

In the second part of the *Chronicle*, Makhairas provides information about the Turks, first describing their actions in Anatolia in the fourteenth century. He cites an important incident in Cypriot history: the defence of the castle in Gorhigos (Κουρίκος), which from 1361 to 1448 remained under protection of the Cypriots,[1524] who in 1367 abandoned the required vigilance.[1525] The ruler of the Karaman emirate, called the 'Great Karaman' in the *Chronicle*, took advantage of this and retook it.[1526] The chronicler notes that he found information about these events in documents 'recorded at the royal court' (γραμμένον εἰς τὴν αὐλὴν τὴν ρηγάτικην). He describes the castle thus:

> *This Gorhigos belonged to the king of Armenia; the episcopal see (ἐπισκοπή) depended upon the metropolitan of Tarsus (ἀπὸ κάτω τοῦ μητροπολίτου τῆς Ταρσοῦ), and this marches with the Land of Promise (μὲ τὴν γῆν τῆς ἐπαγγελίας) and runs down to the east to Little Armenia (εἰς τὸ Ἀρμενάκιν),[1527] stretching on this side to Seleucia (εἰς τὴν Σελευκίαν) and on that side to Sis*

[1521] LM III 304.
[1522] LM III 305, 309.
[1523] After Παυλίδης (Ed.), Λεοντίου Μαχαιρᾶ Χρονικόν, 505 (fn. 1). He was of Circassian (Κιρκάσιος) origin. Cf. Dawkins, Notes, 215.
[1524] Hill, History of Cyprus II, 320–321; Burkiewicz, Polityczna rola królestwa Cypru, 190–191; Dawkins, Notes, 96; Müller-Wiener, Castles of the Crusaders, 79; Stewart, The Armenian Kingdom, 27.
[1525] LM II 112–114.
[1526] Hill, History of Cyprus II, 348; Jones (Ed.), New Cambridge Medieval History, 851. 'Karaman' is actually the name of a territory in Anatolia. A detailed description of the Karamanid dynasty (*Karamān-Oghlu*) in Houtsma (Ed.), E.J. Brill's First Encyclopaedia of Islam, 448–752.
[1527] Little Armenia, that is the Armenian Kingdom of Cilicia. See Ghazarian, The Armenian Kingdom in Cilicia.

('ς τὸ Σίσιν). *And all this the Turks took from us because of our sins, and the town of Gorhigos was* –*left without any Christian service*– (–*ἔμεινεν ἡ χώρα τοῦ Κουρικός*–). (LM II 112)[1528]

And further on:

–[…] *From the church of the Holy Trinity* (Ἀπὲ τὴν ἐκκλησίαν τῆς Ἁγίας Τριάδος) *they enclosed a great space, coming*– *as far as the Pillars* (εἰς τὰ Πιλέργια), *where the customs house was, and down as far as the Jewish quarter, and as far as Gorhigos, that is, to the castle of Gorhigos; and the wall of their castle and the foundations of the towers may be seen to this day.* (LM II 112)

In the *Chronique d'Amadi* Gorhigos (*Corico*) was presented as a harbour in which the Venetians stopped in 1293 to rest and prepare for battle with the Genoese.[1529] This source states that on 15 January 1359 inhabitants of the town requested the protection of King Peter I,[1530] and also discusses the events of 1367 that Makhairas relates.[1531] The last mention concerns 1375, when turcopolier Thibald Belfarage (*Thebat*) asked Peter II to gift him the castle.[1532]

Leontios states that the ethnically diverse community of Gorhigos had in a way been orphaned by its ruler who, expecting an unpleasant turn of events, fled to France. Among the inhabitants of the town he names Christians, such as Greeks and Armenians, calling them 'poor' (πτωχοί), 'orphaned' (ὀρφανοί), 'having no help from anywhere' (δὲν εἶχαν ἀπού πούποτες βοήθειαν) and 'deprived of the opportunity for [normal] life' (νὰ ζήσουν).[1533] In answer to the call for help, Peter I took over the protection of the fortress, and promised on the Bible that he would hold the place according to God's plan, even though the prize had aroused his covetousness (πεθυμημένος):

[…] *he set the Gospel upon the desk* (ἔβαλεν εἰς τὸ ἀναλόγιον τὸ Εὐαγγέλιον), *and all and each of them swore that they would hold the said castle for their lord King Peter, and above all things in the name of the Holy and Life-giving Cross.* (LM II 114)

This motif, well-known from the Alexandrian events, is repeated also in the case of other endeavours. Makhairas shows that an oath on the Bible may be used by a group or an individual to signal its presence in a new location, one that had previously belonged to a people that was part of a different civilisation, as a kind of ceremony or ritual. Peter I, characterised by the traits assigned to him by the author of the *Chronicle*, is constantly accompanied by a certainty that he has the right to items that are not his, obtained peaceably or seized by force, and that such an act is in every instance accompanied by the consent and approbation of God.

Like in the narrative about the siege of Alexandria, also here Makhairas tells of the armies approaching Gorhigos: this time Turkish ones that systematically move 'from place to place' (ἀπού τόπον εἰς τόπον), gradually taking control of 'remotely located houses' (τὰ ἔξω σπιτία) together with 'gardens' (περιβόλαια) and 'belongings of other kinds' (ἄλλα πολλά), until they take over the whole 'territory' (τὴν χώραν). As regards the attitude of the Christians surprised by the Turkish attack, the chronicler writes that because of the real danger some of them fled to Cyprus while others stayed behind in the castle or just outside it, protecting it 'for the love of Christ' (διὰ τὴν ἀγάπην τοῦ Χριστοῦ).

When describing these events, Makhairas emphasises the role of supernatural protection, such as the 'help of God' (ἡ βοήθεια τοῦ Θεοῦ) and the support of the icon of the Kouroukiotissa[1534] located

---

[1528] Nicolaou-Konnari hypothesises that Makhairas had personally seen Gorhigos, arguing as follows: 'The detailed way in which Leontios describes the topography of Gorhigos suggests that he may have visited the area; thanks to La Broquière, *Le Voyage d'Outremer*, p. 106, we know that in 1432 he was on a diplomatic mission in Laranda, a town north of Taurus which he may have reached through the port of Gorhigos.' (Nicolaou-Konnari, 'A poor island…', 131, fn. 34). See Bertrandon de La Broquière, Le voyage d'outremer.
[1529] Mas Latrie (Ed.), Chronique d'Amadi, 232.
[1530] Mas Latrie (Ed.), Chronique d'Amadi, 410–411.
[1531] Mas Latrie (Ed.), Chronique d'Amadi, 416–418.
[1532] Mas Latrie (Ed.), Chronique d'Amadi, 482–483.
[1533] LM II 113.
[1534] LM II 114. This information is missing from Mas Latrie (Ed.), Chronique de Strambaldi, 44.

in the main church (ὁποῦ ἦτον εἰς τὴν καθολικήν),[1535] which the Cypriots used 'for protection against the Turks' (κατὰ πρόσωπα τοὺς Τούρκους). He thus accents the power of the Christian religion, without specifying which rite he means. Having mentioned the icon, he proceeds to present its history in detail: the 'everyday miracles' (καθημερινὰ θαύματα) occurring through its mediation and the many terrifying, improbable phenomena in full revelation (πληροφορία) (LM II 115). To illustrate his claim the author of the *Chronicle* cites the story of a vision (ὅρωμαν) of the Karaman emirate's ruler, that is the 'Great Karaman' (τοῦ Καραμάνου τοῦ μεγάλου), who was blinded by the icon (ἐτύφλωσέν; ἐτυφλῶσεν τον), through 'one Lady of Gorhigos' (μία ἀρχόντισσα ἀπὲ τὸ Κουρίκος). Like in the case of the icon of St Nicholas, which played a significant role in the fighting for Myra, also in this case there ensued various 'terrifying miracles' (φοβερὰ θαύματα): the emir of Karaman 'withdrew his army' (ἐσήκωσεν τὸ φουσάτον του), '[ordered] many fat wax candles to be made' (ἐποῖκεν πολλὰς λαμπάδας –κερένας χοντρές–),[1536] 'three silver lamps' (γ' καντῆλες ἀργυρές) to be hung before the image (ὀμπρός τῆς), provided 'many quarts of olive oil' (–πολλὲς γέρνες λάδιν–) and 'lighted the lamps' (ἐποῖκεν λυγχναψίαν), while singing was be heard all night long (ἐψάλλαν ὅλη νύκτα). Makhairas completes this picture with the words:

> [...] *and on the following day they rubbed cotton over the picture (ἀπὲ τὴν εἰκόναν) and put it on his eyes (ἔβαλάν το εἰς τὰ 'μμάτιά του), and he was at once cured (παραῦτα ἐγίανεν).* (LM II 115)

This passage is a link that connects the legends about miracles from the first part of the *Chronicle* and mentions of other supernatural events. What sets this particular incident apart from those previously discussed is the fact that Makhairas chose a person from outside the Christian world to be the addressee of the Marian vision, even though through most of the narrative he distinctly distinguishes Christian beliefs from Muslim ones, assuming that each of the two civilisations is governed by separate laws, based on its own rules and rituals.

We find no other such examples in the Cypriot work that would show the operation of the subjects of Christian cult, the persons of the Holy Trinity and the Virgin Mary, within another civilisation, and which would demonstrate their impact on the behaviour of people of other religions. In this portrait, Leontios not only goes beyond the perspective of intercivilisational differences, but also transcends the schism between the Orthodox and Catholic faiths, which is why the message of this fragment is so exceptional.

Hill states after Guillaume de Machaut that the situation was wholly different, and the emir of Karaman had actually been wounded.[1537] However, the chronicler attaches such a large importance to Marian iconography, which to him is an evident manifestation of God's action in the earthly world, that he allows himself to emphasise only such information that is consistent with his perception of reality. According to it, Cyprus is an exceptional place for all of Christendom, and thus even Cypriots who live in other lands carry this spiritual element and are protected by Providence.

The retaking of Gorhigos castle was, in the belief of the *Chronicle*'s author, accompanied by 'great joy' (ἐχάρην χαρὰν μεγάλην) and the sound of trumpets (ἐπαῖξαν τὰ τρουμπέττια) and bells (ἐσημάναν τὲς καμπάνες). Makhairas does not hesitate to cite examples of the valiance and ruthlessness of the Cypriots, supported by God:

> [...] *God gave the victory (ἔδωκεν τὸ νῖκος τούς) to the Christians, and they routed the Turks so that they took flight: and they took many of them alive, and many Turks were killed, and the Christians captured much material of war (πολλὰ πολεμικά), and their tents and much gear, and they also gave the Great Karaman many wounds (πολλοὺς κόρπους), and they further took the tower which the Turks had taken.* (LM II 195)

[1535] This information is contained in MS O. See Dawkins (Ed., transl.), Ἐξήγησις/ Recital, 100 (fn. 7); Παυλίδης (Ed.), Λεοντίου Μαχαιρᾶ Χρονικόν, 86 (fn. 2).

[1536] LM II 115. MS O writes that these candles were 'καφουρένες' ('of camphor'). See Dawkins (Ed., transl.), Ἐξήγησις/ Recital, 102 (fn. 1); Παυλίδης (Ed.), Λεοντίου Μαχαιρᾶ Χρονικόν, 86 (fn. 4). The description in Mas Latrie (Ed.), Chronique de Strambaldi, 44: *Et levè il sue essercito et fece più torzi et tre ciciudelli d'argento et le messe inanti alla detta immagine, et fece che avesse quattro zare d'oglio al'anno et assai ducati; et fece orationi tutta una notte, et il giorno seguente, la matina, tuolsero del gotton et lo toccorono sopra la immagine et lo messero sopra li occhi suoi et immediate si sanò; et molti altri miracoli*.

[1537] Hill, History of Cyprus II, 348.

The chronicler uses many devices in the attempt to express his conviction that the deeds of the Cypriots were righteous. Because Providence is a constantly present theme in his narrative and a force that is invariably present in the depicted events, he uses this motif and attributes the Christian success to the intervention of the Virgin Mary. At the same time, he passes over other issues such as the evident lack of mercy in their actions, which according to the worldview he subscribes to is a Divine attribute. Conversely, he firmly repeats that the enslavement and killing of the Turks and capture of the town was rooted in the holy and incontestable will of the Creator. One cannot fail to notice that such a presentation bears the hallmark of manipulation of religious categories in order to assign value to the criminal actions of the Franks.

4.3.2.2. Retaking of Adalia in 1370

The imposing castle of Gorhigos was not the only important target of Cypriots' operations outside the boundaries of their own land. A significant episode, which casts light on Christians-Muslim contacts, involved attempts to retake Turkish Adalia (Ἀταλία), which had been conquered by the Christians in 1361 (LM II 120–129), undertaken by its one-time ruler emir Takka (Τακκᾶς).[1538] The *Chronique d'Amadi* mentions that already in 1363 Takka (*Taca*) had plundered Adalia (*Satalia*) multiple times (*molte fiate*) but had suffered defeat each time.[1539] Makhairas bluntly states that these failures ended with a 'great massacre' (μέγαν μακελλειόν).[1540]

The description of this event in Makhairas' work contains a mention that Takka was vividly interested in the Cypriot situation because he wished to use, at the opportune moment, the internal unrest (μεγάλην ἀνακάτωσιν) on the island and immediately retake Adalia.[1541] It may be ventured that in this period the relations between the Christians from Cyprus and the Turks involved watching each other for signs of lessened attention and signals of rising conflicts, in order to use this knowledge about the 'other' for their own purposes. Furthermore, the Muslims did not hesitate to use arguments of a religious nature, which may on the one hand be interpreted as mockery of foreign religious truths and contempt of others' spiritual traditions, and on the other, as an expression of the awareness – acquired through respect for their own religion – that anything connected to the sacred can penetrate consciousness the most deeply.

Takka took advantage of this particular truth, requesting his Turkish friend to go to Adalia and beg its inhabitants to allow him to be baptised (καὶ ἐπαρακάλεσεν καὶ ἐβαπτίσαν τον). He correctly foresaw the reaction of the populace, who quickly started to trust (ἀποθάρησέν του) the arrival, which led, Makhairas states, to the establishment of close relationships (συγγενάδες) and friendship (φίλοι). The false neophyte enabled the emir to get inside the town 'in the middle of the night' (μονονυκτίς) and set fire to the gates, and as a result to kill people (ἐσκοτῶνναν τους) and take fourteen towers (ἐπῆραν ιδ' πύργους).

The story of the battle of Adalia shows that knowledge of the values that are important to the enemy may provide tools for distracting him and permeating into his world. From the *Chronicle* narrative there emerges an image of Christians who trust in God to such an extent that they drop their vigilance, accepting into their community a new person who declares interest in the values of the Gospel. Leontios does not comment their inattention and carelessness, however, but emphasises the Turks' deceitfulness. Nevertheless, thanks to Providence, which was forced to take action, the Cypriots regained the town. Takka, meanwhile, had to account for his sins at the proper time, and for violating the principles of hospitality in particular. The description of the Christian triumph in the *Chronicle* is very vivid: the victory is announced by the sound of a bell tolled with a hammer (ἐσημάναν τὴν καμπάναν μὲ τὸ σφυρίν) telling of 'the betrayal' (γιὰ παραβουλίαν). Some time later another battle occurred, which once again, 'with God's help' (βοηθῶντος

[1538] Dawkins notes that for the Cypriots Turkey was an equivalent of Asia Minor 'along the southern coast of which there were several points, such as Gorhigos, held sometimes by them, and sometimes by the Turks'. Dawkins also observes the terseness of the description portraying the events of 1361 in the *Chronicle*, a feature that is not seen in other authors such as Froissart. The scholar explains the name 'Takka', writing that the name 'Takka' itself referred to a Turkish state with its capital in Adalia. Persons ruling this area were titled 'Takka Bey' (Dawkins, Notes, 102–103).

[1539] Mas Latrie (Ed.), Chronique d'Amadi, 413.

[1540] LM II 133. This term was taken from MS O. See Dawkins (Ed., transl.), Ἐξήγησις/ Recital, 118 (fn. 2); Παυλίδης (Ed.), Λεοντίου Μαχαιρᾶ Χρονικόν, 98 (fn. 4).

[1541] LM III 317.

τοῦ θεοῦ), was won by the followers of Christ, who killed many Muslims, including a relative of Takka, and left the rest in ignominy.[1542]

As we find out from further parts of Makhairas' work, in 1373 Adalia ultimately passed under Turkish rule. Cyprus' ruler at the time, Peter II, was so occupied with war with the Genoese that he decided to cede the town to Takka on condition that he would uphold the terms of his oath. This decision also followed deep deliberations by the Frankish ruler as to who was a greater threat to Cypriot affairs: the citizens of Genoa or the Muslims. This situation, from Peter II's perspective without a solution, was called 'a great shame for the Christian world' (μεγάλη ἀντροπὴ τῆς χριστιανοσύνης) by Leontios.[1543] It is worth considering what is meant by this shame: is it equivalent to the feeling that God tamed the pride of his fellow countrymen or rather to a sense of shame caused by political defeat, which is free from moral judgement from the point of view of Christian theology? The role that the author attributes to Providence in this chapter of the conflict is unknown, because he includes no information in that respect.

The chronicler vividly describes the moment of departure from Adalia by the Christian population, who out of all their belongings (βιτουαλίες) took with them mainly objects related to ritual and liturgy, such as 'the icon of the Mother of God of Cyprus' (ἡ εἰκόνα τῆς Κύπρου Θεοτόκου), 'all the silver and gold of the Church' (οὗλον τὸ ἀσημοχρούσαφον τοῦ ναοῦ), icons (τῶν εἰκόνων) and 'numerous other relics' (πολλὰ ἄλλα λείψανα).[1544] Equipped with the insignia of their faith, they left the outpost of a foreign civilisation in three senses: in the physical sense they left behind an empty place; in the political sense they lost their influence on the international scene; and in the spiritual and material sense they departed from territory ruled by the Muslims together with their religion. As a result, their domination over that place ceased completely.

4.4. Saracen attacks on Cyprus in the years 1363 and 1424–1426

The *Chronicle* shows that not only did the Cypriots reach Saracen lands, appropriating them for their own use, but also that the followers of Islam organised expeditions to Cyprus to plunder it, murder its inhabitants and seize their belongings. From the perspective of the *Chronicle* this is the fourth such significant presentation of a foreign presence in Makhairas' land, right after the Templars, Franks and representatives of the merchant Republics, although it is the first time that the mentions concern the followers of Islam and the first time that such presence is not connected to permanent settlement. Already LM I 35, telling the legend of St Diomidios, contains the comment 'and the Saracens invaded Cyprus many times' (–ἀποὺ τὲς πολλὲς φορὲς ὅπου 'πῆραν οἱ Σαρακηνοὶ τὴν Κύπρον [...]–).[1545]

The first invasion more extensively described in the *Chronicle* is connected to a plague that devastated the island in 1363 and a visit by the king of France: circumstances taken advantage of by the Turks, who came to Cyprus twice led by Mahomet Reis (Χαμοὺτ Ραῖς). Dawkins observes that fragments LM II 137–144, which depict these events, appear only in Makhairas and Strambaldi,[1546] which shows their particularly Cypriot message. Mahomet encouraged his countrymen to come to the island, which 'was depopulated' (εἶνε εὔκαιρη) and lacked a guard (δὲν πολομοῦν καμίαν βίγλαν).[1547] The Cypriots tried to protect their country on land and sea, burning the ships assaulting them. They univocally called Mahomet the 'enemy of Cyprus' (ὁ ἐχθρὸς τῆς Κύπρου), and unsuccessfully tried to seek the assistance of Emir Melek (Μὲλ ἀμιρᾶς), who declined to intervene and help 'when he saw Turks from Anemouri in chains' (θεωρῶντα τοὺς Τούρκους τοῦ Ἀνεμουρίου κλαππωμένους).[1548]

Kyriacou discusses the folk *Song of Antzoules*, which begins with the words 'Παφούτις εκουρσέψασιν οι Φράντζιοι Ανεμούριν κουρσέψαν χώρες...' ('When the Franks sacked Anemourion they plundered...') and what he believes to be evidence that constant war between Latins and Muslims left 'its imprint

---

[1542] LM III 317. Cf. LM II 195.
[1543] LM III 366–368. Cf. Mas Latrie (Ed.), Chronique d'Amadi, 441.
[1544] LM III 368.
[1545] Dawkins dates St Diomidios to the fourth century, and so this must be when the Saracen attack on Cyprus took place (Dawkins, Notes, 65).
[1546] Dawkins, Notes, 107.
[1547] LM II 139.
[1548] LM II 144.

on the collective memory and folk imagination of the Cypriots'. Kyriacou refers to Henri Grégoire and Hedwig Lüdeke's discovery 'that the song's Cypriot context led to a modification of the initial reference to Amorion (conquered by an Arab army in 838)', and in consequence, as he stresses, the Saracens were 'replaced' by Franks. Such a perspective shows Latins in an unfavourable light. Grivaud finds traces of *The Song of Antzoules* in the *Chronicle* but, importantly, notes that Makhairas put Latins in a position of 'the protagonists instead of the Muslims' and confused 'Amorion, a town in Phrygia, with Anamur, a port on the Cilician coast'.[1549] This discovery raises the questions: whether the Cypriot historiographer did so consciously or unconsciously, and whether this fact could shed light on his identity.

The second invasion in 1424, initiated by the Mamlūk sultan Barsbāy, was the Egyptian response to the fact that the islanders seemingly ignored the bold actions of the pirates who ravaged the coast of Syria, which many Franks profited from. The chronicler names Philip Picquigny, the bailiff of Lemesos, and Sir John Gasel, the commander of Aliki as those who wanted to gain riches at the expense of the attacked. Thanks to the reports of a Saracen slave who managed to flee the island, the Muslims amassed sufficient forces and attacked Lemesos on 26 September. According to Makhairas' account, they invaded the estates of the Venetians, destroyed a Cretan merchant vessel and a pirate galley and, most importantly, burned down the town. Like in the case of other descriptions of contact between or within civilisations, also in his depiction of these events the chronicler does not fail to touch on matters of religion. He points out that God is a judge who...

...does not wait for a man to bring forward his case before he does justice [...]. (LM V 651)

Makhairas thus emphasises his worldview once again, according to which historical events play out on two planes: the human and the divine. People involved in the sequence of events undertake various actions, having access to a restricted perspective of a situation. However, Providence, unlike them completely unhampered but persistent in executing a payment for every deed, functions beyond the complexity of the human world.

The episode that presents the attack on Lemesos also shows that the representatives of two different civilisations who establish contact with each other through pacts and agreements have the right to require the other to be loyal and true to the settlements made. The Cypriots' violation of these rules resulted in a severe punishment: burning down of one of the most distinguished Cypriot towns.[1550]

The third Saracen invasion of Cyprus, in 1425, was still more damaging because they managed to destroy many beautiful Cypriot towns and villages, including Trapeza (Τράπεζα), Kalopsida (Καλοψίδα), Kellia (Κελλία), Aradippou (Ἀραδίππου), Agrinou (Ἀγρίνου), Vromolaxia (Βρωμολαξία) and Kiti (Κίτι). They moved from place to place, setting subsequent settlements on fire. Fighting was also present in Styli (Στύλλοι) and Aliki (Ἀλική).[1551] Thanks to the help of a slave, the invaders managed to enter Lemesos through a hole in the city's walls, but having encountered opposition decided to return to Cairo.[1552]

If the losses suffered by the Cypriots during these invasions are estimated on the basis of the *Chronicle*, it may be concluded that the revenge of the Muslims was not only a pretext to obtain material goods, but that their actions were intended to have a far broader effect. Although the area of Cyprus is not large – the author himself terms it an 'islet' (νησσάκι)[1553] – and the settlements listed above lie at small distances from each other, the scale of the steps taken by the Saracens seems impressive. Equally imposing is the fact that the island's inhabitants were able to force such a powerful invader to withdraw its armies.

In 1426 the sultan Barsbāy, persuaded by the Genoese and Karaman Beg (Μακαράμ Πάκ),[1554] the successor of the 'Great Karaman',[1555] once again sent Egyptian ships, crewed by Mamlūks, Turks and Arabs and led by Tagriverdi Mahomet (Τακριβὲρ ὁ Μεχαμέτ), to the chaos-filled island. Once again, the target of the attack was Lemesos, and more precisely, the castle built within the town by King Janus.[1556]

[1549] Kyriacou, The Byzantine Warrior Hero, 73–74.
[1550] LM V 652.
[1551] LM V 654–657.
[1552] LM V 659.
[1553] LM II 158.
[1554] LM V 671.
[1555] Dawkins, Notes, 221.
[1556] LM V 672.

Makhairas, who participated in these events personally as a wine carrier[1557] was informed by a bowman he encountered that the Muslims had been successful in their mission to take the town.[1558] The aggressors addressed a letter to King Janus with the allegation that he had not received them with due honour and emphasised that 'a new bond and [new] peace conditions' (ἔλθης πρὸς ἐμᾶς νὰ ποίσωμε δῆμμαν κίνούργιον καὶ στοιχήματα τῆς ἀγάπης) were necessary. They demanded the Cypriot ruler to promise the followers of Islam that from then on he would not allow pirates or other bandits to plunder the lands that belonged to them, and would not succour the enemies of Muslims or consider them his friends. With the letter they enclosed a carpet (πεύκιν) to let the king sit upon it before the infidels.[1559] The sense of the letter (ὁ ὄρδινος τοῦ χαρτίου) is a clear signal of contempt and an expression of the Muslims' belief in their advantage.

On 7 July, when people came for wine, the news spread that the Saracens were approaching. From the tale of the constable, Leontios was privy to the whole sequence of the invaders' previous actions. They had reached the castle in Khirokitia (Χεροκοιτία), found there a Muslim servant who had been tortured, killed the prince and then stabbed the king in the forehead with a lance, upon which he shouted 'melek' (μελέκ), which means 'king' in Arabic, probably pointing to himself.[1560] Wreaking great destruction, which included burning down Potamia (Ποταμία), they started to systematically approach Lefkosia, which as the *Chronicle* states, unfolded its stunning beauty before them.

Thanks to the chronicler's detailed description of the fighting that played out at this time on Cyprus, and because he gives the composition of the Cypriot armies, it is possible to recreate the structure of the Christian community on Cyprus that took part in the defence of the island. He lists Rhodian, Catalan and merchant ships that hastened to help the islanders and mentions the dead, who included Genoese, one baptised Saracen, Syrians and also Armenians.[1561] The chronicler wishes all those who died to rest in peace regardless of who they were in life.

In the context of these events, the theme of the agreement concluded between the Venetians and Muslims is emphasised. This pact filled the followers of Islam with evident trust and hope for an easy victory, but the attitude of the representatives of the Republic shows some discord. Some of them turned away from the risky ally, fearfully watching his approach to Lefkosia and then fleeing in panic to Kerynia or taking shelter, together with the town's populace, in the lodge of the Venetian bailiff, while others allowed him to take further control of the town and decided to open the gates to him.[1562] Of the latter, Makhairas says that they:

> [...] *lit candles* (ἄψα λαμπάδες) *and received them* (ἐπροσδέκτησαν τους), *and gave them courage* (ἔδωκάν τους καρδίαν) *to enter the admirable city of Lefkosia* (ἐμπῆκαν εἰς τὴν θαυμαστὴν Λευκωσίαν).
> (LM V 693)

The Venetians, who wished to aid the sultan's emissaries, spread an illusion of security before the inhabitants of Lefkosia, counselling them to return to their daily tasks in peace in order to lull their vigilance.[1563] The Muslims used the opportunity offered to them, burning down the houses of the common folk, stealing possessions and destroying buildings important for Cypriot Christians such as churches and monasteries, and most importantly the church of the Great Cross.[1564] By painting this moving image, Makhairas shows that it was Christians who turned out to be the greatest enemies of Cyprus.

In this portrayal, the chronicler introduces the figure of Khanna of Damascus (Χάννας ὁ Δαμασκηνός) and the lady Pella (ἡ κυρὰ ἡ Πέλλα), who in their way fought against the enslavement of their country. This is one of the few fragments in the *Chronicle*, next to mentions of Galeftira, the prince's cook, and the peasant uprising, that focus of the actions of brave and sensitive representatives of the people. Thus he gives homage and justice to the common people.

Of Khanna and Pella he says this:

[1557] LM V 674.
[1558] LM V 674.
[1559] LM V 676.
[1560] LM V 683.
[1561] LM V 685–686.
[1562] LM V 692.
[1563] LM V 693.
[1564] LM V 694–695.

—And if the fire had lasted, all the town would have been burned,— but (the Christians,) Khanna of Damascus and the lady Pella, the potter's wife (–μουχρουτίνα–), –worked for four days and nights quenching it (ἐσβῆσαν τα).– And (the Saracens) carried off[1565] *the Christians and the plunder, and went away, and a curse be upon them (ἐπῆγαν εἰς τὸ ἀνάθεμμαν).* (LM V 695)

This fragment draws particular attention because of the author's emotional attitude to the situation described, as it contains expressions indicating that the fate of the citizens of his native country was not unimportant to him. Significantly, he also gives the names of members of the Rhomaian community and emphasises the importance of their efforts and the extent of the sacrifice they decided to make in order to save all that was very precious to the Cypriots.

The Saracens' invasions of Cyprus turned out to be exhausting for the island and its inhabitants. They were not conducive to the formation of mutual understanding, and above all they left no doubts as to the distinctness of the two civilisations and the impossibility of effacing the sharp boundaries between them. The Muslims found the island in all its diversity: the defence of the Syrians differed from that of the Venetians. On the basis of this episode it may also be observed that Makhairas notices the differences within the Muslim community, although he is not always able to precisely establish where the dividing lines run. Because of his personal participation in the events he was able to examine the enemy at close range. Distributing wine also became an opportunity for him to obtain valuable information and a broader perspective on the events, and thus to prepare a more precise account.

4.5. Other encounters between Cypriots and Saracens

Christians and Muslims met in the *Chronicle* also when the former captured places belonging to the Turks from Armenia (Τοῦρκοι τῆς Ἀρμενίας) in 1367, such as Valena (Βαλίνα),[1566] Laodicea (Λαδικία), Malo (Μάλος) and Ayasi (Ἀγιάσι),[1567] which is described in a mention concerning two Saracen castles (δύο γεμάτα Σαρακηνούς). In the interpretation of these events Makhairas does not introduce a new perspective, but consistently advocates an unambiguous understanding of them: the actions of the Cypriots are successful because they have the aid of God, who desires the Christian faith to spread. This optic is clearly visible in the wording he uses. We read for example that when the Frankish king arrived with a mighty army,

[...] God helped them, so that in the fight the Saracens kept falling from the walls of the castle in their fear: others fled away and escaped. And they took the town and killed many Saracens [...]. (LM II 212)

In another place there appears a reference to the capture of an enemy ship in Sidon and the transporting of its whole crew of Ammochostos, done 'for the glory of the Venerable Cross' (εἰς τὴν δόξαν τοῦ τιμίου σταυροῦ).[1568]

A separate space in the *Chronicle* narrative is taken by descriptions of clashes between Turks and Christians at sea, though such passages are not numerous. There is an impression that Makhairas' Muslims have some reservations about this type of military activity.

During one such encounter described by Leontios, in 1363, the Muslims attacked the Cypriot peninsula of Karpasi (Καρπάσιν), having first discovered that the island was unguarded (δὲν πολομοῦν καμίαν βίγλαν).[1569] The invaders decided to carry the fight to the very end, until their own ships burned down completely. When they noticed that Sir Francis Spinola's (σὶρ Φραντζικὴ Σπινόλα) galley was unarmed, they said to themselves:

[1565] By night.
[1566] Balenea, later known as 'Μπανιάς', a town in Syria located between Tortosa and Laodicea, after Παυλίδης (Ed.), Λεοντίου Μαχαιρά Χρονικόν, 157.
[1567] Ayasi, located in Alexandretta bay, is present-day İskenderun in south-east Turkey. See Παυλίδης (Ed.), Λεοντίου Μαχαιρά Χρονικόν, 573. In the *Chronicle* it appears in LM V 613, VII 653, 662.
[1568] LM II 213.
[1569] LM II 139.

'We see that the Christians drag us to execution and hang us (κωλοσύρνουν καὶ φουρκίζουν μας), and we have no way of escape (δὲν γλυτώννομεν): let us stand to our arms to the death (ἂ σταθοῦμεν εἰς τ' ἄρματά μας ν' ἀποθάνωμεν), rather than that they drag us at the horse's tail (παρὰ νὰ μᾶς κωλοσύρουν).' And immediately they cut the cable, and take a store of arrows for their bows, and shot and killed the captain, Sir Francis Spinola, and wounded many of the crew and the galley as well. When the rest saw the valour of the Turks, certain (of the Christians) threw themselves into the sea and swam to the other galley, that of Sir Henry de La Couronne, and told him of this, because he was not aware of it. And at once he made his men arm, and turned back and came up to them. And in their fury (ἀπὸ τὸν θυμόν) the Cypriots leaped on the Turkish ship (ἀππηδῆσαν εἰς τὸ τούρκικον) [...]. (LM II 141)

Another time, the sultan, in anger at the 1368 attack on Sarepta (Σαρφές) by John de Colie (σὶρ Τζουὰν τε Κολιές) and at the detainment of his envoys on Cyprus, and also because of the destruction wrought by Genoese ships, sent two Moroccan galleys (κάτεργα μαγραπίτικα) on an expedition against Cyprus, where they seized not only a Venetian merchant ship near Castellorhizo (Καστέλλο Ρούζου), but also two small ships with Christians aboard and took them to Alexandria.[1570]

The encounter, which brought serious consequences, occurred in that same year between two Genoese ships heading for Damietta (εἰς τὸν Δαμιάτην) and two Saracen sailing vessels (νάβες σαρακήνιες), one of which reached the port, while the other was captured and brought to Ammochostos.[1571]

At the end of the *Chronicle* there also appears a description of two pilgrim boats (καραβία πιλιγρίνικα), which in 1426, some time after the kidnapping of the king by the Saracens, sailed into the midst of a Muslim fleet while heading for the Holy Land.[1572]

Like the *Chronique d'Amadi* and Boustronios' text, Makhairas' text includes many short incidents involving sea battles, among which a part are clashes between Christians and followers of Islam. They help to form a complete image of such contacts, permitting their frequency and the diversity of the groups participating in them to be ascertained.

4.6. Cases of conversion

A separate issue that is worth raising when analysing the depiction of interreligious contact in the *Chronicle* is conversion. The Cypriot work contains information that a character had previously been of a different religion and mentions of specific Saracens with the addition of the adjective 'baptised' (βαπτισμένος), suggesting that such a process had occurred. Although religious conversion is actually a certain form of passage, as Diane Austin-Broos writes,[1573] Makhairas does not usually explain the circumstances in which it occurred, concentrating only on its fact. The exception is the attempt to put physical or psychological pressure on individuals, carried out for various purposes, as in the case of the boy who wished to enter the Templar order and of the Carmelite Peter de Thomas. However, there is no way to establish whether the conversion of the followers of Islam was dictated by the desire to regain their freedom or by religious beliefs.[1574]

The Cypriot records instances of conversion both within Christianity and Islam. In the second part of his work he makes a distinction between unbaptised (Σαρακηνοί ἄπιστοι) and baptised Saracens (Σαρακηνοί βαπτισμένοι).[1575] The adjective 'baptised' (βαπτισμένος) neutralises the connotations of the negative term 'Saracen', causing a new category to be distinguished through such a combination.

[1570] LM II 220.
[1571] LM II 222.
[1572] LM V 688.
[1573] The scholar claims that conversion 'is a form of passage, a "turning from and to", that is neither syncretism not absolute breach' (Austin-Broos, The Anthropology of Conversion, 1).
[1574] James Muldoon observes that Muslim slaves looked for opportunities to convert to Christianity in order to regain liberty, while conversions in the opposite direction were something 'less than an intense and personal spiritual experience', in Muldoon, Introduction, 7.
[1575] LM II 193. Dawkins gives 'Σαρακηνὸς ἀβάπτιστος', claiming that the reading 'Σαρακηνοί ἄπιστοι' present in MS V is incorrect. See Dawkins (Ed., transl.), Ἐξήγησις/ Recital, 174 (fn. 3); Παυλίδης (Ed.), Λεοντίου Μαχαιρᾶ Χρονικόν, 142 (fn. 3).

One of the comments in the *Chronicle* concerns a baptised Saracen named Antony.[1576] In another place Leontios mentions the friend of the turcopolier, a Genoese man, Sir de Lort the Usher (σίρε Λουσίερ τε Λόρτ), who converted, probably from Christianity, to Islam (ὅπου ἐμουσθλουμάνισεν), taking a new name, which was 'Nasr-ed-Din' (τον Νασὰρ ελ Τήν) 'in the language of the Saracens' (σαρακηνὸν ἐκράζαν).[1577] Because of his conversion he was able to act as intermediary between the Cypriots and Egyptians, and also to pass messages to the sultan, one of which was:

> *God will send a heavy chastisement* (μεγάλην παίδευσιν) *upon us if you do not make peace, for we know that all the Christians are ready to join together to come against you to wipe you out* (χριστιανοὶ μέλλει νὰ σωρευτοῦσιν νὰ ἔλθουν κατάδικά σου νὰ σὲ ξηλείψουν), *and to destroy also the people of your realm* (νὰ καταλύσουν καὶ τὸν σουλτανικὸν λαόν): *and it seems to us that you are forcing them to do this* (ἀναγγάζεις τους νὰ τὸ ποίσουν). (LM II 203)

Makhairas shows how conversion broadens the possibilities standing before individuals, who gain through it an insight into the internal reality of a different civilisation and the right to comment on what is happening within it, to warn and to counsel.

In yet another place in Leontios' narrative there appears a Saracen slave who was baptised by force (τὸν ἐβαπτίσαν) and was given the name Thomas (Τουμᾶς) upon confirmation. During the Egyptian invasion of Cyprus, after a meeting with a Mamlūk group in Kouvouklia (Κουβουκλία), he 'rejected his baptism' (ἀρνήθην τὸ βάπτισμαν), for which he was punished by the Cypriots by burning.[1578] This case shows that the moment of conversion is equivalent to initiation into a new order, in which much depends on how the neophyte uses their situation. If he remains faithful to his new community, he will become an 'other' and an 'infidel' to his former co-believers. If he reneges on the ritual of conversion, however, he will be doubly repudiated by the community that took him in.

Thomas' example is not the only one in the *Chronicle* to touch on the issue of punishment in the context of conversion. Severe consequences awaited the natives of Gorhigos, Rekouniatos (τὸν Ρεκουνιάτον) and Andronikos (τὸ(ν Ἀντρό)νικον),[1579] martyred in suffering for 'sweet Jesus' (οἱ δύο ἐδῶκαν θάνατον διὰ τὸν γλυκὺν Ἰησοῦν), which Makhairas comments thus:

> *And they chose to die* (ἐδέκτησαν τὸν θάνατον) *in the faith of Christ* (εἰς τὴν πίστιν τοῦ Χριστοῦ) *rather than to live in lies* (παρὰ νὰ χαν ζήσειν εἰς τὰ ψέματα) *and to turn Moslem* (νὰ χαν μουσθλουμανίσειν); *and they reviled* (ἐξητιμάσαν) *the sultan and those who tormented them* (τοὺς ἐκριτηρεῦγαν). *And at the last the sergeant cut off their holy heads* (ἔκοψεν τὰς κεφαλάς τους τὲς ἁγίες), *and they rendered their holy souls* (ἐδῶκαν τὲς ἁγίες τους ψυχές) *into the hands of the living God* (εἰς τὰς χεῖρας τοῦ θεοῦ τοῦ ζῶντος), *and their memory abides for ever. And the church placed them with the martyrs* (ἔσμιξέν τους ἡ ἐκλησία μὲ τοὺς μάρτυρες), *and they were canonized* (ἐκανονίσαν τους). (LM IV 660)

The above example resembles in its structure the legends about martyrs from the first book of the *Chronicle*. As in their case, here also death came at the hands of the Muslims. The chronicler records the moment of their deaths and provides information about what happened to the souls of the victims as a result of the infidel attack. No other saint presented in the Cypriot work is able to choose whether he wants to die for his faith or to convert to Islam: the Saracens usually kill with no heed for a given person's attitude. In this case, however, Rekouniatos and Andronikos get the chance to decide. Makhairas unequivocally gives us to understand that adopting the Muslim faith (μουσθλουμανίσειν) is nothing but 'living in lies' (ζήσειν εἰς τὰ ψέματα). Meanwhile, persevering within the Christian community guarantees the determined persons two primary intangible benefits. One of them is memory (μνήμη) about the heroic individuals, cultivated by members of the community over the centuries, and the other, being accepted after death by the 'living God' (τοῦ θεοῦ τοῦ ζῶντος). The expression 'into the hands' (εἰς τὰς χεῖρας) gives the images of life after death some tangibility. The phrase 'holy [...] souls' (τὲς ἁγίες [...] ψυχές) indicates that the chronicler believes that the souls will remain sanctified for all times. When commenting this

---
[1576] LM V 685.
[1577] More about the person and actions of Nasr-ed-Din may be found in Runciman, *A History of the Crusades* 2, 244, 343–344.
[1578] LM V 652.
[1579] The suggestion that this concerned Andronikos alone comes from Dawkins, *Notes*, 216.

episode, Makhairas emphasises that the Church (ἐκκλησία) as an institution and community of fellow believers numbered (ἔσμιξέν) Rekouniatos and Andronikos among the martyrs (μὲ τοὺς μάρτυρες), and also exalted them: they are therefore the first and only persons in the *Chronicle* to have been officially canonised (ἐκανονίσαν τους).[1580]

In his narrative, Leontios introduces the figure of an old Mamlūk (ἕνας γέρος Μαμουλούκης), a former Christian (ὅπου ἤτον χριστιανός) who ultimately renounced Christ (ἀρνήθην τὸν Χριστόν),[1581] and 'baptised Saracen slaves' (σκλάβους Σαρακηνοὺς βαπτισμένους), watched by the Cypriots to prevent them from joining their former fellow worshippers.[1582] He shows that converts faced specific consequences for leaving the Muslim community, and so they were accompanied by evident fear:

> there were many baptized Saracens (–πολλοὶ ἦσαν Σαρακηνοὶ βαπτισμένοι–) who, (as soon as they heard of the king's defeat,) ran away (from fear) and hid themselves in the mountains, that they might not be caught by the Saracens. (LM V 677)

Further, Makhairas names George of Damat (Τζορτζὴ τε Ταμαθιάνη), who burned powder (ἔψηννεν τὸ παρούτιν) and made syrup (ἐπολόμαν κόλλαν) and carmelised sugar (ἔψηννεν τὸν ζάχαριν), Theodoki (Θεοτοκής),[1583] a royal builder (τοῦ ρηγὸς ὁ κτίστης), Nicholas (Νικολής), the son of an employee at the baths (λουτράρη), Michael (Μίκελλος), a toll collector (ταλιούρης), an emancipated Syrian (Συργιάνος ἐλεύθερος), Paul (Παῦλος), the servant of a bishop (ὁ σκλάβος […] τοῦ ἐπισκόπου), a slave of the Makhairas monastery (ὁ σκλάβος τοῦ μοναστηρίου τοῦ Μαχαιρᾶ), Stavrias (Σταυρίας), a slave from the Great Cross monastery (ὁ σκλάβος […] τοῦ Σταυροῦ τοῦ μεγάλου), and 'others, who preferred to die rather than fall into the hands of the Saracens' (ὅπου ἐπροτιμοῦσα ν' ἀπεθάνουν παρὰ νὰ δοθοῦν εἰς τὰ χέρια τοὺς Σαρακηνούς).[1584]

We do not encounter very many episodes presenting conversion in this narrative, and when they do appear, it is usually in the context of coercion, which is often connected to a later return of such a person to their original faith. In total, the *Chronicle* singles out ten cases of conversion from Islam to Christianity, and one in the opposite direction.

For a Cypriot, conversion to Christianity is equivalent to being baptised. Makhairas does not delve into theological details and does not even use the word 'sacrament'. Neither does he state whether the conversion of a given Muslim was to Orthodoxy or to Catholicism. On the one hand, conversion brings two faiths together the most fully, because the encounter happens within the identity of a single person. On the other, however, acceptance of a new religion is equivalent to abandonment of the former one, and thus with the rejection of the foundations of one's own civilisation. An analysis of the passages of the *Chronicle* that illustrate this phenomenon do not usually provide answers as to the reasons for the decision to convert. However, where we do obtain some fragmentary data, we are able to conclude that the converts were motivated either by the desire to raise their standard of living by integrating into a new community or by fear of losing their lives.

4.7. The letters of the old man of Damascus and the story of the boy George

The *Chronicle* contains two legible warnings against attacking the Saracens addressed to the Cypriots. The first of these is expressed in the form of letters of a God-fearing sheikh of Damascus addressed to the Cypriot ruler Janus in 1425, the other in the form of a parabolic tale about the boy George. They

---

[1580] Aleksander Mień observes that 'canonisation as official inclusion in the group of saints is a relatively late phenomenon. The Eastern Church did not establish a specific canonisation ritual. It was sanctioned by patriarchs, bishops, Councils, Synods and even emperors. Most saints in the liturgical calendar were not formally canonised. The worship given to them by the faithful was initially something elemental, and only later were their names included in the menologion (liturgical calendar).' (Mień, *Sakrament, słowo, obrzęd*, 92. Translated by Kupiszewska).
[1581] LM V 673.
[1582] LM V 677. See Nicolaou-Konnari, *Greeks*, 39.
[1583] Dawkins believes that Tadok Favla (ὁ Θαδόκη ὁ Φαύλα) z LM III 594, also a builder, is the same person (Dawkins, *Notes*, 594).
[1584] LM V 677.

4.7.1. Letters of the old man of Damascus

The presentation in the Cypriot work of an exchange of moderate, peaceful correspondence between the Frankish King Janus and a sheikh (σιεχᾶς) from Damascus who is particularly respected by his fellow worshippers shows that the image of the Saracens is not wholly unambiguous. Namely, an appearance is made by an individual from the hostile religion who turns out to be a positive figure. Despite the different faith that this wise man represents, Makhairas does not hesitate to call him a 'good man' (ἕνας καλὸς ἄνθρωπος).[1585] The sheikh, an opponent of war (δὲν ἦτον πολεμιστής), is aware that the peace negotiations are heading in an undesirable direction, especially as 'in his times the Saracens often attacked the islands' (εἰς τὸν καιρόν του πῶς πολλὲς φορὲς –ἐπῆραν οἱ Σαρακηνοὶ τὰ νησσία–),[1586] formerly and currently (εἰς παλαιόν καιρόν καί τώρα),[1587] which Dawkins interprets as a reference to the Arab attacks on Crete.[1588] The chronicler calls the sheikh's attitude to Janus 'love' several times (ἀγάπησέν τον; τὸν ἠγαπημένον του υἱόν εἰς τὸν ρήγα, LM V 661; πολλά μου ἠγαπημένε; ἡ ἀγάπη ἡ μεγάλη τὴν ἔχω μετά σου; διὰ [...] τελειουμένην ἀγάπην, LM V 664).

The letter is sent at a moment when sultan Barsbāy discovers that counter to his promise, King Janus has established contact with the pirates, which is detrimental to Muslim interests.[1589] The old man attempted to present the might of the Egyptian ruler to the king, underlining that he had subjugated all the kingdoms of Syria, from Ayas to Aleppo (Χαλέπιν), and enjoyed exceptional authority in Damascus, Tripoli (Τρίπολη), Jerusalem (Γεροσόλυμαν), and up to Cairo (Κάργιος), and would not find it difficult, 'if he puts his mind to it' (ἂν βάλη τὸν νοῦν του), that is if it would become the object of his thought and actions, to 'destroy the unhappy island' (θέλει ξηλοθρέψειν τὸ ἄτυχο νησσίν). The sheikh witnessed the sultan uttering words promising that he would burn the 'stinking island of Cyprus' (νὰ κάψω τὸ βρωμονήσσιν τῆς Κύπρου),[1590] and moreover he himself had seen how the Saracens had despoiled the island during his life. The Frankish knights did not want to allow this letter to be transmitted, suspecting trickery; however, George Khatit (σὶρ Τζόρτζε Χατίτ) finally translated it into French (ἐμεταγλώττισέν το φράγγικα).

Leontios introduces the correspondence with the words:

When this news, which stank in our nostrils (βρωμισμένα μαντάτα), went to the godless sultan (τὸν ἄθεον σουλτάνον) and also to Damascus, it came to the ears of a good man whom the Saracens held to be a saint (ἕνας καλὸς ἄνθρωπος τὸν εἴχασιν οἱ Σαρακηνοὶ δι' ἅγιον). (LM IV 661)

The chronicler states that the old man had decided to resolve the relations between the followers of the two religions because he had promised God to use all his power. He addresses the following words to the Cypriot ruler:

[...] My son, I have heard of the graces (χαρίσματα) which God has given you [...]. (LM V 664)

He thus takes a gentle tone as he begins on a longer announcement, containing a radical message and being a display of persuasion that is subtle and yet brooks no opposition. And further:

And wise is (σοφὸς εἶνε) he who endures to be taught by others (ὅπου διαβάζει διδασκαλίαν ἀποὺ ἄλλους), for "wisdom learneth and escapeth punishment." ('μανθάνει ἡ γνῶσι, καὶ λείπεται τὴν παίδευσιν.') Therefore I beg you and beseech you by your Creator (θειορκίζω σε εἰς τὸν πλάστην σου)

[1585] LM V 661.
[1586] LM V 663.
[1587] LM V 663. See Dawkins (Ed., transl.), Ἐξήγησις/ Recital, 640 (fn. 3); Παυλίδης (Ed.), Λεοντίου Μαχαιρᾶ Χρονικόν, 502 (fn. 4).
[1588] Dawkins, Notes, 219.
[1589] LM V 661.
[1590] LM V 661–662.

that so far as may be –you will refuse to take this evil path, by which your island will be led captive and the blood of the Christians– will be shed. (LM V 664)

This show of rhetorical ability seems to have been very well planned: here is a Muslim sage who declares faith and love for one God but invokes the God of another civilisation. It is unknown whether he is simply referring to a category that his addressee is mentally capable of accepting, in which case this would be a purely technical device intended to make the content of the message more accessible or to cause a given reaction, or whether it is a less conscious furnishing of the term meaning the Supreme Being with the possessive pronoun 'your'. At the same time, this is the only place where Makhairas uses the word 'πλάστης' ('Creator'). From his further words it seems that the sheikh places the sultan in second place right after God in the hierarchy of beings and influences:

[…] he is the sole ruler of Islam (μονοκράτωρ τοῦ μουσθλουμανείου), and above all (παρὰ τὰ πάντα) he is far richer than you are (πολλὰ πλούσιος παρὰ σέναν) […]. And do not be unbelieving (μὲν γενῆς ἄπιστος), but believe me. I am acting towards you as a good father acts towards his son (ὡς γοιὸν πολομᾷ καλὸς πατὴρ πρὸς τὸν υἱόν του). (Be sure of this, that if I did not love you, I would not be giving you the advice which I am now giving; wherein I go against my faith and against my master. And I have only one dear son, and because of my love for you, I have sent him to you, in order that you may know my love, whether I love you or not.) I do not know whether God is angry with you (ἂν ἦνε ὁ θεὸς ἀγγκρισμένος μετά σου) and that therefore your councillors hate you and stand in your way, (and have been sent by God to bring you into an affair which will end in your captivity.) And I promise you that from the time of Melek Shah and Barkuk (ἀπὸ τὸν καιρὸν τοῦ Μελὲ Ζὰ καὶ τοῦ Μπάρκου),[1591] God has never sent forth so strong a sultan (δὲν ἔπεψεν ἥτζου δυνατὸν σουλτάνον). I promise you by the Creator of heaven and of earth (εἰς τὸν ποιητὴν τοῦ οὐρανοῦ καὶ τῆς γῆς), that if you do not turn away from this foolish counsel (ἀπὲ τὴν μωρικὴν βουλὴν τούτην), you will be conquered and destroyed and driven out (θέλεις νικηθεῖν, καὶ θέλεις χαλαστεῖν, καὶ θέλεις ἐξοριστεῖν), (and all who are with you,) and afterwards you will repent, but it will avail you nothing (τἄπισα θέλεις τὸ μετανώσειν, καὶ δὲ νὰ 'φεληθῆς). My son, I am going against my conscience and against my faith (πάγω κατάδικα τῆς συνείδησίς μου καὶ κατάδικα τῆς πίστις μου) […], I am advising you against my master, who is a true believer (ἀβιζιάζω σε κατάδικα τοῦ ἀφέντη μου ὀρθοδόξῳ). […] do I hold you for my dear son, God knows, even as if I had begotten you […], I pray God to deliver you from the hands of the Saracens. […] May God grant you many years. (LM V 664)

It is hard to conclude based on the above fragment whether the sage, divided between the need to be faithful to the sultan and the desire to satisfy the values he holds as well as a liking for the Cypriot king is attempting to help Janus or whether he is manipulating him in order to obtain a desired effect. He does not hide his devotion to the Muslim ruler, nor does he hesitate to show fear of the consequences of going against him. He sees the ruler of the sultanate as the only true believer (ὀρθόδοξος), the one who knows the principles of behaviour according to God's requirements. However, he decides to make an exception for the Cypriot king: he thus makes a move towards an individual belonging to a different civilisation. He even goes one step further when he invokes the ties of spiritual kinship, emphasising the categories of 'conscience' or 'moral awareness' (συνείδηση) and 'faith' (πίστις), which are important for understanding and experiencing religion. The statement of the Muslim sheikh is one of the most detailed professions of faith in the *Chronicle*, and very similar in its message to what is presented in Christian churches. It is only this old Saracen, of all the characters, who fully understands who God is and what should be done in order to participate in Divine reality and thus also in order to be a part of a community that holds to the same values, which forms the foundations of civilisation as a whole. The choice of wording presented in this fragment is imposing. Next to the noun 'πλάστης' we have the noun 'ποιητής' ('Doer', 'Creator'),[1592] which puts emphasis on the aspect of God's creativity, his causal force and ability to form matter at will. The use

---

[1591] Dawkins states after Miller and Sathas that these were probably King Shah of the Seljuk dynasty ruling in Persia and Barkuk, progenitor of the Mamlūk line of Burji sultans. See Dawkins, Notes, 219; Παυλίδης (Ed.), Λεοντίου Μαχαιρά Χρονικόν, 505 (fn. 4). 'Malek Shah' appears in Anna Komnene, The Alexiad, 109 (book VI, chapter VIII).
[1592] In Strambaldi's translation some shade of meaning of the first noun disappears because he gives it as *Iddio*. In the second case we have *creator del cielo et délia terra*. See Mas Latrie (Ed.), Chronique de Strambaldi, 272–273.

of such terminology brings the sage's message closer to the way in which representatives of the Christian world usually talk about God, but above all it is consistent with the contents of the Qur'ān, where we read:

He is God, the Creator,
The Evolver,
The Bestower of Forms
(Or Colours).[1593]

According to the Qur'ān God created the world, that is heaven and earth (in the *Chronicle* the sheikh says that God is the 'Creator of heaven and earth', ὁ ποιητὴς τοῦ οὐρανοῦ καὶ τῆς γῆς), which is expressed in many ways:

Praise be God,
Who created the heavens
And the earth,
And made the Darkness
And the light.[1594]

Who has made the earth your couch,
And the heavens your canopy.[1595]

On high hath He raised
Its canopy, and He hath
Given it order and perfection.

Its night doth He
Endow with darkness,
And its splendour doth He
Bring out (with light).

And the earth, moreover,
Hath He extended
(To a wide expanse).[1596]

And he called man to life:

He it is created
You from clay.[1597]

Created man, out of
A (mere) clot
Of congealed blood.[1598]

Nevertheless, this similarity did not move the Cypriots to the extent that would allow them to accept this speech and the suggestions therein, which clearly shows that origins and belonging to a given civilisation determine in advance how a person will be treated. The knights with whom the ruler of Cyprus takes counsel warned Janus against the words of the sheikh, explaining that the Saracens were capable of great, destructive deeds and 'through the astrological arts' (μὲ τὴν τέχνην τῆς ἀστρολογίας) they 'could remove

---

[1593] Sura LIX, *Exile*, [Al-Ḥashr], v. 24, in Ali (Transl.), Quran, 1529.
[1594] Sura VI, *Cattle* [Al-An'ām], v. 1, in Ali (Transl.), Quran, 289.
[1595] Sura II, *The Cow*, [Al-Baqara], v. 22, in Ali (Transl.), Quran, 21.
[1596] Sura LXXIX, *Those who Tear Out* [An-Nāzi'āt], v. 28–30, in Ali (Transl.), Quran, 1683.
[1597] Sura VI, *Cattle* [Al-An'Am], v. 2, in Ali (Transl.), Quran, 289.
[1598] Sura XCVI, *Read!/Proclaim!* [Iqraa] or *The Clot* [Al-'Alaq], v. 2, in Ali (Transl.), Quran, 1761.

[them] from the world' (ἠμποροῦσι νὰ [...] χαλάσουν ἀπὸ τὸν κόσμον).¹⁵⁹⁹ Disappointed, the old man insisted that he had wanted to perform an 'act of kindness' (φιλανθρωπία), but that if the island's inhabitants did not want to receive the gift, they could become slaves of the sultan through their own pride.¹⁶⁰⁰

4.7.2. The story of the boy George

The second motif that plays the role of a warning against conflict with the followers of Islam, in the shape of the tale of the sixteen-year-old Alexandrian lad George and his mother, told in the final parts of the *Chronicle* (LM V 668), somewhat symbolically shows the respective attitudes of Christians and Muslims to the other. It is, Dawkins notes, a local Cypriot legend that does not appear either in the *Chronique d'Amadi* or in Boustronios' work.¹⁶⁰¹

As the legend tells, it was the boy's desire to visit the Holy Sepulchre, and also to go over all the land that Jesus walked on. Fulfilment of this dream was hampered by the fears of his mother, who fearing a Saracen attack (τὸν φόβον τοὺς Σαρακηνούς), addressed the following words to him:

> *My son, you see that the Saracens are hostile (θυμωμένοι) to the Christians and are at war (ἀγκαρρωμένοι) with them; and will you travel among them, going from place to place?* (LM V 668)

He responded:

> *My sweet mother, I beseech you to let me go; and if the Saracens are at enmity (ὀκτρεμένοι) with the Christians, how are we concerned (with them,) we who are the servants of God (δοῦλοι τοῦ θεοῦ) and go –to worship God– for the good of our souls?* (LM V 668)

The chronicler presents an idealised figure of the boy, attributing to him features such as: virtuousness, the ability to lead a good life, persistence in obeying Divine commands, which is consistent with the hagiographical convention, and firmness and tenacity. Meanwhile, he ascribes to the Saracens a propensity to anger (θυμωμένοι) and remaining in a state of war (ἀγκαρρωμένοι) with representatives of other nations.

During their wanderings the heroes of the tale reach a place that Makhairas terms 'beautiful' (ὅμορφος). This word actually appears three times: in the context of a 'beautiful stream' (ηὗραν μίαν ὅμορφην βρύσιν), a 'beautiful tree' (εἶχεν ἕναν ὅμορφον δεντρόν) and a 'beautiful place' (εἰς τὸν ὅμορφον τόπον). This is a simplified description of paradise into which, as into Eden, a serpent has stolen:

> [...] *behold a snake*¹⁶⁰² *came quickly and went up into the tree,* (LM V 669)

which reflects primal, ontic fear (ἐφοβήθην; φοβοῦμαι). In this context, the testimony of the mother is evocative:

> *My son, the Lord who knows all things (ὁ Κύριος, ὁ τὰ πάντα γινώσκει), sees whither we are going (θωρεῖ ποῦ πηγαίννομεν), and he will send his angel of peace to guard us (θέλει πέψειν τὸν ἄγγελόν του τῆς εἰρήνης καὶ θέλει μᾶς φυλάξει).* (LM V 669)

recalling the Biblical guarantees of God's omniscience, evident in the above example.¹⁶⁰³

[1599] LM V 665.
[1600] LM V 667.
[1601] Dawkins, Notes, 219.
[1602] A symbol frequently used in the Bible, e.g. Gen. 3: 2; 2 Cor. 11: 3; Rev. 12: 15; 20: 2; Isa. 27: 1.
[1603] Cf. 1 John 3: 20; 1 Cor. 2: 16 ('"For who has known the mind of the Lord so as to instruct him?" But we have the mind of Christ.'); 1 Cor. 2: 7 ('But we speak God's wisdom, secret and hidden, which God decreed before the ages for our glory. [...]').

At the climax the boy kills the beast (θηρίον) with an arrow from his bow, and 'half of his body becomes paralysed' (-ἐπιάστην- τὸ ἥμισόν του μέλος). The tale culminates with a legible vision (εἶδεν ὅρωμαν) experienced by George, showing three 'young knights, handsome cavalrymen' (παιδίους στρατιῶτες, ὅμορφοι καβαλλάριδες),[1604] who tell him to fear not (Μὲν φοβηθῆς!),[1605] and then, seizing him by the hair, arms and legs, heal him of the paralysis.[1606] Significant words that set out their purpose there are then spoken:

We are sent to help (εἰς τὴν βοήθειαν) the Cypriots against the Saracens. [...] God has commanded us to leave Cyprus (ὥρισέν μας νὰ πᾶμεν ἀπὸ τὴν Κύπρον), because they do not put their hope in God (δὲν ὀρπίζουν εἰς τὸν θεόν), but they hope in their vain weapons (ἀμμὲ ὀλπίζουν εἰς τὰ ψεματινά τους ἄρματα), and this is why we are passing this way. (LM V 670)

The boy and his mother return to their country as God-appointed messengers and relate the matter in secret to their countrymen.[1607]

Like in the case of the legend of St Helena, who supernaturally came into contact with the Creator, also here the assessment of the Cypriots' conduct is revealed in the form of a vision. In this narrative, supernatural signs are one of the main ways of obtaining information on whether specific decisions of individuals are ultimately sanctioned or not. The story of George conclusively shows that according to Makhairas it was the inhabitants of the island that God chose to be the victors, but their own choices became an obstacle.

4.8. Summary

Christians and Muslims are presented in the *Chronicle* as two autonomous worlds. Makhairas places particular emphasis on the feelings and behaviours of rulers and commanders. On the one hand, we encounter an image of the group of Christians of both rites, dominated by Latins, and on the other, the image of the group of followers of Islam, composed primarily of Turks and Egyptians. It is this collective that is in the foreground, because we only later meet specific individuals who are involved in the defence of their land or conquering that of others. Thus the primacy of the image of a community, composed of different nations connected by a network of relationships, allows these wholes to be perceived as civilisations, and their contacts as a clash between them that escapes the framework of peaceful confrontation, a crack, a mismatch that will be inadequate at all points in history. As at the foundation of each of these civilisations there lies an alterity that is insurmountable, it is not even possible to talk of negotiating identities or of commensurability of conceptual and cognitive frameworks, but only of perceptions that bring discomfort during contact with alterity and often, a failure to accept it, which can clearly be seen in the *Chronicle*.

The analysis of fragments in which Makhairas describes the forging of alliances and agreements between members of one community, as in the case of joint action by the Republics and King Peter's cooperation with the brothers of Rhodes[1608] or Emir Takka's coalition with the lord of Alaya and lord of Monovgat[1609] brings the realisation that the chronicler noticed the diversity within these communities. Sometimes, when a break occurs within its fold, such diversity is detrimental to the community in question,

---

[1604] Dawkins, citing Hasluck's research, writes: 'That the boy's name was George and that he saw three knights on horseback, makes it clear that they were of the military saints, and that one of them was his patron St George, especially kind to travellers [...]. St George, like his Islamic parallel Khidr, has a grey or white horse, and St Demetrios a bay or red horse [...]. The third may have been any one of the sainted knights, St Theodore, St Procopios, and so on.' (Dawkins, Notes, 220). The position cited by Dawkins is Hasluck, Hasluck, Christianity and Islam.
[1605] LM V 670.
[1606] As Dawkins shows, the motif of healing via stretching out is probably present in the fifth-century text *Martyrdom and Miracles of St George of Cappadocia* (Dawkins, Notes, 220).
[1607] LM V 670.
[1608] LM II 117, 131, 160–161, 201, 217.
[1609] LM II 116.

which can be seen in the example of the incomplete information held by the Western rulers concerning peace with the sultan.

In the narrative, a lot of space is taken up by a description of peace negotiations between the Christians and the Muslims, which were the only chance for bringing order to the relations between the sides, and where a large role was played by envoys who carried messages, and not infrequently experienced the fate of hostages and were exposed to direct, impulsive reactions of the addressee.[1610] War prisoners, held captive against their will by representatives of a foreign civilisation until the end of the conflict, are also highly important. Their function in the history of humanity is accurately defined by Jarbel Rodriguez, who calls them 'the nexus between hostility and compromise'.[1611]

The distribution of power in the encounters between Christians and Muslims presented by Makhairas is ambiguous. Regardless of whether battles were fought on land or at sea, it is impossible to ultimately assess who really turned out to be best adapted to them. Apart from needs of an economic nature, both powers are driven by the desire to reach the 'infidel' (ἄπιστοι) and a strong need to start interactions with them. They sometimes happen to use moments of inattention of the opponent who is embroiled in chaos, as was the case for example when there were no men schooled in battle in Cyprus or when no commander could be found in Egypt.[1612]

A large influence on the depiction of intercivilisational relations in the *Chronicle* is exerted by the strongly emphasised presence of the Lusignans, who dominated the island and involved the forces of Western countries in a common fight against the enemy. These actions lead the Latin world to unite, but paradoxically they also prompt separate policies towards the Saracens. Namely, the Venetians, disoriented by the consequences that were to directly affect them, started to express uncertainty as to the radical plans of interfering in the internal life of the Muslim community. From this perspective, the colonisation of the island by the Franks had a significant impact on the course of the relations between the Saracens and Cypriots, because it was the Latins who persevered in their intentions to seize further lands, sometimes for the purpose of spreading their faith, and sometimes under its guise. The presence in the *Chronicle* of ideological elements characteristic for the crusaders, evident particularly in the attitudes of Peter I and Peter II, has been proven by Nicolaou-Konnari.[1613] This crusading perspective may be broadened to a colonial perspective because within it there comes to a fore the same dynamic of force, power struggles, sense of superiority and lack of mercy towards 'others', and all this is sanctioned by religious discourse. If the Lusignans were able to occupy Christian Cyprus, why should they not go further, to peoples outside the protection of the same God?

Christian-Muslim contacts in the *Chronicle* show the Cypriots themselves from a different side. They include mainly Franks, Genoese and Venetians, while the Cyprians are overshadowed by the Frankish hegemons, who are shown as needed sometimes as owners of a heritage that is not theirs and sometimes as the victims of Guy and Amaury's old decision, forced to abandon their patrimony and to stay on a small island, facing the terror that the closeness of the followers of Muḥammad provokes in them. They manipulate explanations of their situation, but their statements do not assuage the fact that their presence was forced onto the Rhomaian population.

The atmosphere of the direct clashes described by Leontios is one of cruelty. He shows Muslims as devious people who take advantage of the unfavourable situations the Christians find themselves in, such as plagues,[1614] and who use subterfuge and more or less sophisticated trickery,[1615] and also break oaths. In very few cases do we get the opportunity to find out the names of the unhappy people who lost their lives, while the rest remain nameless.[1616]

[1610] LM V 676.
[1611] Rodriguez, Captivity and Diplomacy, 111.
[1612] LM II 210.
[1613] Nicolaou-Konnari, 'A poor island...'.
[1614] LM II 137.
[1615] LM II 210.
[1616] The most touching situations in which named and unnamed Christians die include: one where Siam Beg cast Philip Provosto off his horse and the Saracens cut off his head and took it to Cairo, LM V 652; the death of a young Flemish furrier, LM V 656; the murder of the falconer Strutos, James of Floury, Thomas Armaratti, craftsman James of Kithraia, Armenian knight Toros of Konsta and Stephen of Vicenzo, the bailiff of Lemesos, LM V 657; death by torture of an envoy LM V 676; the kidnapping of the Catalan, Carceran Suarez, and poor Nicholas, a man who knew the Arab tongue, the killing of everybody along the way, the meeting between a Mamlūk Saracen and a young knight, LM V 683; the stoning of pilgrims by Saracens

4.8. Summary

The element that unifies all the depictions of hostile contacts is always religion: on the material plane implemented via the Saracens' practice of destroying buildings, particularly sacred ones, and on the spiritual plane, by attacking the enemy's religion.

While the *Chronicle* contains frequent references made by each side to the category of God without indicating that 'our God' is meant, there also occur moments of profession of the faith where the Christians directly invoke the glory of Christ's Cross or where a sheikh refers to the might of Islam in his correspondence with King Janus. The chronicler often divides the Muslims into 'baptised' and 'unbaptised',[1617] taking into account the possibility that they might accept the Christian faith. Characteristically, he does not specify whether a given Saracen was baptised in the Greek or the Latin rite.

Also noteworthy is the role of figures such as the sultan, emir or sheikh. Makhairas does not delve into issues such as the inseparability of the sacred and the secular sphere in Islam,[1618] giving only an insight into his own perceptions of the Muslim community, which was actually, as Hamilton Gibb notes, a historiographical trend in the Middle Ages:

> *Mediaeval chronicles [...] suffer from one almost universal defect. They present a narrowly-focussed view of events. Those, the majority, written around the activities of some ruling institution, caliphs, emperors, or sultans, concentrate on the political affairs, undertaken by or relevant to the history of that particular institution, and rarely note things that happened or activities that were going on elsewhere.*[1619]

Naturally the perspective of the *Chronicle* was narrowed down to only one worldview, due to the limitations of its author, who lived in a specific cultural and historical situation. The chronicler provides an example of the untranslatability of one civilisation into another when he tells of the birth of Christianity on the island, of its principles and manifestations, creating a depiction of the community of Cypriots connected by shared values and experiences, without simultaneously making the same effort to understand the principles governing the Muslim world. The Reader, acquainted with descriptions of the travels of Empress Helena, the fates of martyrs and events connected to the development of the young Church, is able to understand what Christian civilisation was for Makhairas, but encounters a distinct obstacle when he tries, with a similar attitude, to find a depiction of the Muslim civilisation in his work.

---

before the eyes of the king, as Makhairas says, 'for entertainment' (διὰ νὰ πάρουν ἀπλαζίριν), LM V 691. This last entry is not featured in the *Chronique d'Amadi* or Strambaldi's chronicle (Dawkins, Notes, 228).

[1617] LM II 193.
[1618] Rosenthal, Political Thought in Medieval Islam, 23.
[1619] Gibb, Studies on the Civilization of Islam, 47.

V. Final conclusions

The depiction of contacts between denominations and religions in Makhairas' *Chronicle* is the product of the author's specific circumstances, formed by the time and place of his life, his family history, personal experiences, knowledge, observations, interests, idiosyncrasies, his strategy of functioning the reality he encountered, his degree of knowledge of the Cypriot dialect and his ability to shape the narrative using it, and also the availability of particular documents and various types of texts (literary, theological, philosophical) in medieval Cyprus. The chronicler, who lived in the fifteenth century, casts a retrospective glance at the origins that were significant for the shaping of the Cypriots' identity and religiosity: the birth of Christianity on the island (fourth century) and the moment of Cyprus' occupation by Guy of the Latin Lusignan dynasty (twelfth century), organising the remaining narrative in chronological, 'dynastic' order, with elements of a 'circular view of time' (time measured in feast days, announcements of future processions).

The concepts used to analyse the *Chronicle* and drawn from the postcolonial toolkit allowed the delimitation of the significant, focal interpretational planes: Leontios' geography of the Mediterranean Basin, the image of the 'other' or 'others', the ways in which individuals and communities come into contact, changing over time, the features of 'colonial' literature revealed in the narrative layer, and also the identity of the author himself. The concepts considered have helped the author delve deeper into the phenomenon of the separateness (in terms of religion, geography, teleology and axiology, that is differing paradigms) of Christian and Muslim identities.

5.1. Imagined geography in the *Chronicle*

Individual rulers of the Lusignan dynasty were able to carry out their crusading plans (religious and economic) thanks to the annexation for their purposes of an island situated in a strategic part of the Mediterranean Sea, which was simultaneously at the sidelines of the Byzantine world. Cyprus' peripheral location with respect to Byzantium is indicated by mentions that it lies near Jerusalem (ἦτον κοντὰ τὸ Ἰεροσόλυμαν εἰς τὴν Κύπρον, LM I 26) and Turkey (ἀμμέ ἡ Τουρκία κοντά μας εἶνε, LM II 264),[1621] and thus at the juncture of two mighty civilisations, as well as by Guy's words addressed to sultan Saladin, ruler of Egypt and Syria: 'by God's grace we are neighbours' (μὲ τὴν χάριν τοῦ θεοῦ εἴμεστεν γειτόνοι, LM I 22). Makhairas also states that 'near Cyprus' (κοντὰ εἰς τὴν Κύπρον) is Beyrout (Βερούτιν), which lies 'one hundred seventy sea miles' (ρο' μιλία τῆς θαλάσσου) away (LM II 177). The island of Rhodes is located closer to Turkish Adalia than Cyprus is (κοντὰ τῆς Ἀταλείας παρὰ τὴν Κύπρον, LM II 135). Makhairas' conviction about the strategic location of Cyprus at the crossroads of pilgrimage routes is evident in the description of the peregrinations of Margaret de Lusignan (Μαργαρίτα Λουζουνία), the spouse of lord Manuel Kantakouzenos (τοῦ κυροῦ Μανουὴλ τοῦ Κατακουζηνοῦ), the basileus of Morea (τοῦ βασιλέως τοῦ Μορέως), who first set off from Cyprus on a pilgrimage (νὰ προσκυνήσῃ) to the Holy Sepulchre (τὸν ἁγιώτατον τάφον), then returned to Cyprus, and afterwards departed for Constantinople (LM III 345, 351). In the *Chronicle* we find few references to contacts with the Greek world apart from several episodes (the appearance of St Helena on Cyprus in LM I 3–8, the matrimonial proposal by John V Palaiologos in LM III 344, King John's wedding with Helena Palaiologina in 1441 in LM VI 709–710).

[1621] Also LM III 370, already mentioned above.

The island's location on Leontios map is in a sense 'hybrid', because it combines aspects of periphery and centrality. Cyprus, 'squeezed' into a space surrounded to a large extent by Muslim territory, perceived by them as a 'rock grown from the sea' (μία πέτρα φυτεμένη εἰς τὴν θάλασσαν, LM V 664) and, interestingly, viewed in the same way by Cypriot Franks (νὰ ἀπλικέψουν εἰς μίαν πέτραν μέσα εἰς τὴν θάλασσαν, LM II 106; εἴμεστεν ἀπλικιμένοι μέσον τοὺς ἀπίστους Τούρκους καὶ Σαρακηνούς, LM III 370), is nevertheless a centre of events and a place where various influences mix. Outside the island's boundaries extends the 'world' that the king's sons so wish to see ('δοῦν τὸν κόσμον, LM I 79). It is from different quarters of this unspecified vastness that saints whose fame later spread 'all around the world' (εἰς οὗλον τὸν κόσμον, LM I 33) arrived on Cyprus. The warriors recruited by Thibald in Venice (LM III 559) were world-famous, while John Palaiologos' daughter was said by envoys to be 'one of the first among beautiful women that the whole earth has issued forth' (ἀπού τὲς πρῶτες ὄμορφες γυναῖκες ὅπου ἔχει οὗλη ἡ γῆ τοῦ κόσμου, LM III 346). A comparison of Cyprus' tininess with the world's immensity appears in a statement by Peter I, who says:

> *Would that God had made me be king of Cyprus with my honour, rather than king of all the world and be put to shame.*[1622] (LM II 251)

A more evident binary between 'centre' and 'periphery' may be found in descriptions of Cyprus itself, where a clearly defined centre was formed by towns (Ammochostos, Lemesos, Lefkosia, Kerynia and Paphos) because that was there that the main events played out, while the peripheries covered a large number of villages famed for the presence of relics and as resting places of saints and martyrs. The chronicler uses spatial designations to sometimes bring out the Frank universe, and at other times, that of the Cyprians. In Leontios' topography we encounter only the names of towns and villages and their vestigial descriptions. There is no direct reference – in the sense of an indication of the mountainous features of the area and giving the name itself – to the Troodos mountains, which are important for the island's religious history, even though the names of villages located in these mountains do appear, including Galata and Omodos (Γαλάτα, Ὅμοδος; LM II 238, 375, IV 620).[1623] Sporadically, in addition to larger islands such as Rhodes and Chios, the *Chronicle* mentions smaller islets along Cyprus' coastline, such as Oxen Island (τὸ νησσὶ τῶν Βοϊδίων) and St Catarina island (τὸ νησσὶ εἰς τὴν Σάντα Κατερίνας),[1624] both in LM III 362, or along the coast of Asia, such as Crambousa (Ραοῦζε) in LM II 171 and Rosetta (τὸ νησσὶ τοῦ Ρισίου) in LM III 288.

Long-term cohabitation of Greeks and Latins in the same land did not involve the replacement of one culture by the other, or the perseverance of two independent cultures alongside one another, but a superimposition of one perspective (Latin) on another (Greek). A reading of the *Chronicle* offers an interesting, rich world in which these two cultures, Western and Eastern, co-create and share one space, intermingling in some places, and remaining impermeable to foreign elements in others, but always dependent on each other in some sense.

Space in the *Chronicle* is also closely connected with time, which is in accordance with the concept of 'literary chronotope' by Mikhail Bakhtin, who, reflecting on time-space in the literary work, states:

> *We understand the chronotope as a formally constitutive category of literature [...]. In the literary artistic chronotope, spatial and temporal indicators are fused into one carefully thought-out, concrete whole. Time, as it were, thickens, takes on flesh, becomes artistically visible; likewise, space becomes charged and responsive to the movements of time, plot and history. The intersection of axes and fusion of indicators characterises the artistic chronotope.*[1625]

The designations of time often used by Leontios (apart from ἡμέρα, καθημερινόν, νύκτα, μονονυκτίς, μηνός, ὥρα, ἔτη) include the nouns: 'year' (χρόνος), given with the relevant date, and 'season', 'occasion' and 'time' (καιρός).[1626]

[1622] 'Νἄχεν ποίσειν ὁ θεὸς νἄχασταιν ῥήγας τῆς Κύπρου τιμημένος καὶ ὄχι ῥήγας ὅλου τοῦ κόσμου καὶ νἆμαι ἀντροπιασμένος.'
[1623] Cf. Dawkins, Notes, 129 (ref. to Galata).
[1624] On this island stood the church of St Catarina (Dawkins, Notes, 153).
[1625] Bakhtin, Dialogic Imagination, 223. An interesting position focused on Bakhtin's concept is Bakhtin's Theory of the Literary Chronotope. Outside from the novel, this theory has been applied among others in Sykes, Time and Space in Haggai-Zechariah.
[1626] The word 'time' (καιρός) is combined in the *Chronicle* with other parts of speech: 'how long' (πόσον καιρόν, LM I 1), 'so much time' (τόσον καιρόν, in LM I 7, II 157), 'at that time' (-εἰς- τὸν καιρὸν ἐκεῖνον; ἐκεῖνον τὸν καιρόν, LM I 70, 73, 77, 84, II 110, 116, 218), 'many years' (πολλὺν καιρόν, LM I 78, II 126, 130, III 317, 552, 563), 'shortly after' (εἰς ὀλλίγον καιρόν,

When writing about the empty Cypriot land at the beginning of the *Chronicle*, Makhairas combines this clear message with the information that the depopulation lasted thirty-six years, thus exacerbating the image of emptiness and multiplying its significance. He emphasises, however, that the repopulation occurred very rapidly, which should be treated as a positive effect of resolving an existential, spiritual and material crisis. The chronicler links this strongly accented start of a new era in the island's history with the declaration that this state of affairs would last 'until the fullness of time' (ἕως τῆς συντελείας) and 'for all times' (εἰς τοὺς αἰῶνας).[1627] The last expression is strongly connected both with the long duration of the earthly world and its end. When Makhairas voices the wish that memory of Rekouniatos and Andronikos should last for 'ages' (αἰωνία), he means the period over which the human ability to preserve knowledge operates. The land of Cyprus is filled with bodies of saints from the past, whose lives Leontios sketches in a brief way that allows to strengthen, via contrast, the weight of their constant presence after death, manifesting itself 'to this day' (ἕως τὴν σήμμερον, LM I 33; μέχρι τὴν σήμμερον, LM I 36). This expression is also used many times in other instances not related to religion (LM I 28–29, 87, II 112, III 473, IV 622). Similarly, the crosses of the thieves are sanctified because they lay next to the Holy Cross 'for such a long time: three hundred and nine years' (τόσον καιρὸν χρόνους τθ´, LM I 7).

The settlements named after saints mentioned in the *Chronicle* resonate with the liturgical calendar used by Leontios. Celebrations are held in a concrete space (mass, processions), which helps call up the desired past or present situations and at the same time, to look forward to their future celebration. This shows the repetitiveness of the very act of celebration and remembrance.

Although Makhairas' work is a chronicle, and as such it recounts with specific dates real events from the history of Cyprus, the degree of condensation of some content, that is the employment of time and space in the narrative, or in other words, 'imagined time-space' depends solely on the author, who lends a supernatural character to historical sequences, giving them a Providentialist explanation. It is the chronicler who fuses past, present and future in such a way that they remain co-dependent, although at the beginning of the *Chronicle* he explicitly separates them one from the other, deciding that the narrative is the only connector and the only link guaranteeing the flow of images and content between them.

5.2. Material reality: tradition, heritage and gifts in the *Chronicle*

In the descriptions of various nations in the *Chronicle* – the Cyprians, Franks, Genoese, Venetians, Egyptians and Turks – it is possible to identify elements that indicate their internal cohesion. Affiliation with a given religion assigns these groups to the Christian or to the Muslim community. The Christians' participation in the lives of different churches divides them into two basic groups: Greeks and Latins. That said, the Latin community is so diverse that the factors integrating each of its subgroups differ.

LM I 37, II 171, III 283, V 641), 'as happened earlier' (ὡς γοιὸν τὸν περασμένον καιρόν; κατὰ τὸν πρῶτον καιρόν, LM II 154), 'since old times' (ἀποῦ παλαιὸν καιρόν, LM II 253), 'in times gone by' (τὸν διαβόντα καιρόν, LM II 255), 'some time' (κἄποσον καιρόν, LM II 257), 'appropriate occasion' (καιρὸς ἐπιτήδειος) in LM II 260, 'bad time' (ἕνας κακὸς καιρός; διὰ κακὸν καιρόν, LM III 285, 382), 'at the right time' (εἰς τὸν πρεπάμενον καιρόν, LM V 686), 'at the same time' (τὸν αὐτὸν καιρόν, LM II 280, III 584, VI 706), as a measure of time that is slightly harder to define. This last noun also appears in expressions such as: 'from time to time' (κατὰ καιρόν, LM I 9), 'if time allows us' (ὡς γοιὸν ὁ καιρὸς νὰ τὸ δώσῃ, LM II 97), 'until the time' (ὡς τὸν καιρόν, LM II 113), 'in advance' (πρὶν τὸν καιρόν, LM II 190, 251), 'in time' (κατὰ τὸν καιρόν, LM II 200), 'at the set time' (κάθα καιρόν, LM III 550), 'for some time' (ἕως τὸν καιρόν, LM II 200), 'since a longer time' (ἀποῦ καιρόν, LM III 584) and in phrases together with verbs such as: the time 'came' (ἔφτασεν, LM II 278, ἐποῖκεν LM III 587), 'went by' (ἐδιάβην) in LM III 319, 443, 'happened' ('βρέθην, LM II 260), 'will come' (θέλει ἔρτειν LM II 225, III 374), 'pass' (διαβαίνοντα, LM II 277, III 544, 563, 567), 'look forward' (ἐγύρευγεν, LM III 407) in the sense 'wait for an opportunity'. Once, in LM II 157, time personified makes an appearance: 'everything that time brings to the kingdom year after year' (ὅσα φέρει ὁ καιρὸς χρόνον πρὸς χρόνον εἰς τὴν ῥηγάδα). Unfavourable circumstances are expressed by the chronicler using the sentences 'time does not favour it' (δὲν τὸ διδεῖ ὁ καιρός, LM II 275, III 348, 371; δὲν τὸ φέρνει ὁ καιρός, LM III 348). Time and space are interconnected in the expressions: 'at the right place and time' (χωρὶς νὰ ἦνε καιρὸς καὶ τόπος, LM II 230), 'to preserve memory about this time and place' (διὰ ἀθύμησιν καιροῦ καὶ τόπου, LM II 274) and 'without saying what I have to say at the right time and place' (χωρὶς τὸ ἔχω νὰ εἰπῶ τίντα τόπος καὶ καιρὸς νὰ ἦνε, LM III 321). The passage of time is shown in the phrase 'from day to day' (ἡμέραν πρὸς ἡμέραν, LM II 260). An interesting adjective is 'long lasting' (παντοτεινός), used in MS O, LM II 264, when the endurance of pleasure derived from contact with dogs is discussed. See Dawkins (Ed., transl.), Ἐξήγησις/ Recital, 244 (fn. 3, 4); Παυλίδης (Ed.), Λεοντίου Μαχαιρᾶ Χρονικόν, 196 (fn. 1, 2). In LM III 296 the word 'καιρός' was used in the meaning of 'spring'.
[1627] LM I 8.

The Orthodox Christian community in the *Chronicle* is united by what may be called 'tradition', though Makhairas does not directly write about tradition itself. He does not use any word such as 'παράδοση' to express it.[1628] Although the implications of events before the schism (the work of St Helena, saints, martyrs) should be considered equally important for both churches, and the actual depiction of the Greeks should be examined only starting from passage LM I 12, which concerns the twelfth century, the chronicler does indicate the continuity of the Cyprians' 'tradition', which should be termed 'Byzantine' after the role played in its establishment by the saints Helena and St Constantine, Byzantine emperors particularly worshipped in the Orthodox Church, and also due to the natural adoption by the Cypriot Rhomaioi – by living in Cyprus – of the early Christian legacy (composed of events of a religious nature, acts of martyrdom, manifestations of holiness, miraculous phenomena and voices from heaven). Furthermore, since Leontios emphasises the fact that the thief's cross was sanctified through its three hundred and nine year-long proximity to Christ's Cross in Jerusalem, the sanctification of the island must have been still greater, since the Relic was present on it for nine centuries, from the visit of St Helena to the coming of Guy de Lusignan. Makhairas, extremely proud of Cyprus' past, seemingly and diplomatically grants the Latins the right to participate in the spiritual wealth of the Greeks, but in actual fact makes available to them only certain content and images, emphasising their true 'Cyprian' affiliation. The past remains set in matter, in the remains of saints, numerous graves, monastic and church buildings and in the earth, pockmarked by burial places: in other words in physical reality, which endures 'to this day' and will endure 'until the fullness of time', which is consistent with the Orthodox concept of tradition as universal and eternal.[1629] And it is on this matter that Orthodox 'spirituality' was built.

The material aspect is important also when searching the text of the *Chronicle* for the depiction of factors responsible for cohesion of the Latin community. In this case Makhairas usually cites the concept of inheritance. He says already at the very start (LM I 1) that the legacy must pass successively from parents to children. Reversing this order would be like 'picking unripe fruit' (καταλυοῦμεν τοὺς καρποὺς ἄγουρους). We encounter 'inheritance' in the material sense, in the meaning of everything possessed by a given person or persons (who remain in a particular relationship with others through their community or through kinship) in the mention about transferring 'all the goods' (ὅλα […] τὰ καλά) and 'heritage' (κλερονομιές) of the Templars to the Hospitallers (LM I 15). Peter I's envoys to the pope argued for the strict rules of inheritance in LM II 106, when the former was defending his right to the throne from being usurped by Hugh de Lusignan. In this case, the scope of the word 'inheritance' includes 'houses' (σπιτία), 'relatives' (συγκενάδες) and 'heritage' (κλερονομιές), and all goods are inherited by (κλερονομίσουν) 'the living children of the deceased' (τὰ παιδία τοὺς ἀποθαμμένους τὰ εὑρίσκουνται ζωντανά). When King Peter I received a message about the betrayal committed by his wife Eleanora, he started to lament that this had occurred as a punishment for his desire to gain new lands instead of being satisfied with the 'natural [inheritance] that his parents had given him' (τὸ ψυσικὸν τὸ μοῦ ἔδωκεν ἀπὸ τοὺς γονεῖς μου). In passage LM II 277 some knights stated that the first Franks to arrive on Cyprus had relinquished their old inheritance, and so had to build new foundations for their functioning. The culmination of this process was the institution of lesser 'agreements and laws' (σασμοὺς καὶ νόμους μεσόν τους), which in turn helped to establish 'customs' (συνηθία) connected to their common faith (ὁ εἷς ὑπὲρ τοῦ ἄλλου εἰς πίστιν). Liberty is also inherited (τόσην ἐλευθερίαν), which was violated by Peter I, who imprisoned Sir Henry and Sir James, who was 'his first recognised heir' (πρῶτος ἐκδεχόμενος τοῦ ψουμιοῦ τοῦ). Another material element uniting the Frankish community is the texts they use, such as the *Assizes*, lesser laws and papal letters.

[1628] The role of the words 'παράδοση' in the sense of 'tradition' and 'παραδίδω' in the sense of 'give', 'offer' and 'do good' is examined in Bebis, Święta Tradycja, 13. The verb 'παραδίδω' (also 'cede') appears for example in Peter II's letter addressed to the constable, in which he asks for the Kerynian castle to be entrusted to Luke d'Antiaume (LM III 513). The chronicler uses the same verb in descriptions of actions connected to giving something, such as those where the regent transferred (ἐπαράδωκεν) the kingdom to Peter II (LM III 323), the constable handed (ἐπαράδωκεν) the keys to the Kerynian castle to the queen (LM III 462), and many passages later (ἐξαναπαράδωκεν) offered Kerynia to the captain during mass (LM III 525); Thibald assigned (ἐπαράδωκεν) positions to various people (LM III 560), Peter II submitted (ἐπαράδωκεν) Thibald, Alexopoulos and the Franks involved in the intrigue to judgement by the viscount and judges, who were to decide on the type of death they were to suffer (LM III 574), and Peter II entrusted his mother to Sir Francis Cassantse (LM III 589). In an intercivilisational perspective, Peter II gave (ἐπαράδωκεν) emir Takka the keys to Adalia and the latter promised to serve him (LM II 125). All these incidents are connected by a special shade of meaning related to the transfer of possessions or duties to someone, placement under somebody's care, which may be indirectly linked to its meaning as tradition, but is a purely linguistic issue. In one instance, this verb is used in the sense 'yield his spirit' with reference to King Janus (LM VI 703).

[1629] Bebis, Święta Tradycja, 18.

The Latins in the *Chronicle* often reached for the inheritance of others without scruple. For example, a Genoese admiral who wished to conquer the island cunningly provoked Peter II in LM III 425, saying that his uncles had 'divided' (ἐδιαμοιράσαν) his kingdom, and so he would become 'poor and deprived of his heritage' (πτωχὸς καὶ ἄκλερος). Also the Genoese in LM III 489 are suspected of the desire to deprive him of his legacy (ἔχετε τὸ θέλημα νὰ καθαρίσετε [...] ἀπὸ τὴν κληρονομίαν του).

Material heritage, connecting people into one community, belongs to a specific space, which is why by leaving that space one also abandons that heritage. The promise of a tangible inheritance may also convince somebody to move from one place to another, which is why the sultan advises Guy to populate Cyprus with Latins in this way (LM I 25–26). The strongest material connotations of heritage are expressed with respect to the Lusignans.

Another physical element that connects characters, which is just as strongly emphasised by Makhairas, is kinship. The Genoese, for instance, as Latins who differ from Cypriot Franks, are connected by – rarely mentioned in the *Chronicle*, however – 'ethnicity (kin group, people)' (γένος) in LM II 153 and V 685 and 'blood ties' (ἀπὲ τὸ αἷμαν μας) in LM II 146. This is not an exclusive attribute of the Latins' depiction, however, because Makhairas himself, a Rhomaios, underlines his kinship with his father and brothers. The Genoese and also the Venetians use many signs that identify them and make them part of their community: namely, in LM III 436 we also encounter the White Genoese (Makhairas does not write about White Venetians). As a result of significant dispersal and mobility, the Genoese define themselves via affiliation with the merchant community and contacts with Genoa (and Venetians, with Venice), their mother-place.

The word 'heritage' is used only once with respect to the Muslims, when in LM V 664 the sheikh of Damascus states that King Janus' people wish to 'loot the heritage' (νὰ δηγοῦν τὲς κλερονομίες) of the Saracens. The term 'Muslim nation' (τὸ γένος τῶν Μουσθλουμάνων) also makes a single appearance, in LM II 196. The Egyptians derive their sense of continuity from the chronicles of the sultans in which their history is recorded.

The material connection between the communities, in particular between civilisations, is gifts exchanged by rulers via their envoys. Particular generosity is demonstrated by Muslims. Saladin himself instructs Guy in LM I 25 that it is better to give 'generous gifts' (δόσια αὐτάρκετα) that attract great people (νὰ φέρῃς μεγάλους ἀνθρώπους), than miserly ones (ὀλλίγα), which alienate the rest (νὰ χάσῃς τὸ δελοιπόν). Christians receive gifts 'from the sultan' (τὰ κανισκία τοῦ σουλτάνου) for example in LM V 646. The lord of Monovgat, knowing that Peter I is heading towards Ousgat, is anxious and sends him 'gifts' (κανισκία) (LM II 125). Takka offers Peter II's envoys part of a 'silver tableware set' (μερτικὸν ἀγκεῖα ἀργυρά), including an 'extremely precious and very heavy silver chalice that the Turks usually used during feasts' (ἕναν ποτήριν ἀργυρὸν πολλὰ τιμημένον καὶ πολλὰ βαρύν, τὸ ἔχουν οἱ Τοῦρκοι εἰς τὴν παρδιάβασιν καὶ μεσώννουν τὸ κρασίν) (LM III 368). Emir Melek was also generous (LM II 144). In LM V 647 John Podocataro presented one of the Saracens with 'precious gifts' (πλούσια κανισκία), and later together with Thomas Provosto in LM V 661 gave further 'suitable presents' (ἀκριβὰ κανισκία).

Matter is particularly important to Makhairas because it permits storage and the strengthening of spiritual heritage and culture in human awareness, as well as communication between civilisations. Far less effective is memory, which when not fixed in writing has no chance of survival.

5.3. Depiction of denominations and religions in the *Chronicle*

The narrative about the Orthodox components of the world presented in the *Chronicle* has the most markedly spiritual nature. A large role in it is played by references to high-ranking church dignitaries such as the patriarchs of Constantinople and Antioch (LM I 40, 77), and also references to representatives of the Greek clergy and to legends about numerous saints and martyrs.

Makhairas devotes far less attention to the spiritual dimension of Catholicism, which appears on the island together with the settlers, and rather in the context of their annexation of the Greek clergy's estates and possessions than in terms of doctrine. The exception is a mention of two ways of pardoning sins (LM I 73) and the large emphasis placed on the importance of mass (LM II 172, III 523). Information is woven into the *Chronicle* narrative about Latin priests and Roman church buildings. A significant role in this optic is played by specific persons of popes, who primarily influence decisions of a political nature. Subordination to the pope places the Lusignans next to the Genoese and the Venetians, which makes it possible to recreate on the basis of the *Chronicle* the natural, though not overly emphasised connection between them.

The last of the groups discussed, the Muslims, is defined by the chronicler to a large extent as – via references to Christians – unchristian, and thus composed of 'infidel' individuals, rather than as having clear features of a separate religion. It is only the intervention of the Damascene sage who advises King Janus of the greatness and importance of the sultan and who explicitly cites the Qur'ān that introduces elements of the Islamic faith into the narrative.

5.4. Function of religion in the *Chronicle*

The perspective adopted by Leontios is theocentric. Religion, as a main element of the narrative, holds specific functions in the *Chronicle*. It is an important component of tradition and a key element that defines a civilisation, determining primarily the identity of Cypriots (Franks and Cyprians) and the inhabitants of Muslim lands. It impacts the perception of time because in Leontios' work we primarily encounter the liturgical calendar. The chronicler explains the course of events and interprets various phenomena with the help of religion and it is the point of departure in forming judgements about individuals and whole communities. It is most fully expressed in the material, practical, experiential and emotional spheres (cf. Roderick Ninian Smart, pp. 20, 78).

Life in a space of religious references mobilises the faithful to intensive practice of thanksgiving and supplicatory prayer. Makhairas expresses this action through various verbs: 'pray' (προσεύχομαι), 'worship' (προσκυνέω) and 'beg' (παρακαλῶ) and the phrase 'offer prayers' (ποιέω παρακάλεσες). The expected effect of such activities is the revelation of God's will, as expressed in the sentence 'the monk asked God to reveal himself to him' (Ὁ μοναχὸς ἐζήτησεν τοῦ θεοῦ νὰ τοῦ ἀποκαλύψῃ, LM I 76).

The God of Christians is presented in the *Chronicle* not only as the Creator of matter (heaven and earth), but also as the source of life. The chronicler writes of the 'Living God' (τοῦ θεοῦ τοῦ ζῶντος, LM I 5, 13) twice. The conviction that He has the ability to influence life expectancy is conveyed in the words of Emperor John Palaiologos' envoys, who wish Peter II that the Lord may 'multiply [his] years' (ν' αὐξήσῃ τὰ ἔτη, LM III 346). Creative force, giving man the power to create, is the domain of the Holy Spirit, because it is through its inspiration that Leontios writes his *Chronicle*. The Holy Cross is 'life-giving' (ζωοποιός) (LM I 5, 8, 67, 70–71, 73–75, II 114), and in addition to 'giving life' on the metaphysical level, seen in the healing of people and the Christians community through their physical and moral restoration, manifests a certain 'vitality' and 'decision-making ability' because, as we read in LM I 68, it 'came down from above of itself' (μοναχός του ἦλθεν κάτω τοῦ ὄρου), which happened in 1426 when the Saracens arrived. Through the presence of the Cross the community of Cyprians and then the Cypriots is constantly revitalised.

God, who in Makhairas' world is clearly transcendental, shapes man's cognitive faculties. Thanks to him St Helena 'recognised' (ἀγρώνισεν) the Holy Cross, distinguishing it from the crosses of the thieves (LM I 5). It was he who redirected the attention of the Saracens, providing them with a distraction (ἔδωκέν τους [...] σκόλισιν) to let Diomidios steal away the head of St Triphyllios (LM I 35). John de Monstri addresses Peter I as the 'Majesty whom God endowed with a clear mind' (ἡ ἀφεντιά σου ὅπου σοῦ ἐχάρισεν ὁ θεὸς τὸν νοῦν καθαρόν, LM II 273). Irene, the daughter of John Palaiologos, is endowed by God with imposing knowledge (τόσην γνῶσιν), which fortified via a careful education (παίδευσιν) is reflected in the Byzantine princess' skills, such as proficiency in writing (διδασκαλεμένη γραμμάτων, LM III 346). In MS O we read that God has the power to enlighten (νὰ μᾶς/ σᾶς φωτίσῃ) man (LM II 252, 253).[1630] Next to the mind, it is the heart that is the centre for reception of supernatural power. The Creator 'hardened' (ἐσκλέρυνεν) the heart of the Pharaoh and did the same to Peter I (LM II 189). He can make 'the same that is on the lips' (ὡς γοιὸν τὸ εἶπαν τὰ χείλη σου) be in the heart, which is why one knight says to the Genoese admiral Peter de Campo Fregoso (LM III 491) that it would be good 'if [God] made a window in every [man]' (μακάρι νἄχεν ποίσειν τοῦ πα(σα)νοῦ παραθύριν), 'so that one could open it and look at their hearts' (νὰ τ' ἀνοῖγαν νὰ 'θωροῦσαν τὲς καρδιές τους) and check 'whether things are

---

[1630] Dawkins (Ed., transl.), Ἐξήγησις/ Recital, 232 (fn. 1 and 5); Παυλίδης (Ed.), Λεοντίου Μαχαιρά Χρονικόν, 182 (fn. 2 and 6).

5.4. FUNCTION OF RELIGION IN THE *CHRONICLE*

as the lips say they are' (ἂν ἔνι ὡς γοιὸν λαλοῦν τὰ χείλη). Finally, the spirit inspired both the mind and the heart of Thibald, which is explored extensively in Subchapter 2.4 (LM III 556). Satan reaches human beings through the same way, as he 'hardened' (ἐσκλέρυνεν) the hearts of Amaury's supporters (LM I 52) and 'entered' (ἐμπῆκεν) the heart of John of Morphou, awaking in him the forbidden love of Queen Eleanora (LM II 239). Both these faculties, mind and heart, played an important role in the thought of early Christian theologians. Evagrius Ponticus (fourth century) and Maximus the Confessor (sixth century) may serve as examples: the first placed the mind at the centre of his deliberations, while the second made the heart the source of anthropology.[1631]

In the *Chronicle*, God influences events through their causal connections, which is why his depiction is interpreted in this book as a depiction of 'Providence', although the chronicler does not use this term. The most evident example of providential mechanics is 'God's response' (ἦτον παραχώρησις θεοῦ) to human sin. Persons in the depicted world employ the conviction that God works in such a way to strengthen the force and effectiveness of their statements. They invoke God (θεός) or the Lord (Κύριος) (LM I 32, 35, 40). They refer to him (or other persons of the Holy Trinity) as 'almighty' (παντοδύναμος, LM I 14, II 243), 'omnibenevolent' (πανάγαθος, LM II 253[1632]) and 'most holy' (παναγίος, LM I 2, II 254,[1633] III 512). Both in the comments of the narrator and in statements by figures of the *Chronicle* there appear many references to his will,[1634] and particularly to Divine features and attributes (such as knowledge,[1635] mercy,[1636] the ability to judge and assess human behaviour[1637]), actions (such as revealing himself,[1638] influencing human decisions and cognitive faculties,[1639] bringing help,[1640] preserving,[1641] saving towns and objects from destruction and individuals from death,[1642] granting victory,[1643] meting out punishment[1644]) and to his chief emotion, namely anger.[1645] Less frequent are references to the Holy Spirit.[1646] God also plays an important state-building role because he designates a specific person to be the ruler, as Peter I observes.[1647] People react to events with faith in God[1648] and by enriching their knowledge,[1649] and also often transgress the Divine commandments (ἀπὸ τὴν μισητείαν διαβαίννουν τὴν ἐντολὴν τοῦ θεοῦ, LM II 273). According to such a perspective even unfavourable circumstances may have a deeper significance, which is seen in the passage in which Makhairas writes of a 'blessed plague of locusts' (εὐλογημένη ἀκρίδα, LM I 66). Great importance is assigned to doing something 'in the name' of the Holy Trinity or one of its persons (LM I 1, 15, II 172, 198, 241, 279, III 392, 509, 539), and even of the Holy Cross (LM II 114), speaking this name (LM I 35), praising it (LM I 28) and swearing an oath on it (LM II 278). Muslims also use the expression 'in the name of God' (LM V 662, 664). Sometimes there appear in the text abstract references to the mechanism of influencing events and reacting to them. For example, the chronicler personifies fate, understood as a providential instance, in the sentence 'the Saracens asked God to send somebody who would bring peace, but fate did not wish it' (παρακαλοῦν τὸν θεὸν οἱ Σαρακηνοὶ νὰ

[1631] Meyendorff, Teologia bizantyjska, 87–89.
[1632] In MS O. See Dawkins (Ed., transl.), Ἐξήγησις/ Recital, 232 (fn. 5); Παυλίδης (Ed.), Λεοντίου Μαχαιρά Χρονικόν, 186 (fn. 6).
[1633] In MS O. See Dawkins (Ed., transl.), Ἐξήγησις/ Recital, 234 (fn. 1); Παυλίδης (Ed.), Λεοντίου Μαχαιρά Χρονικόν, 188 (fn. 1).
[1634] The phrase 'ἐθέλησεν ὁ θεὸς ν᾿ ἁγιτιάσῃ' in LM V 631.
[1635] The phrase 'ὁ θεὸς τὸ γινώσκει' in LM III 566.
[1636] The expression 'διὰ τὸ ἔλεος τοῦ θεοῦ' in LM III 320, 521.
[1637] God as a judge (κριστής) whose ability is judgement (κρισίς) in LM I 50, 52, III 574; 'ὁ θεὸς νὰ ποίσῃ κρίσιν' in LM II 271; God who assigns value (ὁ θεὸς νὰ μὲν τὸν ἀξιώσῃ) in LM III 566, 'ὁ θεὸς εἶνε κριτής' in LM V 651.
[1638] The expression 'δι᾿ ἀποκαλύψεως θεοῦ' in LM I 34.
[1639] Phrases 'ἐχάρισεν ὁ θεὸς τὸν νοῦν καθαρόν' in LM II 273; 'νὰ βάλῃ ὁ θεὸς εἰς τὴν καρδιάν σου' in LM III 566; 'ἐθέλησεν ὁ θεὸς νὰ σηκώσῃ τὸν νοῦν' in LM V 677.
[1640] The expression 'με καταυγόδιον βοηθῶντος θεοῦ' in LM II 236.
[1641] The phrase 'νὰ τὸν μαντενιάζῃ ὁ θεός' in LM III 574.
[1642] Phrases 'ὁ θεὸς ἐγλύτωσέν το' in LM II 234; 'ὁ θεὸς νὰ μὲ σκεπάσῃ' in LM III 566.
[1643] Phrases 'μὲ τὴν δύναμιν τοῦ θεοῦ ἐνίκησέν' in LM II 126; 'ὁ θεὸς ἔδωκεν τὸ νῖκος' in LM II 195; 'ἔχω θάρος εἰς τὸν θεὸν νὰ μοῦ δώσῃ τὸ νίκος' in LM II 230; 'βοηθῶντος τοῦ θεοῦ ἐνίκησαν' in LM III 317.
[1644] The phrase 'ὁ θεὸς ἐπαιδεύσεν με διὰ νὰ τζακκίσῃ τὴν σουπερπίαν μου' in LM II 251.
[1645] Phrases 'ὀργιστῇ τους ὁ θεός' in LM I 52; 'ὁ θεὸς ἀγκρίστην μετά μας' in LM IV 623.
[1646] The phrase 'νὰ σᾶς δώσῃ χάριν καὶ γνῶσιν τὸ ἅγιον πνεῦμα' in LM II 251.
[1647] Peter I observes twice in one statement that God has appointed him to be the ruler (Ὁ θεὸς ἐποῖκεν με ρήγαν τῆς Κύπρου; ποίσειν ὁ θεὸς νάχάσταιν ρήγας τῆς Κύπρου) in LM II 251.
[1648] The phrase 'θαροῦμεν εἰς τὸν θεόν' in LM III 520.
[1649] The phrase ''Εμάθαμεν διὰ τὸ ἔλεος τοῦ θεοῦ' in LM III 521.

ξαποστείλη τινὰν νὰ τοὺς ποίσουν ἀγάπη, καὶ ἡ τύχη δὲν ἔθελεν, LM V 682). Elsewhere, the narrator states: 'may their way [Saracens – note M.G.] be accursed' (ἐπῆγαν εἰς τὸ ἀνάθεμμαν, LM V 695).

In the *Chronicle*, religion serves as the most important narrative element used in the description of the 'colonial' situation and the clash of different worlds.

5.5. 'Others' in the *Chronicle*

The episode describing Cyprus' occupation by the Franks, and thus signalising a 'colonial' situation, commences the *Chronicle* narrative that provides a sequence of images showing the process of 'othering' (in the meaning used by Spivak)[1650] of certain individuals or groups versus others. Makhairas constructs the portrait of the Lusignans as others in order to more fully define the religious and cultural identity of the Cyprians through this otherness. He places the Genoese in such a position as to bring the Franks and the Cyprians teleologically closer (in terms of a commonality of goals), and give a deeper dimension to the Muslims' otherness. He needs the Muslims as others in order to unite all Christians (Greeks and Latins) in recognition of their common religious identity. Finally, the Greeks are others for the Templars, Guy and Peter de Thomas. From this perspective, identity has many shades, depending on the relative perception of differences. Makhairas also 'examines himself' in his *Chronicle*, creating a depiction of his own understanding of the Cypriot historical reality, and also addresses the potential reader as an other, seeing himself in the 'mirror' of the reader's awareness. The Lacanian 'big Other', the symbolical object that each 'colonised' must confront, is the collectively understood community of the 'Franks' and what they brought with them, namely the French language (Makhairas chooses to use the Cypriot dialect instead of the French language which he knows) and the *Assizes*. For the Greeks, moral otherness is represented in its various shades by the Templars, Genoese and Muslims.

Specific scopes of meaning are also held by words expressing 'otherness', such as ξένος, ξενικός and their derivatives, often used by the chronicler to designate 'foreigners' (LM II 192, 258, III 310, 486, 510, V 685). Foreigners (ξενικός) came with the Lusignans to monitor matters on Cyprus (LM II 99). The author of the *Chronicle* uses this term for Syrians who are killed, for example (LM II 111). The Rhomaioi Alexopoulos is an 'outlander' (ξένος), as he comes from a place other than Cyprus, which in his case is a mitigating circumstance, because he is 'uninformed' (ἄπρακτος) about the situation and evidently, according to Makhairas, has the right to be so (LM III 573). The Venetians, harried by the Genoese, say of themselves in their lamentations, 'woe to us, poor foreigners (in the sense of "living in exile")' (Οὐαί μας τοὺς πτωχοὺς τοὺς ξένους, LM III 593). When speaking of the Genoese, one of the knights comforts King James that 'the foreigners will depart, the locals will stay' (οἱ ξένοι θέλουν πάγειν, καὶ οἱ τοπικοὶ θέλουν μείνειν, LM III 492). A 'foreign thing' (πρᾶμαν ξένον), something that did not belong to them, namely Cyprus, was sold by the Templars (LM III 527). The young Peter and John de Lusignan associate the West with a foreign (τὴν ξενιτείαν) but desirable place (LM I 79). Queen Charlotte opened a shelter on Cyprus for 'foreign' (τοὺς ξένους) arrivals (LM V 642). The sheikh of Damascus obtained news about Janus both from his own people and from 'foreigners' (γροικῶ ἀποὺ ξένους, LM V 664). 'Foreignness' was usually related to belonging to place other than the one in which one currently was. The exception is the concept of 'foreignness' that Leontios uses to explain the need for detachment when he writes that 'foreign doctors' (ξένοι ἰατροί) and 'foreign judges' (ξένοι κριτάδες) would be better able to resolve a difficult matter than those who are emotionally connected to the needy (LM II 253).

[1650] Ashcroft, Griffiths, Tiffin, Post-colonial Studies, 156–158. Sune Quotrup Jensen notes that in this strategy, Spivak is inspired by several other intellectual traditions besides the Lacanian, such as Hegel's master-slave dialectic, Simone de Beauvoir's theory which offers a view of the relationship between 'self' and 'other' from the perspective of gender and Said's 'imagined geographies' concept, which perceives, as Jensen says, 'the Orient as other in a reductionist, distancing and pathologizing way' (Jensen, Othering, 64).

5.6. Nature of relations in the *Chronicle*

The depiction created by Makhairas presents interpersonal relations only through dialogues and action, and the latter are the most difficult to capture due to their dynamics. The only 'static' elements of the narrative, imbued with religious significance, are mentions of material objects such as church buildings and icons. Schryver is right that it is impossible to analyse the contacts between Franks and Cyprians on Cyprus in a binary way because one would need to simultaneously consider the aspect of integration, that is the assimilation of certain elements of the other (e.g. joint processions by the Greeks and Latins in the *Chronicle*), and the aspect of segregation, that is either excluding others from one's own heritage, or taking the decision to abide by it during confrontations with representatives of another worldview (e.g. the reaction of the bishops to the attempts made by Peter de Thomas to convert them). In effect, elements may emerge that do not fit the newly-formed whole and upset its internal balance (e.g. the Greeks who were forced to convert).

In the article about the work of Makhairas and Philippe de Mézières already mentioned in the *Introduction*, Nicolaou-Konnari writes of 'three-century cohabitation' in a limited space. According to this scholar, a detailed investigation of the complex image of intercultural contacts on the island in the texts of the writers named above may lead to the conclusion that in their opinion there occurred on it 'the disappearance or redefinition of ethnic and cultural identity'.[1651] Nicolaou-Konnari also mentions the phenomenon of 'the adoption of another' and 'the paradoxical coexistence of cultural conservatism and adaptability', factors that impacted 'self-perception and the perception of the Other', simultaneously underlining that in this perspective the 'criteria of identification and alterity' were religion, and also language.[1652] In the *Chronicle* we certainly encounter the expansion of the meaning of the terms 'Cyprians' (Κυπριῶτες) and 'Cyprian' (Κυπριώτης). We may speak of a certain adaptation by the Greeks to the new circumstances and of overt forms of coexistence with the Latins, but fragments that would help to explain exactly what such an adoption of another would entail are few.

The vision of events created in the *Chronicle* shows that among representatives of Christian denominations, the opponents of Latins were almost always other Latins. Similarly, alliances were forged within the Latin community. This may be seen in the fact that the Lusignans can call on the help of the rulers of the Western world without difficulty, to which the 'colonial' situation on the island contributed.

Meanwhile, the depiction of the followers of Islam in the Cypriot text and the narrative presenting Christian attempts to comprehend and name them are permeated with elements indicating that they treated the Muslim world as homogeneous, assigning it attributes that were unambiguously negative in moral terms, even though they were able to discern the groups within it. Makhairas reveals his attitude towards both civilisations through hyperbolic terms, calling the representative of Christians the 'Most Holy Father the Pope' (ὁ ἁγιώτατος πατὴρ ὁ πάπας), and the sultan, 'thrice damned' (περὶ τοῦ τρισκατάρατου σουλτάνου) (LM III 284).

It should be emphasised that the relations between the Cyprians and the Franks, the Cypriots (Lusignans, sporadically Cyprian) and the Genoese and Venetians, and also between Christians and Muslims described in the *Chronicle* change over time. We may therefore consider that this is a case of a processual narrative which describes transforming denominational and religious communities that come into contact with each other, and such contact takes various forms.

In this context, terms such as 'negotiations' and 'hybridisation' find a reflection. Both suggest the presence of a process where elements that do not fit try to find themselves a space in their mutual presence and form a whole that will function despite obvious differences. Frankish authorities in the Cypriot work initially deprive the Greek clergy of their land, to later defend them when they are harassed by the Carmelite. The sultan sometimes imprisons western captives, demonstrating hostility, and at other times sends his own envoys with gifts or receives emissaries hospitably.

Leontios does not show all the forms of joint presence, and thus recreating the consecutive phases of the transition is not fully possible.

[1651] Nicolaou-Konnari, Alterity and identity, 38.
[1652] Nicolaou-Konnari, Alterity and identity, 38–39.

5.7. Perception, words and emotions: ways of contacting the 'other' in the *Chronicle*

The interdenominational and interreligious relations presented in the *Chronicle*, as well as intradenominational ones, may be investigated by analysing aspects of contact expressed in three dimensions: perceptual, verbal and emotional.

Christians and Muslims usually have the opportunity to see the opponent as being formed into an army (φουσάτον, LM II 226, 229, V 672) or approaching from the sea in the form of a fleet (ἁρμάδα, more rarely στόλος). Western forces usually use galleys (κάτεργον),[1653] but also other transport units,[1654] and the Muslims, different types of ships.[1655] Christians are often accompanied by horses (ἄλογα). Direct meetings between the two groups usually occur as part of embassies, during which gifts are exchanged, in which hostility or hospitality is most fully expressed.

Characters contact each other using words: by transmitting information through various means (ἐποῖκε νῶσιν; ἀγγαλέσῃ; ἀγγαλίω; ἀγγαλίζει), correspondence, through envoys and directly. Proclamations (διαλαλημός) by one group about another are sometimes issued (e.g.: LM II 148). Expressions and references of a religious nature are frequently woven into statements, often to manipulate the interlocutor: this is a permanent rhetorical element. Within the *Chronicle*, it is possible to distinguish a large spectrum of responses, from the positive through the manipulated to the negative (ἀντίλογος). Periods of misunderstanding occur, for example in the case of contradictory communications expressed by rulers. The Alexandrians, for instance, use words that are full of arrogance (πολλὰ ἄπρεπα λογία καὶ σουπέρπια, LM II 171). Makhairas calls the turcopolier's words severe (σκλερά), uncouth (ἄπρεπα) and characterised by arrogance (ἐφουμίζετον) (LM II 202).[1656]

The role of envoys is particularly important here because it is they who step outside the world known to them and cross lands to fulfil their mission (τὴν μαντατοφοριάν), directly confronting the addressee of the message. Sentences referring to the real or desired features of envoys are sometimes included in the *Chronicle*. For example, in LM I 25 Saladin advises Guy to send only 'clever' (φρενίμους) envoys and not 'helpless' (ἄτυχους) ones, because he could lose a lot (χάσῃς πολλά). The Genoese admiral voices a thought that has the nature of a maxim:

> […] *many times wise envoys* (σοφοὶ μαντατοφόροι) *soften down the wrath of their master* (καταπαύγουν τὸν θυμὸν τοῦ ἀφέντη τους), *for the masters in their wrath say much* (λαλοῦν πολλά), *although they may do but little* (πολομοῦν ὀλλίγα), *and the envoys shift it* (ἀλλάσσουν) *and make what was hard soft* (πολομοῦν τὰ σκληρὰ εἰς μαλακτοσύνην), *and in this way peace is made in the world* (οὕτως γίνεται ἡ ἀγάπη εἰς τὸν κόσμον). […] (LM III 488)

They have the ability of selecting the 'appropriate' (πρεπάμενα) words, transmitting the message in 'a far gentler form than [it was] transmitted [to them]' (μαλακτόττερα παρὰ ποῦ […] 'παράγγειλαν πολλά). In LM III 492 a knight calms Peter II down by saying:

> […] *be not troubled at all by what we say, for this is the way of envoys* (συνήθιν εἶνε εἰς τοὺς μαν(τα)τοφόρους): *they often make speeches, which the people indeed think are true* (λαλοῦν λογία, ὅπου

[1653] Examples of expressions: 'ἕναν κάτεργον ἁρματωμένον' (LM II 101), 'τὰ κάτεργα οἱ Γενουβίσοι' (LM III 549), 'ἕναν κάτεργον γενουβίσικον' (LM II 145), 'τῆς περδέσκας τῶν κατέργων' (LM III 498), 'οἱ λοιποὶ καραβοκυροὶ τῶν κατέργων τῶν Γενουβίσων' (LM III 515), 'τὴν βλέπισιν τοῦ κατέργου τοῦ ρηγός' (LM II 141, 171, 220, III 484, 515, 543).

[1654] Words: 'ξύλον', LM II 120, 140–143, 213, III 463, V 699; 'γριππαρία', LM I 13; 'γρίππον', LM II 146, 220; 'σατίες', LM II 143, 162, 177, 190, 205, 220; 'καραβία', LM II 91, 103, 150, 154, 162, 167, 190, 205, 213, III 367, V 686, 688; 'περιστιρία', LM II 162; 'ταφουρέντζες', LM II 205; 'λουσέργια', LM II 205.

[1655] Words: 'τζέρμες', LM V 671–672; 'νάβαν', LM II 192, 219, III 592; 'σαρακήνικην', LM II 219; 'μαγραπίτικην', LM II 288; 'τὸ τούρκικον', LM II 140–142, 152; 'τζούρμαν', LM III 515, IV 660. Cf. 'μὲ ρν' ξύλα, τζέρμες, καὶ κάτεργα, καὶ καραβία, μὲ φ' Μαμουλούκιδες καὶ β χαρφούσιδες, καὶ χ ἀράπιδες', LM V 672. The need for comprehensive, interdisciplinary research on medieval watercraft is the subject of the paper Christides, Naval History, 309–332.

[1656] Voice itself is also important (φωνή), sometimes appearing as a manifestation of Divine intervention as a 'voice from Heaven' (φωνὴ ἀπὸ τὸν οὐρανόν, LM I 8), sometimes as a piece of news that spread (βγῇ ἡ φωνή) after the death of King Janus in LM VI 703, sometimes as a human reaction to events: the cry of the boy who saw the Cross in the crown of the carob tree (ἔβαλε φωνές) in LM I 70 or the Bulgarians who fell upon the Genoese (ἐβάλαν φωνήν) in LM III 455–456, the proud words shouted by the Saracens (ἐσυντύχαν) in LM II 171, the wild scream (ἄγριαν φωνήν) of the sentries who saw the attacking Turks in LM III 317.

φαίνεται τοὺς λᾶς καὶ εἶνε ἀλήθεια), and where you see great strife (κ' ἐκεῖ ὅπου νὰ 'δῆς μεγάλες ταραχές), there you will see presently peace and friendship (ἐκεῖ θέλεις ἰδεῖν καὶ ἀγάπην καὶ φιλίαν), for after the storm comes fair weather. [...]

An important element of the portrait of individuals and specific groups, and also of the depiction of contacts between them are emotions, and their designations frequently appear in the *Chronicle*.[1657] Makhairas also describes behaviours that reflect these states. Characters have an impact on one another, feel different emotions and cause them in others. The Templars are racked by grief (ἡ λύπη καὶ τὸ κλάμαν; ἐλυπήθησαν, LM I 12). Diomidios feels fear of the Saracens (ἐφοβήθην, LM I 35). The Orthodox population of Cyprus is angry at the Carmelite (ἐρίψαν τὸ πανπάκιν καὶ ἐπτύσαν το, LM II 101). The Catholics envy the Orthodox their access to the mystery of the Holy Cross (ἐζηλεῦγαν; φθονοῦν; διὰ φθόνον, LM I 67, 72). Inhabitants of Alexandria tremble in fear (ἐτρομάξαν) in the face of the Christian threat (LM II 171). The Genoese and Venetians intimidate each other (ἐφοβέριζεν ἕναν κουμούνιν τὸ ἄλλον, LM III 328). When leaving Cyprus, the former are filled with sadness (θλιμμένοι), 'moaning' (μὲ ἀναστεναγμούς) and full of pain (μὲ πόνους) (LM III 458). The Christians experience 'great joy' (χαρὰν μεγάλην) after taking Gorhigos and the Alexandrian port (LM II 171, 195). Western forces zealously march out (ἐζηλέψαν) to conquer Syria (LM II 175). Followers of Islam are also depicted as quick to anger (θυμωμένοι, LM V 668).

Makhairas constructs the descriptions of events through designations of human actions, including nouns such as 'work' (ἔργον), 'doings' (ἔργατα), 'deed' (πρᾶξις), 'effort' and 'toil' (κόπος), and the verbs: 'ἐργάζομαι', 'ποιέω', 'πράττω', and through characters' statements, and persons are characterised mainly via the use of morally-marked words (decisions taken by them, their deeds and the consequences of those deeds are marked thus, e.g. 'πταῖσμαν', 'παρανομία', LM II 239) and words expressing emotions. Portrayals of characters, like mentions of nature and town architecture, lack visuality and vividness, though exceptions do happen. A detailed description of King Peter I is found in MS O, in LM II 249,[1658] and of an object, in LM V 694.[1659] Apart from the story in which a large role was played by a carob tree, we learn somewhat more about nature in Cyprus from LM V 637–639, which contains exceptionally precise descriptions of a locust attack in the years 1409 and 1411 that, as the chronicle notes, attacked 'all the vegetation on the ground' (οὔλην τὴν χλόην τῆς γῆς), fields (χωραφία), orchards (περιβολία), trees (δέντρη), lemon (κιτρομηλίες), olive (ἐλιές) and carob trees (κερατζιές), vineyards (ἀμπελία) and rushes (καλαμερά). While Makhairas usually passes over the natural beauties of Cyprus in the *Chronicle*, in this one passage he reveals to the reader the Cypriot fields and allows him to glimpse the Mediterranean arboretum, familiarising him slightly with the features of its natural wealth – which he surely encountered every day – albeit shown in dramatic circumstances.

As regards descriptions of characters, in Leontios' work a man is what he says and what he does and thus, to borrow the words of Alexandar Mihailovic, which he used when discussing Bakhtin's work, 'the person turns into an event'.[1660] This is in accordance with the Byzantine intuition, expressed by John Meyendorff, that a human being who is 'a dynamic reality' builds their identity in a constant relation with God.[1661] A man participates in the sacred through his or her deeds, not through linguistic images and sophisticated philosophical analysis. This premise is in line with the explanations of Maximus the Confessor, who writes in *Ad Thalassium* 60:

[1657] Kyrris judges: 'the feeling is the dominant constituent element of motivation of the narrative' (Kyrris, Some Aspects, 202).
[1658] 'Καὶ κείνου ἡ καρδιά του δὲν ἐπίστευσεν, διότι ἡ ὀσκιά του ἦτον ἕνας λιόντας, καὶ ὅμορφον κορμὶν καὶ βαλτίσιμος ἄνθρωπος καὶ γνωστικὸς καὶ σοφὸς καὶ χατιτωμένος ἀποὺ τόν Θεὸν καὶ φανταστικός.' 'And in his own heart he did not believe them, for very fittingly was he matched with a lion: he was handsome in body and a valiant man of sense and wisdom, and full of the grace of God and of good wit.' See Dawkins (Ed., transl.), Ἐξήγησις/ Recital, 228 (fn. 3); Παυλίδης (Ed.), Λεοντίου Μαχαιρᾶ Χρονικόν, 182 (fn. 9). Dawkins' translation.
[1659] 'ἡ πανθαύμαστος αὐλή; νοῦς ἀνθρώπου δέν εἶνε νά πῇ τινὰς τὴν μεγαλότητάν του καὶ τὴν ὀμορφιάν του· δέτε ἄν ἦτον μέγας, καὶ εἴχεν μέσα δ' ἐκλησίες διὰ τούς δουλευτάδες καὶ λαόν τόν εἶχεν.' See 'There is no man who can say how big it was: it contained four churches for the servants and for the people who were there.' Dawkins (Ed., transl.), Ἐξήγησις/ Recital, 672 (fn. 1); Παυλίδης (Ed.), Λεοντίου Μαχαιρᾶ Χρονικόν, 526 (fn. 8). Dawkins' translation.
[1660] Mihailovic, Bachtinowska koncepcja słowa, 113. Quoted phrase translated by Kupiszewska.
[1661] Meyendorff, Teologia bizantyjska, 6. Quoted phrase translated by Kupiszewska.

For the sages say that it is impossible for rational knowledge (λόγος) of God to coexist with the direct experience (πεῖρα) of God, or for conceptual knowledge (νόησις) of God to coexist with immediate perception (αἴσθησις) of God.[1662]

'Experience', together with 'perception' and 'participation' (μέθεξις),[1663] determines the chronicler's optic. Such a shaping of the narrative contains the conviction that at the deepest level, divine reality is 'ineffable', which means that neither concepts nor verbal references can reflect the hidden nature of Godhead.

Only sometimes does the chronicler add an epithet indicating some special feature of a character, such as 'one-eyed' (μονόφθαλμος) or 'with his nose cut off' (τοῦ κουτζομούττα) (LM V 686), even if it is secondary to the events presented in the narrative. Instead, there is a 'concretist' focus on objects, shown for instance in the description of the hiding place of a relic (LM II 115) or the mention of the riches and clothing of Queen Valentina (LM III 580), as well as a 'beautiful saddle decorated from top to bottom with pearls' (μίαν σέλλαν ὄμορφην μαργ(αρ)ιταρένην ἀπουπάνω ὡς κάτω), prepared for her and King Peter II by Thibald as prenuptial 'gifts' (χάρισμα) (LM III 578), provided that they serve the narrative.

It is using these tools of description that Leontios shows interdenominational, interreligious and also intradenominational relations. The reader discovers the motivations, actions and endeavours of individuals and groups, but has no opportunity to imagine what the 'other' looked like or what the lands that he inhabited looked like.

5.8. Heretics, pagans and infidels in the *Chronicle*

Makhairas' Cypriots believe both the Genoese and the Saracens to be ἄπιστοι, although (as in the case of the ambiguous term 'Κυπριώτης') the first of them should be termed 'dissenters', because according to the Cypriots they betray the Christian God, while the latter should be referred to with the noun 'infidels', because they do not know the God of the Christians at all, or the noun 'pagans' because they invoke another, their 'own God' (e.g. the sheikh of Damascus). In MS O (in LM II 131, 169, 175) the form 'ἀλλόπιστοι' ('other-believers') is used with reference to the followers of Islam.[1664] Leontios also talks of the 'Godless Agarenes' (ἄθεοι -Ἀγαρηνοί-, LM I 32) and the 'Godless sultan' (ἄθεος σουλτάνος, LM V 661). The adjective ἄθεος may indicate someone who does not know God, but also a 'wicked' person, because that is what he calls Queen Eleanora: 'Godless' (ἄθεη, LM II 235). Finally, 'unrighteous' (ἄνομος) is the designation given to the Turk who conquered the 'City' (τὴν Πόλιν), i.e. Constantinople, in 1453 (LM VI 711).

In MS O (LM III 414) the Genoese ask whether the Cypriots treat them (κρατεῖτε μας) as Christians (χροστιανούς), as enemies of God (διὰ ἐχθρούς τοῦ θεοῦ), or as dogs (ὡς γοιὸν σκύλλους), because they 'do not respect any of their (lit. our) requests' (δὲν ἀντετιάζετε τὸν ὁρισμόν μας).[1665]

Only in two places in his work does Leontios use the term 'heresy' (αἰρετικία): when he describes the pope's outrage at the news of the hidden practices of the Templars, who during initiation use the symbols of Christianity for their own purposes (LM I 13), and when talking of the envious resentment of the Latins, who claim that the Greeks 'lead the people to heresy' (βάλλουν τους εἰς αἱρεσίαν), tell 'lies' (ψέματα) and are like the 'pagans' (ὡς γοιὸν τοὺς Ἕλληνες) (LM I 73). The term 'pagans' (Ἕλληνες) appears in LM I 31 and may mean the Saracens who occupied Cyprus in the seventh century.[1666]

The chronicler therefore sees heresy as the adoption of certain behaviours and gestures derived from the Christian sacred sphere and using them in a manner contrary to what they were intended for by the Church, and the case of the Templars indicates that this was done in a secluded place, not easily

---

[1662] Maximus the Confessor, On the Cosmic Mystery of Jesus Christ, 126.
[1663] Maximus the Confessor, On the Cosmic Mystery of Jesus Christ, 126.
[1664] Dawkins (Ed., transl.), Ἐξήγησις/ Recital, 116 (fn. 1), 150 (fn. 3), 156 (fn. 2); Παυλίδης (Ed.), Λεοντίου Μαχαιρᾶ Χρονικόν, 96 (fn. 5), 124 (fn. 1), 128 (fn. 2). Strambaldi does not retain this meaning, translating the word as *li infideli*. See Mas Latrie (Ed.), Chronique de Strambaldi, 51.
[1665] Dawkins (Ed., transl.), Ἐξήγησις/ Recital, 394 (fn. 4); Παυλίδης (Ed.), Λεοντίου Μαχαιρᾶ Χρονικόν, 304 (fn. 3).
[1666] Pavlidis briefly explains the specific meaning of the word Ἕλληνες: 'Στο κείμενο Ἕλληνες, εννοεί τους αρχαίους Ἕλληνες που πίστευαν στους 12 θεούς, που ἦσαν, δηλαδή, ειδωλολάτρες. Τους σύγχρονούς του Ἕλληνες ονομάζει Ρωμαίους (=Ρωμιούς).' 'In the work [the word] Ἕλληνες means the Ancient Greeks, who worshipped twelve gods, who were, in other words, idolaters. He calls modern Greeks Rhomaioi (i.e. Romans).' See Παυλίδης (Ed.), Λεοντίου Μαχαιρᾶ Χρονικόν, 57 (fn. 5). Kupiszewska's translation from the Polish translation by the author.

accessible for outsiders. That which is 'heretical' is 'dirty' (βρωμισμένη), practiced 'in secret' (εἰς τὸ κρυφόν), 'under cover of night' (τῇ νύκταν) and goes beyond 'the truth of the Church' (τὴν ἀλήθειαν τῆς ἐκκλησίας). The adjective 'heretical' (αἱρετικός) appears with respect to Thibald and to deliberations of whether conversion is justified, but Makhairas does not call even the Genoese, who have no qualms against making false oaths during mass, by the term. In turn, the Muslims treat Christians with the same contempt that the Christians treat Muslims: the first mention indicating this is contained already in LM I 23. These two religions lack a common foundation such as a holy book recognised by both sides or comparable religious practices. Nowhere does Leontios use the word 'schism' (σχίσμα) or 'schismatic' (σχισματικός).

The opposite of the negative, marked designations discussed above is the word 'orthodox' (ὀρθόδοξος), which Makhairas uses in the *Chronicle* three times with respect to individuals. He uses it in LM III 579 in discussions of conversion from the Greek to the Latin denomination, as the opposite of 'heretic' (αἱρετικός), suggesting that an orthodox person has no need to change denominations. This adjective is also uttered in LM II 216 by Florimond de Lesparre, who standing before the pope calls King Peter I an 'orthodox Christian' (ὀρθόδοξος χριστιανός), as well as using other positive designations related to religion such as 'good' (καλός) and 'champion of the Holy Church' (κυνηγὸς τῆς ἁγίας ἐκκλησίας). Interestingly, this term is not reserved for Christians only, because in a letter to King Janus the sheikh of Damascus terms the sultan thus in the fragment 'against my lord, the orthodox' (κατάδικα τοῦ ἀφέντη μου ὀρθοδόξου, LM V 664).[1667] This particular usage is an attempt by Leontios to find, in a representative of a foreign religion, and therefore a foreign civilisation, some traces of a way of thinking similar to what he knew from the Christian mentality.

5.9. Leontios Makhairas' identity

Leontios' religious identity is disputed by scholars, as discussed in the introduction to this monograph. The Cypriot chronicler created a narrative that should be read 'contrapuntally', with a focus not only on what he devotes the most space to (the deeds of the Lusignans, the colonial ethos of the conquering king), but also on what seems to emerge between the layers of a text that has a clearly pro-Latin message (e.g. the way he describes the cult elements important to the Greeks). Like in colonial literature, where we encounter the phenomenon of a 'metonymic gap', which deprives the colonisers of the capacity to fully understand a text written by the representative of the colonised language – although in many respects adapted to their understanding or even pretending to be deliberately tailored to their need to understand (or simply to their pleasure) – due to the use of single words in the native language of the colonised ('unglossed words, phrases or passages from a first language, or concepts, allusions or references which may be unknown to the reader'),[1668], in this case due to the use of the Cypriot dialect the 'obscuring' of the text covers the *Chronicle* as a whole.

> *The metonymic gap is that cultural gap formed when appropriations of a colonial language insert unglossed words, phrases or passages from a first language, or concepts, allusions or references which may be unknown to the reader. Such words become synecdochic of the writer's culture – the part that stands for the whole – rather than representations of the world, as the colonial language might. Thus the inserted language 'stands for' the colonized culture in a metonymic way, and its very resistance to interpretation constructs a 'gap' between the writer's culture and the colonial culture.*[1669]

Although Makhairas treated the tale of St Helena as a story that had really happened, the description of the Cyprus christianised by the empress has overtones of 'mythic occupation of space'. In many places he says of churches and relics from the distant Byzantine past that they have survived 'to this day' (σήμερα). Of Rekouniatos and Andronikos, martyred by the Saracens, he writes that 'their memory will last for ever' (LM V 660). In LM III 579, when he speaks of Thibald who converted, he voices an attachment

---

[1667] Miller and Sathas preserve this element of meaning, translating it as: *contre mon seigneur l'orthodoxe*. See Sathas, Miller (Eds, transl.), Chronique de Chypre, 373.
[1668] Ashcroft, Post-Colonial Transformation, 75.
[1669] Ashcroft, Post-Colonial Transformation, 75.

to the 'faith of his fathers' (ἡ πατρική του πίστη), and he mentions the importance of heritage (κληρονομιά) already in LM I 1, that is at the very start of the *Chronicle*. He additionally signals that 'love for the king' (ἡ ἀγάπη τοῦ ῥηγός) cannot be the reason for converting. After all, he himself respected the representatives of the Frankish dynasty. He pays a lot of attention to reflecting on the 'fall' of Thibald, whose morals deteriorated after his conversion, leading to his perdition and death. In LM II 158, when he explains the Byzantine division of authority between the secular ruler and the spiritual ruler, he emphasises that it ceased to apply on the island when the Latin Lusignans took power (πρὶν τὴν πάρουν οἱ Λατῖνοι; 'πῆραν τὸν τόπον οἱ Λαζανιάδες), which 'commenced the Latin period' (ἄρκεψεν τὸ λατίνικον).[1670] MS O underlines the fact that

> *the royal court (ἡ αὐλὴ ἡ ρηγάτικη) was a foundation (κτίσμαν) of the Greek emperor, and there the dukes lived [...]. (LM II 158)*[1671]

When he writes that before the coming of the Latins the Cyprians had to know common Greek (διὰ τοῦτον ἦτον χρῆσι νὰ ξεύρωμεν ῥωμαϊκὰ καθολικά) and Syriac (συριάνικα) due to contacts with the emperor of Constantinople and the patriarch of Antioch,[1672] Leontios uses the first person plural, and thus declares his acceptance of this heritage. He continues his argument, claiming that later Greek came to be corrupted ('βαρβαρίσαν τὰ ῥωμαϊκά), and that such a state of affairs persisted to his time (ὡς γοιὸν καὶ σήμερον). In the light of these words the fact that he consciously decided to write the *Chronicle* in the Cypriot dialect even though he knew French and held a high post at the Lusignan court takes on a special significance. The chronicler's orthodox identity is also supported by the fact that he describes the beginnings of Frankish rule in the first part of the *Chronicle* rather succinctly, placing them in the context of a quite expansively depicted Byzantine past of the island and elaborating on the subject of its heritage. Perhaps he was aware of the slow decline of the dynasty and the need to emphasise that which indicated the island's inviolate identity, and so he decided to pen his account in the Cypriot dialect, which he treated as a tool for transmitting and putting into practice the Cypriot ideal (see Vassiliou, p. 37). He may also have been working from the assumption that the language of the local population reflected the transformations that the island had undergone over the centuries and wanted to preserve all these influences as the most important component of Cyprus' heritage. Through the choice of this particular language, which formed a certain integral whole, he created an original world, impossible to recreate in any other language (as even the translations of fragments of the *Chronicle* in the *Chronique d'Amadi* and *Chronique de Strambaldi* prove). Undoubtedly the fact that he lived at the meeting point of two powerful cultures, his awareness that Cypriot culture had become hybrid and difficult for others to understand (ὅτι εἰς τὸν κόσμον δὲν ἠξεύρουν ἴντα συντιχάννομεν) provided him with tools for capturing these transformations, but also for distinguishing a permanent core.

Nevertheless, Makhairas does not hide his admiration for the conquests of the Lusignans. He follows the fates of the rulers, cites the story of Peter I's romance, relates in detail the course of the conflict with the Genoese and shows how the Franks managed in difficult situations. He is proud that the whole population of Cypriots defeated the Muslims. He accepts the Frankish rulers, treating them as part of 'one body' (ἕναν κορμίν) with the people inhabiting the island. In a comparison meant to illustrate this unity, Peter I is compared to a bird (ἕναν ὄρνεον; ὄρνιθα; MS O ἕνας ἀετός[1673]), and his subjects to 'wings' (πτερά) (LM II 255). In a letter to the constable, Peter II calls himself the 'king of Cyprus and Jerusalem by the grace of the Holy Spirit' (διὰ τῆς χάριτος τοῦ παναγίου πνεύματος ῥήγας Ἱεροσολύμου καὶ Κύπρου, LM III 512). Also in LM I 23 the sultan writes in a letter to Guy that God grants authority to rule (ἔδωκεν τὴν ἐξουσίαν). Peter I, commenting in a letter the behaviour of the sultan who delays the peace agreement, writes that sovereignty (ἀφεντία) may be obtained 'by birth' (ἀπὸ γεννήσεώς τους) and because 'fate so ordered it' (ὅπου σ' ἐψήλωσεν ἡ τύχη), but always through the direction of God (LM II 230). In turn the sheikh of Damascus shows that it can be taken by force (περφόρτζα), which does not stop him from considering such a sultan legitimate (LM V 664). Makhairas' respect for the Frankish

---

[1670] Statement present in MS O. See Dawkins (Ed., transl.), Ἐξήγησις/ Recital, 142 (fn. 3); Παυλίδης (Ed.), Λεοντίου Μαχαιρά Χρονικόν, 116 (fn. 6).

[1671] Dawkins (Ed., transl.), Ἐξήγησις/ Recital, 142 (fn. 2); Παυλίδης (Ed.), Λεοντίου Μαχαιρά Χρονικόν, 116 (fn. 5).

[1672] In MS O we read that Syriac was used 'because of the patriarch' (διὰ τὸν πατριάρχην). See Dawkins (Ed., transl.), Ἐξήγησις/ Recital, 142 (fn. 1); Παυλίδης (Ed.), Λεοντίου Μαχαιρά Χρονικόν, 116 (fn. 4).

[1673] Dawkins (Ed., transl.), Ἐξήγησις/ Recital, 234 (fn. 7); Παυλίδης (Ed.), Λεοντίου Μαχαιρά Χρονικόν, 188 (fn. 5).

rulers, and particularly for Peter I, may be observed in his returning to the subject of Peter's murder, which he treats as one of the Cypriots' greatest sins, for which Ammochostos and even all of Cyprus should be taken away from them (LM III 482).

In their edition of the translation of the *Chronique d'Amadi*, Edbury and Coureas carefully note the differences between it and Makhairas' text, distinguishing fragments that in their opinion contain an anti-Latin message, particularly in the accounts of the theft of the Holy Cross by the Latin priest John Santamarin or the Carmelite Peter de Thomas,[1674] and also many places that are present in one text but not the other. This may be partly due to the fact that the two authors did not have access to certain information. For example, in LM V 695 Leontios does not describe the details of the Saracen attack on Stavro Vouni monastery (τὸν Σταυρὸν τὸν Μέγαν) in 1426, though knowing his attitude to the infidels he would certainly have provided more details of Saracen cruelty, which we can read about in the *Chronique d'Amadi*.[1675] Sometimes Makhairas does not give the names of some Latins, including the Catholic confessor of Queen Eleanora, Glimin of Narbonne.[1676] This is not an indication of his dislike for the Latins however, because he gives the names of other Frankish clergymen. Fragments about John Santamarin and Peter de Thomas undoubtedly show Leontios' anxiety that stems from the fact that Latins take without asking for permission that which is at the core of Greek identity (belonging to the Orthodox faith, the Cross of Togni linked to Cypriot land), as well as his love for a narrative that is rich in details. They also say much about the person (or persons) who selected information when creating the *Chronique d'Amadi*.

However, in no place does the chronicler refer to the Franks unambiguously negatively, as for example the Constantinople-born Melkite monk Nikon of the Black Mountain (i.e. Mount Amanus near Antioch) did after Antioch was captured from the Turks by 'Franks' in 1098. In his work *Τακτικόν* (Military treatise), he discourses about 'the Franconian people and its errors' (ἐπὶ τὸ γένος τῶν Φραγγῶν καὶ τῶν αὐτῶν πτωμάτων).[1677]

In the case of bygone authors the only way of reaching the aspects of their identity is to analyse the narrative of the texts they wrote in terms of what it says 'directly' and also of what it can 'suggest'. Paul Ricouer, discussing 'the notion of narrative identity' understands it as 'the sort of identity to which a human being has access thanks to the mediation of the narrative function'.[1678] If the author – compelled to adopt, consciously or not, one of the strategies of functioning in a multicultural collective – does not state their beliefs directly, the scholar's task is difficult, because they must confront the overlapping elements of the reality described in the work and his own interpretational skills and attitude. If we examine a work using concepts 'borrowed' from theories of the postcolonial school, we should use the opportunity afforded by this method to gain an understanding of the identity of an author who has found themselves in a 'colonial' situation. Namely, the identity of such a person, experiencing constant tackling of 'otherness' and undergoing a natural metamorphosis, combines 'precolonial' elements such as a link with their ancestors' culture (that is, their religion, language, place of residence, history) and 'colonial' elements resulting from the individual's reaction to the multi-layered, splintered cultural reality. This attitude often takes the form of **ambivalence** (Bhabha's term), in a case of which, as Ashcroft, Griffiths and Tiffin underline, 'complicity and resistance exist in a fluctuating relation within the colonial subject'.[1679]

The narrative presence of Greek and Latin elements with variously distributed accents allows us to venture on an interpretation of Makhairas' identity, taking into account several types of identities of this

---

[1674] Coureas, Edbury (Transl.), The Chronicle of Amadi, 371 (fn. 4, ref. to § 804), 373 (fn. 2, ref. to § 814).
[1675] Coureas, Edbury (Transl.), The Chronicle of Amadi, 463 (fn. 3, ref. to § 1071).
[1676] Coureas, Edbury (Transl.), The Chronicle of Amadi, 424 (fn. 6, ref. to § 953).
[1677] Levy-Rubin, 'The Errors of the Franks', 422–423.
[1678] Ricouer, Narrative Identity, 79.
[1679] Ashcroft, Griffiths, Tiffin, Post-colonial Studies, 10.

kind: that is, one which is simultaneously influenced by distinctly differing factors. Here the 'mixed',[1680] 'rhizomatic',[1681] 'catalytic'[1682] and 'hybrid'[1683] types are included.[1684]

An analysis of the *Chronicle* allows the conclusion that its contrapuntal composition is not only a sum of Greek and Latin elements (which would indicate that the chronicler's identity was mixed), but a varied structure that shows the author's somewhat non-coherent though process, shown quite 'freely' in a text that very probably alludes to the oral tradition. Neither is the work complex enough for us to be able to see an expansion of co-dependent motifs like a rhizome in it (rhizomatic identity). The ongoing dispute whether Makhairas was a Greek or a Latin may be reformulated into the question whether he had a catalytic identity, that is whether despite the coexistence of foreign elements within his identity (an internalisation of otherness at some level) he had fixed core identity (Greek or Latin), or a hybrid identity, which would mean that the coexistence of these elements had formed a new whole that cannot be reduced to their sum.

Clues leading to discovery of the author's identity may be found not only in how he presents various phenomena appearing at the juncture of cultures and civilisations on the lexical and descriptive level, though this is very important, but in a detailed analysis of fragment LM III 579, where Makhairas comments Thibald's conversion. Namely, it is possible to cite many arguments showing that some of his statements and his way of presenting events are constructed as if they had been made by someone who was a Greek at heart – not least those mentioned above. Quite a few arguments supporting the claim that the chronicler shows Latin inclinations could also be found in the *Chronicle*. This is because he usually presents actions and does not concern himself with extended descriptions of characters or happenings, and so does not declare anything. It may also be because he is not interested in revealing his identity.

However, when Makhairas comments Thibald's deed, his tone expresses surprise at the futility of somebody abandoning their denomination for another within a single religion. This surprise seems to indicate that he himself has a well-grounded sense of belonging, and that the choice had been made for him by his ancestors. This is so obvious to him that he does not explicitly state it. The sentence 'I do not condemn Latins' (δὲν καταδικάζω τοὺς Λατίνους) comes closest to revealing the truth, as if Leontios were distancing himself from them, showing that he did not belong to them. This may, however, have been an simple device by the chronicler, who wanted to preserve religious neutrality in the reader's eyes.

We should be aware that Makhairas may have manipulated the narrative in the places that concern himself or his family. Although he writes his work in the Cypriot dialect, and thus it is intended for the mass audience, the people (ὄχλος, πτωχός), he does not glorify the people itself and does not pay to it much attention. This may be seen for example in references to the peasant rebellion of 1426–1427. This reticence was likely due to his brother Peter's participation in the suppression of the rebellion (LM V 696–697). Leontios practically ignores the fact that the group of people who went out to greet the Muslims in Lefkosia included Badin Goneme, his relative. Dawkins identifies the persons who affiliated themselves with the attacking Saracens as belonging to Rhomaian Cypriot families.[1685] Meanwhile, when analysing Thibald's moral fall, Makhairas may have had mixed feelings towards him because like him he was a non-

---

[1680] Collins Cobuild English Dictionary for Advanced Learners gives several definitions of use of the term 'mixed'. One of them says: 'Mixed is used to describe something which includes or consists of different things of the same general kind.' (McMahon, Seaton, Collins Cobuild English Dictionary, 991).

[1681] The concept of rhizome is well known from Deleuze, Guattari, A Thousand Plateaus. Deleuze and Guattari describe it in the following way: 'A rhizome has no beginning or end; it is always in the middle, between things, interbeing, *intermezzo*. The tree is filiation, but the rhizome is alliance, uniquely alliance. The tree imposes the verb "to be," but the fabric of the rhizome is the conjunction, "and… and… and…" This conjunction carries enough force to shake and uproot the verb "to be."' (Deleuze, Guattari, A Thousand Plateaus, 25).

[1682] The concept of catalysis, adopted in (post)colonial discourse by Denis Williams, refers to a change in certain external forms of the individual's or the community's functioning (manifestation of culture) in such a way as to make them fit the customs dominant in the surrounding world, without undergoing any change at the deepest level of identity. Such a catalyst is 'a body which changes its surrounding substance without itself undergoing any change' (Ashcroft, Griffiths, Tiffin, Post-colonial Studies, 30–31).

[1683] The concept of hybrydity, most often used by Bhabha and sometimes replaced by the concept of 'synergy', is used to express deeper changes in culture, and thus also in the identities of individuals and whole communities, because it refers to a phenomenon that is the resultant of various factors that interplay, leading to the formation of a new paradigm (Ashcroft, Griffiths, Tiffin, Post-colonial Studies, 108–109).

[1684] In her interesting discussion of the topic of 'multiple identities' Cristina-Georgiana Voicu names four types of cultural identities: the 'nested/embedded', 'marble-cake/mixed', 'cross-cutting/overlapping', 'separate/exclusive' (Voicu, Exploring Cultural Identities, 20).

[1685] Dawkins, Notes, 229.

Frankish 'local burgher' (βουργέσης τοπικός, LM III 403) who had become close to Peter II, whom Leontios himself served, and advanced rapidly, which the chronicler may have envied. Furthermore Thibald killed his relative, the priest Philip, which undoubtedly threw a shadow over the *Chronicle* author's judgement. It is interesting that the account of Thibald and Alexopoulos is slightly more expanded in the *Chronique d'Amadi*, to include passages about the latter.[1686] Restricting the narrative to Thibald shows that the Cypriot chronicler wanted to make this specific person more visible in order to expound his attitude towards conversion from one's inherited faith.

At the very level of the *Chronicle*'s narrative it is possible to consider the features of a hybrid or catalytical 'narrative identity'. Both these types assume a certain hierarchy of 'native' and 'foreign' elements in the aspects of identity expressed. Both 'catalysis' and 'hybridity' are some of the most difficult forms of adjustment to new realities depicted in the literary text.[1687] In the **catalytical 'narrative identity'**, although signs of identification with elements of one's own culture and the imposed culture do occur, one particular core linked to one of these cultures is apparent. In the **hybrid 'narrative identity'** we encounter a new quality, composed of selected elements of the two cultures which form an original configuration that is subject to constant change.[1688]

Indications derived from the *Chronicle* allow to conjecture that Makhairas was at his core a Cyprian, but he does not allow himself to be fully defined, does not say so unambiguously, manipulates the text so that the reader has trouble drawing conclusions, misleads where he has just started to reveal something. Data thus exist which suggest that the *Chronicle*'s author may have represented a 'catalytical identity' type, which despite combining Greek and Latin elements in various configurations (shaped through a tradition of many years' standing wherein Cyprus was shared by the Orthodox and the Catholics), would nevertheless give primacy to the Orthodox faith. What Makhairas shows in his work may, however, be classified rather as a 'hybrid narrative identity', because in his narrative he only resorts to stronger accenting of Greek predilections.

The element that undoubtedly determines identity according to the chronicler, and which is certainly expressed in the *Chronicle*, is permanent (longer than passing residence) affiliation with a place, in his case with the island of Cyprus. This is why in almost all his work starting from LM I 33 up to LM V 671 he consistently uses the term 'Κυπριῶτες' to designate all the inhabitants of Cyprus, both before the appearance of the Lusignans and after. This term does not include those who have lived on the island for too short a period or live between two places (such as the Genoese and Venetians, who maintain permanent contact with Genoa and Venice, respectively, return there, etc.). However, it does include those who, despite embarking on distant expeditions to the West and East, return home. The Syrians in LM II 111 are according to MS O 'those who came from outside' (κείνοι ὁποῦ φέραν) when compared to the local Cypriots (τοπικοί).[1689] Muslims are affiliated with overseas territories, which is why Saracen converts living in Cypriot peripheries remain Saracens, though deracinated and hybrid. In a sense, in Makhairas' narrative Cyprus, unlike the Holy Land, is in a privileged position, because the constant civilisational, centrifugal fight for influence did not occur within its territory.

In the hierarchy of the main factors that determine identity, after affiliation with a place comes affiliation with a religion. In the *Chronicle*, Cyprus is Christian from the very start and remains so, which is why even the appearance of the Franks does not change its identity, though it introduces polyphony and subtle levels of otherness that – thanks to transforming space of the contacts – allow individuals to more fully identify themselves.

[1686] Coureas, Edbury (Transl.), The Chronicle of Amadi, 439 (fn. 3, ref. to §§ 989–990).
[1687] Cf. Young, Constructing 'England', iii.
[1688] The changing nature of hybrid forms is discussed in Voicu, Exploring Cultural Identities, 18.
[1689] Dawkins (Ed., transl.), Εξήγησις/ Recital, 96 (fn. 6); Παυλίδης (Ed.), Λεοντίου Μαχαιρά Χρονικόν, 82 (fn. 6).

Appendixes

Appendix 1.

Cyprus: location and chronology (1191–1432)[1690]

This *Appendix* consists of two parts. In the first part Cyprus' special location is described in order to illustrate the cause of the island's role in the medieval Christian-Muslim universe. Next, in the second part a chronology of events from the fourth to the fifteenth century (that is the period delimited by the *Chronicle*'s narrative) is presented, with an indication of the most important events in the history of Christianity and of Cyprus. The events that Makhairas includes in his *Chronicle* are written in bold. This will help the Reader to note what Leontios passes over, permitting a better acquaintance with him.

Location of Cyprus

Located in the eastern part of the Mediterranean Sea, Cyprus (Κύπρος) has an area of around 9,250 km², making it the third-largest island in this basin after Sicily (25,711 km²)[1691] and Sardinia (24,000 km²).[1692] Its distance to Turkey is only 70 km (64 km, 75 km),[1693] to the shores of Syria, around 150 km, and to the African coastline, around 380 km.[1694] To get there from Rhodes and Karpathos, one has to travel around 380 km by sea,[1695] while moving in the north-west direction it is 772 km to mainland Greece.[1696]

The island has five capes: on the eastern side this is Arnaoutis (Ακρωτήριο Αρναούτι), on the southern, Gata (Κάβο Γάτα), on the western, Greko (Κάβο Γκρέκο), on the northern, Kormakitis (Ακρωτήρι Κορμακίτη) and on the north-eastern side, Apostolos Andreas (Ακρωτήρι Αποστόλου Ανδρέα). Taking a bird's eye view of the island, one may see the Rizokarpaso (Ριζοκάρπασο) peninsula emerging from its north-eastern part, while the island's coastline is shaped by the following bays: Morphou Bay (Κόλπος Μόρφου) in the north-west, Famagusta Bay (Κόλπος της Αμμοχώστου) in the east, Akrotiri Bay (Κόλπος Ακρωτηρίου) to the south, Episkopi Bay (Κόλπος Επισκοπής) to the south-west, and Coral Bay (Κόλπος των Κοραλλίων) and Fontana Amorosa Bay (Κόλπος Φοντάνα Αμορόζα)[1697] north of Paphos (Πάφος).

As Misztal indicates, this coastline engenders comparisons of the island's shape to a violin, a frying pan or a clenched fist, which many scholars do.[1698] Przemysław Kordos sees a similarity to a 'prehistoric idol',[1699] and Luigi Palma di Cesnola cites the associations of the ancients: 'The shape of this island was not inappropriately compared by the ancients to that of a deer's skin or a fleece spread out.'[1700]

The surface of Cyprus is intersected by two mountain ranges: the Troodos (Τρόοδος) mountains located in the south-west, with Olympus (Όλυμπος) as their highest peak (1,951 m a.s.l.) and the Kyrenia

---

[1690] Chronological range from the occupation of Cyprus by the Franks to the probable year of Makhairas' death.
[1691] After Privitera, Combining Organic Agiculture and Recreation, 310.
[1692] Webster, A Prehistory of Sardinia, 28.
[1693] First figure after Kordos, Geografia, klimat i przyroda Cypru, 19; second after Spilling, Cyprus, 7; third after Delipetrou *et al.*, Cyprus, 171.
[1694] Both values after Kordos, Geografia, klimat i przyroda Cypru, 19.
[1695] Delipetrou *et al.*, Cyprus, 171.
[1696] After Spilling, Cyprus, 7.
[1697] Cf. Sibthorp *et al.*, Journal, 332.
[1698] Misztal, Historia Cypru, 9.
[1699] Kordos, Geografia, klimat i przyroda Cypru, 19 (after Prof. Dariusz Maliszewski).
[1700] Cesnola, Cyprus, 5.

Mountains, also called 'Five-fingers' (Πενταδάκτυλος), stretched out along the northern shore with their distinctive peak of Kyparissovouno (Κυπαρισσόβουνο; Mount Selvili) standing at 1,024 m a.s.l. The Mesaoria (Μεσαορία) plain is spread to the north-east, and the remaining territory consists of coastal plains.

Thanks to its characteristic geographical location, Cyprus played a special role in international relations for centuries, as noted by Vassiliou, who writes: 'The geographical position of Cyprus and its natural resources were the two main reasons for its turbulent history.'[1701]

On the one hand, the island's location attracted pilgrims voyaging to the Holy Land, and on the other, it shifted the Cypriot land away from the centre of events occurring in the Mediterranean world. Above all, however, because of its small surface and favourable location in the maritime space between Europe, Africa and Asia, Cyprus was conquered consecutively by: the Phoenicians (ca. 1200 BCE), Assyrians (725–575 BCE), Persians (525–425 BCE, 350–325 BCE), the king of Salamis, Evagoras (411–374 BCE), by Alexander the Great (325 BCE), which heralded the Hellenistic period of the island's history (300–50 BCE), through the Romans (58 BCE–330 CE), the Byzantine Empire (325–1191 CE), up to the Franks (1192 CE–1489 CE). After the period important for the *Chronicle*, Cyprus witnessed the following periods: Venetian (1489–1571 CE), Turkish (1571–1878 CE) and British (1878–1960) up to the conclusion in 1960 of an agreement between the United Kingdom, Cyprus and Turkey, which decided that the island would be divided into a Cypriot and a Turkish part.[1702]

In terms of the degree of subjugation to other, larger political entities the history of Cyprus may be compared to that of Crete, an island with an area of 8336 km², located in the Mediterranean Sea, which from 67 BCE was a Roman province, belonged to the Byzantine empire from 395 CE to 1204 CE (with an Arab episode in the years 832–961), later passed to Venetian (1204–1669) and then Turkish hands (1771–1897) with a period of Egyptian rule (1821–1833). In 1913 Crete became part of Greece.[1703]

Chronology of Cypriot history 324–1458[1704]

Period from 324 to 1358

324–337 – reign of St Constantine as emperor of East and West[1705]

325 – first universal (ecumenical) Greek-Latin Council in Nicaea, with the participation of: Cyril, bishop of Paphos, Gelasius, bishop of Salamis, and the miracle worker Spyridon of Trimythos (during it, Arianism was condemned)[1706]

325–330 – St Helena's activity in Palestine[1707]

326/327 – discovery of the Sepulchre of Christ and the Holy Cross relic by St Helena[1708]

330 – founding of Constantinople[1709]

330–964/965 – neutral period during which Cyprus was the location of collisions between Byzantine and Arab influence[1710]

[1701] Vassiliou, The Word Order of Medieval Cypriot, 13.
[1702] Misztal, Historia Cypru, 421, 435.
[1703] Allbaugh, Crete, 5.
[1704] Period dictated by the timeframe of the *Chronicle*. The chronology was prepared fully based on: Burkiewicz, Polityczna rola królestwa Cypru; Edbury, The Kingdom of Cyprus; Hill, The History of Cyprus II; Misztal, Historia Cypru, 164–240; Runciman, A History of the Crusades 1, 2, 3; Schwakopf, Chronologia 1, 2, 3; Setton, Wolff, Hazard, The Later Crusades. The starting date of the Byzantine period on Cyprus has been given after Raszewski, Cypr w okresie bizantyńskim, 227.
[1705] Schwakopf, Chronologia 1, 329.
[1706] Hackett, A History of the Orthodox Church of Cyprus, 7; Bebis, Święta Tradycja, 20.
[1707] Schwakopf, Chronologia 1, 329.
[1708] Schwakopf, Chronologia 1, 329.
[1709] Schwakopf, Chronologia 1, 329.
[1710] Raszewski uses the term 'condominium', in Raszewski, Cypr w okresie bizantyńskim, 227.

381/382 – second ecumenical council in Constantinople, with the participation of prelates: Julius of Paphos, Theopompus of Trimythos, Tycho of Tamassos, Mnemonius of Kition (condemnation of Apollinarianism)[1711]

431 – third ecumenical council in Ephesus; with Cypriot participants: archbishop Reginos, Saprikios, the bishop of Paphos, Zeno, bishop of Kourion, Evagrius, bishop of Solia, and the Protopapas Caesarius (obtaining of autocephaly by the Cypriot church, i.e. independence from the Antiochian church; condemnation of Nestorianism)[1712]

451 – fourth ecumenical council in Chalcedon, in which the prelates Epiphanios of Solia, Epaphroditos of Tamassos and Soter of Theodosiana took part (condemnation of monophysitism)[1713]

553 – fifth ecumenical council in Constantinople, convened by Justinian I (condemnation of the teachings of Theodore of Mopsuestia, Theodoret of Cyrus (Cyrrhus) and Ibas of Edessa, belonging to the School of Antioch)[1714]

6th c. – return of Jews to Cyprus after the Jewish revolt in 116 CE[1715]

609–610 – Muḥammad's revelation in the cave of Hira[1716]

632 – taking of Kition by Abū Bakr, immediate successor of Muḥammad[1717]

649 – attack of Muʿāwiya, governor of Syria, on Cyprus[1718]

653 – second Arab maritime campaign against Cyprus[1719]

680–681 – sixth ecumenical council in Constantinople, with the participation of: Tychon of Kition, Stratonik of Solia, Theodore of Trimythos (condemnation of monothelitism)[1720]

692 – 'ecumenical' council in Trullo in Constantinople, during which the Eastern bishops announced the disciplinary canons collected and drawn up after the fifth and sixth ecumenical councils[1721]

787 – last ecumenical council in Nicaea (condemnation of iconoclasm)[1722]

867 – start of the schism of the Churches[1723]

964/965 – liberation of Cyprus and Asia Minor from Arab influence through the involvement of Byzantine Emperor Nikephoros II Phokas[1724]

965–1191 – period of Byzantine domination, incursions by Seljuk Turks[1725]

1054 – schism between the Greek and the Latin Church[1726]

1096–1099 – first crusade at the instigation of Urban II[1727]

1099 – conquest of Jerusalem by Western forces (Godfrey de Bouillon, king of France Philip and emperor of Constantinople Alexios I Komnenos)[1728]

1110–1118 – reign of Baldwin of Boulogne in Jerusalem[1729]

[1711] Hackett, A History of the Orthodox Church of Cyprus, 7; Bebis, Święta Tradycja, 20.

[1712] Year 382 according to Kuczara, Kościół prawosławny, 318; Bebis, Święta Tradycja, 20; Hackett, A History of the Orthodox Church of Cyprus, 16–19.

[1713] Hackett, A History of the Orthodox Church of Cyprus, 32–33; Bebis, Święta Tradycja, 21.

[1714] Hackett, A History of the Orthodox Church of Cyprus, 33; Bebis, Święta Tradycja, 21.

[1715] Schabel, Religion, 162.

[1716] Haylamaz, Khadija, 90. Hackett comments the event: 'In A.D. 609 began at Mecca that strange religious upheaval, which eventually transformed the illiterate camel-driver of the Koreish into the Prophet of God. For more than two hundred years the island became the battle-ground between the opposing forces of the Cross and the Crescent [...]. During that disastrous period the ruthless warriors of Islam are reported to have carried fire and sword into it on more than twenty-four occasions [...].' (Hackett, A History of the Orthodox Church of Cyprus, 33).

[1717] Hackett, A History of the Orthodox Church of Cyprus, 33.

[1718] Raszewski, Cypr w okresie bizantyńskim, 227; Misztal, Historia Cypru, 120–121; Beihammer, The First Naval Campaigns, 47–68; Browning, Byzantium and Islam, 101–116; Hackett, A History of the Orthodox Church of Cyprus, 33.

[1719] Beihammer, The First Naval Campaigns, 47–68; Browning, Byzantium and Islam, 101–116.

[1720] Hackett, A History of the Orthodox Church of Cyprus, 35–36; Bebis, Święta Tradycja, 21.

[1721] Bebis, Święta Tradycja, 21.

[1722] Schaff, Schmidt (Eds), 'History of the Christian Church...', 149; Bebis, Święta Tradycja, 21.

[1723] Schwakopf, Chronologia, 329.

[1724] Misztal, Historia Cypru, 117; Raszewski, Cypr w okresie bizantyńskim, 234–235.

[1725] Raszewski cites the 1042 uprising initiated by Theophilos Erotikos and a 1091 rebellion led by Rapsomatis, in Raszewski, Cypr w okresie bizantyńskim, 235–236.

[1726] Edbury, The Kingdom of Cyprus, 1.

[1727] Schwakopf, Chronologia 1, 330.

[1728] Schwakopf, Chronologia 1, 330.

[1729] Misztal, Historia Cypru, 633.

1118–1131 – reign of Baldwin of Bourg in Jerusalem[1730]
1131–1143 – reign of Fulk the Younger in Jerusalem[1731]
1136–1137 – Emperor John II Komnenos resettles the Armenian population from Tall Hamdun in Cilician Armenia to Cyprus[1732]
1143–1163 – reign of Baldwin III in Jerusalem[1733]
1147–1149 – second crusade (King Louis VII the Young of France, King Conrad III Hohenstauf of Germany)[1734]
1163–1174 – reign of Amaury I in Jerusalem[1735]
1174–1185 – reign of Baldwin IV the Leper in Jerusalem[1736]
1182 – massacre of the Latins in Constantinople[1737]
1183/1184 – arrival of Isaac Doukas Komnenos, relative of Emperor Manuel I Komnenos on Cyprus, together with an army composed of Armenians, who was recognised as the island's governor and then independent emperor[1738]
– contacts with Muslims, including Saladin of the Ayyūbid dynasty[1739]
1185–1186 – reign of Baldwin V the Child in Jerusalem[1740]
1186–1190 – reign of Sybil in Jerusalem[1741]
1186–1190 – reign of Guy de Lusignan in Jerusalem[1742]
1187 – defeat of Guy's army at the Arab village of Hittin, as a result of which the Muslims took the Holy Cross[1743]
1189–1192 – third crusade (German Emperor Frederick I Barbarossa, King Philip II Augustus of France, King Richard Cœur de Lion of England)[1744]
1191 – encounter between Richard's and Isaac's forces at Trimythos in Cyprus[1745]
– purchase of Cyprus from Richard by the Templars for 100,000 Saracen bezants[1746]
1192 – Cypriot rebellion against the Templars[1747]
– purchase of Cyprus from the Templars by Guy de Lusignan, who became Richard's vassal[1748]
– first wave of refugees (Latins, Christian Syrians, Maronites and Armenians), who came to Cyprus from lands conquered by the Muslims[1749]
– emigration of the Templars to Syria[1750]
– emigration of part of the Rhomaian aristocracy from Cyprus[1751]
1190–1205 – reign of Isabella I in Jerusalem[1752]

[1730] Misztal, Historia Cypru, 633.
[1731] Misztal, Historia Cypru, 643.
[1732] Schabel, Religion, 166.
[1733] Misztal, Historia Cypru, 633.
[1734] Misztal, Historia Cypru, 167; Conte, The 14th and Final Crusade, 5.
[1735] Misztal, Historia Cypru, 630.
[1736] Misztal, Historia Cypru, 633.
[1737] Schabel, Religion, 191.
[1738] Misztal, Historia Cypru, 164–165; Edbury, The Kingdom of Cyprus, 3.
[1739] Ayyūbids – a Kurdish dynasty that ruled from 1174 to the fifteenth century. See Setton, Wolff, Hazard, The Later Crusades, 600; Misztal, Historia Cypru, 167–180.
[1740] Misztal, Historia Cypru, 633.
[1741] Misztal, Historia Cypru, 674.
[1742] Misztal, Historia Cypru, 645.
[1743] Misztal, Historia Cypru, 169–170; Runciman, A History of the Crusades 2, 486–491; Schwakopf, Chronologia 2, 470; Edbury, The Kingdom of Cyprus, 23; Burkiewicz, Na styku chrześcijaństwa i islamu, 8.
[1744] Edbury, The Kingdom of Cyprus, 5; Misztal, Historia Cypru, 170.
[1745] Misztal, Historia Cypru, 173–174; Mirbagheri, Historical Dictionary of Cyprus, 151.
[1746] Misztal, Historia Cypru, 175–176.
[1747] Edbury, The Kingdom of Cyprus, 28; Hill, A History of Cyprus II, 36–37.
[1748] Misztal, Historia Cypru, 179; Hill, A History of Cyprus II, 37–38; Edbury, The Kingdom of Cyprus, 8–9.
[1749] Misztal, Historia Cypru, 180. Cf. LM I 26–27.
[1750] Dawkins, Notes, 52.
[1751] Nicolaou-Konnari, Greeks, 42.
[1752] Misztal, Historia Cypru, 650.

1194–1205 – reign of Amaury de Lusignan (Amaury I) in Cyprus[1753]

1196 – Pope Celestine III's bull addressed to the clergy and citizens of Cyprus permitting the presence of the Latin Church in Cyprus[1754]

1198–1205 – reign of Amaury de Lusignan (Amaury II) in Jerusalem[1755]

1202–1204 – fourth crusade (Boniface of Montferrat, Baldwin of Flanders, Enrico Dandolo)[1756]

1204 – conquest of Constantinople, as a result of which Byzantium stopped supporting Syria, Palestine and Cyprus[1757]

– extension by Amaury II of the cease-fire with sultan Abū Bakr al-'Ādil I, called Sayf ad-Dīn, for another six years, through which gained access to Jerusalem and Nazareth for pilgrims[1758]

1205–1218 – reign of Hugh I, son of Amaury and Echive d'Ibelin[1759]

1205–1212 – reign of Maria of Montferrat in Jerusalem (together with John of Brienne)[1760]

1206 – attempts made by the Cypriots to support Christians present in Adalia, important for trade with the Levant, in their defence against the sultan of Iconium, Ghiyāth al-Dīn Kaykhusraw, resulting in the Cypriots' failure[1761]

1212 – children's crusade[1762]

1217 – fifth crusade (King Andrew II of Hungary, prince Bohemond IV the One-eyed of Antioch and Leopold VI of Austria and Hugh I) upon the initiative of Pope Honorius III[1763]

1218–1253 – reign of Henry I, son of Hugh I and Alice of Champagne[1764]

1220–1222 – proclamation of an agreement between the Latin clergy and Frankish nobility regarding tithing[1765]

– regulation of issues concerning admission to monastic orders, reduction of Greek bishoprics to four[1766]

1229–1233 – civil war in Cyprus[1767]

1229 – signing of a ten-year peace treaty according to which Christians could keep Jerusalem, Bethlehem, Nazareth and west Galilee as well as a strip of land from Lydda to Jaffa, while the Muslims retained access to the Dome on the Rock and Al-Aqsa Mosque[1768]

1231 – execution of thirteen monks from Kantara, described in the document *Martyrion Kyprion*[1769]

1232 – attack on Cyprus by Richard Filangieri, Emperor Frederick II's marshal[1770]

1233 – Henry's confirmation of the privileges granted by Alice and Philip to the Genoese[1771]

1238 – Pope Gregory IX's letter to Latin prelates in eastern lands in which he demands that the Greek clergy submit to the authority of the pope[1772]

1240 – voluntary exile of Greek monks in Armenia[1773]

1244 – loss of Jerusalem by the Franks to the Khwarazmians[1774]

1247 – release by Pope Innocent IV from an oath of loyalty made to Frederick II (in 1228)[1775]

[1753] Hill, A History of Cyprus II, 44–66.
[1754] Hill, A History of Cyprus II, 46; Kuczara, Kościół prawosławny na Cyprze, 320.
[1755] Misztal, Historia Cypru, 630.
[1756] Schwakopf, Chronologia 3, 513.
[1757] Hill, A History of Cyprus II, 65; Misztal, Historia Cypru, 185.
[1758] Misztal, Historia Cypru, 185.
[1759] Hill, A History of Cyprus II, 73–83; Misztal, Historia Cypru, 648.
[1760] Misztal, Historia Cypru, 191, 662.
[1761] Misztal, Historia Cypru, 186.
[1762] Schwakopf, Chronologia 3, 513.
[1763] Schwakopf, Chronologia 3, 513; Hill, A History of Cyprus II, 81. Dating of the popes after Dopierała, Księga papieży.
[1764] Hill, A History of Cyprus II, 83–137; Misztal, Historia Cypru, 189–191, 646.
[1765] Misztal, Historia Cypru, 189–191.
[1766] Schabel, Religion, 191.
[1767] Edbury, Kingdom of Cyprus, 13.
[1768] Misztal, Historia Cypru, 194.
[1769] Schabel, Religion, 159, 196; Burkiewicz, Sztuka dla wychowania, 3.
[1770] Misztal, Historia Cypru, 195–197; Edbury, Kingdom of Cyprus, 13.
[1771] Misztal, Historia Cypru, 199.
[1772] Schabel, Religion, 197.
[1773] Schabel, Religion, 188.
[1774] Hill, History of Cyprus II, 138–139; Edbury, Kingdom of Cyprus, 14, 84; Misztal, Historia Cypru, 197–198.
[1775] Nicolaou-Konnari, Schabel, Introduction, 1–2.

– Pope Innocent IV's declaration of Cyprus' lack of dependence on the Western Empire[1776]

1248 – sixth crusade[1777]

– presence of French King Louis IX in Cyprus, as well as forces from England and Scotland, the Hospitallers, Templars and Syrian barons[1778]

1251 – decree addressed to the Greeks concerning the requirement to conduct mixed marriages according to the Latin rite[1779]

ca. 1252 (and ca. 1280) – warning issued by the Latin bishops of Nicosia addressed to Christians against using the services of Jewish and Muslim doctors[1780]

1253–1261 – regency of Cyprus assumed by Plaisance[1781]

1254 – Pope Innocent IV's letter to the legate cardinal Odo of Châteauroux, in which he expressed his acceptance for Greek practices provided that they are not detrimental to the spiritual dimension of experiencing faith[1782]

1260 – *Bulla Cypria* issued by Pope Alexander IV, making Solia, Arsinoe, Karpasi and Lefkara bishops' seats and subjugating the Greek Church to the pope and Latin clergy in Cyprus[1783]

1261–1267 – regency of Cyprus assumed by Hugh of Antioch[1784]

1263–1272 – reduction of the number of Latin states in the East by the sultan of Egypt, Baybars al-Bunduqdārī[1785]

1263 – Pope Urban IV informs the Cypriots about Michael VIII Palaiologos' and Baybars' plans to capture Cyprus for their own ends[1786]

1267–1284 – reign of Hugh III (Hugh of Antioch), son of Henry of Antioch and Isabella de Lusignan in Cyprus[1787]

1270 – seventh crusade (King Louis IX of France, Prince Edward I of England)[1788]

1277 – Hugh loses the Jerusalem crown[1789]

1280s – synod in Nicosia during which marriages between Greeks and Latins in the Greek rite were forbidden[1790]

1284–1285 – reign of John, son of Hugh III and Isabella d'Ibelin on Cyprus[1791]

1285–1324 – reign of Henry II, son of Hugh III and Isabella d'Ibelin in Cyprus[1792]

1286–1324 – reign of Henry II in Jerusalem[1793]

1291 – fall of Acre[1794]

– arrival of the second wave of refugees on Cyprus[1795]

– return of the Templars to Cyprus[1796]

1292 – Henry II's unsuccessful attempts to invade Alexandria[1797]

1298 – archbishop Gerard's decision decreeing that sexual contact with Jewish or Muslim women would be considered a crime[1798]

[1776] Edbury, Franks, 71.
[1777] Schwakopf, Chronologia 3, 514.
[1778] Misztal, Historia Cypru, 198.
[1779] Nicolaou-Konnari, Greeks, 59.
[1780] Schabel, Religion, 162.
[1781] Misztal, Historia Cypru, 669.
[1782] Schabel, Religion, 198.
[1783] Nicolaou-Konnari, Greeks, 16, 55, 59; Schabel, Religion, 203–210; Coureas, The Latin Church in Cyprus, 184.
[1784] Misztal, Historia Cypru, 648.
[1785] Edbury, Kingdom of Cyprus, 87.
[1786] Hill, History of Cyprus II, 158–178; Misztal, Historia Cypru, 202.
[1787] Misztal, Historia Cypru, 203. According to LM I 41 the start of his reign was in 1269.
[1788] Schwakopf, Chronologia 3, 515.
[1789] Misztal, Historia Cypru, 205–206.
[1790] Nicolaou-Konnari, Greeks, 59.
[1791] Hill, History of Cyprus II, 179; Misztal, Historia Cypru, 651.
[1792] Hill, History of Cyprus II, 179–190, 261–285; Edbury, Kingdom of Cyprus, 101–140; Misztal, Historia Cypru, 647.
[1793] Misztal, Historia Cypru, 647.
[1794] Schwakopf, Chronologia 3, 515.
[1795] Nicolaou-Konnari, Greeks, 14.
[1796] Haag, Templars, 204.
[1797] Misztal, Historia Cypru, 210–211.
[1798] Schabel, Religion, 162.

APPENDIX 1

1306–1310 – **usurper Amaury of Tyre, son of Hugh III and Isabella d'Ibelin, takes the Cypriot throne**[1799]

1307 – Pope Clement V issues the bull *Pastoralis Praeeminentiae* ordering the Templars on Cyprus to be arrested[1800]

1310 – **Amaury's murder by Simon de Montolif**[1801]

1311–1312 – Pope Clement V issues the bull *Vox in excelso*, in which he **dissolves the Templar order and commands that their estates be given to the Hospitallers**[1802]

1313 – riots provoked by papal legate Peter de Pleine Chassagne[1803]

1314 – Jacques de Molay, grand master of the Templar order, burned at the stake[1804]

1320 etc. – the pope starts to issue permits for trading with the Muslims[1805]

1324–1359 – **reign of Hugh IV, son of Guy de Lusignan and Echive d'Ibelin in Cyprus in Jerusalem (as Hugh II)**[1806]

1330 – forty-day procession composed of Latins, Greeks, Armenians, Nestorians, Jacobites and Maronites led through Cyprus by John of Conti, a Dominican and the archbishop of Nicosia after the river Pedieos flooded[1807]

1334 – Cypriots join the Holy League; victory over the Turks[1808]

1340 – council in Nicosia during which Greek bishops agreed to the use of unleavened bread for consecration and accepted the *filioque* issue[1809]

1347–1348 – **plague epidemic on Cyprus,** leading to the deaths of a large part of the island's population[1810]

1280s and 1353 – synod in Nicosia during which (once again) marriages between Greeks and Latins in the Greek rite were forbidden[1811]

Reign of Peter I

1358–1369 – **reign of Peter I, son of Hugh IV and Alice d'Ibelin, as the king of Cyprus**[1812]

1360 – Peter's coronation as king of Jerusalem by Peter de Thomas[1813]

– Peter de Thomas arrives in Cyprus and attempts to convert the Greek clergy[1814]

– inhabitants of the Armenian Gorhigos, ruled by Constantine IV, **voluntarily surrender to Peter I**[1815]

1361 – capture of Adalia at the centre of the Takka emirate, and then surrender of the emirs of Alaya and Monovgat[1816]

1362–1365 – Peter I's visit to the West (**Venice, Genoa, Avignon,** Flanders, Brabant, **Germany,** London, Prague, Cracow, Vienna and **Venice again**)[1817]

1362–1363 – **Turkish attacks on Cyprus in 1362 and 1363**[1818]

[1799] Hill, History of Cyprus II, 218–260; Misztal, Historia Cypru, 211–212.
[1800] Edbury, Kingdom of Cyprus, 121.
[1801] Edbury, Kingdom of Cyprus, 125–126; Misztal, Historia Cypru, 211–212.
[1802] Burkiewicz, Templariusze, 9.
[1803] Schabel, Religion, 159.
[1804] Misztal, Historia Cypru, 9.
[1805] Edbury, Kingdom of Cyprus, 150.
[1806] Hill, History of Cyprus II, 285–307; Misztal, Historia Cypru, 216.
[1807] Schabel, Religion, 160.
[1808] Hill, History of Cyprus II, 308–178; Misztal, Historia Cypru, 219.
[1809] Schabel, Religion, 198.
[1810] Nicolaou-Konnari, Greeks, 16.
[1811] Nicolaou-Konnari, Greeks, 59.
[1812] Hill, History of Cyprus II, 308–369; Misztal, Historia Cypru, 219.
[1813] LM II 104.
[1814] Schabel, Religion, 159.
[1815] Misztal, Historia Cypru, 222–223; LM II 114 gives the date 1360.
[1816] Misztal, Historia Cypru, 222–223.
[1817] Burkiewicz, Podróż króla Cypru, 3–29; Misztal, Historia Cypru, 223–224.
[1818] LM II 126–144.

1362 – Peter de Thomas leads an intercessory procession in order to ward off the plague in Famagusta (participants: Greeks, Armenians, Nestorians, Jacobites, Georgians, Nubians, Indians, Ethiopians, as well as Muslims and Jews)[1819]
1365 – **agreement between Cyprus and Genoa**[1820]
    – **Peter I and Western forces capture Alexandria**[1821]
1367 – **Peter I captures Tripoli**[1822]
    – **long period of negotiations between the Cypriots and the Egyptian ruler** Yalbughā al-Khāṣṣakī[1823]
1368 – **Peter's coronation as ruler of Cilician Armenia**[1824]
1369 – **Peter I's murder by Philip d'Ibelin, Henry de Giblet and John de Gaurelle**[1825]

Reign of Peter II

1369–1382 – **reign of Peter II, son of Peter I and Eleanora of Aragon in Cyprus**[1826]
1372 – **proposal made by John V Palaiologos, emperor of Constantinople, for Peter II to marry his daughter Irene**[1827]
1373–1374 – **Venetian-Genoese conflict in Cyprus**[1828]
    – destruction of the Jewish community in Cyprus[1829]
1373 – **Genoese attack on Cyprus with the consent of Pope Gregory XI**[1830]
    – **first peasant rebellion in Cyprus**[1831]
1374 – **conclusion of peace between Cyprus and Genoa**[1832] (**possible conflict between the Genoese Guelph and Ghibelline families?**[1833])
    – **Adalia returned to the Turks in exchange for an annual tribute**[1834]
1378 – **Peter II's marriage to Valentina, daughter of the lord of Milan, Barnabo Visconti**[1835]

Reign of James I

1372 – **marriage of James, son of Hugh IV and Alice d'Ibelin, and Helvis of Brunswick**[1836]
1382–1398 – **James' reign in Cyprus**[1837]
1382–1398 – **James' reign in Jerusalem**[1838]
1385 – **James ransomed from Genoese captivity**[1839]

[1819] Schabel, Religion, 157–158.
[1820] Hill, History of Cyprus II, 314.
[1821] LM II 168–175; Guillaume de Machaut, La prise d'Alexandrie.
[1822] LM II 210.
[1823] Misztal, Historia Cypru, 226.
[1824] Misztal, Historia Cypru, 226.
[1825] Misztal, Historia Cypru, 227–228.
[1826] Hill, History of Cyprus II, 370–430.
[1827] LM III 334.
[1828] Misztal, Historia Cypru, 228–229.
[1829] Schabel, Religion, 163.
[1830] Misztal, Historia Cypru, 230.
[1831] Nicolaou-Konnari, Greeks, 20.
[1832] Coureas, Economy, 109; Hill, History of Cyprus II, 413.
[1833] Dawkins reads these names from LM III 519. He justifies this as follows: 'The names in the text are corrupt and beneath them lie concealed Guelf and Ghibelline, as may be seen from the parallel passages in Amadi, p. 471.' (Dawkins, Notes, 181–182, note 1 to LM III 519).
[1834] Misztal, Historia Cypru, 230–231.
[1835] LM III 305.
[1836] Hill, History of Cyprus II, 431–446.
[1837] Misztal, Historia Cypru, 650.
[1838] Misztal, Historia Cypru, 650.
[1839] Misztal, Historia Cypru, 232; Luke, The Kingdom of Cyprus, 368.

1392–1393 – plague epidemic breaks out[1840]
1396–1398 – James' reign in Armenia[1841]

Reign of Janus

1392 – Janus, son of James and Helvis, ransomed from Genoese captivity[1842]
1399 – Janus accepts the crown of Cyprus, Jerusalem and Antioch[1843]
1402, 1404 – attempts to take Famagusta made by Janus[1844]
1409, 1419, 1420, 1422 – plague epidemics break out[1845]
1409–1412 – plague of locusts appears[1846]
1424–1426 – Egyptian attacks on Cyprus; Larnaka and Lemesos destroyed[1847]
1426 – **battle of Khirokitia**[1848]
    – Egyptians loot the monastery on Mount Stavro Vouni[1849]
    – Lefkosia surrenders[1850]
    – **Janus is taken captive** and ransomed among others using the assets of the Genoese Benedict Pernessin and the Cypriot John Podocataro and through the support of Pope Martin V[1851]
1426–1427 – peasant rebellion[1852]
1432 – Janus sends a diplomatic embassy to the king of Poland, Ladislaus II Jagiello, headed by the marshal of Jerusalem Badin de Nores, with a request for a loan of 100 thousand florins that he could use in the war with the sultan[1853]
    – plans for a marriage between John, son of Janus and Hedwig, the daughter of Ladislaus, ending in failure due to Hedwig's death in 1431[1854]

Reign of John II[1855]

1432–1458 – reign of John, son of Janus and Charlotte in Cyprus[1856]
1438 – plague epidemic breaks out[1857]
1442 – John's marriage to Helena Palaiologina, which allowed the Greek Church to regain part of its influence[1858]
1453 – **capture of Constantinople** and fall of the Byzantine Empire[1859]
1470 – plague epidemic breaks out[1860]
1472 – second, smaller peasant rebellion (intended to kill King James and place Charlotte on the throne)[1861]

[1840] Misztal, Historia Cypru, 234.
[1841] Misztal, Historia Cypru, 650.
[1842] Misztal, Historia Cypru, 235.
[1843] Hill, History of Cyprus II, 447–496.
[1844] Misztal, Historia Cypru, 235. Makhairas does not give the precise dates, see LM V 630–635.
[1845] Misztal, Historia Cypru, 236.
[1846] Misztal, Historia Cypru, 236.
[1847] LM V 651–695.
[1848] LM V 674–685.
[1849] LM V 695.
[1850] Misztal, Historia Cypru, 236.
[1851] Misztal, Historia Cypru, 237.
[1852] Nicolaou-Konnari, Greeks, 16.
[1853] Misztal, Historia Cypru, 238; Burkiewicz, Two Cypriot royal missions.
[1854] Burkiewicz, Σχέσεις Κύπρου-Πολωνίας, 18–47.
[1855] The part of the *Chronicle* that covers these events was probably written after Makhairas' death, by a different person.
[1856] Misztal, Historia Cypru, 239.
[1857] Nicolaou-Konnari, Greeks, 16.
[1858] Kuczara, Kościół prawosławny na Cyprze, 321.
[1859] Schwakopf, Chronologia 3, 515; LM VI 711.
[1860] Nicolaou-Konnari, Greeks, 16.
[1861] Nicolaou-Konnari, Greeks, 20.

Appendix 2. Maps

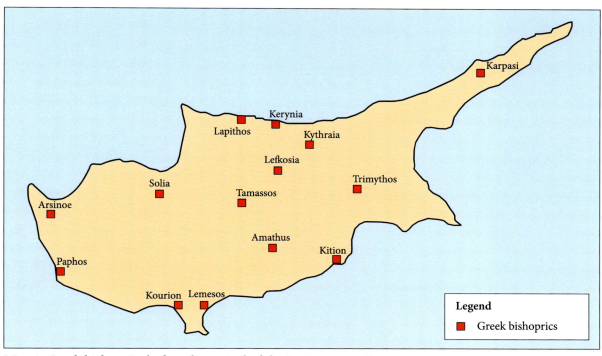

Map 1. Greek bishoprics before the arrival of the Lusignans in Cyprus

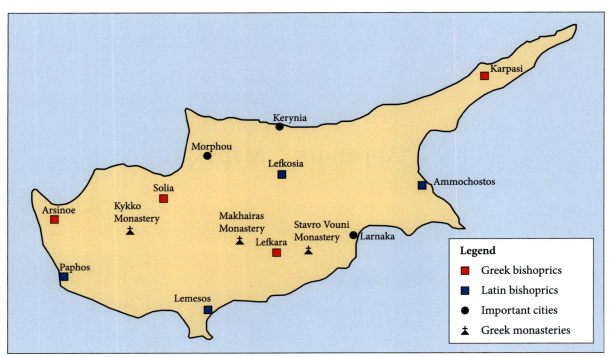

Map 2. Greek and Latin bishoprics after the Lusignan takeover of Cyprus

References

Greek sources

A. Editions and translations of the *Chronicle* of Leontios Makhairas

Dawkins (Ed., transl.), Εξήγησις/ Recital
Λ. Μαχαιράς, Εξήγησις της γλυκείας χώρας Κύπρου η οποία λέγεται Κρόνακα τουτέστιν Κρόνικον/ Recital Concerning the Sweet Land of Cyprus entitled 'Chronicle', R.M. Dawkins (Ed., transl.), 2 Vols, Oxford 1932

Machieras, Wykład o słodkiej ziemi Cypru
L. Machieras, Wykład o słodkiej ziemi Cypru Cronaca, to jest Kroniką zwany, przełożyła z dialektu cypryjskiego, wstępem, przypisami, słownikiem i indeksami opatrzyła Małgorzata Borowska, Warszawa [forthcoming]

Νικολάου-Κονναρή, Πιερής (Eds), Παράλληλη διπλωματική έκδοση
Λ. Μαχαιράς, Χρονικό της Κύπρου. Παράλληλη διπλωματική έκδοση των χειρογράφων, Ά. Νικολάου-Κονναρή, Μ. Πιερής (Eds), Λευκωσία 2003

Παυλίδης (Ed.), Λεοντίου Μαχαιρά Χρονικόν
Ά. Παυλίδης (Ed.), Λεοντίου Μαχαιρά Χρονικόν, Λευκωσία 1995

Σάθας (Ed.), Χρονογράφοι Βασιλείου Κύπρου
Κ.Ν. Σάθας (Ed.), Χρονογράφοι Βασιλείου Κύπρου, *Μεσαιωνική Βιβλιοθήκη*, Τόμος Β, Βενετία 1873

Sathas, Miller (Eds, transl.), Chronique de Chypre
Κ.Ν. Sathas, E. Miller (Eds, transl.), Λεοντίου Μαχαιρά Χρονικόν Κύπρου/ Léonce Makhairas, Chronique de Chypre, *Publications de l'École des Langues Orientales Vivantes. IIe série*, II–III, Paris 1882
Other editions and translations:
    Λ. Μαχαιράς, Χρονικόν Κύπρου [Microforme]/ Chronique de Chypre, E. Miller, C. Sathas (Eds, transl.), Paris 1973
    Λ. Μαχαιράς, Χρονικόν Κύπρου/ Chronique de Chypre, E. Miller, C. Sathas (Eds, transl.), Athènes 2004

B. Works Inspired by the *Chronicle* of Leontios Makhairas

Μαχαιράς, Αναξαγόρου (Elab.), Εξηγήσεις δια αθύμησιν καιρού και τόπου
Λ. Μαχαιράς, Ν. Αναξαγόρου (Elab.), Εξηγήσεις δια αθύμησιν καιρού και τόπου/ Exegeses in Remembrance of Time and Place, Αθήνα 2013

Μαχαιράς, Πιερής (Ed.), Χρονικό της Κύπρου
Λ. Μαχαιράς, Ά. Πιερής (Ed.), Χρονικό της Κύπρου, Λευκωσία 2000

C. Other Greek sources

Βουστρόνιος, Διήγησις κρόνικας Κύπρου
Γ. Βουστρόνιος, Διήγησις κρόνικας Κύπρου, Γ. Κεχαγιόλου (Ed.), Λευκωσία 2002

Schmitt (Ed.), The Chronicle of Morea
J. Schmitt (Ed.), Το χρονικόν του Μορέως. The Chronicle of Morea. A History in Political Verse, Relating the Establishment of Feudalism in Greece by the Franks in the Thirteenth Century, edited in Two Parallel Texts from the MSS of Copenhagen and Paris, with Introduction, Critical Notes and Indices by John Schmitt, London 1904

Ζωναράς, Τα ευρισκόμενα πάντα
Ι. Ζωναράς, Τα ευρισκόμενα πάντα/ Joannis Zonarae Opera Omnia. Historica, Canonica, Dogmatica, accedunt Eustathii Thessalonicensis Scripta ad Rem Christianam Spectantia, J.-P. Migne (Ed.), *Bibliothecae Cleri Universe*, Paris 1864

Other sources and translations

A. Editions of translations of the *Chronicle* and texts based (directly and indirectly) on the *Chronicle*

Bustron, Chronique de l'Île de Chypre
F. Bustron, Chronique de l'Île de Chypre, [in:] R. de Mas Latrie (Ed.), *Mélanges historiques*, Vol. 5, Paris 1886

Bustron, Historia overo Commentarii de Cipro
F. Bustron, Historia overo Commentarii de Cipro, Nicosia 1998

Cervellin-Chevalier (Ed., transl.), Édition critique et traduction française
I. Cervellin-Chevalier (Ed., Transl.), Édition critique et traduction française annotée du manuscrit de Venise de la Chronique de Leontios Machairas, Villeneuve d'Ascq 2002

Cervellin-Chevalier (Transl.), Une histoire du doux pays de Chypre
I. Cervellin-Chevalier (Transl.), Une histoire du doux pays de Chypre: traduction du manuscrit de Venise de Leontios Machairas, vol. publ. sous la dir. d'Andréas Chatzisavas, *Collection Lapithos*, Besançon 2002

Coureas (Transl.), A Narrative of the Chronicle of Cyprus
G. Boustronios, A Narrative of the Chronicle of Cyprus 1456–1489, N. Coureas (Transl.), Nicosia 2005

Coureas, Edbury (Transl.), The Chronicle of Amadi
N. Coureas, P. Edbury (Transl.), The Chronicle of Amadi, *Texts and Studies in the History of Cyprus* LXXIV, Nicosia 2015

Dawkins (Transl., int.), The Chronicle of George Boustronios
R.M. Dawkins (Transl., int.), The Chronicle of George Boustronios 1456–89, Publication No. 2, University of Melbourne Cyprus Expedition, Parkville, Vic., Australia 1964

Mas Latrie (Ed.), Chronique d'Amadi
R. de Mas Latrie (Ed.), Chronique d'Amadi, [in:] R. de Mas Latrie (Ed.), Chroniques d'Amadi et de Strambaldi, Publiées par René de Mas Latrie, Vol. 1, *Collection de documents inédits sur l'histoire de France*, Paris 1891

Mas Latrie (Ed.), Chroniques d'Amadi et de Strambaldi
R. de Mas Latrie (Ed.), Chroniques d'Amadi et de Strambaldi, Publiées par René de Mas Latrie, Vol. 1, 2, *Collection de documents inédits sur l'histoire de France*, Paris 1891

Mas Latrie (Ed.), Chronique de Strambaldi
R. de Mas Latrie (Ed.), Chronique de Strambaldi, [in:] R. de Mas Latrie (Ed.), Chroniques d'Amadi et de Strambaldi, Publiées par René de Mas Latrie, Vol. 2, *Collection de documents inédits sur l'histoire de France*, Paris 1891

Stephen de Lusignan, Lusignan's Chorography
Stephen de Lusignan, Lusignan's Chorography and Brief General History of the Island of Cyprus (A.D. 1573), A.G. Orphanides, P.W. Wallace (Eds), O. Pelosi (Transl.), Albany, New York 2001

B. Editions and translations of other sources

Ali (Transl.), Quran
A.Y. Ali (Transl.), Quran, Birmingham 1946

Alighieri, Inferno
D. Alighieri, Inferno, H.W. Longfellow (Transl.), Mineola, New York 2011

Anna Komnene, The Alexiad
Anna Komnene, The Alexiad, E.A.S. Dawes (Transl.), *Byzantine Series*, Cambridge, Ontario 2000

Al-Atir, Kompletna księga historii
'Alī 'Izz ad-Dīn Ibn al-Aṯir', Kompletna księga historii. Z czynów sułtana Saladyna. al-kāmil fī al-tārīḫ min afʿāl as-sulṭān Ṣalāḥ ad-Dīn, M.F. Horbowski, J. Maćkowiak, D. Małgowski (Transl.), Z. Pentek (Ed., int., com.), Poznań 2007

Bertrandon de La Broquière, Le Voyage d'Outremer
Bertrandon de La Broquière, Le Voyage d'Outremer de Bertrandon, Premier Écuyer Tranchant et Conseiller de Philippe le Bon, Duc de Bourgogne, publié et annoté par Ch. Schefer, Paris 1892 (https://gallica.bnf.fr/ark:/12148/bpt6k1037921.texteImage, accessed 10 December 2021)

Borowska (Transl.), Dijenis Akritas
M. Borowska (Transl.), Dijenis Akritas. Opowieść z kresów, Warszawa 1998

Buchon (Ed.), Les Chroniques de Sire Jean Froissart
J.A.C. Buchon (Ed.), Les Chroniques de Sire Jean Froissart, 3 Vols, Paris 1835

Al-Bukhārī, Ṣaḥīḥ al-Bukhārī
Muḥammad ibn Ismāʿīl Bukhārī, Ṣaḥīḥ al-Bukhārī, Vol. 1, Book 2, Hadith 18 (https://sunnah.com/bukhari/2/11#!, accessed 8 December 2021)

Chimenz (Ed.), Tutte le opera
S.A. Chimenz (Ed.), Tutte le opera. La Divina Commedia di Dante Alighieri, Torino 2003

Choniates, O City of Byzantium
N. Choniates, O City of Byzantium: Annals of Niketas Choniatēs, H.J. Magoulias (Ed.), Detroit 1984

Cobham (Ed.), Excerpta Cypria
C.D. Cobham (Ed.), Excerpta Cypria: materials for a history of Cyprus; tr. and transcribed, with an appendix on the bibliography of Cyprus, Cambridge 1908[1], 1969

Coureas (Transl.), The Assizes
N. Coureas (Transl.), The Assizes of the Lusignan Kingdom of Cyprus, Nicosia 2002

Crawford (Ed.), 'Templar of Tyre'
P. Crawford (Ed.), The 'Templar of Tyre', [in:] P. Crawford (Ed.), 'Deeds of the Cypriots', Part III, Aldershot 2003

Danecki (Select., elab.), Klasyczna poezja arabska
J. Danecki (Select., elab.), Klasyczna poezja arabska. Poezja epoki Abbasydów (VIII–XIII w.), Warszawa 1988

Delehaye (Ed.), Synaxarium ecclesiae Constantinopolitanae
H. Delehaye (Ed.), Synaxarium ecclesiae Constantinopolitanae e codice Sirmondiano nunc Berolinensi adiectis synaxariis selectis, Bruxellis 1902 (1954)

Estienne de Lusignan, Description de toute l'isle de Cypre
Estienne de Lusignan, Description de toute l'isle de Cypre: et des roys, princes et seigneurs, tant payens que chrestiens qui ont commandé en icelle, Paris 1580

Euringer (Ed., transl.), Die äthiopischen Anaphoren
S. Euringer (Ed. transl.), Die äthiopishen Anaphoren des hl. Evangelisten Johannes de Donnersohnes und des hl. Jacobus von Sarug drei bzw. vier Handschriften, *Orientalia Christiana* 33, 1, Roma 1934

Filippo da Novara, Guerra di Federico II in Oriente
Filippo da Novara, Guerra di Federico II in Oriente (1223–1242), S. Melani (Ed.), Napoli 1994

George Akropolites, The History
George Akropolites, The History, R. Macrides (Int., ed., transl.), Oxford 2007

Gilmour-Bryson (Ed.), The Trial of the Templars in Cyprus
A. Gilmour-Bryson (Ed.), The Trial of the Templars in Cyprus, Melbourne 1998

Goldast, Collectio constitutionum imperialium
M. Goldast, Collectio constitutionum imperialium, Vol. 1, Frankfurt am Main 1673

Grégoire de Tours, Histoire Ecclésiastique des Francs
Grégoire de Tours, Histoire Ecclésiastique des Francs par Georges Florent Grégoire, évêque de Tours, en dix livres, Vol. 1, Paris 1836

Gregory of Tours, The History of the Franks
Gregory Bishop of Tours, The History of the Franks, Selections translated with notes by Ernest Brehaut, *Columbia University Records of Civilization, Sources and Studies*, general editor W.T.H. Jackson, New York, London 1969

Guibert of Nogent, The Deeds of God Through the Franks
Guibert of Nogent, The Deeds of God Through the Franks, R. Levine (Ed.), Lexington, KY 1997 (https://www.gutenberg.org/cache/epub/4370/pg4370.html, accessed 12 January 2021)

Guillaume de Machaut, La prise d'Alexandrie
Guillaume de Machaut, La prise d'Alexandrie, ou Chronique du roi Pierre Ier de Lusignan / par Guillaume de Machaut, publiée pour la première fois pour la Société de l'Orient latin par M.L. de Mas-Latrie, Genève 1877

Guillaume de Tyr, L'estoire de Eracles [...] la translation
Guillaume de Tyr, L'estoire de Eracles empereur et la conqueste de la Terre d'Outremer: c'est la translation de l'Estoire de Guillaume arcevesque de Sur, *Recueil des historiens des croisades: Historiens occidentaux* 1, Paris 1844

Guillaume de Tyr, L'estoire de Eracles [...] la continuation
Guillaume de Tyr, L'estoire de Eracles empereur et la conqueste de la Terre d'Outremer: c'est la continuation de l'Estoire de Guillaume arcevesque de Sur, *Recueil des historiens des croisades: Historiens occidentaux* 2, publié par Arthur Beugnot et A. Langlois, Paris 1859, 1–481

Hagenmeyer (Ed.), Gesta Francorum et Aliorum Hierosolymitanorum
H. Hagenmeyer (Ed.), [Anonymi] Gesta Francorum et Aliorum Hierosolymitanorum, Heildelberg 1890

Ibn Battuta, Osobliwości miast i dziwy podróży
Ibn Battuta, Osobliwości miast i dziwy podróży 1325–1354, T. Majda, H. Natorf (Select., transl.), Warszawa 1962

Ibn Chaldun, Wybór pism
Ibn Chaldun, Wybór pism, [in:] J. Bielawski, Ibn Chaldun, Myśli i ludzie, Warszawa 2000

Jacques de Vitry, La traduction de l'Historia Orientalis
Jacques de Vitry, La traduction de l'Historia Orientalis de Jacques de Vitry, C. Buridant (Ed.), Paris 1986

Jean d'Arras, Melusine
Jean d'Arras, Melusine; or, the Noble History of Lusignan, D. Maddox, S. Sturm-Maddox (Eds), University Park, Philadelphia 2012

Kelly, Early Christian Creeds
J.N.D. Kelly, Early Christian Creeds, New York 2008
(https://pl.scribd.com/document/161118009/Early-Christian-Creeds-J-N-D-Kelly, accessed 22 November 2021)

King (Ed.), The Rule, Statutes and Customs of the Hospitallers
E.J. King (Ed.), The Rule, Statutes and Customs of the Hospitallers, 1099–1310, London 1934

Luce, Raynaud, Mirot (Eds), Chroniques de J. Froissart
S. Luce, G.L. Raynaud, A. Mirot (Eds), Chroniques de J. Froissart, 14 Vols, Paris 1869–1875

Macaulay (Ed.), Bourchier, Berners (Transl.), The Chronicles of Froissart
G.C. Macaulay (Ed.), J. Bourchier, L. Berners (Transl.), The Chronicles of Froissart (Les Chroniques de Froissart), reduced into one volume, London 1924
(https://ehistory.osu.edu/books/froissart, accessed 9 December 2021)

Mas Latrie, Histoire de l'île de Chypre I, II, III
L. Mas Latrie, Histoire de l'île de Chypre sous le règne des princes de la maison de Lusignan, Paris, Vol. I, 1861, Vol. II, 1852, Vol. III, 1855

Maximus the Confessor, On the Cosmic Mystery of Jesus Christ
St Maximus the Confessor, On the Cosmic Mystery of Jesus Christ, Selected Writings from St Maximus the Confessor, P.M. Blowers, R.L. Wilken (Transl.), Crestwood, New York 2003

Minervini (Ed.), Cronaca del Templare de Tiro
L. Minervini (Ed.), Cronaca del Templare de Tiro (1243–1314): La caduta degli Stati Crociati nel racconto di un testimone oculare, Napoli 2000

Nesbitt (Ed.), Byzantine Authors
J.W. Nesbitt (Ed.), Byzantine Authors: Literary Activities and Preoccupations. Texts and Translations dedicated to the Memory of Nicolas Oikonomides, Leiden 2003

New Revised Standard Version
New Revised Standard Version (NRSV) of the Bible, 1989
(https://www.biblegateway.com/versions/New-Revised-Standard-Version-NRSV-Bible/#vinfo, accessed 10 December 2021)

Palmer (Ed., transl.), La Prise D'Alixandre
R.B. Palmer (Ed., transl.), Guillaume de Machaut, La Prise D'Alixandre: The Taking of Alexandria, New York, London 2002

Paprocki (Transl.), Liturgie Kościoła prawosławnego
H. Paprocki (Transl.), Liturgie Kościoła prawosławnego, *Biblioteka Ojców Kościoła* nr 20, Kraków 2014

Paris, Mas Latrie (Eds), Les Gestes des Chiprois
G. Paris, L. de Mas Latrie (Eds), Les Gestes des Chiprois, [in:] Recueil des historiens des croisades. Documents arméniens, Vol. 2, Paris 1906, 651–872

Philippe de Mézières, The life of Saint Peter Thomas
Philippe de Mézières, The life of Saint Peter Thomas, J. Smet (Ed.), Rome 1954

Philippe de Mézières, Le Songe
Philippe de Mézières, Le Songe du Vieil Pelerin, G.W. Coopland (Ed.), Vol. 1, Cambridge 1969

Röhricht, Reynaud (Eds), Annales de Terre Sainte
R. Röhricht, G. Reynaud (Eds), Annales de Terre Sainte, *Archives de l'Orient latin* 2, Documents, Paris 1884, 427–461

Σάθας (Ed.), Ασίζαι
Κ.Ν. Σάθας (Ed.), Ασίζαι του Βασιλείου των Ιεροσολύμων και της Κύπρου, *Μεσαιωνική Βιβλιοθήκη Τόμος ΣΤ′*, Βενετία 1877

Schabel (Ed.), Bullarium Cyprium 1
C.D. Schabel (Ed.), Bullarium Cyprium: Papal letters concerning Cyprus, 1196–1261, Nicosia 2010

Schabel (Ed.), Bullarium Cyprium 2
C.D. Schabel (Ed.), Bullarium Cyprium: Papal letters concerning Cyprus, 1261–1314, Nicosia 2010

Schabel, Perrat (Eds), Bullarium Cyprium 3
C.D. Schabel, C. Perrat (Eds), Bullarium Cyprium: Lettres papales relatives à Chypre, 1316–1378, Nicosia 2010

Seferis, Three mules
G. Seferis, Three mules (1955), [in:] George Seferis, Edmund Keeley and Philip Sherrard, *Poetry*, Vol. 105, No. 1 (Oct., 1964), 48–49

Shiapkara-Pitsillides (Ed.), Le Pétrarchisme en Chypre
Th. Shiapkara-Pitsillides (Ed.), Le Pétrarchisme en Chypre. Poèmes d'amour en dialecte chypriote, d'après un manuscrit du XVIe siècle, Biblioteca Nazionale di San Marco App. G. IX, 32, *Collection Connaissance de la Grèce*, Athènes 1952

Smith Lewis (Ed., transl.), Apocrypha Syriaca
A. Smith Lewis (Ed., transl.), Apocrypha Syriaca. The Protevangelium Jacobi and Transitus Mariae, *Studia Sinaitica* 11 (1902)

Stephanos Byzantios, Ethnicorum quæ supersunt
Stephanos Byzantios, Ethnicorum quæ supersunt. Ex recensione Augusti Meinekii, Berollini 1849

Usama Ibn Munkiz, Kitab al I'tibar
Usama Ibn Munkiz, Kitab al I'tibar. Księga pouczających przykładów dzieło Usamy Ibn Munkidha, J. Bielawski (Transl.), Wrocław 1975

Wallis Budge (Transl.), The Book of the Saints of the Ethiopian Church
E.A. Wallis Budge, The Book of the Saints of the Ethiopian Church: A Translation of the Ethiopic Synaxarium (Mashafa Senkesar): made from the mss. Oriental 660 and 661 in the British Museum, Cambridge 1928

Wincenty Kadłubek, Kronika polska
Mistrz Wincenty (tzw. Kadłubek), Kronika polska, B. Kürbis (Transl., elab.), Warszawa, Kraków 2008 (edition based on *Seria I Biblioteki Narodowej* nr 277, 1996)

Scientific studies

A. Scientific studies in Greek

Γιαγκουλλης, Θησαυρός της Κυπριακής Διαλέκτου
Κ.Γ. Γιαγκουλλης, Θησαυρός της Κυπριακής Διαλέκτου. Ερμηνευτικό, Ετυμολογικό, Φρασεολογικό και Ονοματολογικό Λεξικό της Μεσαιονικής και Νεότερης Κυπριακής Διαλέκτου, δ.φ. Βιβλιοθήκη Κυπρίων Λαικών Ποιητών, απ. 70. Διευθυντής-Επιμελητής, Δπ. Κ.Γ. Γιαγκουλλής, Λευκωσία 2009

Εγγλεζάκης, Είκοσι μελέται
Β. Εγγλεζάκης, Είκοσι μελέται δια την Εκκλησία της Κύπρου (4ος–20ος αι.), Αθήνα 1996

Καρυολαίμου, Τι απέγινε η κυπριακή διάλεκτος
Κ. Καρυολαίμου, Τι απέγινε η κυπριακή διάλεκτος, *Κείμενο που δημοσιεύτηκε στην Επετηρίδα Κέντρου Επιστημονικών Ερευνών* XXXIV, Λευκωσία 2008, 451–492

Καρυολαίμου, Γλωσσική πολιτική
Κ. Καρυολαίμου, Γλωσσική πολιτική και γλωσσικός σχεδιασμός στην Κύπρο, [in:] Α. Βοσκός, Δ. Γούτσος, Α. Μόζερ (Eds), Η ελληνική γλώσσα στην Κύπρο από την αρχαιότητα ως σήμερα, Αθήνα 2010, 242–261

Καρυολαίμου, Le chypriote
Κ. Καρυολαίμου, Le chypriote: dialecte ou idiome, [in:] Α.-Φ. Χριςτίδης *et al.* (Eds), Η ελληνική γλώσσα και οι διάλεκτοί της, Αθήνα 2000, 111–115

Κεχαγιόγλου, Παπαλεοντιόυ, Το γραμματειακό 'πολυσύστημα'
Γ. Κεχαγιόγλου, Λ. Παπαλεοντίου, Το γραμματειακό 'πολυσύστημα' του ύστερου Μεσαίωνα και η ποικιλία της ελληνόγλωσσης λόγιας, ημιλόγιας, δημώδοις και ιδωματικής λογοτεχνίας ώς το τέλος της φραγκοκρατίας (12ος αι.–1489), [in:] Γ. Κεχαγιόγλου, Λ. Παπαλεοντίου, Η ιστορία της νεότερης κυπριακής λογοτεχνίας, Λευκωσία 2016

Κουκουλές, Παροιμίαι καὶ γνωμικά
Φ. Κουκουλές, Παροιμίαι καὶ γνωμικά ἐν τῷ Χρονικῷ τοῦ Λεοντίου Μαχαιρᾶ, *Ἀθηνᾶ* 57–8 (1953–1954), 235–242

Κριαρᾶς, Ἕνα νέο χειρόγραφο
Ἐ. Κριαρᾶς, Ἕνα νέο χειρόγραφο τοῦ Χρονικοῦ τοῦ Λεοντίου Μαχαιρᾶ, *Ἐπιστημονικὴ Ἐπετηρίδα Φιλοσοφικῆς Σχολῆς Πανεπιστημίου Θεσσαλονίκης* 7 (1957), 43–47 (http://epet.nlg.gr/db/icon/1957/57_04.pdf, accessed 10 December 2021)

Κριαρᾶς, Λεξικο
Ε. Κριαρᾶς, Λεξικο της Μεσαιωνικης Ελληνικης δημωδους γραμματειας, 1100–1669, Vol. 1, Hypourgeio Ethnikēs Paideias kai Thrēskeumatōn, Thessaloniki 1968

Κωμοδίκης, Οι Πληροφορίες των Βραχέων Χρονικών
Κ. Κωμοδίκης, Οι Πληροφορίες των Βραχέων Χρονικών για την Κύπρο. Η Κατάταξη και ο Σχολιασμός τους, Λευκωσια 2006

Λαγάκος, Ο Σεφέρης και η Κύπρος
Τ. Λαγάκος, Ο Σεφέρης και η Κύπρος, Αθήνα 1984

Νικολάου-Κονναρή, Η διασκευή
Α. Νικολάου-Κονναρή, Η διασκευή του χειρογράφου της Ραβέννας της Εξήγησης του Λεοντίου Μαχαιρά και η Narratione του Διομήδη Strambali, [in:] P. Agapetos, M. Pieris (Eds), «Τ' ἀδόνιν κεῖνον ποὺ γλυκὰ θλιβᾶται». Εκδοτικά και ερμηνευτικά ζητήματα της δημώδους ελληνικής λογοτεχνίας στο πέρασμα από τον Μεσαίωνα στην Αναγέννηση (1400–1600), Acts of the Fourth International Conference Neograeca Medii Aevi (Nicosia, November 1997), Herakleion 2002, 287–315

Παυλάκου, Εξήγησις της γλυκειάς χώρας Κύπρου
Δ. Παυλάκου, Εξήγησις της γλυκειάς χώρας Κύπρου Λεόντιος Μαχαιράς «Χρονικό της Κύπρου». Δραματική προσαρμογή Μιχάλας Πιερής, Θεατρικό Εργαστήρι του Πανεπιστημίου Κύπρου, η κυριακάτικη ΑΥΓΗ 27, 26 ιουλίου 1998, Λευκωσία 1998
(http://digital.lib.auth.gr/record/7030/files/npa-2004-6775.pdf?version=1, accessed 22 November 2021)

Πιερής, Για μια νέα κριτική έκδοση
Μ. Πιερής, Για μια νέα κριτική έκδοση του Χρονικου του Μαχαιρά, «Αρχές της Νεοελληνικής Λογοτεχνίας». Πρακτικά του Δεύτερου Διεθνούς Συνεδρίου «Neograeca Medii Aevi», Ἀνάτοπο ἀπὸ τὸν Α' τόμο, Βενετία 1993, 343–348

Πιερής, Σταθμοί
Μ. Πιερής, Σταθμοί της κυπριακής λογοτεχνίας. Λεόντιος Μαχαιράς, Βασίλης Μιχαηλίδης, Κώστας Μόντης, Ελληνισμός της διασποράς άγνωστοι γείτονες Κυπριακά ανάτυπον από τον τόμο 12 των διαλέξεων του Λαϊκού Πανεπιστημίου, Λευκωσία 2000, 169–197

Χατζηδημητρίου, Ιστορία της Κύπρου
Κ. Χατζηδημητρίου, Ιστορία της Κύπρου, Λευκωσία 2005

Χριστόδουλος, Γλωσσικὰ Ζητήματα
Μ. Χριστόδουλος, Γλωσσικὰ Ζητήματα, *Κυπρακαὶ Σπουδαί* 33 (1969), 237–248

B. Scientific studies in Polish

Bal, Wędrujące pojęcia
M. Bal, Wędrujące pojęcia w naukach humanistycznych. Krótki przewodnik, M. Bucholc (Transl.), Warszawa 2012

Balard, Łaciński Wschód
M. Balard, Łaciński Wschód, XI–XV wiek, W. Ceran (Transl.), Kraków 2010

Bebis, Święta Tradycja
G.S. Bebis, Święta Tradycja, [in:] K. Leśniewski, J. Leśniewska (Eds), Prawosławie. Światło wiary i zdrój doświadczenia, Lublin 1999, 13–24

Bielecki, Kłopoty z innością
M. Bielecki, Kłopoty z innością, Universitas, Kraków 2011

Borowska, Katabaza Bergadisa
M. Borowska, Katabaza Bergadisa, [in:] M. Borowska (Ed.), Arcydzieła literatury nowogreckiej, t. 1, Warszawa 2004, 45–51

Borowska, Kreta okresu renesansu
M. Borowska, Kreta okresu renesansu, [in:] M. Borowska (Ed.), Arcydzieła literatury nowogreckiej, t. 1, Warszawa 2004, 12-44

Borowska, Panorama greckojęzycznej literatury cypryjskiej
M. Borowska, Panorama greckojęzycznej literatury cypryjskiej, [in:] M. Borowska, P. Kordos, D. Maliszewski (Eds), Cypr, dzieje, literatura, kultura, t. 2, Warszawa 2015, 43-170

Burkiewicz, Podróż króla Cypru
Ł. Burkiewicz, Podróż króla Cypru Piotra I z Lusignan po Europie w latach 1362-1365 i jego plany krucjatowe, *Studia Historyczne*, Nr 197, Z. 1 (2007), 3-29 (with English summary, 29)

Burkiewicz, Na styku chrześcijaństwa i islamu
Ł. Burkiewicz, Na styku chrześcijaństwa i islamu. Krucjaty i Cypr w latach 1191-1291, Kraków 2008 (with English summary, 155-156)

Burkiewicz, Templariusze
Ł. Burkiewicz, Templariusze i ich wpływ na politykę wewnętrzną Królestwa Cypru w przededniu kasaty zakonu, *Studia Historyczne*, Nr 205, Z. 1 (2009), 3-18 (with English summary, 17-18)

Burkiewicz, Two Cypriot royal missions
Ł. Burkiewicz, Two Cypriot royal missions to Poland in 1364 and 1432, Επετηρίς της Κυπριακής Εταιρείας Ιστορικών Σπουδών 9 (2010), 21-40

Burkiewicz, Σχέσεις Κύπρου-Πολωνίας
Ł. Burkiewicz, Σχέσεις Κύπρου-Πολωνίας κατά το Μεσαίωνα και την Αναγέννηση (ΙΔ' – ΙΣΤ' αι.)/ Polska i Cypr – relacje w średniowieczu i renesansie XIV-XVI w., [in:] Γ. Γεωργής, Γ. Καζαμίας/J. Jeorgis, J. Kazamias (Eds), Πολωνία-Κύπρος. Από τη χώρα του Σοπέν στο νησί της Αφροδίτης Σχέσεις Ιστορίας και Πολιτισμού/ *Polska – Cypr. Z kraju Szopena na wyspę Afrodyty. Relacje historyczne i kulturowe*, Λευκωσία/ Nikozja 2011, 18-47

Burkiewicz, Polityczna rola królestwa Cypru
Ł. Burkiewicz, Polityczna rola królestwa Cypru w XIV wieku, Kraków 2013 (with English summary, 331-334)

Burkiewicz, Sztuka dla wychowania
Ł. Burkiewicz, Sztuka dla wychowania. Architektura gotycka w średniowiecznym Cyprze jako element latynizacji, *Cywilizacja* 46 (2013), 175-181

Burzyńska, Markowski (Eds), Teorie literatury XX wieku
A. Burzyńska, M.P. Markowski (Eds), Teorie literatury XX wieku. Antologia, Kraków 2006

Calivas, Oddawanie czci Bogu
A. Calivas, Oddawanie czci Bogu, [in:] K. Leśniewski, J. Leśniewska (Eds), Prawosławie. Światło wiary i zdrój doświadczenia, Lublin 1999, 51-68

Cervera, Teologia i duchowość
J.C. Cervera, Teologia i duchowość świętej ikony Kościoła w świetle KKK, [in:] K. Pek (Ed.), Ikona liturgiczna: ewangelizacyjne przesłanie ikonografii maryjnej, Warszawa 1999, 40-51

Charkiewicz, Relikwie świętych w prawosławiu
J. Charkiewicz, Relikwie świętych w prawosławiu, Warszawa 2010

Charkiewicz, Ikony Matki Bożej
J. Charkiewicz, Ikony Matki Bożej typu «Hodegetria» w prawosławiu i ich obecność w polskich cerkwiach, *Rocznik Teologiczny*, LVIII, z. 2 (2016), 153–171

Czernik, Tożsamość jednostkowa
T. Czernik, Tożsamość jednostkowa w wielokulturowej przestrzeni w procesie dyfuzji kultur, *Perspectiva. Legnickie Studia Teologiczno-Historyczne*, rok VII, nr 1 (12) (2008), 35–47

Czerwiński, Semiotyka dyskursu historycznego
M. Czerwiński, Semiotyka dyskursu historycznego. Chorwackie i serbskie syntezy dziejów narodu, Kraków 2012

Dąbrowska, Bizancjum, Francja i Stolica Apostolska
M. Dąbrowska, Bizancjum, Francja i Stolica Apostolska w drugiej połowie XIII wieku, *Acta Universitatis Lodziensis, Folia Historica* 27, Łódź 1987

Dopierała, Księga papieży
K. Dopierała, Księga papieży, Poznań 1996

Dziekan, Klasyczna kultura arabsko-muzułmańska
M.M. Dziekan, Klasyczna kultura arabsko-muzułmańska. Zagadnienia podstawowe, *Zarządzanie w kulturze* 12, Kraków 2011, 235–249

Frale, Templariusze
B. Frale, Templariusze, P. Dyrda (Transl.), Warszawa 2008

Freud, Kultura jako źródło cierpień
Z. Freud, Kultura jako źródło cierpień, Warszawa 1995

Glinicka, To idē to thaūma
M. Glinicka, To idē to thaūma – zjawisko cudu w I księdze Kroniki Leoncjusza Machierasa, *Teologia i Człowiek*, Vol. 30, Nr 2 (2015), 59–78

Głodek, Utopia Europy zjednoczonej
M. Głodek, Utopia Europy zjednoczonej: Życie i idee Filipa de Mezieres (1327–1405), Słupsk 1997

Handke, Oddziaływanie literatury
R. Handke, Oddziaływanie literatury w perspektywie odbiorcy, *Teksty: teoria literatury, krytyka, interpretacja* 6 (18) (1974), 90–106

Jazurek-Gutek *et al.*, Zapomniane walory
B. Jazurek-Gutek, S. Grundas, J. Laskowski, J. Sadkiewicz, Zapomniane walory funkcjonalne mączki ze strąków szarańczynu (Ceratonia siliqua L.) oraz nowe możliwości jej zastosowania jako prozdrowotnego dodatku do pieczywa, *Acta Agrophysica* 15(2) (2010), 305–313

Jurewicz, Historia literatury bizantyńskiej
O. Jurewicz, Historia literatury bizantyńskiej. Zarys, Wrocław 2007

Kijas, Perspektywy ekumeniczne
Z.J. Kijas, Perspektywy ekumeniczne ikonografii maryjnej, [in:] K. Pek (Ed.), Ikona liturgiczna: ewangelizacyjne przesłanie ikonografii maryjnej, Warszawa 1999, 72–89

Kordos, Geografia, klimat i przyroda Cypru
P. Kordos, Geografia, klimat i przyroda Cypru, [in:] M. Borowska, P. Kordos, D. Maliszewski (Eds), Cypr: dzieje, literatura, kultura, Vol. 1, Warszawa 2015, 19–30

Kuczara, Kościół prawosławny na Cyprze
K. Kuczara, Kościół prawosławny na Cyprze, [in:] M. Borowska, P. Kordos, D. Maliszewski (Eds), Cypr: dzieje, literatura, kultura, Vol. 2, Warszawa 2015, 370–330

Lacan, Stadium zwierciadła
J. Lacan, Stadium zwierciadła jako czynnik kształtujący funkcję Ja, w świetle doświadczenia psychoanalitycznego, J. Aleksandrowicz (Transl.), Referat na XVI Międzynarodowym Kongresie Psychoanalitycznym, Zurich, 17 lipca 1949, *Psychoterapia*, Nr 4 (63) (1987), 5–9

Luhmann, Funkcja religii
N. Luhmann, Funkcja religii, Kraków 2007

Łosski, Teologia Mistyczna
W. Łosski, Teologia Mistyczna Kościoła Wschodniego, I. Brzeska (Transl.), Kraków 2007

Łukasiewicz, Opatrzność Boża
D. Łukasiewicz, Opatrzność Boża, wolność, przypadek. Studium z analitycznej filozofii religii, Poznań 2014

Łukaszuk, Wcielenie fundamentem ikony
T.D. Łukaszuk, Wcielenie fundamentem ikony i jej teologii, [in:] K. Pek (Ed.), Ikona liturgiczna: ewangelizacyjne przesłanie ikonografii maryjnej, Warszawa 1999, 25–39

Madeyska, Historia świata arabskiego
D. Madeyska, Historia świata arabskiego. Okres klasyczny od starożytności do roku 750, Warszawa 1999

Meyendorff, Teologia bizantyjska
J. Meyendorff, Teologia bizantyjska. Historia i doktryna, J. Prokopiuk (Transl.), Warszawa 1984

Mień, Sakrament, słowo, obrzęd
A. Mień, Sakrament, słowo, obrzęd. Prawosławna służba Boża, Z. Podgórzec, Łuków 1992

Mihailovic, Bachtinowska koncepcja słowa
A. Mihailovic, Bachtinowska koncepcja słowa, [in:] D. Ulicka (Ed.), Ja – Inny. Wokół Bachtina, t. 2, Kraków 2009, 81–116

Misztal, Historia Cypru
M. Misztal, Historia Cypru, Kraków 2013

Moroz, Czy Alfred Tarski jest relatywistą aletycznym?
J. Moroz, Czy Alfred Tarski jest relatywistą aletycznym?, *Analiza i Egzystencja* 23 (2013), 99–118

Mrożek-Dumanowska, Islam a Zachód
A. Mrożek-Dumanowska, Islam a Zachód, Warszawa 1991

Muchowski, Polityka pisarstwa historycznego
J. Muchowski, Polityka pisarstwa historycznego. Refleksja teoretyczna Haydena White'a, Warszawa, Toruń 2015

Nalborczyk, Obraz Europejczyka
A.S. Nalborczyk, Obraz Europejczyka w świecie arabsko-muzułmańskim a wojny krzyżowe. Przeszłość, która ożywa we współczesnej propagandzie, [in:] Tacy sami a jednak inni. VIII Festiwal Nauki, Warszawa 2004, 17–25

Nowosielski, Inność prawosławia
J. Nowosielski, Inność prawosławia, Białystok 1998

Pelikan, Tradycja chrześcijańska 1
J. Pelikan, Tradycja chrześcijańska. Historia rozwoju doktryny: Powstanie wspólnej tradycji (100–600), M. Höffner (Transl.), Kraków 2008

Pelikan, Tradycja chrześcijańska 2
J. Pelikan, Tradycja chrześcijańska. Historia rozwoju doktryny: Duch wschodniego chrześcijaństwa (600–1700), M. Piątek (Transl.), Kraków 2009

Pelikan, Tradycja chrześcijańska 3
J. Pelikan, Tradycja chrześcijańska. Historia rozwoju doktryny: Rozwój teologii średniowiecznej (600–1300), J. Pociej (Transl.), Kraków 2009

Pelikan, Tradycja chrześcijańska 4
J. Pelikan, Tradycja chrześcijańska. Historia rozwoju doktryny: Reformacja Kościoła i dogmatów (1300–1700), M. Król (Transl.), Kraków 2010

Płuciennik, Karczewski, Prawda w literaturze
J. Płuciennik, L. Karczewski, Prawda w literaturze to może być tylko prawda pragmatyczna, [in:] A. Tyszczyk, J. Borowski, I. Piekarski (Eds), Prawda w literaturze: studia, Lublin 2009, 83–100

Raszewski, Cypr w okresie bizantyńskim
J. Raszewski, Cypr w okresie bizantyńskim (330–1191), [in:] M. Borowska, P. Kordos, D. Maliszewski (Ed.), Cypr: dzieje, literatura, kultura, Warszawa 2015, 227–242

Rygorowicz-Kuźma, Terminologia prawosławna
A. Rygorowicz-Kuźma, Terminologia prawosławna w języku polskim (na przykładzie nazw osób duchownych), *Acta Polono-Ruthenica* 16 (2011), 403–413

Schwakopf, Chronologia 1
J. Schwakopf, Chronologia, [in:] S. Runciman, Dzieje wypraw krzyżowych, t. 1, Pierwsza krucjata i założenie Królestwa Jerozolimskiego, J. Schwakopf (Transl.), Poznań 1951, 329–330

Schwakopf, Chronologia 2
J. Schwakopf, Chronologia od panowania Baldwina I do podbojów Saladyna 1187–1189, [in:] S. Runciman, Dzieje wypraw krzyżowych, t. 2, Królestwo Jerozolimskie i frankijski Wschód 1100–1187, J. Schwakopf (Transl.), Poznań 1951, 467–470

Schwakopf, Chronologia 3
J. Schwakopf, Chronologia od III krucjaty do upadku państw krzyżowych, [in:] S. Runciman, Dzieje wypraw krzyżowych, t. 3, Królestwo Akki i późniejsze krucjaty, J. Schwakopf (Transl.), Poznań 1951, 513–516

Sourdel, Cywilizacja Islamu
J.D. Sourdel, Cywilizacja Islamu, Warszawa 1980

Tambiah, Racjonalność, relatywizm, przekład
S.J. Tambiah, Racjonalność, relatywizm, przekład a współmierność kultur, [in:] Badanie kultury. Elementy teorii antropocentrycznej – Kontynuacje, Warszawa 2006, 54–86

Tarski, Pojęcie prawdy
A. Tarski, Pojęcie prawdy w językach nauk dedukcyjnych (1933), [in:] A. Tarski, Pisma logiczno-filozoficzne. Prawda, t. 1, Warszawa 1995

Tokarska-Bakir, Obraz osobliwy
J. Tokarska-Bakir, Obraz osobliwy: hermeneutyczna lektura źródeł etnograficznych. Wielkie opowieści, Kraków 2000

Vasiliadis, Misterium śmierci
N. Vasiliadis, Misterium śmierci, Białystok 2004

C. Scientific studies in other languages

Abulafia, The Great Sea
D. Abulafia, The Great Sea: A Human History of the Mediterranean, Oxford, New York 2011

Ainsworth, Configuring Transience
P. Ainsworth, Configuring Transience: Patterns of Transmission and Transmissibility in the Chroniques (1395–1995), [in:] D. Maddox, S. Sturm-Maddox (Eds), Froissart Across the Genres, Gainesville 1998, 15–39

Akbari, Seeing through the Veil
S.C. Akbari, Seeing through the Veil: Optical Theory and Medieval Allegory, Toronto 2004

Akbari, (rev.) Medievalisms in the postcolonial world
S.C. Akbari, (rev.) Medievalisms in the postcolonial world, by K. Davis, N. Altschul, *Studies in the Age of Chaucer* 33 (2011), 328–331

Akbari, Idols in the East
S.C. Akbari, Idols in the East: European Representations of Islam and the Orient, 1100–1450, Ithaca 2012

Alföldi, The Conversion of Constantine
A. Alföldi, The Conversion of Constantine and Pagan Rome, Oxford 1969

Allbaugh, Crete
L.G. Allbaugh, Crete, Princeton 2015

Altschul, Postcolonialism and the Study of the Middle Ages
N.R. Altschul, Postcolonialism and the Study of the Middle Ages, *History Compass* 6(2) (2006), 588–606

Anaxagorou, Narrative and Stylistic Structures
N. Anaxagorou, Narrative and Stylistic Structures in the Chronicle of Leontios Machairas, Nicosia 1998

Andrews, Santa Sophia
J.M. Andrews, Santa Sophia in Nicosia: the Sculpture of the Western Portals and its Reception, *Comitatus: A Journal of Medieval and Renaissance Studies* 39 (1999), 63–80

Andrews, Conveyance and Convergence
J.M. Andrews, Conveyance and Convergence: Visual Culture in Medieval Cyprus, [in:] H.E. Grossman, A. Walker (Eds), Mechanisms of Exchange: Transmission in Medieval Art and Architecture of the Mediterranean, ca. 1000–1500, Leiden 2013, 115–148

Angold, Church and Society
M. Angold, Church and Society in Byzantium Under the Comneni, 1081–1261, Cambridge 2000

Arbel, Intercultural Contacts
B. Arbel, Intercultural Contacts in the Medieval Mediterranean: Studies in Honour of David Jacoby, London 2013

Arbel, Venice's Maritime Empire
B. Arbel, Venice's Maritime Empire in the Early Modern Period, [in:] E. Dursteler (Ed.), A Companion to Venetian History, 1400–1797, Leiden 2013, 125–253

Ashcroft, Griffiths, Tiffin, Post-colonial Studies
B. Ashcroft, G. Griffiths, H. Tiffin, Post-colonial Studies. The Key Concepts. Second edition, London, New York 2007

Ashcroft, Post-Colonial Transformation
B. Ashcroft, Post-Colonial Transformation, London, New York 2013

Austin-Broos, The Anthropology of Conversion
D. Austin-Broos, The Anthropology of Conversion: An Introduction, [in:] A. Buckser, S.D. Glazier (Eds), The Anthropology of Religious Conversion, Lanham, MD 2003, 1–14

Baek, Tadao Ando
J. Baek, Tadao Ando: Nothingness and Sacred Space, London 2009

Baert, A Heritage Of Holy Wood
B. Baert, A Heritage Of Holy Wood: The Legend Of The True Cross In Text And Image, Leiden, Boston 2004

Baert, Santing, Introduction
B. Baert, C. Santing, Introduction, [in:] B. Baert, A. Traninger, C. Santing (Eds), Disembodied Heads in Medieval and Early Modern Culture, Leiden, Boston 2013, 1–13

Baglioni, Language and identity
D. Baglioni, Language and identity in Late Medieval Cyprus, [in:] T. Papacostas, G. Saint-Guillain (Eds), Identity/Identities in Late Medieval Cyprus, Papers given at the ICS Byzantine Colloquium, London, 13–14 June 2011, Nicosia 2014, 27–36

Bakarat, The Arab World
H. Bakarat, The Arab World. Society, Culture, and State, Berkeley 1993

Bakhtin, Dialogic Imagination
M.B. Bakhtin, The Dialogic Imagination, Four Essays, M. Holquist (Ed.), C. Emerson, M. Holquist (Transl.), Austin 1981

Bartlett, The Making of Europe
R. Bartlett, The Making of Europe: Conquest, Colonization, and Cultural Change, 950–1350, Princeton 1994

Battle, Tous, Carob tree
I. Battle, J. Tous, Carob tree: Ceratonia siliqua L. – Promoting the conservation and use of underutilized and neglected crops 17, Rome 1997

Baum, Winkler, Apostolic Churches
W. Baum, D.W. Winkler, Apostolic Churches of the East: A Concise History, London 2003

Beaton, 'Digenes Akrites'
R. Beaton, 'Digenes Akrites' and Modern Greek Folk Song: A Reassessment, *Byzantion. Revue Internationale des Études Byzantines* 4 (1981), 22–43

Beihammer, The First Naval Campaigns
A.D. Beihammer, The First Naval Campaigns of the Arabs Against Cyprus (649, 653): A Reexamination of the Oriental Source Material, [in:] G.K. Livadas (Ed.), Graeco-Arabica Festschrift in Honour of V. Christides, Τιμητικός τόμος Βασιλείου Χρηστίδη, Vol. IX–X, Athens 2004, 47–68

Bekker-Nielsen, The Roads of Ancient Cyprus
T. Bekker-Nielsen, The Roads of Ancient Cyprus, Copenhagen 2004

Belting, Likeness and Presence
H. Belting, Likeness and Presence: A History of the Image Before the Era of Art, Chicago 1996

Benrabah, Language Conflict in Algeria
M. Benrabah, Language Conflict in Algeria: From Colonialism to Post-Independence, *Multilingual Matters*, Bristol 2013

Benthien, Wulf, Körperteile
C. Benthien, C. Wulf, Körperteile. Eine kulturelle Anatomie, Reinbek bei Hamburg 2001

Bevan, Symbolism and Belief
E. Bevan, Symbolism and Belief: Gifford Lectures, London 2014

Bevans, Models of Contextual Theology
S.B. Bevans, Models of Contextual Theology, *Missiology: An International Review*, Vol. XIII, No. 2 (1985), 185–202 (http://hiebertglobalcenter.org/blog/wp-content/uploads/2013/03/Reading-1-Bevans-Models-of-Contextual-Theology.pdf, accessed 10 December 2021)

Bhabha, The Location of Culture
H.K. Bhabha, The Location of Culture, London 1994

Biddick, The Shock of Medievalism
K. Biddick, The Shock of Medievalism, Durham, North Carolina 1998

Biosca, Alfonso Buenhombre
A. Biosca, Alfonso Buenhombre, [in:] D. Thomas, A. Mallett (Eds), Christian-Muslim Relations. A Bibliographical History, Vol. 5 (1350–1500), Leiden, Boston 2013, 67–70

Bliznyuk, Diplomatic Relations
S.V. Bliznyuk, Diplomatic Relations Between Cyprus and Genoa in the Light of the Genoese Juridical Documents: ASG, Diversorum Communis Ianue, 1375–1480, [in:] A.D. Beihammer, M.G. Parani, C.D. Schabel (Eds), Diplomatics in the Eastern Mediterranean 1000–1500: Aspects of Cross-Cultural Communication (The Medieval Mediterranean Peoples, Economies and Cultures, 400–1500, Vol. 74), Leiden, Boston 2008, 275–292

Blumenfeld-Kosinski, Petkov (Eds), Philippe de Mézières and His Age
R. Blumenfeld-Kosinski, K. Petkov (Eds), Philippe de Mézières and His Age, Leiden, Boston 2011

Boas, Crusader Archaeology
A.J. Boas, Crusader Archaeology: The Material Culture of the Latin East, London 2005

Boehmer, Colonial and Postcolonial Literature
E. Boehmer, Colonial and Postcolonial Literature, Oxford 1995

Bohls, Romantic Literature and Postcolonial Studies
E.A. Bohls, Romantic Literature and Postcolonial Studies, *Postcolonial Literary Studies*, Edinburgh 2013

Brann, The Moors?
R. Brann, The Moors?, *Medieval Encounters*, No. 15 (2009), 307–318

Brantlinger, Victorian Literature and Postcolonial Studies
P. Brantlinger, Victorian Literature and Postcolonial Studies, Edinburgh 2009

Brauer, Boundaries and Frontiers
R.W. Brauer, Boundaries and Frontiers in Medieval Muslim Geography, Philadelphia, Pennsylvania 1995

Bredero, Christendom and Christianity
A.H. Bredero, Christendom and Christianity in the Middle Ages, Grand Rapids, Michigan 1994

Browning, Byzantium and Islam
R. Browning, Byzantium and Islam in the Early Medieval Cyprus, Ἐπετηρὶς τοῦ Κέντρου Ἐπιστημονικῶν Ἐρευνῶν, Vol. IX, Λευκωσία 1977–1979, 101–116

Brownlee, The Figure of Peter I
K. Brownlee, The Figure of Peter I and the Status of Cyprus in Le Songe du Vieil Pelerin: Crusade Ideology, Salvation History, and Authorial Self-Representation, [in:] R. Blumenfeld-Kosinski, K. Petkov (Eds), Philippe de Mézières and His Age: Piety and Politics in the Fourteenth Century, Leiden, Boston 2011, 165–188

Buckley, The Alexiad
P. Buckley, The Alexiad of Anna Komnene: Artistic Strategy in the Making of a Myth, Cambridge 2014

Budden, True Stories Fom Ancient History
M.E.H. Budden, True Stories From Ancient History: Chronologically Arranged from the Creation of the World to the Death of Charlemagne, London 1837

Burgtorf, The Central Convent of Hospitallers and Templars
J. Burgtorf, The Central Convent of Hospitallers and Templars: History, Organization, and Personnel (1099/1120–1310), Leiden, Boston 2008

Burke, Tamm (Eds), Debating New Approaches to History
P. Burke, M. Tamm (Eds), Debating New Approaches to History, London, New York 2018

Buzwell, Saints in Medieval Manuscripts
G. Buzwell, Saints in Medieval Manuscripts, Toronto 2005

Byerly, Timbs (Eds), The Mirror of Literature
Th. Byerly, J. Timbs (Eds), The Mirror of Literature, Amusement, and Instruction, Vol. 16, London 1830

Bynum, Fragmentation and Redemption
C.W. Bynum, Fragmentation and Redemption: Essays on Gender and the Human Body in Medieval Religion, Michigan 1991

Callin, A Poet at the Fountain
W. Callin, A Poet at the Fountain: Essays on the Narrative Verse of Guillaume de Machaut, Kentucky 2015

Cardinali, Costa, Dizionario della lingua italiana
F. Cardinali, P. Costa, Dizionario della lingua italiana (per cura di Paolo Costa e Francesco Cardinali), Masi 1826

Carr, Morrocco, A Byzantine Masterpiece
A.W. Carr, L.J. Morrocco, A Byzantine Masterpiece Recovered: The Thirteenth-Century Murals of Lysi, Cyprus, Austin 1991

Cesnola, Cyprus
L.P. di Cesnola, Cyprus: Its Ancient Cities, Tombs, and Temples, Cambridge 2015

Chandler, Munday, A Dictionary of Media&Communication
D. Chandler, R. Munday, A Dictionary of Media&Communication, Oxford, Current Online Version 2016 (eISBN: 9780191800986, DOI: 10.1093/acref/9780191800986.001.000, accessed 12 November 2021)

Christides, Naval History
V. Christides, Naval History and Naval Technology in Medieval Times. The Need for Interdisciplinary Studies, *Byzantion*, Vol. 58, No. 2 (1988), 309–332

Christo, Martyrdom
G.G. Christo, Martyrdom According to John Chrysostom: "To Live is Christ, To Die is Gain", Lewiston 1997

Clackson, Language and Society
J. Clackson, Language and Society in the Greek and Roman Worlds, Cambridge 2015

Cohen (Ed.), Monster Theory
J.J. Cohen (Ed.), Monster Theory: Reading Culture, Minneapolis 1996

Cohen, Of Giants
J.J. Cohen, Of Giants: Sex, Monsters, and the Middle Ages, Vol. 17, Medieval Cultures, Minneapolis, London 1999

Cohen, Midcolonial
J.J. Cohen, Midcolonial, [in:] J.J. Cohen (Ed.), The Postcolonial Middle Ages, New York 2001 (another edition New York 2000)

Coldstream, Preface
N. Coldstream, Preface, [in:] M.J.K. Walsh, N. Coureas, P. W. Edbury (Eds), Medieval and Renaissance Famagusta: Studies in Architecture, Art and History, Farnham 2012

Collenberg, État et origine
W.R. de Collenberg, État et origine du haut clergé de Chypre avant le Grand Schisme d'après les Registres des Papes du XIIIe et du XIVe siècle, *Mélanges de l'Ecole française de Rome. Moyen-Age, Temps modernes*, No. 1, Vol. 91 (1979), 197–332

Commemoration of Holy Equals of the Apostles
Commemoration of Holy Equals of the Apostles the Emperor Constantine & the Empress Helena (https://www.ponomar.net/maktabah/MenaionLambertsenMay2000/0521470.html, accessed 22 November 2021)

Constanelos, Christian Faith and Cultural Heritage
D.J. Constanelos, Christian Faith and Cultural Heritage: Essays from a Greek Orthodox Perspective, Boston 2005

Conte, The 14th and Final Crusade
J.J. Conte, The 14th and Final Crusade to the Middle East: Crusades from the 11th Century to the 21st Century, Bloomington 2008

Coopland, General Introduction
G.W. Coopland, General Introduction, [in:] Philippe de Mézières, Le Songe du Vieil Pelerin, G.W. Coopland (Ed.), Vol. 1, Cambridge 1969, 1–80

Coopland, Synopsis
G.W. Coopland, Synopsis and Commentary to Book I, [in:] Philippe de Mézières, Le Songe du Vieil Pelerin, G.W. Coopland (Ed.), Vol. 1, Cambridge 1969

Couchman, The Mystery of the Cross
J. Couchman, The Mystery of the Cross: Bringing Ancient Christian Images to Life, Downers Grove, Illinois 2010

Coureas, The Latin Church in Cyprus
N.S.H. Coureas, The Latin Church in Cyprus, 1195–1312, Aldershot 1997

Coureas, Economy
N.S.H. Coureas, Economy, [in:] A. Nicolaou-Konnari, C.D. Schabel (Eds), Cyprus: Society And Culture 1191–1374, Leiden, Boston 2005, 103–156

Coureas, Taverns in Medieval Famagusta
N.S.H. Coureas, Taverns in Medieval Famagusta, [in:] M.J.K. Walsh, N.S.H. Coureas, P.W. Edbury (Eds), Medieval and Renaissance Famagusta: Studies in Architecture, Art and History, Farnham 2012, 65–74

Coureas, Religion and ethnic identity
N.S.H. Coureas, Religion and ethnic identity in Lusignan Cyprus: How the Various Groups Saw Themselves and Were Seen by Others, [in:] T. Papacostas, G. Saint-Guillain (Eds), Identity/Identities in Late Medieval Cyprus, Papers given at the ICS Byzantine Colloquium, London, 13–14 June 2011, Nicosia 2014, 13–25

Coureas, Edbury, Annexe 4
Coureas, Edbury (Transl.), Annexe 4: *Amadi*'s Sources: a Synopsis, [in:] N. Coureas, P. Edbury (Transl.), The Chronicle of Amadi, *Texts and Studies in the History of Cyprus* LXXIV, Nicosia 2015

Coureas, Edbury, Introduction
Coureas, Edbury, Introduction, [in:] N. Coureas, P. Edbury (Transl.), The Chronicle of Amadi, *Texts and Studies in the History of Cyprus* LXXIV, Nicosia 2015

Crone, Medieval Islamic Political Thought
P. Crone, Medieval Islamic Political Thought, Edinburgh 2005

Çakmak (Ed.), Islam
C. Çakmak (Ed.), Islam: A Worldwide Encyclopedia, 4 Vols, Santa Barbara, California 2017

Dadoyan, Armenians in the Medieval Islamic World
S.B. Dadoyan, The Armenians in the Medieval Islamic World: The Arab Period in Armnyah Seventh to Eleventh Centuries, New Brunswick, NJ 2011

Dan (Ed.), Studies in Jewish Thought
J. Dan (Ed.), Studies in Jewish Thought, Westport, Connecticut 1989

Dascal, Colonizing and decolonizing minds
M. Dascal, Colonizing and decolonizing minds, Tel Aviv 2007

Davis, Altschul, Medievalisms in the postcolonial world
K. Davis, N. Altschul, Medievalisms in the postcolonial world: The idea of 'the Middle Ages' outside Europe, Baltimore 2009

Davy, Panayotou, French loans in Cypriot Greek
J. Davy, A. Panayotou, French loans in Cypriot Greek, Actes du colloque tenu à Lyon, 1997, Université Lumière-Lyon 2, Université de Chypre, *Publications de la Maison de l'Orient et de la Méditerranée* 31 (2000), 113–125

Dawkins, Glossary
R.M. Dawkins, Glossary, [in:] Λ. Μαχαιράς, Εξήγησις της γλυκείας χώρας Κύπρου η οποία λέγεται Κρόνακα τουτέστιν Κρόνικον/ Recital Concerning the Sweet Land of Cyprus entitled 'Chronicle', R.M. Dawkins (Ed., transl.), 2 Vols, Oxford 1932, 235–276

Dawkins, Index of Names of Persons
R.M. Dawkins, Index of Names of Persons, [in:] Λ. Μαχαιράς, Εξήγησις της γλυκείας χώρας Κύπρου η οποία λέγεται Κρόνακα τουτέστιν Κρόνικον/ Recital Concerning the Sweet Land of Cyprus entitled 'Chronicle', R.M. Dawkins (Ed., transl.), 2 Vols, Oxford 1932, 277–310

Dawkins, Introduction
R.M. Dawkins, Introduction, [in:] Λ. Μαχαιράς, Εξήγησις της γλυκείας χώρας Κύπρου η οποία λέγεται Κρόνακα τουτέστιν Κρόνικον/ Recital Concerning the Sweet Land of Cyprus entitled 'Chronicle', R.M. Dawkins (Ed., transl.), 2 Vols, Oxford 1932, 1–24

Dawkins, Notes
R.M. Dawkins, Notes, [in:] Λ. Μαχαιράς, Εξήγησις της γλυκείας χώρας Κύπρου η οποία λέγεται Κρόνακα τουτέστιν Κρόνικον/ Recital Concerning the Sweet Land of Cyprus entitled 'Chronicle', R.M. Dawkins (Ed., transl.), 2 Vols, Oxford 1932, 41–234

Dawkins, Vocabulary of the Mediaeval Cypriot Chronicle
R.M. Dawkins, The Vocabulary of the Mediaeval Cypriot Chronicle of Leontios Makhairas, *Transactions of the Philological Society* (1925–1930), 300–330

Dawkins, The Nature of the Cypriot Chronicle
R.M. Dawkins, The Nature of the Cypriot Chronicle of Leontios Makhairas, Oxford 1945 [other editions Chicago 1980 (1946^1)]

Deanesly, A History of the Medieval Church
M. Deanesly, A History of the Medieval Church: 590–1500, London, New York 1969

Dede, Islamism
A.Y. Dede, Islamism, State Control Over Religion and Social Identity: Turkey and Egypt, Michigan 2008

Deleuze, Guattari, A Thousand Plateaus
G. Deleuze, F. Guattari, A Thousand Plateaus. Capisalism and Schizophrenia, B. Massumi (Transl.), Minneapolis, London 1987

Delipetrou *et al.*, Cyprus
P. Delipetrou, J. Makhzoumi, P. Dimopoulos, K. Georghiou, Cyprus, [in:] I. Vogiatzakis, G. Pungetti, A.M. Mannion (Eds), Mediterranean Island Landscapes. Natural and Cultural Approaches, Heidelberg 2008, 170–203

Dittenberger, Orientis Graeci Inscriptiones Selectae
C.F.W. Dittenberger, Orientis Graeci Inscriptiones Selectae: Supplementum Sylloges Insciptionum Graecarum, Hildesheim 1960

Donadey, Between Amnesia and Anamnesis
A. Donadey, Between Amnesia and Anamnesis: Re-Membering the Fractures of Colonial History, *Studies in 20th Century Literature*, Vol. 23, Issue 1 (1999), 111–116
(https://newprairiepress.org/cgi/viewcontent.cgi?article=1457&context=sttcl, accessed 23 March 2021)

Dorninger, The Island of Cyprus
M.E. Dorninger, The Island of Cyprus in Travel Literature of the Fourteenth Century, [in:] A. Grafetstätter, S. Hartmann, J.M. Ogier (Eds), Islands and Cities in Medieval Myth, Literature, and History: Papers Delivered at the International Medieval Congress, University of Leeds 2005, 2006, 2007, Bern 2011, 67–82

Drijvers, Helena Augusta, the Mother of Constantine
J.W. Drijvers, Helena Augusta, the Mother of Constantine the Great and the Legend of Her Finding of the True Cross, Leiden, Boston 1992

Drijvers, Marutha of Maipherquat
J.W. Drijvers, Marutha of Maipherquat on Helena Augusta, Jerusalem and the Council of Nicea, [in:] E.J. Yarnold, M.F. Wiles (Eds), Historia, Biblica, Theologica et Philosophica, *Papers presented at the Thirteenth International Conference on Patristic Studies held in Oxford 1999, Studia patristica*, Vol. XXXIV, Leuven, Paris 2001, 51–64

Drijvers, Helena Augusta: the Cross and the Myth
J.W. Drijvers, Helena Augusta: the Cross and the Myth: Some New Reflections, [in:] W. Brandes (Ed.), Millennium 8. Yearbook on the Culture and History of the First Millennium C.E., Berlin, Boston 2011, 125–174

Dunphy, Bratu (Eds), The Encyclopedia of the Medieval Chronicle
G. Dunphy, C. Bratu (Eds), The Encyclopedia of the Medieval Chronicle Online, Leiden, Boston 2014–2021 (https://referenceworks.brillonline.com/browse/encyclopedia-of-the-medieval-chronicle, accessed 30 December 2021)

Dupré, Symbols of the Sacred
L.K. Dupré, Symbols of the Sacred, Grand Rapids, Michigan 2000

Edbury, The Kingdom of Cyprus
P.W. Edbury, The Kingdom of Cyprus and the Crusades, 1191–1374, Cambridge 1991

Edbury, The Military Orders in Cyprus
P.W. Edbury, The Military Orders in Cyprus in the Light of Recent Scholarship, [in:] Z. Hunyadi, J. Laszlovszky (Eds), The Crusades and the Military Orders Expanding the Frontiers of Medieval Latin Christianity, Budapest 2001, 101–107

Edbury, Franks
P.W. Edbury, Franks, [in:] A. Nicolaou-Konnari, C.D. Schabel (Eds), Cyprus: Society and Culture 1191–1374, Leiden, Boston 2005, 63–102

Edbury, Machaut, Mézières, Makhairas and Amadi
P.W. Edbury, Machaut, Mézières, Makhairas and Amadi: Constructing the Reign of Peter I (1359–1369), [in:] R. Blumenfeld-Kosinski, K. Petkov (Eds), Philippe de Mézières and His Age: Piety and Politics in the Fourteenth Century, Leiden, Boston 2011, 349–358

Efthimiou, Greeks and Latins
M. Efthimiou, Greeks and Latins on Cyprus in the Thirteenth Century, Brookline, Massachussets 1987

Eisenberg, Jewish Traditions
R.L. Eisenberg, Jewish Traditions: A JPS Guide, Philadelphia, Pennsylvania 2010

El-Cheikh, Byzantium through the Islamic Prism
N.M. El-Cheikh, Byzantium through the Islamic Prism from the Twelfth to the Thirteenth Century, [in:] A.E. Laiou, R.P. Mottahedeh (Eds), The Crusades from the Perspective of Byzantium and the Muslim World, Washington 2001, 53–70

El-Cheikh, Byzantium Viewed by the Arabs
N.M. El-Cheikh, Byzantium Viewed by the Arabs, Harvard Middle Eastern Monographs 36, Cambridge, Massachussetts, London 2004

Eliade, The Sacred and the Prophane
M. Eliade, The Sacred and the Prophane. The Nature of religious myth, symbolism and ritual within life and culture, New York 1963

Ellenblum, Frankish Rural Settlement
R. Ellenblum, Frankish Rural Settlement in the Latin Kingdom of Jerusalem, Cambridge 1998

Ellenblum, Frankish Castles
R. Ellenblum, Frankish Castles, Muslim Castles, and the Medieval Citadel of Jerusalem, [in:] I. Shagrir, R. Ellenblum, J.S.C. Riley-Smith (Eds), In Laudem Hierosolymitani, Aldershot 2007, 93–110

Emmerson (Ed.), Key Figures
R.K. Emmerson (Ed.), Key Figures in Medieval Europe: An Encyclopedia, London, New York 2013

Englezakis, Cyprus
B. Englezakis, Cyprus, Nea Justinianoupolis: sixth annual lecture on history and archaeology, Nicosia 1990

Englezakis, Studies and Documents
B. Englezakis, Studies and Documents Relating to the History of the Church of Cyprus from the Fourth to the Twentieth Centuries, Aldershot, Hampshire, Brookfield, Vt. 1995

Epstein, Genoa and the Genoese
S. Epstein, Genoa and the Genoese, 958–1528, Chapel Hill 2001

Faletra, Wales and the Medieval Colonial Imagination
A.M. Faletra, Wales and the medieval colonial imagination: the matters of Britain in the twelfth century, *The New Middle Ages*, New York 2014

Fanon, Black Skin, White Masks
F. Fanon, Black Skin, White Masks, C.L. Markmann (Transl.), London 2008

Farrelly, The Trinity
J. Farrelly, The Trinity: Rediscovering the Central Christian Mystery, Lanham, MD 2005

Foxe, The Acts and Monuments of the Church
J. Foxe, The Acts and Monuments of the Church, Containing the History and Sufferings of the Martyrs, A new ed., revised, corrected, and condensed by M.H. Seymour, Chestnut Hill 1838

Frankopan, Byzantine Trade Privileges to Venice
P. Frankopan, Byzantine Trade Privileges to Venice in the Eleventh Century: the Chrysobull of 1092, *Journal of Medieval History*, Vol. 30, Issue 2 (2004), 135–160
(https://doi.org/10.1016/j.jmedhist.2004.03.005, accessed 22 November 2021)

Frazee, Catholics and Sultans
Ch.A. Frazee, Catholics and Sultans: The Church and the Ottoman Empire 1453–1923, Cambridge 2006

Freeman-Grenville, Chronology of World History
G.S.P. Freeman-Grenville, Chronology of World History: A Calendar of Principal Events from 3000 BC to AD 1976, Lanham, Maryland 1978

Frojmovic, Karkov (Eds), Postcolonising the Medieval Image
E. Frojmovic, C.E. Karkov (Eds), Postcolonising the Medieval Image, London, New York 2017

Fromherz, Ibn Khaldun
A.J. Fromherz, Ibn Khaldun: Life and Times, Edinburgh 2011

Galatariotou, The Making of a Saint
C. Galatariotou, The Making of a Saint: The Life, Times and Sanctification of Neophytos the Recluse, Cambridge 2004

Gaunt, Can the Middle Ages Be Postcolonial?
S. Gaunt, Can the Middle Ages Be Postcolonial?, *Comparative Literature*, Vol. 61, No. 2 (2009), 160–176

Gaunt, Kay, Introduction
S. Gaunt, S. Kay, Introduction, [in:] S. Gaunt, S. Kay (Eds), The Cambridge Companion to Medieval French Literature, Cambridge 2008, 1–18

Geary, Living with the Dead in the Middle Ages
J.P. Geary, Living with the Dead in the Middle Ages, Ithaca 1994

Geary (Ed.), Readings in Medieval History
J.P. Geary (Ed.), Readings in Medieval History, Toronto 2015

Ghazarian, The Armenian Kingdom in Cilicia
J.G. Ghazarian, The Armenian Kingdom in Cilicia During the Crusades: The Integration of Cilician Armenians with the Latins, 1080–1393, London 2000

Giampapa, The Politics of Identity
F. Giampapa, The Politics of Identity, Representation, and the Discourses of Self-identification: Negotiating the Periphery and the Center, [in:] A. Pawlenko, A. Blackledge (Eds), Negotiation of Identities in Multilingual Contexts, *Multilingual Matters*, Bristol 2004, 192–218

Gibb, Studies on the Civilization of Islam
H.A.R. Gibb, Studies on the Civilization of Islam, Princeton 2014

Gilmour-Bryson, Testimony of Non-Templar Witnesses in Cyprus
A. Gilmour-Bryson, Testimony of Non-Templar Witnesses in Cyprus, [in:] M. Barber (Ed.), The Military Orders. Fighting for the Faith and Caring for the Sick, Aldershot 1994, 205–211

Gilmour-Bryson, Introduction
Gilmour-Bryson, Introduction, [in:] The Trial of the Templars in Cyprus, A. Gilmour-Bryson (Ed.), Melbourne 1998

Gingrich, Conceptualising Identities
A. Gingrich, Conceptualising Identities; Anthropological Alternatives to Essentialising Difference and Moralizing about Othering, [in:] G. Baumann, A. Gingrich (Eds), Grammars of Identity/alterity: A Structural Approach, New York 2005

Given, The Archaeology of the Colonized
M. Given, The Archaeology of the Colonized, London, New York 2004

Goddart, A History of Christian-Muslim Relations
H. Goddart, A History of Christian-Muslim Relations, Lanham, Maryland 2000

Godiwala, Postcolonial Desire
D. Godiwala, Postcolonial Desire: Mimicry, Hegemony, Hybridity, [in:] J. Kuortti, J. Nyman (Eds), Reconstructing Hybridity: Post-colonial Studies in Transition, Amsterdam 2007, 59–80

Gräb, Spiritualität
W. Gräb, Spiritualität – die Religion der Individuen, [in:] W. Gräb (Ed.), Individualisierung – Spiritualität – Religion: Transformationsprozesse auf dem religiösen Feld in interdisziplinärer Perspektive, Münster 2008, 31–44

Griffel, Al-Ghazali's Philosophical Theology
F. Griffel, Al-Ghazali's Philosophical Theology, Oxford 2009

Grivaud, Literature
G. Grivaud, Literature, [in:] A. Nicolaou-Konnari, Ch.D. Schabel (Eds), Cyprus: Society And Culture 1191–1374, Leiden, Boston 2005, 219–284

Grypeou, Kitāb al-majāll
E. Grypeou, Kitāb al-majāll, [in:] D. Thomas, A. Mallett (Eds), Christian-Muslim Relations. A Bibliographical History, Vol. 5 (1350–1500), Leiden, Boston 2013, 634–639

Guignery, Introduction
V. Guignery, Introduction. Hybridity, Why it Still Matters, [in:] V. Guignery, C. Pesso-Miquel, F. Specq (Eds), Hybridity: Forms and Figures in Literature and the Visual Arts, Cambridge 2011, 1–8

Haag, Templars
M. Haag, Templars: History and Myth: From Solomon's Temple to the Freemasons, New York 2009

Hackett, A History of the Orthodox Church of Cyprus
J. Hackett, A History of the Orthodox Church of Cyprus: From the Coming of the Apostles Paul and Barnabas to the Commencement of the British Occupation (A.D. 45–A.D. 1878): Together with Some Account of the Latin and Other Churches Existing in the Island, London 1901

Hadjidemetriou, A History of Cyprus
K. Hadjidemetriou, A History of Cyprus, C. Hadjigeorgiou (Transl.), Nicosia 2002

Hadjioannou, The Medieval Dialect of Cyprus
K.P. Hadjioannou, The Medieval Dialect of Cyprus, Τὰ ἐν Διασπορᾷ, Vol. 3 (1979–1989), 59–76

Hahn, Objects of Devotion and Desire
C. Hahn, Objects of Devotion and Desire. Medieval Relic to Contemporary Art, New York 2011 (http://www.academia.edu/1504272/Objects_of_Devotion_and_Desire_Medieval_Relic_to_Contemporary_Art, accessed 10 December 2021)

Harvey, Scenting Salvation
A. Harvey, Scenting Salvation: Ancient Christianity and the Olfactory Imagination, Berkeley, Los Angeles, London 2006

Hasluck, Hasluck, Christianity and Islam
F.W. Hasluck, M.M. Hasluck, Christianity and Islam under the Sultans, 2 Vols, Oxford 1929

Haylamaz, Khadija
R. Haylamaz, Khadija: the First Muslim and the Wife of the Prophet Muhammad, H. Coşar (Transl.), Somerset, NJ 2007

Hedges, Controversies in Interreligious Dialogue
P. Hedges, Controversies in Interreligious Dialogue and the Theology of Religions, Norwich 2010

Heid, Ursprung der Helenalegende
S. Heid, Der Ursprung der Helenalegende im Pilgerbetrieb Jerusalems, *Jahrbuch für Antike und Christentum* 32 (1989), 41–71

Hendrich, Negotiating and Rebuilding Religious Sites in Cyprus
B. Hendrich, Negotiating and Rebuilding Religious Sites in Cyprus, Cologne 2013

Heraclides *et al.*, Y-chromosomal analysis of Greek Cypriots
A. Heraclides, E. Bashiardes, E. Fernández-Domínguez, S. Bertoncini, M. Chimonas, V. Christofi, J. King, B. Budowle, P. Manoli, and M.A. Cariolou, Y-chromosomal analysis of Greek Cypriots reveals a primarily common pre-Ottoman paternal ancestry with Turkish Cypriots, C.-C. Wang (Ed.), *PLoS One* 12(6) (2017) (https://www.ncbi.nlm.nih.gov/pmc/articles/PMC5473566/, accessed 13 December 2021)

Higgins, John Mandeville
I.M. Higgins, John Mandeville, [in:] D. Thomas, A. Mallett (Eds), Christian-Muslim Relations. A Bibliographical History, Vol. 5 (1350–1500), Leiden, Boston 2013, 147–164

Hill, A History of Cyprus I
G. Hill, A History of Cyprus, Vol. I, To the Conquest by Richard Lion Heart (1940), Cambridge 2010

Hill, A History of Cyprus II
G. Hill, A History of Cyprus, Vol. II, The Frankish Period 1192–1432 (1948), Cambridge 2010

Hill, A History of Cyprus III
G. Hill, A History of Cyprus, Vol. III, The Frankish Period 1432–1572 (1948), Cambridge 2010

Hill, A History of Cyprus IV
G. Hill, A History of Cyprus, Vol. IV, The Ottoman Province, The British Colony 1571–1948 (1948), Cambridge 2010

Hillman, Mazzio, The Body in Parts
D. Hillman, C. Mazzio, The Body in Parts: Fantasies of Corporeality in Early Modern Europe, London, New York 2013

Hirschler, Medieval Arabic Historiography
K. Hirschler, Medieval Arabic Historiography: Authors as Actors, London, New York 2011

Hirschler, Ibn Wāṣil
K. Hirschler, Ibn Wāṣil: An Ayūbbid Perspective on Frankish Lordships and Crusades, [in:] A. Mallett (Ed.), Medieval Muslim Historians and the Franks in the Levant, Vol. II, Leiden, Boston 2014, 136–160

Hofrichter, The Anaphora of Addai and Mari
P.L. Hofrichter, The Anaphora of Addai and Mari. An Early Witness to Apostolic Tradition, Paper presented in Kottayam/Kerala at a Conference: 'Orientalium Ecclesiarum. Its Recepetion in the Syro-Malabar Church' Missionary Orientation Center (MOC) Manganam, Kottayam, Kerala, October 9th, 2004
(https://www.academia.edu/37288113/The_Anaphora_of_Addai_and_Mari_An_Early_Witness_to_Apostolic_Tradition_delivered_2004, accessed 10 December 2021)

Holsinger, Medieval Studies, Postcolonial Studies
B.W. Holsinger, Medieval Studies, Postcolonial Studies, and the Genealogies of Critique, *Speculum*, Vol. 77, No. 4 (Oct., 2002), 1195–1227

Holsinger, The Premodern Condition
B.W. Holsinger, The Premodern Condition: Medievalism and the Making of Theory, Chicago, London 2005

Holsinger, Neomedievalism
B.W. Holsinger, Neomedievalism, Neoconservatism, and the War on Terror, Chicago 2007

Horrocks, Greek
G. Horrocks, Greek: A History of the Language and its Speakers, Hoboken, New Jersey 2009

Horst, Pious Long-Sleepers
P.W. van der Horst, Pious Long-Sleepers in Greek, Jewish, and Christian Antiquity, [in:] M. Kister, H. Newman, M. Segal, R. Clements (Eds), Tradition, Transmission, and Transformation from Second Temple Literature through Judaism and Christianity in Late Antiquity, Proceedings of the Thirteenth International Symposium of the Orion Center for the Study of the Dead Sea Scrolls and Associated Literature, Jointly Sponsored by the Hebrew University Center for the Study of Christianity, 22–24 February 2011, Leiden, Boston 2015

Houtsma (Ed.), E.J. Brill's First Encyclopaedia of Islam
M.Th. Houtsma (Ed.), E.J. Brill's First Encyclopaedia of Islam, Vol. 4, London, Boston 1913–1936

Huot, Postcolonial Fictions
S. Huot, Postcolonial Fictions in the 'Roman de Perceforest' Cultural Identities and Hybridities, Cambridge 2013

Iacovou, 'Greeks', 'Phoenicians', 'Eteocypriots'
M. Iacovou, "Greeks", "Phoenicians", "Eteocypriots". Ethnic Identities in the Cypriote Kingdoms, [in:] J. Chrysostomides, C. Dendrinos (Eds), "Sweet Land…". Lectures on the History and Culture of Cyprus, Camberley 2006, 27–59

Illieva, The Suppression of the Templars in Cyprus
A. Illieva, The Suppression of the Templars in Cyprus According to the Chronicle of Leontios Makhairas, [in:] M. Barber (Ed.), The Military Orders Fighting for the Faith and Caring for the Sick, London 1994, 212–219

Ingham, Contrapuntal Histories
P. Ingham, Contrapuntal Histories, [in:] P.C. Ingham, M.R. Warren (Eds), Postcolonial Moves: Medieval through Modern, New York 2003
(https://doi.org/10.1057/9781403980236_3, accessed 23 March 2021)

Ingham, Warren, Introduction
P.C. Ingham, M.R. Warren, Introduction, [in:] P.C. Ingham, M.R. Warren (Eds), Postcolonial Moves: Medieval through Modern, New York 2003, 1–15

Iorga, Philippe de Mézières
N. Jorga, Philippe de Mézières, 1327–1405, La croisade au XIV siècle, Paris 1896

Jacoby, Byzantium, the Italian Maritime Powers
D. Jacoby, Byzantium, the Italian Maritime Powers, and the Black Sea Before 1204, A. Berger (Ed.), *Byzantinische Zeitschrift*, Vol. 100, Issue 2 (2008), 677–699
(https://doi.org/10.1515/BYZS.2008.677, accessed 22 November 2021)

Jagessar, Burns, Christian Worship
M.N. Jagessar, S. Burns, Christian Worship: Postcolonial Perspectives, London, New York 2014

Jeanrond, Toward an Interreligious Hermeneutics
W.G. Jeanrond, Toward an Interreligious Hermeneutics of Love, [in:] C. Cornille, Ch. Conway (Eds), Interreligious Hermeneutics, Eugene, Oregon 2010, 44–60

Jeffreys (Ed., transl.), Digenis Akritis
E. Jeffreys (Ed., transl.), Digenis Akritis: The Grottaferrata and Escorial Versions, Cambridge 1998

Jensen, Othering
S.Q. Jensen, Othering, identity formation and agency, *Qualitative Studies* 2 (2011), 63–78

Jensen, Towards Contemporary Islamic Concepts
J.S. Jensen, Towards Contemporary Islamic Concepts of the Person, [in:] H.G. Kippenberg, Y.B. Kuiper, A.F. Sanders (Eds), Concepts of Person in Religion and Thought: A–Et, Berlin, Boston 2012, 177–216

Joh, Heart of the Cross
W.A. Joh, Heart of the Cross: A Postcolonial Christology, Louisville 2006

Jones, Constantine and the Conversion of Europe
A.H.M. Jones, Constantine and the Conversion of Europe, Toronto 1962

Jones (Ed.), The New Cambridge Medieval History
M. Jones (Ed.), The New Cambridge Medieval History, Vol. 6, (1300–1415), Cambridge 2015

Jones, Martindale, Morris, The Prosopography of the Later Roman Empire
A.H.M. Jones, J.R. Martindale, J. Morris, The Prosopography of the Later Roman Empire, Vol. 3, Cambridge 1971

Jouanno, Shared Spaces
C. Jouanno, Shared Spaces: 1 Digenis Akritis, The Two-Blood Border Lord, [in:] C. Cupane, B. Krönung (Eds), Fictional Storytelling in the Medieval Eastern Mediterranean and Beyond, Leiden, Boston 2016, 260–284

Kabir, Williams, Introduction
A.J. Kabir, D. Williams, Introduction: a return to wonder, [in:] A.J. Kabir, D. Williams (Eds), Postcolonial Approaches to the European Middle Ages: Translating Cultures, Cambridge 2005, 1–22

Kahane, Kahane, The Western Impact on Byzantium
H., R. Kahane, The Western Impact on Byzantium: The Linguistic Evidence, *Dumbarton Oaks Papers*, Vol. 36 (1982), 127–153

Karyolemou, Le chypriote
M. Karyolemou, Le chypriote: dialecte ou idiome, [in:] A.-Φ. Χριςτίδης *et al.* (Eds), Η ελληνική γλώσσα και οι διάλεκτοί της, Αθήνα 2000, 111–115

Karyolemou, Goutsos (Eds), The Sociolinguistics of Cyprus
M. Karyolemou, D. Goutsos (Eds), The sociolinguistics of Cyprus: Studies from the Greek sphere, Vol. 1, Berlin 2004

Kaul, Eighteenth-Century British Literature and Postcolonial Studies
S. Kaul, Eighteenth-Century British Literature and Postcolonial Studies, Edinburgh 2009

Kearney, Taylor, Introduction
R. Kearney, J. Taylor, Introduction, [in:] R. Kearney, J. Taylor (Eds), Hosting the Stranger: Between Religions, New York 2011, 1–8

Kieckhefer, Imitators of Christ
R. Kieckhefer, Imitators of Christ: Sainthood in the Christian Tradition, [in:] R. Kieckhefer, G.D. Bond (Eds), Sainthood: Its Manifestations in World Religions, Berkeley, Los Angeles, London 1990, 1–42

Kim, Introduction
Y.R. Kim, Introduction, [in:] St. Epiphanius of Cyprus, Ancoratus, Washington 2014, 3–50

Kinoshita, Medieval Boundaries
S. Kinoshita, Medieval Boundaries; Rethinking Difference in Old French Literature, *The Middle Ages Series*, Philadelphia 2006

Kinoshita, Deprovincializing the Middle Ages
S. Kinoshita, Deprovincializing the Middle Ages, [in:] R. Wilson, C.L. Connery (Eds), The Worlding Project: Doing Cultural Studies in the Era of Globalization, Santa Cruz 2007, 75–89

Kirk, Civilization without Religion?
R. Kirk, Civilization without Religion?, Washington 1992

Klein, Eastern Objects and Western Desires
H.A. Klein, Eastern Objects and Western Desires: Relics and Reliquaries between Byzantium and the West, *Dumbarton Oaks Papers* 58 (2004), 283–314

Kleinhenz (Ed.), Routledge Revivals
C. Kleinhenz (Ed.), Routledge Revivals: Medieval Italy (2004): An Encyclopedia, Vol. I, London, New York 2017

Knight, Britain in India
L. Knight, Britain in India, 1858–1947, London 2012

Kolditz, Barsbāy
S. Kolditz, Barsbāy, [in:] D. Thomas, A. Mallett (Eds), Christian-Muslim Relations. A Bibliographical History, Vol. 5 (1350–1500), Leiden, Boston 2013, 366–369

Konstantinu, Aporias of Identity
K.M. Konstantinu, Aporias of Identity. Bicommunalism, Hybridity and the 'Cyprus Problem', *Cooperation and Conflict: Journal of the Nordic International Studies Association*, Vol. 42(3) (2007), 247–270 (http://fbemoodle.emu.edu.tr/pluginfile.php/47356/mod_resource/content/1/Cooperation%20and%20 Conflict-2007-Constantinou-247-70.pdf, accessed 22 November 2021)

Korobeinikov, Byzantium and the Turks
D. Korobeinikov, Byzantium and the Turks in the Thirteenth Century, Oxford 2014

Kouneni, The Kykkotissa Virgin
L. Kouneni, The Kykkotissa Virgin and Its Italian Appropriation, *Artibus et Historiae*, Vol. 29, No. 57 (2008), 95–107

Kristeva, Powers of Horror
J. Kristeva, Powers of Horror. An Essay on Abjection, L.S. Roudiez (Ed.), New York 1982

Krueger, The Religion of Relics
D. Krueger, The Religion of Relics in Late Antiquity and Byzantium, [in:] M. Bagnoli *et al.* (Eds), Treasures of Heaven: Saints, Relics, and Devotion in Medieval Europe, New Haven 2010, 5–17

Kyriacou, The Byzantine Warrior Hero
Ch. Kyriacou, The Byzantine Warrior Hero: Cypriot Folk Songs as History and Myth, 965–1571, *Byzantium: A European Empire and Its Legacy*, Lanham 2020

Kyrris, Some Aspects
K.P. Kyrris, Some Aspects of Leontios Makhairas' Ethnoreligious Ideology, Cultural Identity and Historiographic Method, Στασίνος 10 (1989–1993)

Kyrris, Cypriot Identity
K.P. Kyrris, Cypriot Identity, Byzantium and the Latins (1192–1489), *History of European Ideas* 19(4–6) (1994), 563–573

Kyrris, History of Cyprus
K.P. Kyrris, History of Cyprus, Nicosia 1985, 1996²

Labossiere, Chosen Champions
J.T. Labossiere, Chosen Champions: Medieval and Early Modern Heroes as Postcolonial Reactions to Tensions between England and Europe, 2016, Graduate Theses and Dissertations (https://scholarcommons.usf.edu/etd/6289/, accessed 23 March 2021)

Laliwala, Islamic Philosophy of Religion
J.I. Laliwala, Islamic Philosophy of Religion: Synthesis of Science Religion and Philosophy, New Delhi 2005

Lampert-Weissig, Medieval Literature and Postcolonial Studies
L. Lampert-Weissig, Medieval Literature and Postcolonial Studies, Edinburgh 2010

Lanfer, Allusion to and Expansion of the Tree of Life
P.T. Lanfer, Allusion to and Expansion of the Tree of Life and Garden of Eden in Biblical and Pseudepigraphal Literature, [in:] C.A. Evans, H.D. Zacharias (Eds), Early Christian Literature and Intertextuality, Vol. 1, Thematic Studies, New York 2009, 96–108

Larkin, The Coeur-de-Lyon Romances
Larkin, The Coeur-de-Lyon Romances, [in:] D. Thomas, A. Mallett (Eds), Christian-Muslim Relations. A Bibliographical History, Vol. 5 (1350–1500), Leiden, Boston 2013, 268–277

Lasareff, Studies in the Iconography
V. Lasareff, Studies in the Iconography of the Virgin, *The Art Bulletin*, Vol. 20, No. 1 (Mar., 1938), 26–65

Latif, Religion and Ethical Education
D. Latif, Religion and Ethical Education in Divided Societies. The Case of Cyprus, [in:] A.B. Seligman (Ed.), Religious Education and the Challenge of Pluralism, Oxford 2014, 45–69

Lauxterman, Byzantine Poetry
M.D. Lauxterman, Byzantine Poetry from Pisides to Geometers. Texts and Contexts, Vol. 1, Wien 2003

Levine, Introduction
R. Levine, Introduction, [in:] R. Levine (Ed.), Guibert of Nogent, The Deeds of God Through the Franks, Lexington, Kentucky 1997

Levy-Rubin, 'The Errors of the Franks'
M. Levy-Rubin, "The Errors of the Franks" by Nikon of the Black Mountain: Between Religious and Ethno-cultural Conflict, *Byzantion*, Vol. 71, No. 2 (2001), 422–437

Liddell, Scott, A Greek-English Lexicon
H.G. Liddell, R. Scott, A Greek-English Lexicon, revised and augmented throughout by Sir H.S. Jones, with the assistance of R. McKenzie, Oxford 1940

Liddell, Scott, An Intermediate Greek-English Lexicon
H.G. Liddell, R. Scott, An Intermediate Greek-English Lexicon, Oxford 1889

Lieu, Introduction
S. Lieu, Introduction. Pagan and Byzantine Historical Writing on the Reign of Constantine, [in:] S. Lieu, D. Montserrat (Eds), From Constantine to Julian: Pagan and Byzantine Views: A Source History, London, New York 2002, 1–38

Lionett, Autobiographical Voices
F. Lionett, Autobiographical Voices: Race, Gender, Self-Portraiture, Ithaca 1989

Lock, The Franks in the Aegean
P. Lock, The Franks in the Aegean: 1204–1500, New York 2014

Loomba, Colonialism/Postcolonialism
A. Loomba, Colonialism/Postcolonialism, The New Critical Idiom, London, New York 2005

Lorenti, Geographia
N. Lorenti, Geographia (Geographia neograece), Vol. 3, Benko 1839

Luke, The Kingdom of Cyprus
H. Luke, The Kingdom of Cyprus 1369–1489, [in:] H.W. Hazards, K.N. Setton (Eds), A History of the Crusades: The fourteenth and fifteenth centuries, Vol. III, Madison 1969

Luttrell, Sugar and Schism
A. Luttrell, Sugar and Schism. The Hospitallers in Cyprus from 1378 to 1386, [in:] A. Bryer, G. Georghallides (Eds), "The Sweet Land of Cyprus": Papers given at the 25th jubilee spring symposium of Byzantine studies, Nicosia 1993, 157–166

MacDonald, The Life of Al-Ghazzali
D. MacDonald, The Life of Al-Ghazzali, Piscataway Township, New Jersey 2010

MacEvitt, The Crusades
Ch. MacEvitt, The Crusades and the Christian World of the East. Rough Tolerance, Philadelphia 2008

MacPhee, Postwar British Literature and Postcolonial Studies
G. MacPhee, Postwar British Literature and Postcolonial Studies, Edinburgh 2011

Maddox, Sturm-Maddox, Introduction
D. Maddox, S. Sturm-Maddox, Introduction, [in:] Jean d'Arras, Melusine; or, the Noble History of Lusignan, D. Maddox, S. Sturm-Maddox (red.), University Park, Philadelphia 2012

Magoulias, Introduction
H.J. Magoulias (Ed.), Introduction, [in:] N. Choniates, O City of Byzantium: Annals of Niketas Choniatēs, H.J. Magoulias (Ed.), Detroit 1984, ix–xxviii

Maio et al., Ambiguitas Constantiniana
M. di Maio, J. Zeuge, N. Zoton, Ambiguitas Constantiniana: the Caeleste Signum Dei of Constantine the Great, *Byzantion* 58 (1988), 333–360

Mallett, Usāma ibn Munqidh
A. Mallett, Usāma ibn Munqidh, [in:] D. Thomas, A. Mallett (Eds), Christian-Muslim Relations. A Bibliographical History, Vol. 3 (1050–1200), Leiden, Boston 2011, 764–768

Mallette, European Modernity and the Arab Mediterranean
K. Mallette, European Modernity and the Arab Mediterranean: Toward a New Philology and a Counter-Orientalism, Philadelphia, Pennsylvania 2010

Marcdante, Nelson Pediatria
K. Marcdante, Nelson Pediatria, Vol. 1, Wrocław 2013

Masad, The Medieval Islamic Apocalyptic Tradition
M.A. Masad, The Medieval Islamic Apocalyptic Tradition: Divination, Prophecy and the End of Time in the 13th Century Eastern Mediterranean, *Retrospective Theses and Dissertations* 21, Washington 2008 (https://openscholarship.wustl.edu/etd_restrict/21, accessed 22 November 2021)

Mas Latrie, Guillaume de Machaut et la prise d'Alexandrie
L. Mas Latrie, Guillaume de Machaut et la prise d'Alexandrie, *Bibliothèque de l'école des chartes, Année*, Vol. 37, No 1 (1876), 445–470
(http://www.persee.fr/doc/bec_0373-6237_1876_num_37_1_446707, accessed 22 November 2021)

McCleery, What is 'colonial' about medieval colonial medicine?
I. McCleery, What is 'colonial' about medieval colonial medicine? Iberian health in global context, *Journal of Medieval Iberian Studies*, 7(2) (2015), 151–175

McMahon, Seaton, Collins Cobuild English Dictionary
C. McMahon, M. Seaton, Collins Cobuild English Dictionary for Advanced Learners, Glasgow 2001

Melichar, God, Slave and a Nun
P. Melichar, God, Slave and a Nun: a Case from Late Medieval Cyprus, *Byzantion. Revue Internationale des Études Byzantines*, t. LXXIX (2009), 180–291

Memon, The Struggles of Ibn Taymīya
M.U. Memon, The Struggles of Ibn Taymīya Against Popular Religion: With an Annotated Translation of His Kitāb Iqtiḍā' Aṣ-ṣirāṭ Al-mustaqīm Mukhalafat Aṣḥāb Al-jahīm, Los Angeles 1971

Merry, Encyclopedia of Modern Greek Literature
B. Merry, Encyclopedia of Modern Greek Literature, Westport, Connecticut 2004

Mersch, Hybridity
M. Mersch, Hybridity in late medieval ecclesiastical architecture on Cyprus and the difficulties of identifying Saint Peter and Paul of Famagusta, [in:] T. Papacostas, G. Saint-Guillain (Eds), *Identity/Identities in Late Medieval Cyprus, Papers given at the ICS Byzantine Colloquium*, London, 13–14 June 2011, Nicosia 2014, 241–280

Meyer, Il dialetto delle Cronache di Cipro
G. Meyer, Il dialetto delle Cronache di Cipro di Leonzio Machera e Giorgio Bustron, *Rivista di Filologia e d'Istruzione Classica* 4 (1876), 255–286

Millar, Rome's 'Arab' Allies
F. Millar, Rome's «Arab» Allies in Late Antiquity. Conceptions and Representations from within the Frontiers of the Empire, [in:] H. Börm, J. Wiesehöfer (Eds), Commutatio et contentio, Düsseldorf 2010, 199–226

Mirbagheri, Historical Dictionary of Cyprus
F. Mirbagheri, Historical Dictionary of Cyprus, Lanham 2009

Momma, Medievalism
H. Momma, Medievalism – Colonialism – Orientalism: Japan's Modern Identity in Natsume Soseki's Moboroshi no Tate and Kairo-ko, [in:] K. Davis, N. Altschul (Eds), Medievalisms in the Postcolonial World: The Idea of "the Middle Ages" Outside Europe, Baltimore, Maryland 2009, 141–173

Montgomery, Securing the Sacred Head
S. Montgomery, Securing the Sacred Head: Cephalophory and Relic Claims, [in:] Disembodied Heads in Medieval and Early Modern Culture, London, Leiden 2013, 77–116

Moravcsik, Byzantinoturcia
G. Moravcsik, Byzantinoturcia, Vol. 1, Budapest 1942

Morosini, Giovanni Bocaccio
R. Morosini, Giovanni Bocaccio, [in:] D. Thomas, A. Mallett (Eds), Christian-Muslim Relations. A Bibliographical History, Vol. 5 (1350–1500), Leiden, Boston 2013

Mouriki, A Thirteenth-Century Icon
D. Mouriki, A Thirteenth-Century Icon with A Wariant of the Hodegetria in the Byzantine Museum of Athens, *Dumbarton Oaks Papers*, Vol. 41, Studies on Art and Archeology in Honor of Ernst Kitzinger on His Seventy-Fifth Birthday (1987), 403–414

Moyaert, Fragile Identities
M. Moyaert, Fragile Identities: Towards a Theology of Interreligious Hospitality, Amsterdam 2011

Möhring, Saladin
H. Möhring, Saladin, the Sultan and His Times, 1138–1193, D.S. Bachrach (Transl.), Baltimore, Maryland 2008

Muldoon, Introduction
J. Muldoon, Introduction: The Conversion of Europe, [in:] J. Muldoon (Ed.), Varieties of Religious Conversion in the Middle Ages, Gainesville 1997, 1–10

Müller-Wiener, Castles of the Crusaders
W. Müller-Wiener, Castles of the Crusaders, New York 1966

Nagel, The Afterlife of the Reliquary
A. Nagel, The Afterlife of the Reliquary, [in:] M. Bagnoli, H.A. Klein, C.G. Mann, J. Robinson (Eds), Treasures of Heaven: Saints, Relics, and Devotion in Medieval Europe, New Haven 2010, 211–222

Nandy, The Intimate Enemy
A. Nandy, The Intimate Enemy: Loss and Recovery of Self under Colonialism, New Delhi 1983

Nasr, Ideals and Realities of Islam
S.H. Nasr, Ideals and Realities of Islam, Chicago, Illinois 2000 (http://traditionalhikma.com/wp-content/uploads/2015/02/Ideals-and-Realities-of-Islam.pdf, accessed 9 November 2021)

Nasr, The Heart of Islam
S.H. Nasr, The Heart of Islam. Enduring Values for Humanity, PDF edition, San Francisco, California 2002

Nazmi, The Muslim Geographical Image
A. Nazmi, The Muslim Geographical Image of the World in the Middle Ages. A Source Studies, Warszawa 2007

Neocleous, Imagining Isaak Komnenos of Cyprus
S. Neocleous, Imagining Isaak Komnenos of Cyprus (1184–1191) and the Cypriots: Evidence from the Latin Historiography of the Third Crusade, *Byzantion. Revue Internationale des Études Byzantines*, Vol. LXXXIII (2013), 297–338

Nicholson, Templars, Hospitallers, and Teutonic Knights
H. Nicholson, Templars, Hospitallers, and Teutonic Knights: Images of the Military Orders, 1128–1291, Leicester, New York 1993

Nicolaou-Konnari, Literary Languages
A. Nicolaou-Konnari, Literary Languages in the Lusignan Kingdom of Cyprus in the Thirteenth-Century, *Μολυβδο-κονδυλο-πελεκητής* 7 (2000), 7–27

Nicolaou-Konnari, Ethnic Names
A. Nicolaou-Konnari, Ethnic Names and the Construction of Group Identity in Medieval and Early Modern Cyprus: The Case of *Κυπριώτης*, Κυπριακαί Σπουδαί: Δελτίον της Εταιρείας Κυπριακών Σπουδών, Τομος ξδ'-ξε', Λευκωσία 2000–2001, 259–275

Nicolaou-Konnari, Greeks
A. Nicolaou-Konnari, Greeks, [in:] A. Nicolaou-Konnari, C.D. Schabel (Ed.), Cyprus: Society And Culture 1191–1374, Leiden, Boston 2005, 13–62

Nicolaou-Konnari, Apologists or Critics?
A. Nicolaou-Konnari, Apologists or Critics? The Reign of Peter I of Lusignan (1359–1369) Viewed by Philippe de Mézières (1327–1405) and Leontios Makhairas (ca. 1360/1380–after 1432) [in:] R. Blumenfeld-Kosinski, K. Petkov (Eds), Philippe de Mézières and His Age: Piety and Politics in the Fourteenth Century, Leiden, Boston 2011, 359–402

Nicolaou-Konnari, 'A poor island…'
A. Nicolaou-Konnari, 'A poor island and an orphaned realm…, built upon a rock in the midst of the sea…, surrounded by the infidel Turks and Saracens': The Crusader Ideology in Leontios Makhairas's Greek Chronicle of Cyprus, *Crusades* 10 (2011), 119–145

Nicolaou-Konnari, Alterity and identity
A. Nicolaou-Konnari, Alterity and identity in Lusignan Cyprus from ca. 1350 ca. 1450: the testimonies of Philippe de Mézières and Leontios Makhairas, [in:] T. Papacostas, G. Saint-Guillain (Eds), Identity/Identities in Late Medieval Cyprus, Papers given at the ICS Byzantine Colloquium, London, 13–14 June 2011, Nicosia 2014, 37–66

Nicolaou-Konnari, Leontios Makhairas's Greek Chronicle
A. Nicolaou-Konnari, Leontios Makhairas's Greek Chronicle of the 'Sweet Land of Cyprus': History of Manuscripts and Intellectual Links [in:] I. Afanasyev, J. Dresvina, E.S. Kooper (Eds), The Medieval Chronicle X, Leiden 2016, 163–201

Nicolaou-Konnari, Schabel, Limmasol
A. Nicolaou-Konnari, C. Schabel, Limmasol under Lartin Rule, [in:] Lemesoss: A History of Limassol in Cyprus from Antiquity to the Ottoman Conquest, Cambridge 2015, 195–361

Nicolle, Crusader Castles in Cyprus
D. Nicolle, Crusader Castles in Cyprus, Greece and the Aegean 1191–1571, Oxford 2013

Noyes, Colonial Space
J.K. Noyes, Colonial Space. Spatiality in the Discourse of German Southwest-Africa 1884–1915, London, New York 2012

Odahl, Constantine and the Christian Empire
Ch. Odahl, Constantine and the Christian Empire, London, New York 2003

Okumura, Living by Vow
S. Okumura, Living by Vow: A Practical Introduction to Eight Essential Zen Chants and Texts, Somerville 2012

Olsen, The Templar Papers
O. Olsen, The Templar Papers: Ancient Mysteries, Secret Societies, and the Holy Grail, Franklin Lakes, New Jersey 2006

Olympios, Shared devotions
M. Olympios, Shared devotions: non-Latin responses to Latin sainthood in late medieval Cyprus, *Journal of Medieval History*, London, New York 2013, 1–21

(http://www.academia.edu/4867860/Shared_devotions_non-Latin_responses_to_Latin_sainthood_in_late_medieval_Cyprus_Journal_of_Medieval_History_39_3_2013_321–341, accessed 22 November 2021)

Olympios, Institutional identities
M. Olympios, Institutional identities in late medieval Cyprus: The case of Nicosia Cathedral, [in:] T. Papacostas, G. Saint-Guillain (Eds), Identity/Identities in Late Medieval Cyprus, Papers given at the ICS Byzantine Colloquium, London, 13–14 June 2011, Nicosia 2014, 195–240

Ong, Orality and Literacy
W.J. Ong, Orality and Literacy, London, New York 2002 (https://monoskop.org/images/d/db/Ong_Walter_J_Orality_and_Literacy_2nd_ed.pdf, accessed 10 November 2021)

Orlandos, Ἡ Μονὴ Σαγματᾶ
A.K. Orlandos, 'Ἡ Μονὴ Σαγματᾶ', Ἀρχεῖον Βυζαντινῶν Μνημείων τῆς Ἑλλάδος Z', 1948

Ouspensky, Lossky, The Meaning of Icons
L. Ouspensky, V. Lossky, The Meaning of Icons, Crestwood, New York 1982

Özkutlu, Medieval Famagusta
S. Özkutlu, Medieval Famagusta: Socio-economic and Socio-cultural Dynamics (13th to 15th Centuries), A thesis submitted to the University of Birmingham for the degree of Doctor of Philosophy 2014 (http://etheses.bham.ac.uk/6111/1/Ozkutlu15PhD.pdf, accessed 22 November 2021)

Pahlitzsch, Manuel Gabalas
J. Pahlitzsch, Manuel Gabalas, [in:] D. Thomas, A. Mallett (Eds), Christian-Muslim Relations. A Bibliographical History, Vol. 5 (1350–1500), Leiden, Boston 2013, 71–75

Papacostas, Saint-Guillain, Preface and Aknowledgement
T. Papacostas, G. Saint-Guillain, Preface and Aknowledgement, [in:] T. Papacostas, G. Saint-Guillain (Eds), Identity/Identities in Late Medieval Cyprus, Papers given at the ICS Byzantine Colloquium, London, 13–14 June 2011, Nicosia 2014

Parker, Peter I de Lusignan
K.S. Parker, Peter I de Lusignan, the Crusade of 1365, and the Oriental Christians of Cyprus and the Mamluk Sultanate, [in:] S. Rogge, M. Grünbart (Eds), Medieval Cyprus: a Place of Cultural Encounter, Münster, New York 2015, 53–72

Paschali, Negotiating identities
M. Paschali, Negotiating identities in fourteenth-century Famagusta: Saint George of the Greeks, the liturgy of the Latins, [in:] T. Papacostas, G. Saint-Guillain (Eds), Identity/Identities in Late Medieval Cyprus, Papers given at the ICS Byzantine Colloquium, London, 13–14 June 2011, Nicosia 2014, 281–302

Patke, Modernist Literature and Postcolonial Studies
R.S. Patke, Modernist Literature and Postcolonial Studies, Edinburgh 2013

Pears, Doing Contextual Theology
A. Pears, Doing Contextual Theology, London, New York 2009

Peckruhn, Of Bodily Anamnesis
H. Peckruhn, Of Bodily Anamnesis. Postcolonial, Queer, Religious Analysis, [in:] D.L. Boisvert, J.E. Johnson (Eds), Queer Religion, t. 2, Santa Barbara, California 2011, 193–226

Pepper, World Hypotheses
S.C. Pepper, World Hypotheses: A Study in Evidence, Berkeley, Los Angeles, London 1942

Petersen, Can Ἀρσενοκοῖται be Translated by 'Homosexuals'?
L. Petersen, Can Ἀρσενοκοῖται be Translated by 'Homosexuals'? (1 Cor 6:9, 1 Tim 1:10) [in:] J. Krans, J. Verheyden (Eds), Patristic and Text-Critical Studies: The Collected Essays of William L. Petersen, Leiden, Boston 2012, 62–66

Petre, The Fortifications of Cyprus
J. Petre, The Fortifications of Cyprus under the Lusignans: 1191–1489, PhD Thesis, Cardiff University (http://orca.cf.ac.uk/54199/1/U564882.pdf, accessed 22 November 2021)

Pieris, The Medieval Cypriot Chronicler
M. Pieris, The Medieval Cypriot Chronicler Leontios Makhairas. Comments on his life and work, [in:] S. Rogge, M.-E. Mitsou, J.G. Deckers (Eds), Beiträge zur Kulturgeschichte Zyperns von der Spätantike bis zur Neuzeit, Münster 2005, 107–148

Plaza, Paradigmas en contacto
L.C. Plaza, Paradigmas en contacto: el medievalismo en diálogo con la literatura comparada y la literatura mundial, *Revistes científiques de la Universitat de Barcelona* 20 (2019), 55–66

Pratt, Arts of the Contact Zone
M.L. Pratt, Arts of the Contact Zone, *Profession* (1991), 33–40
(http://www.jstor.org/stable/25595469, accessed 22 November 2021)

Prawer, The Crusaders' Kingdom
J. Prawer, The Crusaders' Kingdom: European Colonialism in the Middle Ages, New York 1972

Prawer, Latin Kingdom of Jerusalem
J. Prawer, Latin Kingdom of Jerusalem: European Colonialism in the Middle Ages, London 1973

Privitera, Combining Organic Agriculture and Recreation
D. Privitera, Combining Organic Agriculture and Recreation: Evidence from Italy, [in:] G. Popescu (Ed.), Agricultural Management Strategies in a Changing Economy, Hershey, Pennsylvania 2015, 301–317

Puchner, The Crusader Kingdom of Cyprus
W. Puchner, The Crusader Kingdom of Cyprus – A Theatre Province of Medieval Europe? Including a Critical Edition of the Cyprus Passion Cycle and the 'Represaesentatio figurata' of the Presentation of the Virgin in the Temple, with the advice of Nicolaos Conomis, Texts and Documents of Early Modern Greek Theatre, Vol. 2, Athens 2006

Quigley, Skulls and Skeletons
C. Quigley, Skulls and Skeletons: Human Bone Collections and Accumulations, Jefferson, North Carolina 2001

Rabasa, Decolonizing Medieval Mexico
J. Rabasa, Decolonizing Medieval Mexico, [in:] K. Davis, N. Altschul (Eds), Medievalisms in the postcolonial world: The idea of 'the Middle Ages' outside Europe, Baltimore 2009, 27–50

Raman, Renaissance Literatures and Postcolonial Studies
Sh. Raman, Renaissance Literatures and Postcolonial Studies, Edinburgh 2011

Rapti, Painted Books
I. Rapti, Painted Books in Late Medieval Cyprus, [in:] T. Papacostas, G. Saint-Guillain (Eds), Identity/Identities in Late Medieval Cyprus, Papers given at the ICS Byzantine Colloquium, London, 13–14 June 2011, Nicosia 2014, 303–330

Renard, Islam and Christianity
J. Renard, Islam and Christianity: Theological Themes in Comparative Perspective, Berkeley 2011

Ricoeur, Narrative Identity
P. Ricoeur, Narrative Identity, *Philosophy Today*, Vol. 31, No. 1 (1991), 73–81

Rigby, Knight
S.H. Rigby, The Knight, [in:] S.H. Rigby, A.J. Minnis (Eds), Historians on Chaucer: The 'General Prologue' to the Canterbury Tales, Oxford 2014, 42–62

Riley-Smith, Hospitallers
J.S.C. Riley-Smith, Hospitallers: the History of the Order of St. John, London 1999

Riley-Smith, The Knights Hospitaller in the Levant
J.S.C. Riley-Smith, The Knights Hospitaller in the Levant, C. 1070–1309, Basingstoke 2012

Robinson, Beer, Harnden (Eds), Common Ground
J. Robinson, L. de Beer, A. Harnden (Eds), Common Ground: Reliquaries and the Lower Classes in Late Medieval Europe, from A Matter of Faith: An Interdisciplinary Study of Relics and Relic Veneration in the Medieval Period, London 2014, 110–115

Rodriguez, Captivity and Diplomacy
J. Rodriguez, Captivity and Diplomacy in the Late Medieval Crown of Aragon, [in:] K.L. Jansen, G. Geltner, A.E. Lester (Eds), Center and Periphery: Studies on Power in the Medieval World in Honor of William Chester Jordan, Leiden, Boston 2013, 107–117

Rogge, Grünbart (Eds), Medieval Cyprus
S. Rogge, M. Grünbart (Eds), Medieval Cyprus: a Place of Cultural Encounter, Münster, New York 2015, 53–72

Rohrbacher, Storia universale della Chiesa cattolica
F.R. Rohrbacher, Storia universale della Chiesa cattolica dell'abate Renato-Francesco Rohrbacher, Vol. 2, Firenze 1859

Rollo, (rev.) Wales and the Medieval Colonial Imagination
D. Rollo, (rev.) Wales and the Medieval Colonial Imagination (https://michaelfaletra.weebly.com/wales-and-the-medieval-colonial-imagination.html, accessed 22 November 2021)

Rosenthal, Political Thought in Medieval Islam
E. Rosenthal, Political Thought in Medieval Islam: An Introductory Outline, Cambridge 1958

Runciman, A History of the Crusades 1
S. Runciman, A History of the Crusades, Vol. 1, The First Crusade and the Foundation of the Kingdom of Jerusalem, Cambridge 1951

Runciman, A History of the Crusades 2
S. Runciman, A History of the Crusades, Vol. 2, The Kingdom of Jerusalem and the Frankish East, 1100–1187, Cambridge 1951

Runciman, A History of the Crusades 3
S. Runciman, A History of the Crusades, Vol. 3, The Kingdom of Acre and the Later Crusades, Cambridge 1951

Russell, Lucifer
J.B. Russell, Lucifer. The Devil in the Middle Ages, Ithaca, London 1984

Ryder, Micromosaic Icons
C. Ryder, Micromosaic Icons of the Late Byzantine Period, New York 2007

Said, Culture and Imperialism
E.W. Said, Culture and Imperialism, New York 1994

Said, Orientalism
E.W. Said, Orientalism, Poznań 2005

Al-Saidi, Post-colonialism Literature
A.A.H. Al-Saidi, Post-colonialism Literature the Concept of self and the other in Coetzee's Waiting for the Barbarians: An Analytical Approach, *Journal of Language Teaching and Research*, Vol. 5, No. 1 (2014), 95–105
(https://www.academypublication.com/issues/past/jltr/vol05/01/12.pdf accessed 10 December 2021)

Sansaridou-Hendrickx, The World View of the Anonymous Author
T. Sansaridou-Hendrickx, The World View of the Anonymous Author of the Greek *Chronicle of the Tocco*, Johannesburg 2000
(https://core.ac.uk/download/pdf/18220112.pdf, accessed 22 November 2021)

Saradi, Space in Byzantin Thought
H. Saradi, Space in Byzantin Thought, [in:] S. Ćurčić, E. Hadjitryphonos (Eds), Architecture as Icon: Perception and Representation of Architecture in Byzantine Art, Exhibition at the Princeton University Art Museum: March 6, 2010–June 6, 2010, New Haven, Connecticut, 2010, 73–111

Sarrió Cucarella, Muslim-Christian Polemics
D.R. Sarrió Cucarella, Muslim-Christian Polemics across the Mediterranean: The Splendid Replies of Shihāb al-Dīn al-Qarāfī, Leiden, Boston 2015

Saunders, A History of Medieval Islam
J.J. Saunders, A History of Medieval Islam, London, New York 2002

Savvides, Some Notes
A.G.K. Savvides, Some Notes on the Terms Agarenoī, Ismaelītai and Sarakenoī in Byzantine Sources, *Byzantion*, Vol. LXVII, Fas. 1 (1997), 89–96

Savvides, Byzantino-Normannica
A.G.K. Savvides, Byzantino-Normannica: The Norman Capture of Italy (to A. D. 1081) and the First Two Invasions in Byzantium (A.D. 1081–1085 and 1107–1108), Leuven 2007

Schabel, Religion
C.D. Schabel, Religion, [in:] A. Nicolaou-Konnari, C.D. Schabel (Eds), Cyprus: Society And Culture 1191–1374, Leiden, Boston 2005, 157–218

Schabel, Greeks, Latins and the Church
C.D. Schabel, Greeks, Latins and the Church in Early Frankish Cyprus, Farnham 2010

Schaff, Schmidt (Eds), 'History of the Christian Church...'
P. Schaff, M.W.G.A. Schmidt (Eds), "And on this Rock I Will Build My Church". A new Edition of Philip Schaff's 'History of the Christian Church': From Nicene and Post-Nicene Christianity to Medieval Christianity A.D. 311–1073, [Hamburg] 2017

Schädel, Die Häupter der Heiligen
S. Schädel, Die Häupter der Heiligen in Ost und West, [in:] Knotenpunkt Byzanz. Wissensformen und kulturelle Wechselbeziehungen, hg. von Andreas Speer und Philipp Steinkrüger, *Miscellanea Mediaevalia/ Veröffentlichungen des Thomas-Instituts der Universität Köln* 36, Berlin, Boston 2012, 655–678

Schriemer (Ed.), Relieken
Inge Schriemer (Ed.), Relieken: Krachtbronnen verweven met verhalen, Zwolle, Utrecht 2018

Schryver, Colonialism or Conviviencia...?
J.G. Schryver, Colonialism or Conviviencia in Frankish Cyprus?, [in:] I.W. Zartman (Ed.), Understanding Life in the Borderlands: Boundaries in Depth and in Motion, Athens 2010, 133–159

Schryver, Excavating the identities
J.G. Schryver, Excavating the identities of Frankish Cyprus, [in:] T. Papacostas, G. Saint-Guillain (Eds), Identity/Identities in Late Medieval Cyprus, Papers given at the ICS Byzantine Colloquium, London, 13–14 June 2011, Nicosia 2014, 1–11

Schumm, Stoltzfus, Disability in Judaism, Christianity, and Islam
D. Schumm, M. Stoltzfus, Disability in Judaism, Christianity, and Islam: Sacred Texts, Historical Traditions, and Social Analysis, Basingstoke 2011

Segen, The Dictionary of Modern Medicine
J.C. Segen, The Dictionary of Modern Medicine, Boca Raton, Florida 1992

Setton, Wolff, Hazard, The Later Crusades
K.M. Setton, R.L. Wolff, H.W. Hazard, The Later Crusades, 1189–1311, Madison, Wisconsin 1969

Shabliy, Representations of the Blessed Virgin Mary
E.V. Shabliy, Representations of the Blessed Virgin Mary in World Literature and Art, Latham 2017

Shawcross, Oral Residue and Narrative Structure
T. Shawcross, Oral Residue and Narrative Structure in the Chronicle of Morea, *Byzantion. Revue Internationale des Études Byzantines*, Vol. LXXV (2005), 310–333

Schmitt, Introduction
J. Schmitt, Introduction, [in:] J. Schmitt (Ed.), The Chronicle of Morea. To chronikon tou moreos. A History in Political Verse, Relating the Establishment of Feudalism in Greece by the Franks in the Thirteenth Century, edited in Two Parallel Texts from the MSS of Copenhagen and Paris, with Introduction, Critical Notes and Indices by John Schmitt, London 1904, xv–lxvi

Shoemaker, Ancient Traditions
S. Shoemaker, Ancient Traditions of the Virgin Mary's Dormition and Assumption, *Oxford Early Christian Studies*, Oxford 2002

Shoemaker, A Peculiar Version of the Inventio crucis
S. Shoemaker, A Peculiar Version of the Inventio crucis in the Early Syriac Dormition Traditions, *Studia Patristica* 41 (2006), 75–81

Sibthorp *et al.*, Journal
J. Sibthorp, C.W.M. Leake, Hume, D. Sestini, W.G. Browne, Journal, [in:] C.D. Cobham (Ed.), Excerpta Cypria: materials for a history of Cyprus; tr. and transcribed, with an appendix on the bibliography of Cyprus, Cambridge 1908, 323–343

Simpson, Efthymiadis, Niketas Choniates
A. Simpson, S. Efthymiadis, Niketas Choniates: A Historian and a Writer, Genève 2009

Simpson, Niketas Choniates
A. Simpson, Niketas Choniates: A Historiographical Study, Oxford 2013

Slack, The Quest for Gain
C. Slack, The Quest for Gain: Were the First Crusaders Proto-Colonists?, [in:] A.J. Andrea, A. Holt (Eds), Seven Myths of the Crusades, Indianapolis, Cambridge, 2015, 70–90

Smart, Ninian Smart on World Religions
N. Smart, Ninian Smart on World Religions: Selected Works, Vol. 1, Aldershot 2009

Smith, Wells, Introduction
K.A. Smith, S. Wells, Introduction: Penelope D. Johnson, The Boswell Thesis And Negotiating Community and Difference in Medieval Europe, [in:] K.A. Smith, S. Wells (Eds), Negotiating Community and Difference in Medieval Europe: Gender, Power, Patronage, and the Authority of Religion in Latin Christendom, Leiden, Boston 2009, 1–13

Spetsieris, The Hermitess Photini
J. Spetsieris, The Hermitess Photini, Florence, Arizona 2000

Spiegel, The Past as Text
G. Spiegel, The Past as Text: The Theory and Practice of Historiography, Baltimore 1997

Spiegel, (rev.) Medievalisms in the Postcolonial World
G. Spiegel, (rev.) Medievalisms in the Postcolonial World: the Idea of 'The Middle Ages 'Outside Europe', *Rethinking History* 15(4) (2011), 617–625

Spilling, Spilling, Cyprus
M. Spilling, J-A. Spilling, Cyprus, Singapur 2010

Spivak, Adamson, Post-Colonial Critic
G.C. Spivak, W. Adamson, Post-Colonial Critic. Interviews, Strategies, Dialogues, S. Harasym (Ed.), New York, London 1990

Stavrakos, Chalkondyles, Laonikos
Ch. Stavrakos, Chalkondyles, Laonikos, [in:] G. Dunphy, C. Bratu (Eds), Encyclopedia of the Medieval Chronicle, Leiden, Boston 2014–2021
(http://dx.doi.org/10.1163/2213-2139_emc_SIM_01656, accessed 30 December 2021)

Steele, A Linguistic History of Ancient Cyprus
P.M. Steele, A Linguistic History of Ancient Cyprus: The Non-Greek Languages and their Relations with Greek, c. 1600–300 BC, Cambridge 2013

Steenbergen, The Alexandrian Crusade
J.V. Steenbergen, The Alexandrian Crusade (1365) and the Mamlūk Sources. Reassessment of the Kitāb Al-Ilmām An-Nuwayrī al-Iskandarānī (D. A.D. 1372), [in:] K.N. Ciggaar, H.G.B. Teule (Eds), East and West in the Crusader States: Context, Contacts, Confrontations: Acta of the Congress Held at Hernen Castle in September 2000, Leuven 2003, 123–137
(http://www.academia.edu/4510935/_The_Alexandrian_Crusade_1365_and_the_Mamluk_Sources_reassessment_of_the_Kitab_al-Ilmam_of_an-Nuwayri_al-Iskandarani_d._1372_AD_, accessed 22 November 2021)

Stetkevych, The Poetics of Islamic Legitimacy
S.P. Stetkevych, The Poetics of Islamic Legitimacy: Myth, Gender, and Ceremony in the Classical Arabic Ode, Bloomington, Indiana 2002

Stewart, The Armenian Kingdom
A.D. Stewart, The Armenian Kingdom and the Mamluks: War and Diplomacy During the Reigns of Hetʿum II (1289–1307), Leiden, Boston 2001

Stewart, Domes of Heaven
C.A. Stewart, Domes of Heaven: The Domed Basilicas of Cyprus, Bloomington 2008

Stewart, The First Vaulted Churches in Cyprus
C.A. Stewart, The First Vaulted Churches in Cyprus, *Journal of the Society of Architectural Historians*, Vol. 69, No. 2 (2010), 162–189

Swann, The Forgotten Desert Mothers
L. Swann, The Forgotten Desert Mothers: Sayings, Lives, and Stories of Early Christian Women, New York 2001

Swanson, The Copto-Arabic Synaxarion
M.N. Swanson, The Copto-Arabic Synaxarion, [in:] D. Thomas, A. Mallett (Eds), Christian-Muslim Relations. A Bibliographical History, Vol. 5 (1350–1500), Leiden, Boston 2013, 92–100

Swanson, The Martyrdom of Rizq Allāh ibn Nabaʿ of Tripoli
M.N. Swanson, The Martyrdom of Rizq Allāh ibn Nabaʿ of Tripoli, [in:] D. Thomas, A. Mallett (Eds), Christian-Muslim Relations. A Bibliographical History, Vol. 5 (1350–1500), Leiden, Boston 2013, 526–528

Swanson, The rite of the Jar
M.N. Swanson, The rite of the Jar, [in:] D. Thomas, A. Mallett (Eds), Christian-Muslim Relations. A Bibliographical History, Vol. 5 (1350–1500), Leiden, Boston 2013, 177–181

Sykes, Time and Space in Haggai-Zechariah
S. Sykes, Time and Space in Haggai-Zechariah 1–8: A Bakhtinian Analysis of a Prophetic Chronicle, Bern 2002

Taboada, 'Reconquista'
H.G.H. Taboada, 'Reconquista' and the 'Three Religion Spain', Baltimore, Maryland 2009, 123–140

Taft, Women at Church in Byzantium
R.F. Taft, Women at Church in Byzantium: Where, When-And Why?, *Dumbarton Oaks Papers*, Vol. 52 (1998), 27–87

Teule, East and West in the Crusader States
G.B. Teule, East and West in the Crusader States: Context, Contacts, Confrontations: Acta of the Congress Held at Hernen Castle in September 2000, Leuven 2003

Thomas, Saʿīd ibn Ḥasan al-Iskandarānī
D. Thomas, Saʿīd ibn Ḥasan al-Iskandarānī, [in:] D. Thomas, A. Mallett (Eds), Christian-Muslim Relations. A Bibliographical History, Vol. 4 (1200–1350), Leiden, Boston 2012, 775–777

Todt, John V Cantacuzenus
K.-P. Todt, John V Cantacuzenus, [in:] D. Thomas, A. Mallett (Eds), Christian-Muslim Relations. A Bibliographical History, Vol. 5 (1350–1500), Leiden, Boston 2013, 165–178

Tongeren, Exaltation of the Cross
L. Tongeren, Exaltation of the Cross: Toward the Origins of the Feast of the Cross and the Meaning of the Cross in Early Medieval Liturgy, Leuven 2000

Tziovas, Decolonizing Antiquity
D. Tziovas, Decolonizing Antiquity, Heritage Politics, and Performing the Past, [in:] D. Tziovas (Ed.), Re-Imagining the Past: Antiquity and Modern Greek Culture, Oxford 2014, 1–26

Uhlig, Quand 'Postcolonial' et 'Global' riment avec 'Médiéval'
M. Uhlig, Quand 'Postcolonial' et 'Global' riment avec 'Médiéval': sur quelques approches théoriques anglo-saxonnes, *Perspectives médiévales* 35 (2014), 1–24
(http://journals.openedition.org/peme/4400, accessed 10 February 2021)

Valiavitcharska, Rhetoric and Rhythm in Byzantium
V. Valiavitcharska, Rhetoric and Rhythm in Byzantium: The Sound of Persuasion, Cambridge 2013

Van Millingen, Byzantine Constantinople
A. Van Millingen, Byzantine Constantinople: The Walls of the City and Adjoining Historical Sites, Cambridge 2010

Vaporis (Ed.), The Divine Liturgy
Fr.N. Michael Vaporis (Ed.), The Divine Liturgy of Saint Basil the Great
(https://www.goarch.org/-/the-divine-liturgy-of-saint-basil-the-great, accessed 24 November 2021)

Varella, Language Contact
S. Varella, Language Contact and the Lexicon in the History of Cypriot Greek, Bern 2006

Vassiliou, The Word Order of Medieval Cypriot
E. Vassiliou, The Word Order of Medieval Cypriot, Bundoora, Victoria 2002
(http://arrow.latrobe.edu.au:8080/vital/access/manager/Repository/latrobe:19667, accessed 22 November 2021)

Visotzky, Sage Tales
B.L. Visotzky, Sage Tales: Wisdom and Wonder from the Rabbis of the Talmud, Woodstock, Vermont 2014

Voicu, Exploring Cultural Identities
C.-G. Voicu, Exploring Cultural Identities in Jean Rhys' Fiction, Berlin 2014

Voskarides *et al.*, Y-chromosome phylogeographic analysis of the Greek-Cypriot population
K. Voskarides, S. Mazières, D. Hadjipanagi, J. Di Cristofaro, A. Ignatiou, C. Stefanou, R.J. King, P.A. Underhill, J. Chiaroni (corresponding author), C. Deltas (corresponding author), Y-chromosome phylogeographic analysis of the Greek-Cypriot population reveals elements consistent with Neolithic and Bronze Age settlements, *Investigative Genetics* 7: 1 (2016)
(https://investigativegenetics.biomedcentral.com/articles/10.1186/s13323-016-0032-8, accessed 13 December 2021)

Waardenburg, Muslims and Others
J.J. Waardenburg, Muslims and Others: Relations in Context, Berlin 2003

Waldman, Mason, Encyclopedia of European Peoples
C. Waldman, C. Mason, Encyclopedia of European Peoples, Vol. 2, New York 2006

Walsh, Introduction
M.J.K. Walsh, Introduction: The Armenian Church Project: Heritage Welfare in an Unrecognized State, [in:] M.J.K. Walsh (Ed.), The Armenian Church of Famagusta and the Complexity of Cypriot Heritage: Prayers Long Silent, Basingstoke 2017, 1–40

Ward, History of the Cross
H.D. Ward, History of the Cross, the Pagan Origin, and Idolatrous Adoption and Worship of the Image, Oxford 1871

Warren, History on the Edge
M.R. Warren, History on the Edge: Excalibur and the Borders of Britain, 1100–1300, Minneapolis 2000

Watkins, Reyerson, Mediterranean Identities
J. Watkins, K.L. Reyerson, Mediterranean Identities in the Premodern Era: Entrepôts, Islands, and Empires, [in:] J. Watkins, K.L. Reyerson (Eds), Mediterranean Identities in the Premodern Era: Entrepôts, Islands, Empires, Farnham 2014, 1–11

Webster, A Prehistory of Sardinia
G.S. Webster, A Prehistory of Sardinia, 2300–500 BC, Sheffield 1996

Weiss, El postcolonialismo medieval
J. Weiss, El postcolonialismo medieval: líneas y pautas en la investigación de un problema histórico, [in:] N.F. Rodríguez, M.F. Ferreiro (Eds), Literatura medieval y renacentista en España: líneas y pautas, Salamanca 2012, 177–200

White, The Historical Text
H. White, The Historical Text as Literary Artifact, [in:] V.B. Leitch (Ed.), The Norton Anthology of Theory and Criticism, New York 2001

Wispelwey, Biographical Index
B. Wispelwey, Biographical Index of the Middle Ages/ Biographischer Index des Mittelalters/ Index Biographique du Moyen-Âge, Berlin 2008

Woods, Encountering Icons
K. Woods, Encountering Icons: Byzantine Icons in the Netherlands, Bohemia and Spain During the Fourteenth and Fifteenth Centuries, [in:] A. Lymberopolou, R. Duits (Eds), Byzantine Art and Renaissance Europe, Farnham 2013, 135–157

Wright, The Departure of My Lady Mary
W. Wright, The Departure of My Lady Mary from This World, Edited from Two Syriac MSS. in the British Museum, and Translated by W. Wright, reprinted from *The Journal of Sacred Literature and Biblical Record* 6–7 (1865), London 1965

Wrisley, Historical Narration and Digression
D.J. Wrisley, Historical Narration and Digression in al-Nuwairī al-Iskandarānī's Kitāb al-Ilmām, [in:] R. Blumenfeld-Kosinski, K. Petkov (Eds), Philippe de Mézières and His Age: Piety and Politics in the Fourteenth Century, Leiden, Boston 2011, 451–476

Yakinthou, Political Settlements
Ch. Yakinthou, Political Settlements in Divided Societies: Consociationalism and Cyprus, Berlin 2009

Yarbrough, Ibn al-Durayhim
L. Yarbrough, Ibn al-Durayhim, [in:] D. Thomas, A. Mallett (Eds), Christian-Muslim Relations. A Bibliographical History, Vol. 5 (1350–1500), Leiden, Boston 2013, 138–144

Young, Constructing 'England'
H.V. Young, Constructing 'England' in the Fourteenth Century: A Postcolonial Interpretation of Middle English Romance, contributor G. Barnes, Lewiston 2010

Yousey-Hindes, Living the Middle Life
J.B. Yousey-Hindes, Living the Middle Life, Secular Priests and Their Communities in Thirteenth-century Genoa, PhD Thesis, Stanford University 2010

Websites

https://apostolosvarnavas.weebly.com/, accessed 10 December 2021
http://www.saint.gr/1513/saint.aspx, accessed 22 November 2021
http://www.saint.gr/4341/saint.aspx, accessed 22 November 2021
http://www.saint.gr/4338/saint.aspx, accessed 22 November 2021
http://liturgia.cerkiew.pl/pages/File/docs/festum-30-konstantyn.pdf, accessed 23 December 2021
http://www.wordreference.com, accessed 2013–2021

Indices

Geographical index

A
Acre 144, 242
Adalia 47, 60, 61, 62, 82, 150, 188, 192, 198, 201, 202, 217, 241, 243, 244
Aegean Sea 139
Africa 21, 184, 237, 238
Agrinou 203
Akaki 110
Akrotiki 107, 154
Akrotiri Bay 237
Alaya 60, 106, 107, 213, 243
Aleppo 179, 209
Alexandria 50, 56, 62, 130, 137, 142, 174, 179, 188, 189, 190, 191, 192, 199, 206, 212, 226, 227, 242, 244
Algeria 20
Aliki 62, 203
Amanus, Mount, see Black Mountain
Ammochostos (see also Famagusta) 29, 33, 47, 49, 59, 60, 61, 62, 63, 82, 108, 116, 121, 127, 131, 132, 143, 145, 148, 149, 152, 153, 154, 158, 164, 166, 167, 181, 191, 205, 206, 218, 231, 248
Amorion 203
Anamur, see also Anemouri 203
Anatolia 198
Anemouri 60, 202
Antioch 47, 52, 58, 59, 84, 85, 110, 118, 147, 152, 221, 230, 231, 239, 241, 242, 245
Apostolos Andreas, Cape 237
Arabia 175, 185
Aradippou 203
Aragon 61, 62, 69, 149, 154, 162, 244
Armenia, Cilician 55, 60, 62, 80, 83, 90, 140, 198, 205, 240, 241, 244, 245
Arnaoutis 237
Arsinoe 127, 242
Arsuf 142
Ascalon 46, 97, 113, 179
Asia 21, 38, 41, 106, 218, 238, 239
Athens 50

Avignon 60, 74, 164, 243
Avra 115
Ayas 62, 140, 209
Ayasi 60, 205

B
Babylon 69, 196, 197
Baḥr ar-Rūm, see also Mediterranean Sea 178
Barcelona 149
Bari 104
Bethlehem 241
Beyrout (Beirut) 49, 62, 217
Black Mountain (Mount Amanus) 231
Boutron 62
Brabant 243
Byzantium (Byzantine Empire) 28, 35, 41, 50, 70, 80, 92, 99, 109, 178, 179, 180, 187, 217, 238, 241, 245

C
Cairo 58, 69, 164, 165, 187, 203, 209
Calicut 189
Carmel, Mount 128
Casa Piphani 104
Castellorhizo 206
Catalonia 69, 99
Catarina, St 218
Chalcedon 119, 239
China 55, 189
Chioggia 62, 144, 145, 166, 169
Chios 140, 218
Cilicia 198
Constantinople 35, 43, 45, 70, 83, 84, 98, 109, 113, 122, 124, 136, 139, 165, 179, 180, 181, 217, 221, 228, 230, 231, 238, 239, 240, 241, 244, 245
Coral Bay 237
Corinth 139
Coron 131
Cracow 243
Crambousa (Gramvousa) 189, 218
Crete 41, 80, 139, 209, 238

D
Damascus 68, 179, 182, 204, 205, 208, 209, 221, 224, 228, 229, 230
Damietta 206
Dometios, St 80, 118

E
East 23, 45, 53, 75, 90, 91, 145, 164, 174, 185, 233, 238, 242
Egypt 42, 73, 113, 181, 185, 194, 197, 214, 217, 242
Elia 132
England 48, 58, 69, 99, 113, 240, 242
Englistra 109
Ephesus 180, 239
Epirus 98
Episkopi Bay 237
Europe 20, 21, 23, 91, 119, 238

F
Famagusta (see also Ammochostos) 29, 48, 49, 82, 121, 140, 141, 142, 147, 148, 150, 244, 245
Famagusta Bay 237
Farfa 119
Flanders 48, 241, 243
Fontana Amorosa, Bay 237
France 29, 48, 55, 57, 60, 69, 70, 99, 135, 194, 199, 202, 239, 240, 242

G
Galata 218
Galilee 59, 61, 149, 241
Gascony 139
Gata 237
Genoa 29, 33, 42, 60, 61, 62, 98, 139, 140, 141, 142, 143, 144, 145, 146, 148, 151, 152, 153, 154, 156, 157, 158, 159, 160, 162, 163, 164, 169, 170, 171, 191, 192, 202, 221, 233, 243, 244
Giblet (Jubail) 33, 61, 62, 70, 244
Glyphia 104
Gorhigos 60, 67, 82, 123, 132, 188, 192, 198, 199, 200, 201, 207, 227, 243
Greece 37, 131, 237, 238
Greko 237

H
Hattin 113
Hilarion, St, the Castle of 157
Hira 239
Holy Land 52, 53, 79, 84, 91, 99, 136, 162, 206, 233, 238

I
Iconium (Konya) 35, 241
India 20, 55, 59, 189

J
Jaffa 241
Jerusalem 15, 33, 41, 49, 57, 58, 59, 62, 63, 69, 70, 79, 85, 87, 91, 92, 98, 99, 113, 126, 138, 182, 185, 186, 209, 217, 220, 230, 239, 240, 241, 242, 243, 244, 245

K
Kalamoulli 90, 115
Kalopsida 203
Kantara 241
Karpasi 60, 127, 154, 242, 247, 248
Karpathos 237
Kaulam (Quilon) 189
Kellia 203
Kerynia 33, 59, 60, 62, 104, 116, 129, 150, 152, 153, 154, 156, 157, 158, 166, 204, 218, 247, 248
Khirokitia (Kherokitia) 33, 34, 63, 65, 204, 245
Kiti, Kition (see also Larnaka) 102, 203, 239, 247
Klavdia 107
Kormakitis 237
Kouka 114
Kourion 127, 239, 247
Koutsovendi 110
Kouvouklia 207
Kykko 109, 123, 248
Kyparissovouno 238
Kyrenia (Kerynia) Mountains 237, 238
Kythraia 245

L
Lajjun 97
Laodicea 60, 62, 126, 205
Lapithos 247
Larnaka (see also Kiti, Kition) 102, 104, 245, 248
Lefkosia (see also Nicosia) 29, 33, 59, 62, 63, 90, 93, 97, 106, 107, 108, 118, 127, 129, 138, 142, 153, 154, 155, 158, 163, 167, 181, 204, 218, 232, 245
Lemesos (Lemeso, see also Limassol) 29, 62, 101, 107, 127, 153, 203, 218, 245, 247, 248
Levant 99, 140, 179, 180, 241
Limassol (see Lemesos) 141, 142,
Liondis, St 111
Lombardy 61
London 18, 241
Lydda 241

M
Maghreb 184
Mala Paga 160
Malo 60, 205
Mandraki 159
Marathasa 109, 111, 123
Marrakesh 181

Mediterranean Sea (Basin) 26, 35, 63, 70, 85, 140, 141, 163, 165, 178, 179, 190, 191, 217, 237, 238
Meniko 110
Mesaoria (Mesaria) 48, 127, 153, 238
Mesoamerica 25
Messenia 139
Messina, Strait 140
Middle East 24, 37, 69, 141, 162, 165, 173, 175
Monovgat 60, 221
Morea 50, 63, 98, 217
Morphou (Edessa, see also Rukha) 61, 66, 107, 149, 223, 248
Morphou, Bay 237
Mosul 179
Myra 60, 104, 124, 200

N
Napa, St 191
Naples 40, 79
Navarre 139
Nazareth 239
Nicosia (see also Lefkosia) 29, 242, 243
Nubia 55

O
Olympia (see also Stavro Vouni) 89, 116
Olympus (see also Stavro Vouni) 88, 237
Omodos 114, 218
Ousgat 48, 221
Oxen, Island of the 149, 218
Oxford 17, 18, 19, 33

P
Palestine 183, 238, 241
Palokythro 124
Paphos 17, 40, 60, 62, 85, 97, 125, 153, 191, 218, 237, 238, 239, 247, 248
Paris 55
Pedieos, river 243
Pendaskinon 111
Pendaskinos (Pentaschinos), river 114
Persia 91, 185
Petra 132
Phinika 62
Phrygia 203
Plakoundoudi 111
Poitou 29
Poland 245
Potamia 118, 204
Prague 243
Provence 42, 79
Psoka 114

R
Ravenna 17
Rhodes (Rhodos) 43, 60, 61, 62, 63, 94, 97, 98, 150, 158, 159, 164, 167, 171, 189, 191, 213, 217, 218, 237
Rizokarpaso 237
Rome 52, 56, 60, 61, 68, 126, 131, 161, 162, 163, 179, 191
Rosetta 218
Rubin, river 48
Rukha (Edessa, see also Morphou) 149

S
Salamis 40, 85, 238
Sardinia 237
Sarepta 60, 194, 206
Scandinavia 55
Scotland 48, 242
Seleucia 85, 198
Sevasteia 118
Sicily 237
Sidon 60, 62, 205
Sis 198
Solia 239, 242, 247, 248
Spain 25, 48, 92, 179
Stavro Vouni (see also Olympia, Olympus) 88, 114, 116, 190, 231, 245, 248
Styli 203
Sudaqin 189
Syria 42, 60, 62, 67, 68, 73, 88, 110, 113, 162, 164, 165, 189, 191, 198, 203, 209, 217, 227, 237, 239, 240, 241

T
Tamassos 239, 247
Tarsus 198
Tartary 83
Thebes 139
Thessaloniki (Saloniki) 43
Tenis, river 48
Togni 53, 70, 88, 89, 113, 114, 116, 136, 231
Tortosa 60, 62, 124, 192
Toulouse 94
Trakhona 155
Trapeza 203
Trimithia 132
Trimythos 40, 238, 239, 240, 247
Tripoli 58, 60, 181, 192, 209, 244
Troodos, Mountains 34, 109, 218, 237
Trullo 239
Turkey 60, 70, 217, 237, 238
Tyre 53, 58, 97, 144, 243

V
Valena 60, 205
Venice 17, 29, 34, 42, 57, 60, 62, 139, 144, 145, 159, 164, 165, 169, 192, 218, 221, 235, 243
Vienna 243
Voni 155
Vromolaxia 203

W
West 23, 25, 26, 28, 55, 60, 69, 75, 142, 165, 174, 193, 196, 197, 224, 233, 238, 243
Western Sea 178

Z
Zaitun 189
Zotia 104

Index of persons

A

Abū Bakr, immediate successor of Muḥammad 239
Abū Bakr al-ʿĀdil I (Sayf ad-Dīn) 241
Abulafia, David 140
Abū Tammām 177, 178
Adam 149
Afxivios, St 102
Agatha, St 125
Akbari, Suzanne Conklin 25
Alegi, Tariq 15
Alexander IV, pope 74, 161, 242
Alexander the Great, king of Macedonia 74, 161, 242
Alexandrians 190, 192, 226
Alexios I Komnenos, Byzantine emperor 142
Alexis, self-appointed ruler 40
Alexopoulos (Alexis), Cretan 66, 133, 224, 233
Algra, Keimpe 89
Alice of Champagne, wife of Hugh I 117, 141, 241
Alice d'Ibelin, wife of Hugh IV 141, 142
Alighieri, Dante 139
Altschul, Nadia 25
Amadeus VI, count of Savoy 165
Amadi, Francesco 53
Amaury, lord of Tyre and Toron 53, 58, 66, 67, 68, 82, 142, 223, 243
Amaury I, king of Jerusalem 57, 69, 192, 240
Amaury (Aimery) de Lusignan, king of Cyprus and Jerusalem 58, 101, 126, 214, 241
Amazons 49
Anaxagorou, Nadia (Νάτια Αναξαγόρου) 16, 35, 36, 39, 40, 44, 45, 47, 48, 50, 63, 67
Andrew II, king of Hungary 241
Andronikos of Kanakaria, St 107
Angold, Michael 109
Anna Komnene (Ἄννα Κομνηνή) 43, 44, 46, 48
Antony, St 125, 181
Antony de Negrone 144
Apostles 85, 101, 126
Arabs 92, 184, 203
'Ardent Desire' 55, 83
Aristotle 47, 64

Armenians 15, 74, 79, 80, 127, 144, 146, 171, 199, 204, 240, 243, 244
Arodaphnousa 41
Arslan, Alp 199
Ashcroft, Bill 26, 231
Al-Ašraf Zayn ad-Dīn Šaʿbān 165
Assyrians 238
Athanasios Pendaskinitis, St 111, 114
Al-Aṯir (ʿAlī ʿIzz ad-Dīn Ibn al-Aṯir) 47, 173, 182
Austin-Broos, Diane 206
Ayyūbid (Banū Ayyūb), dynasty 182, 240

B

Babai the Great 86
Babin, Raymond 149
Badin de Nores 245
Baglioni, Daniele 76
Bahri, Deepika 23
Bakarat, Halim 176
Bakhtin, Michail 218, 227
Baldwin I of Bouillon (Boulogne), king of Jerusalem 57, 69, 239
Baldwin II d'Aiguillon, king of Jerusalem 57, 69, 92, 240
Baldwin III, the Old, king of Jerusalem 57, 69, 113, 240
Baldwin IV, the Leper, king of Jerusalem 57, 69, 240
Baldwin V, the Child, king of Jerusalem 58, 69, 240
Baldwin of Flanders 241
Balian d'Ibelin 97
Barkuk (Barquq), bourgeois sultan 210
Barnabas, Apostle 85, 101
Barsbāy, sultan of Egypt 181, 198, 203
Baybars al-Bunduqdārī 242
Basil (Vasileios) Digenis Akritas (Βασίλειος Διγενής Ἀκρίτας) 41
Baxis (see also Makhairas, Antony) 34
Beauvoir, Simone de 21
Bekker-Nielsen, Tønnes 40
Belfarage, Thibald 62, 66, 131, 132, 133, 134, 135, 165, 166, 199, 218, 223, 228, 229, 230, 232, 233

Belting, Hans 123
Benedict XI, pope 160
Berenger, Raymond, grand master of Rhodes 94
Bergadis (Μπεργαδής) 55
Bertrandon de La Broquière 34
Bevan, Edwyn 89
Bevans, Stephen 20, 28, 77
Bhabha, Homi 27, 75, 135, 231
Bili, George 33
Bili, Nicholas 33
Bilis 31
Boccaccio, Giovanni 181
Bochard, Arnold (Arnaud Bouchart) 93
Boehmer, Elleke 24, 27
Bohemond IV the One-eyed, prince of Antioch and count of Tripoli 241
Bonaventure of Savio 140
Boniface VIII, pope 160
Boniface of Montferrat, marquis of Montferrat and king of Thessalonica 241
Borowska, Małgorzata 17, 19, 38, 41, 46
Boustronios, George (Τζορτζής [Μ]πουστρούς[1862])
17, 57, 79, 80, 90, 97, 112, 126, 139, 140, 160, 206, 212
Bragamains, peoples in *La Songe...* 83
Brownlee, Kevin 54
Buenhombre, Alfons 181
Bulgarians 66, 79, 157, 158
Burkiewicz, Łukasz 30, 92
Burns, Stephen 27
Busat, Nicol 33
Bustron, Florio 54, 185
Byzantines 37, 135, 139, 154, 187

C

Caesarius, Protopapas 239
Campo Fregoso, Peter de, Genoese admiral 167, 222
Cassi (Cassin), Peter de 62
Cassirer, Ernst 16
Catalans 79, 139, 165, 196
Cattaneo, Damian 153
Celestine III, pope 126, 160, 161, 241
Celestine IV, pope 161
Celestines 55
Cervera, Jesús Castellano OCD 124
Cesnola, Luigi Palma di 237
Charlemagne, king of the Franks and Emperor of the Holy Roman Empire 56, 192, 194
Charles VI, emperor of the Holy Roman Empire 55
Charlotte de Lusignan, queen of Cyprus 63, 224, 245
Chrétien de Troyes 25
Christinus, St 183

Christopher, St, Martyr 124
Clari, Robert de 44
Claudius, Roman emperor 86
Clement V, pope 57, 78, 94, 95, 96, 97, 243
Clement VI, pope 59, 160
Clovis I, king of the Franks 100
Cobham, Claude Delaval 19
Cohen, Jeffrey Jerome 21, 22, 23
Coldstream, Nicola 148
Conrad III Hohenstauf, German king 240
Constantine I the Great, St, Byzantine emperor 14, 35, 57, 70, 83, 84, 85, 86, 87, 89, 90, 91, 113, 116, 120, 238
Constantine IV the Younger, Byzantine emperor 243
Coopan, Vilashini 23
Coopland, George William 54
Copts 73, 74, 83
Cornaro, Catarina, queen of Cyprus 57
Coureas, Nicholas (Νίκος Κουρέας) 15, 20, 31, 33, 46, 115, 131, 231
Cretans 80, 166
Cyprian, St 110
Cyprians 29, 35, 39, 69, 70, 74, 75, 77, 79, 80, 87, 94, 99, 100, 101, 102, 103, 104, 106, 112, 119, 120, 129, 134, 135, 137, 139, 146, 170, 174, 214, 218, 219, 220, 222, 224, 225, 230
Cypriots 14, 26, 29, 35, 37, 38, 59, 60, 62, 63, 75, 77, 80, 82, 93, 94, 96, 98, 120, 124, 128, 136, 138, 142, 146, 147, 148, 150, 151, 153, 154, 157, 159, 160, 162, 163, 164, 165, 166, 167, 168, 169, 170, 171, 174, 177, 179, 185, 186, 187, 188, 189, 190, 192, 198, 200, 201, 202, 203, 205, 206, 207, 208, 211, 213, 214, 215, 217, 222, 225, 228, 230, 231, 233, 241, 242, 243, 244
Cyriac (Judas Kyriakos), St 64, 86, 87
Cyril, bishop of Paphos 238
Czernik, Tomasz, rev. 75
Czerwiński, Maciej 14

D

Aḏ-Ḏāhir, caliph of the Abbasyd dynasty 192
Dampierre, Galio de 33
Dandolo, Enrico 241
Davis, Kathleen 25
Dąbrówka, Andrzej 11, 137
Devotion 83
Dimitrios Daniel 62
Diomidios, St 64, 105, 106, 108, 112, 202, 222, 227
Dometios, St 118
Dominic, St 125, 126
Doukas, family 41, 45
Drijvers, Jan Willem 86
Dupré, Louis 89
Dziekan, Marek 176

[1862] After Borowska, *Panorama greckojęzycznej literatury cypryjskiej*, 80.

E

Echive d'Ibelin, queen of Cyprus 241, 243
Echive de Lusignan 58, 61
Echive de Scandelion, mistress of Peter I 61, 66
Edbury, Peter 20, 53, 54, 115, 231
Edward I, king of England 242
Egyptians 174, 175, 176, 184, 185, 188, 190, 192, 193, 195, 196, 198, 207, 213, 219, 221, 245
Eirenikos of Zotia, St 104
El Bogha el Azizi 194
El-Cheikh, Nadia Maria 179
Eleanora of Aragon, queen of Cyprus 33, 61, 62, 64, 66, 69, 133, 149, 154, 155, 162, 163, 220, 223, 228, 231, 244
Eliade, Mircea 89
Elias, priest 168, 170
Eliezer, rabbi 166
Englishmen 166
Epaphroditos of Tamassos, prelate 239
Ephraim (Ἐφραίμ) 43
Epiphanios, archbishop of Salamis 40, 118
Epiphanios, St 110
Epiphanios of Solia, prelate 239
Epstein, Steven 77
Ernoul 126
Estienne de Lusignan 42
Eteocypriots 13
Ethiopians 244
Eudoxia 86
Eugene III, pope 110
Euthymios, St 118
Evagoras, king of Salamis 238
Evagrius, bishop of Solia, prelate 239
Evagrius Ponticus 223
Eve 149

F

Faletra, Michael 25
Fanon, Frantz 27
Fatimid, dynasty 194
fertility goddess 13
Filangieri, Richard, Emperor Frederick II's marshal 241
Florentines 79
Florimond, Sieur de Lesparre 229
Folly 83
Fra Marco, Catholic bishop of Ammochostos 116, 121, 127, 136
Franks 14, 15, 26, 28, 29, 35, 36, 39, 50, 51, 56, 58, 61, 66, 69, 70, 71, 74, 75, 76, 77, 79, 80, 94, 98, 99, 100, 101, 102, 103, 105, 119, 120, 126, 127, 128, 129, 131, 133, 134, 135, 136, 137, 138, 139, 140, 142, 143, 145, 146, 148, 150, 158, 166, 169, 170, 171, 173, 174, 179, 180, 182, 183, 186, 187, 189, 191, 201, 202, 203, 214, 218, 219, 220, 221, 222, 224, 225, 230, 231, 233, 238, 241
Frederick II Hohenstaufen, emperor of the Holy Roman Empire 92, 241
Freud, Sigmund 174
Froissart, John 48, 189
Fulk V the Younger, king of Jerusalem 57

G

Gabriel, monk 70, 116, 117, 118
Galatariotou, Katia (Κάτια Γαλαταριώτου) 36
Galeftira, cook 152, 204
Gandhi, Leela 76
Ġanġara (Ğanġara, Janghara) 190
Gasel, John 203
Gaunt, Simon 24
Gaurelle, John de 244
Al-Ġazālī, Abū Ḥāmid 177, 180
Gelasius, bishop of Salamis 238
Genette, Gérard 16
Genoese 8, 26, 27, 28, 31, 33, 34, 47, 49, 52, 53, 55, 60, 61, 62, 63, 68, 70, 79, 82, 97, 98, 99, 110, 132, 134, 137, 139, 140, 141, 142, 143, 144, 145, 146, 147, 148, 149, 150, 151, 152, 153, 154, 155, 156, 157, 158, 159, 160, 162, 163, 164, 165, 166, 167, 168, 169, 170, 171, 174, 176, 196, 198, 199, 202, 203, 204, 206, 207, 214, 219, 221, 222, 224, 225, 226, 227, 228, 229, 230, 233, 241, 243, 245
Geoffrey of Monmouth 25
Geoffrey of Villehardouin 44, 50
George, St 121, 183
George (see also Gabriel, monk) 116, 117
George, Christian lad of Alexandria 137, 208, 212, 213
George of the Birds, St 49
George of Damat 208
George the Exiler, St 80
George of Kalamoulli 115
George Khatit 209
George of the Pulans, St 49, 125
George of Rhodos 43
George slain by the Sword, St 111
Georgians 83, 244
Georgios Akropolites (Γεώργιος Ακροπολίτης) 43
Georgios Lapithes (Γεώργιος Λαπίθης) 42
Georgios Pachymeres (Γεώργιος Παχυμέρης) 43, 44
Gerald of Wales 25
Gerard, archbishop 242
Ghiyāth al-Dīn Kaykhusraw, sultans of Rûm 241
Ghosh, Amitav 25
Gibb, Hamilton 215
Giblet, Henry de 33, 70, 244
Giustiniani, Peter 165
Glimin of Narbonne 231

Goddart, Hugh 173
Godfrey de Bouillon 57, 69, 79, 80, 239
Godiwala, Dimple 77
Goneme, Badin 33, 42, 232
good thief 87, 88
Goytisolo, Juan 25
Grandclaude, Maurice 42
Greek Cypriots 45
Greeks (see also Rhomaioi) 14, 15, 26, 27, 28, 29, 31, 33, 35, 42, 51, 56, 61, 69, 70, 73, 74, 75, 76, 78, 79, 80, 93, 94, 98, 100, 102, 119, 120, 121, 122, 124, 125, 127, 128, 129, 130, 131, 133, 134, 135, 136, 137, 156, 165, 171, 178, 179, 186, 187, 193, 199, 218, 219, 220, 224, 225, 228, 229, 242, 243
Grégoire, Henri 203
Gregory, brother 63
Gregory II, patriarch of Constantinople 40
Gregory IX, pope 162, 239
Gregory XI, pope 143, 145, 158, 161, 162, 163, 244
Gregory of Tours 51
Griffiths, Gareth 26, 231
Grivaud, Gilles 42, 203
Guibert of Nogent 46, 47, 48
Guignery, Vanessa 77
Guillaume de Machaut 56, 123, 161, 162, 189, 190, 191, 192, 200
Guy de Lusignan, king of Jerusalem 19, 35, 58, 94, 98, 187, 220, 240, 243

H

Hadjidemetriou, Katia (Κάτια Χατζηδημητρίου) 19, 30
Hadjioannou, Kyriakos 42
Hagarenes 184, 187
Hahn, Cynthia 105
Al-Ḥākim bi-Amr Allāh 194
Halliday, Michael 16
Hareris 31
Hārūn ar-Rašīd 192, 194
Hasan, Ruqaiya 16
Haughtiness 83
Haume de Seliers 92
Hebrews 52
Hedges, Paul 119
Hedwig, daughter of Ladislaus 245
Heidegger, Martin 21
Helena, St, mother of Constantine the Great 28, 57, 58, 70, 77, 84, 85, 86, 87, 88, 89, 90, 91, 92, 94, 96, 113, 114, 116, 137, 179, 185, 213, 215, 217, 220, 222, 229, 238
Helena Palaiologina (Palaiologos), Byzantine princess 14, 63, 71, 90, 245
Helvis of Brunswick, queen of Cyprus and Armenia 90, 244, 245

Henana of Adiabene 86
Henry of Antioch 242
Henry de Giblet 33, 70, 244
Henry de La Couronne 206
Henry I de Lusignan, king of Cyprus 58, 241
Henry II de Lusignan, king of Cyprus 49, 58, 66, 68, 82, 144, 242
Herakleides, St 118
Heraklios, Byzantine emperor 53, 91, 175
Hill, George 19, 30, 35, 79, 126, 127, 141, 190, 200
Hirschler, Konrad 183
Honi (Ḥoni) 116
Honorius II, pope 92
Honorius III, pope 241
Hopelessness 83
Horrocks, Geoffrey 37
Hospitallers, Knights of the Hospital 8, 27, 79, 92, 97, 98, 122, 158, 220, 242, 243
Hugh de Lusignan, cardinal 63
Hugh de Lusignan, son of Guy de Lusignan, prince of Galilee 61, 149, 220
Hugh I de Lusignan, king of Cyprus 58, 241
Hugh II de Lusignan, king of Cyprus 58
Hugh III de Lusignan (Hugh of Antioch), king of Cyprus 58, 242, 243
Hugh IV de Lusignan, king of Cyprus 40, 54, 58, 59, 61, 70, 124, 136, 149, 243, 244
Hungarians 166
Huntington, Samuel 174
Husserl, Edmund 21

I

Ibas of Edessa 239
Ibn Baṭṭūṭa 189
Ibn al-Durayhim ('Alī Ibn Muḥammad Ibn ad-Durayhim) 181
Ibn Ḥaldūn 176, 177, 178, 179
Ibn al-Ḥaṭṭāb, 'Umar 183
Ibn Qayyim al-Ǧawziyya 180
Ibn Taymīya 180
Ibn Wāṣil 182, 189
Ibrahim Beg 34
Ibrahim Beg, 'Grand Karaman', the emir of Karaman, lord of Alaya, and the lord of Monovgat 34, 60, 61 198, 200
Ignatios, patriarch of Antioch 58, 118
Indians 244
Ingham, Patricia Clare 21, 22, 23
'Innocent' (properly Urban V) 60
Innocent IV, pope 161, 241, 242
Innocent VI, pope 61, 129, 161
Ioannes Anagnostes (Ἰωάννης Ἀναγνώστης) 43
Ioannes Kananos (Ἰωάννης Κανανός) 43

Ioannes VI Kantakouzenos (Ἰωάννης Καντακουζηνός) 43, 44, 181
Ioannes Kinnamos (Ἰωάννης Κίνναμος) 43
Ioannes Klimakos (Ἰωάννης τῆς Κλίμακος) 64
Ioannes Malalas 44
Ioannes Zonaras (Ἰωάννης Ζωναρᾶς) 43
Irene, John V Palaiologos' daughter 222, 244
Irene Doukaina, Byzantine empress 41
Isaac (I) Doukas Komnenos, ruler of Cyprus 82, 240
Isabella d'Ibelin, mother of Henry II 68, 242, 243
Isabella I of Jerusalem, queen of Jerusalem 240
Isabella de Lusignan 242
Isaiah 89
Ishmaelites 184

J
Jacob of Sarug/Serugh 86, 152
Jacobites 29, 74, 80, 83, 243, 244
Jagessar, Michael 27
James de Giblet 61
James I de Lusignan, king of Cyprus 57, 58, 61, 62, 63, 90, 147, 152, 154, 159, 164, 224, 244, 245
James II de Lusignan, king of Cyprus 57
James de Nores 195
James de St Michel 153
Janus de Lusignan 19, 33, 35, 57, 63, 68, 144, 174, 198, 203, 204, 208, 209, 210, 211, 215, 221, 222, 224, 229, 245
Jeanrond, Werner 20, 174
Jeffreys, Elizabeth 41
Jensen, J.S. 178
Jews 86, 239, 244
Joanna L'Aleman 41, 61, 66, 110
Joel (Ἰωήλ) 43, 90
John, (arch)bishop of Cyprus 74
John, St 102, 118, 125
John the Almsgiver, St 40
John de Arsuf 143
John of Brienne 241
John Carmaïn 60, 61
John Chrysostom, St 133, 152
John de Colie 206
John of Conti 243
John de Gaurelle 244
John d'Ibelin 96
John of Jerusalem, St 92
John II Komnenos, Byzantine emperor 240
John Lambadistis 111
John Lombard 58
John de Lusignan, prince of Antioch and constable of Cyprus 58, 142, 152, 167, 224
John I de Lusignan, king of Cyprus 58
John II de Lusignan, king of Cyprus 14, 63, 217, 218, 242, 245

John de Montfort, St 106, 112
John de Monstri 60, 62, 222
John of Morphou 61, 66, 149, 223
John de Neuville 33
John de Nores 33, 34
John V Palaiologos (Kaloyoanni) 35, 122, 135, 165, 187, 217, 222, 244
John of Salisbury 25
John de Sur 147
John of Verona 42, 59
Judas 96, 149
Julius of Paphos, prelate 239
Jurewicz, Oktawiusz 29, 43
Justina, St 110
Justinian I, Byzantine emperor 239

K
Kabir, Ananya Jahanara 23, 25
Kalorites, Makarios 110
Karaman Beg 203
Karczewski, Leszek 14
Kassia 73
Kassianos, St (Glyphia) 104
Kazhdan, Alexander 44
Kearney, Richard 120
Kechagioglou (Kekhagioglou), Giorgos (Γιώργος Κεχαγιόγλου) 41
Khanna of Damascus 204, 205
Khatziani 60
Khosrow II Parviz, Sasanian king of Iran 91
Khwarazmians 241
Kieckhefer, Richard 112
Kijas, Zdzisław Józef OFMConv 124
Kinoshita, Sharon 21
Kirk, Russell 174
Komodikis, Konstantinos (Κωνσταντίνος Κωμοδίκης) 90, 114, 122, 135
Konstantinos Anagnostes (Κωνσταντίνος Ἀναγνώστης) 42
Konstantinos Manasses (Κωνσταντίνος Μανασσής) 43
Kordos, Przemysław 11, 19, 237
Kornacka, Małgorzata 11
Kriaras, Emmanuel (Εμμανουήλ Κριαρᾶς) 17
Kuczara, Konrad 11
Kyriacou, Chrystovalantis (Χρυσοβαλάντης Κυριάκου) 40, 108, 202, 203
Kyrris, Kostas (Κώστας Κύρρης) 16, 31, 32, 36, 37, 38, 44, 45, 46, 50

L
Lacan, Jacques 22
Ladislaus II Jagiello, king of Poland 245
Lakha, Francis 34, 59, 80

Lakha, Nicholas 80
Lampert-Weissig, Lisa 20, 22, 25
Lanitis, Nikos (Νίκος Λανίτης) 36
Laonikos Chalkokondyles (Λαόνικος Χαλκοκονδύλης) 43
Lazaros, bishop of Kition 102
Lebov, William 16
Lefkis, Giannis (Γιάννης Λεύκης) 35
Leon d'Antiaume 60
Leontios, bishop of Naples (Λεόντιος) 40
Leopold VI of Austria 239
Le Petit, Peter 162
Lescure Brother (Raymond) de 94
Levine, Robert 47
Lindbeck, George 120
Lithuanians 83
Lock, Peter 139
Lombards 58, 98, 149, 166
Loomba, Ania 24, 27
Lort the Usher, Sir de 207
Lossky, Vladimir 113
Louis VII the Young, king of France 240
Louis IX, St, king of France 113, 242
Lüdeke, Hedwig 203
Luhmann, Niklas 91
Luke d'Antiaume 153
Luke, Apostle 123, 124, 125
Lusignans 26, 28, 29, 35, 51, 57, 59, 70, 76, 77, 92, 98, 99, 100, 101, 102, 119, 120, 130, 134, 135, 136, 140, 142, 143, 144, 147, 148, 149, 153, 154, 158, 160, 165, 169, 179, 189, 214, 221, 222, 224, 225, 229, 230, 233, 247

M
MacEvitt, Christopher 179, 180
'Machis' (see also Makhairas, Peter) 33
Mahomet, Tagriverdi 203
Mahomet Reis 202
Makhairas, Antony (see also Baxis) 34, 207
Makhairas, Cosmas (Kosmas) 34
Makhairas, Nicholas 33
Makhairas, Paul 33
Makhairas, Peter (see also 'Machis') 33, 232
Makhairas, Stavrinos 31, 32, 33, 122
Makhairotissa 34
Mamas, St 64, 106, 107, 112, 120, 125
Mamlūk, old Saracen 208
Mamlūks, the Mamlūk dynasty 165, 184, 188, 193, 198, 203, 207
Mandeville, John 181
Mantzas, priest 129
Manuel Gabalas (Μανουὴλ Γαβαλάς) 180
Manuel Kantakouzenos (Μανουὴλ Καντακουζηνός), Byzantine emperor 217
Margaret de Lusignan 217
Maria d'Ibelin (see also Maria of Plisie) 58
Maria of Montferrat 241
Maria of Plisie (see also Maria d'Ibelin) 58
Maronites 29, 42, 73, 74, 240, 243
Marshal, Paul 33
Martin, St 126
Martin V, pope 245
Martyrs of Sevasteia 118
Mary, Virgin 34, 74, 86, 109, 123, 124, 125, 128, 200, 201
Mas Latrie, Louis de 19, 126
Matthew, St 85
Maximus the Confessor 223, 227
McCleery, Iona 26
Medea 63
Melek Bekhna 60, 221
Melek Shah 210
Mersch, Margit 121
Michael, toll collector 208
Michael II Andronikos (Μιχαὴλ Ἀνδρόνικος), Byzantine emperor 40
Michael Glykas (Μιχαὴλ Γλυκάς) 43
Michael Kritoboulos (Μιχαὴλ Κριτοβούλος) 43, 45
Michael VIII Palaiologos (Μιχαὴλ Παλαιολόγος), Byzantine emperor 242
Michael Panaretos (Μιχαὴλ Πανάρετος) 43
Michailidis, Vasilis (Βασίλης Μιχαηλίδης) 45, 46
Michalopoulos, Fanis (Φάνης Μιχαλόπουλος) 36
Mihailovic, Alexandar 227
Miller, Emmanuel 18
Misztal, Mariusz 11, 19, 30, 190, 237
Mnemonius of Kition, prelate 239
Molay, Jacques de 97, 243
Momma, Haruko 25
Monstri, Peter 164
Montis, Kostas (Κώστας Μόντης) 45, 46
Moors 184
Moses 56
Mouriki, Doula 123
Moyaert, Marianne 120, 131, 135
Mrożek-Dumanowska, Anna 180
Muʿāwiya, caliph of Ummayad dynasty 178, 239
Muḥammad 175, 178, 181, 182, 183, 186, 190, 214, 239
Muʿīn ad-Dīn 182
Al-Muqtadir, caliph of the Abbasyd dynasty 180
Muṣūr, emir 41
Al-Mutawakkil, caliph of the Abbasyd dynasty 180

N
Nasr-ed-Din (see also Lort the Usher) 207
Nazmi, Ahmad 178
Neophytos the Recluse, St 64, 109, 110, 134

Nestorians 29, 73, 74, 79, 80, 83, 243, 244
Nicholas, St 21, 59, 104, 124, 125, 151, 200
Nicholas, the merchant 41
Nicholas, the son of an employee at the baths 208
Nicholas I (Mystikos), patriarch of Constantinople 180
Nicholas IV, pope 162
Nicolaou-Konnari, Angel (Άγγελ Νικολάου-Κονναρή) 15, 16, 17, 18, 19, 26, 28, 34, 35, 38, 42, 44, 54, 56, 70, 131, 134, 146, 188, 192, 193, 214, 225
Nikephoros Gregoras (Νικηφόρος Γρηγοράς) 43, 44
Nikephoros Kallistos Xanthopoulos (Νικηφόρος Κάλλιστος Ξανθόπουλος) 43
Nikephoros II Phokas, Byzantine empire 239
Niketas Choniates (Νικήτας Χωνιάτης) 43, 44, 46
Nikon of the Black Mountain 231
Nowosielski, Jerzy 90, 103
Noyes, John 22
Nubians 244
Nūr ad-Dīn 49, 192
An-Nuwayrī al-Iskandarānī, Muḥammad ibn Qāsim 189

O
Odo of Châteauroux 242
Olympas 114, 116
Olympios, Michalis (Μιχάλης Ολύμπιος) 77
Order of the Passion of Christ 89, 93
Orlandos, Anastasios 34
Özkutlu, Seyit 134

P
Pallis, Alexandros (Αλέξανδρος Πάλλης) 36
Papadopoulos, Christos (Χρήστος Παπαδόπουλος) 19
Papaleontiou, Lefteris (Λευτέρης Παπαλεοντίου) 41
Paschali, Maria 75, 121
Paul, St 51
Paul, the servant of a bishop 208
Pavlakou, Dimitra (Δήμητρα Παυλάκου) 31
Pavlidis, Antros (Άντρος Παυλίδης) 18, 94, 96, 132, 158, 184
Pears, Angie 20, 28, 78
Peckruhn, Heike 76
Pelestri, James 94
Pella 204, 205
Pepper, Stephen Coburn 20, 78
Pernessin, Benedict 245
Persians 238
Peter of Aragon 162
Peter de Campo Fregoso 167, 222
Peter de Cassi 62
Peter the Hermit 52, 88
Peter I de Lusignan, king of Cyprus 15, 41, 53, 54, 57, 58, 59, 60, 61, 62, 64, 65, 66, 67, 68, 69, 70, 71, 74, 82, 83, 110, 122, 123, 128, 130, 131, 132, 138, 142, 144, 149, 154, 155, 158, 159, 161, 164, 165, 167, 170, 175, 188, 189, 190, 192, 193, 195, 196, 197, 199, 213, 214, 218, 220, 221, 222, 223, 224, 227, 229, 230, 231, 243, 244
Peter II de Lusignan, king of Cyprus 33, 44, 51, 54, 57, 61, 62, 71, 122, 132, 133, 135, 138, 143, 144, 145, 149, 150, 151, 153, 155, 156, 157, 162, 164, 187, 199, 202, 214, 221, 222, 226, 228, 230, 233, 244
Peter de Pleine Chassagne 243
Peter de Thomas, legate of the pope 35, 54, 59, 129, 130, 135, 190, 206, 224, 225, 231, 243, 244
Pharaoh 195, 222
Philip, priest 33, 122, 132, 233
Philip I, king of France 57, 239
Philip II Augustus, king of France 113, 240
Philip d'Ibelin 241, 244
Philip of Novara 53
Philippe de Mézières 15, 20, 54, 55, 56, 74, 81, 83, 102, 112, 113, 130, 134, 140, 175, 190, 225
Phoenicians 238
Picquigny, Philip 203
Photios, St 106
Photios I the Great, patriarch of Constantinople 180
Pieris, Michael (Μιχάλης Πιερής) 18, 35, 37, 45, 46, 68, 69
Pikatoros, Ioannis (Ιωάννης Πικατόρος) 55
Pisani, Victor 145
Pisans 49, 140, 144
Plaisance 240
Plato 89
Płuciennik, Jarosław 14
Podocataro, John 221, 245
Pride 83
Protonike, Claudius' wife 86
Provosto, Thomas 221
Psilidi (Psichidis) 156

Q
Al-Qarāfī 180

R
Rabasa, José 25
Rapti, Ioanna 75
Reginos, bishop of Skopelos 239
Reinhart, Tanya 16
Rekouniatos 207, 208, 219, 229
Rey, Emmanuel 179
Reyerson, Kathryn 74
Rhodians 62, 79, 94, 98, 158, 159, 160

Rhomaioi 15, 26, 28, 29, 31, 33, 42, 51, 56, 61, 69, 70, 74, 75, 76, 78, 79, 80, 93, 98, 100, 120, 125, 131, 135, 136, 137, 156, 165, 186, 220, 224
Richard Cœur de Lion, Kind of England 58, 74, 113, 126, 181, 240
Ricouer, Paul 231
Rinald, bishop of Ostia, see Aleksander IV 161
Rodriguez, Jarbel 214
Romanites 79
Romanos III Argyros, Byzantine emperor 192
Romanos IV Diogenes, Byzantine emperor 192
Rosenthal, Erwin 175, 176, 177
Runciman, Steven 19
Rushdie, Salman 25

S

Sabas, St 144
Said, Edward 26, 27
Saʿīd ibn Ḥasan al-Iskandarānī 180
Saladin, sultan of Cairo 58, 99, 113, 173
Sansaridou-Hendrickx, Thekla 183
Santamarin, John 58, 114, 120, 231
Saprikios, bishop of Paphos 239
Saracens 33, 59, 60, 67, 70, 80, 92, 94, 103, 106, 108, 111, 112, 113, 116, 131, 133, 147, 148, 150, 151, 164, 166, 175, 179, 183, 184, 185, 186, 189, 190, 193, 194, 196, 197, 198, 202, 203, 204, 205, 206, 207, 208, 209, 210, 211, 212, 213, 214, 215, 221, 222, 223, 224, 227, 228, 229, 232, 233
Saradi, Helen 89
Sassanid, dynasty 91
Sathas, Konstantinos (Κωνσταντίνος Σάθας) 18, 32, 35
Saul 85
Saunders, John 176
Savoy, People of 166
Schmitt, John 50, 51
Schryver, James 26, 71, 76, 225
Sebacs 31
Seljuk, dynasty 185, 192, 239
Seshadri-Crooks, Kalpana 23
Shoemaker, Stephen 86
Simeon the Holy Fool, St 40
Simon de Montolif 243
Smart, Roderic Ninian 20, 78, 222
Smith, Katherine Allen 106
Solomon from the order of St Dominic, bishop of Tortosa 92
Soter of Theodosiana, prelate 239
Sourdel, Dominique 178
Sozomenoi 31
Sozomenos, St 118
Sozondas, St 111
Spiegel, Gabriela 25
Spinola, Francis 60, 205, 206
Spivak, Gayatri Chakravorty 21, 27, 224
Spyridakis, Konstantinos (Κωνσταντίνος Σπυριδάκης) 35
Spyridon of Trimythos 40, 238
Stavrias, slave of the Church of the Holy Cross 208
Stephen of La Ferté 92
Strambaldi, Diomede 18, 54, 202
Stratonik of Solia 239
Suarez, Carceran 42
Sudheim, Ludolf von 79
Sulaymān, sultan of the Ottoman dynasty 178
Sybil of Jerusalem 240
Syrians 15, 49, 59, 73, 79, 80, 100, 113, 135, 155, 157, 158, 171, 204, 205, 224, 233, 240

T

Taboada, Hernán G.H. 25
Takka, emir 60, 62, 82, 104, 150, 201, 202, 213, 221, 243
Tarasios, St, patriarch of Constantinople 124
Tatars 79, 80, 175
Taylor, James 120
Templars 27, 69, 70, 74, 79, 92, 93, 94, 95, 96, 97, 98, 99, 100, 113, 122, 123, 136, 182, 202, 220, 224, 227, 228, 240, 242, 243
Teutonic Knights 92
Theodoki, royal builder 208
Theodore of Mopsuestia 239
Theodore II Palaiologos 63
Theodore of Paphos 40
Theodoret of Cyrus 239
Theodoxia 86
Theopompus of Trimythos, prelate 239
Thomas, baptised Saracen 207
Thomas Aquinas, St 166
Tiffin, Helen 26, 231
Tillich, Paul 91
Tivčev, Petar 36
Tocco, family 98, 183
Tokarska-Bakir, Joanna 91
Trari, Bertolacci 33
Triphyllios, St, bishop of Lefkosia 66, 106, 108, 118, 222
Truth ('Queen Truth') 55, 56, 83
Tryphon, St, Martyr 124
Tsarra 97
Tsetsious 34, 59, 97
Tsoles 34, 59
Turks 18, 35, 60, 61, 107, 122, 131, 148, 150, 151, 166, 174, 175, 176, 183, 184, 185, 186, 188, 189, 193, 198, 199, 200, 201, 202, 203, 205, 206, 213, 219, 221, 231, 239, 243, 244
Tycho of Tamassos, prelate 239

Tychon of Kition 239
Tykhikos, bishop of Lemesos 101
Tziovas, Dimitris 74

U
Umayyad, dynasty 178
Urban II, pope 46, 52, 57, 160, 161, 239
Urban IV, pope 242
Urban V (see also 'Innocent'), pope 61, 144, 161, 165, 191, 192
Usāma Ibn Munqiḏ 20, 181

V
Valentina 62, 228, 244
Varella, Stavroula 37
Vasiliadis, Nikolas 113
Vassiliou, Erma 17, 18, 37, 39, 42, 230, 238
Venetians 26, 28, 49, 60, 61, 63, 68, 70, 79, 133, 137, 139, 140, 141, 142, 143, 144, 145, 149, 164, 165, 166, 169, 171, 174, 179, 189, 190, 192, 196, 199, 203, 204, 205, 214, 219, 221, 222, 224, 225, 227, 233
Vignol 158
Vincent Kadłubek, bishop of Cracow 52
Vergilina (Virginella) 156
Visconti, Barnabo 244
Visconti, John 61, 66, 82
Vitry, Jacques de 53
Voutoumitis, Manuel 109

W
Waardenbur, Jean Jacques 178, 180
Al-Walīd, caliph of Ummayad dynasty 178
Warren, Michelle R. 21
Watkins, John 74
Wells, Scott 106
White, Hayden 14
Wichrowska, Elżbieta 11
William of Charni 162
William of Palerme 25
William of Tyre 53
Williams, Deanne 23, 25
Wilmot, brother 122
Wolfram von Eschenbach 25

X
Xenos Romanites 43

Y
Yalbughā al-Khāṣṣakī 244
Young, Helen 20, 22, 25
Yousey-Hindes, John 140, 147

Z
Zacharias 42
Zeno, bishop of Kourion 239
Zeno, Carlo 145
Zoras, Georgios (Γεώργιος Ζώρας) 36

PLATES

List of figures

Fig. 1. The Church of Saint Paraskevi (Αγία Παρασκευή), Geroskipou (Γεροσκήπου), village east of Paphos, 9th c. (photo by M. Glinicka)

Fig. 2. The Church of Saint Lazarus (Άγιος Λαζάρος), Larnaca (Λάρνακα), 9th c. (photo by B. Lichocka)

Fig. 3. The Church of Panagia Angeloktisti ('The Church of Our Lady built by Angels', Παναγία Αγγελόκτιστη), Kiti (Κίτι), village in the Larnaca District, 11th c. (photo by B. Lichocka)

Fig. 4. The Church of Panagia Angeloktisti ('The Church of Our Lady built by Angels', Παναγία Αγγελόκτιστη), Kiti (Κίτι), village in the Larnaca District, 11th c., architectural detail (photo by B. Lichocka)

Fig. 5. The Church of Panagia Odigitria ('The Church of Our Lady the Guide', Παναγία Οδηγήτρια), Kouklia (Κούκλια), village in the Paphos District, 12th c. (photo by P. Kordos)

Fig. 6. Bellapaïs Abbey, near Kyrenia (Κερύνεια), 12th c. (photo by M. Wojdak)

Fig. 7. Lusignan Manor, Kouklia (Κούκλια), village in the Paphos District, 13th c. (photo by B. Lichocka)

Fig. 8. The Church of Saint Kyriaki (Αγία Κυριακή) / The Basilica of Panagia Chrysopolitissa ('The Basilica of Our Lady of the Golden City', Παναγία Χρυσοπολίτισσα), around the 13th c., and the remains of the 4th c. basilica, Paphos (Πάφος) (photo by P. Kordos)

Fig. 9. The Church of Saint George of the Latins (Άγιος Γεώργιος των Λατίνων), Famagusta (Αμμόχωστος), 13th c. (photo by P. Kordos)

Fig. 10. The Church of Saint Catherine (Αγία Αικατερίνη), Nicosia (Λευκωσία), 14th c., from the 16th c. the Mosque of Haydar Pasha (Haydarpaşa Camii) (© Republic of Cyprus Press and Information Office)

Fig. 11. The Cathedral of Saint Sophia (Αγία Σοφία), Nicosia (Λευκωσία), 13/14th c., from the 16th c. the Mosque of Selim (Selimiye Camii) (© Republic of Cyprus Press and Information Office)

Fig. 12. The Church of Saint George of the Greeks (Άγιος Γεώργιος των Ελλήνων), Famagusta (Αμμόχωστος), 14th c. (© Republic of Cyprus Press and Information Office)

Fig. 13. The Cathedral of Saint Nicholas (Άγιος Νικολάος), Famagusta (Αμμόχωστος), 13/14th c., from the 16th c. the Mosque of Lala Mustafa Pasha (Lala Mustafa Paşa Camii) (photo by B. Lichocka)

Fig. 14. The Cathedral of Saint Nicholas (Άγιος Νικολάος), Famagusta (Αμμόχωστος), 13/14th c., from the 16th c. the Mosque of Lala Mustafa Pasha (Lala Mustafa Paşa Camii), fragment of a side façade (photo by M. Wojdak)

Fig. 15. The Church of Saints Peter and Paul (Άγιοι Πέτρος και Παύλος), Famagusta (Αμμόχωστος), 14th c., from the 16th c. the Mosque of Sinan Pasha (Sinan Paşa Camii) (© Republic of Cyprus Press and Information Office)

Fig. 16. The Church of the Transfiguration of the Saviour (Μεταμόρφωση του Σωτήρος), Kakopetria (Κακοπετριά), village of the Nicosia District, 16th c. (photo by M. Wojdak)

Fig. 1. The Church of Saint Paraskevi, Geroskipou

Fig. 2. The Church of Saint Lazarus, Larnaca

Fig. 3. The Church of Panagia Angeloktisti, Kiti

Fig. 4. The Church of Panagia Angeloktisti, Kiti, architectural detail

Fig. 5. The Church of Panagia Odigitria, Kouklia

Fig. 6. Bellapaïs Abbey, near Kyrenia

Fig. 7. Lusignan Manor, Kouklia

Fig. 8. The Church of Saint Kyriaki / The Basilica of Panagia Chrysopolitissa, Paphos

Fig. 9. The Church of Saint George of the Latins, Famagusta

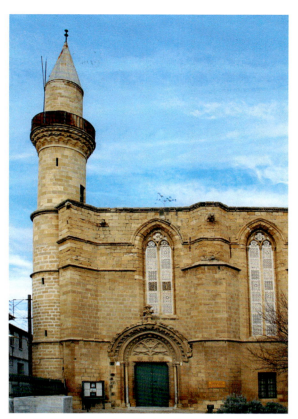

Fig. 10. The Church of Saint Catherine, Nicosia

Fig. 11. The Cathedral of Saint Sophia, Nicosia

Fig. 12. The Church of Saint George of the Greeks, Famagusta

Fig. 13. The Cathedral of Saint Nicholas, Famagusta

Fig. 14. The Cathedral of Saint Nicholas, Famagusta, fragment of a side façade

Fig. 15. The Church of Saints Peter and Paul, Famagusta

Fig. 16. The Church of the Transfiguration of the Saviour, Kakopetria